BIRDS OF PREY:

BLACK CANARY

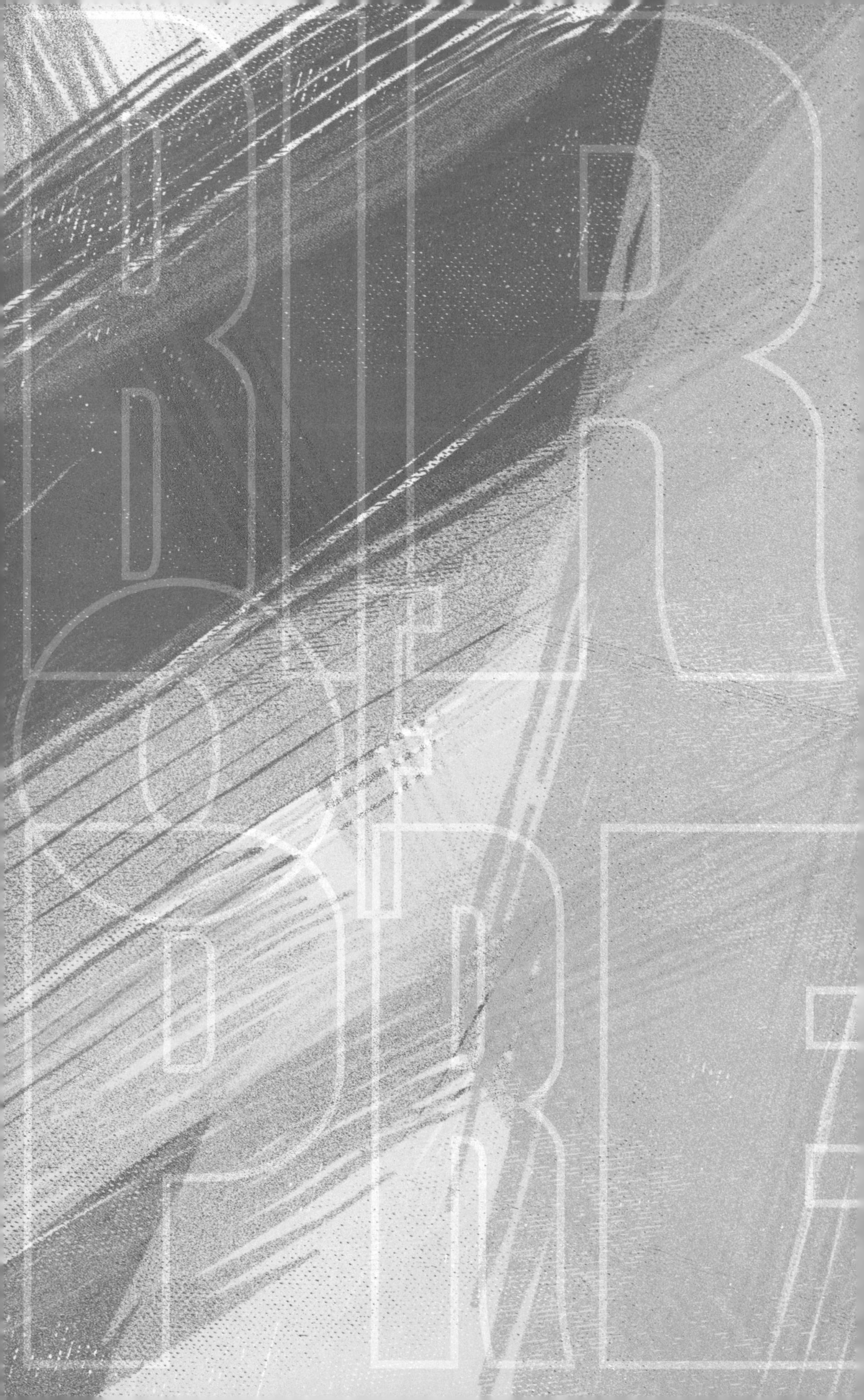

BRENDEN FLETCHER
MATTHEW ROSENBERG
WRITERS

ANNIE WU
SANDY JARRELL
PIA GUERRA
MORITAT
WAYNE FAUCHER
ARTISTS

BLACK CANARY

LEE LOUGHRIDGE
SERGE LaPOINTE
COLORISTS

STEVE WANDS
MARILYN PATRIZIO
LETTERERS

TULA LOTAY
COLLECTION COVER ARTIST

CHRIS CONROY editor – original series
DAVE WIELGOSZ assistant editor – original series
JEB WOODARD group editor – collected editions
ERIKA ROTHBERG editor – collected edition
STEVE COOK design director – books
MONIQUE NARBONETA publication design
DANIELLE DIGRADO publication production

BOB HARRAS senior vp – editor-in-chief, dc comics
PAT McCALLUM executive editor, dc comics

DAN DiDIO publisher
JIM LEE publisher & chief creative officer
BOBBIE CHASE vp – new publishing initiatives & talent development
DON FALLETTI vp – manufacturing operations & workflow management
LAWRENCE GANEM vp – talent services
ALISON GILL senior vp – manufacturing & operations
HANK KANALZ senior vp – publishing strategy & support services
DAN MIRON vp – publishing operations
NICK J. NAPOLITANO vp – manufacturing administration & design
NANCY SPEARS vp – sales
MICHELE R. WELLS vp & executive editor, young reader

BIRDS OF PREY: BLACK CANARY

DC Comics, 2900 West Alameda Ave., Burbank, CA 91505
Printed by LSC Communications, Owensville, MO, USA. 12/13/19. First Printing.
ISBN: 978-1-4012-9891-3

Library of Congress Cataloging-in-Publication Data is available.

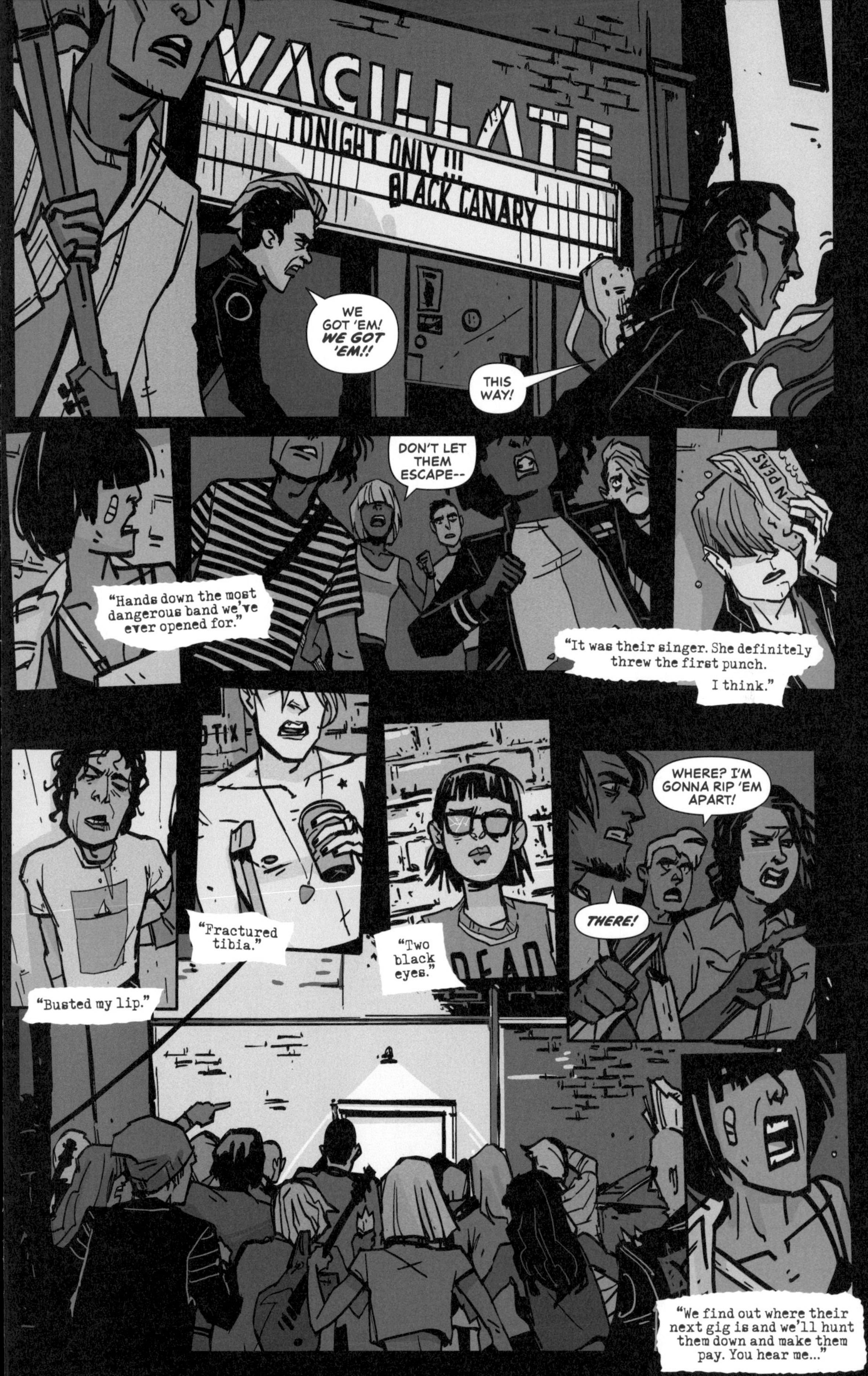

VACILLATE
TONIGHT ONLY !!!
BLACK CANARY
WE GOT 'EM! WE GOT 'EM!!
THIS WAY!
"Hands down the most dangerous band we've ever opened for."
DON'T LET THEM ESCAPE--
"It was their singer. She definitely threw the first punch.
I think."
"Busted my lip."
TIX
"Fractured tibia."
"Two black eyes."
DEAD
WHERE? I'M GONNA RIP 'EM APART!
THERE!
"We find out where their next gig is and we'll hunt them down and make them pay. You hear me..."

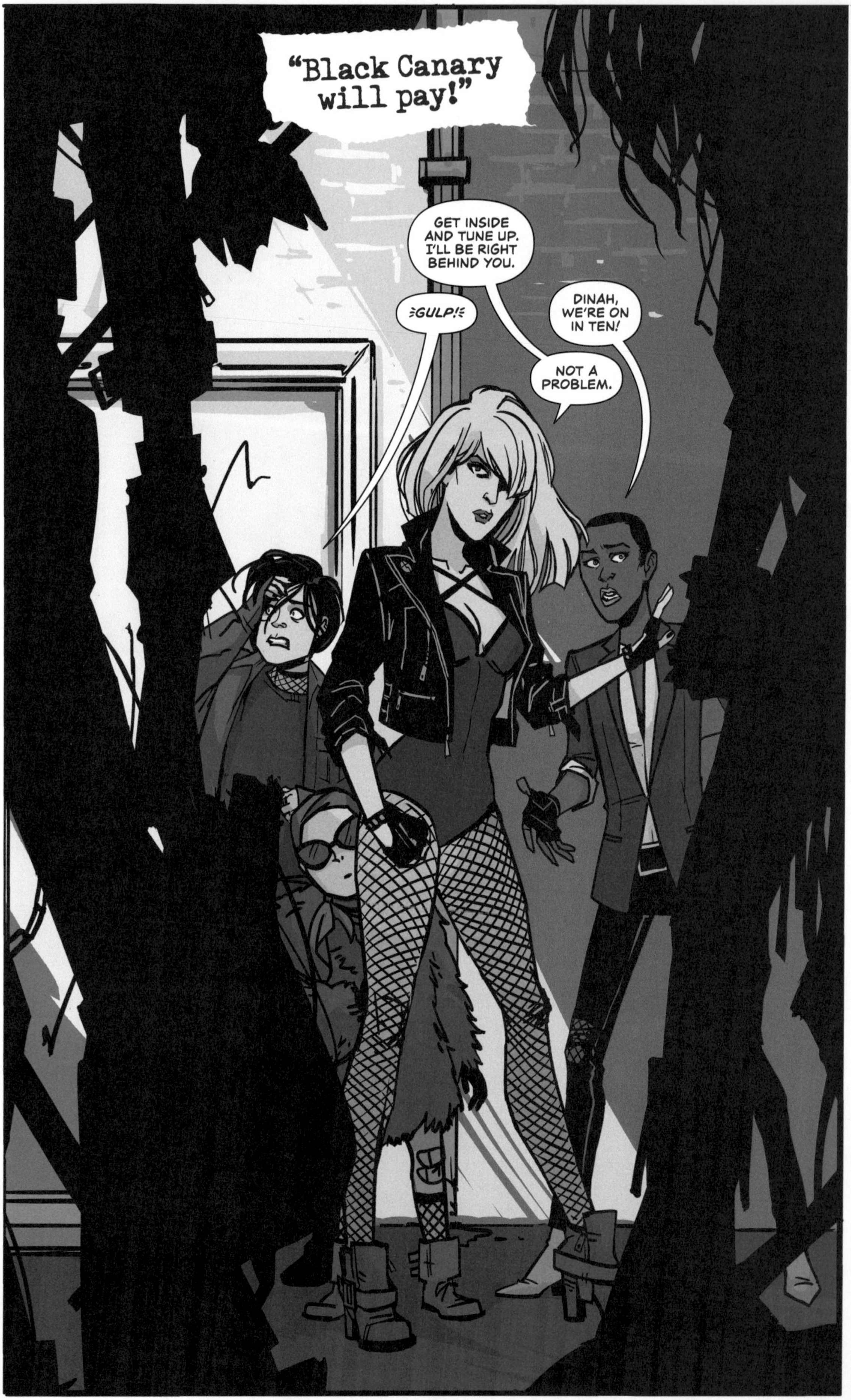
"Black Canary will pay!"
GET INSIDE AND TUNE UP. I'LL BE RIGHT BEHIND YOU.
GULP!
DINAH, WE'RE ON IN TEN!
NOT A PROBLEM.

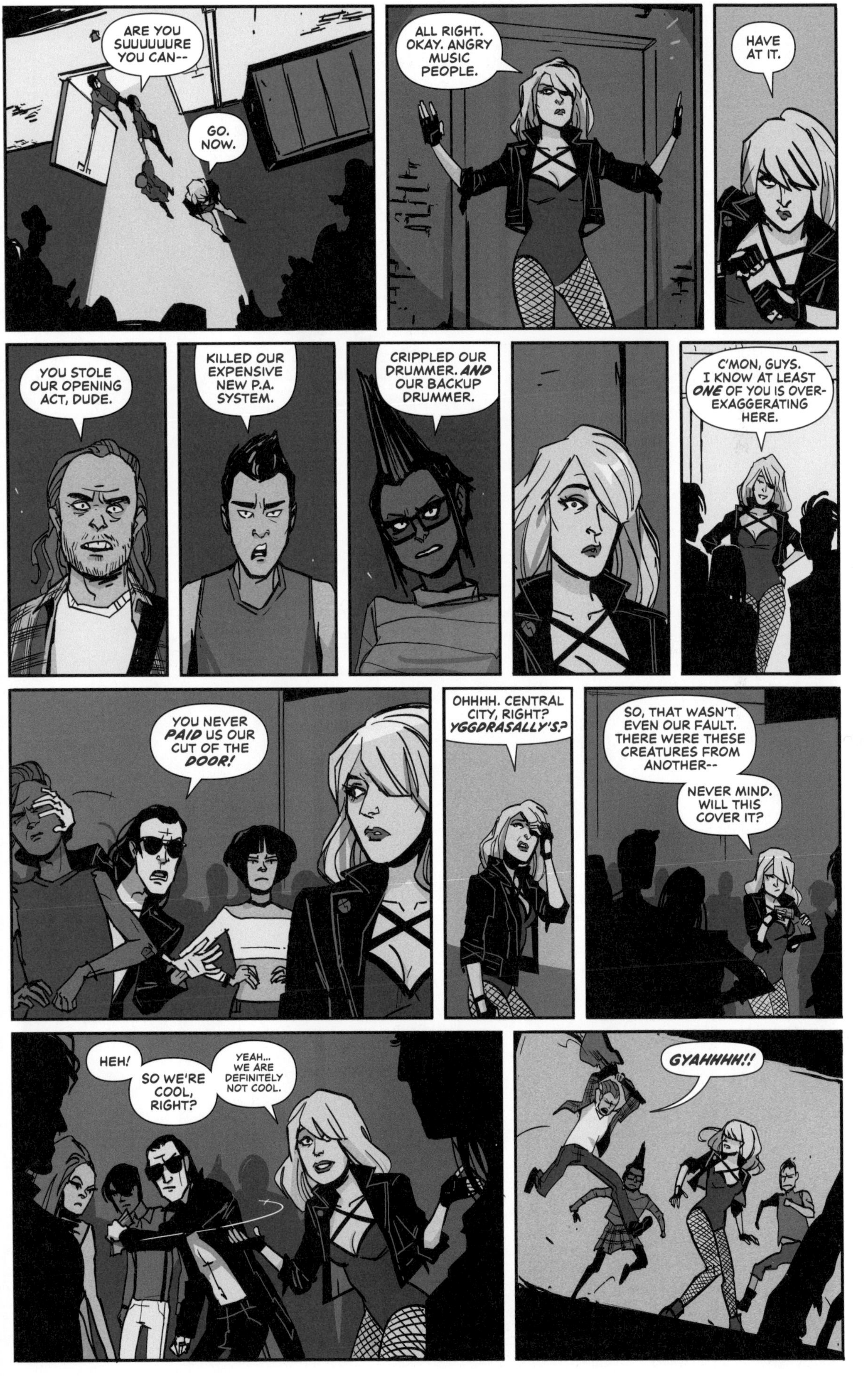

ARE YOU SUUUUUURE YOU CAN--
GO. NOW.
ALL RIGHT. OKAY. ANGRY MUSIC PEOPLE.
HAVE AT IT.
YOU STOLE OUR OPENING ACT, DUDE.
KILLED OUR EXPENSIVE NEW P.A. SYSTEM.
CRIPPLED OUR DRUMMER. AND OUR BACKUP DRUMMER.
C'MON, GUYS. I KNOW AT LEAST ONE OF YOU IS OVER-EXAGGERATING HERE.
YOU NEVER PAID US OUR CUT OF THE DOOR!
OHHHH. CENTRAL CITY, RIGHT? YGGDRASALLY'S?
SO, THAT WASN'T EVEN OUR FAULT. THERE WERE THESE CREATURES FROM ANOTHER--
NEVER MIND. WILL THIS COVER IT?
HEH!
SO WE'RE COOL, RIGHT?
YEAH... WE ARE DEFINITELY NOT COOL.
GYAHHHH!!

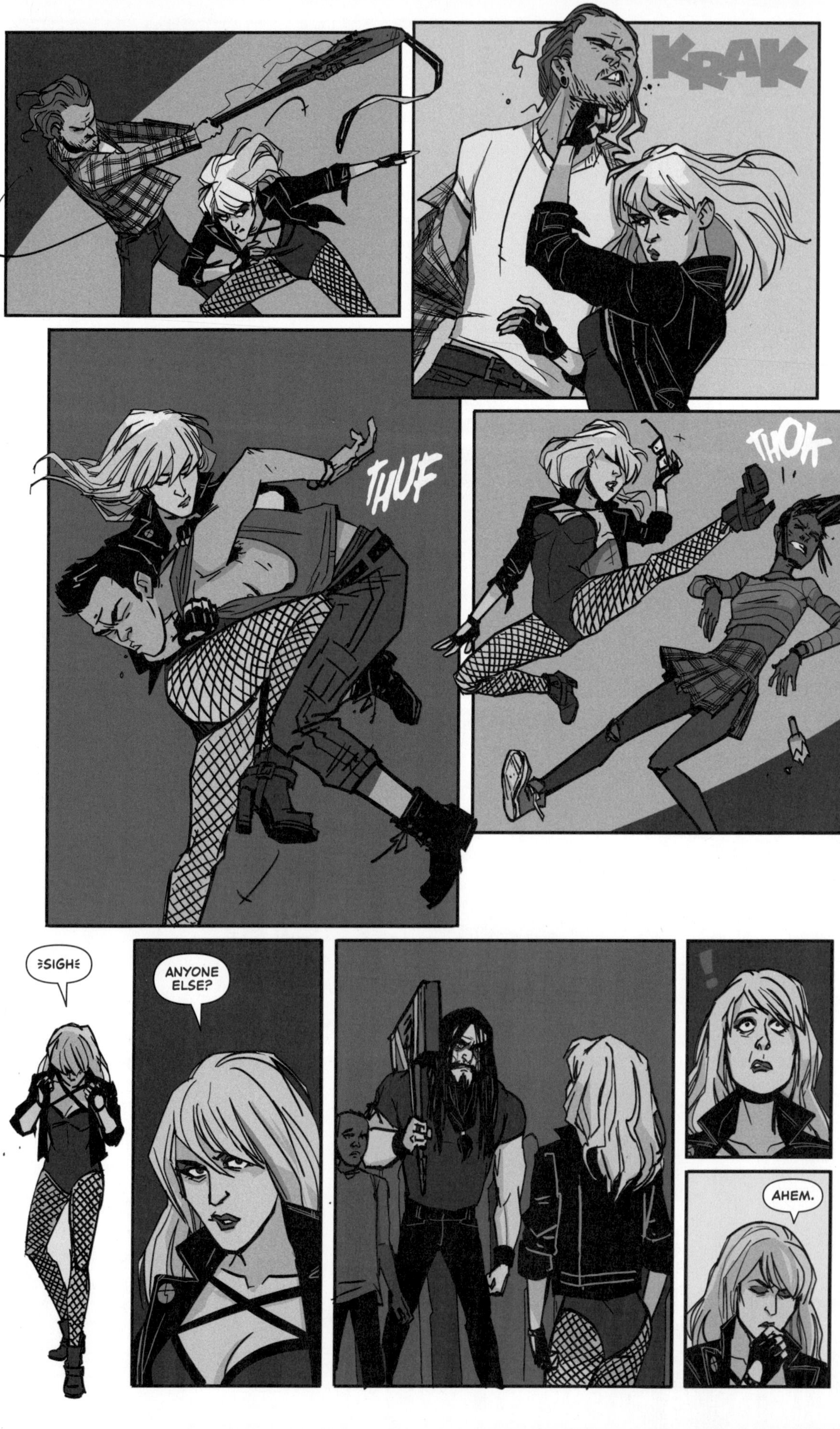
KRAK
THUF
THOK
SIGH
ANYONE ELSE?
!
AHEM.

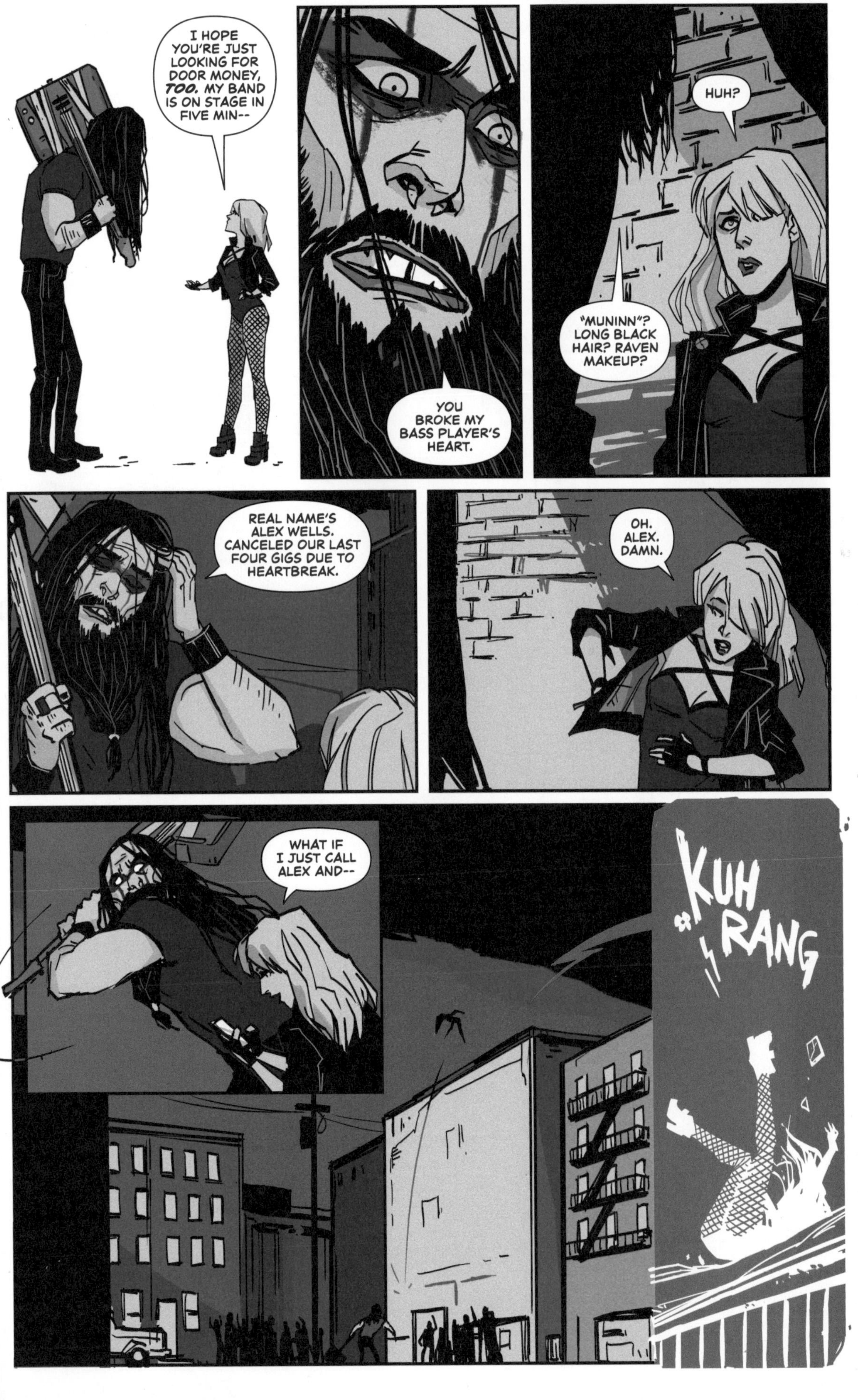
I HOPE YOU'RE JUST LOOKING FOR DOOR MONEY, TOO. MY BAND IS ON STAGE IN FIVE MIN--
YOU BROKE MY BASS PLAYER'S HEART.
HUH?
"MUNINN"? LONG BLACK HAIR? RAVEN MAKEUP?
REAL NAME'S ALEX WELLS. CANCELED OUR LAST FOUR GIGS DUE TO HEARTBREAK.
OH. ALEX. DAMN.
WHAT IF I JUST CALL ALEX AND--
KUH RANG

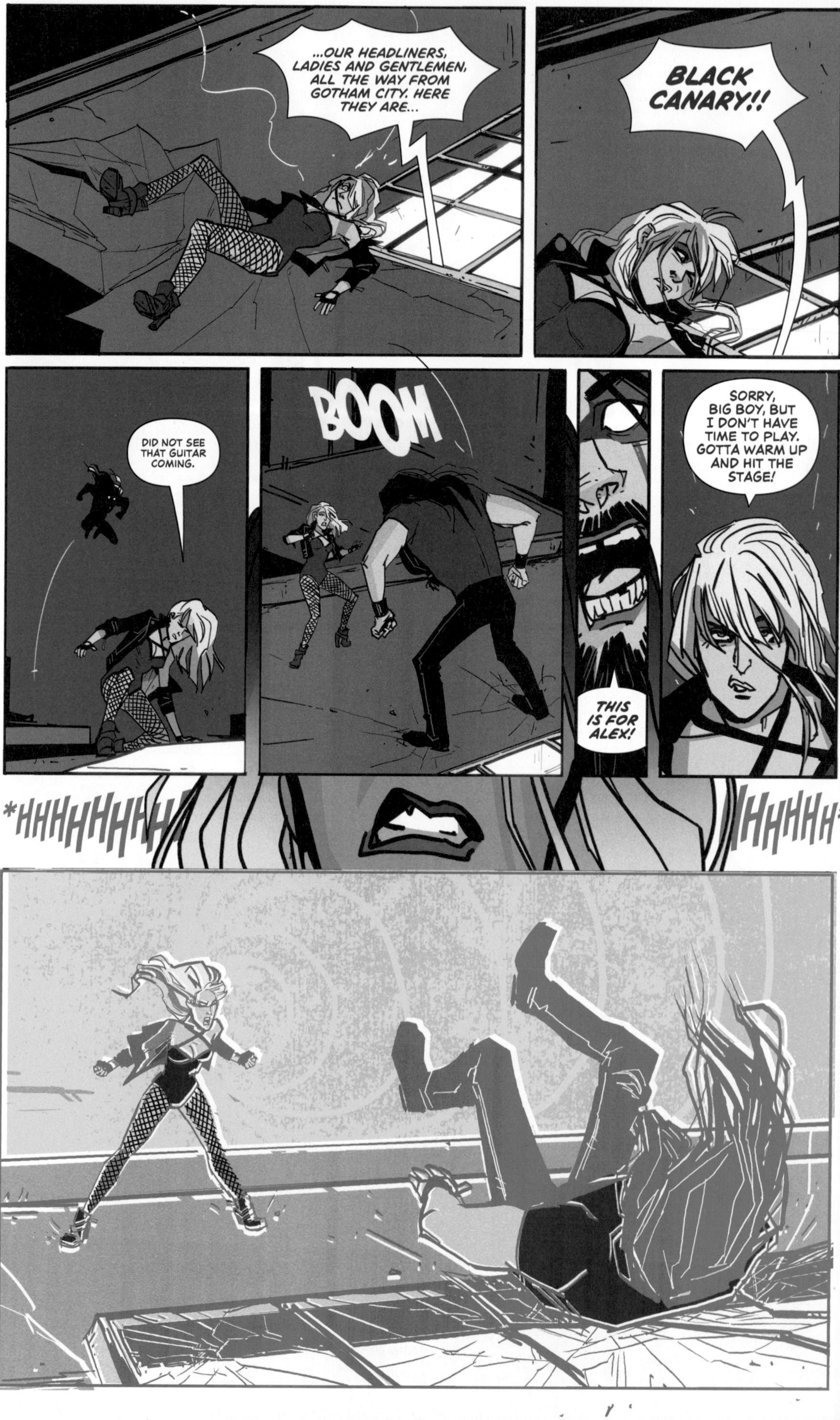
...OUR HEADLINERS, LADIES AND GENTLEMEN, ALL THE WAY FROM GOTHAM CITY. HERE THEY ARE...
BLACK CANARY!!
DID NOT SEE THAT GUITAR COMING.
BOOM
THIS IS FOR ALEX!
SORRY, BIG BOY, BUT I DON'T HAVE TIME TO PLAY. GOTTA WARM UP AND HIT THE STAGE!
HHHHHHHHHHHHHHHHH

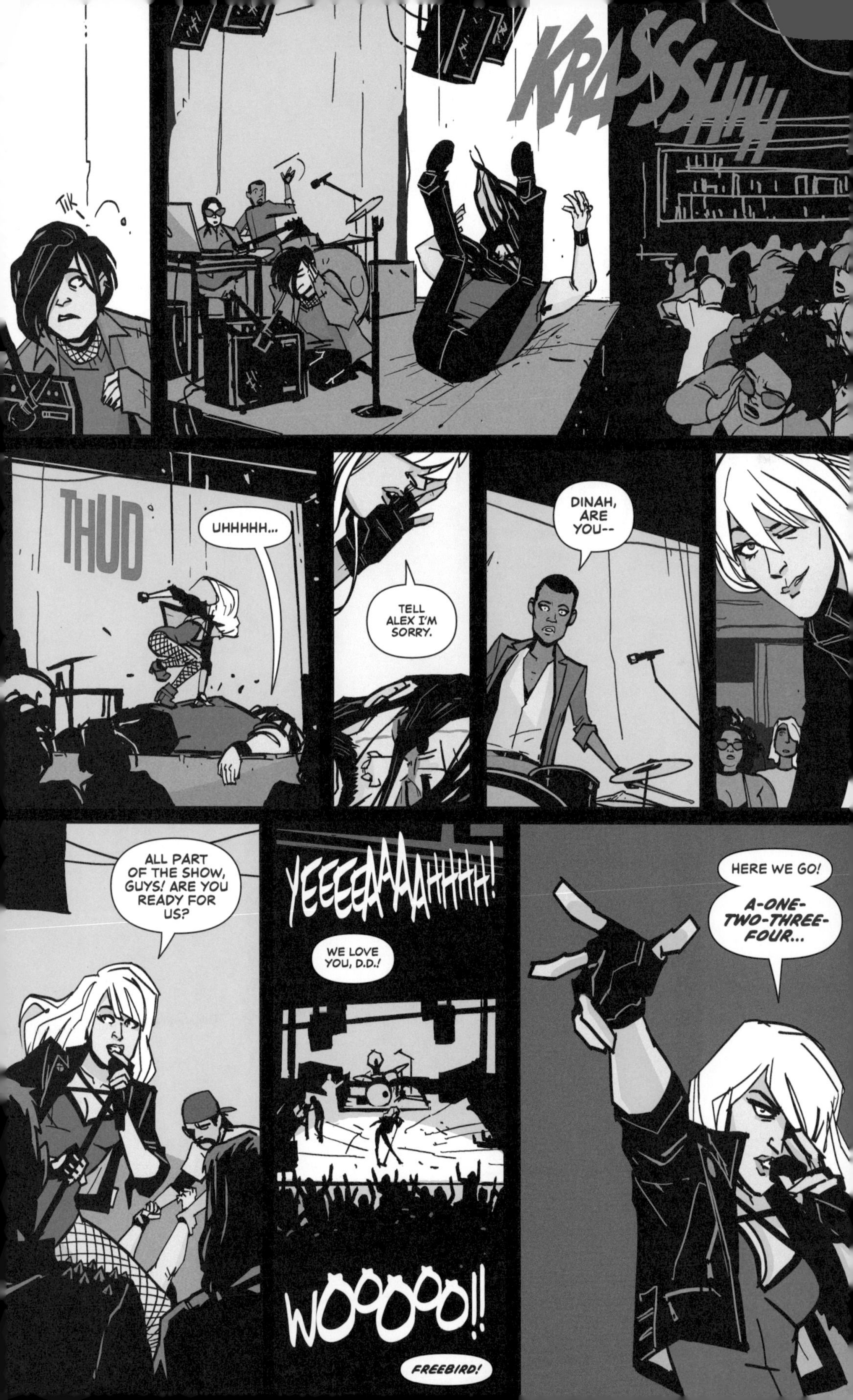
TIK
KRASSHHH
THUD
UHHHHH...
TELL ALEX I'M SORRY.
DINAH, ARE YOU--
ALL PART OF THE SHOW, GUYS! ARE YOU READY FOR US?
YEEEEAAAAHHHH!
WE LOVE YOU, D.D.!
WOOOOO!!
FREEBIRD!
HERE WE GO!
A-ONE-TWO-THREE-FOUR...

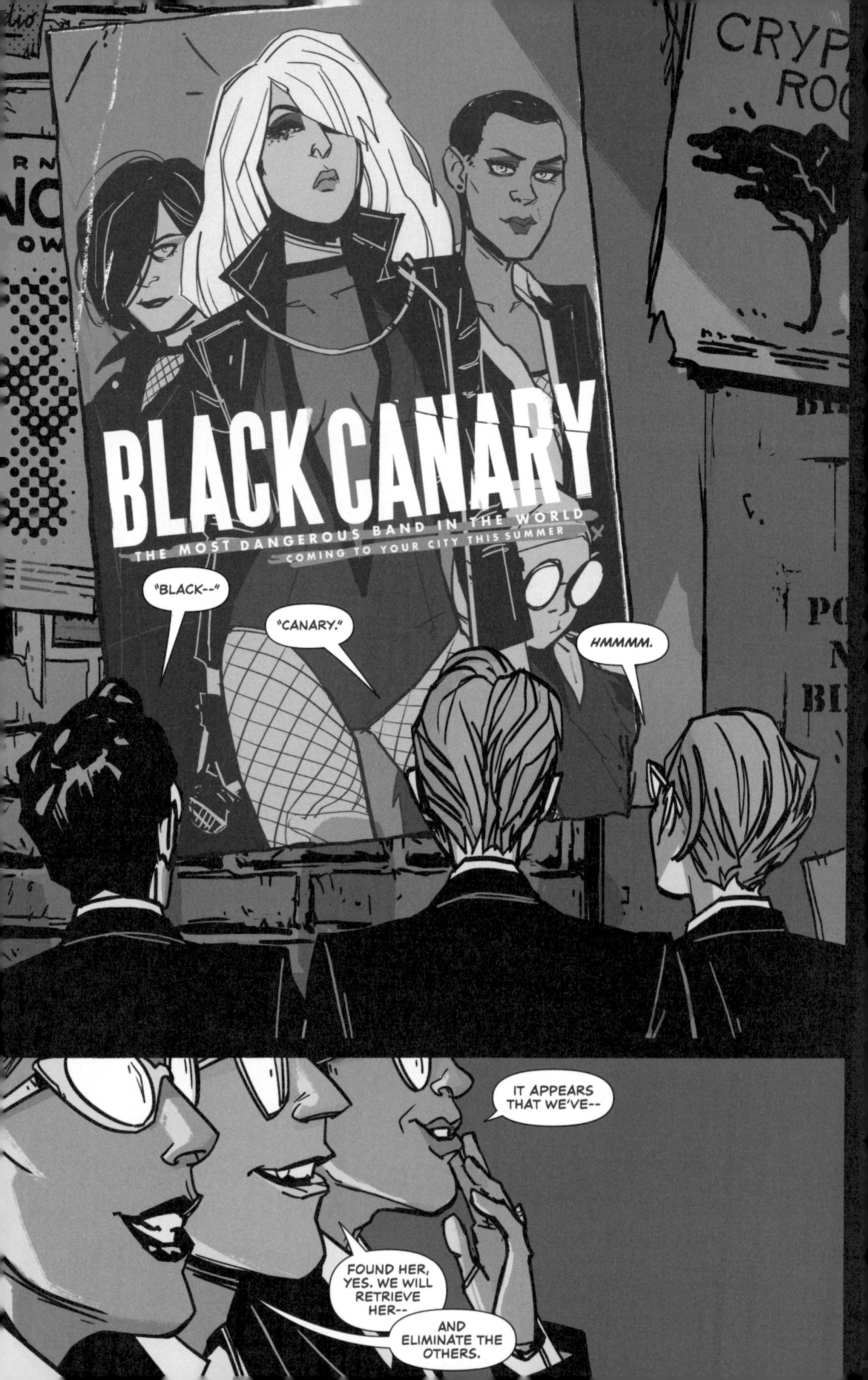
BLACK CANARY
THE MOST DANGEROUS BAND IN THE WORLD
COMING TO YOUR CITY THIS SUMMER
"BLACK--"
"CANARY."
HMMMM.
IT APPEARS THAT WE'VE--
FOUND HER, YES. WE WILL RETRIEVE HER--
AND ELIMINATE THE OTHERS.

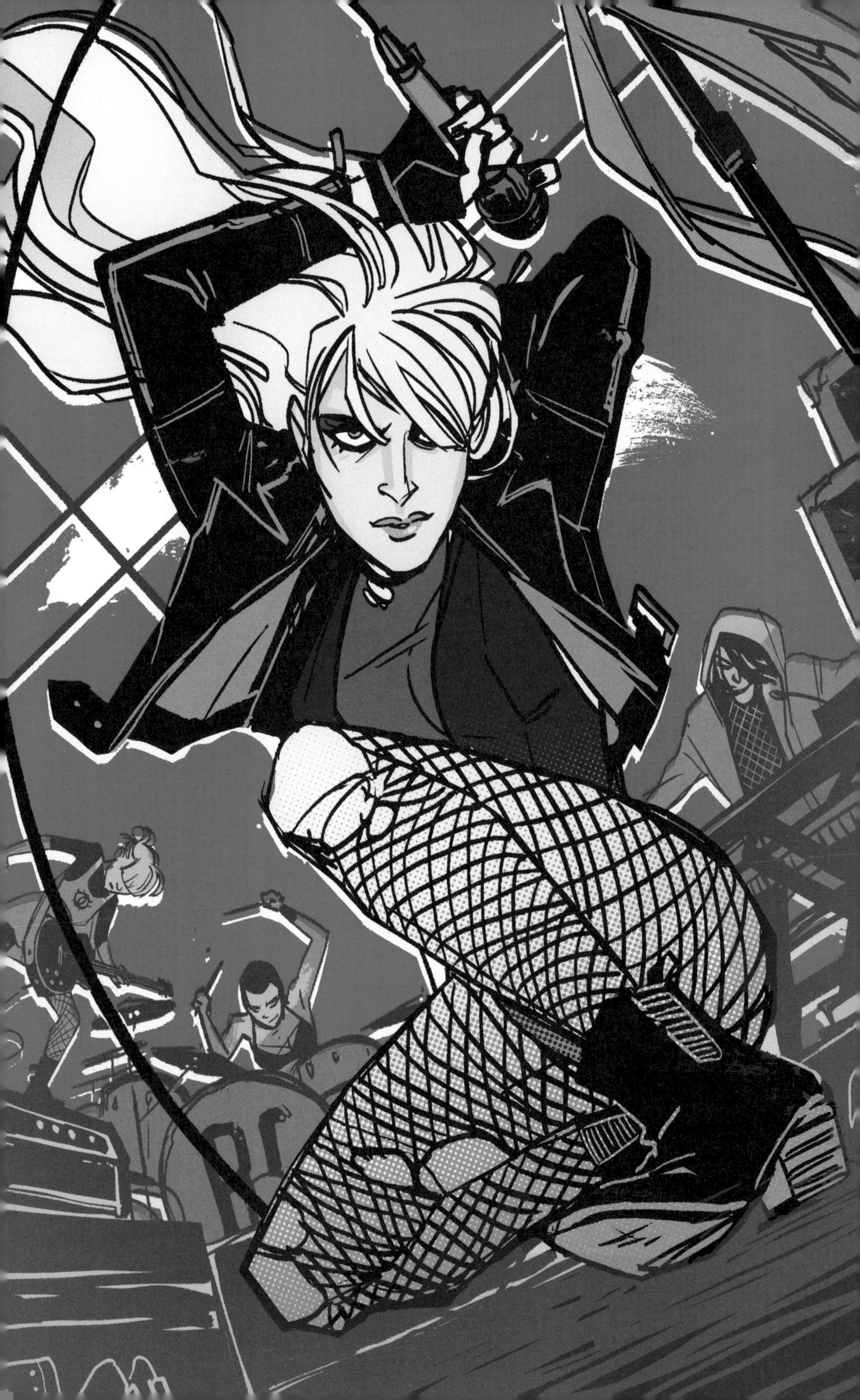

WHERE BLACK CANARY GOES, TROUBLE FOLLOWS

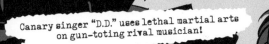
Canary singer "D.D." uses lethal martial arts on gun-toting rival musician!

A BURNSIDE TOFU EXCLUSIVE BY TANTOO LA BICHE

Gotham City-based four-piece band Black Canary have been tearing up the road on tour--literally! Five of their last seven shows have reportedly ended in violence, with witnesses at last month's EXE Festival outside Central City describing mysterious frontwoman "D.D." as "more of a UFC fighter than a singer," after she single-handedly stopped a group of armed gunmen.

Full story on page 2

BURNSIDE TOFU The zine for people with the right kind of taste

Editor in Chief
TANTOO LA BICHE

Photo Editor
TANTOO LA BICHE

Staff Writer
TANTOO LA BICHE

Social Media Director
TANTOO LA BICHE

Audience member Sasha S. shows off souvenirs.

This guy sucked.

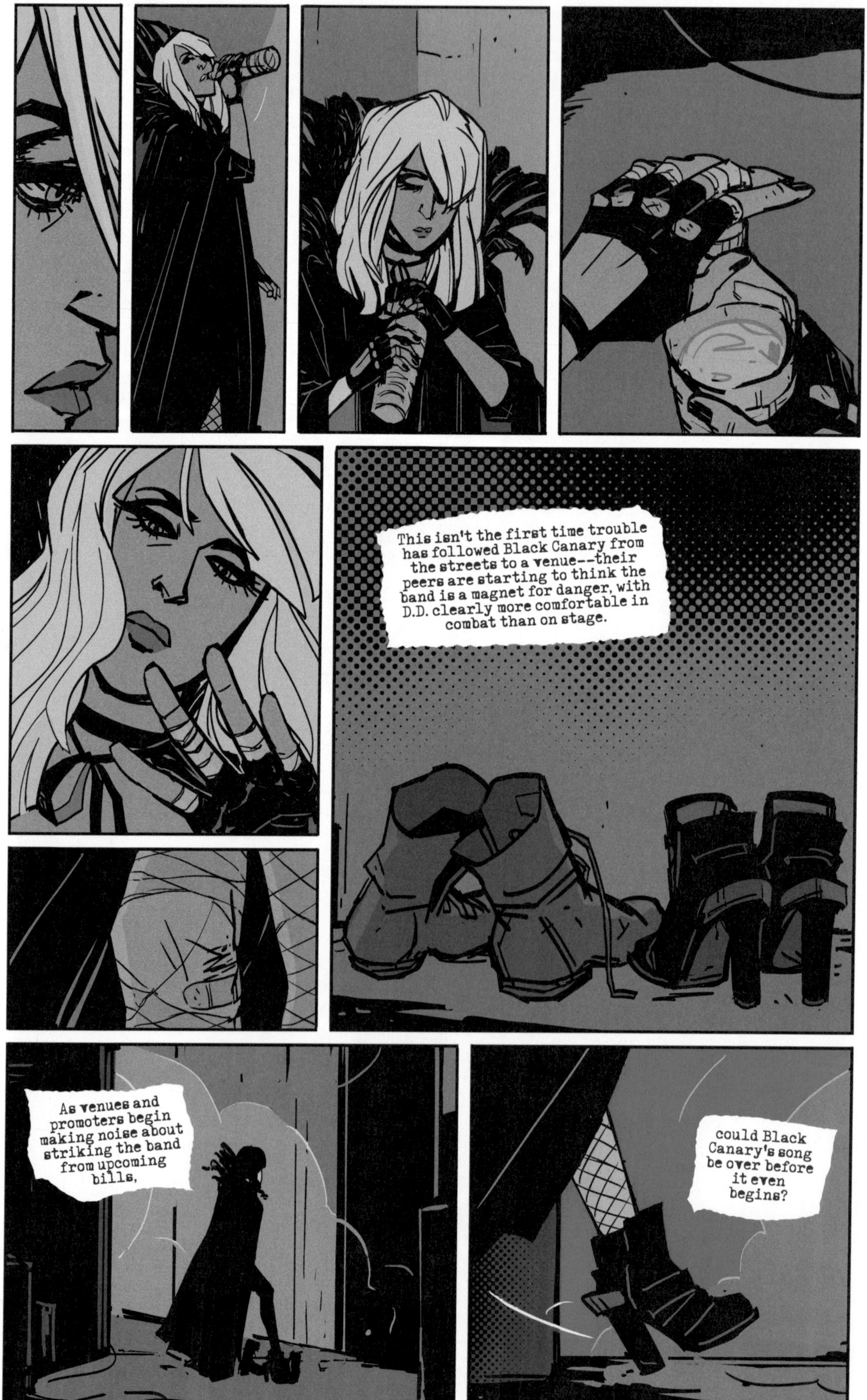
This isn't the first time trouble has followed Black Canary from the streets to a venue--their peers are starting to think the band is a magnet for danger, with D.D. clearly more comfortable in combat than on stage.
As venues and promoters begin making noise about striking the band from upcoming bills,
could Black Canary's song be over before it even begins?

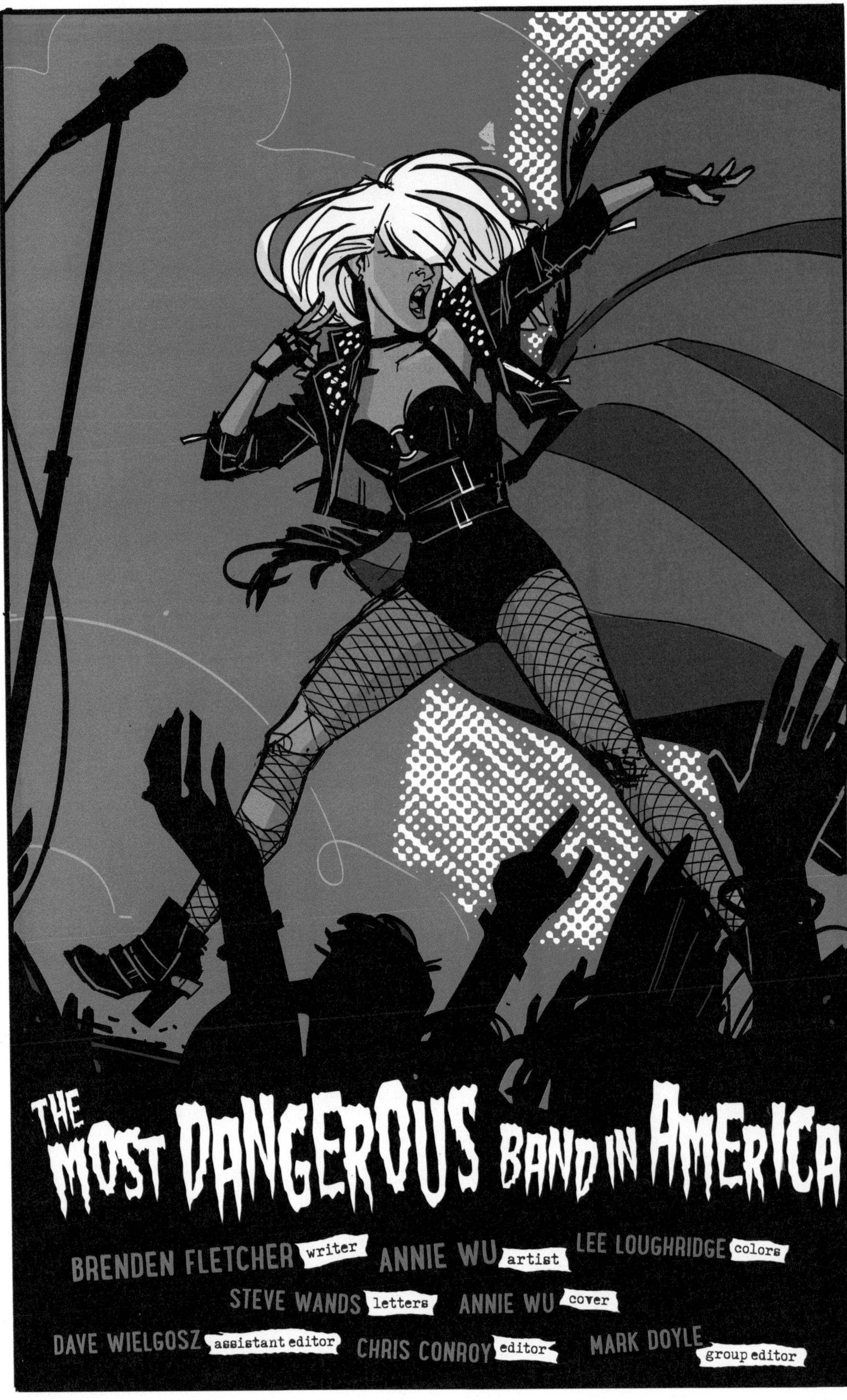

THE MOST DANGEROUS BAND IN AMERICA
BRENDEN FLETCHER writer
ANNIE WU artist
LEE LOUGHRIDGE colors
STEVE WANDS letters
ANNIE WU cover
DAVE WIELGOSZ assistant editor
CHRIS CONROY editor
MARK DOYLE group editor

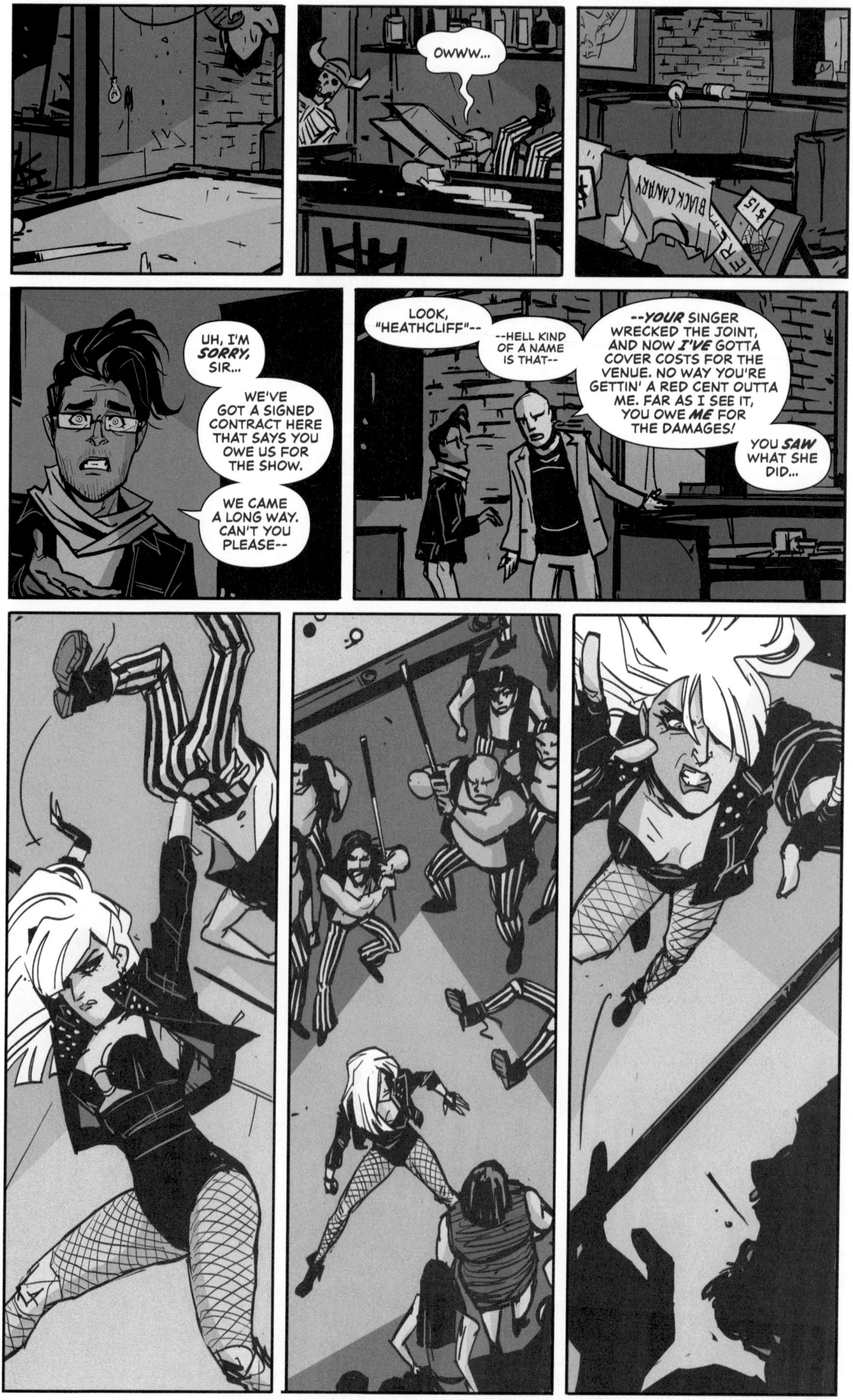
OWWW...
BLACK CANARY
$15
UH, I'M SORRY, SIR...
WE'VE GOT A SIGNED CONTRACT HERE THAT SAYS YOU OWE US FOR THE SHOW.
WE CAME A LONG WAY. CAN'T YOU PLEASE--
LOOK, "HEATHCLIFF"--
--HELL KIND OF A NAME IS THAT--
--YOUR SINGER WRECKED THE JOINT, AND NOW I'VE GOTTA COVER COSTS FOR THE VENUE. NO WAY YOU'RE GETTIN' A RED CENT OUTTA ME. FAR AS I SEE IT, YOU OWE ME FOR THE DAMAGES!
YOU SAW WHAT SHE DID...

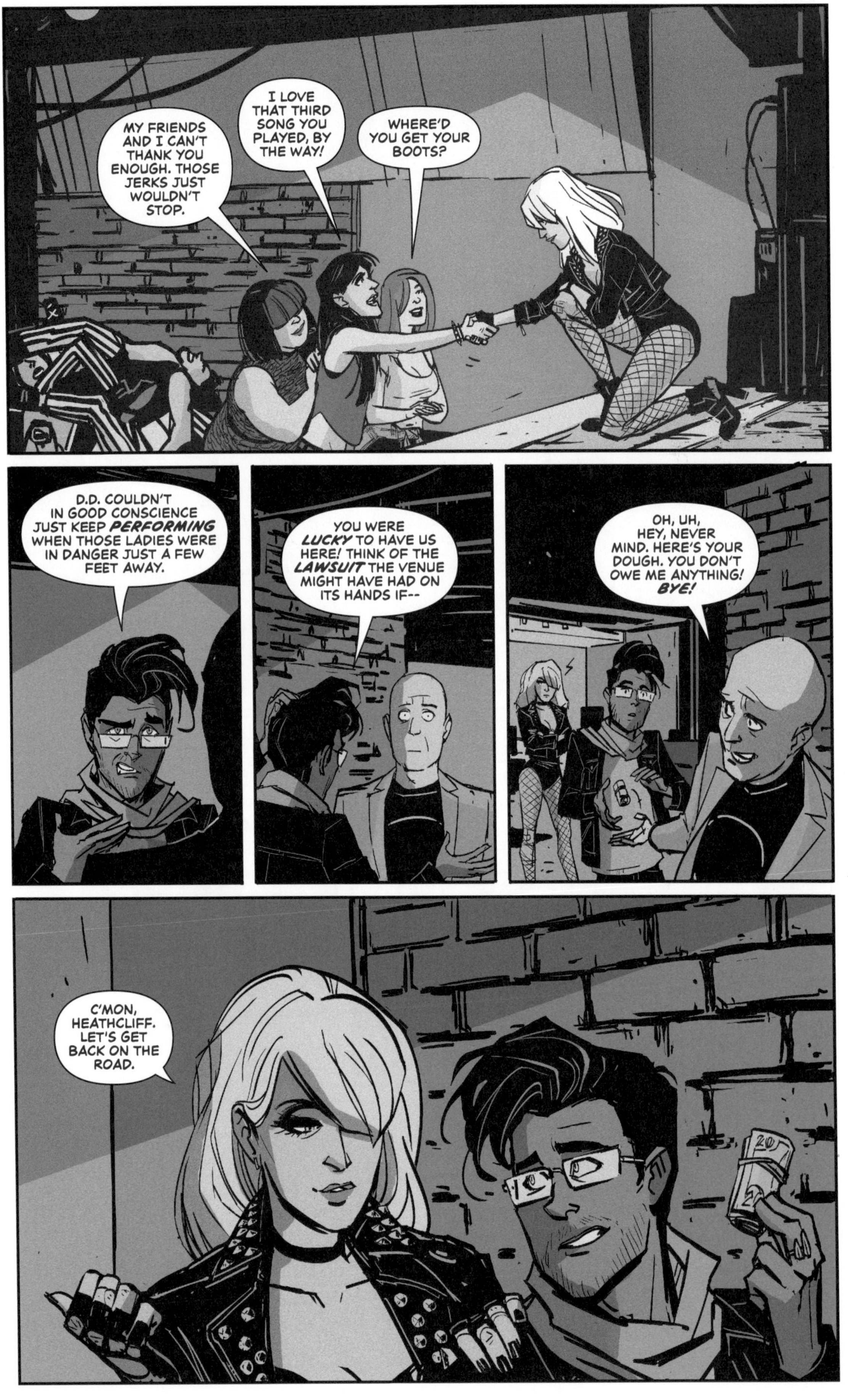
MY FRIENDS AND I CAN'T THANK YOU ENOUGH. THOSE JERKS JUST WOULDN'T STOP.
I LOVE THAT THIRD SONG YOU PLAYED, BY THE WAY!
WHERE'D YOU GET YOUR BOOTS?
D.D. COULDN'T IN GOOD CONSCIENCE JUST KEEP PERFORMING WHEN THOSE LADIES WERE IN DANGER JUST A FEW FEET AWAY.
YOU WERE LUCKY TO HAVE US HERE! THINK OF THE LAWSUIT THE VENUE MIGHT HAVE HAD ON ITS HANDS IF--
OH, UH, HEY, NEVER MIND. HERE'S YOUR DOUGH. YOU DON'T OWE ME ANYTHING! BYE!
C'MON, HEATHCLIFF. LET'S GET BACK ON THE ROAD.

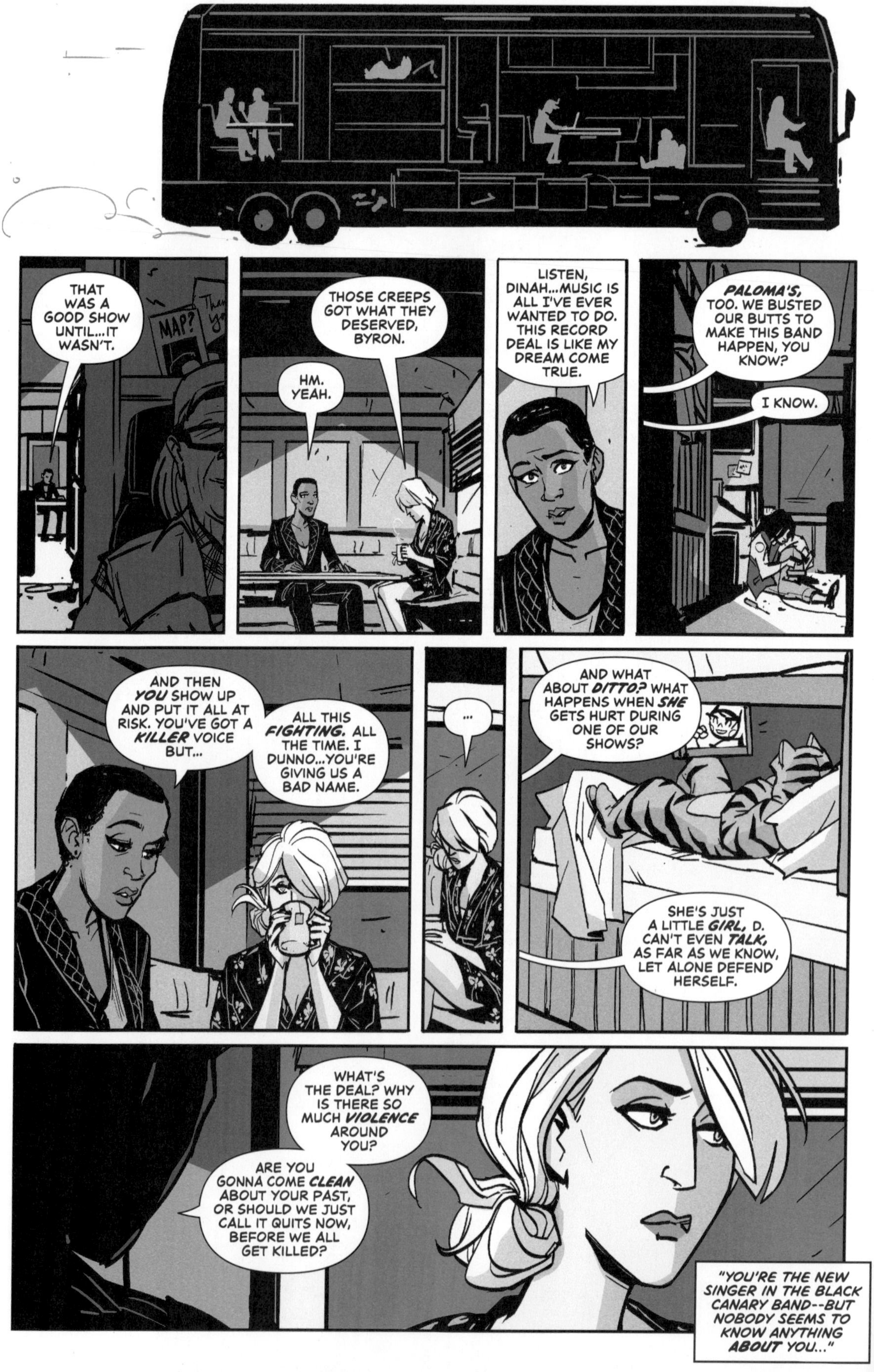
THAT WAS A GOOD SHOW UNTIL...IT WASN'T.
THOSE CREEPS GOT WHAT THEY DESERVED, BYRON.
HM. YEAH.
LISTEN, DINAH...MUSIC IS ALL I'VE EVER WANTED TO DO. THIS RECORD DEAL IS LIKE MY DREAM COME TRUE.
PALOMA'S, TOO. WE BUSTED OUR BUTTS TO MAKE THIS BAND HAPPEN, YOU KNOW?
I KNOW.
AND THEN YOU SHOW UP AND PUT IT ALL AT RISK. YOU'VE GOT A KILLER VOICE BUT...
ALL THIS FIGHTING. ALL THE TIME. I DUNNO...YOU'RE GIVING US A BAD NAME.
...
AND WHAT ABOUT DITTO? WHAT HAPPENS WHEN SHE GETS HURT DURING ONE OF OUR SHOWS?
SHE'S JUST A LITTLE GIRL, D. CAN'T EVEN TALK, AS FAR AS WE KNOW, LET ALONE DEFEND HERSELF.
WHAT'S THE DEAL? WHY IS THERE SO MUCH VIOLENCE AROUND YOU?
ARE YOU GONNA COME CLEAN ABOUT YOUR PAST, OR SHOULD WE JUST CALL IT QUITS NOW, BEFORE WE ALL GET KILLED?
"YOU'RE THE NEW SINGER IN THE BLACK CANARY BAND--BUT NOBODY SEEMS TO KNOW ANYTHING ABOUT YOU..."

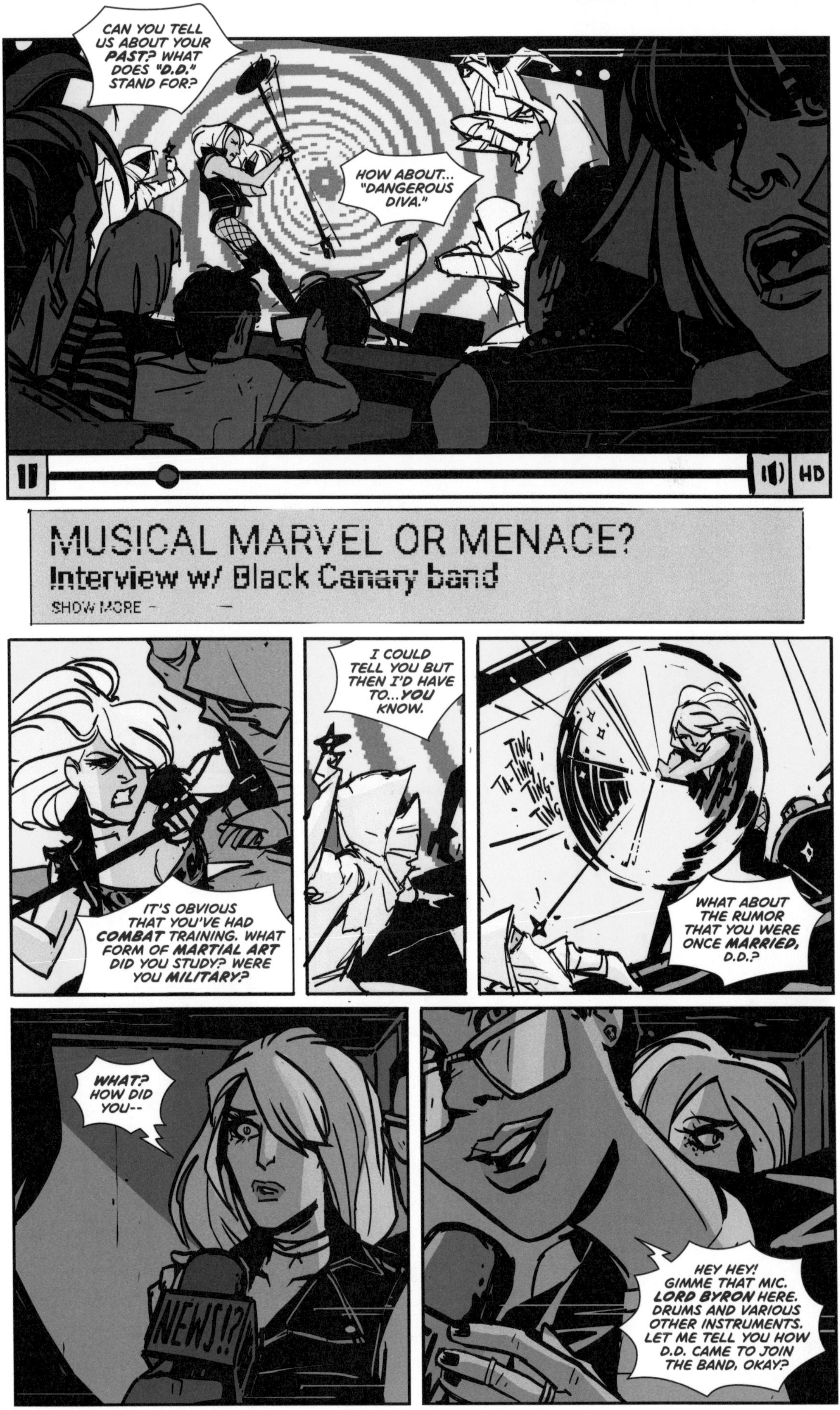
CAN YOU TELL US ABOUT YOUR PAST? WHAT DOES "D.D." STAND FOR?
HOW ABOUT... "DANGEROUS DIVA."
HD
MUSICAL MARVEL OR MENACE?
Interview w/ Black Canary band
SHOW MORE
IT'S OBVIOUS THAT YOU'VE HAD COMBAT TRAINING. WHAT FORM OF MARTIAL ART DID YOU STUDY? WERE YOU MILITARY?
I COULD TELL YOU BUT THEN I'D HAVE TO...YOU KNOW.
TING TA-TING TING-TING
WHAT ABOUT THE RUMOR THAT YOU WERE ONCE MARRIED, D.D.?
WHAT? HOW DID YOU--
NEWS!?
HEY HEY! GIMME THAT MIC. LORD BYRON HERE. DRUMS AND VARIOUS OTHER INSTRUMENTS. LET ME TELL YOU HOW D.D. CAME TO JOIN THE BAND, OKAY?

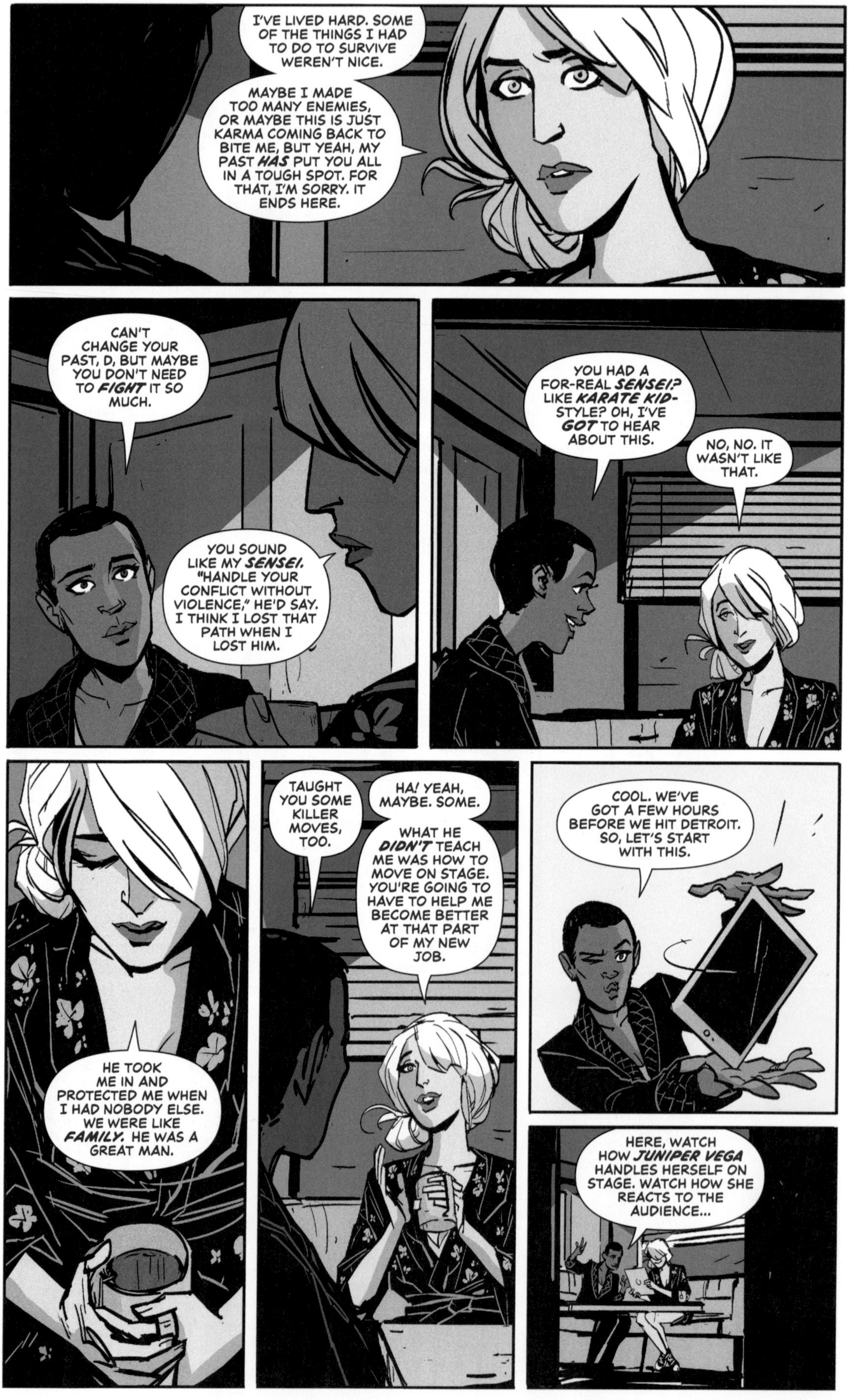

I'VE LIVED HARD. SOME OF THE THINGS I HAD TO DO TO SURVIVE WEREN'T NICE.
MAYBE I MADE TOO MANY ENEMIES, OR MAYBE THIS IS JUST KARMA COMING BACK TO BITE ME, BUT YEAH, MY PAST *HAS* PUT YOU ALL IN A TOUGH SPOT. FOR THAT, I'M SORRY. IT ENDS HERE.
CAN'T CHANGE YOUR PAST, D, BUT MAYBE YOU DON'T NEED TO *FIGHT* IT SO MUCH.
YOU SOUND LIKE MY *SENSEI.* "HANDLE YOUR CONFLICT WITHOUT VIOLENCE," HE'D SAY. I THINK I LOST THAT PATH WHEN I LOST HIM.
YOU HAD A FOR-REAL *SENSEI?* LIKE *KARATE KID*-STYLE? OH, I'VE *GOT* TO HEAR ABOUT THIS.
NO, NO. IT WASN'T LIKE THAT.
HE TOOK ME IN AND PROTECTED ME WHEN I HAD NOBODY ELSE. WE WERE LIKE *FAMILY.* HE WAS A GREAT MAN.
TAUGHT YOU SOME KILLER MOVES, TOO.
HA! YEAH, MAYBE. SOME.
WHAT HE *DIDN'T* TEACH ME WAS HOW TO MOVE ON STAGE. YOU'RE GOING TO HAVE TO HELP ME BECOME BETTER AT THAT PART OF MY NEW JOB.
COOL. WE'VE GOT A FEW HOURS BEFORE WE HIT DETROIT. SO, LET'S START WITH THIS.
HERE, WATCH HOW *JUNIPER VEGA* HANDLES HERSELF ON STAGE. WATCH HOW SHE REACTS TO THE AUDIENCE...

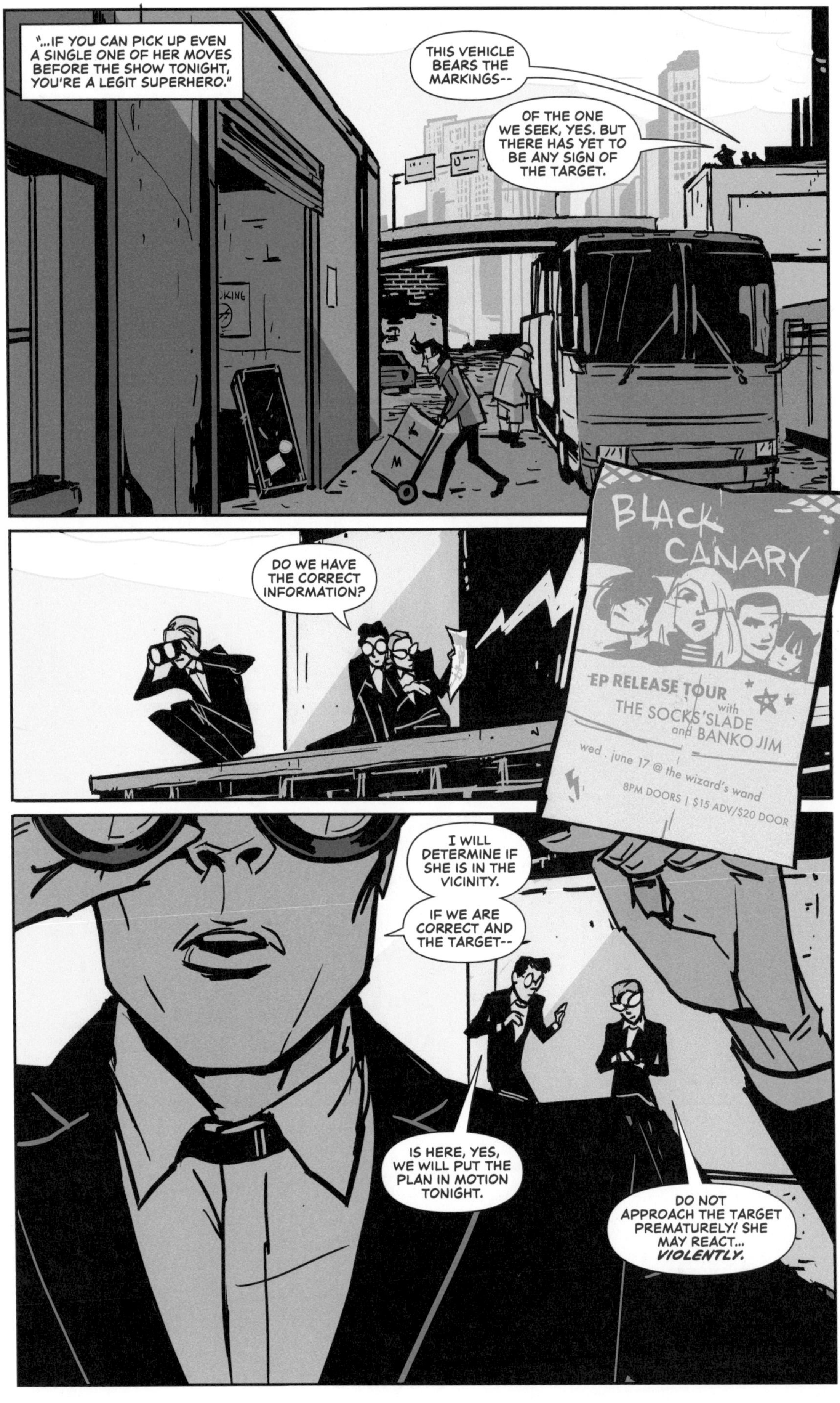
"...IF YOU CAN PICK UP EVEN A SINGLE ONE OF HER MOVES BEFORE THE SHOW TONIGHT, YOU'RE A LEGIT SUPERHERO."
THIS VEHICLE BEARS THE MARKINGS--
OF THE ONE WE SEEK, YES. BUT THERE HAS YET TO BE ANY SIGN OF THE TARGET.
DO WE HAVE THE CORRECT INFORMATION?
BLACK CANARY
EP RELEASE TOUR
with THE SOCKS'SLADE and BANKO JIM
wed . june 17 @ the wizard's wand
8PM DOORS | $15 ADV/$20 DOOR
I WILL DETERMINE IF SHE IS IN THE VICINITY.
IF WE ARE CORRECT AND THE TARGET--
IS HERE, YES, WE WILL PUT THE PLAN IN MOTION TONIGHT.
DO NOT APPROACH THE TARGET PREMATURELY! SHE MAY REACT... *VIOLENTLY.*

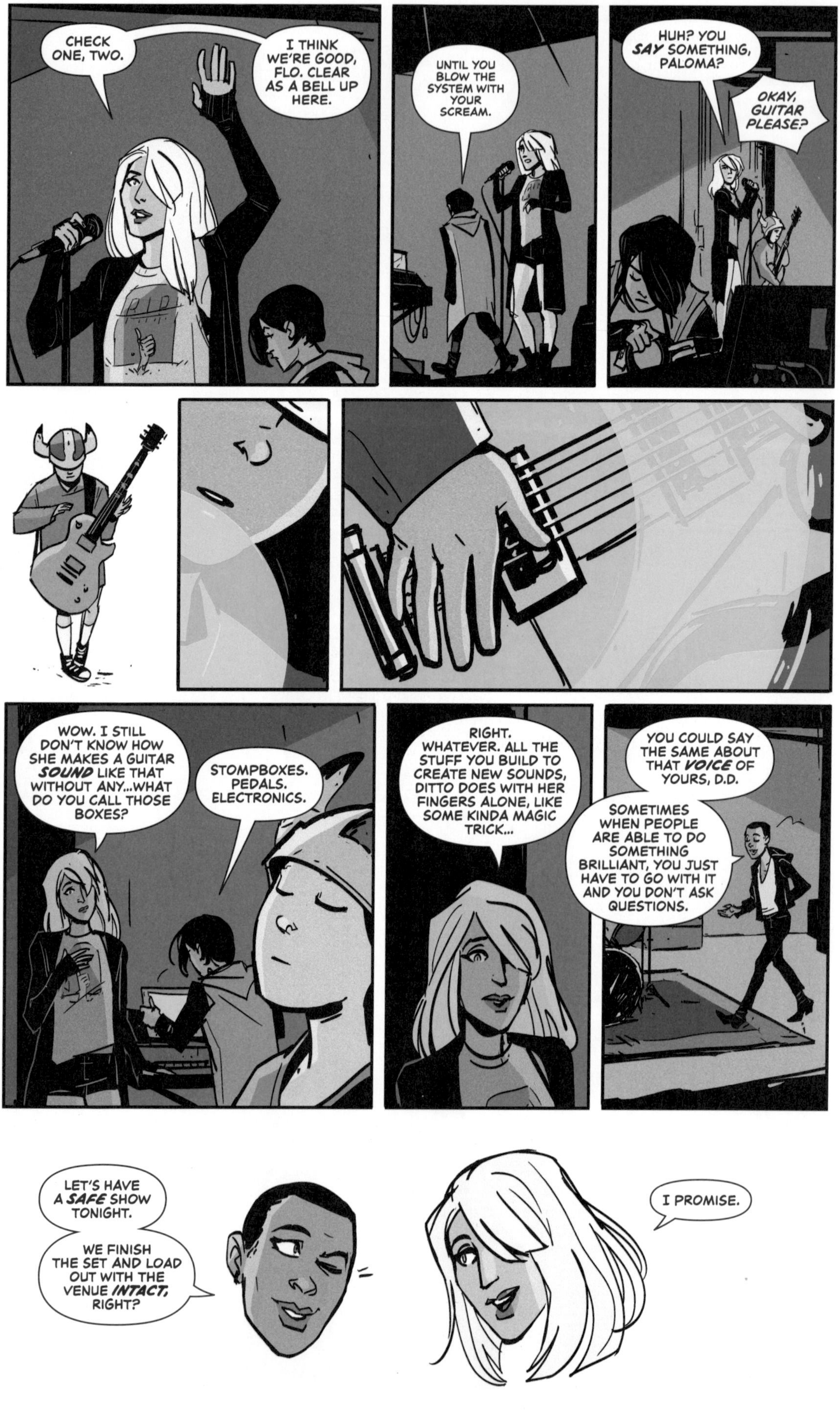
CHECK ONE, TWO.
I THINK WE'RE GOOD, FLO. CLEAR AS A BELL UP HERE.
UNTIL YOU BLOW THE SYSTEM WITH YOUR SCREAM.
HUH? YOU SAY SOMETHING, PALOMA?
OKAY, GUITAR PLEASE?
WOW. I STILL DON'T KNOW HOW SHE MAKES A GUITAR SOUND LIKE THAT WITHOUT ANY...WHAT DO YOU CALL THOSE BOXES?
STOMPBOXES. PEDALS. ELECTRONICS.
RIGHT. WHATEVER. ALL THE STUFF YOU BUILD TO CREATE NEW SOUNDS, DITTO DOES WITH HER FINGERS ALONE, LIKE SOME KINDA MAGIC TRICK...
YOU COULD SAY THE SAME ABOUT THAT VOICE OF YOURS, D.D.
SOMETIMES WHEN PEOPLE ARE ABLE TO DO SOMETHING BRILLIANT, YOU JUST HAVE TO GO WITH IT AND YOU DON'T ASK QUESTIONS.
LET'S HAVE A SAFE SHOW TONIGHT.
WE FINISH THE SET AND LOAD OUT WITH THE VENUE INTACT, RIGHT?
I PROMISE.

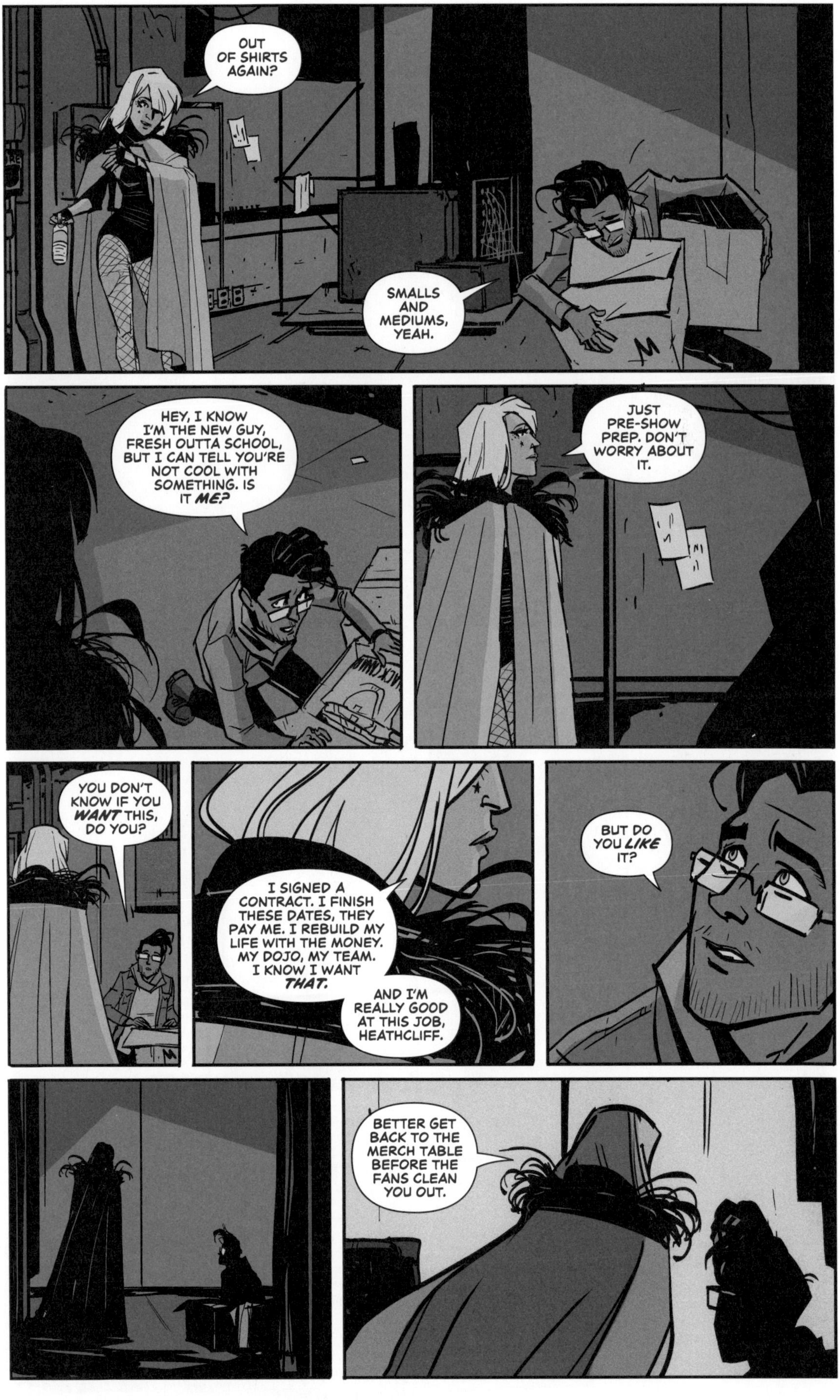
OUT OF SHIRTS AGAIN?
SMALLS AND MEDIUMS, YEAH.
HEY, I KNOW I'M THE NEW GUY, FRESH OUTTA SCHOOL, BUT I CAN TELL YOU'RE NOT COOL WITH SOMETHING. IS IT *ME?*
JUST PRE-SHOW PREP. DON'T WORRY ABOUT IT.
YOU DON'T KNOW IF YOU *WANT* THIS, DO YOU?
I SIGNED A CONTRACT. I FINISH THESE DATES, THEY PAY ME. I REBUILD MY LIFE WITH THE MONEY. MY DOJO, MY TEAM. I KNOW I WANT *THAT.*
AND I'M REALLY GOOD AT THIS JOB, HEATHCLIFF.
BUT DO YOU *LIKE* IT?
BETTER GET BACK TO THE MERCH TABLE BEFORE THE FANS CLEAN YOU OUT.

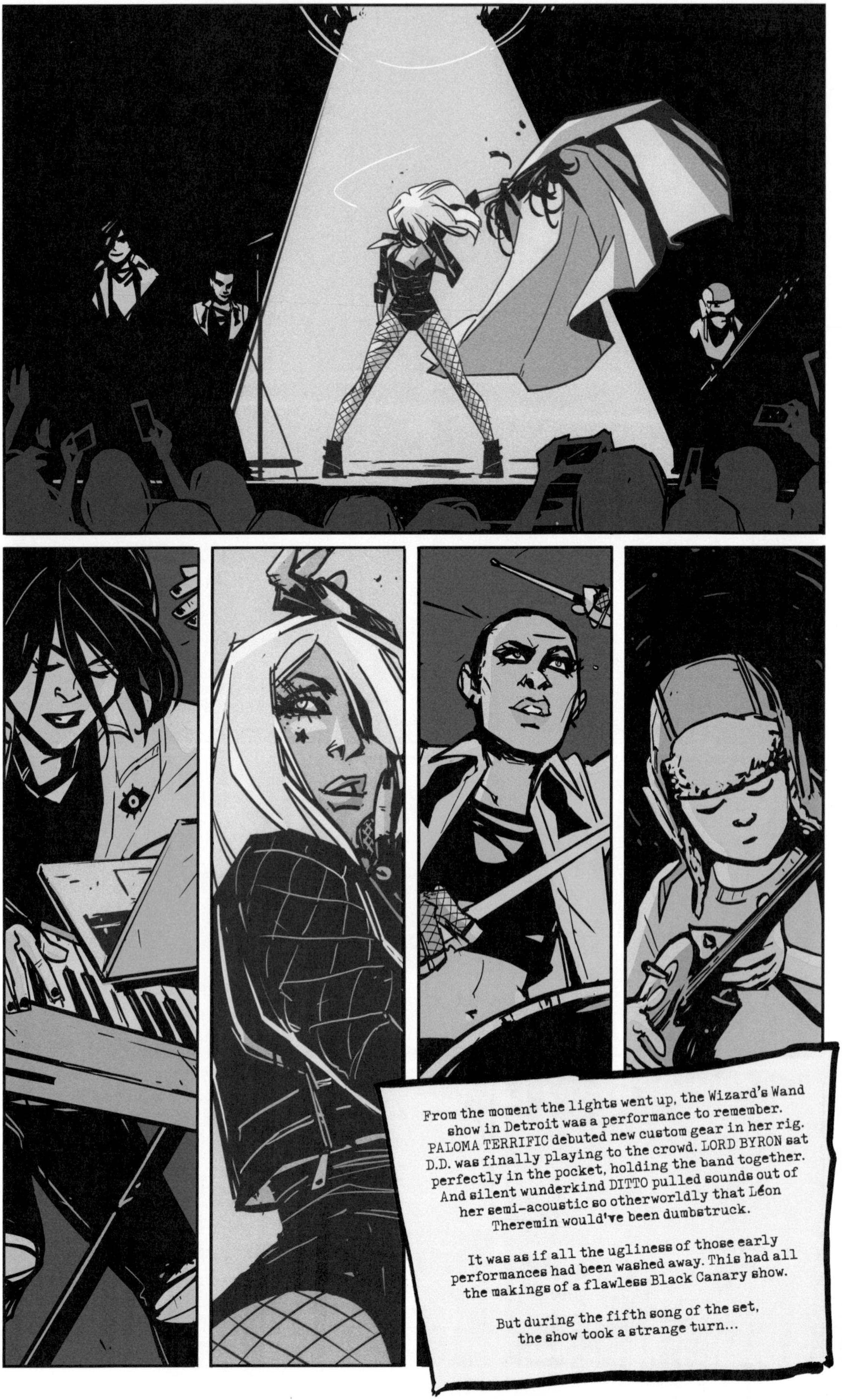
From the moment the lights went up, the Wizard's Wand show in Detroit was a performance to remember. PALOMA TERRIFIC debuted new custom gear in her rig. D.D. was finally playing to the crowd. LORD BYRON sat perfectly in the pocket, holding the band together. And silent wunderkind DITTO pulled sounds out of her semi-acoustic so otherworldly that Léon Theremin would've been dumbstruck.
It was as if all the ugliness of those early performances had been washed away. This had all the makings of a flawless Black Canary show.
But during the fifth song of the set, the show took a strange turn...

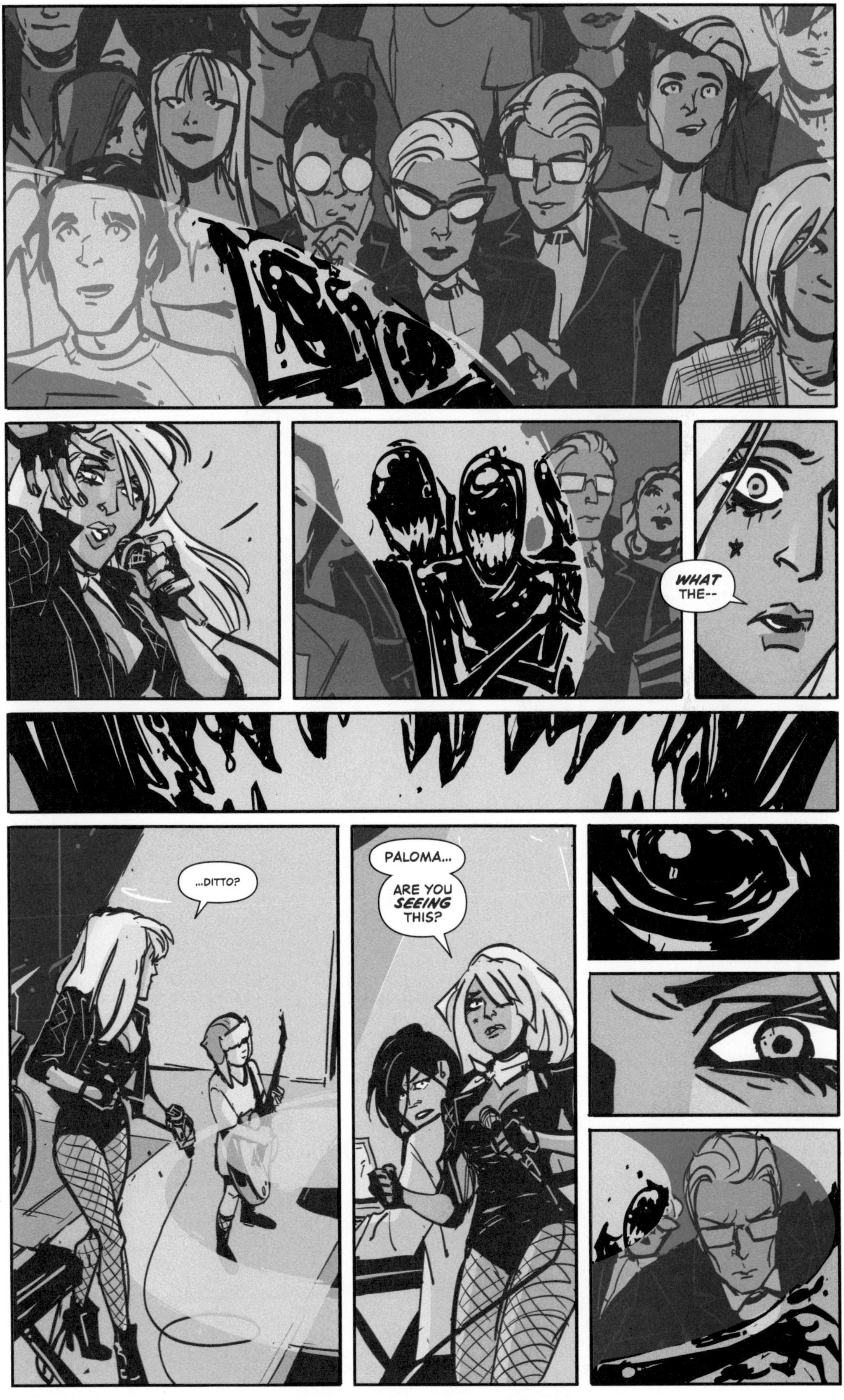
WHAT THE--
...DITTO?
PALOMA...
ARE YOU SEEING THIS?

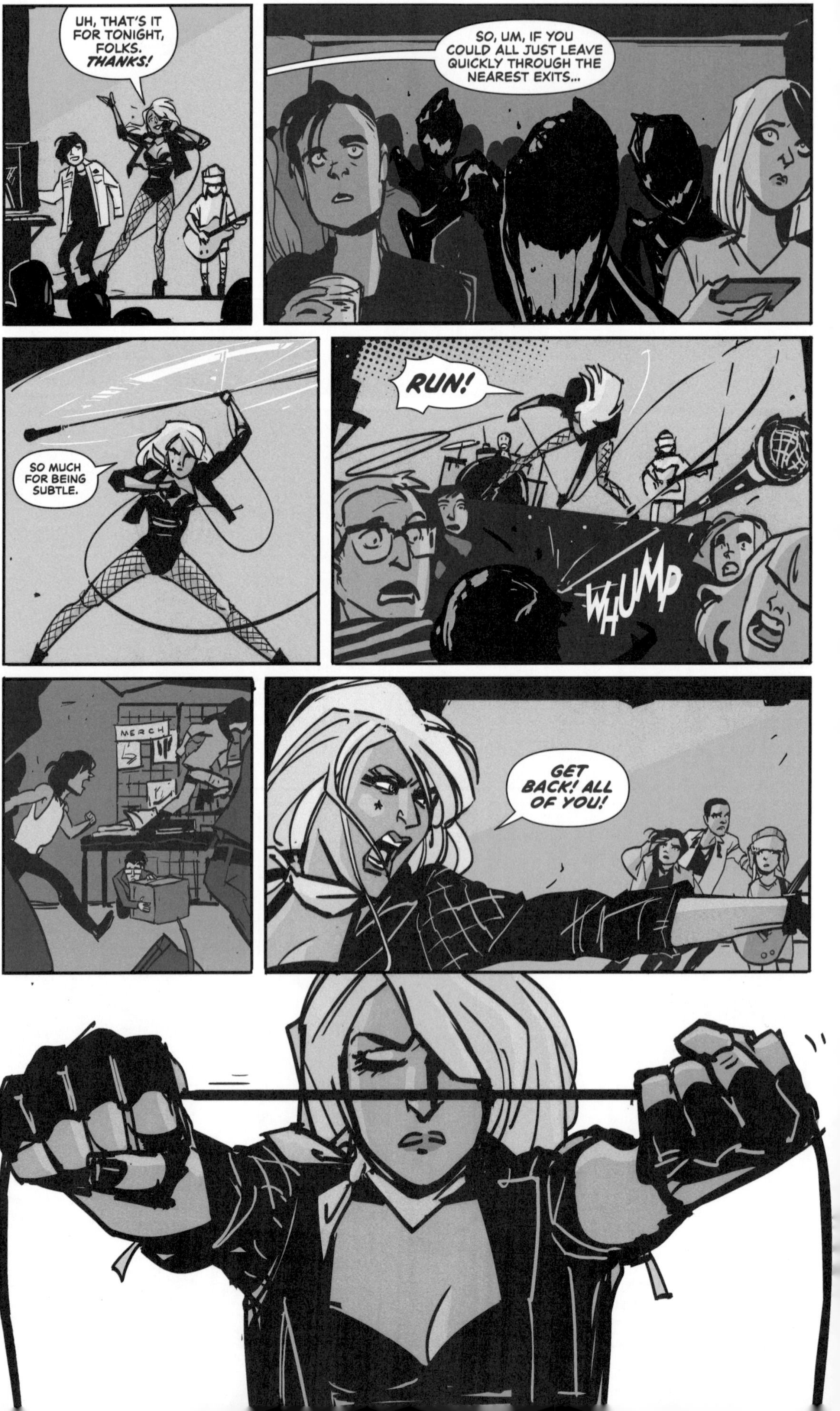
UH, THAT'S IT FOR TONIGHT, FOLKS. THANKS!
SO, UM, IF YOU COULD ALL JUST LEAVE QUICKLY THROUGH THE NEAREST EXITS...
SO MUCH FOR BEING SUBTLE.
RUN!
WHUMP
MERCH
GET BACK! ALL OF YOU!

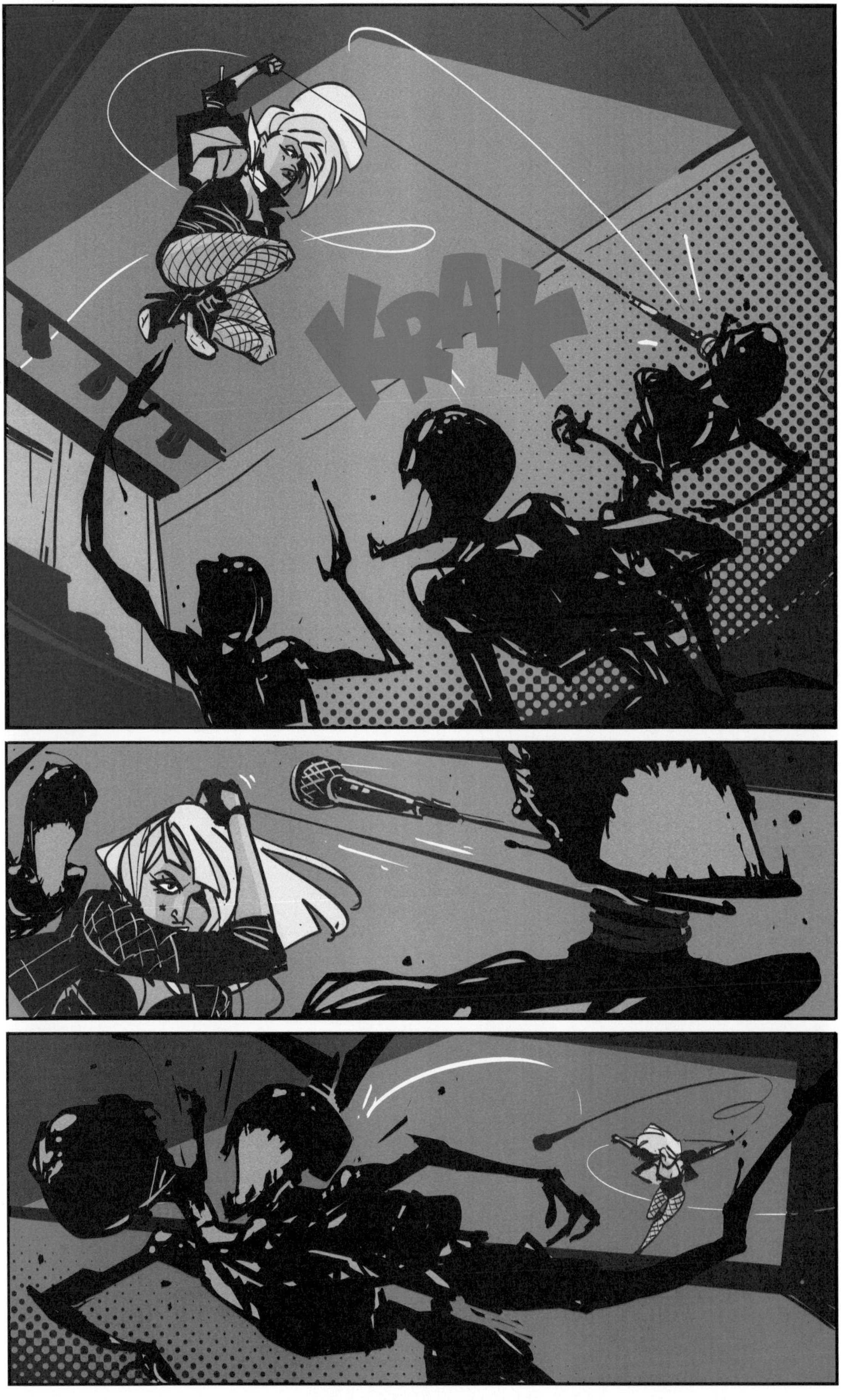
KRAK

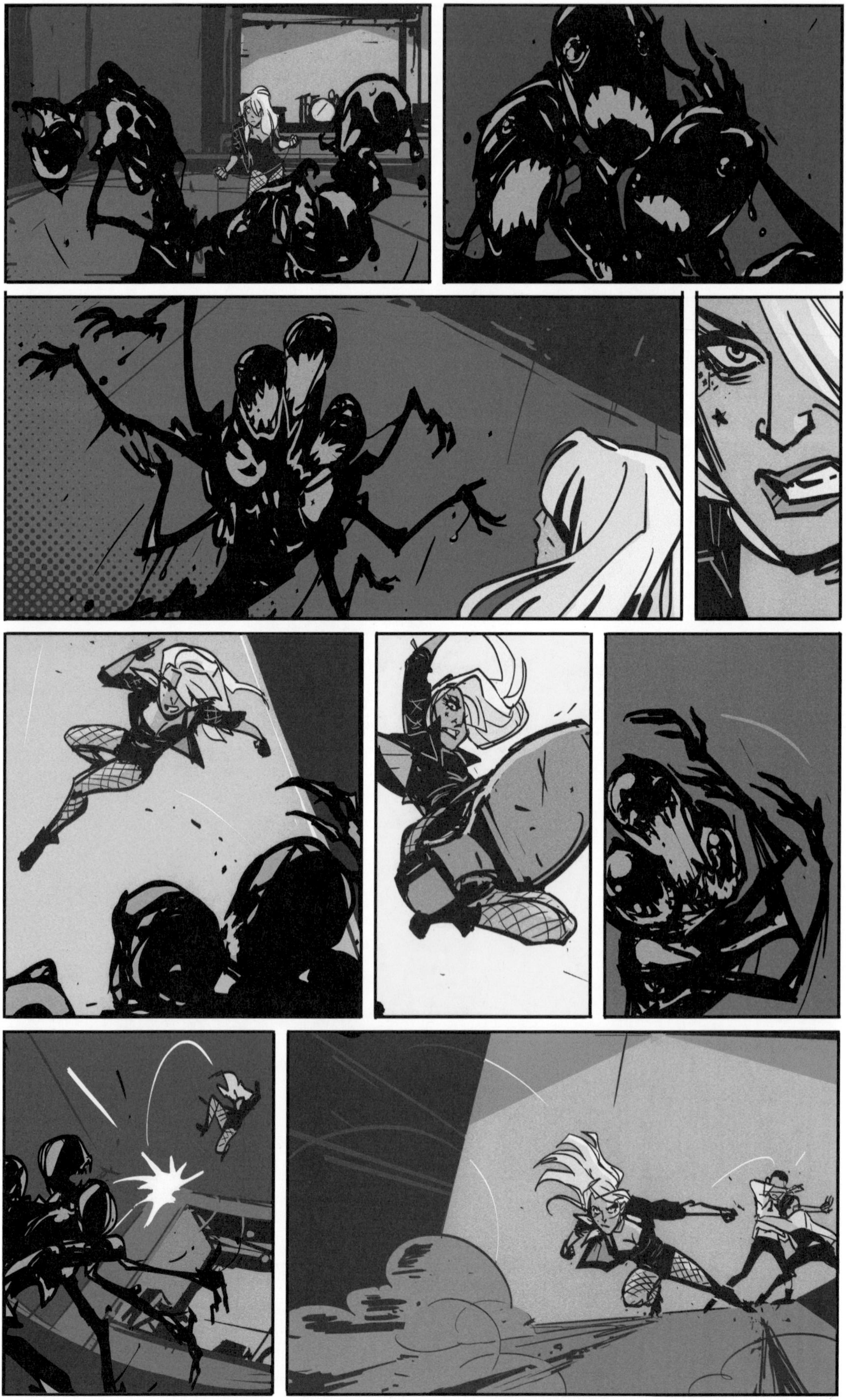

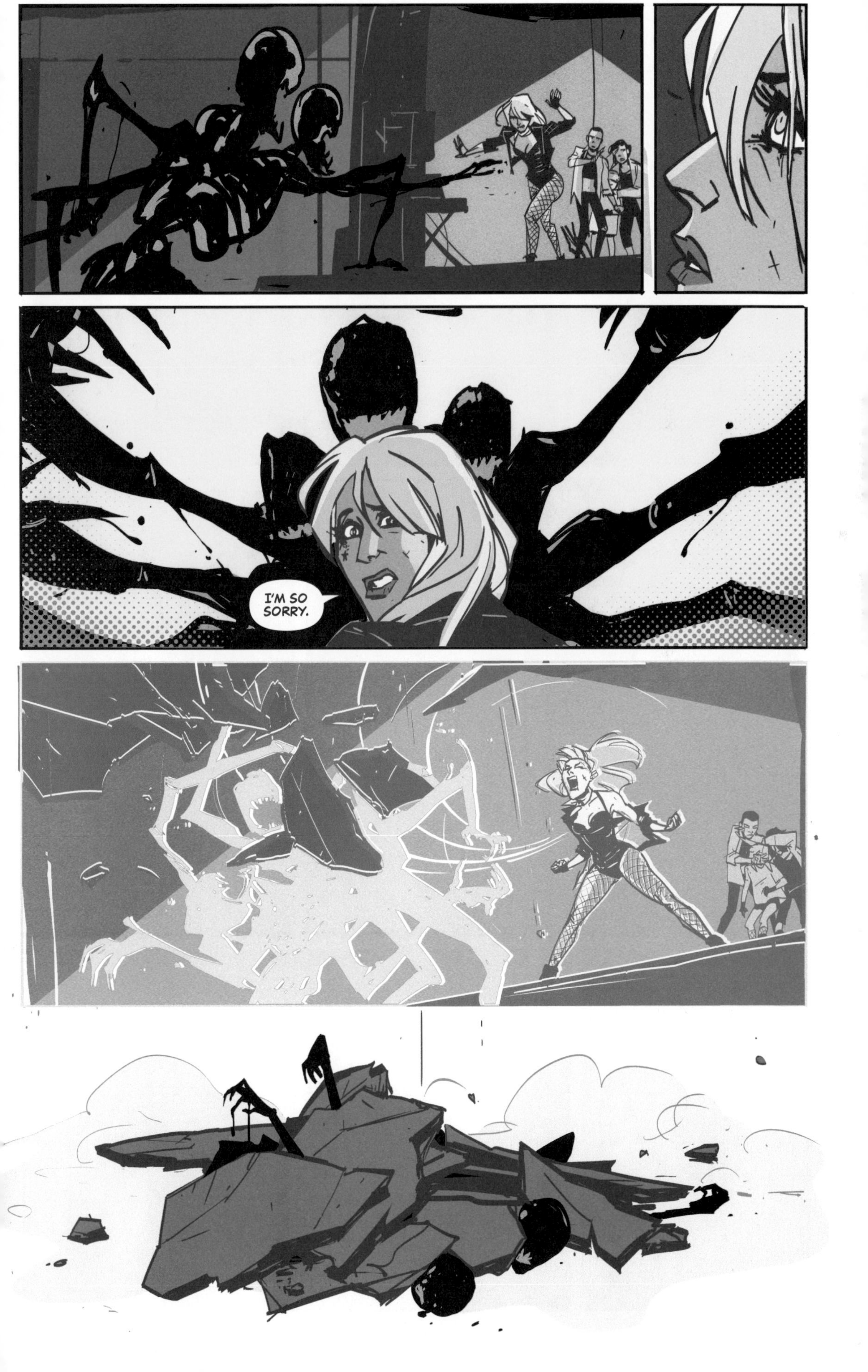
I'M SO SORRY.

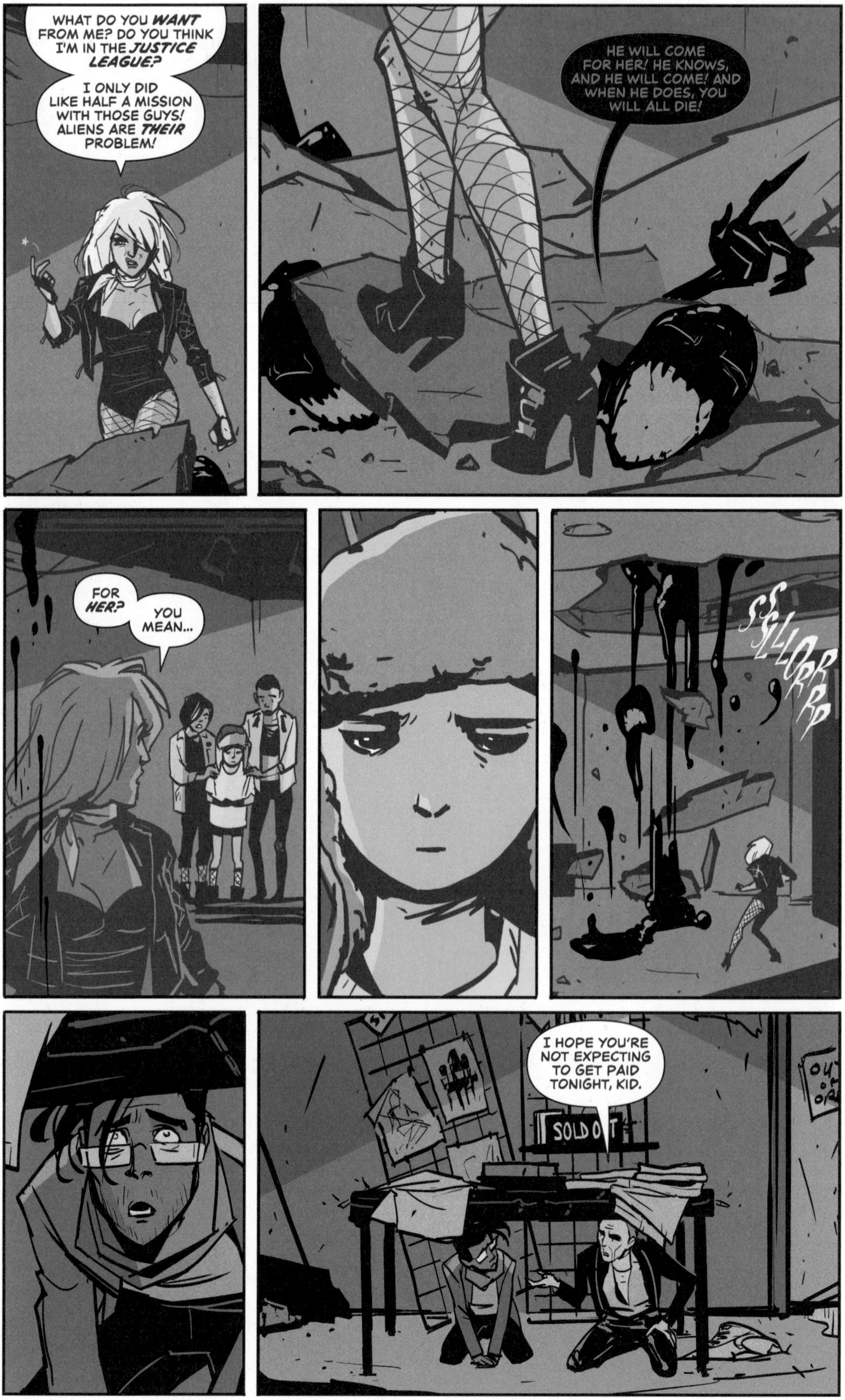
WHAT DO YOU *WANT* FROM ME? DO YOU THINK I'M IN THE *JUSTICE LEAGUE?*
I ONLY DID LIKE HALF A MISSION WITH THOSE GUYS! ALIENS ARE *THEIR* PROBLEM!
HE WILL COME FOR HER! HE KNOWS, AND HE WILL COME! AND WHEN HE DOES, YOU WILL ALL DIE!
FOR *HER?*
YOU MEAN...
SSLLORRRP
I HOPE YOU'RE NOT EXPECTING TO GET PAID TONIGHT, KID.
SOLD OUT

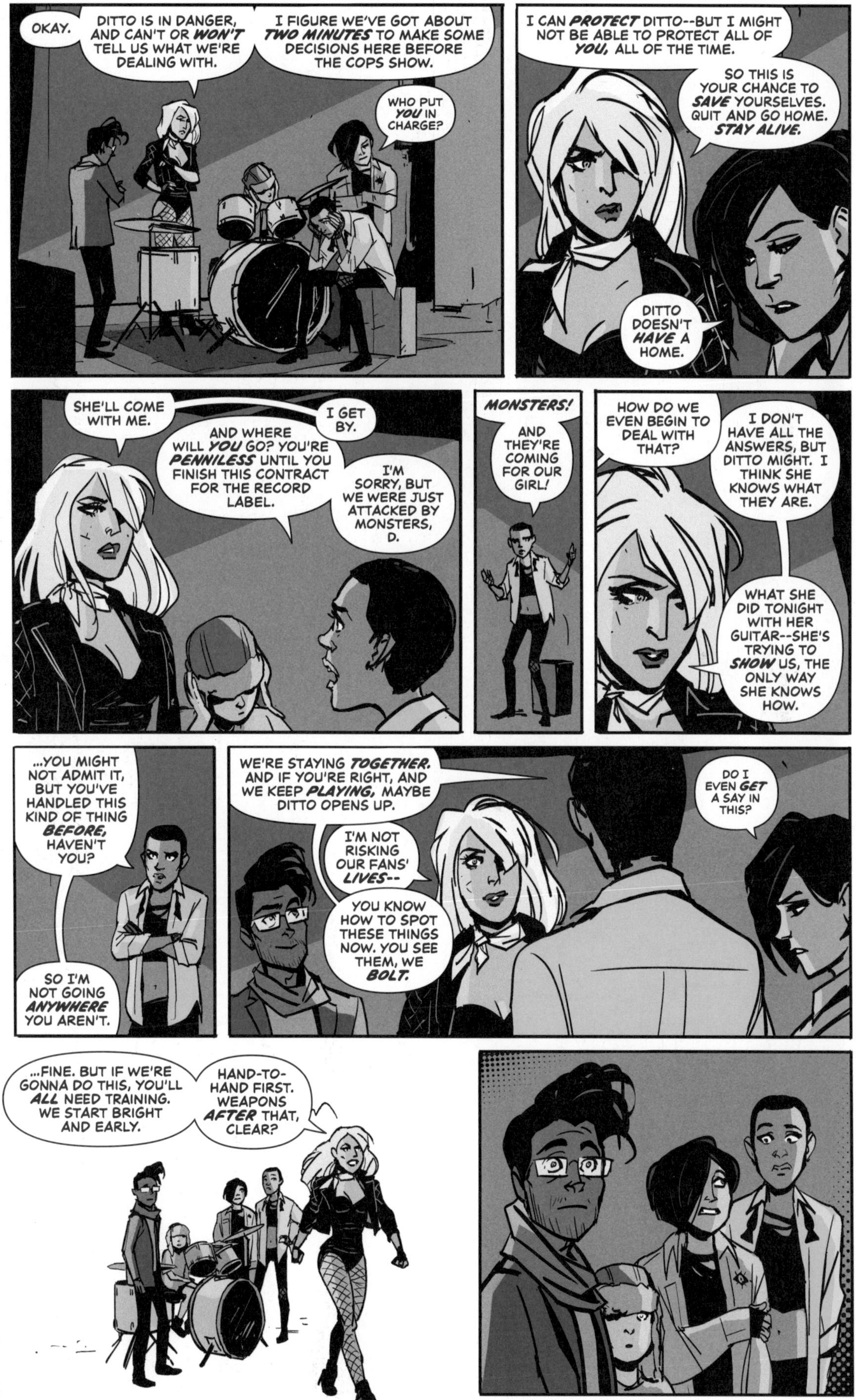
OKAY.
DITTO IS IN DANGER, AND CAN'T OR WON'T TELL US WHAT WE'RE DEALING WITH.
I FIGURE WE'VE GOT ABOUT TWO MINUTES TO MAKE SOME DECISIONS HERE BEFORE THE COPS SHOW.
WHO PUT YOU IN CHARGE?
I CAN PROTECT DITTO--BUT I MIGHT NOT BE ABLE TO PROTECT ALL OF YOU, ALL OF THE TIME.
SO THIS IS YOUR CHANCE TO SAVE YOURSELVES. QUIT AND GO HOME. STAY ALIVE.
DITTO DOESN'T HAVE A HOME.
SHE'LL COME WITH ME.
I GET BY.
AND WHERE WILL YOU GO? YOU'RE PENNILESS UNTIL YOU FINISH THIS CONTRACT FOR THE RECORD LABEL.
I'M SORRY, BUT WE WERE JUST ATTACKED BY MONSTERS, D.
MONSTERS!
AND THEY'RE COMING FOR OUR GIRL!
HOW DO WE EVEN BEGIN TO DEAL WITH THAT?
I DON'T HAVE ALL THE ANSWERS, BUT DITTO MIGHT. I THINK SHE KNOWS WHAT THEY ARE.
WHAT SHE DID TONIGHT WITH HER GUITAR--SHE'S TRYING TO SHOW US, THE ONLY WAY SHE KNOWS HOW.
...YOU MIGHT NOT ADMIT IT, BUT YOU'VE HANDLED THIS KIND OF THING BEFORE, HAVEN'T YOU?
SO I'M NOT GOING ANYWHERE YOU AREN'T.
WE'RE STAYING TOGETHER. AND IF YOU'RE RIGHT, AND WE KEEP PLAYING, MAYBE DITTO OPENS UP.
I'M NOT RISKING OUR FANS' LIVES--
YOU KNOW HOW TO SPOT THESE THINGS NOW. YOU SEE THEM, WE BOLT.
DO I EVEN GET A SAY IN THIS?
...FINE. BUT IF WE'RE GONNA DO THIS, YOU'LL ALL NEED TRAINING. WE START BRIGHT AND EARLY.
HAND-TO-HAND FIRST. WEAPONS AFTER THAT, CLEAR?

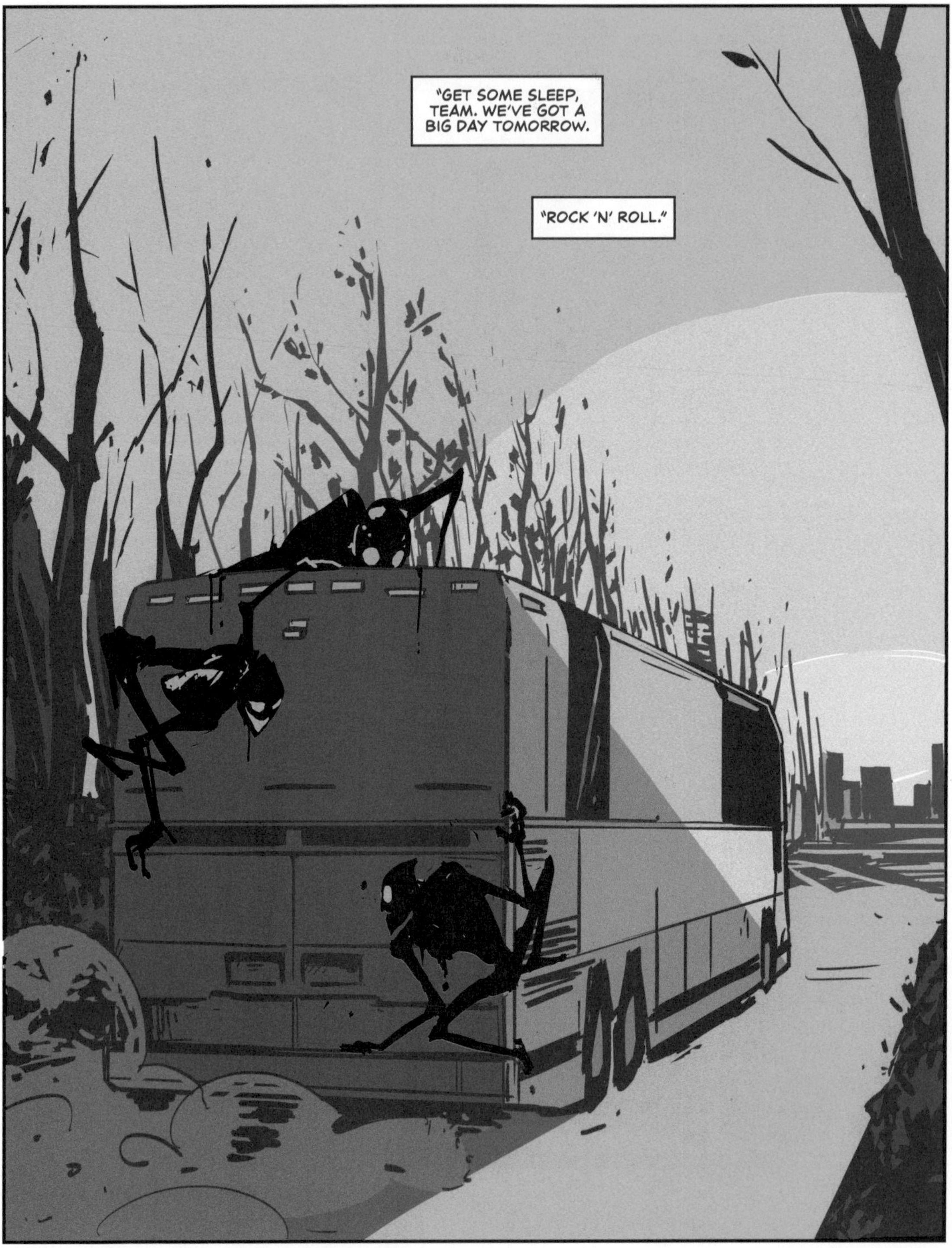
"GET SOME SLEEP, TEAM. WE'VE GOT A BIG DAY TOMORROW.
"ROCK 'N' ROLL."

BLACK CANARY

PLAYLIST: UP NEXT!

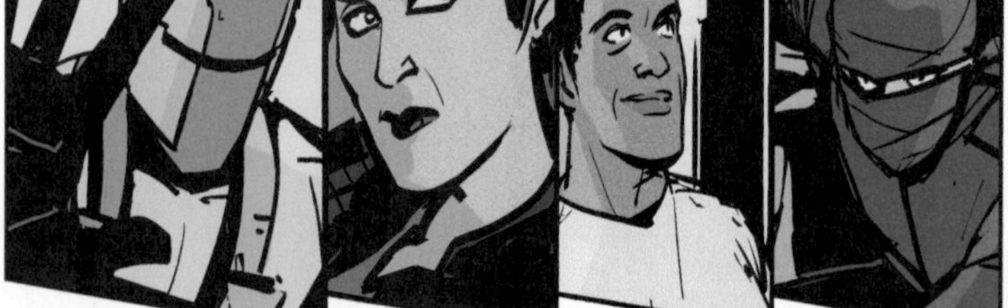

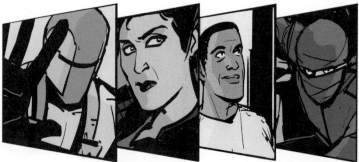

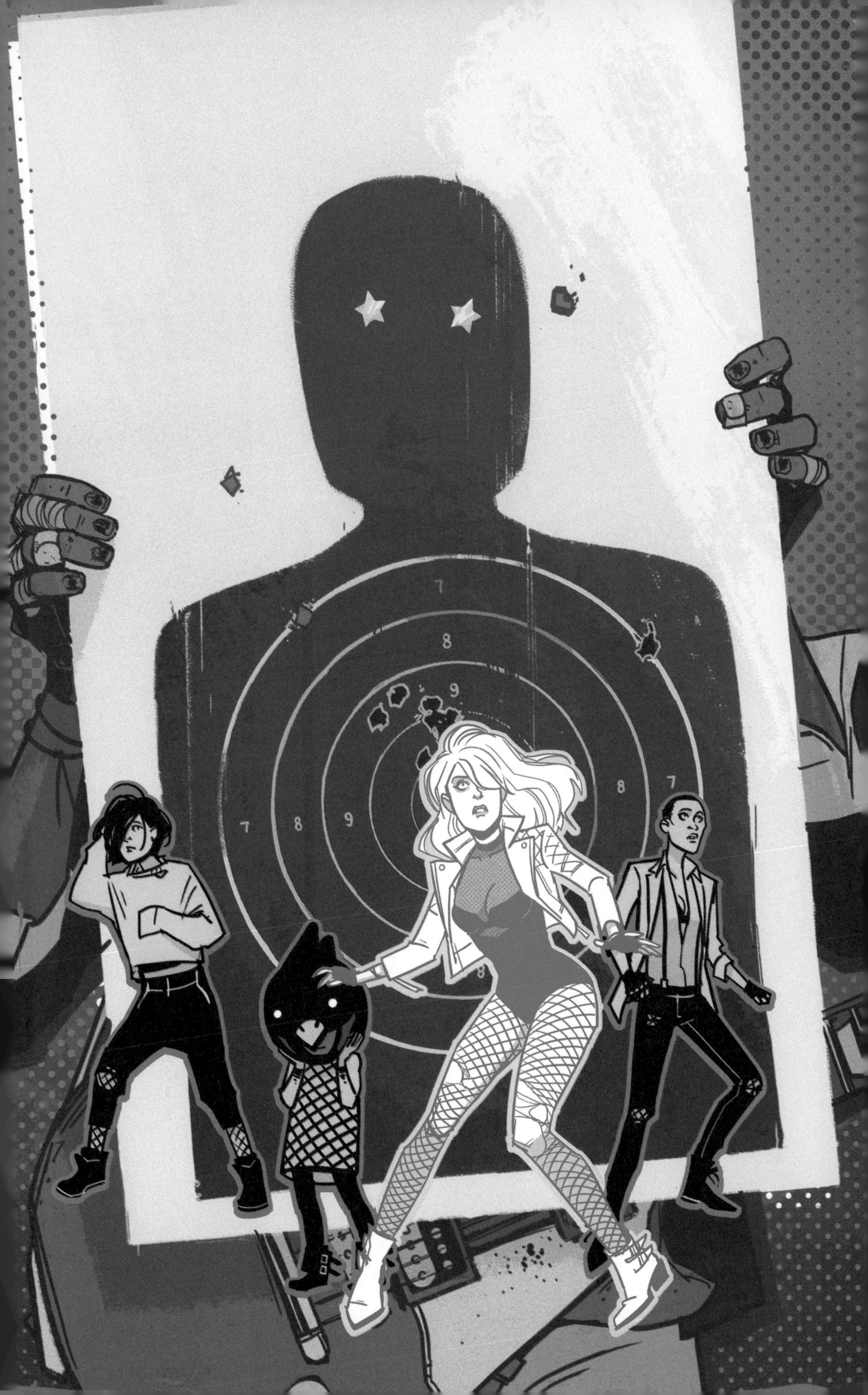

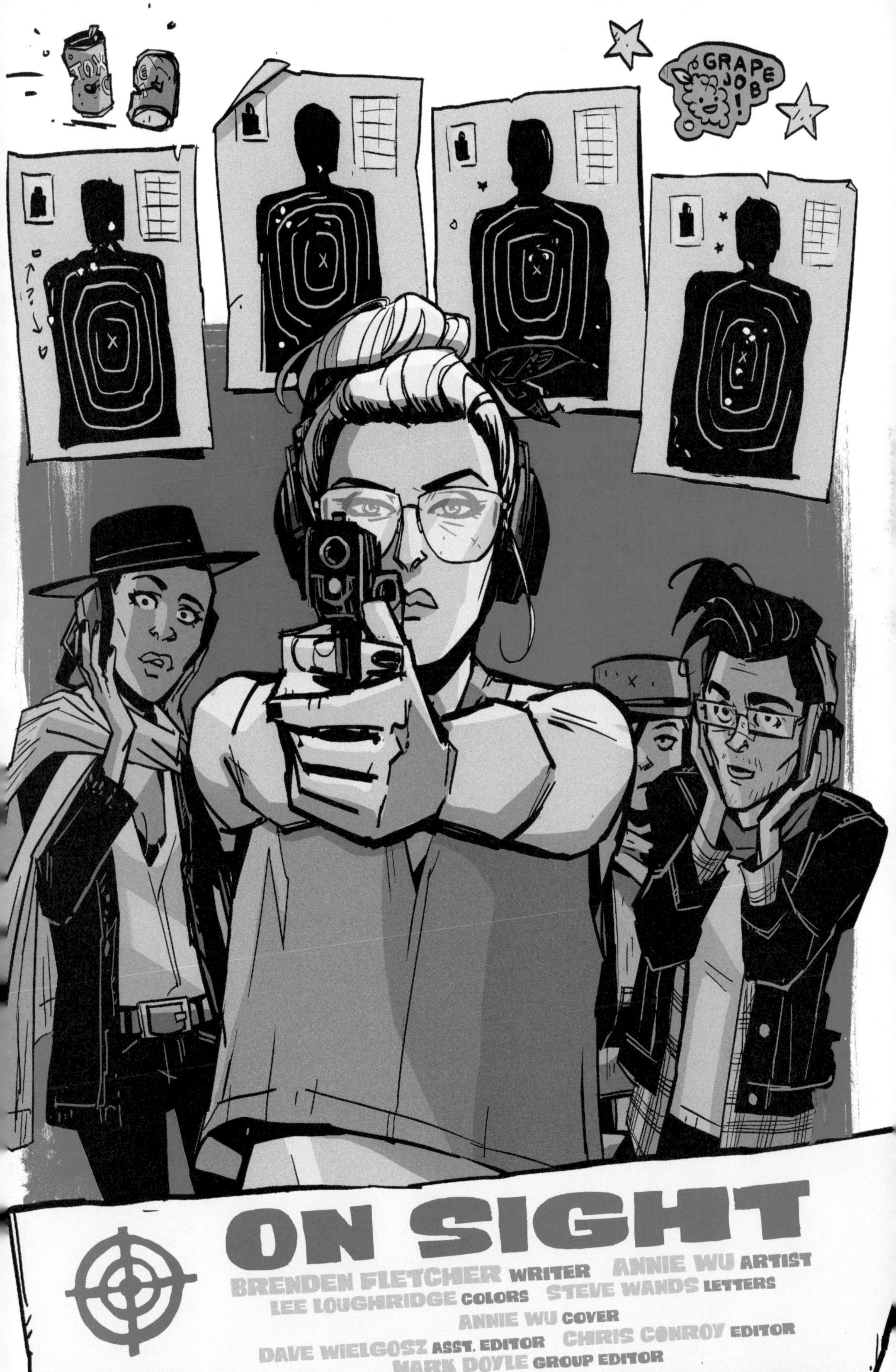
GRAPE JOB!

ON SIGHT

BRENDEN FLETCHER WRITER ANNIE WU ARTIST
LEE LOUGHRIDGE COLORS STEVE WANDS LETTERS
ANNIE WU COVER
DAVE WIELGOSZ ASST. EDITOR CHRIS CONROY EDITOR
MARK DOYLE GROUP EDITOR

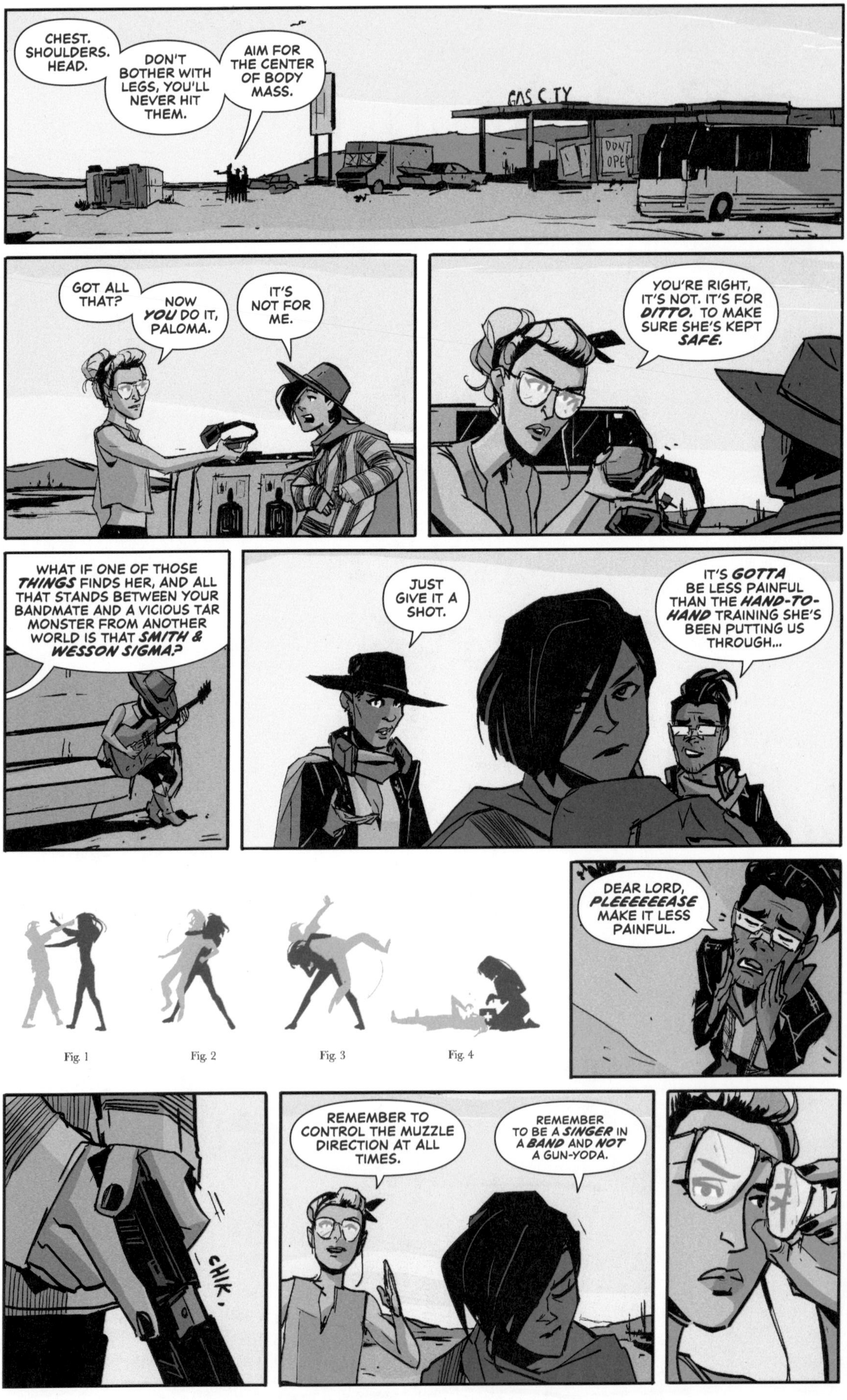
CHEST. SHOULDERS. HEAD.
DON'T BOTHER WITH LEGS, YOU'LL NEVER HIT THEM.
AIM FOR THE CENTER OF BODY MASS.
GAS C TY
GOT ALL THAT?
NOW *YOU* DO IT, PALOMA.
IT'S NOT FOR ME.
YOU'RE RIGHT, IT'S NOT. IT'S FOR *DITTO.* TO MAKE SURE SHE'S KEPT *SAFE.*
WHAT IF ONE OF THOSE *THINGS* FINDS HER, AND ALL THAT STANDS BETWEEN YOUR BANDMATE AND A VICIOUS TAR MONSTER FROM ANOTHER WORLD IS THAT *SMITH & WESSON SIGMA?*
JUST GIVE IT A SHOT.
IT'S *GOTTA* BE LESS PAINFUL THAN THE *HAND-TO-HAND* TRAINING SHE'S BEEN PUTTING US THROUGH...
Fig. 1
Fig. 2
Fig. 3
Fig. 4
DEAR LORD, *PLEEEEEEASE* MAKE IT LESS PAINFUL.
CHIK
REMEMBER TO CONTROL THE MUZZLE DIRECTION AT ALL TIMES.
REMEMBER TO BE A *SINGER* IN A *BAND* AND *NOT* A GUN-YODA.

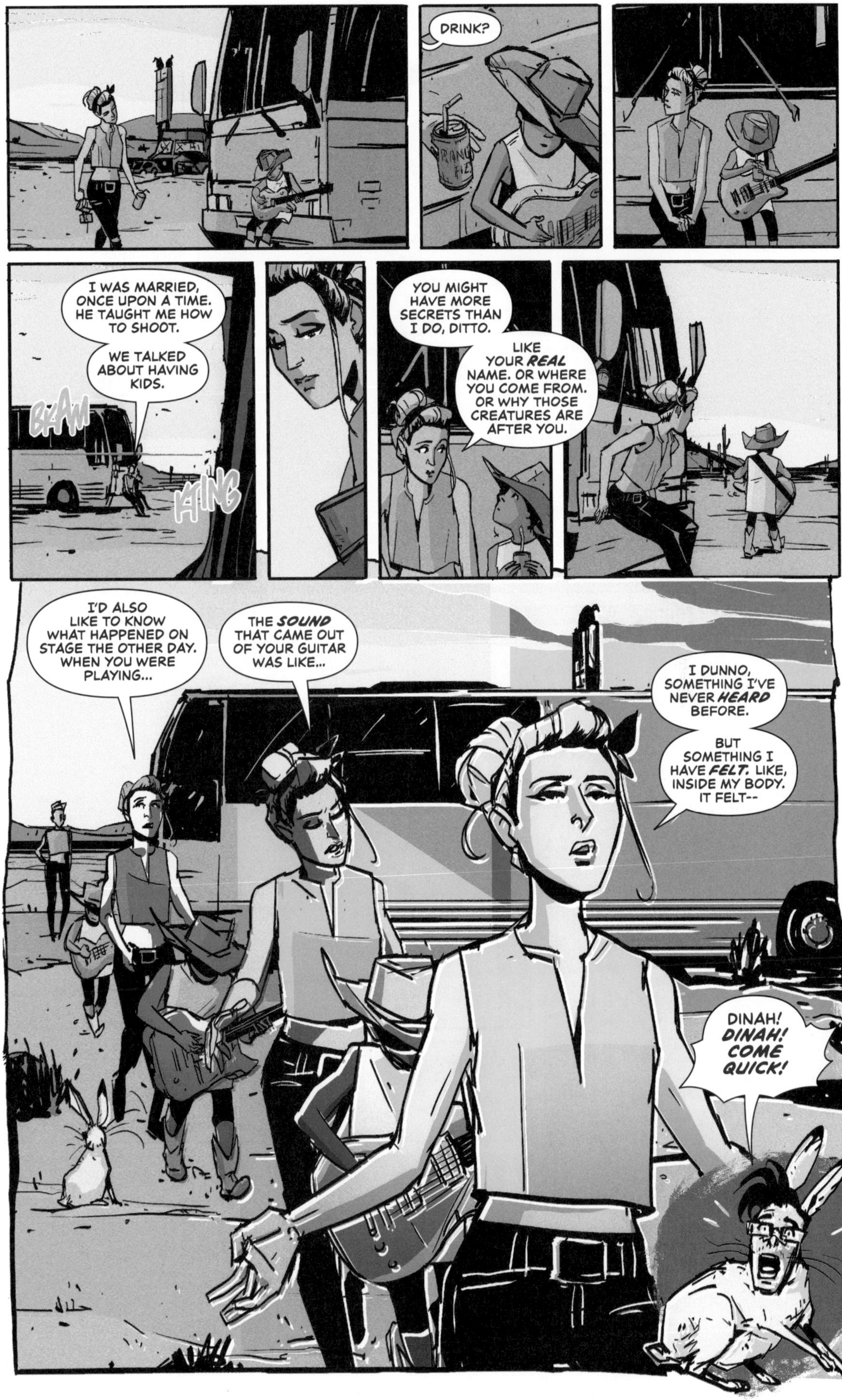
DRINK?
I WAS MARRIED, ONCE UPON A TIME. HE TAUGHT ME HOW TO SHOOT.
WE TALKED ABOUT HAVING KIDS.
BKAM
KATING
YOU MIGHT HAVE MORE SECRETS THAN I DO, DITTO.
LIKE YOUR *REAL* NAME. OR WHERE YOU COME FROM. OR WHY THOSE CREATURES ARE AFTER YOU.
I'D ALSO LIKE TO KNOW WHAT HAPPENED ON STAGE THE OTHER DAY. WHEN YOU WERE PLAYING...
THE *SOUND* THAT CAME OUT OF YOUR GUITAR WAS LIKE...
I DUNNO, SOMETHING I'VE NEVER *HEARD* BEFORE.
BUT SOMETHING I HAVE *FELT*. LIKE, INSIDE MY BODY. IT FELT--
DINAH! *DINAH! COME QUICK!*

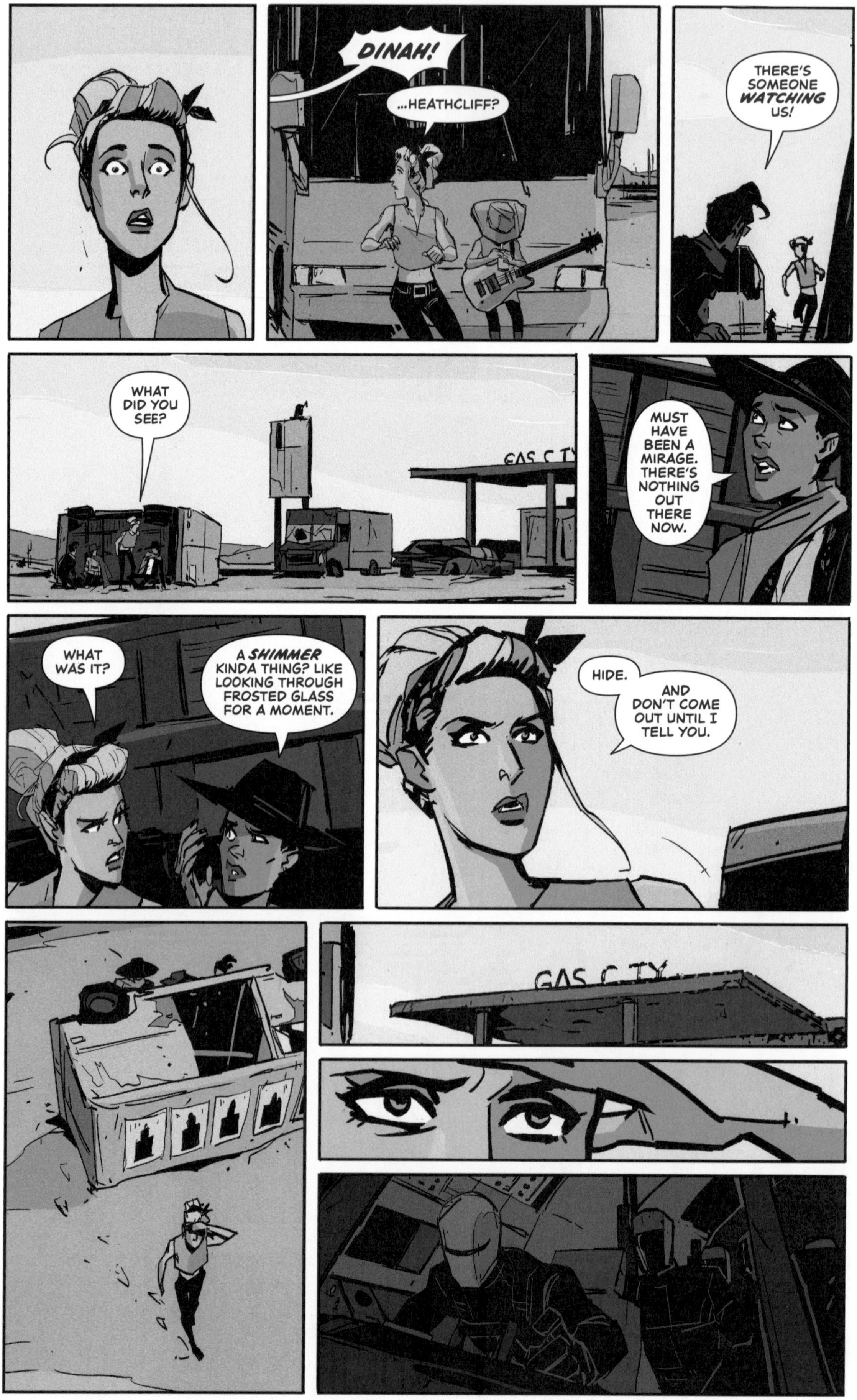
DINAH!
...HEATHCLIFF?
THERE'S SOMEONE WATCHING US!
WHAT DID YOU SEE?
GAS C TY
MUST HAVE BEEN A MIRAGE. THERE'S NOTHING OUT THERE NOW.
WHAT WAS IT?
A SHIMMER KINDA THING? LIKE LOOKING THROUGH FROSTED GLASS FOR A MOMENT.
HIDE.
AND DON'T COME OUT UNTIL I TELL YOU.
GAS C TY

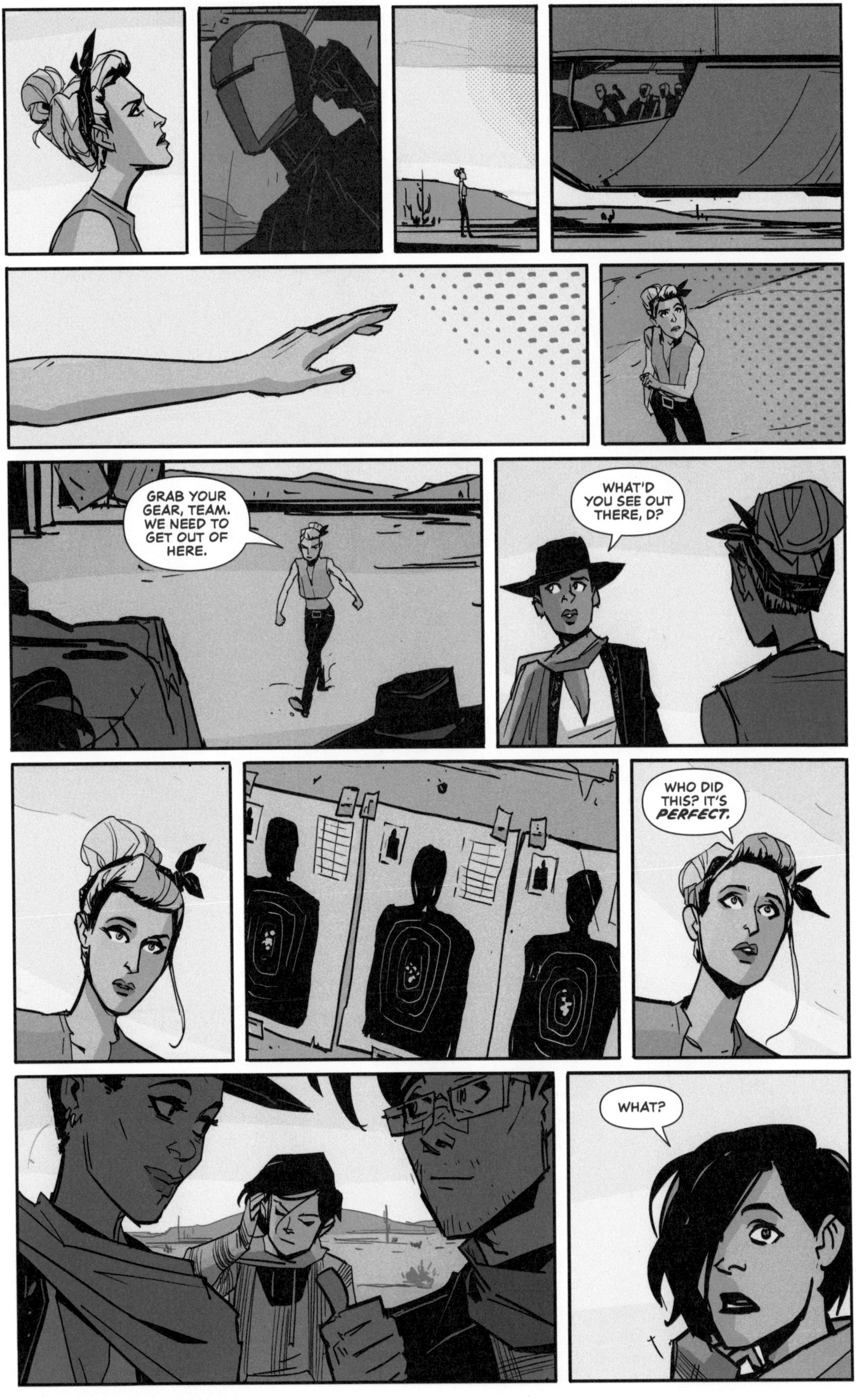
GRAB YOUR GEAR, TEAM. WE NEED TO GET OUT OF HERE.
WHAT'D YOU SEE OUT THERE, D?
WHO DID THIS? IT'S *PERFECT.*
WHAT?

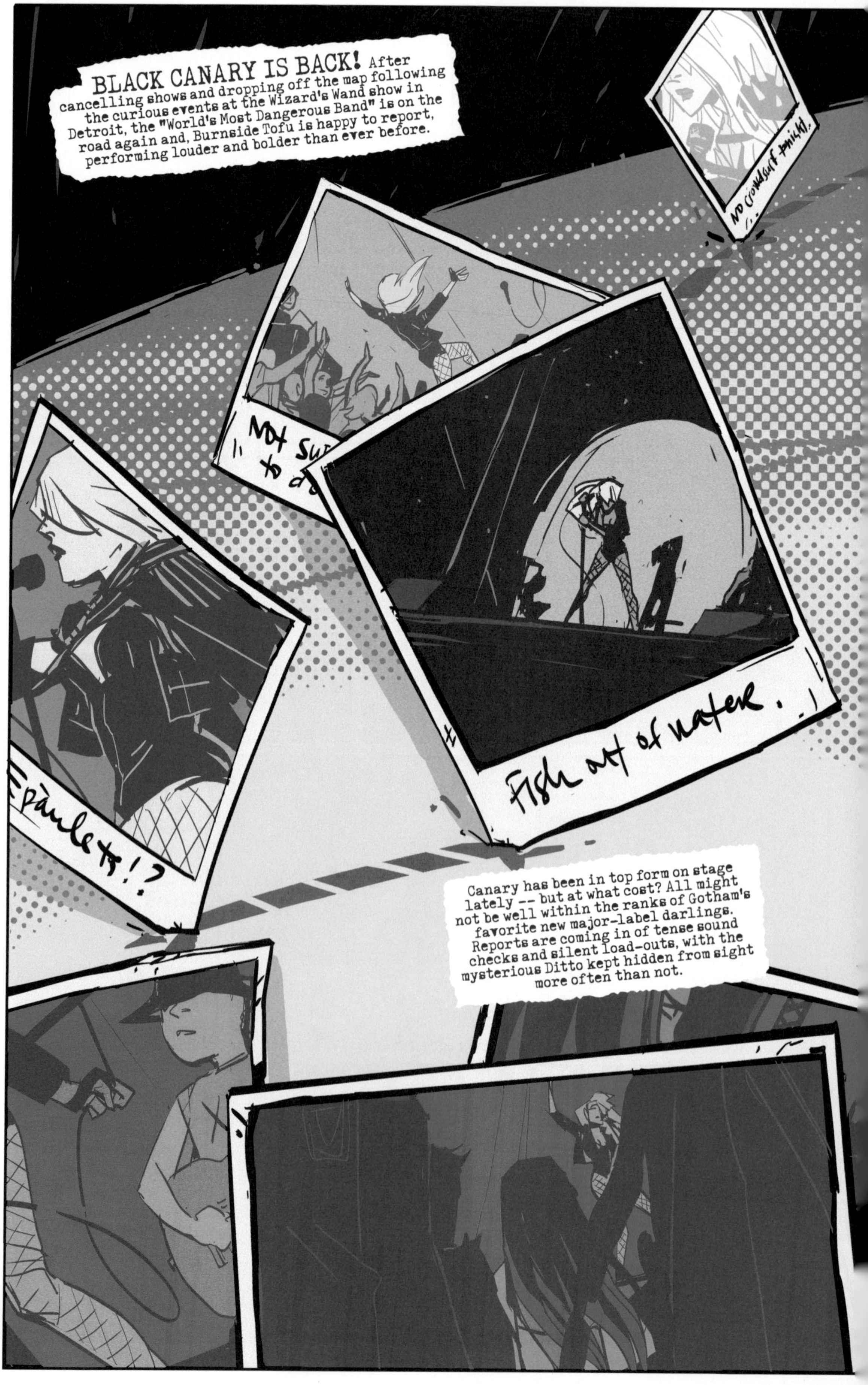
BLACK CANARY IS BACK! After cancelling shows and dropping off the map following the curious events at the Wizard's Wand show in Detroit, the "World's Most Dangerous Band" is on the road again and, Burnside Tofu is happy to report, performing louder and bolder than ever before.
NO crowdsurf
Fish out of water.
Epaulets!?
Canary has been in top form on stage lately -- but at what cost? All might not be well within the ranks of Gotham's favorite new major-label darlings. Reports are coming in of tense sound checks and silent load-outs, with the mysterious Ditto kept hidden from sight more often than not.

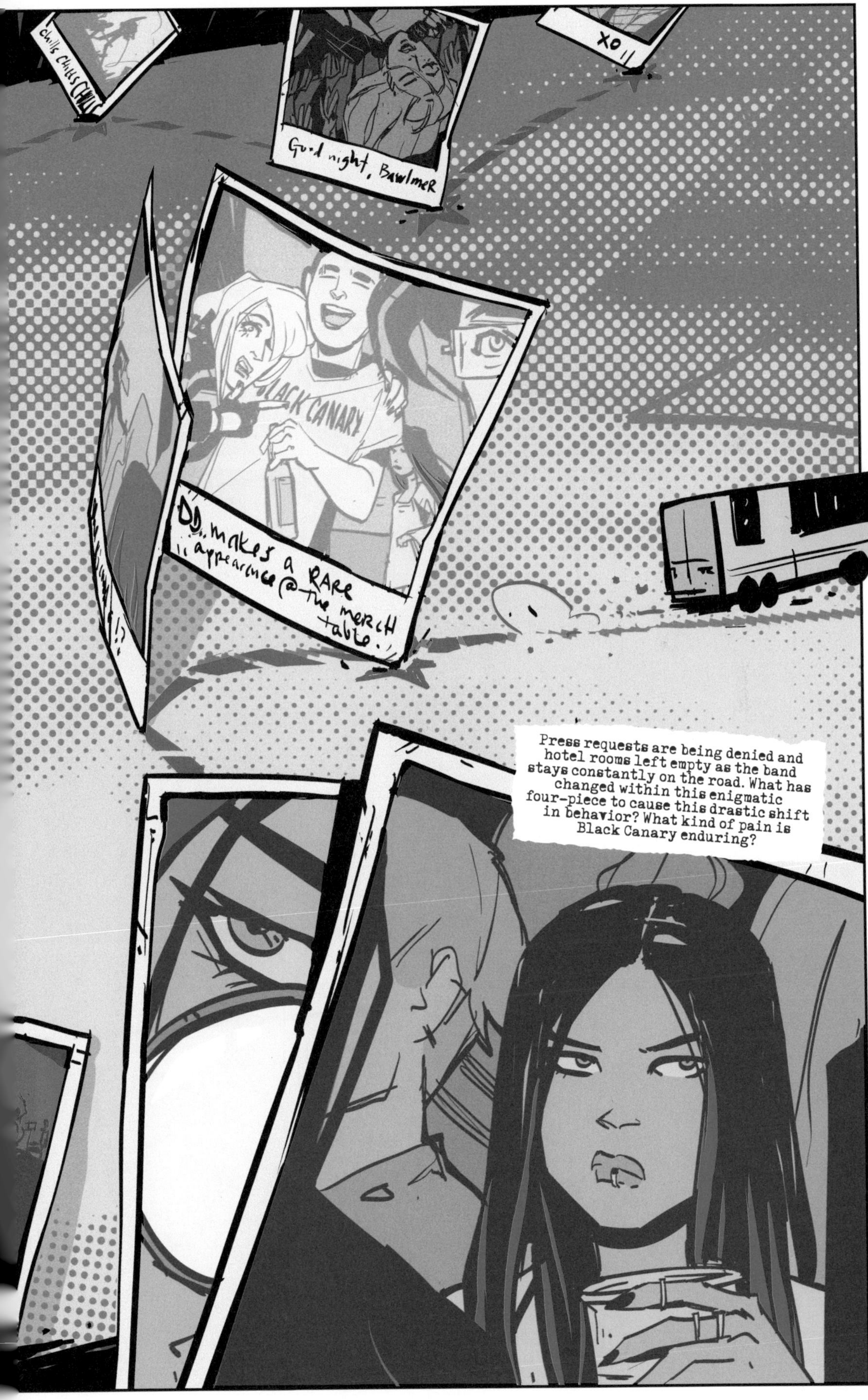
Chills Chills CHILL
Good night, Bawlmer
XO
BLACK CANARY
DD makes a RARE appearance @ the merch table.
Press requests are being denied and hotel rooms left empty as the band stays constantly on the road. What has changed within this enigmatic four-piece to cause this drastic shift in behavior? What kind of pain is Black Canary enduring?

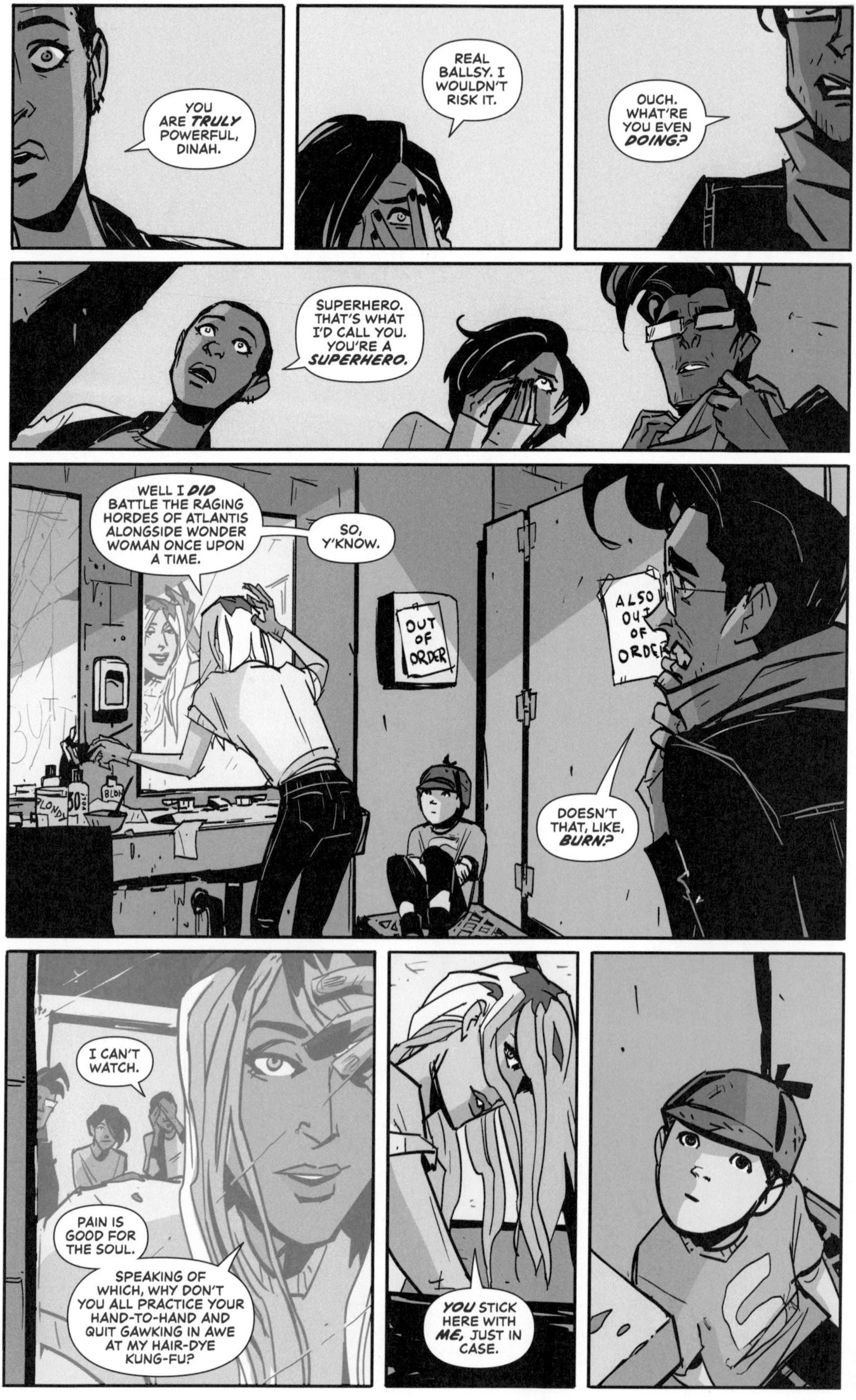

YOU ARE TRULY POWERFUL, DINAH.
REAL BALLSY. I WOULDN'T RISK IT.
OUCH. WHAT'RE YOU EVEN DOING?
SUPERHERO. THAT'S WHAT I'D CALL YOU. YOU'RE A SUPERHERO.
WELL I DID BATTLE THE RAGING HORDES OF ATLANTIS ALONGSIDE WONDER WOMAN ONCE UPON A TIME.
SO, Y'KNOW.
OUT OF ORDER
ALSO OUT OF ORDER
DOESN'T THAT, LIKE, BURN?
I CAN'T WATCH.
PAIN IS GOOD FOR THE SOUL.
SPEAKING OF WHICH, WHY DON'T YOU ALL PRACTICE YOUR HAND-TO-HAND AND QUIT GAWKING IN AWE AT MY HAIR-DYE KUNG-FU?
YOU STICK HERE WITH ME, JUST IN CASE.

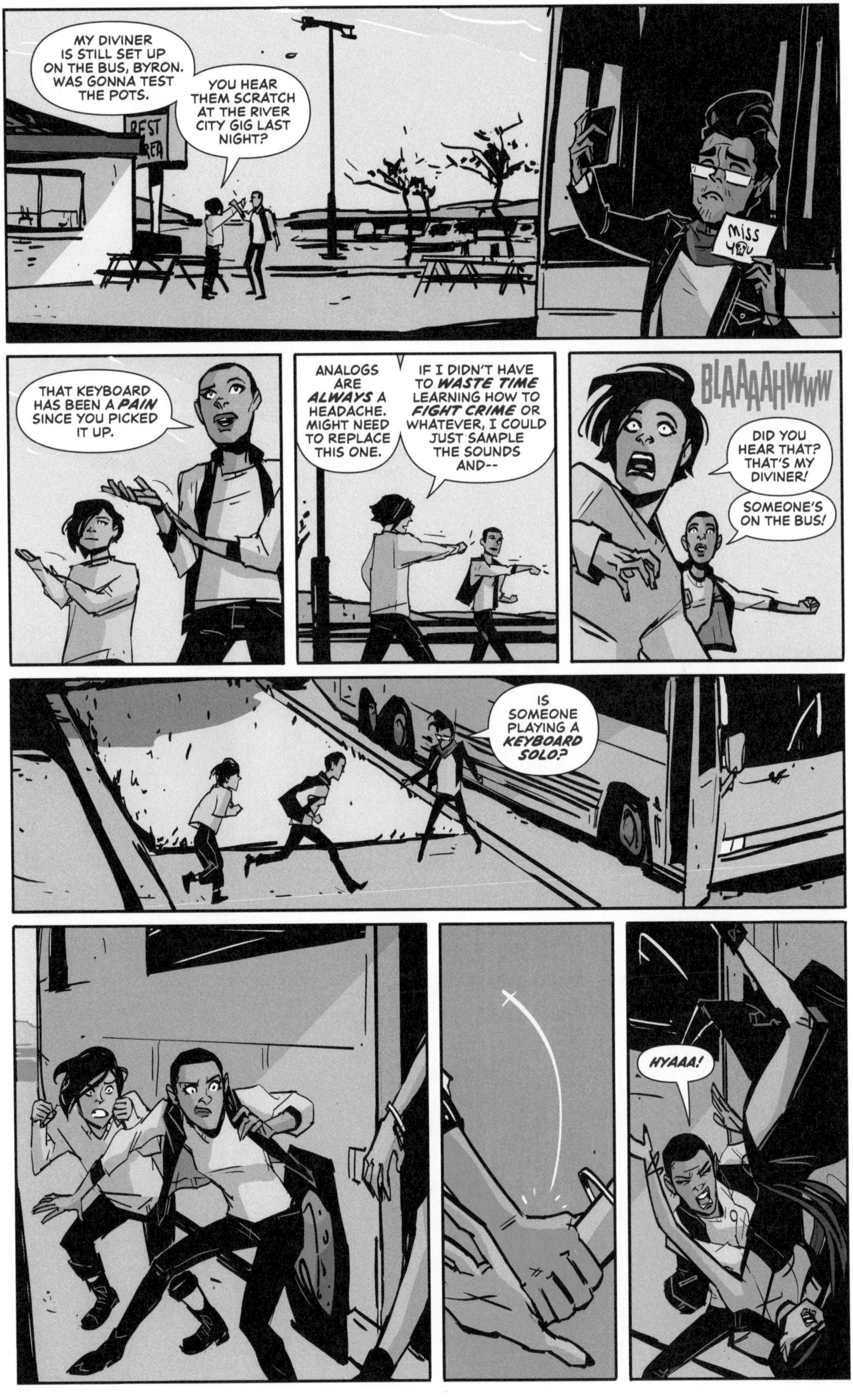
MY DIVINER IS STILL SET UP ON THE BUS, BYRON. WAS GONNA TEST THE POTS.
YOU HEAR THEM SCRATCH AT THE RIVER CITY GIG LAST NIGHT?
REST AREA
MISS YOU
THAT KEYBOARD HAS BEEN A PAIN SINCE YOU PICKED IT UP.
ANALOGS ARE ALWAYS A HEADACHE. MIGHT NEED TO REPLACE THIS ONE.
IF I DIDN'T HAVE TO WASTE TIME LEARNING HOW TO FIGHT CRIME OR WHATEVER, I COULD JUST SAMPLE THE SOUNDS AND--
BLAAAAHWWW
DID YOU HEAR THAT? THAT'S MY DIVINER!
SOMEONE'S ON THE BUS!
IS SOMEONE PLAYING A KEYBOARD SOLO?
HYAAA!

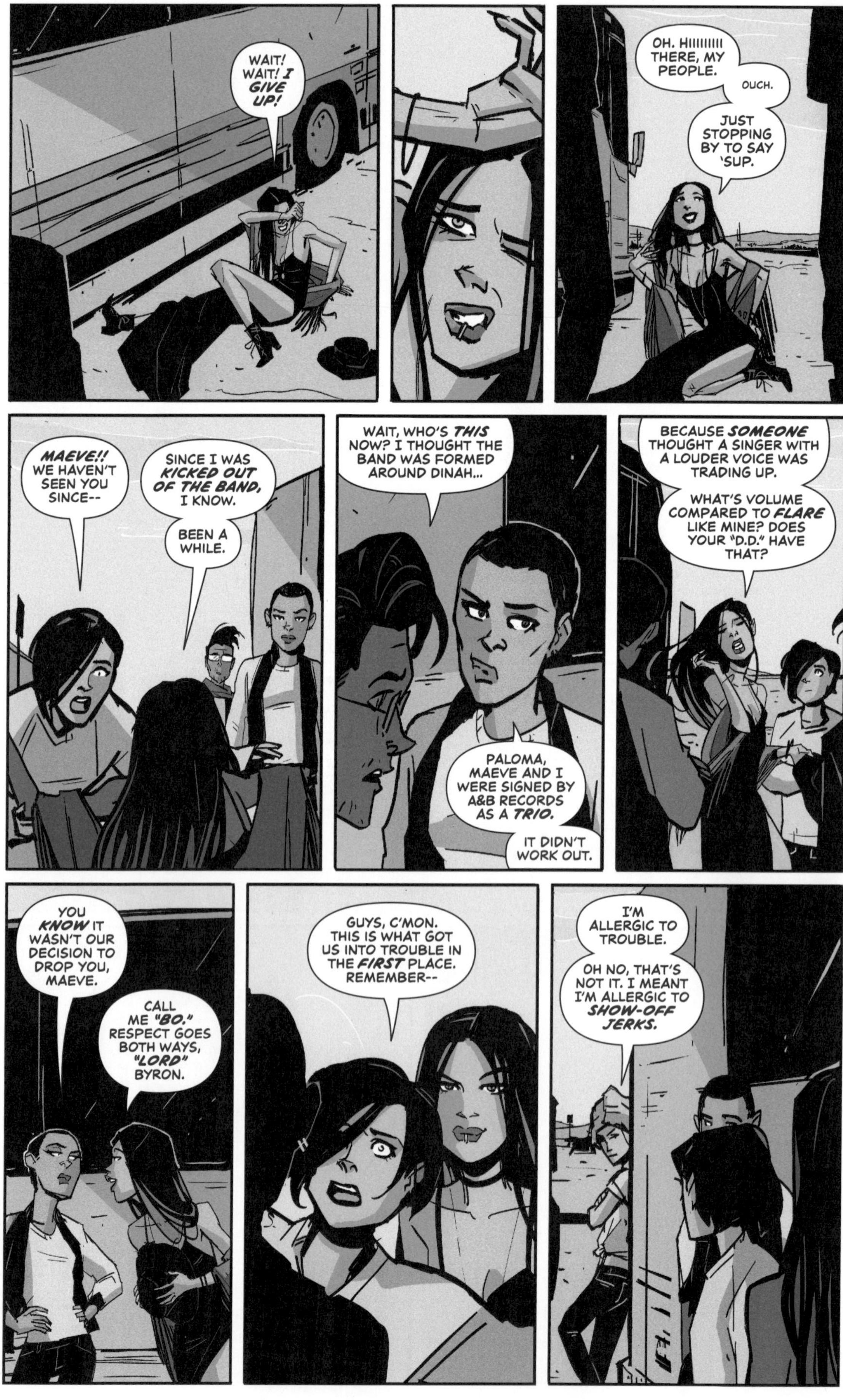
WAIT! WAIT! I GIVE UP!
OH. HIIIIIIIII THERE, MY PEOPLE.
OUCH.
JUST STOPPING BY TO SAY 'SUP.
MAEVE!! WE HAVEN'T SEEN YOU SINCE--
SINCE I WAS KICKED OUT OF THE BAND, I KNOW.
BEEN A WHILE.
WAIT, WHO'S THIS NOW? I THOUGHT THE BAND WAS FORMED AROUND DINAH...
PALOMA, MAEVE AND I WERE SIGNED BY A&B RECORDS AS A TRIO.
IT DIDN'T WORK OUT.
BECAUSE SOMEONE THOUGHT A SINGER WITH A LOUDER VOICE WAS TRADING UP.
WHAT'S VOLUME COMPARED TO FLARE LIKE MINE? DOES YOUR "D.D." HAVE THAT?
YOU KNOW IT WASN'T OUR DECISION TO DROP YOU, MAEVE.
CALL ME "BO." RESPECT GOES BOTH WAYS, "LORD" BYRON.
GUYS, C'MON. THIS IS WHAT GOT US INTO TROUBLE IN THE FIRST PLACE. REMEMBER--
I'M ALLERGIC TO TROUBLE.
OH NO, THAT'S NOT IT. I MEANT I'M ALLERGIC TO SHOW-OFF JERKS.

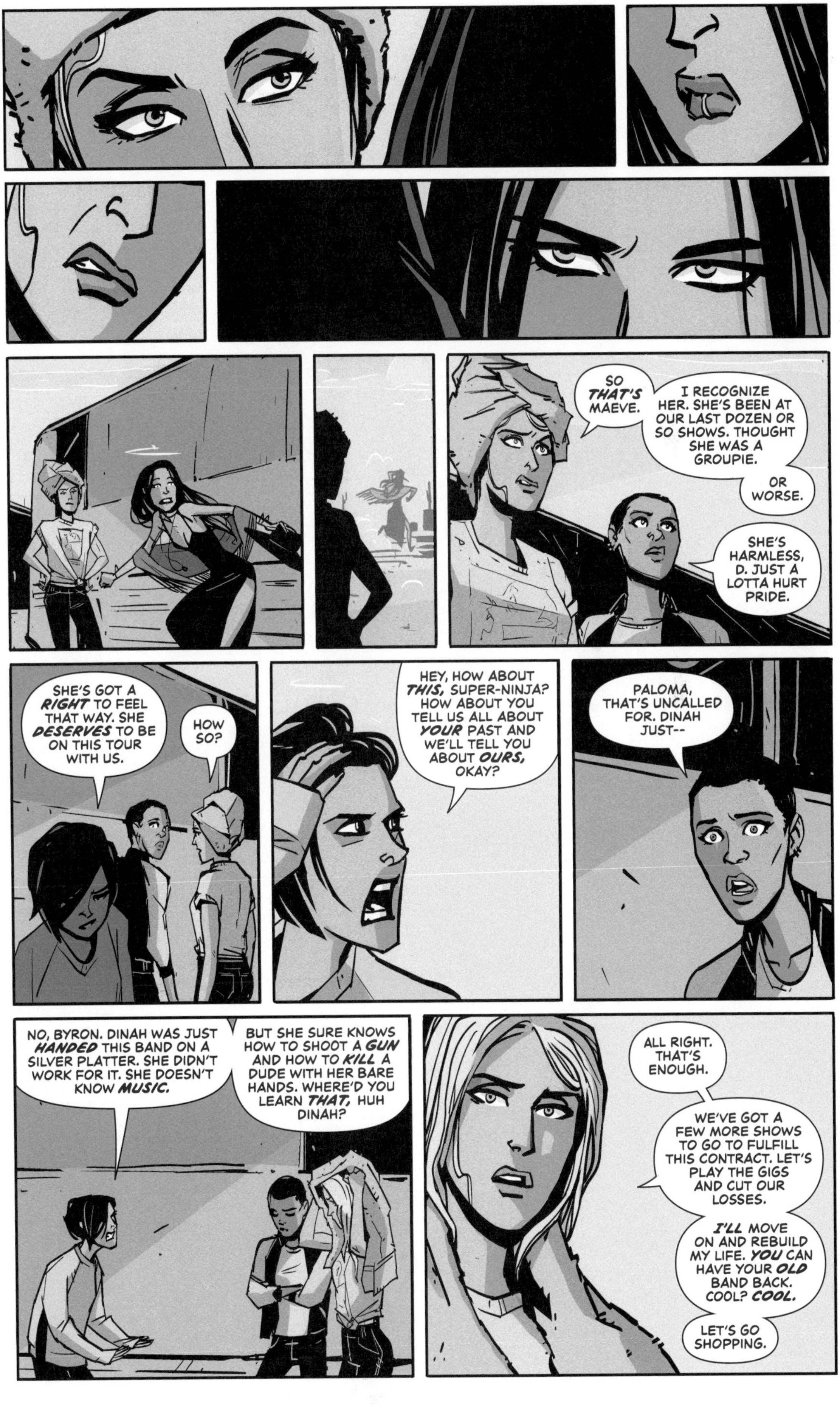
SO THAT'S MAEVE.
I RECOGNIZE HER. SHE'S BEEN AT OUR LAST DOZEN OR SO SHOWS. THOUGHT SHE WAS A GROUPIE.
OR WORSE.
SHE'S HARMLESS, D. JUST A LOTTA HURT PRIDE.
SHE'S GOT A RIGHT TO FEEL THAT WAY. SHE DESERVES TO BE ON THIS TOUR WITH US.
HOW SO?
HEY, HOW ABOUT THIS, SUPER-NINJA? HOW ABOUT YOU TELL US ALL ABOUT YOUR PAST AND WE'LL TELL YOU ABOUT OURS, OKAY?
PALOMA, THAT'S UNCALLED FOR. DINAH JUST--
NO, BYRON. DINAH WAS JUST HANDED THIS BAND ON A SILVER PLATTER. SHE DIDN'T WORK FOR IT. SHE DOESN'T KNOW MUSIC.
BUT SHE SURE KNOWS HOW TO SHOOT A GUN AND HOW TO KILL A DUDE WITH HER BARE HANDS. WHERE'D YOU LEARN THAT, HUH DINAH?
ALL RIGHT. THAT'S ENOUGH.
WE'VE GOT A FEW MORE SHOWS TO GO TO FULFILL THIS CONTRACT. LET'S PLAY THE GIGS AND CUT OUR LOSSES.
I'LL MOVE ON AND REBUILD MY LIFE. YOU CAN HAVE YOUR OLD BAND BACK. COOL? COOL.
LET'S GO SHOPPING.

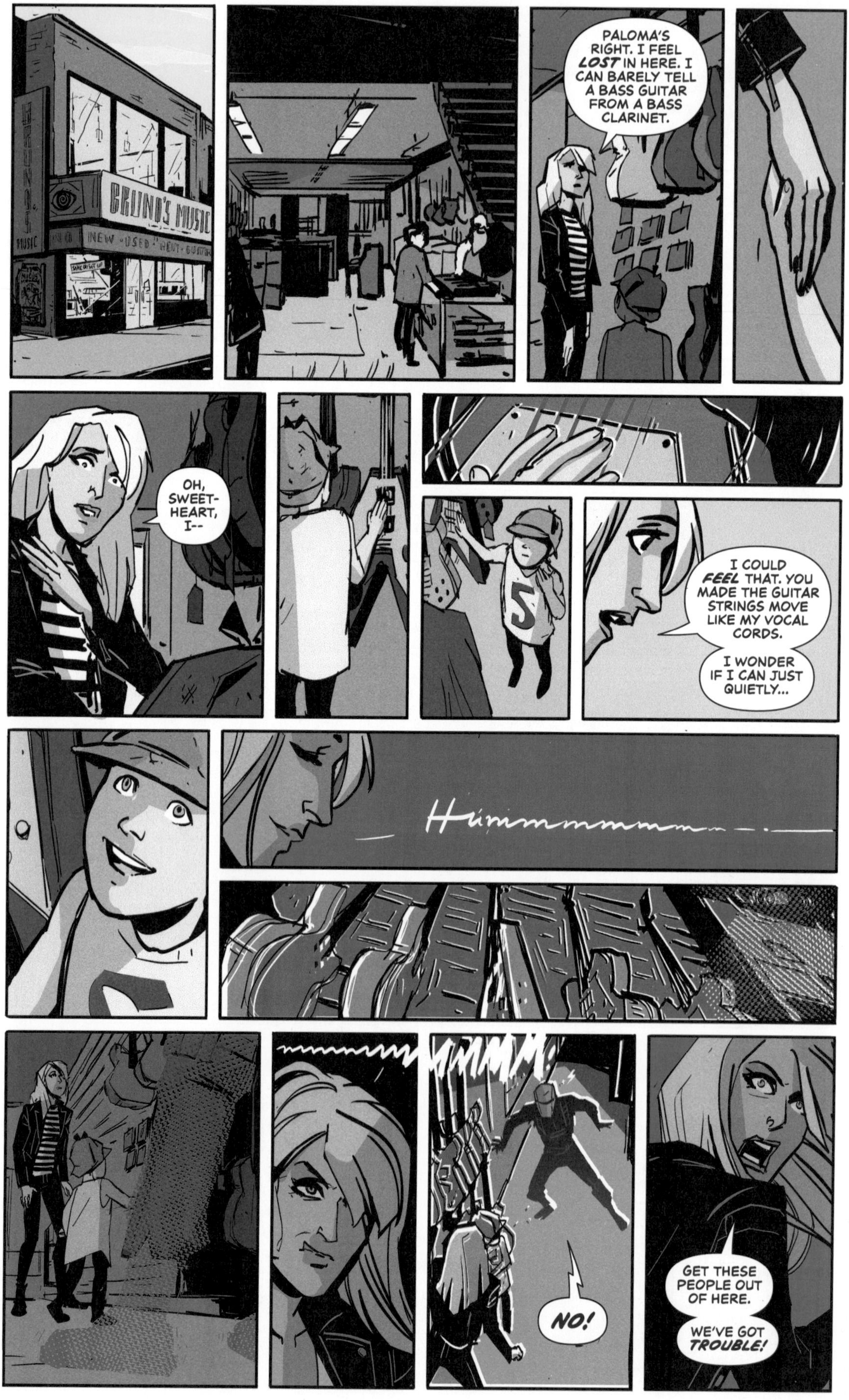
BRUNO'S MUSIC
NEW · USED · RENT · GUITAR
MUSIC
PALOMA'S RIGHT. I FEEL *LOST* IN HERE. I CAN BARELY TELL A BASS GUITAR FROM A BASS CLARINET.
OH, SWEET-HEART, I--
I COULD *FEEL* THAT. YOU MADE THE GUITAR STRINGS MOVE LIKE MY VOCAL CORDS.
I WONDER IF I CAN JUST QUIETLY...
Hummmmmmm
NO!
GET THESE PEOPLE OUT OF HERE.
WE'VE GOT *TROUBLE!*

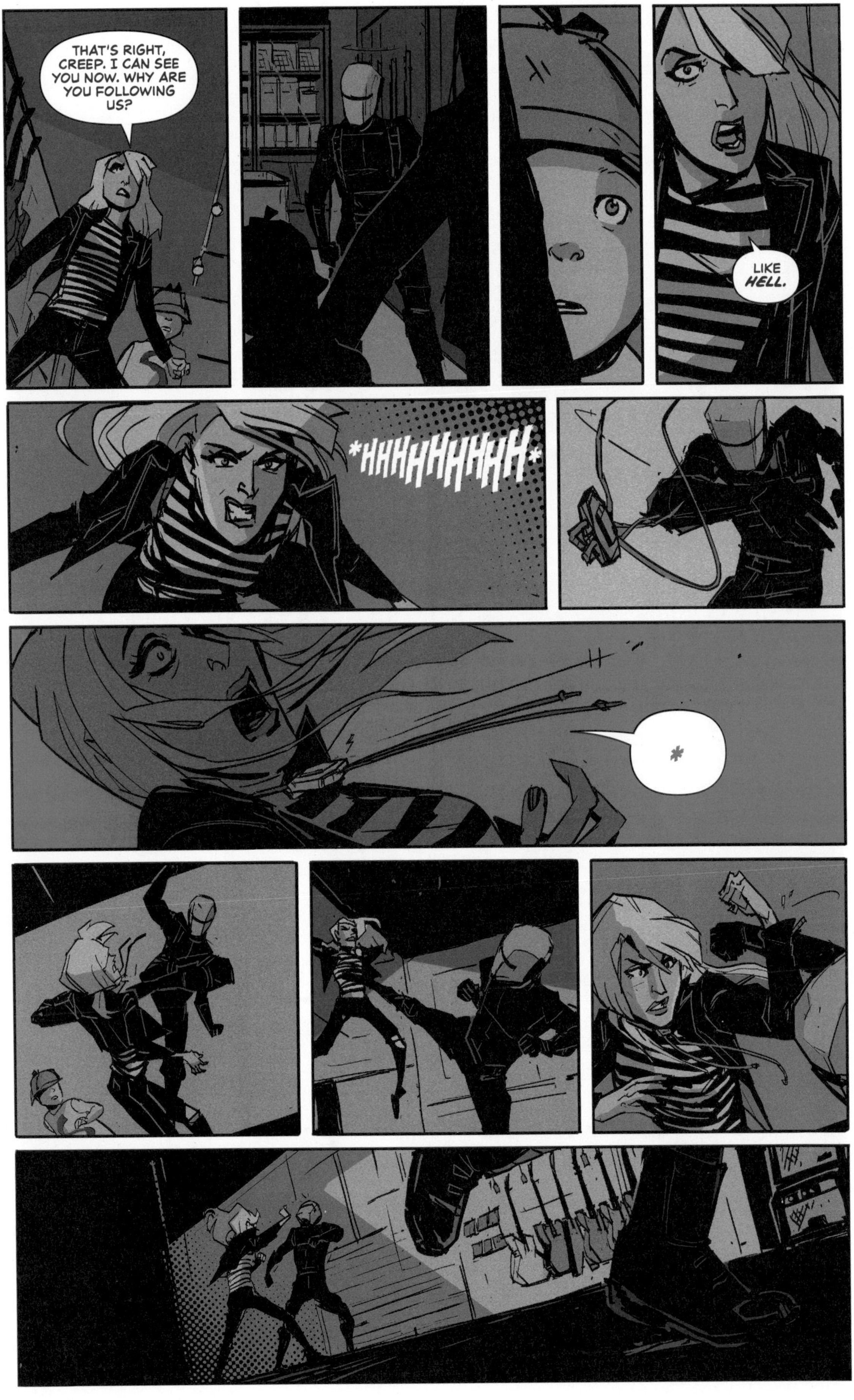
THAT'S RIGHT, CREEP. I CAN SEE YOU NOW. WHY ARE YOU FOLLOWING US?
LIKE *HELL.*
HHHHHHHHH
*

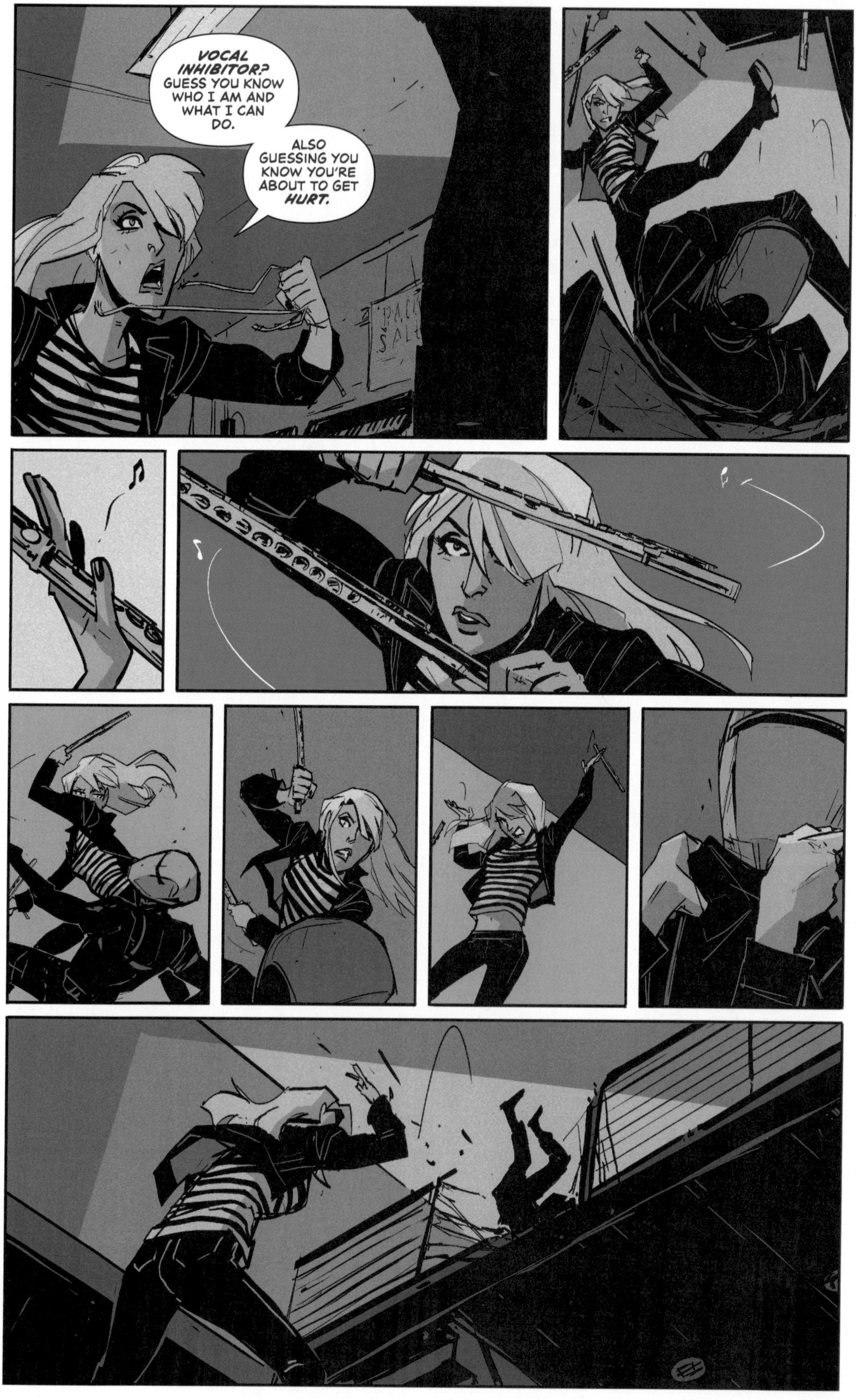
VOCAL INHIBITOR? GUESS YOU KNOW WHO I AM AND WHAT I CAN DO.
ALSO GUESSING YOU KNOW YOU'RE ABOUT TO GET HURT.

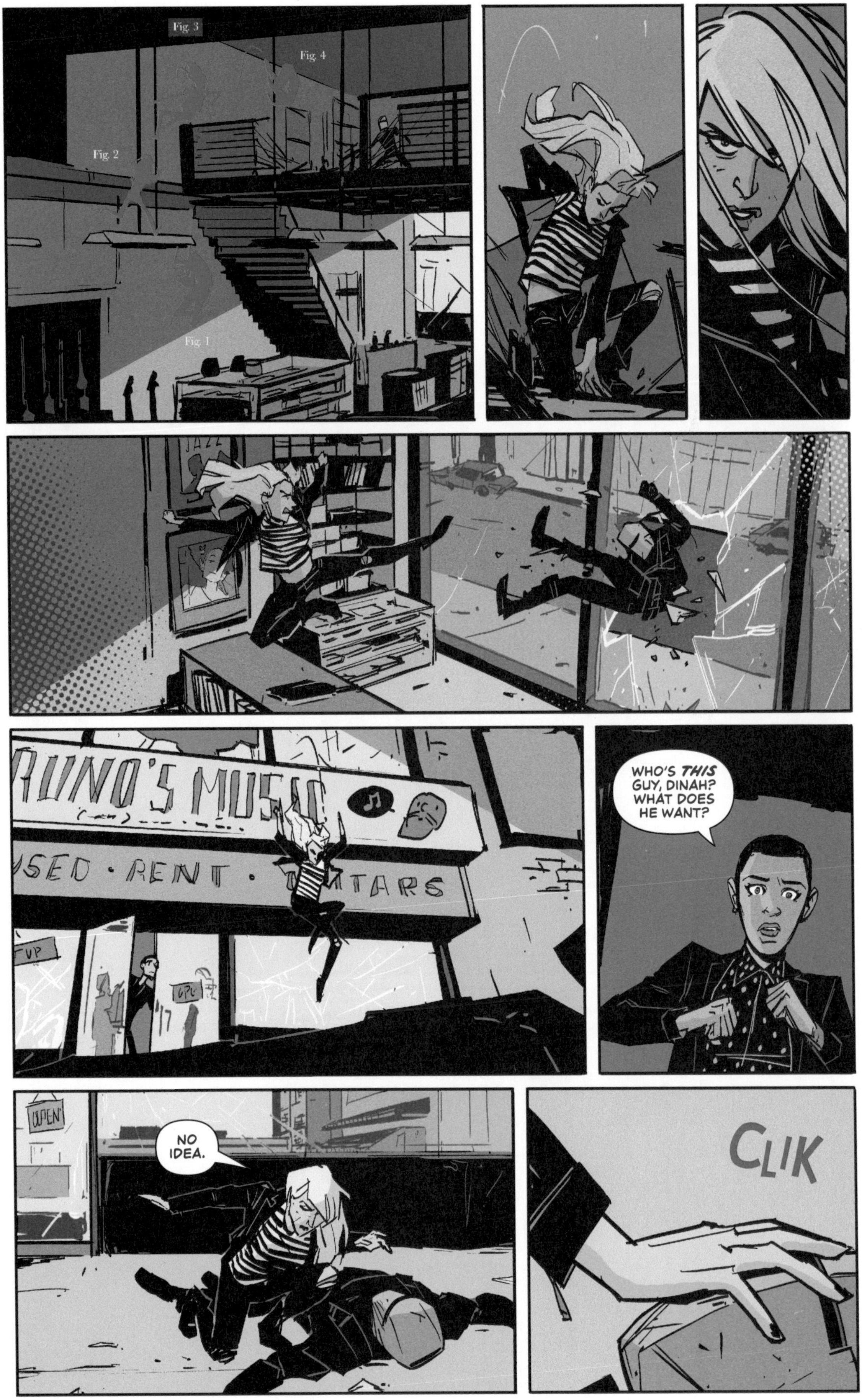
Fig. 3
Fig. 4
Fig. 2
Fig. 1
WHO'S *THIS* GUY, DINAH? WHAT DOES HE WANT?
NO IDEA.
CLIK

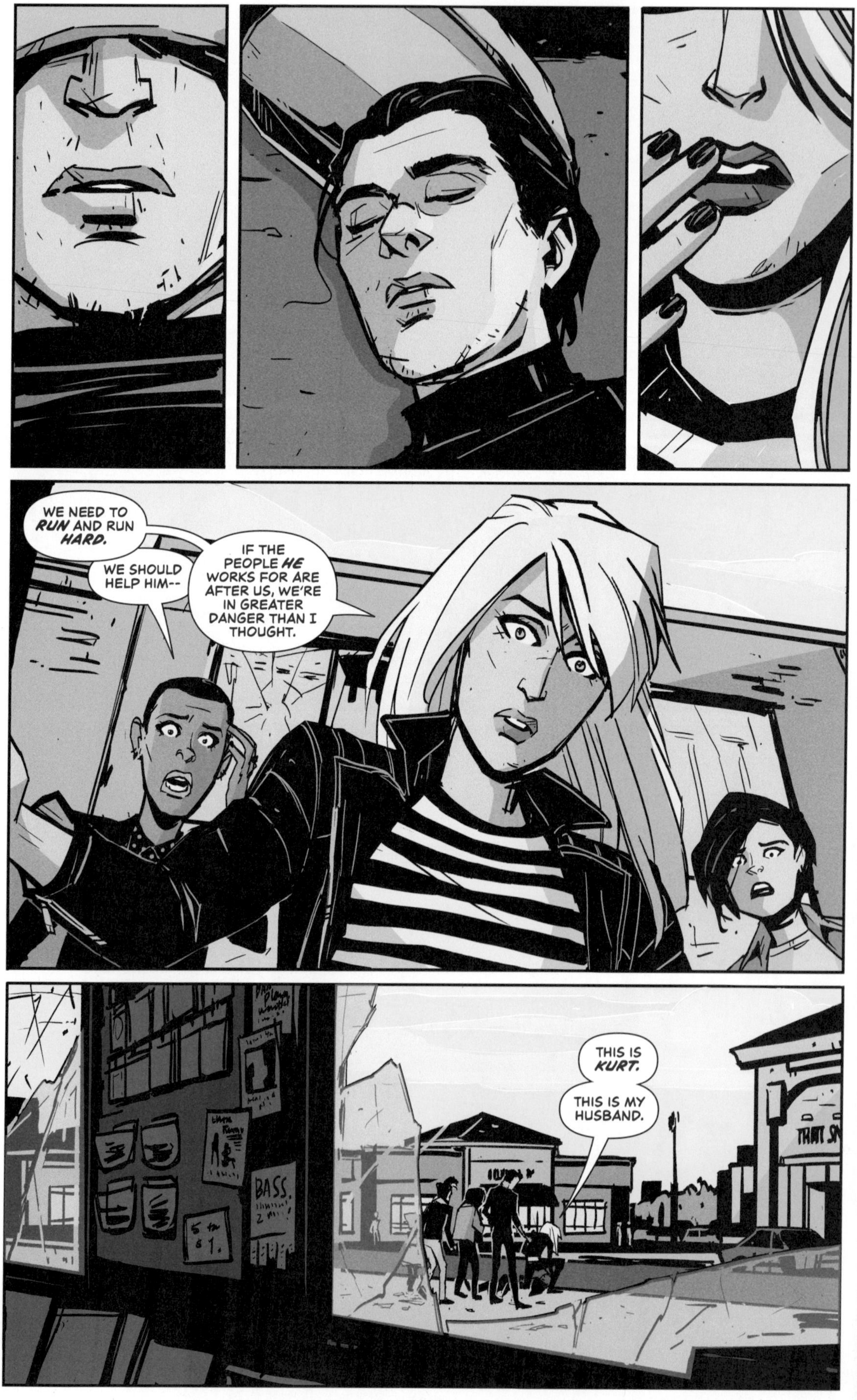
WE NEED TO RUN AND RUN HARD.
WE SHOULD HELP HIM--
IF THE PEOPLE HE WORKS FOR ARE AFTER US, WE'RE IN GREATER DANGER THAN I THOUGHT.
BASS
THIS IS KURT.
THIS IS MY HUSBAND.

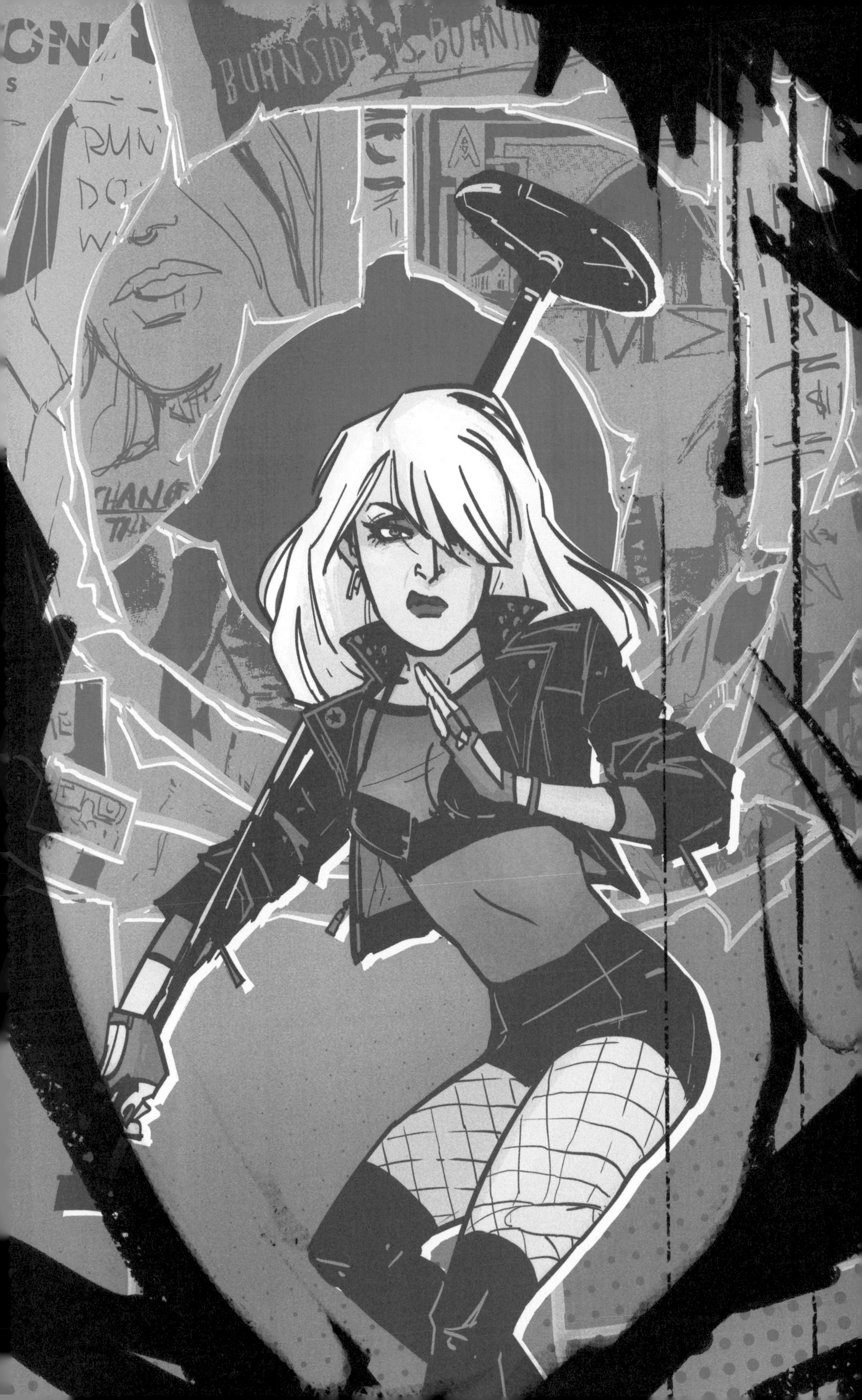
BURNSIDE

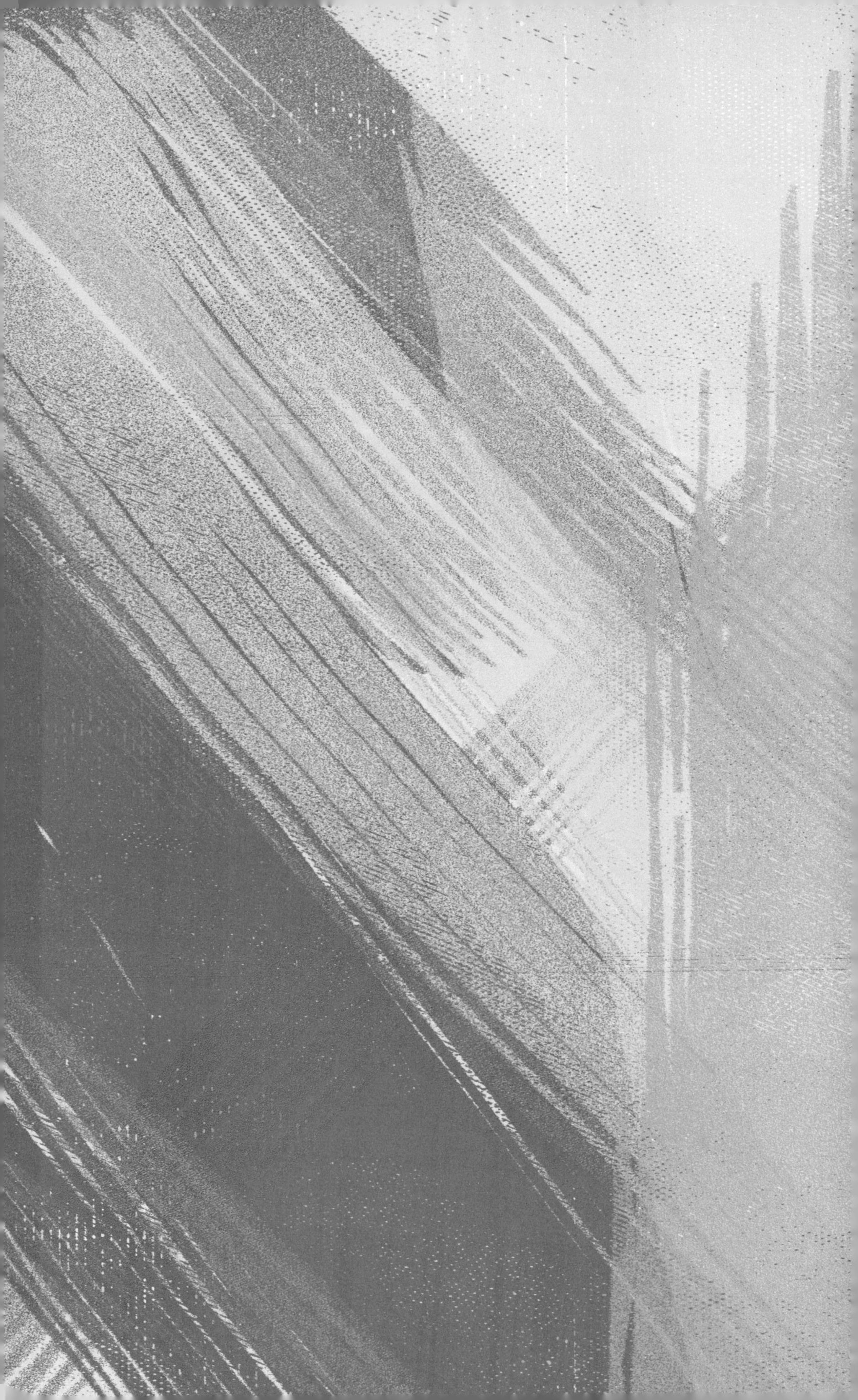

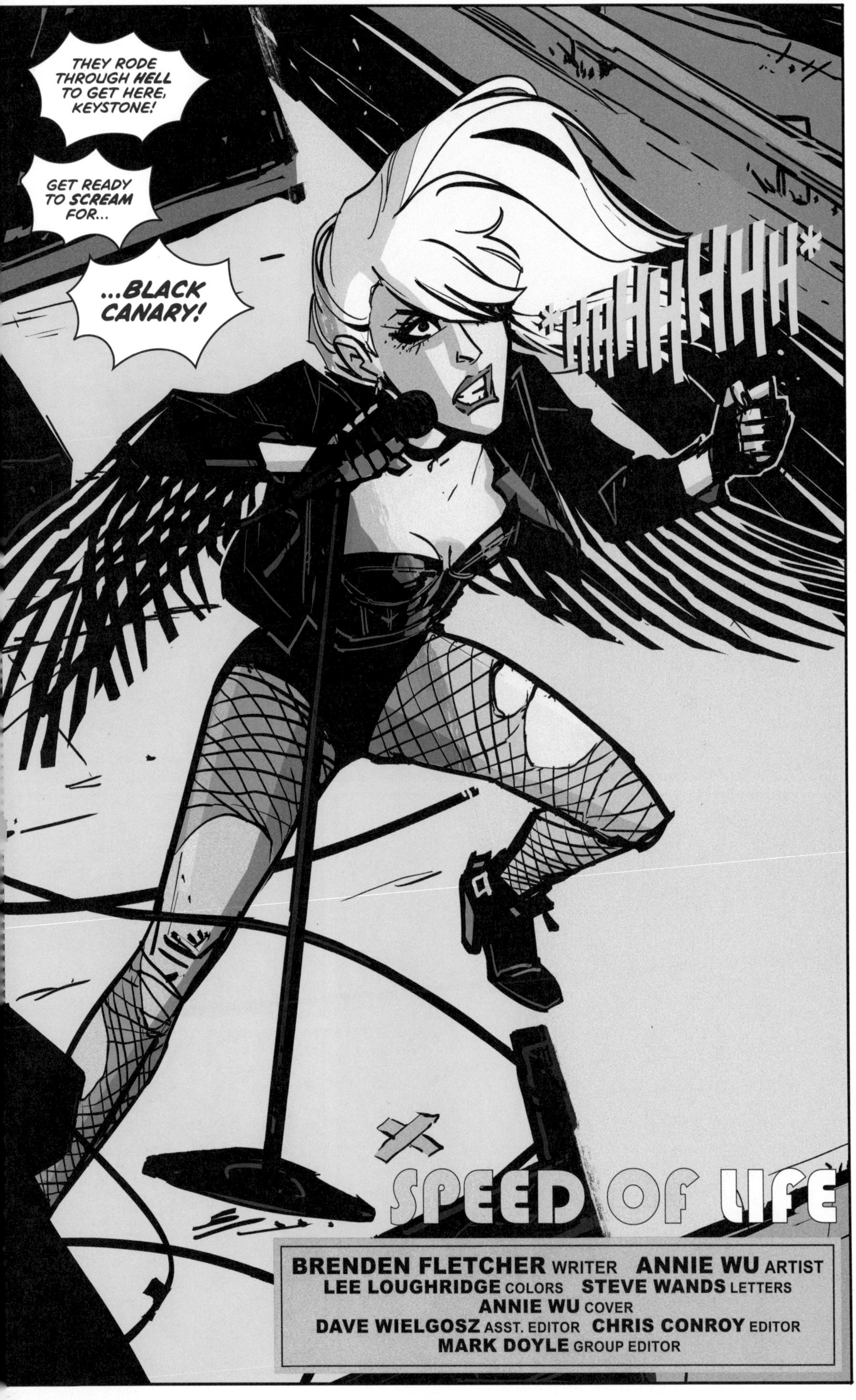
THEY RODE THROUGH HELL TO GET HERE, KEYSTONE!
GET READY TO SCREAM FOR...
...BLACK CANARY!
HHHHHHHHH
SPEED OF LIFE
BRENDEN FLETCHER WRITER ANNIE WU ARTIST
LEE LOUGHRIDGE COLORS STEVE WANDS LETTERS
ANNIE WU COVER
DAVE WIELGOSZ ASST. EDITOR CHRIS CONROY EDITOR
MARK DOYLE GROUP EDITOR

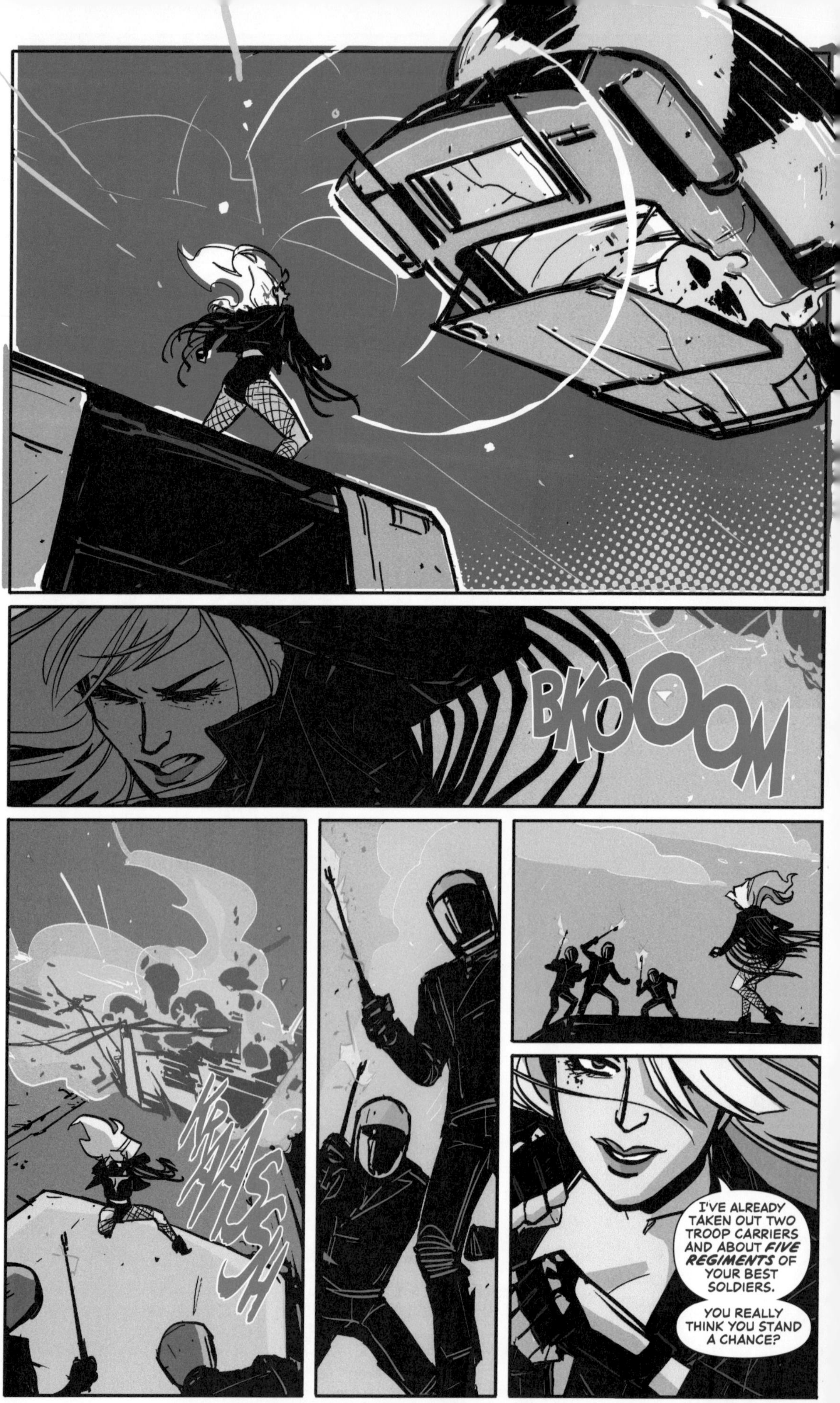
BKOOOOM
KRASH
I'VE ALREADY TAKEN OUT TWO TROOP CARRIERS AND ABOUT *FIVE* *REGIMENTS* OF YOUR BEST SOLDIERS.
YOU REALLY THINK YOU STAND A CHANCE?

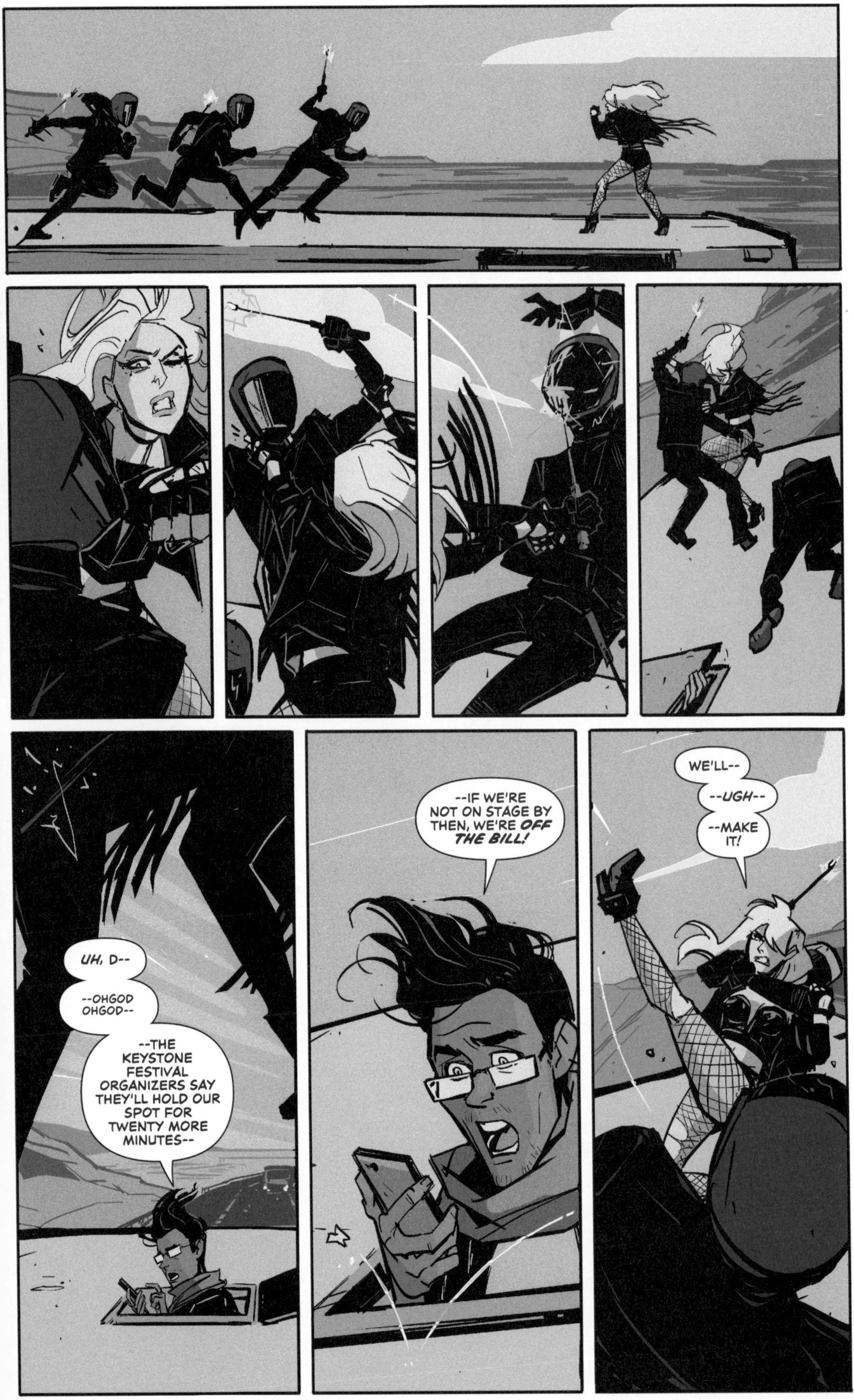
UH, D--
--OHGOD OHGOD--
--THE KEYSTONE FESTIVAL ORGANIZERS SAY THEY'LL HOLD OUR SPOT FOR TWENTY MORE MINUTES--
--IF WE'RE NOT ON STAGE BY THEN, WE'RE OFF THE BILL!
WE'LL--
--UGH--
--MAKE IT!

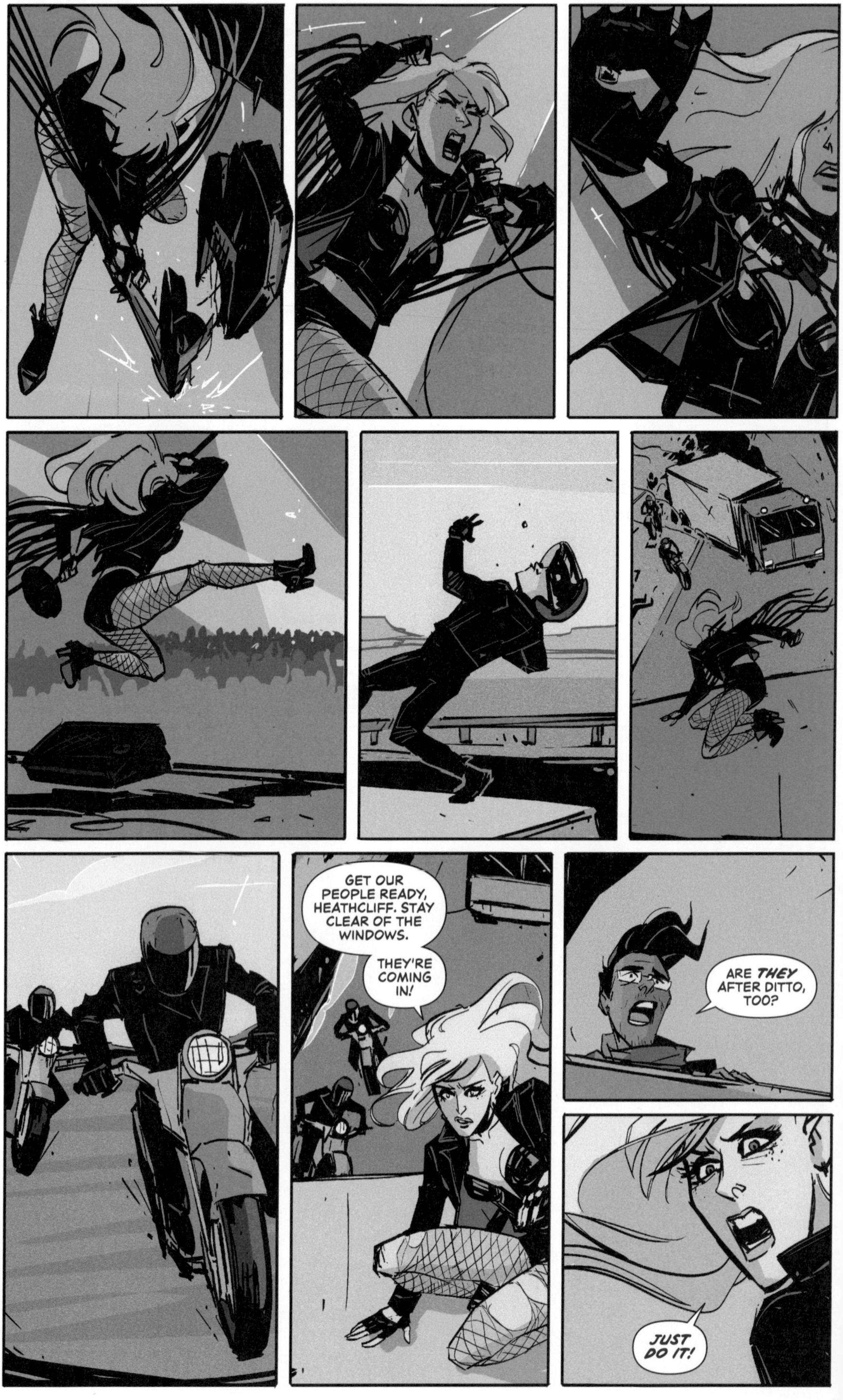
GET OUR PEOPLE READY, HEATHCLIFF. STAY CLEAR OF THE WINDOWS.
THEY'RE COMING IN!
ARE THEY AFTER DITTO, TOO?
JUST DO IT!

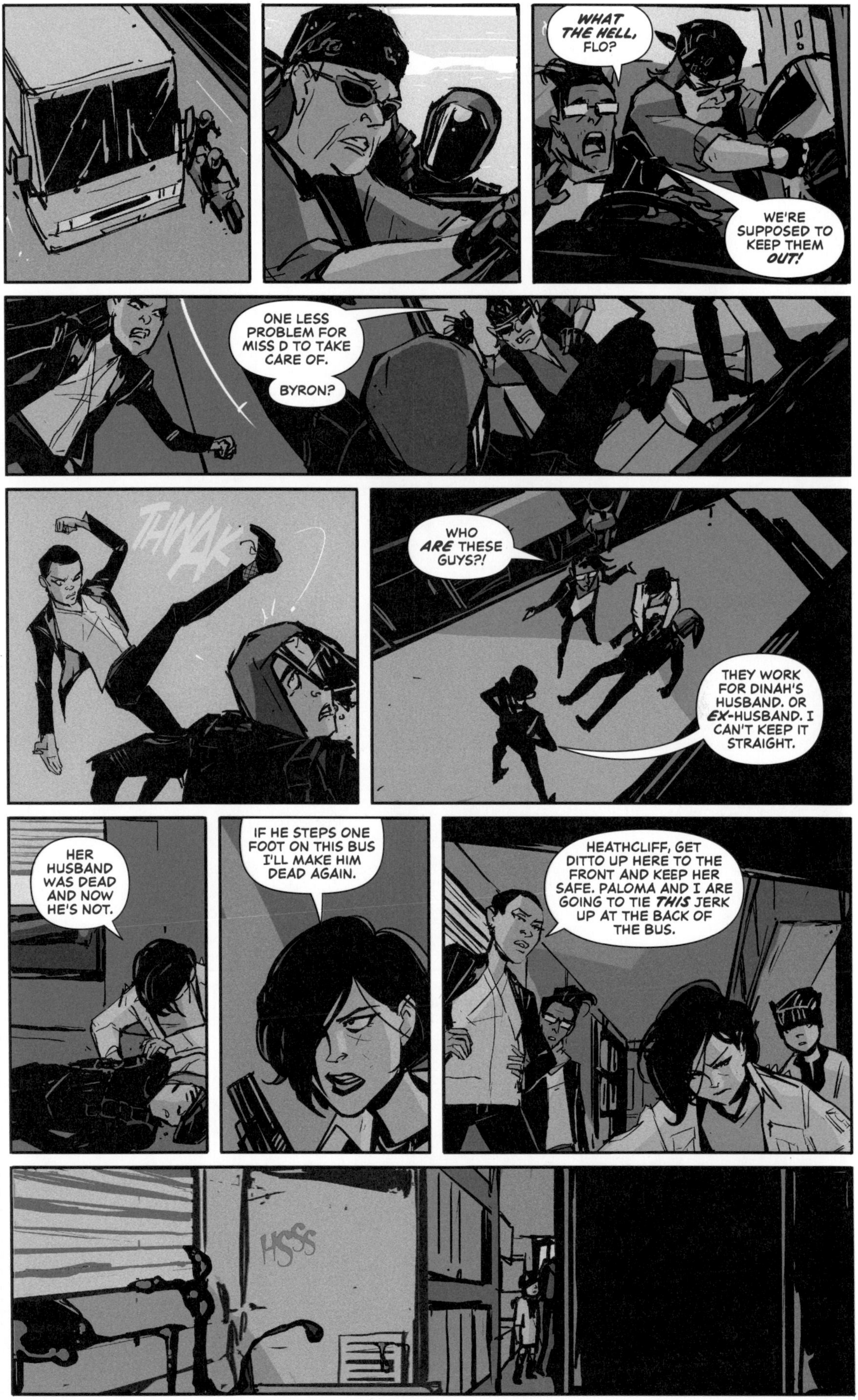
WHAT THE HELL, FLO?
WE'RE SUPPOSED TO KEEP THEM OUT!
ONE LESS PROBLEM FOR MISS D TO TAKE CARE OF.
BYRON?
THWAK
WHO ARE THESE GUYS?!
THEY WORK FOR DINAH'S HUSBAND. OR EX-HUSBAND. I CAN'T KEEP IT STRAIGHT.
HER HUSBAND WAS DEAD AND NOW HE'S NOT.
IF HE STEPS ONE FOOT ON THIS BUS I'LL MAKE HIM DEAD AGAIN.
HEATHCLIFF, GET DITTO UP HERE TO THE FRONT AND KEEP HER SAFE. PALOMA AND I ARE GOING TO TIE THIS JERK UP AT THE BACK OF THE BUS.
HSSS

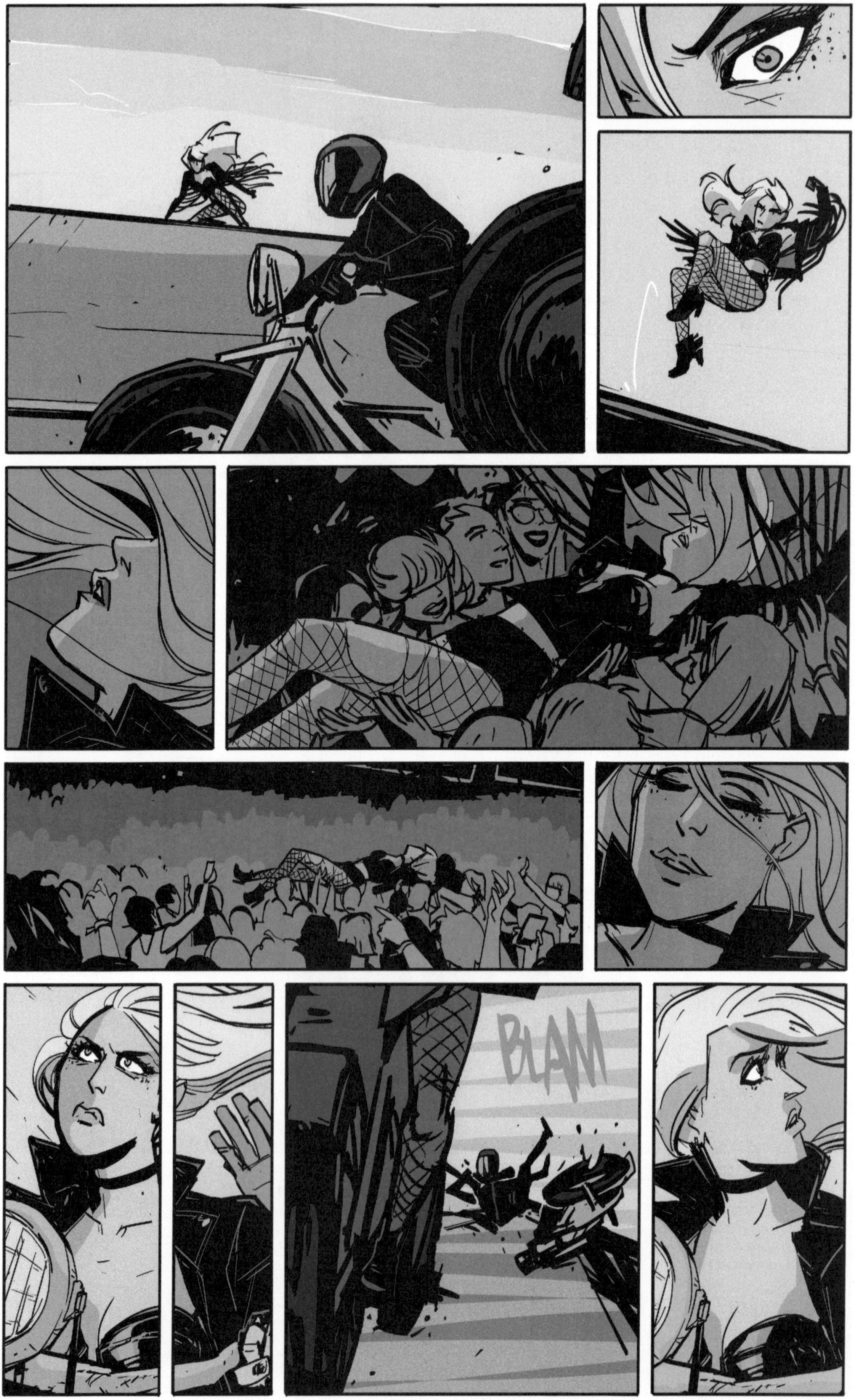
BLAM

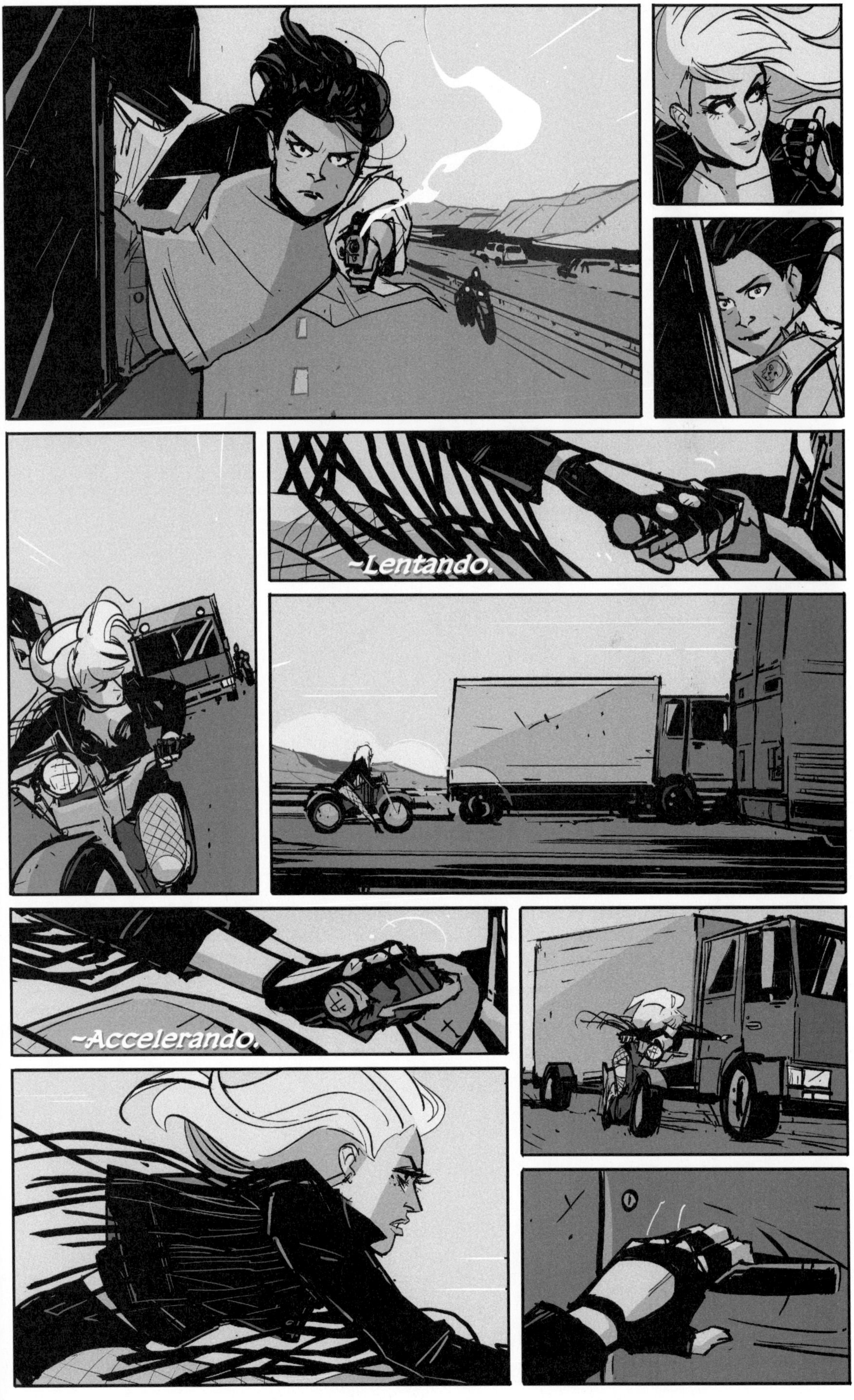
~Lentando.
~Accelerando.

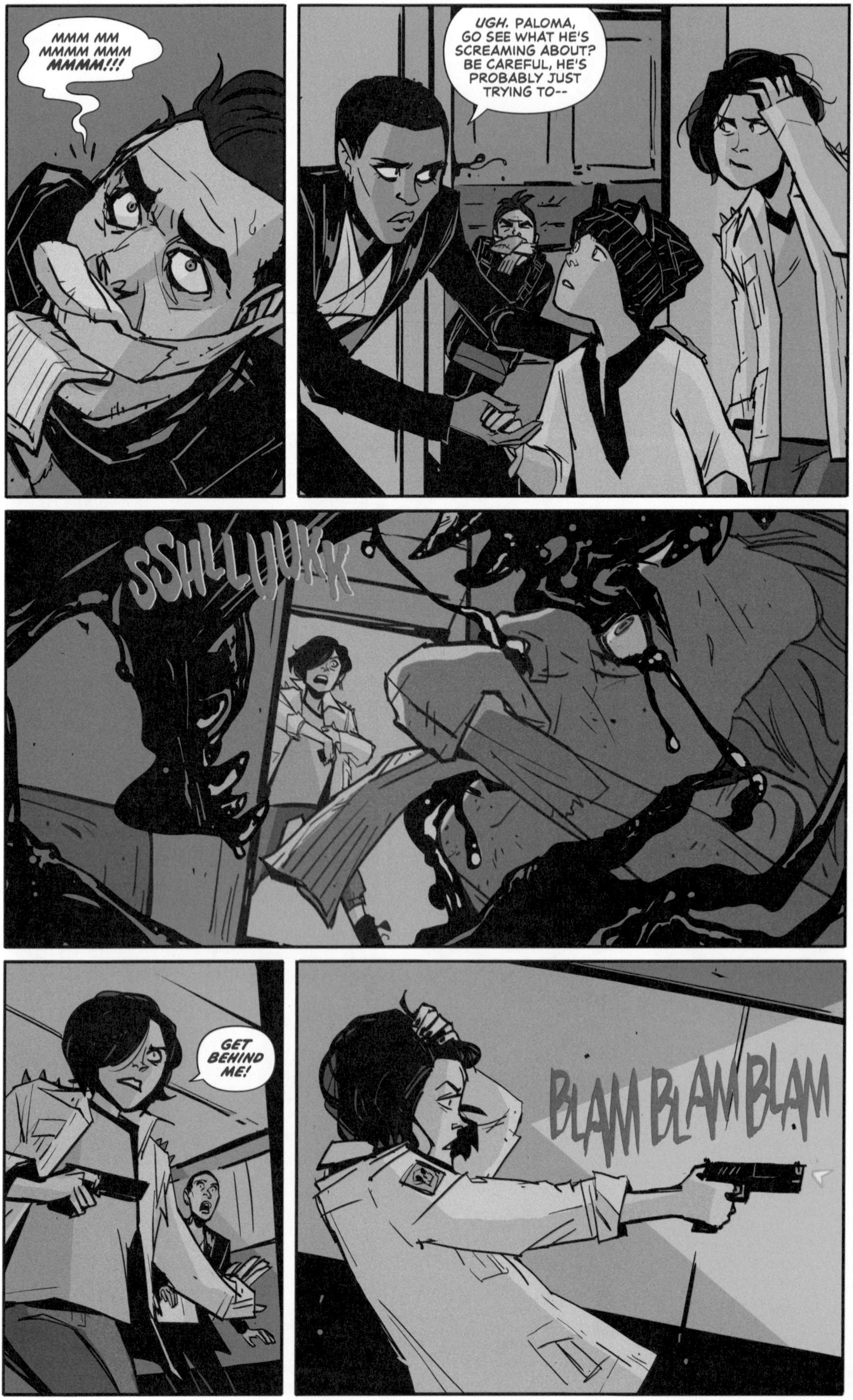
MMM MM MMMM MMM MMMM!!!
UGH. PALOMA, GO SEE WHAT HE'S SCREAMING ABOUT? BE CAREFUL, HE'S PROBABLY JUST TRYING TO--
SSHLLUUKK
GET BEHIND ME!
BLAM BLAM BLAM

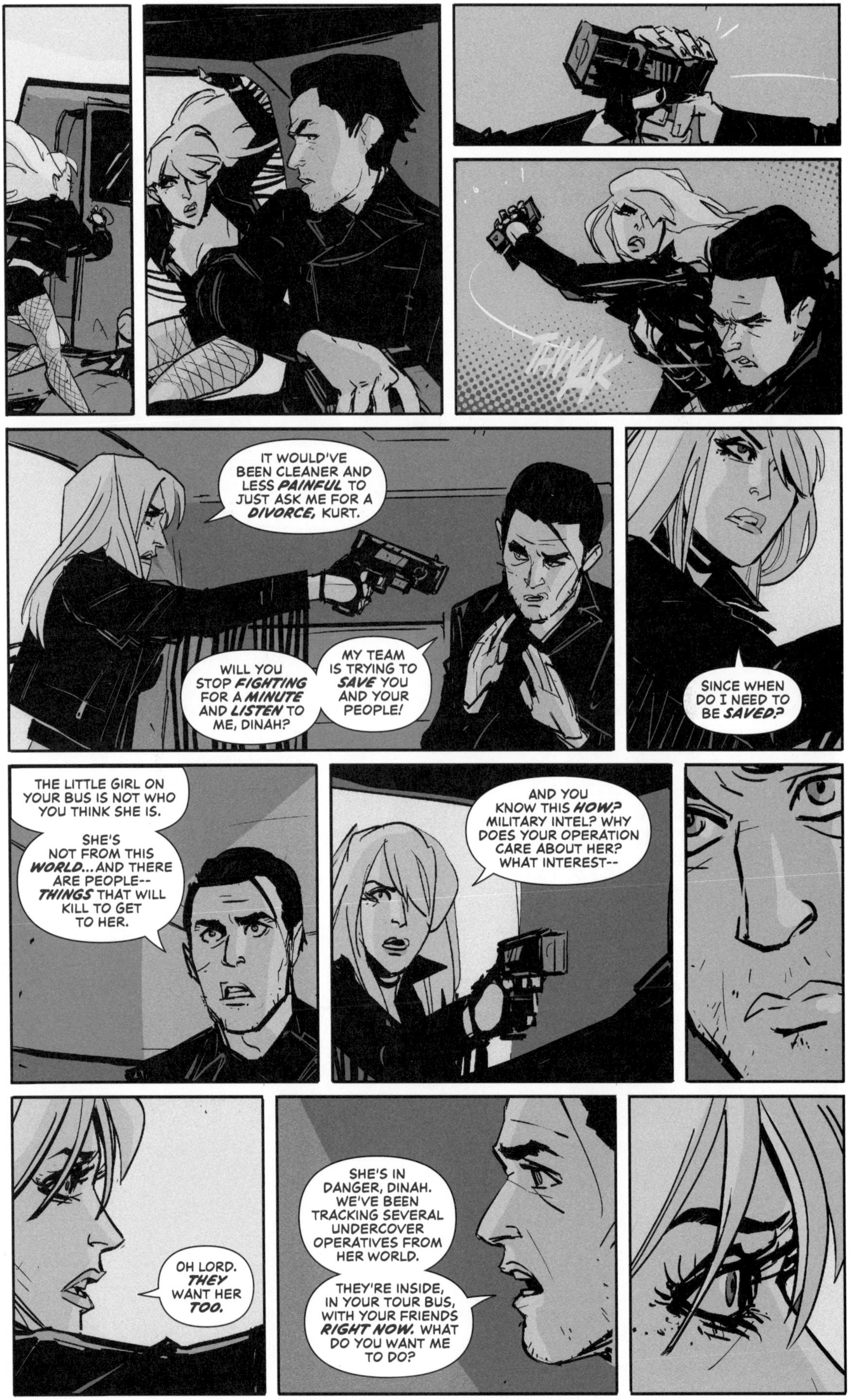
THWAK
IT WOULD'VE BEEN CLEANER AND LESS PAINFUL TO JUST ASK ME FOR A DIVORCE, KURT.
WILL YOU STOP FIGHTING FOR A MINUTE AND LISTEN TO ME, DINAH?
MY TEAM IS TRYING TO SAVE YOU AND YOUR PEOPLE!
SINCE WHEN DO I NEED TO BE SAVED?
THE LITTLE GIRL ON YOUR BUS IS NOT WHO YOU THINK SHE IS.
SHE'S NOT FROM THIS WORLD... AND THERE ARE PEOPLE-- THINGS THAT WILL KILL TO GET TO HER.
AND YOU KNOW THIS HOW? MILITARY INTEL? WHY DOES YOUR OPERATION CARE ABOUT HER? WHAT INTEREST--
OH LORD. THEY WANT HER TOO.
SHE'S IN DANGER, DINAH. WE'VE BEEN TRACKING SEVERAL UNDERCOVER OPERATIVES FROM HER WORLD.
THEY'RE INSIDE, IN YOUR TOUR BUS, WITH YOUR FRIENDS RIGHT NOW. WHAT DO YOU WANT ME TO DO?

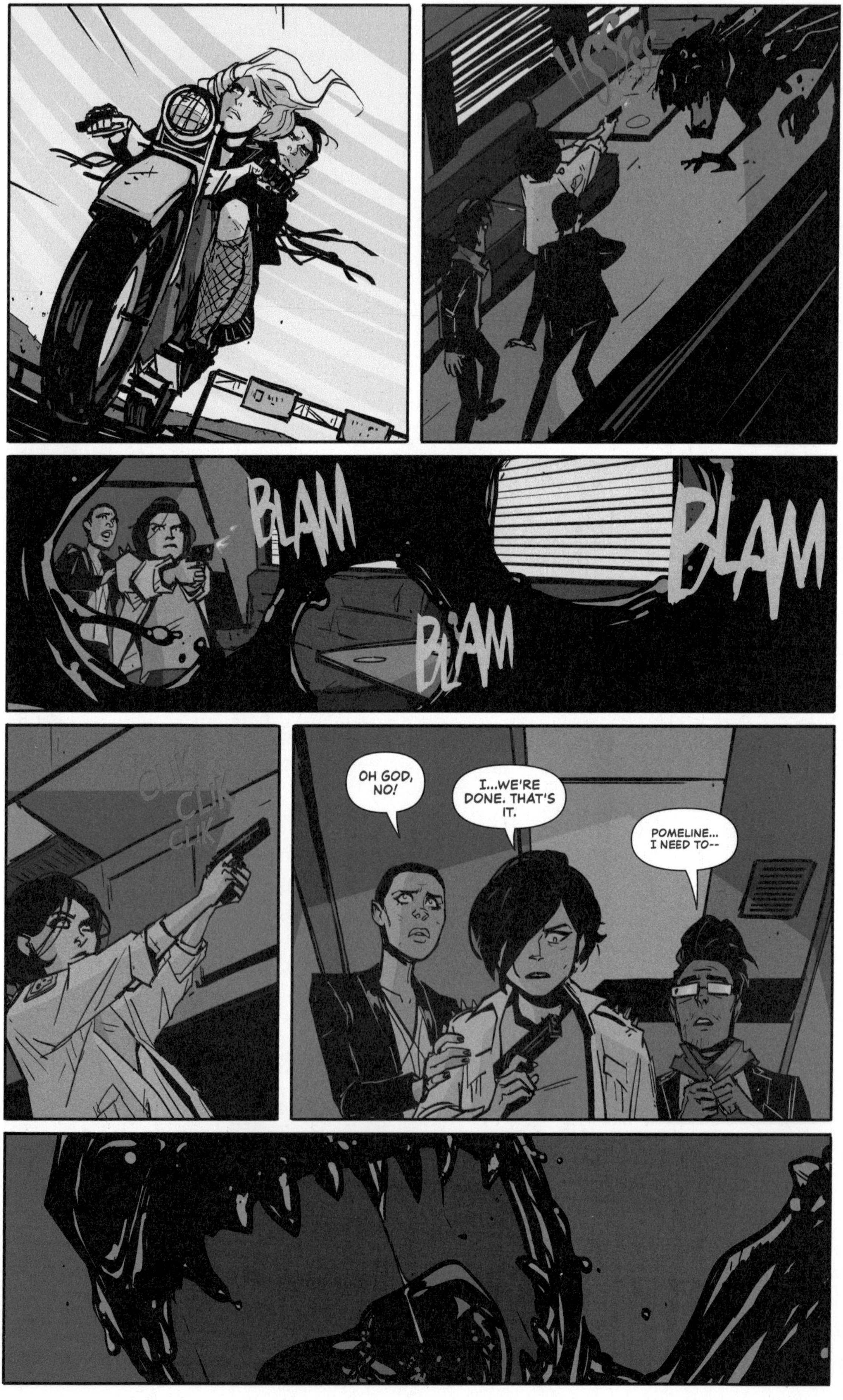
HSSSS
BLAM
BLAM
BLAM
CLIK
CLIK
CLIK
OH GOD, NO!
I...WE'RE DONE. THAT'S IT.
POMELINE... I NEED TO--

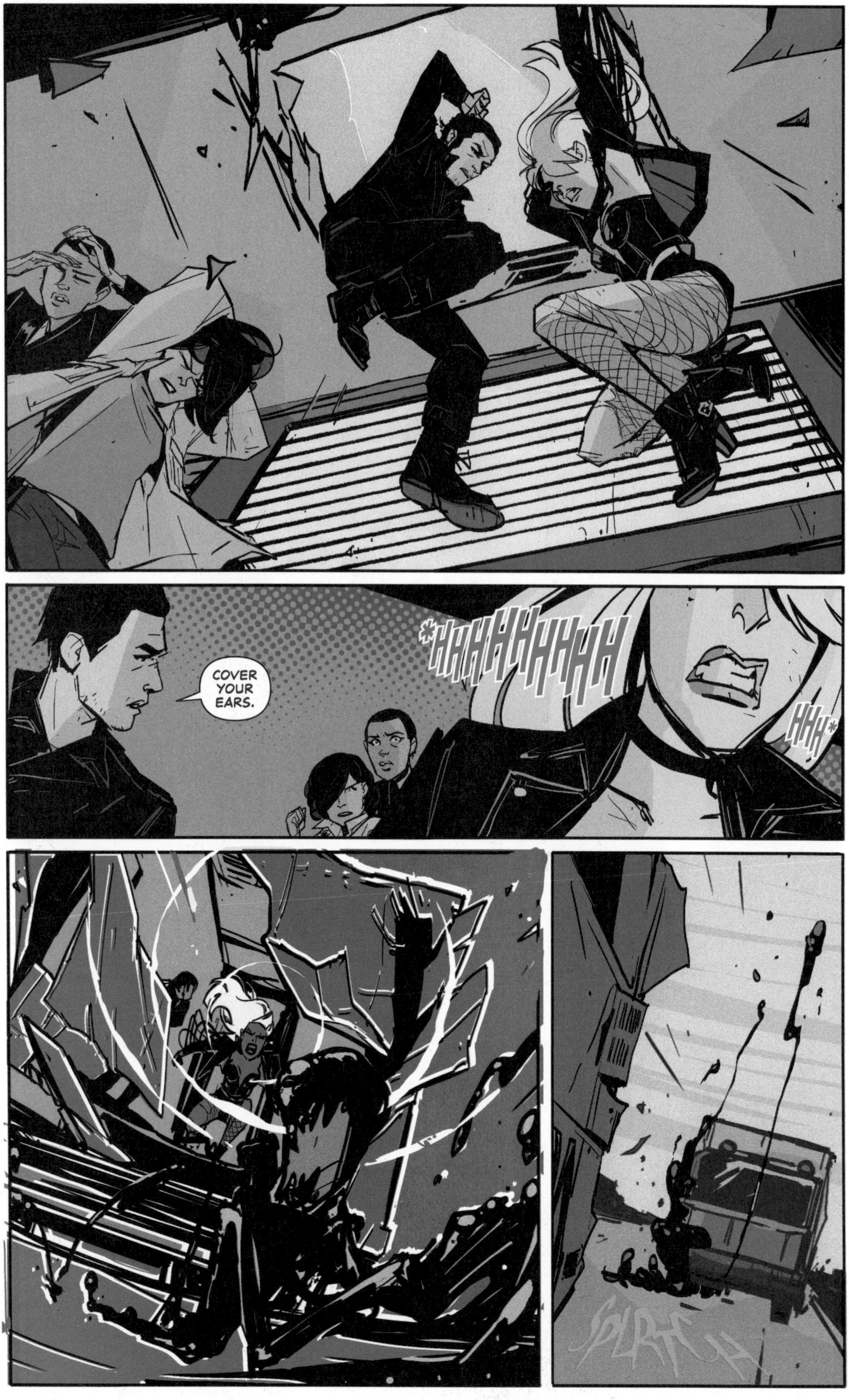
COVER YOUR EARS.
*HHHHHHHHHH
HHH*
SPLRTCH

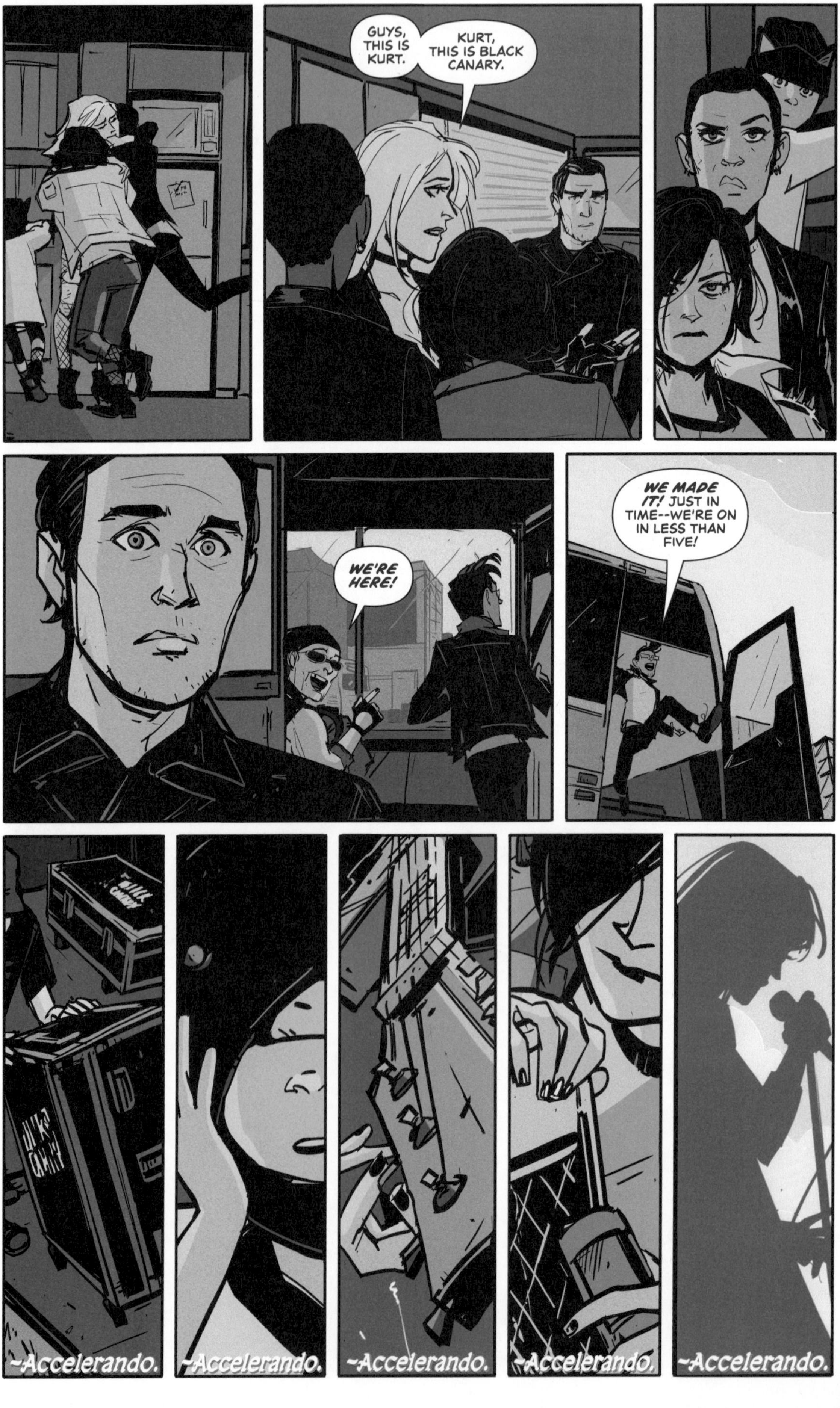
GUYS, THIS IS KURT.
KURT, THIS IS BLACK CANARY.
WE'RE HERE!
WE MADE IT! JUST IN TIME--WE'RE ON IN LESS THAN FIVE!
~Accelerando.
~Accelerando.
~Accelerando.
~Accelerando.
~Accelerando.

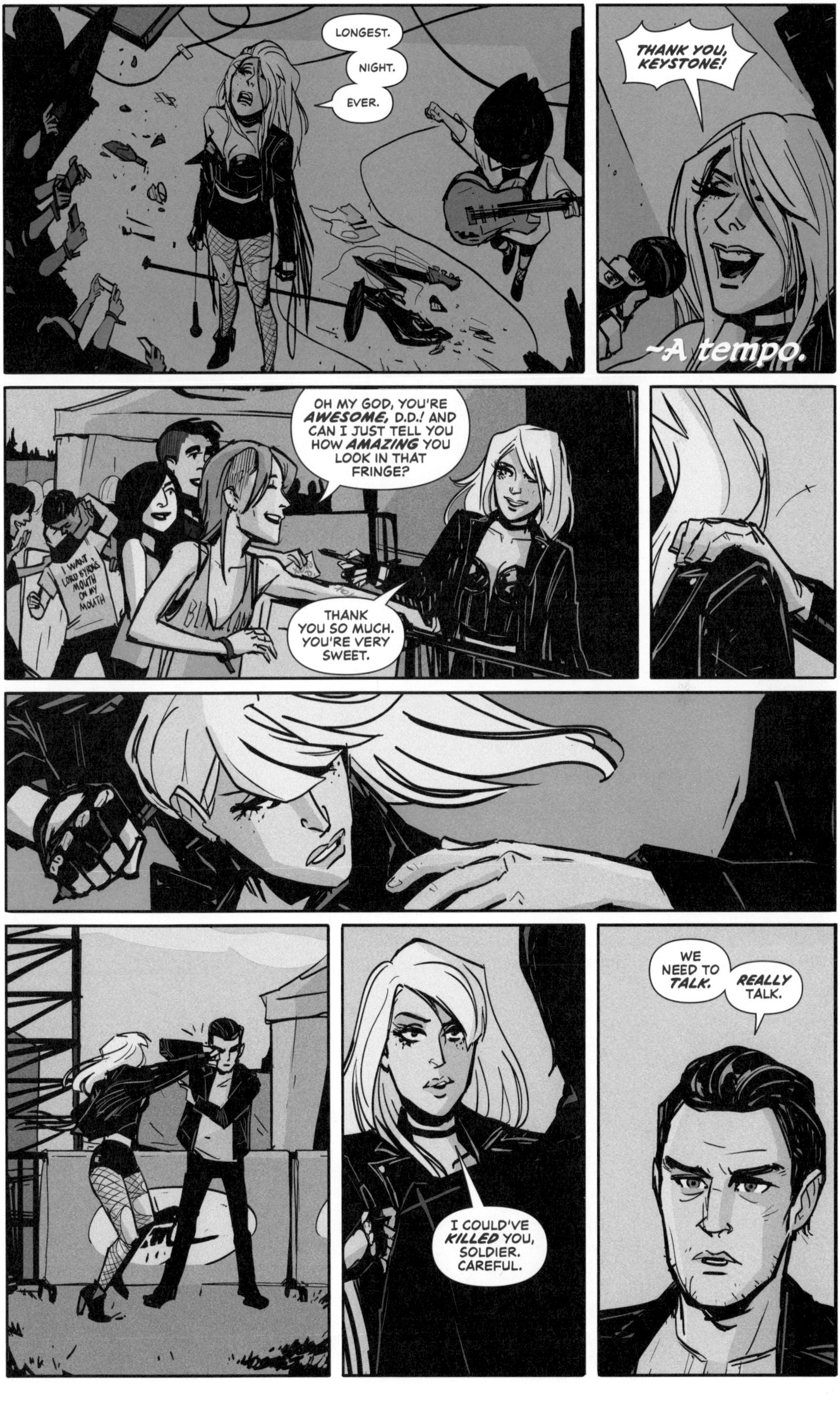
LONGEST.
NIGHT.
EVER.
THANK YOU, KEYSTONE!
~A tempo.
OH MY GOD, YOU'RE *AWESOME,* D.D.! AND CAN I JUST TELL YOU HOW *AMAZING* YOU LOOK IN THAT FRINGE?
I WANT LORD BYRON'S MOUTH ON MY MOUTH
THANK YOU SO MUCH. YOU'RE VERY SWEET.
I COULD'VE *KILLED* YOU, SOLDIER. CAREFUL.
WE NEED TO *TALK.*
REALLY TALK.

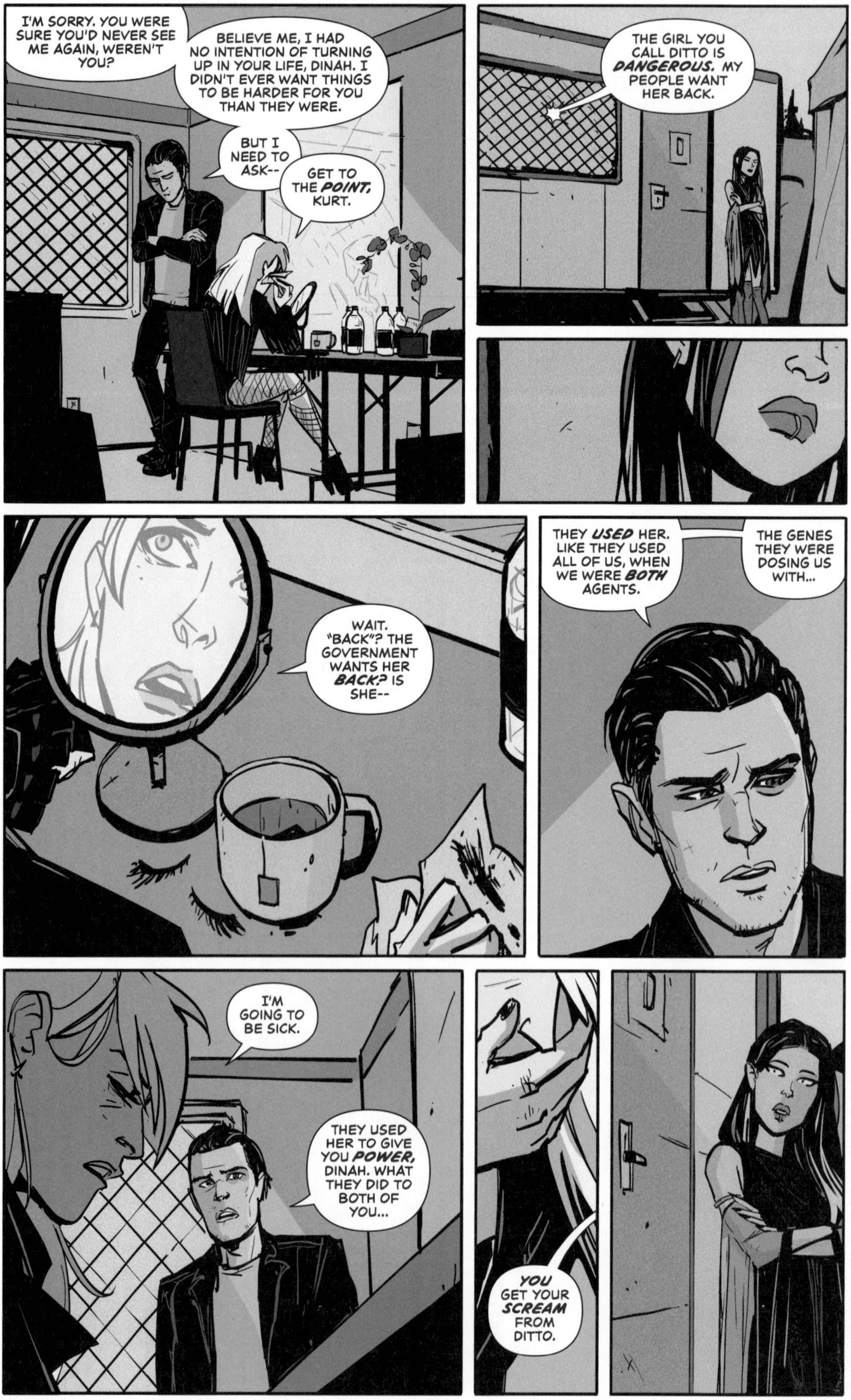
I'M SORRY. YOU WERE SURE YOU'D NEVER SEE ME AGAIN, WEREN'T YOU?
BELIEVE ME, I HAD NO INTENTION OF TURNING UP IN YOUR LIFE, DINAH. I DIDN'T EVER WANT THINGS TO BE HARDER FOR YOU THAN THEY WERE.
BUT I NEED TO ASK--
GET TO THE POINT, KURT.
THE GIRL YOU CALL DITTO IS DANGEROUS. MY PEOPLE WANT HER BACK.
WAIT. "BACK"? THE GOVERNMENT WANTS HER BACK? IS SHE--
THEY USED HER. LIKE THEY USED ALL OF US, WHEN WE WERE BOTH AGENTS.
THE GENES THEY WERE DOSING US WITH...
I'M GOING TO BE SICK.
THEY USED HER TO GIVE YOU POWER, DINAH. WHAT THEY DID TO BOTH OF YOU...
YOU GET YOUR SCREAM FROM DITTO.

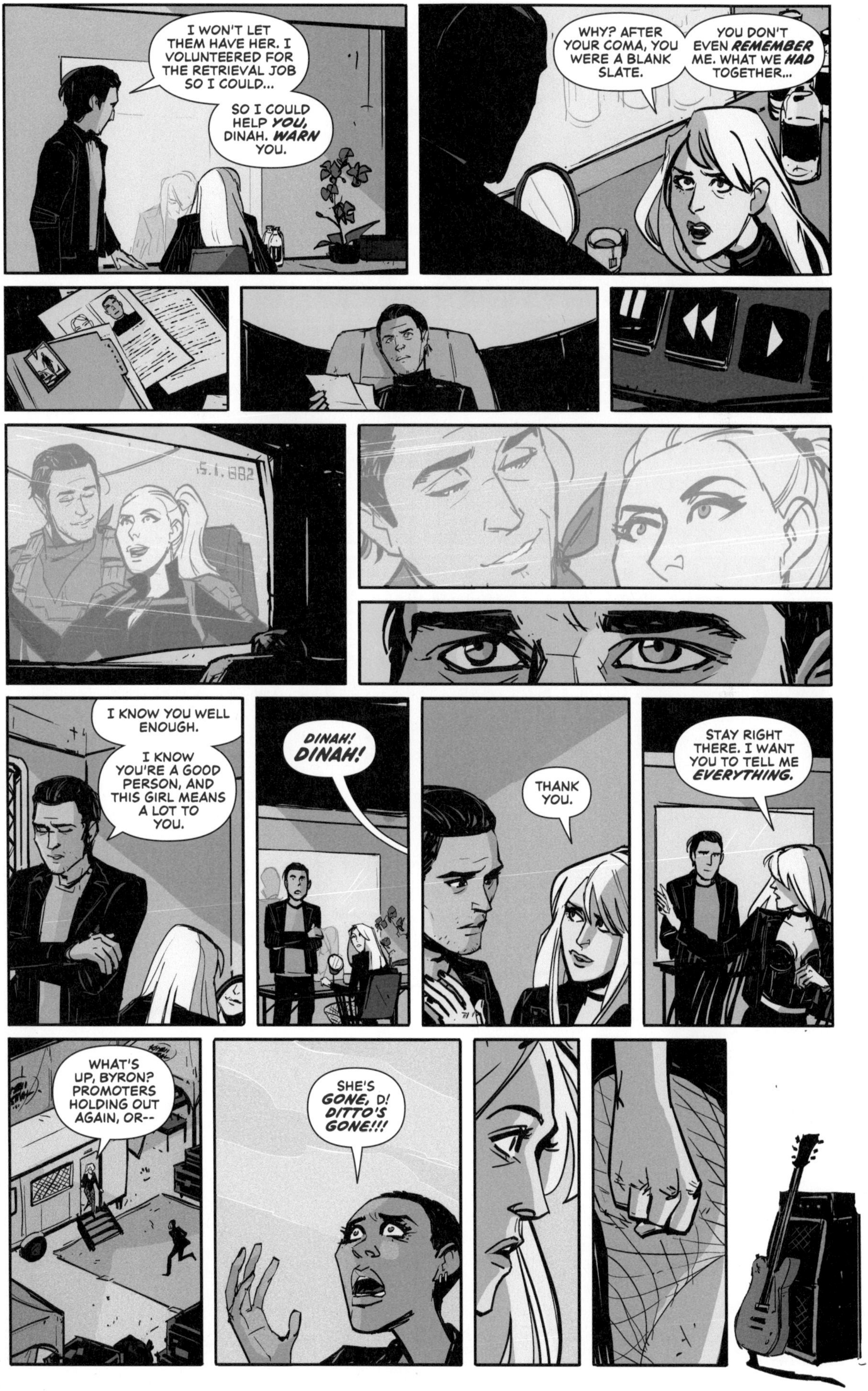
I WON'T LET THEM HAVE HER. I VOLUNTEERED FOR THE RETRIEVAL JOB SO I COULD...
SO I COULD HELP ***YOU,*** DINAH. ***WARN*** YOU.
WHY? AFTER YOUR COMA, YOU WERE A BLANK SLATE.
YOU DON'T EVEN ***REMEMBER*** ME. WHAT WE ***HAD*** TOGETHER...
I KNOW YOU WELL ENOUGH.
I KNOW YOU'RE A GOOD PERSON, AND THIS GIRL MEANS A LOT TO YOU.
DINAH! DINAH!
THANK YOU.
STAY RIGHT THERE. I WANT YOU TO TELL ME ***EVERYTHING.***
WHAT'S UP, BYRON? PROMOTERS HOLDING OUT AGAIN, OR--
SHE'S ***GONE,*** D! ***DITTO'S GONE!!!***

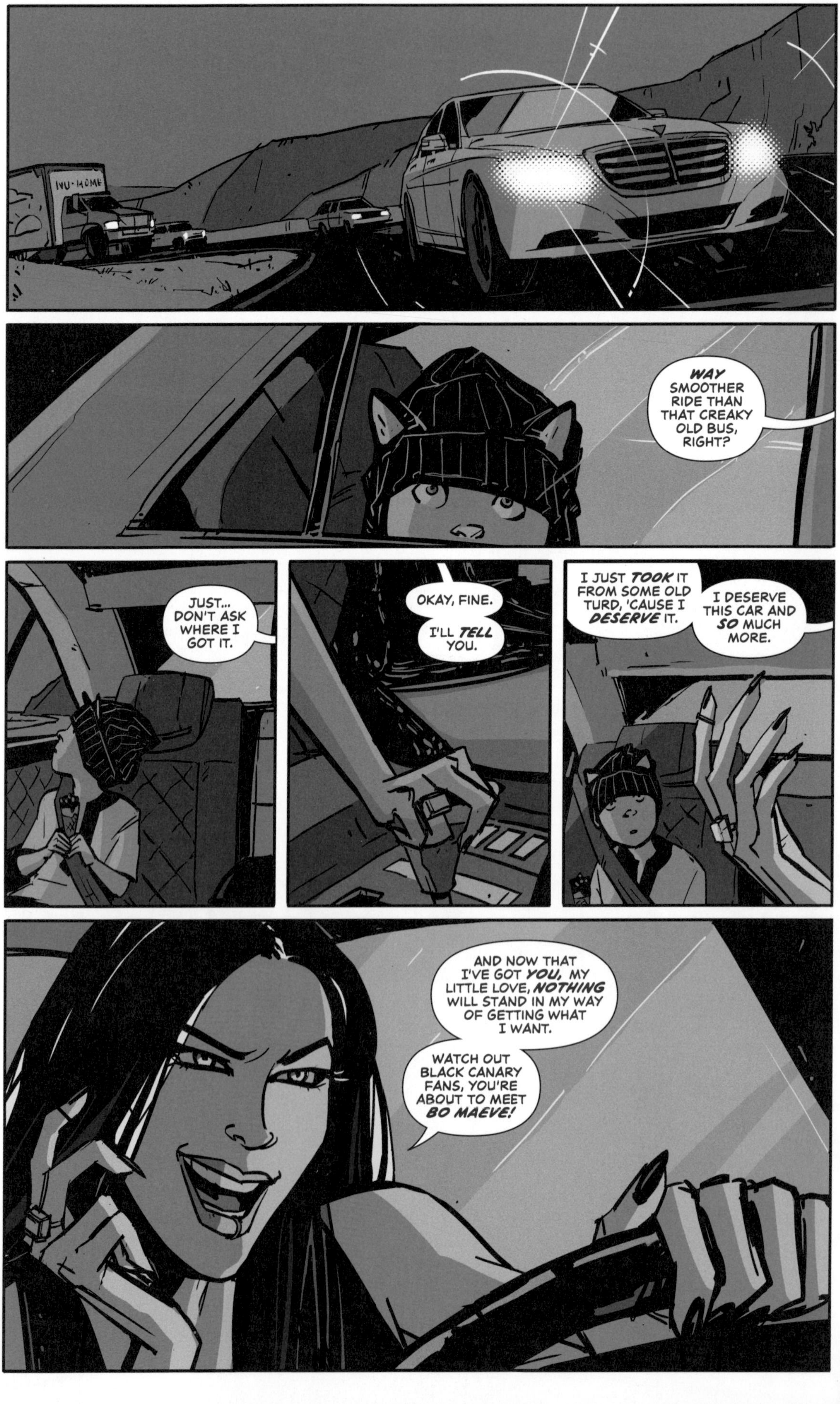
IVU-HOME
WAY SMOOTHER RIDE THAN THAT CREAKY OLD BUS, RIGHT?
JUST... DON'T ASK WHERE I GOT IT.
OKAY, FINE.
I'LL TELL YOU.
I JUST TOOK IT FROM SOME OLD TURD, 'CAUSE I DESERVE IT.
I DESERVE THIS CAR AND SO MUCH MORE.
AND NOW THAT I'VE GOT YOU, MY LITTLE LOVE, NOTHING WILL STAND IN MY WAY OF GETTING WHAT I WANT.
WATCH OUT BLACK CANARY FANS, YOU'RE ABOUT TO MEET BO MAEVE!

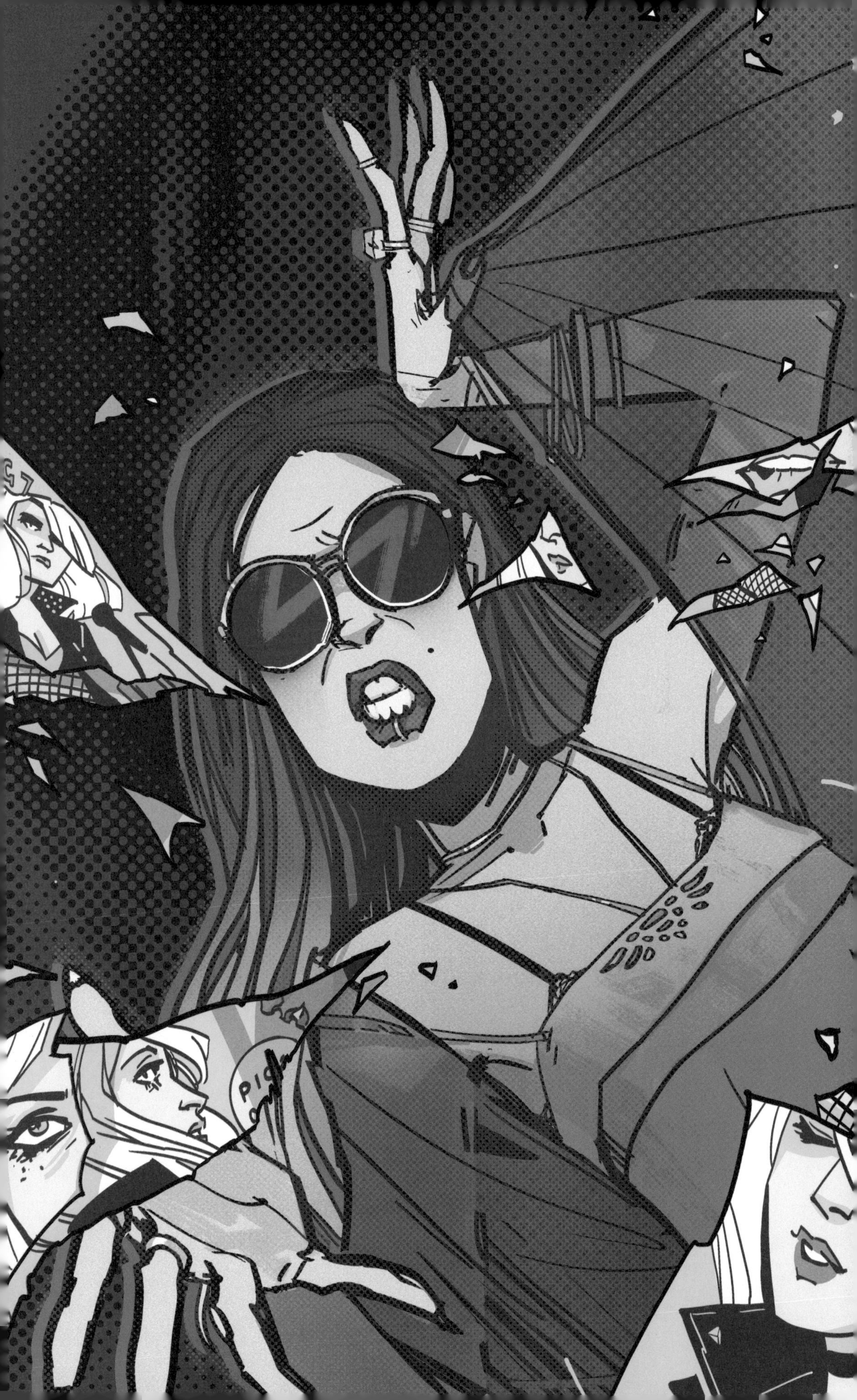

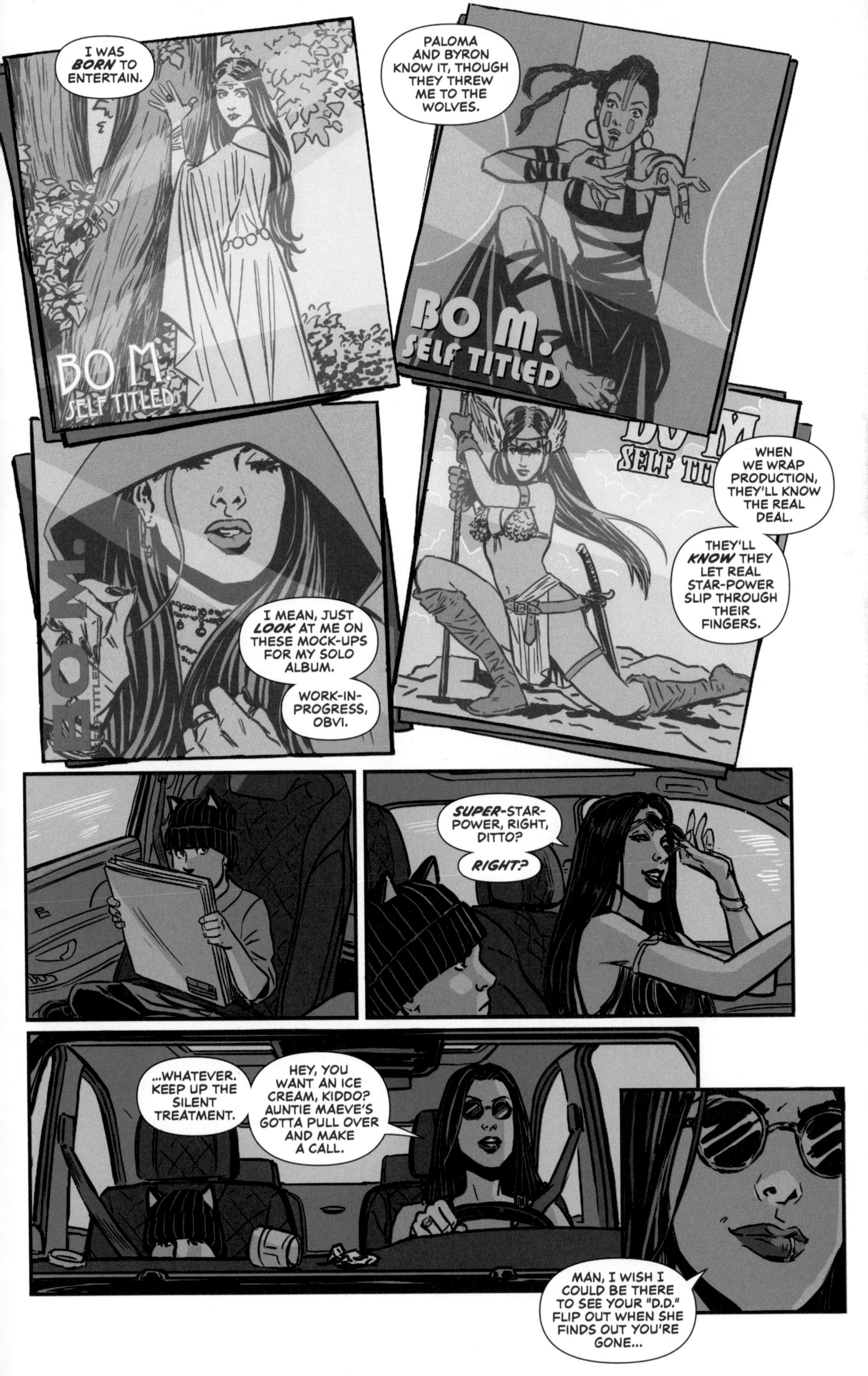
I WAS BORN TO ENTERTAIN.
BO M. SELF TITLED
PALOMA AND BYRON KNOW IT, THOUGH THEY THREW ME TO THE WOLVES.
BO M. SELF TITLED
I MEAN, JUST LOOK AT ME ON THESE MOCK-UPS FOR MY SOLO ALBUM.
WORK-IN-PROGRESS, OBVI.
WHEN WE WRAP PRODUCTION, THEY'LL KNOW THE REAL DEAL.
THEY'LL KNOW THEY LET REAL STAR-POWER SLIP THROUGH THEIR FINGERS.
SUPER-STAR-POWER, RIGHT, DITTO?
RIGHT?
...WHATEVER. KEEP UP THE SILENT TREATMENT.
HEY, YOU WANT AN ICE CREAM, KIDDO? AUNTIE MAEVE'S GOTTA PULL OVER AND MAKE A CALL.
MAN, I WISH I COULD BE THERE TO SEE YOUR "D.D." FLIP OUT WHEN SHE FINDS OUT YOU'RE GONE...

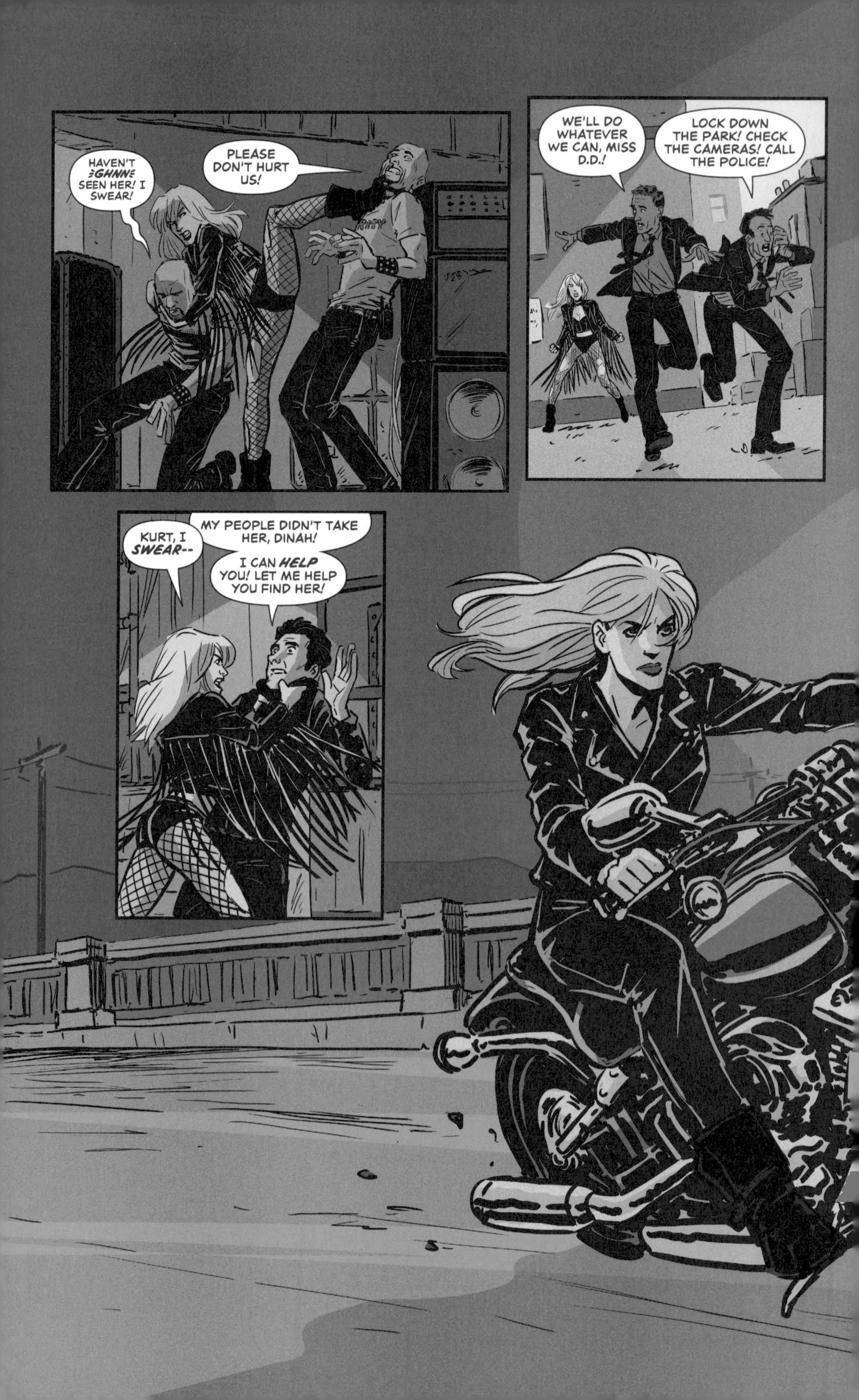
HAVEN'T *GHNN* SEEN HER! I SWEAR!
PLEASE DON'T HURT US!
WE'LL DO WHATEVER WE CAN, MISS D.D.!
LOCK DOWN THE PARK! CHECK THE CAMERAS! CALL THE POLICE!
KURT, I *SWEAR*--
MY PEOPLE DIDN'T TAKE HER, DINAH!
I CAN *HELP* YOU! LET ME HELP YOU FIND HER!

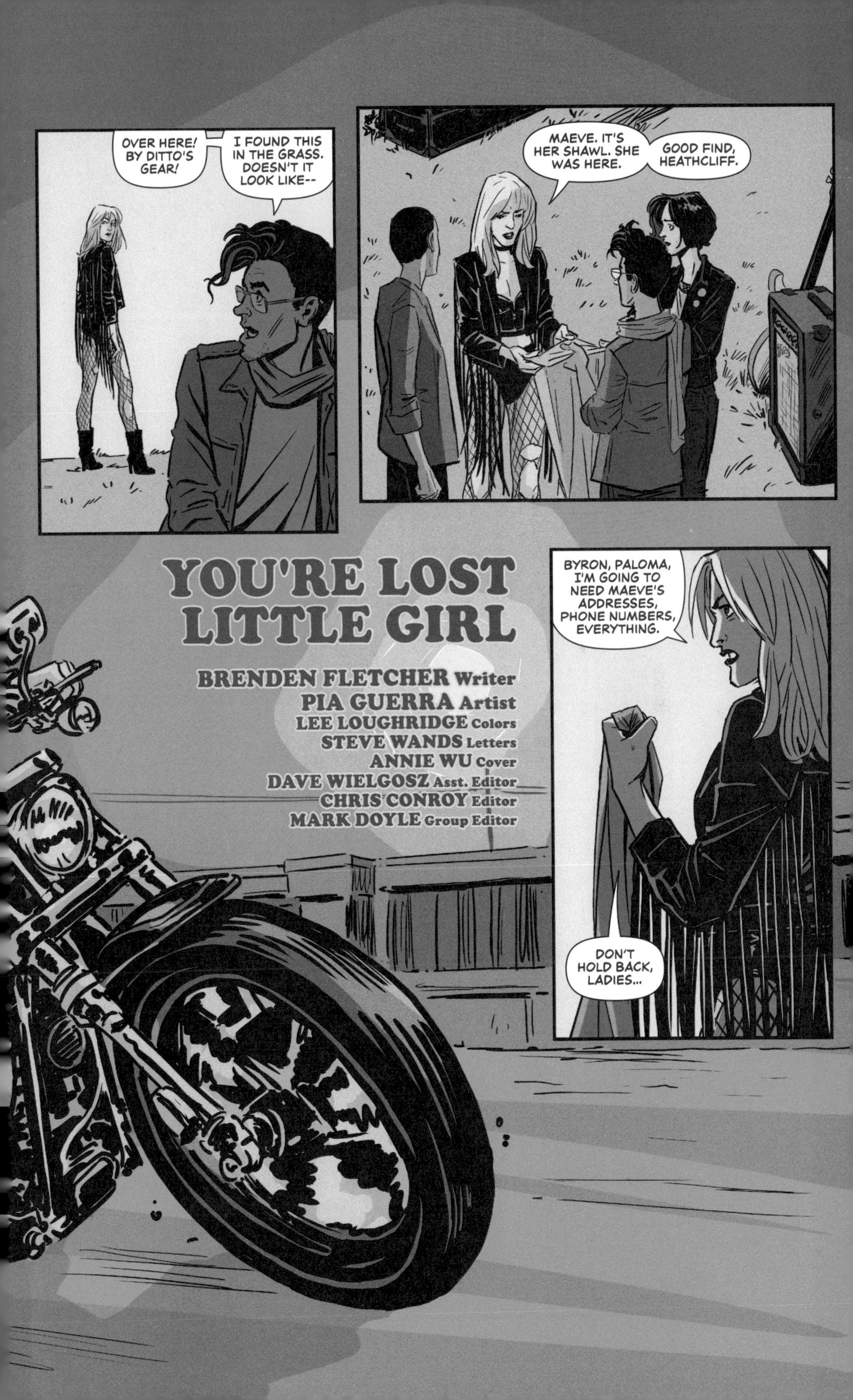
OVER HERE! BY DITTO'S GEAR!
I FOUND THIS IN THE GRASS. DOESN'T IT LOOK LIKE--
MAEVE. IT'S HER SHAWL. SHE WAS HERE.
GOOD FIND, HEATHCLIFF.
YOU'RE LOST LITTLE GIRL
BRENDEN FLETCHER Writer
PIA GUERRA Artist
LEE LOUGHRIDGE Colors
STEVE WANDS Letters
ANNIE WU Cover
DAVE WIELGOSZ Asst. Editor
CHRIS CONROY Editor
MARK DOYLE Group Editor
BYRON, PALOMA, I'M GOING TO NEED MAEVE'S ADDRESSES, PHONE NUMBERS, EVERYTHING.
DON'T HOLD BACK, LADIES...

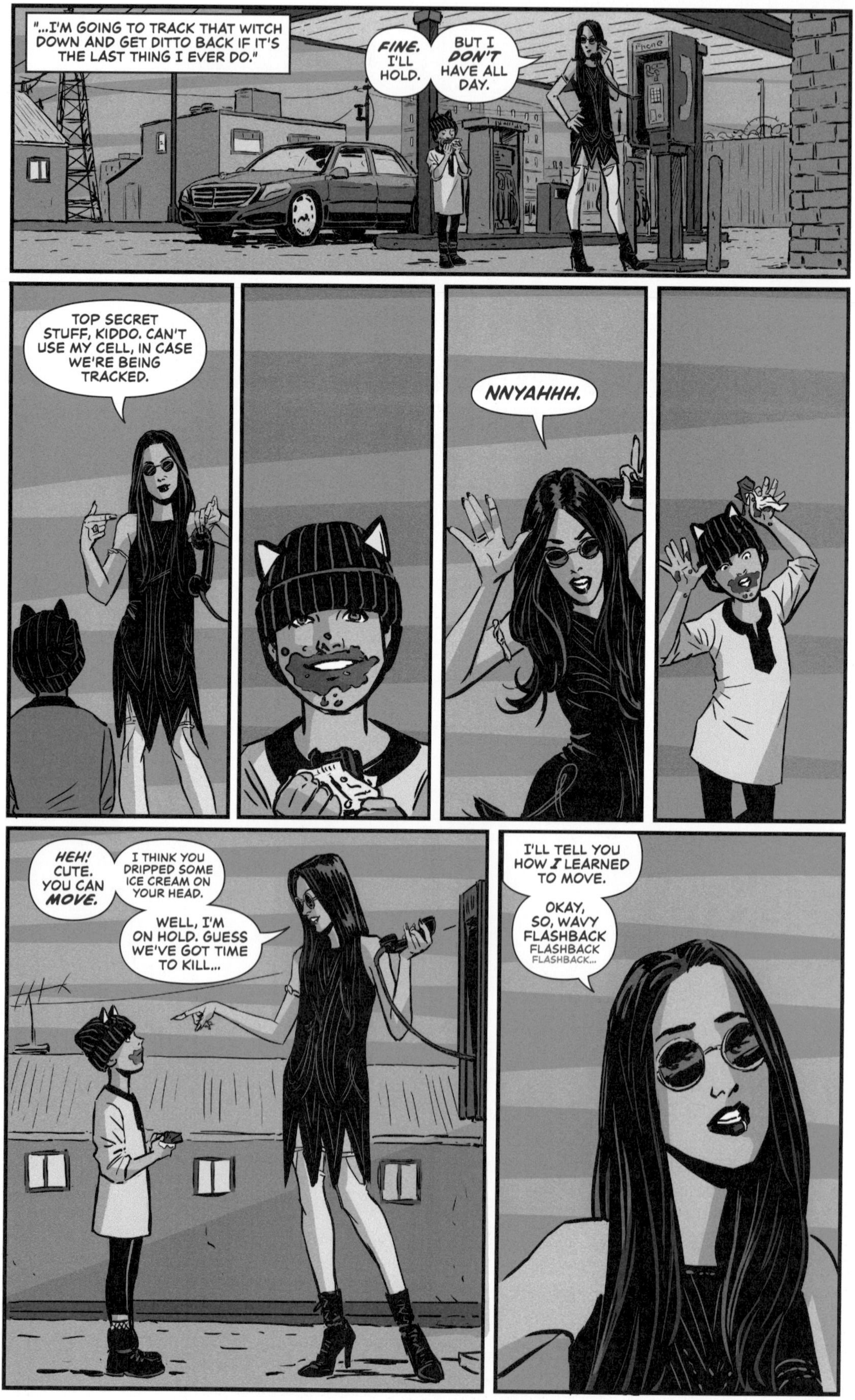

"...I'M GOING TO TRACK THAT WITCH DOWN AND GET DITTO BACK IF IT'S THE LAST THING I EVER DO."
FINE. I'LL HOLD.
BUT I DON'T HAVE ALL DAY.
TOP SECRET STUFF, KIDDO. CAN'T USE MY CELL, IN CASE WE'RE BEING TRACKED.
NNYAHHH.
HEH! CUTE. YOU CAN MOVE.
I THINK YOU DRIPPED SOME ICE CREAM ON YOUR HEAD.
WELL, I'M ON HOLD. GUESS WE'VE GOT TIME TO KILL...
I'LL TELL YOU HOW I LEARNED TO MOVE.
OKAY, SO, WAVY FLASHBACK FLASHBACK FLASHBACK...

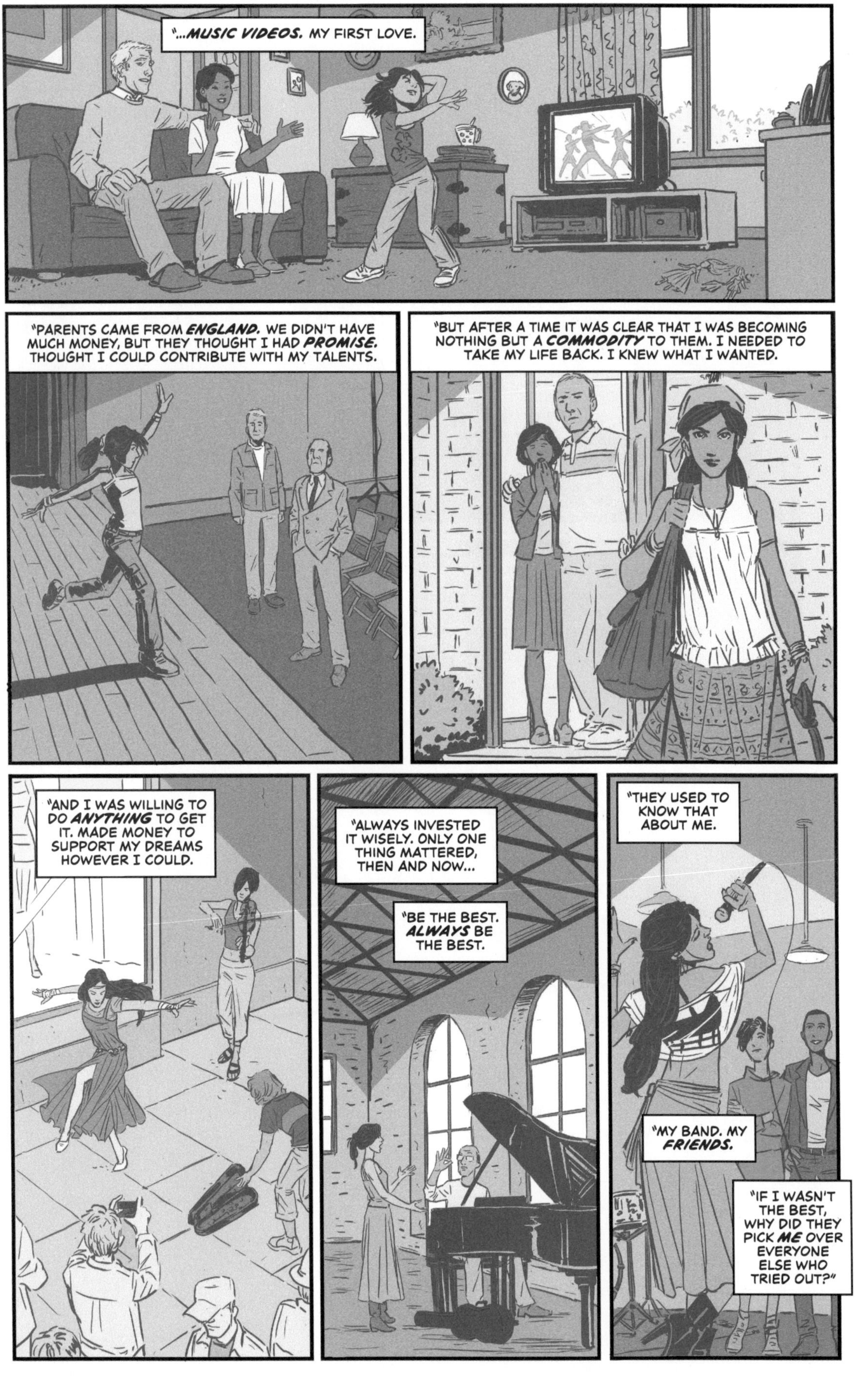
"...MUSIC VIDEOS. MY FIRST LOVE.
"PARENTS CAME FROM ENGLAND. WE DIDN'T HAVE MUCH MONEY, BUT THEY THOUGHT I HAD PROMISE. THOUGHT I COULD CONTRIBUTE WITH MY TALENTS.
"BUT AFTER A TIME IT WAS CLEAR THAT I WAS BECOMING NOTHING BUT A COMMODITY TO THEM. I NEEDED TO TAKE MY LIFE BACK. I KNEW WHAT I WANTED.
"AND I WAS WILLING TO DO ANYTHING TO GET IT. MADE MONEY TO SUPPORT MY DREAMS HOWEVER I COULD.
"ALWAYS INVESTED IT WISELY. ONLY ONE THING MATTERED, THEN AND NOW...
"BE THE BEST. ALWAYS BE THE BEST.
"THEY USED TO KNOW THAT ABOUT ME.
"MY BAND. MY FRIENDS.
"IF I WASN'T THE BEST, WHY DID THEY PICK ME OVER EVERYONE ELSE WHO TRIED OUT?"

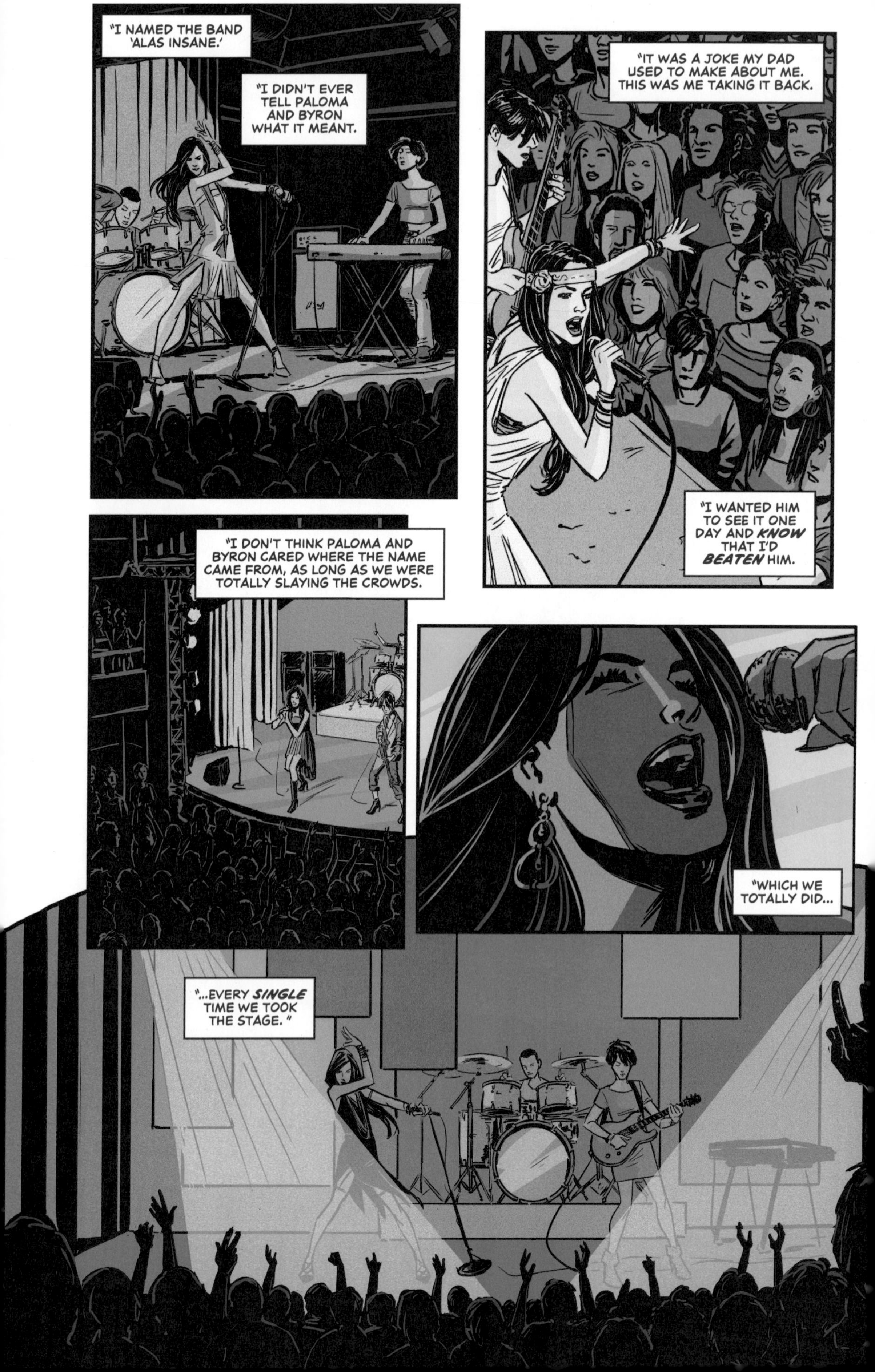
"I NAMED THE BAND 'ALAS INSANE.'
"I DIDN'T EVER TELL PALOMA AND BYRON WHAT IT MEANT.
"IT WAS A JOKE MY DAD USED TO MAKE ABOUT ME. THIS WAS ME TAKING IT BACK.
"I WANTED HIM TO SEE IT ONE DAY AND *KNOW* THAT I'D *BEATEN* HIM.
"I DON'T THINK PALOMA AND BYRON CARED WHERE THE NAME CAME FROM, AS LONG AS WE WERE TOTALLY SLAYING THE CROWDS.
"WHICH WE TOTALLY DID...
"...EVERY *SINGLE* TIME WE TOOK THE STAGE."

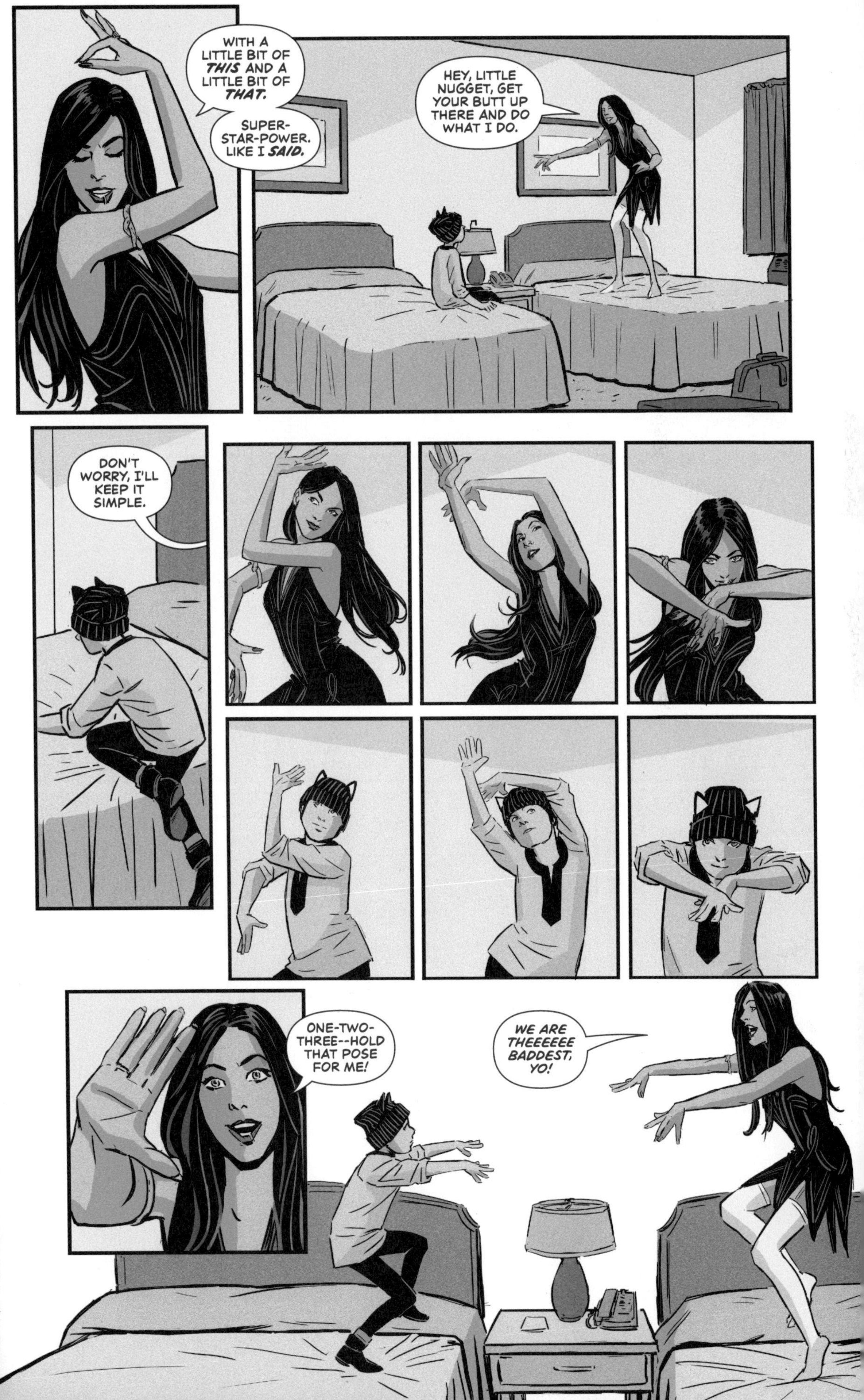

WITH A LITTLE BIT OF *THIS* AND A LITTLE BIT OF *THAT.*
SUPER-STAR-POWER. LIKE I *SAID.*
HEY, LITTLE NUGGET, GET YOUR BUTT UP THERE AND DO WHAT I DO.
DON'T WORRY, I'LL KEEP IT SIMPLE.
ONE-TWO-THREE--HOLD THAT POSE FOR ME!
WE ARE THEEEEEE BADDEST, YO!

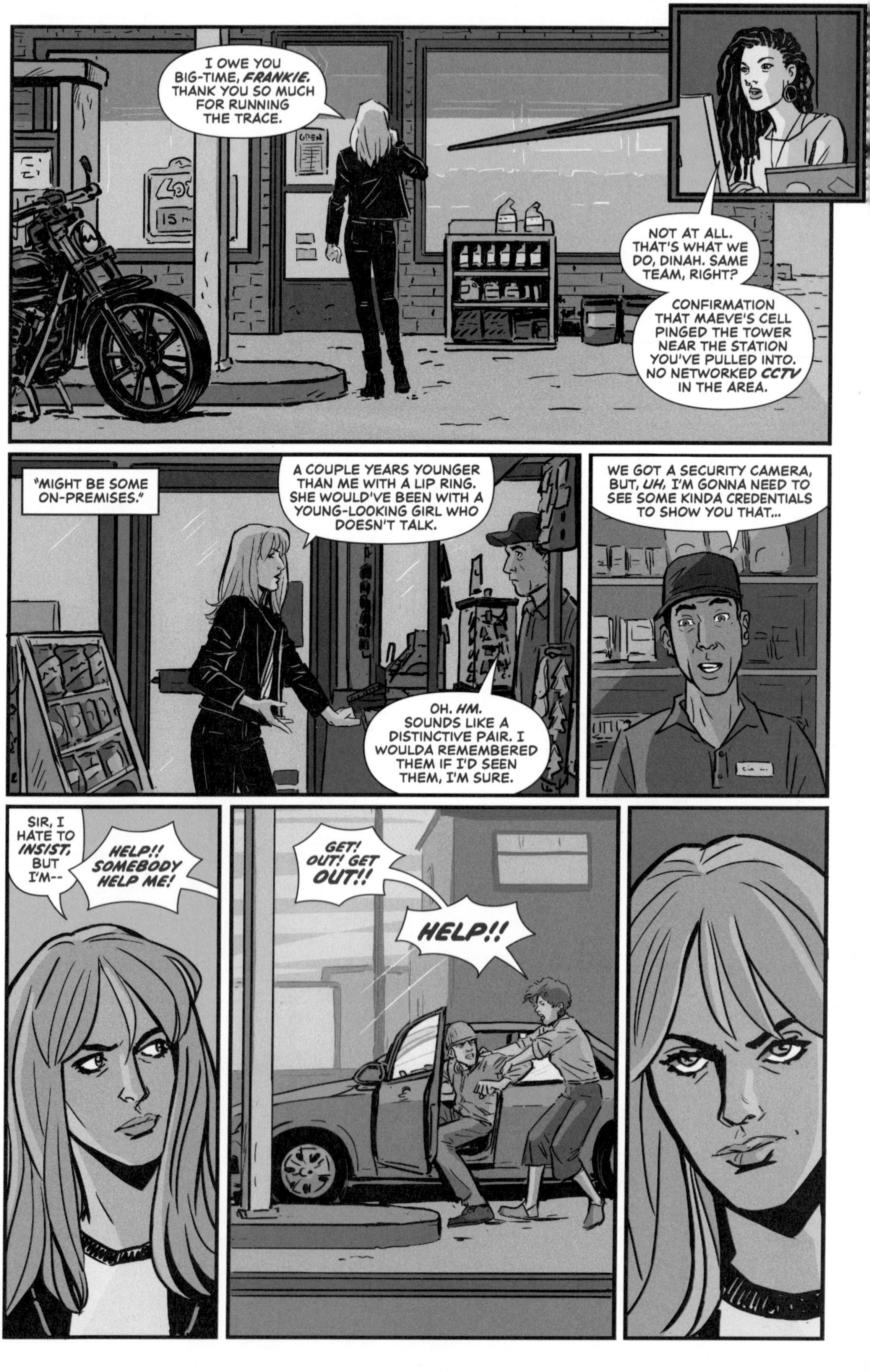
I OWE YOU BIG-TIME, ***FRANKIE.*** THANK YOU SO MUCH FOR RUNNING THE TRACE.
NOT AT ALL. THAT'S WHAT WE DO, DINAH. SAME TEAM, RIGHT?
CONFIRMATION THAT MAEVE'S CELL PINGED THE TOWER NEAR THE STATION YOU'VE PULLED INTO. NO NETWORKED ***CCTV*** IN THE AREA.
"MIGHT BE SOME ON-PREMISES."
A COUPLE YEARS YOUNGER THAN ME WITH A LIP RING. SHE WOULD'VE BEEN WITH A YOUNG-LOOKING GIRL WHO DOESN'T TALK.
OH. ***HM.*** SOUNDS LIKE A DISTINCTIVE PAIR. I WOULDA REMEMBERED THEM IF I'D SEEN THEM, I'M SURE.
WE GOT A SECURITY CAMERA, BUT, *UH,* I'M GONNA NEED TO SEE SOME KINDA CREDENTIALS TO SHOW YOU THAT...
SIR, I HATE TO ***INSIST,*** BUT I'M--
HELP!! SOMEBODY HELP ME!
GET! OUT! GET OUT!!
HELP!!

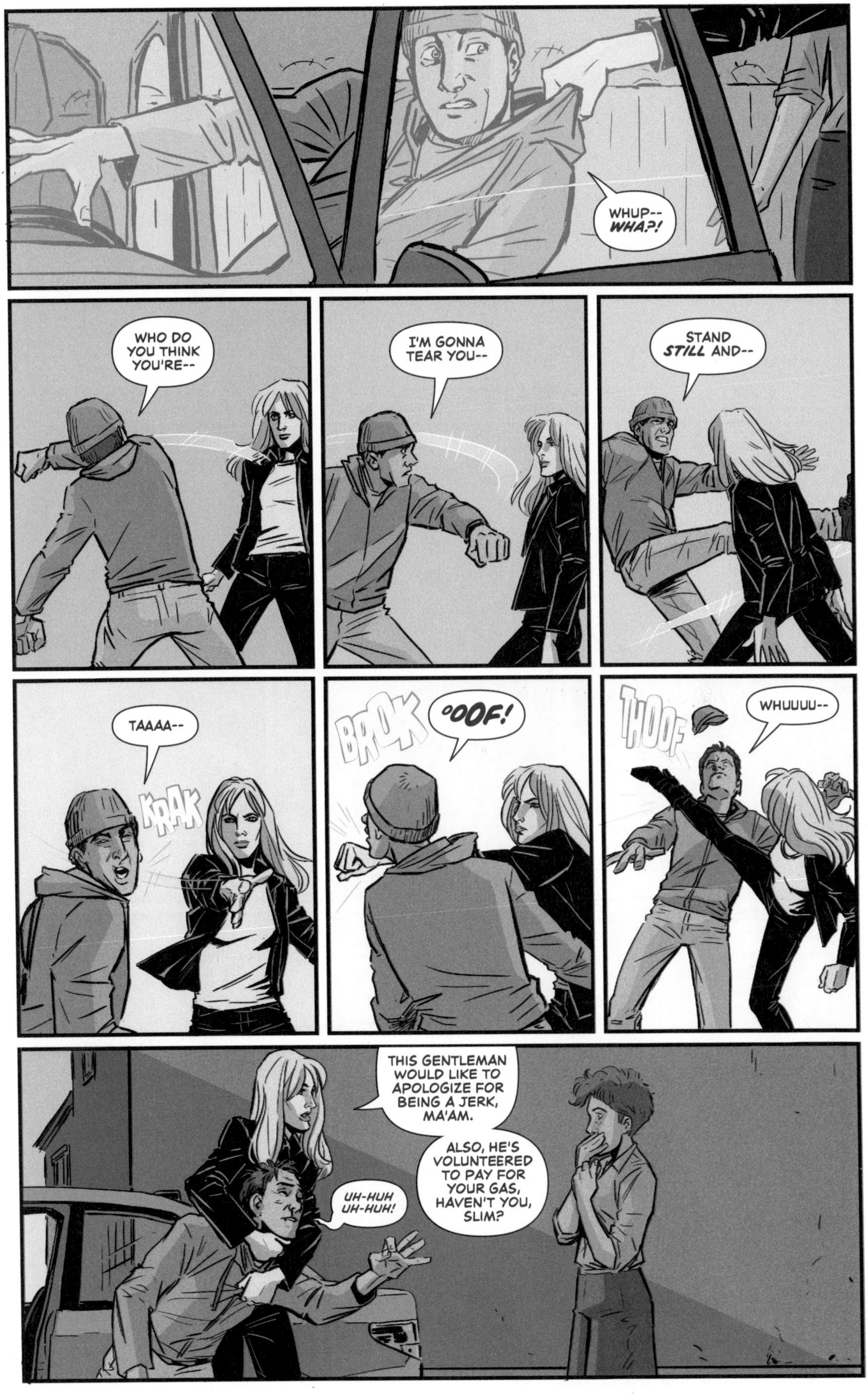
WHUP--
WHA?!
WHO DO YOU THINK YOU'RE--
I'M GONNA TEAR YOU--
STAND STILL AND--
TAAAA--
KRAK
BROK
OOF!
THOOF
WHUUUU--
THIS GENTLEMAN WOULD LIKE TO APOLOGIZE FOR BEING A JERK, MA'AM.
ALSO, HE'S VOLUNTEERED TO PAY FOR YOUR GAS, HAVEN'T YOU, SLIM?
UH-HUH UH-HUH!

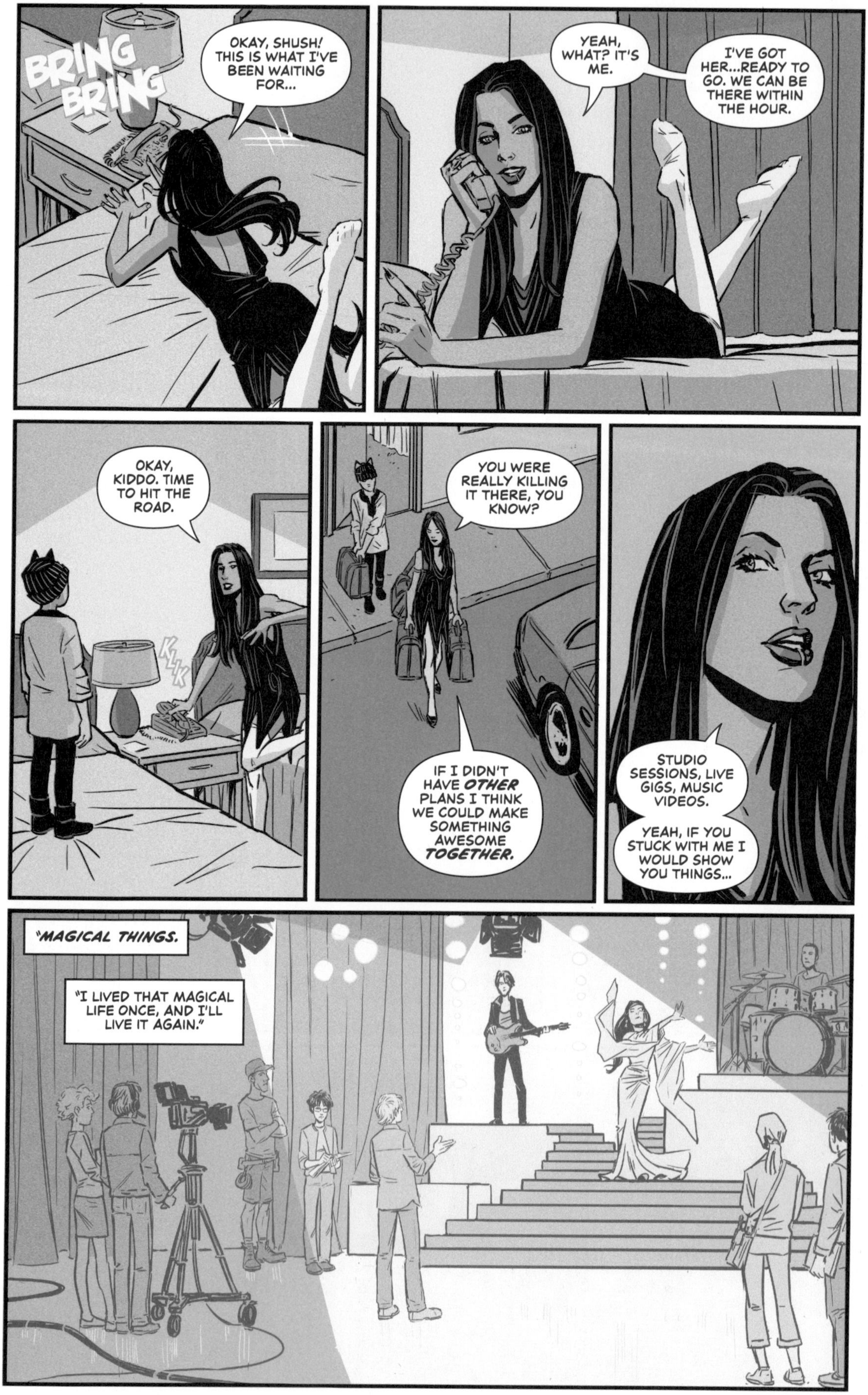
BRING BRING
OKAY, SHUSH! THIS IS WHAT I'VE BEEN WAITING FOR...
YEAH, WHAT? IT'S ME.
I'VE GOT HER...READY TO GO. WE CAN BE THERE WITHIN THE HOUR.
OKAY, KIDDO. TIME TO HIT THE ROAD.
KLIK
YOU WERE REALLY KILLING IT THERE, YOU KNOW?
IF I DIDN'T HAVE *OTHER* PLANS I THINK WE COULD MAKE SOMETHING AWESOME *TOGETHER.*
STUDIO SESSIONS, LIVE GIGS, MUSIC VIDEOS.
YEAH, IF YOU STUCK WITH ME I WOULD SHOW YOU THINGS...
"*MAGICAL THINGS.*
"I LIVED THAT MAGICAL LIFE ONCE, AND I'LL LIVE IT AGAIN."

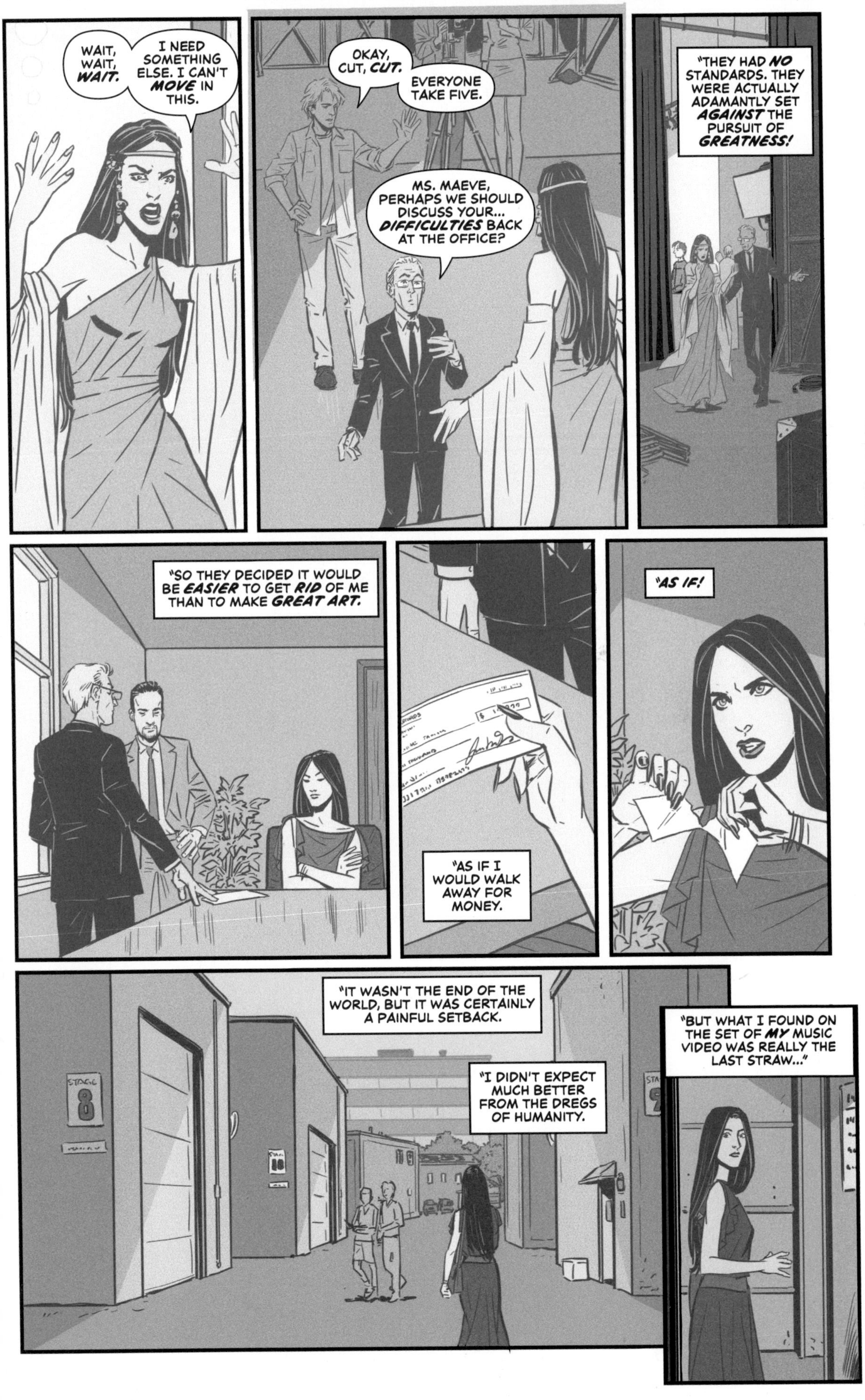
WAIT, WAIT, WAIT.
I NEED SOMETHING ELSE. I CAN'T MOVE IN THIS.
OKAY, CUT, CUT.
EVERYONE TAKE FIVE.
MS. MAEVE, PERHAPS WE SHOULD DISCUSS YOUR... DIFFICULTIES BACK AT THE OFFICE?
"THEY HAD NO STANDARDS. THEY WERE ACTUALLY ADAMANTLY SET AGAINST THE PURSUIT OF GREATNESS!
"SO THEY DECIDED IT WOULD BE EASIER TO GET RID OF ME THAN TO MAKE GREAT ART.
"AS IF I WOULD WALK AWAY FOR MONEY.
"AS IF!
"IT WASN'T THE END OF THE WORLD, BUT IT WAS CERTAINLY A PAINFUL SETBACK.
"I DIDN'T EXPECT MUCH BETTER FROM THE DREGS OF HUMANITY.
STAGE 8
"BUT WHAT I FOUND ON THE SET OF MY MUSIC VIDEO WAS REALLY THE LAST STRAW..."

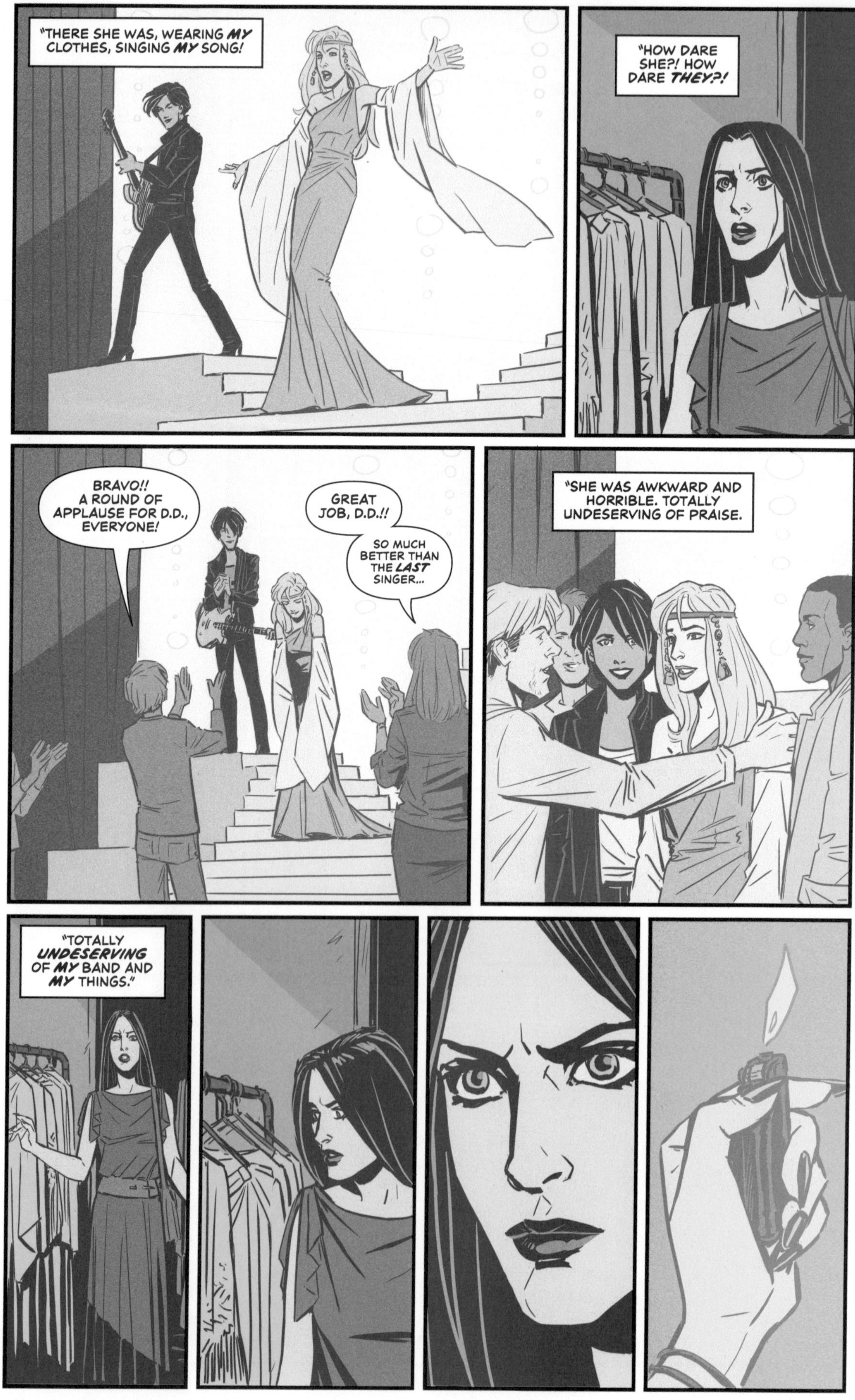
"THERE SHE WAS, WEARING MY CLOTHES, SINGING MY SONG!
"HOW DARE SHE?! HOW DARE THEY?!
BRAVO!! A ROUND OF APPLAUSE FOR D.D., EVERYONE!
GREAT JOB, D.D.!!
SO MUCH BETTER THAN THE LAST SINGER...
"SHE WAS AWKWARD AND HORRIBLE. TOTALLY UNDESERVING OF PRAISE.
"TOTALLY UNDESERVING OF MY BAND AND MY THINGS."

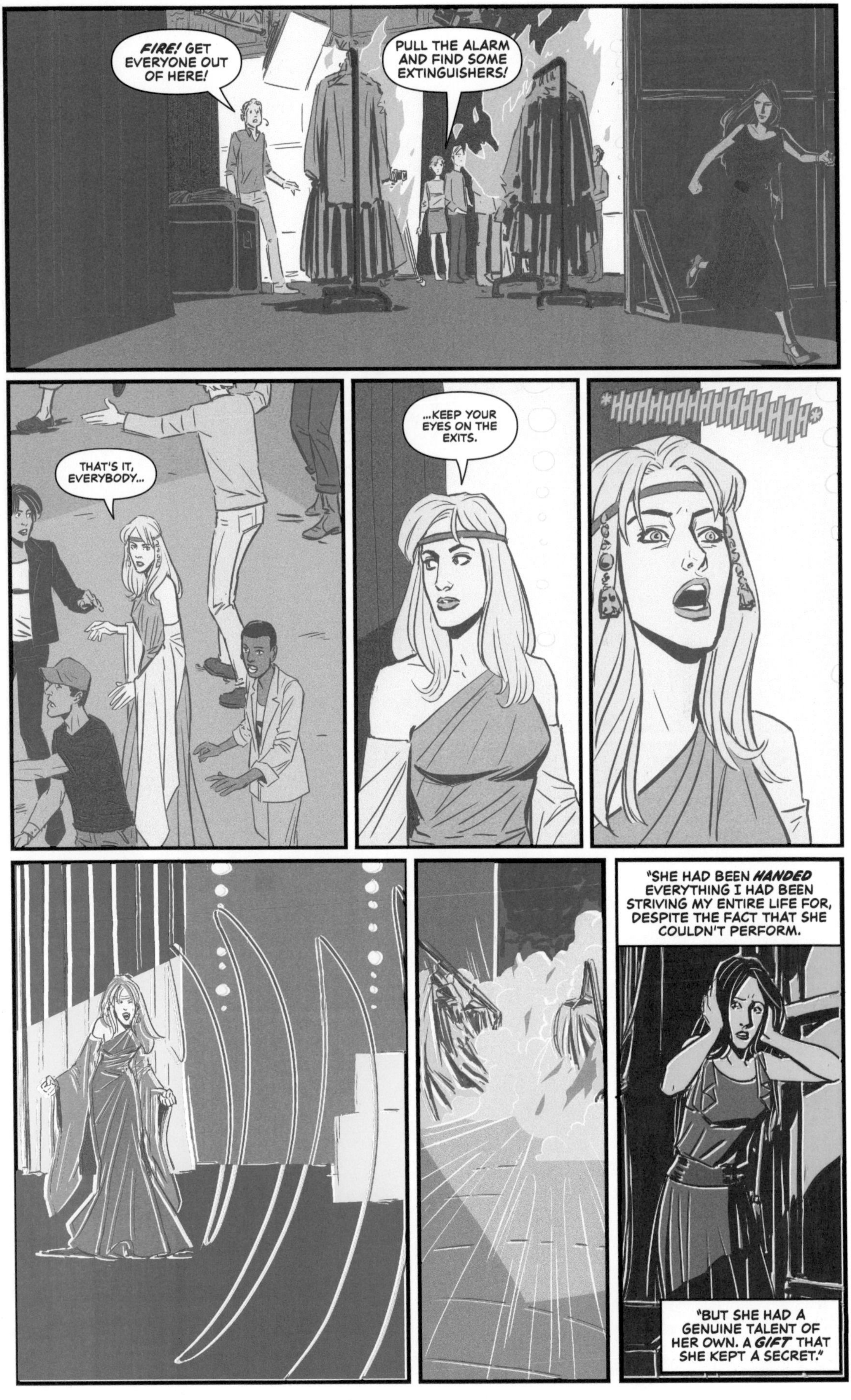
FIRE! GET EVERYONE OUT OF HERE!
PULL THE ALARM AND FIND SOME EXTINGUISHERS!
THAT'S IT, EVERYBODY...
...KEEP YOUR EYES ON THE EXITS.
HHHHHHHHHHHHHHHH
"SHE HAD BEEN HANDED EVERYTHING I HAD BEEN STRIVING MY ENTIRE LIFE FOR, DESPITE THE FACT THAT SHE COULDN'T PERFORM.
"BUT SHE HAD A GENUINE TALENT OF HER OWN. A GIFT THAT SHE KEPT A SECRET."

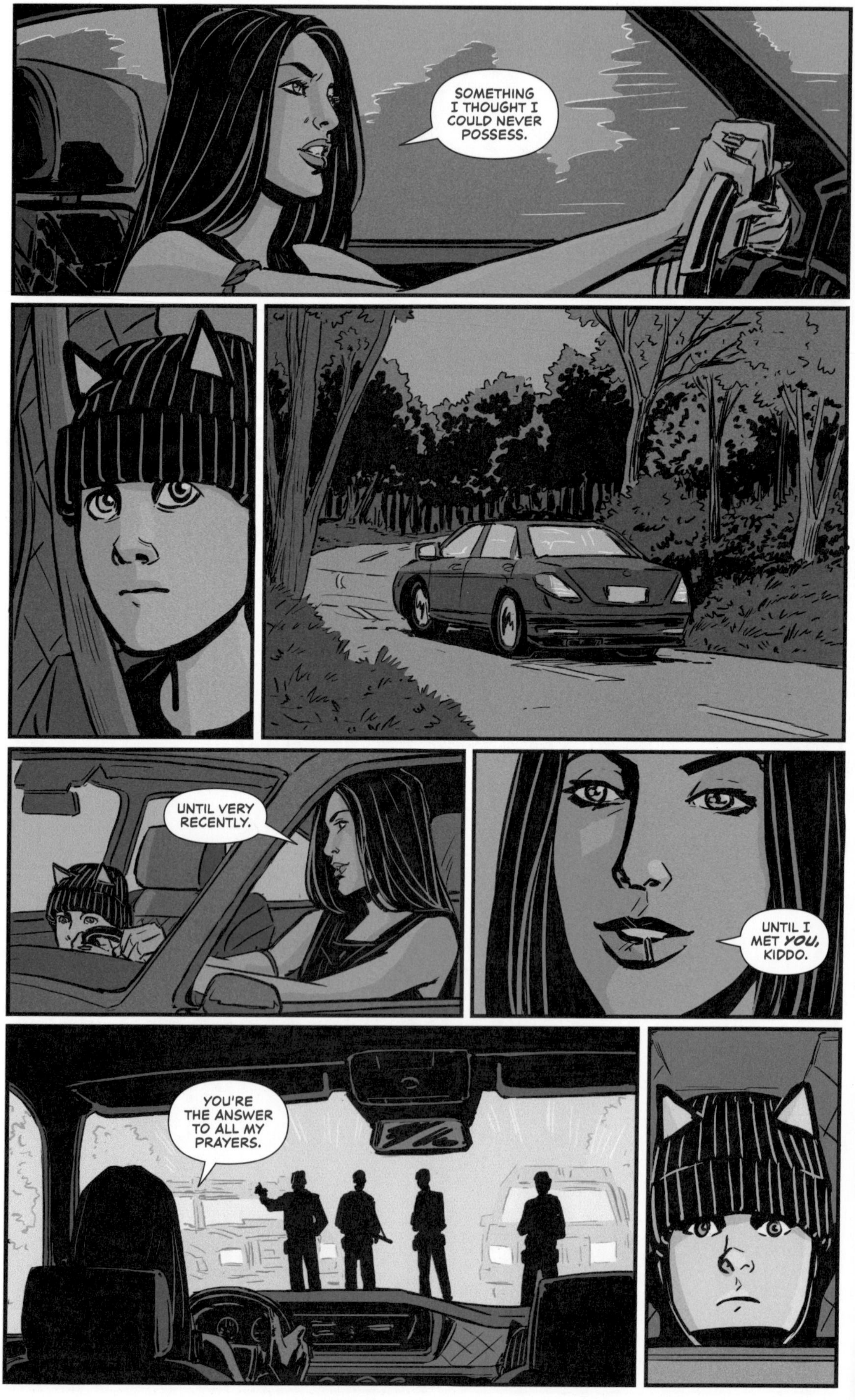
SOMETHING I THOUGHT I COULD NEVER POSSESS.
UNTIL VERY RECENTLY.
UNTIL I MET *YOU*, KIDDO.
YOU'RE THE ANSWER TO ALL MY PRAYERS.

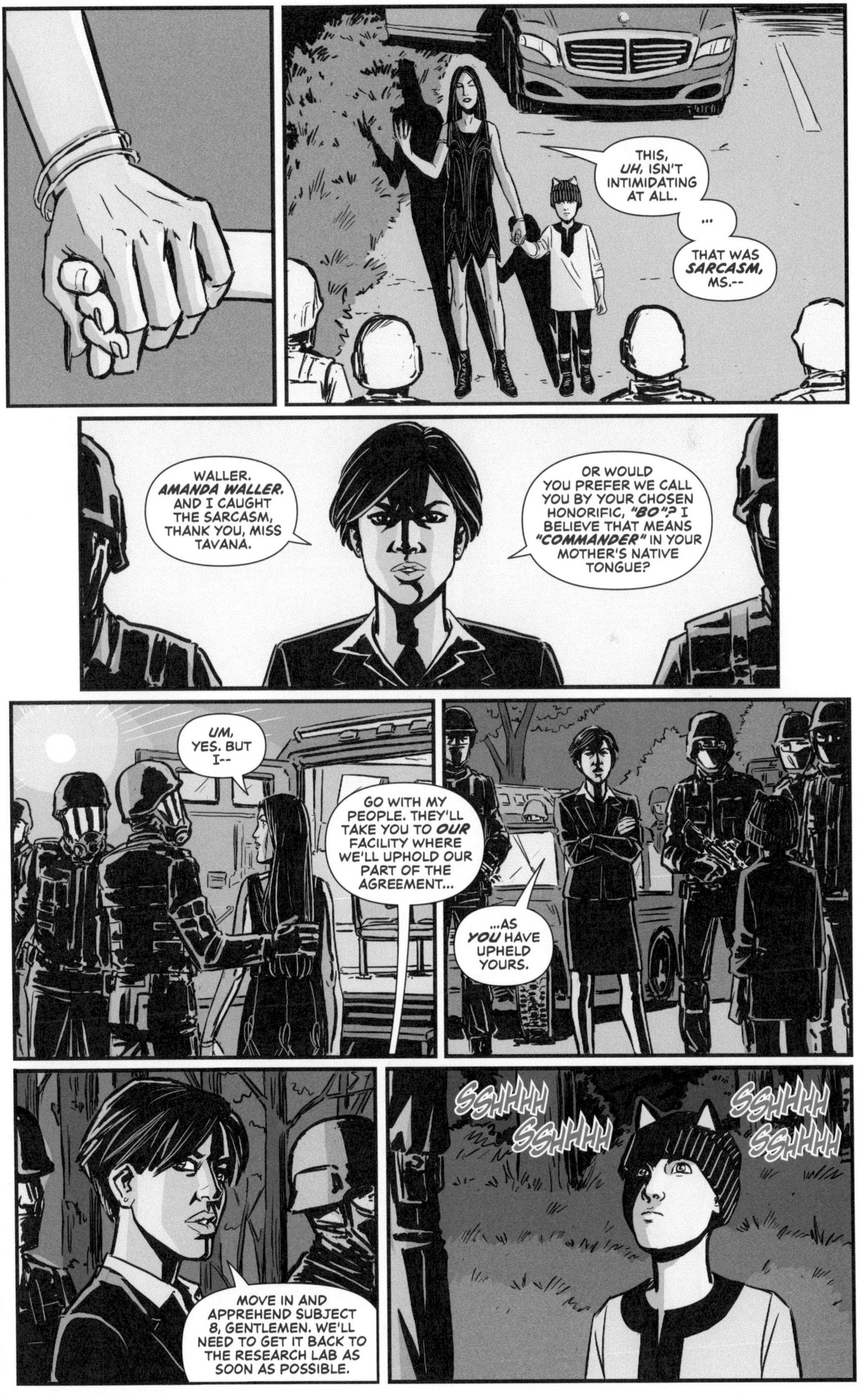
THIS, UH, ISN'T INTIMIDATING AT ALL.
...
THAT WAS SARCASM, MS.--
WALLER. AMANDA WALLER. AND I CAUGHT THE SARCASM, THANK YOU, MISS TAVANA.
OR WOULD YOU PREFER WE CALL YOU BY YOUR CHOSEN HONORIFIC, "BO"? I BELIEVE THAT MEANS "COMMANDER" IN YOUR MOTHER'S NATIVE TONGUE?
UM, YES. BUT I--
GO WITH MY PEOPLE. THEY'LL TAKE YOU TO OUR FACILITY WHERE WE'LL UPHOLD OUR PART OF THE AGREEMENT...
...AS YOU HAVE UPHELD YOURS.
MOVE IN AND APPREHEND SUBJECT 8, GENTLEMEN. WE'LL NEED TO GET IT BACK TO THE RESEARCH LAB AS SOON AS POSSIBLE.
SSHHHH
SSHHHH
SSHHHH
SSHHHH

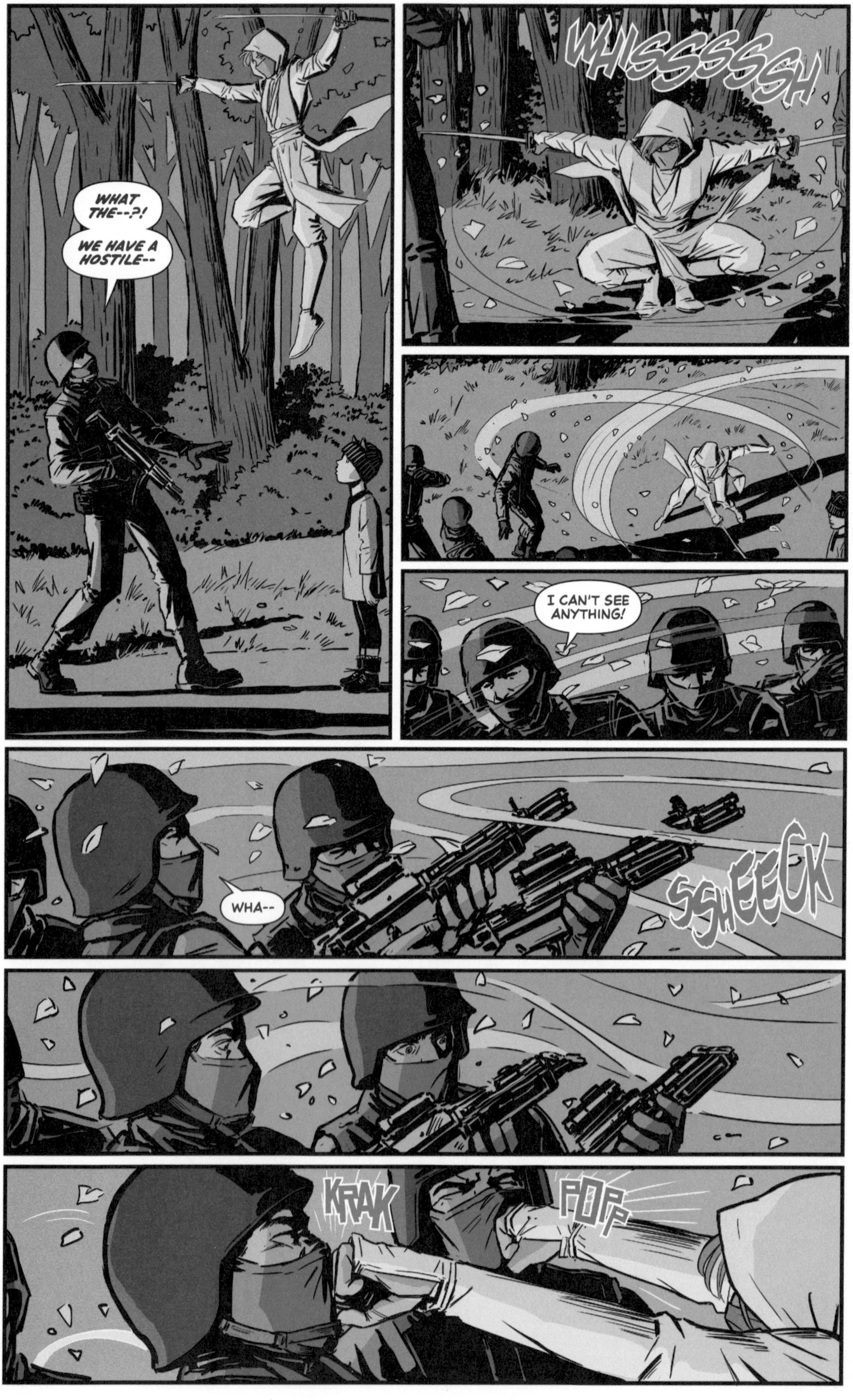
WHAT THE--?!
WE HAVE A HOSTILE--
WHISSSSSH
I CAN'T SEE ANYTHING!
WHA--
SSHEEECK
KRAK
POP

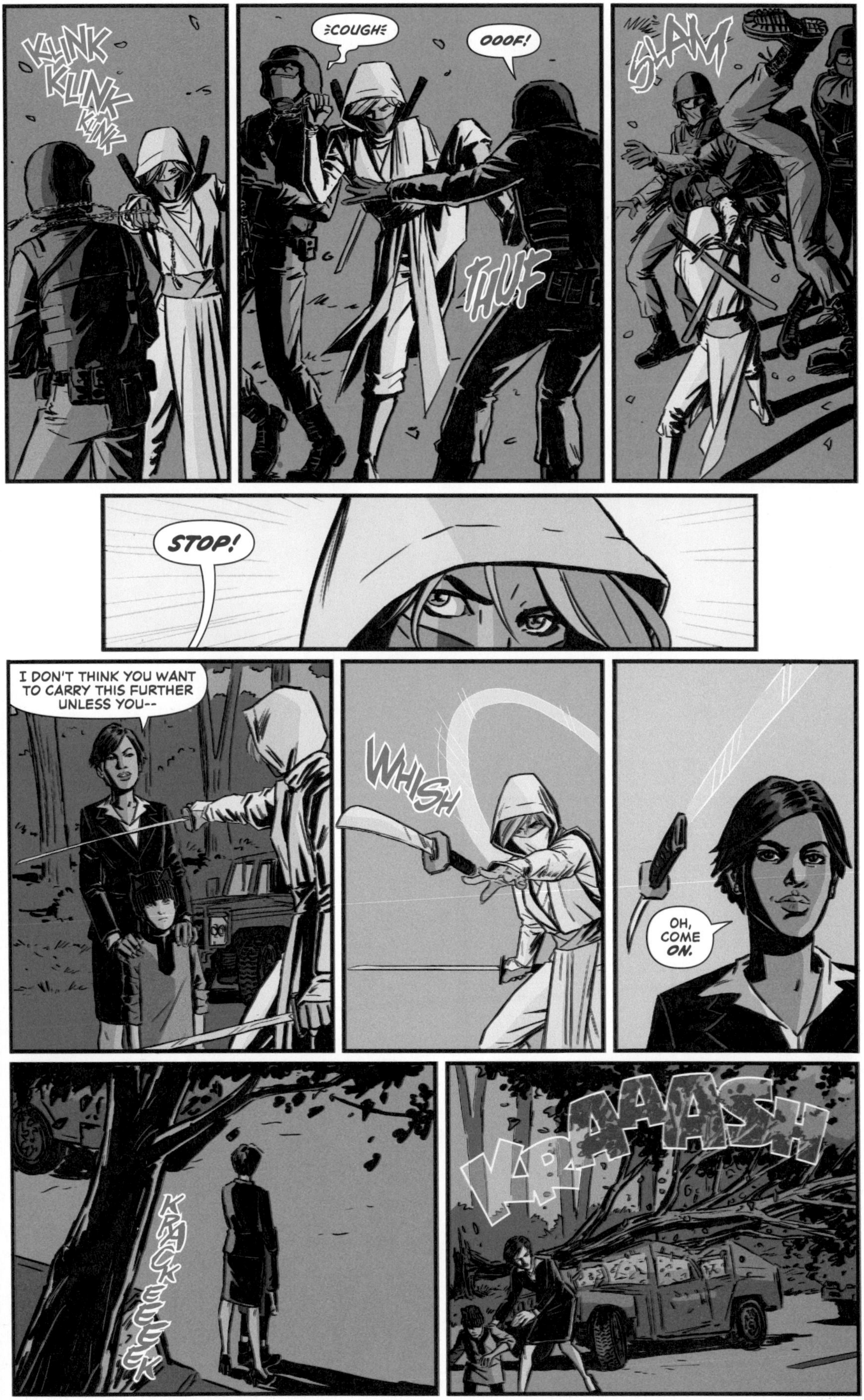
KLINK KLINK KLINK
COUGH
OOOF!
THUF
SLAM
STOP!
I DON'T THINK YOU WANT TO CARRY THIS FURTHER UNLESS YOU--
WHISH
OH, COME ON.
KRACKEEEEK
KRAAAASH

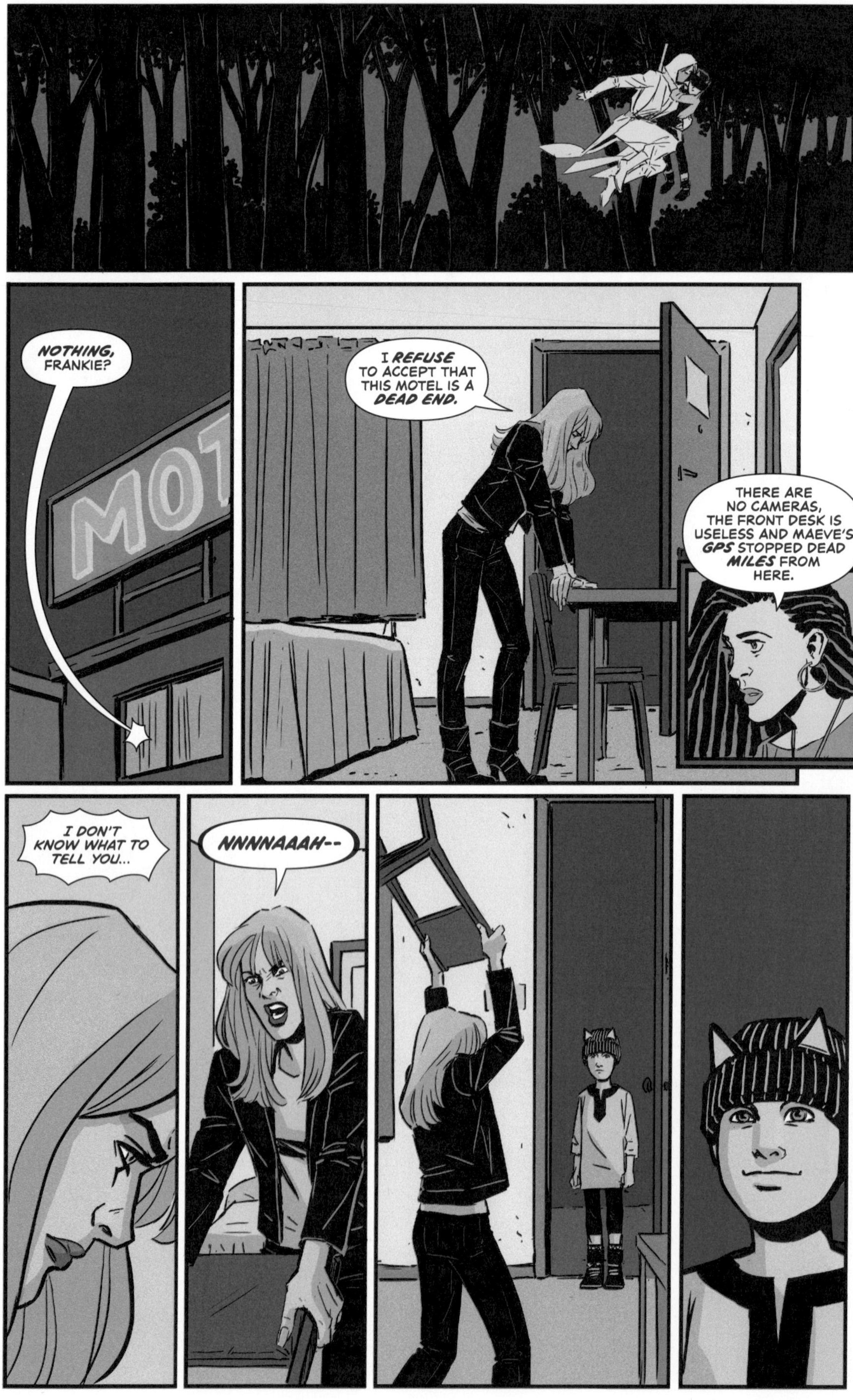

NOTHING, FRANKIE?
MOT
I REFUSE TO ACCEPT THAT THIS MOTEL IS A DEAD END.
THERE ARE NO CAMERAS, THE FRONT DESK IS USELESS AND MAEVE'S GPS STOPPED DEAD MILES FROM HERE.
I DON'T KNOW WHAT TO TELL YOU...
NNNNAAAH--

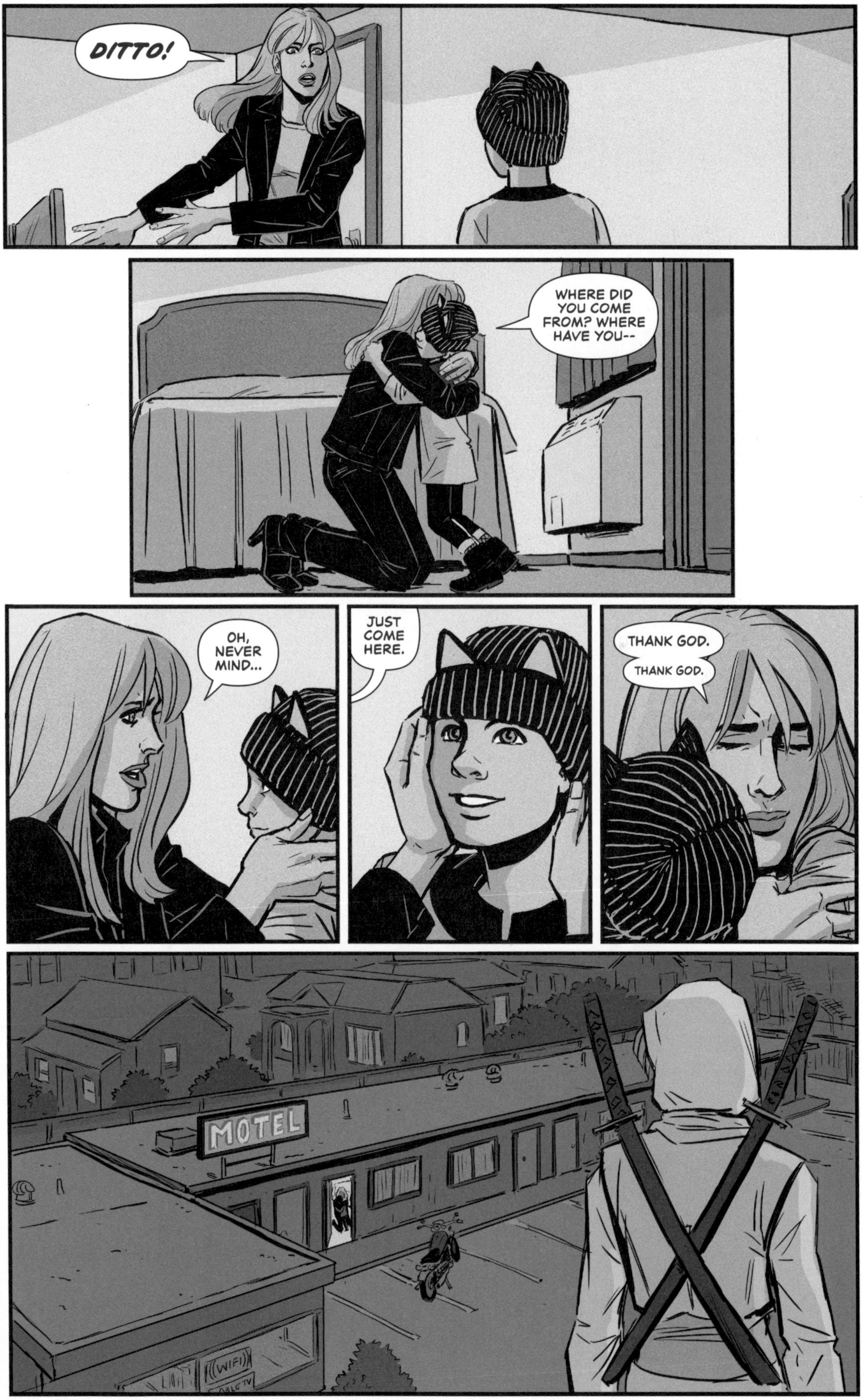
DITTO!
WHERE DID YOU COME FROM? WHERE HAVE YOU--
OH, NEVER MIND...
JUST COME HERE.
THANK GOD.
THANK GOD.
MOTEL
WIFI

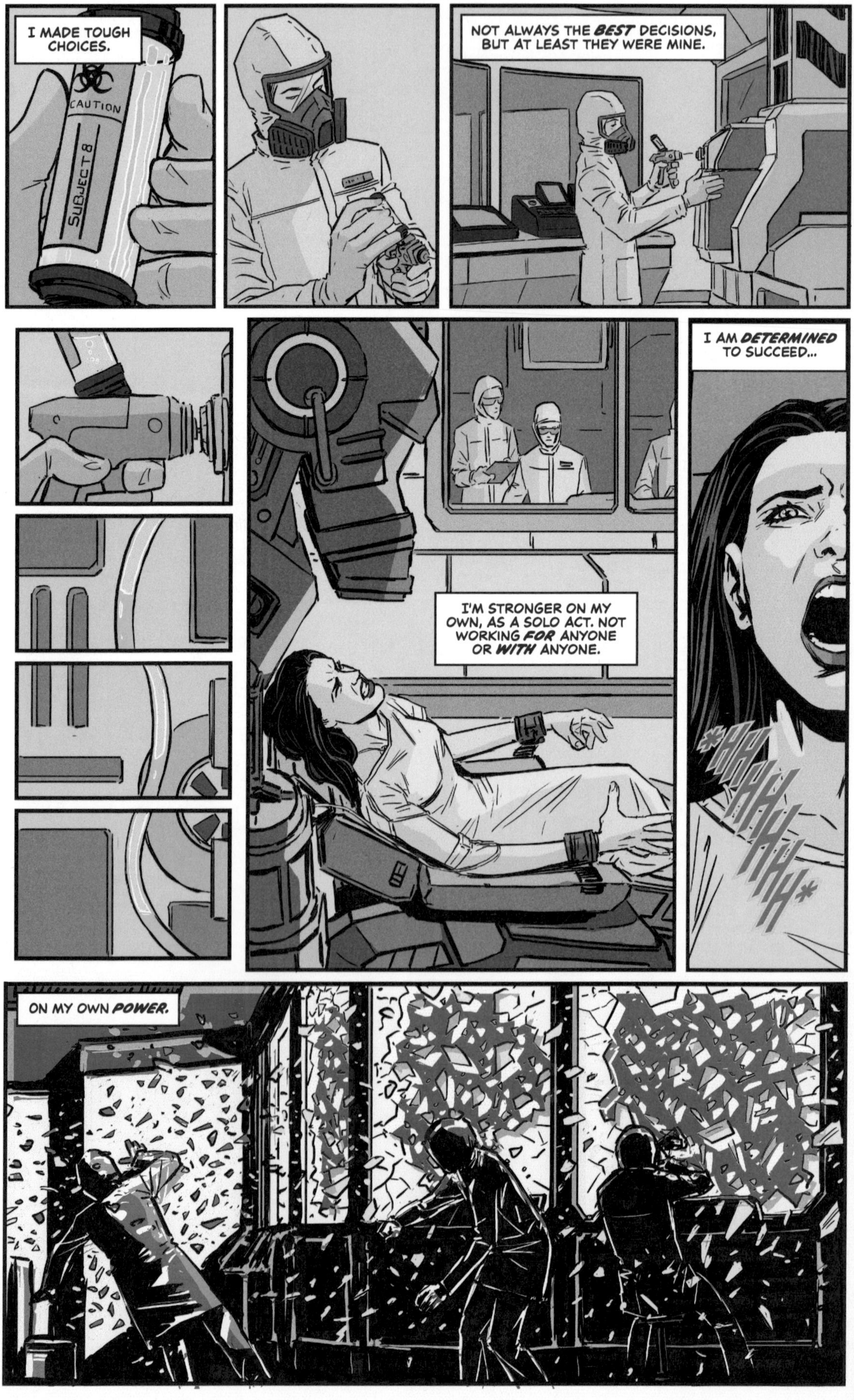
I MADE TOUGH CHOICES.
CAUTION
SUBJECT 8
NOT ALWAYS THE BEST DECISIONS, BUT AT LEAST THEY WERE MINE.
I'M STRONGER ON MY OWN, AS A SOLO ACT. NOT WORKING FOR ANYONE OR WITH ANYONE.
I AM DETERMINED TO SUCCEED...
AHHHHHHH
ON MY OWN POWER.

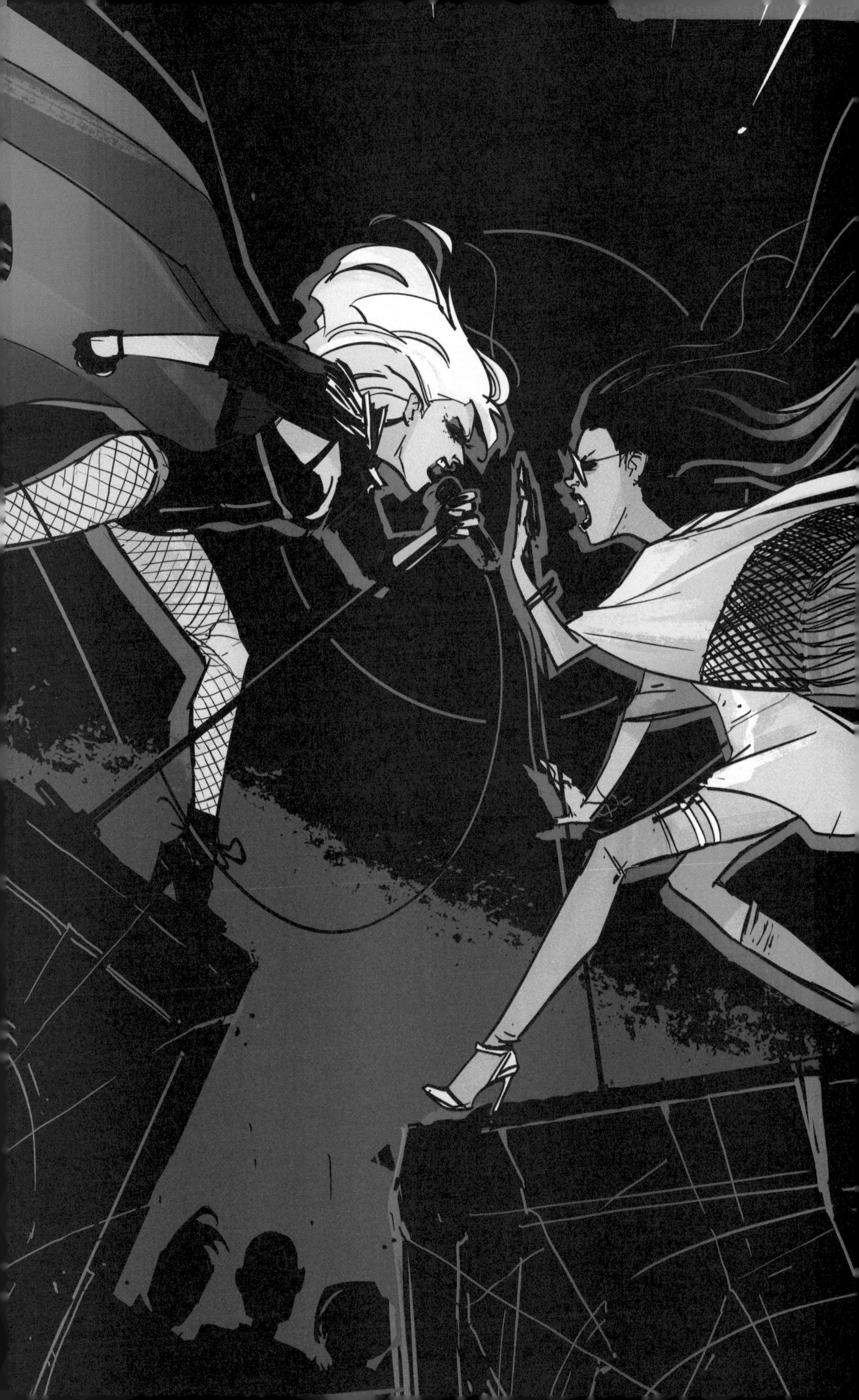

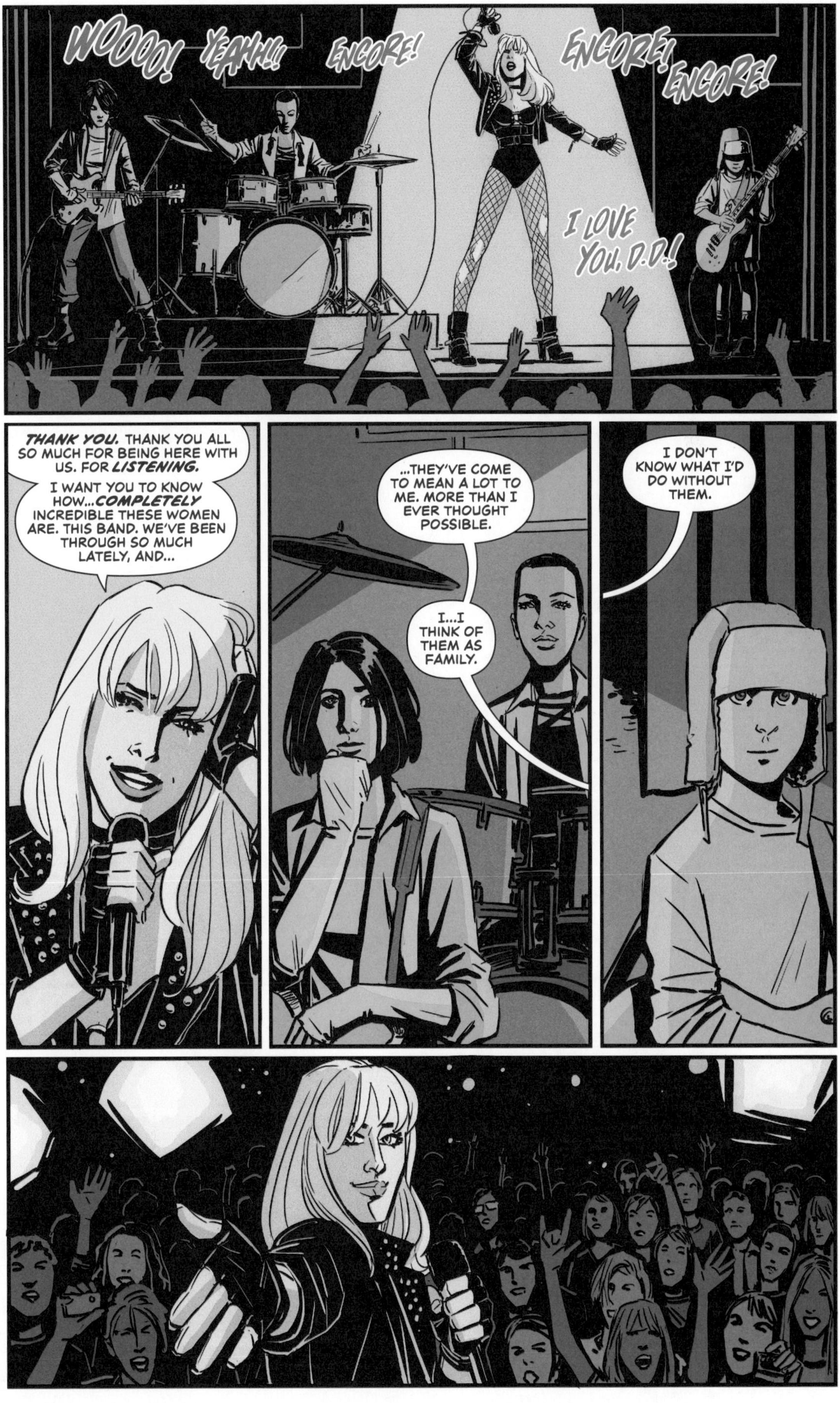
WOOOO! YEAHH!! ENCORE!
ENCORE! ENCORE!
I LOVE YOU, D.D.!
THANK YOU. THANK YOU ALL SO MUCH FOR BEING HERE WITH US. FOR LISTENING.
I WANT YOU TO KNOW HOW...COMPLETELY INCREDIBLE THESE WOMEN ARE. THIS BAND. WE'VE BEEN THROUGH SO MUCH LATELY, AND...
...THEY'VE COME TO MEAN A LOT TO ME. MORE THAN I EVER THOUGHT POSSIBLE.
I...I THINK OF THEM AS FAMILY.
I DON'T KNOW WHAT I'D DO WITHOUT THEM.

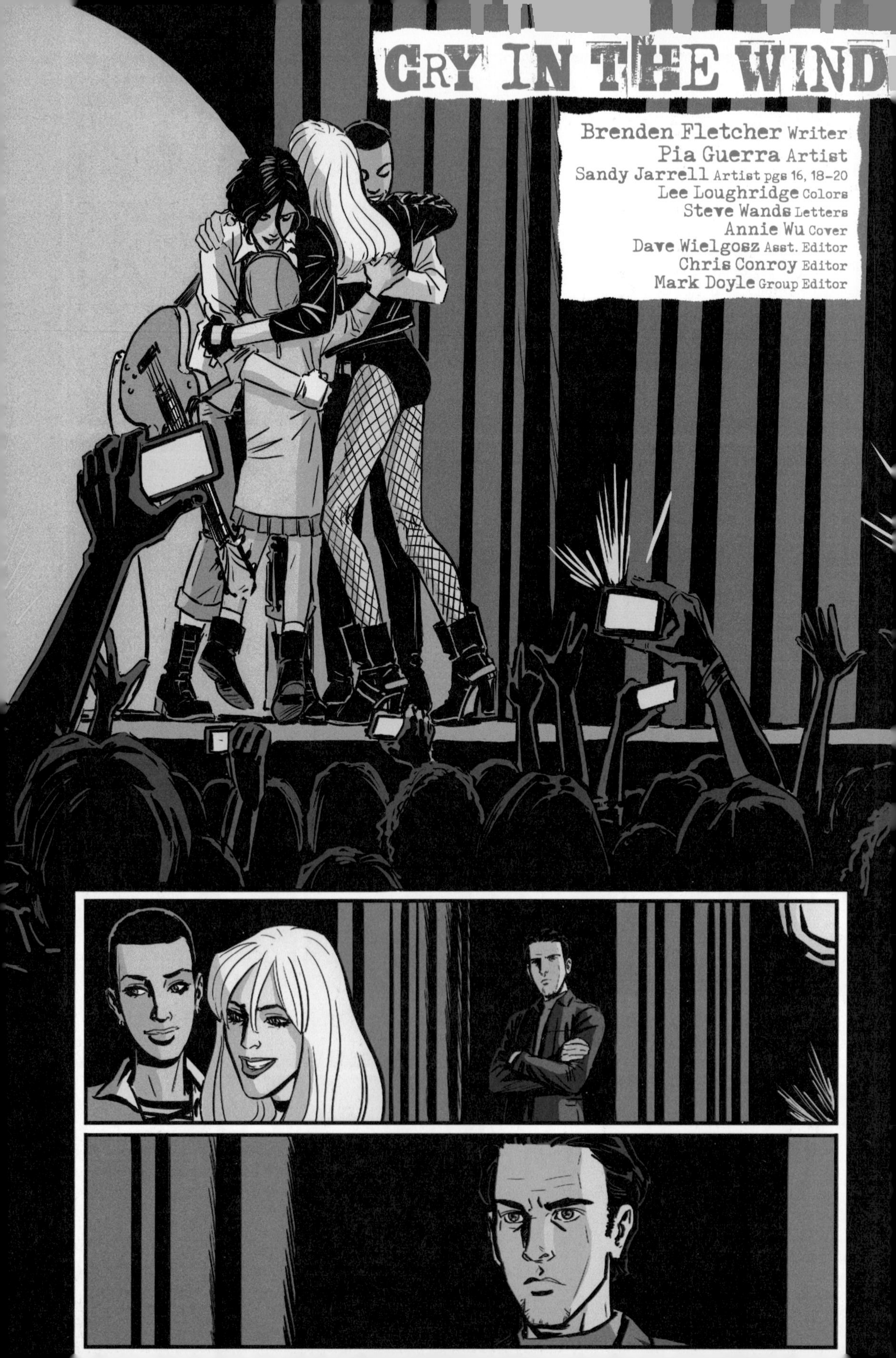
CRY IN THE WIND
Brenden Fletcher Writer
Pia Guerra Artist
Sandy Jarrell Artist pgs 16, 18-20
Lee Loughridge Colors
Steve Wands Letters
Annie Wu Cover
Dave Wielgosz Asst. Editor
Chris Conroy Editor
Mark Doyle Group Editor

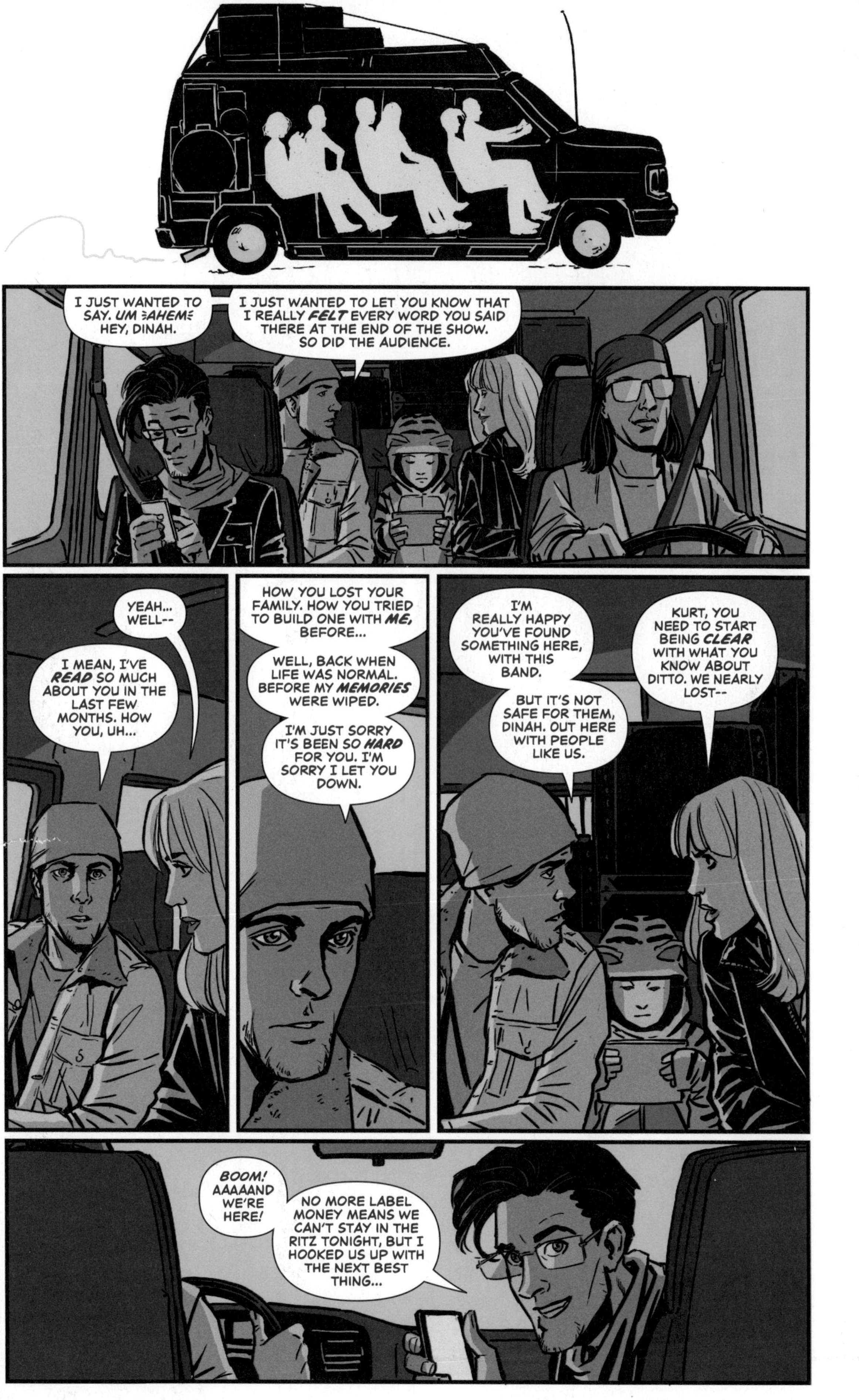
I JUST WANTED TO SAY. UM *AHEM* HEY, DINAH.
I JUST WANTED TO LET YOU KNOW THAT I REALLY FELT EVERY WORD YOU SAID THERE AT THE END OF THE SHOW. SO DID THE AUDIENCE.
YEAH... WELL--
I MEAN, I'VE READ SO MUCH ABOUT YOU IN THE LAST FEW MONTHS. HOW YOU, UH...
HOW YOU LOST YOUR FAMILY. HOW YOU TRIED TO BUILD ONE WITH ME, BEFORE...
WELL, BACK WHEN LIFE WAS NORMAL. BEFORE MY MEMORIES WERE WIPED.
I'M JUST SORRY IT'S BEEN SO HARD FOR YOU. I'M SORRY I LET YOU DOWN.
I'M REALLY HAPPY YOU'VE FOUND SOMETHING HERE, WITH THIS BAND.
BUT IT'S NOT SAFE FOR THEM, DINAH. OUT HERE WITH PEOPLE LIKE US.
KURT, YOU NEED TO START BEING CLEAR WITH WHAT YOU KNOW ABOUT DITTO. WE NEARLY LOST--
BOOM! AAAAAND WE'RE HERE!
NO MORE LABEL MONEY MEANS WE CAN'T STAY IN THE RITZ TONIGHT, BUT I HOOKED US UP WITH THE NEXT BEST THING...

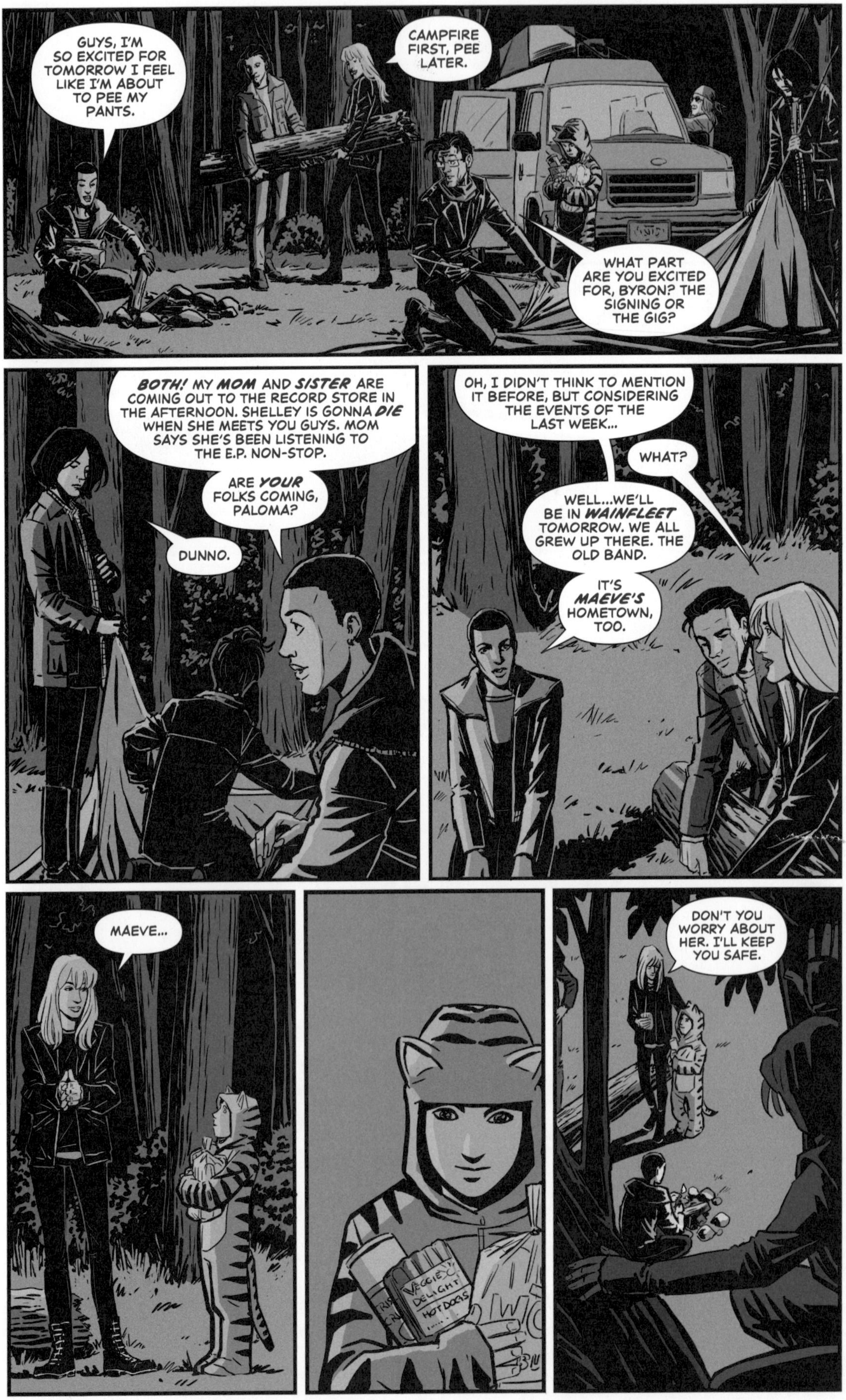
GUYS, I'M SO EXCITED FOR TOMORROW I FEEL LIKE I'M ABOUT TO PEE MY PANTS.
CAMPFIRE FIRST, PEE LATER.
WHAT PART ARE YOU EXCITED FOR, BYRON? THE SIGNING OR THE GIG?
BOTH! MY MOM AND SISTER ARE COMING OUT TO THE RECORD STORE IN THE AFTERNOON. SHELLEY IS GONNA DIE WHEN SHE MEETS YOU GUYS. MOM SAYS SHE'S BEEN LISTENING TO THE E.P. NON-STOP.
ARE YOUR FOLKS COMING, PALOMA?
DUNNO.
OH, I DIDN'T THINK TO MENTION IT BEFORE, BUT CONSIDERING THE EVENTS OF THE LAST WEEK...
WHAT?
WELL...WE'LL BE IN WAINFLEET TOMORROW. WE ALL GREW UP THERE. THE OLD BAND.
IT'S MAEVE'S HOMETOWN, TOO.
MAEVE...
VEGGIE DELIGHT HOT DOGS
DON'T YOU WORRY ABOUT HER. I'LL KEEP YOU SAFE.

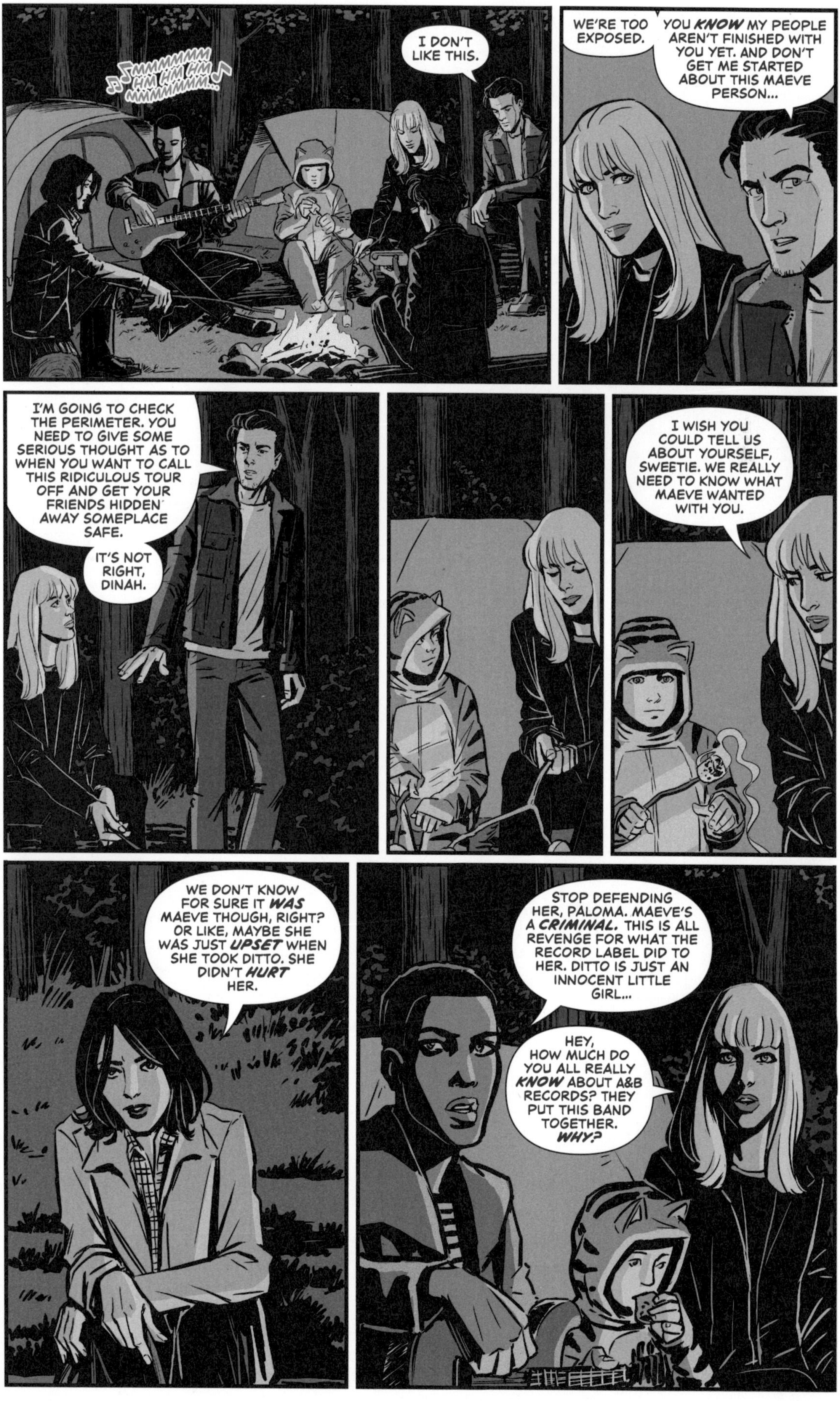
♪MMMMMMM HM HM HM MMMMMMM...♪
I DON'T LIKE THIS.
WE'RE TOO EXPOSED.
YOU KNOW MY PEOPLE AREN'T FINISHED WITH YOU YET. AND DON'T GET ME STARTED ABOUT THIS MAEVE PERSON...
I'M GOING TO CHECK THE PERIMETER. YOU NEED TO GIVE SOME SERIOUS THOUGHT AS TO WHEN YOU WANT TO CALL THIS RIDICULOUS TOUR OFF AND GET YOUR FRIENDS HIDDEN AWAY SOMEPLACE SAFE.
IT'S NOT RIGHT, DINAH.
I WISH YOU COULD TELL US ABOUT YOURSELF, SWEETIE. WE REALLY NEED TO KNOW WHAT MAEVE WANTED WITH YOU.
WE DON'T KNOW FOR SURE IT WAS MAEVE THOUGH, RIGHT? OR LIKE, MAYBE SHE WAS JUST UPSET WHEN SHE TOOK DITTO. SHE DIDN'T HURT HER.
STOP DEFENDING HER, PALOMA. MAEVE'S A CRIMINAL. THIS IS ALL REVENGE FOR WHAT THE RECORD LABEL DID TO HER. DITTO IS JUST AN INNOCENT LITTLE GIRL...
HEY, HOW MUCH DO YOU ALL REALLY KNOW ABOUT A&B RECORDS? THEY PUT THIS BAND TOGETHER. WHY?

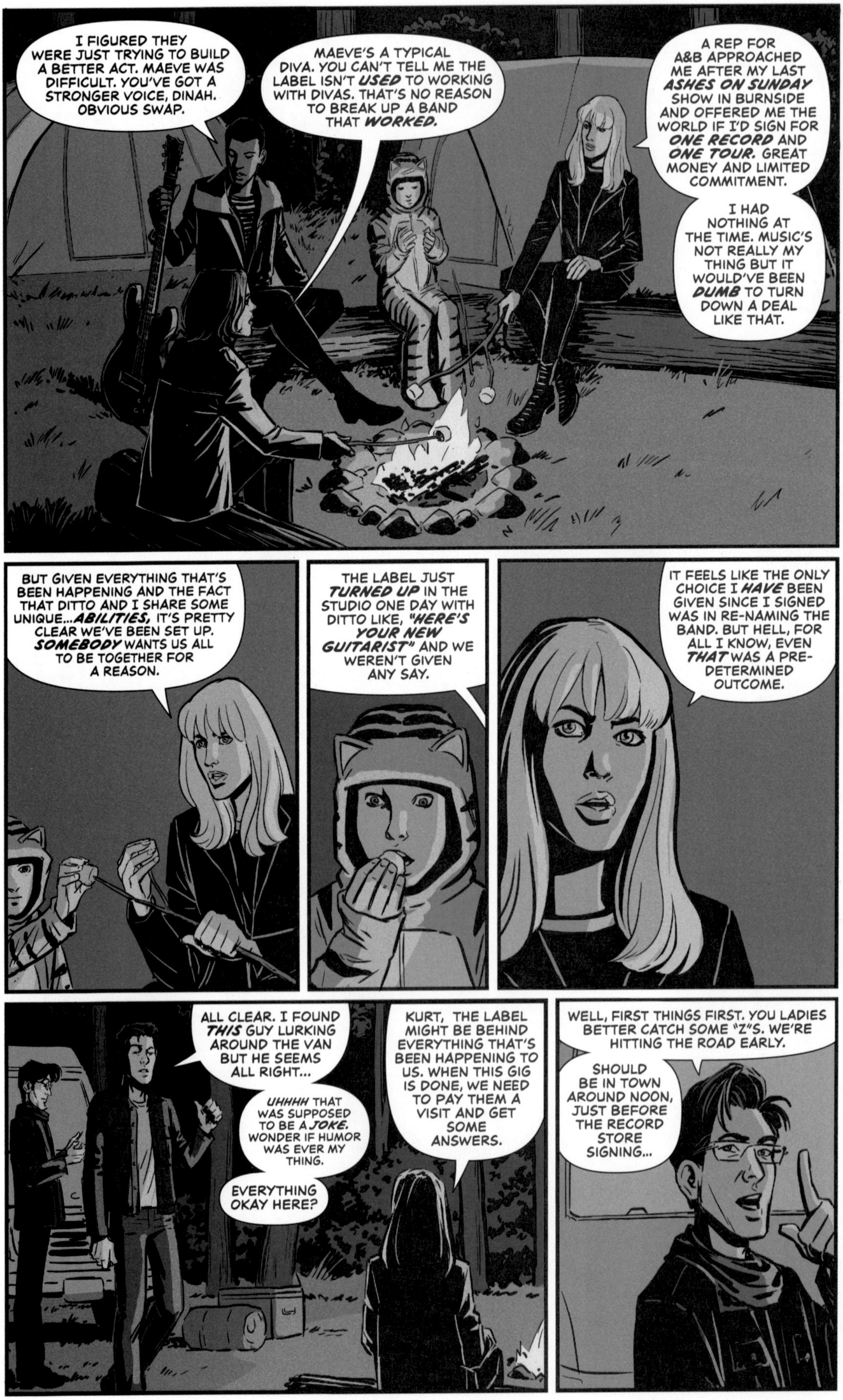
I FIGURED THEY WERE JUST TRYING TO BUILD A BETTER ACT. MAEVE WAS DIFFICULT. YOU'VE GOT A STRONGER VOICE, DINAH. OBVIOUS SWAP.
MAEVE'S A TYPICAL DIVA. YOU CAN'T TELL ME THE LABEL ISN'T USED TO WORKING WITH DIVAS. THAT'S NO REASON TO BREAK UP A BAND THAT WORKED.
A REP FOR A&B APPROACHED ME AFTER MY LAST ASHES ON SUNDAY SHOW IN BURNSIDE AND OFFERED ME THE WORLD IF I'D SIGN FOR ONE RECORD AND ONE TOUR. GREAT MONEY AND LIMITED COMMITMENT.
I HAD NOTHING AT THE TIME. MUSIC'S NOT REALLY MY THING BUT IT WOULD'VE BEEN DUMB TO TURN DOWN A DEAL LIKE THAT.
BUT GIVEN EVERYTHING THAT'S BEEN HAPPENING AND THE FACT THAT DITTO AND I SHARE SOME UNIQUE...ABILITIES, IT'S PRETTY CLEAR WE'VE BEEN SET UP. SOMEBODY WANTS US ALL TO BE TOGETHER FOR A REASON.
THE LABEL JUST TURNED UP IN THE STUDIO ONE DAY WITH DITTO LIKE, "HERE'S YOUR NEW GUITARIST" AND WE WEREN'T GIVEN ANY SAY.
IT FEELS LIKE THE ONLY CHOICE I HAVE BEEN GIVEN SINCE I SIGNED WAS IN RE-NAMING THE BAND. BUT HELL, FOR ALL I KNOW, EVEN THAT WAS A PRE-DETERMINED OUTCOME.
ALL CLEAR. I FOUND THIS GUY LURKING AROUND THE VAN BUT HE SEEMS ALL RIGHT...
UHHHH THAT WAS SUPPOSED TO BE A JOKE. WONDER IF HUMOR WAS EVER MY THING.
EVERYTHING OKAY HERE?
KURT, THE LABEL MIGHT BE BEHIND EVERYTHING THAT'S BEEN HAPPENING TO US. WHEN THIS GIG IS DONE, WE NEED TO PAY THEM A VISIT AND GET SOME ANSWERS.
WELL, FIRST THINGS FIRST. YOU LADIES BETTER CATCH SOME "Z"S. WE'RE HITTING THE ROAD EARLY.
SHOULD BE IN TOWN AROUND NOON, JUST BEFORE THE RECORD STORE SIGNING...

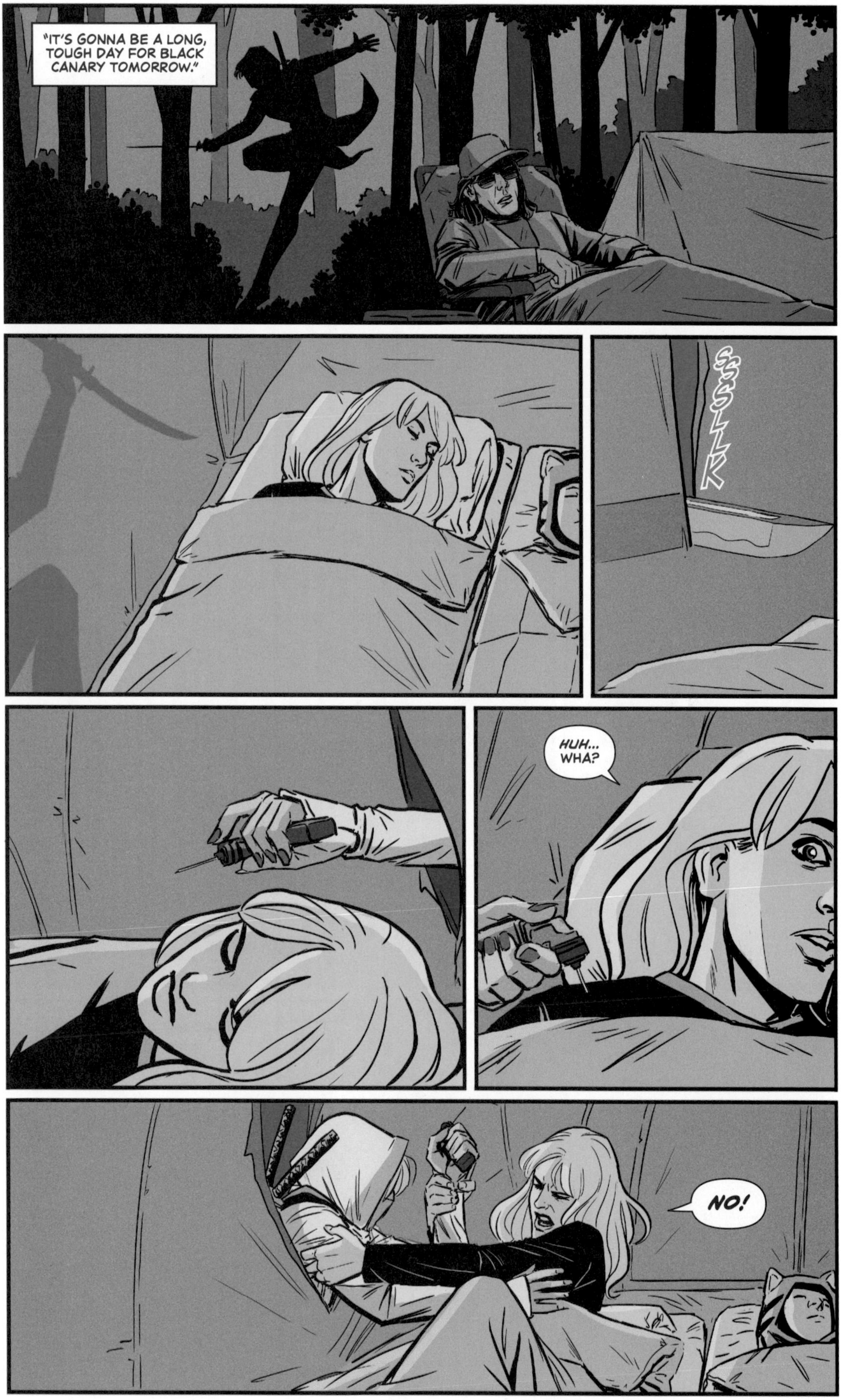
"IT'S GONNA BE A LONG, TOUGH DAY FOR BLACK CANARY TOMORROW."
SSSLLK
HUH... WHA?
NO!

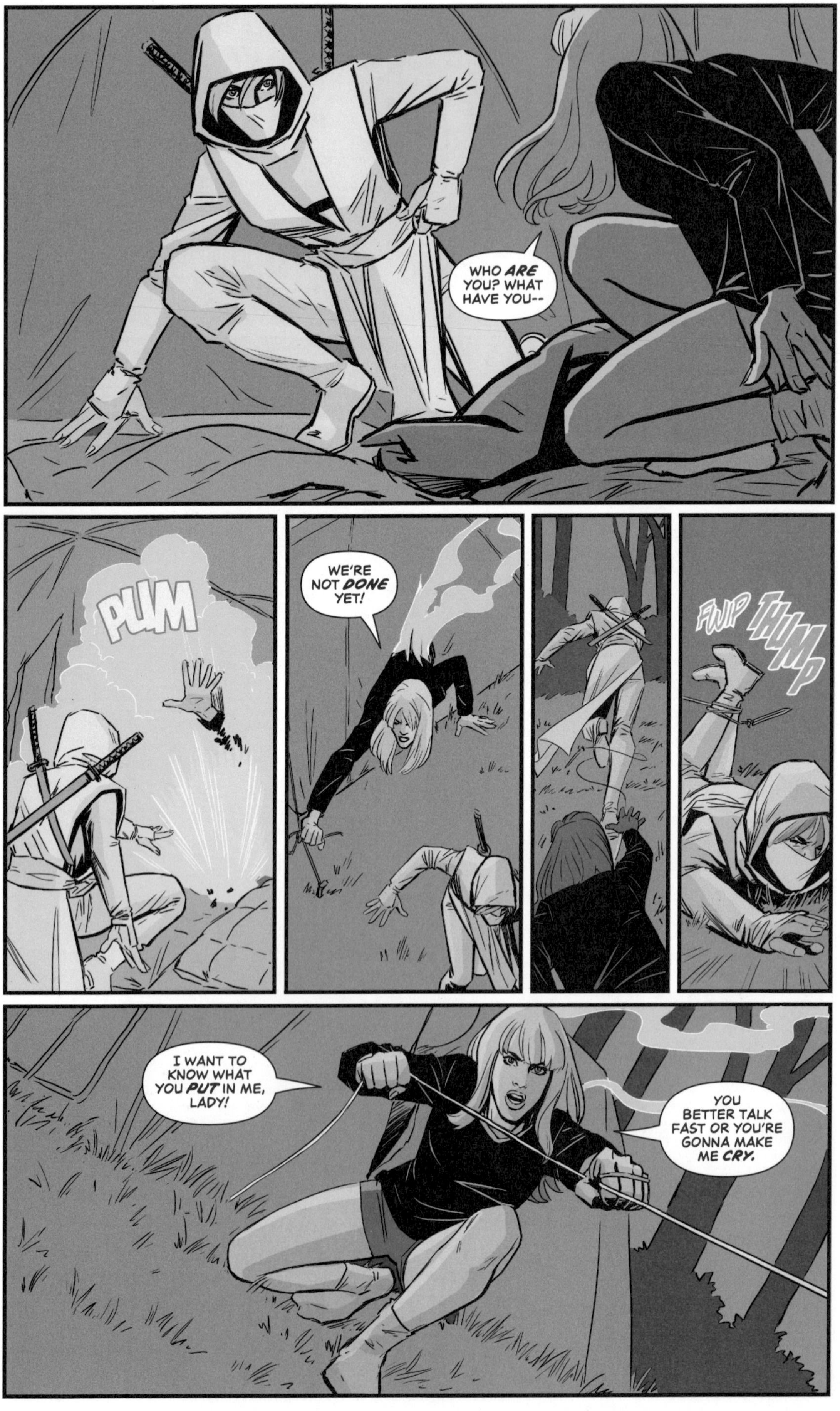
WHO *ARE* YOU? WHAT HAVE YOU--
PUM
WE'RE NOT *DONE* YET!
FWIP THUMP
I WANT TO KNOW WHAT YOU *PUT* IN ME, LADY!
YOU BETTER TALK FAST OR YOU'RE GONNA MAKE ME *CRY.*

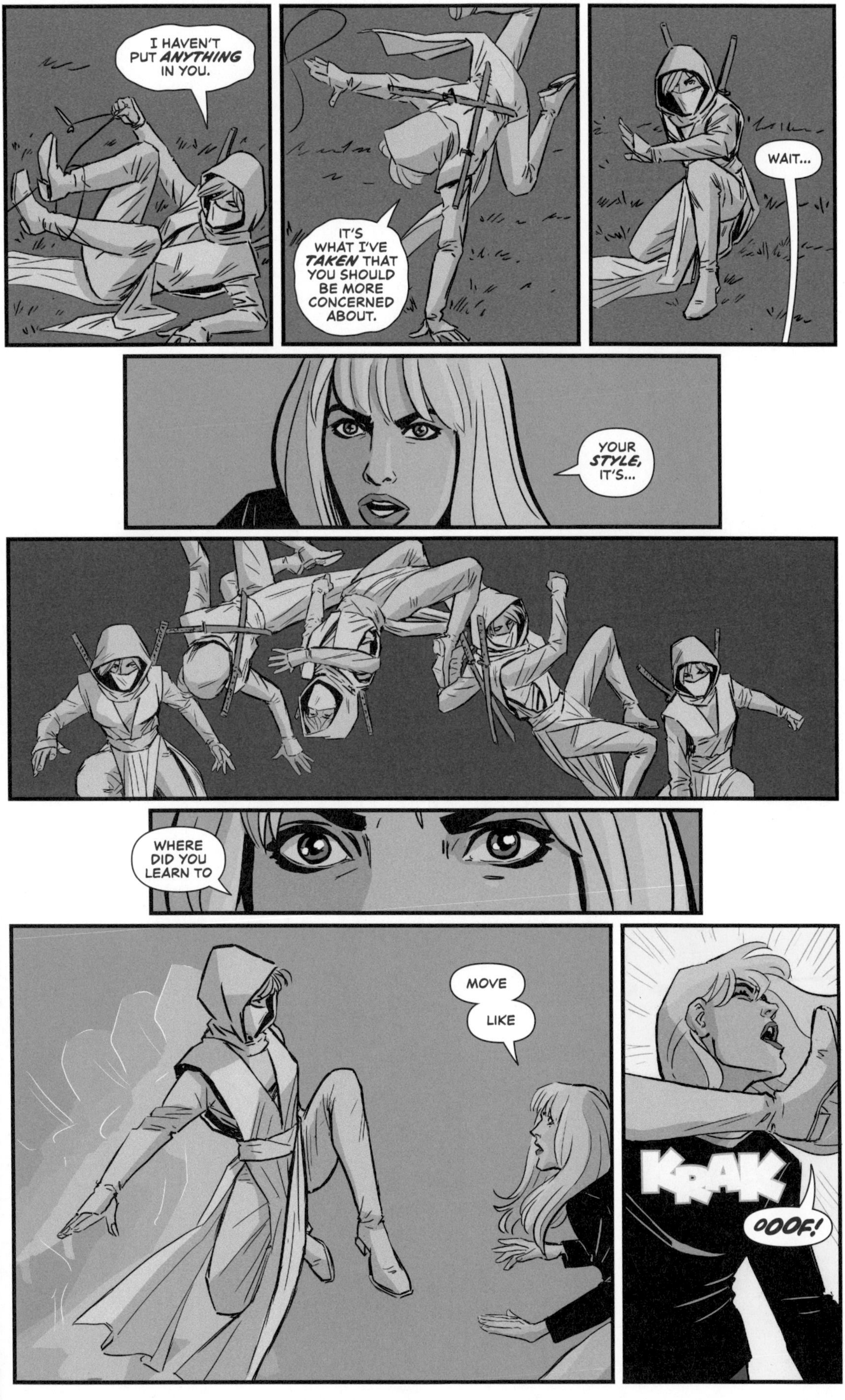
I HAVEN'T PUT ANYTHING IN YOU.
IT'S WHAT I'VE TAKEN THAT YOU SHOULD BE MORE CONCERNED ABOUT.
WAIT...
YOUR STYLE, IT'S...
WHERE DID YOU LEARN TO
MOVE
LIKE
KRAK
OOOF!

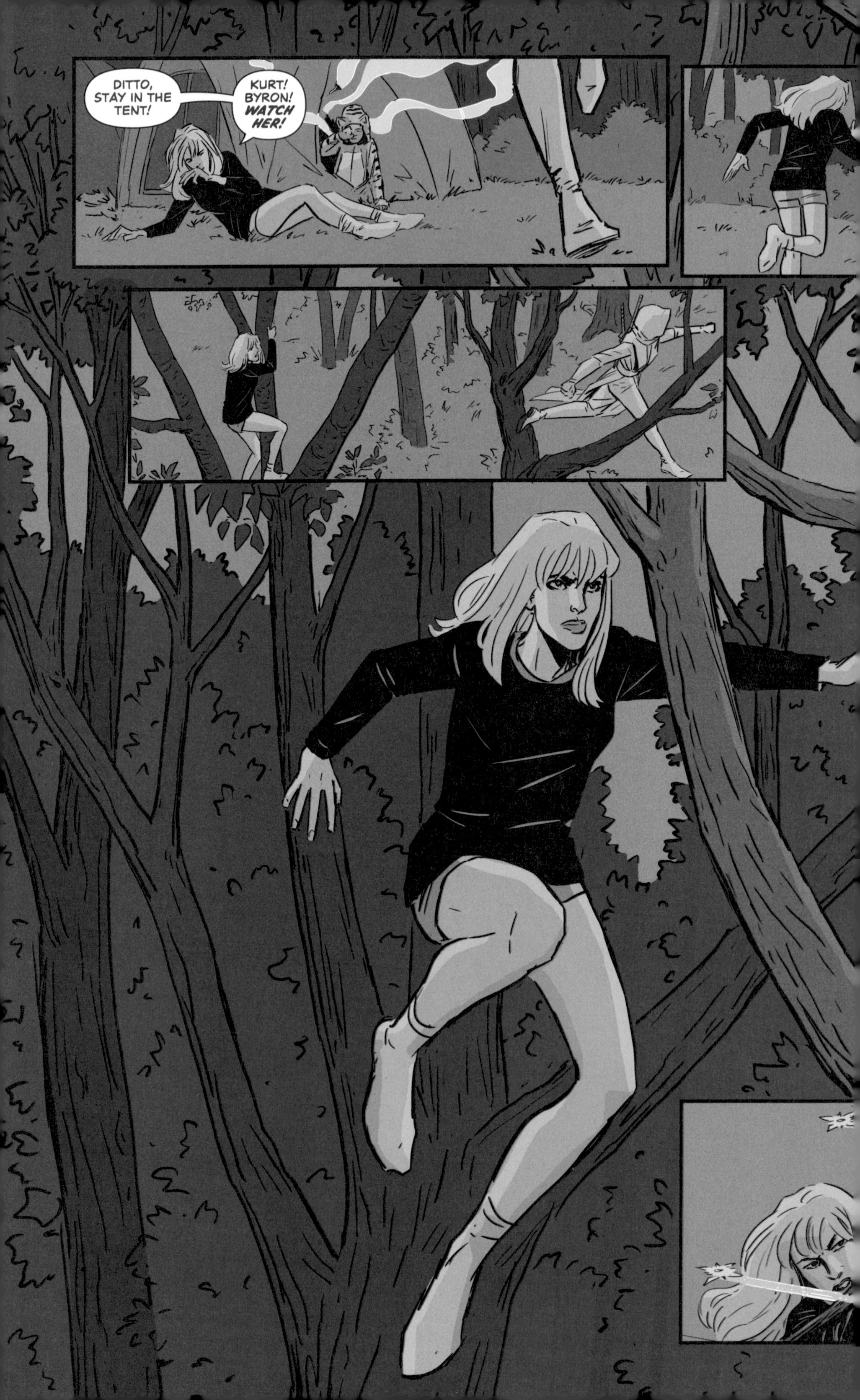
DITTO, STAY IN THE TENT!
KURT! BYRON! WATCH HER!

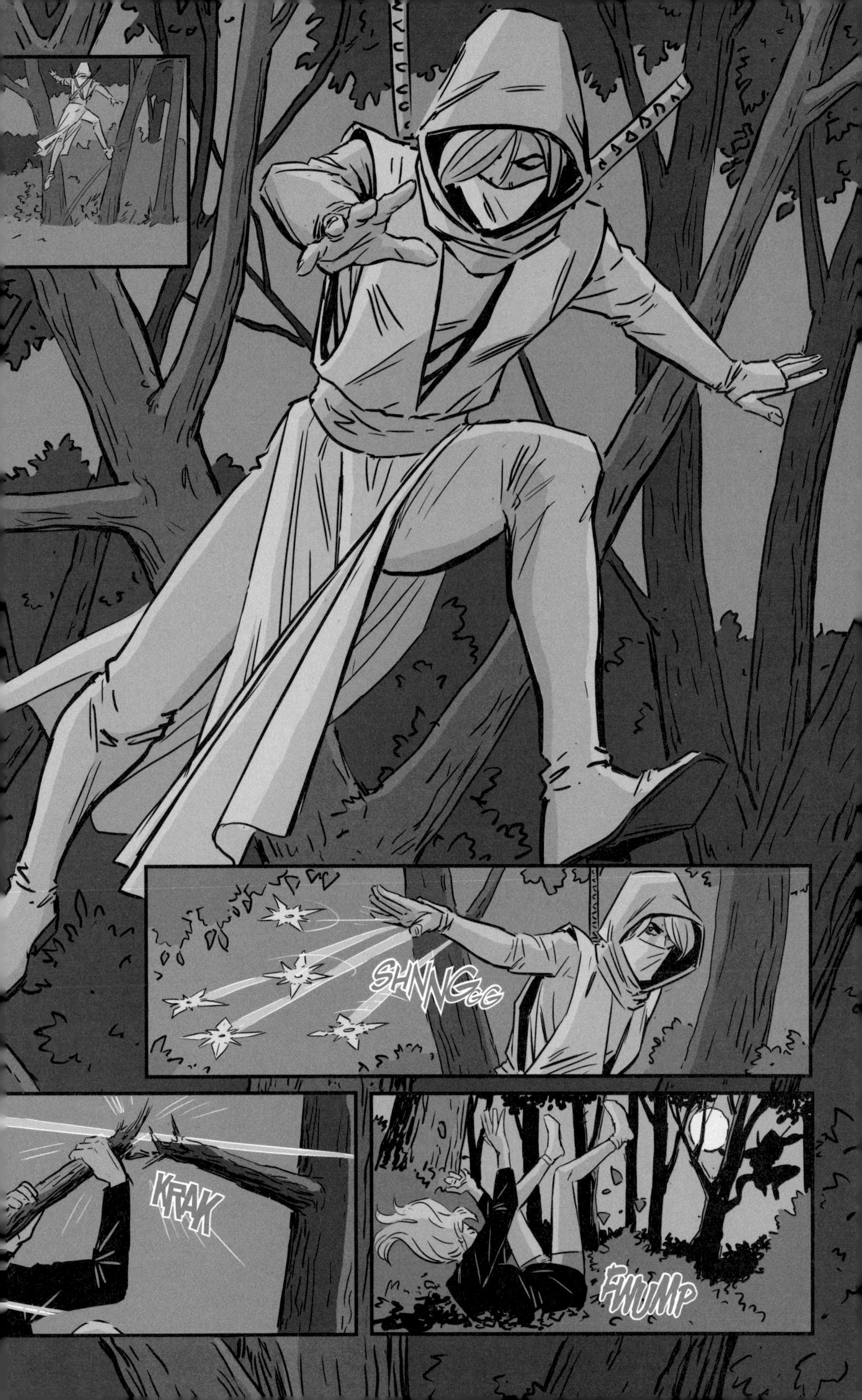
SHNNGGG
KRAK
FWUMP

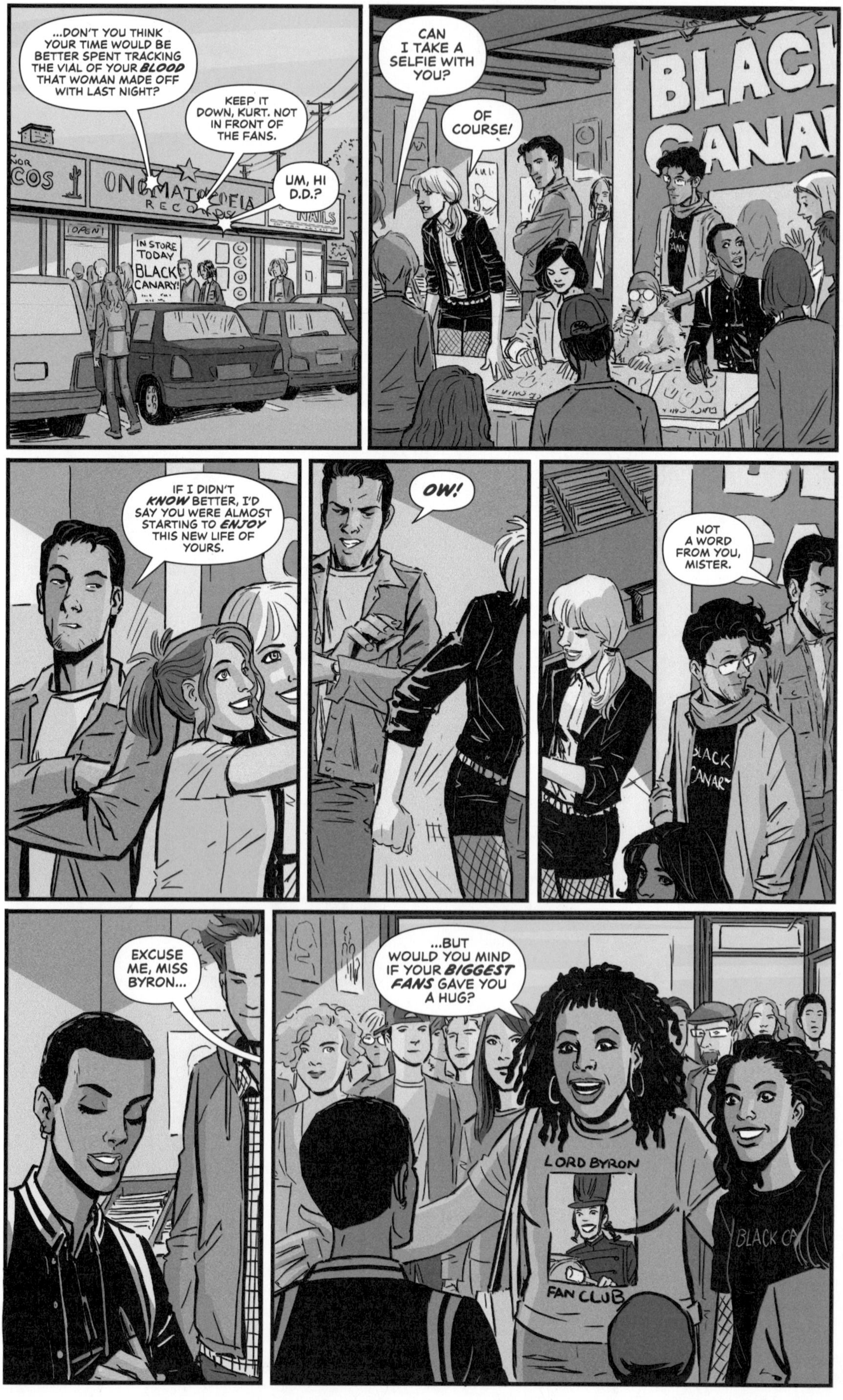

...DON'T YOU THINK YOUR TIME WOULD BE BETTER SPENT TRACKING THE VIAL OF YOUR *BLOOD* THAT WOMAN MADE OFF WITH LAST NIGHT?
KEEP IT DOWN, KURT. NOT IN FRONT OF THE FANS.
UM, HI D.D.?
ONOMATOPOEIA RECORDS
NAILS
OPEN
IN STORE TODAY BLACK CANARY!
CAN I TAKE A SELFIE WITH YOU?
OF COURSE!
BLACK CANA
IF I DIDN'T *KNOW* BETTER, I'D SAY YOU WERE ALMOST STARTING TO *ENJOY* THIS NEW LIFE OF YOURS.
OW!
NOT A WORD FROM YOU, MISTER.
BLACK CANARY
EXCUSE ME, MISS BYRON...
...BUT WOULD YOU MIND IF YOUR *BIGGEST FANS* GAVE YOU A HUG?
LORD BYRON
FAN CLUB
BLACK CA

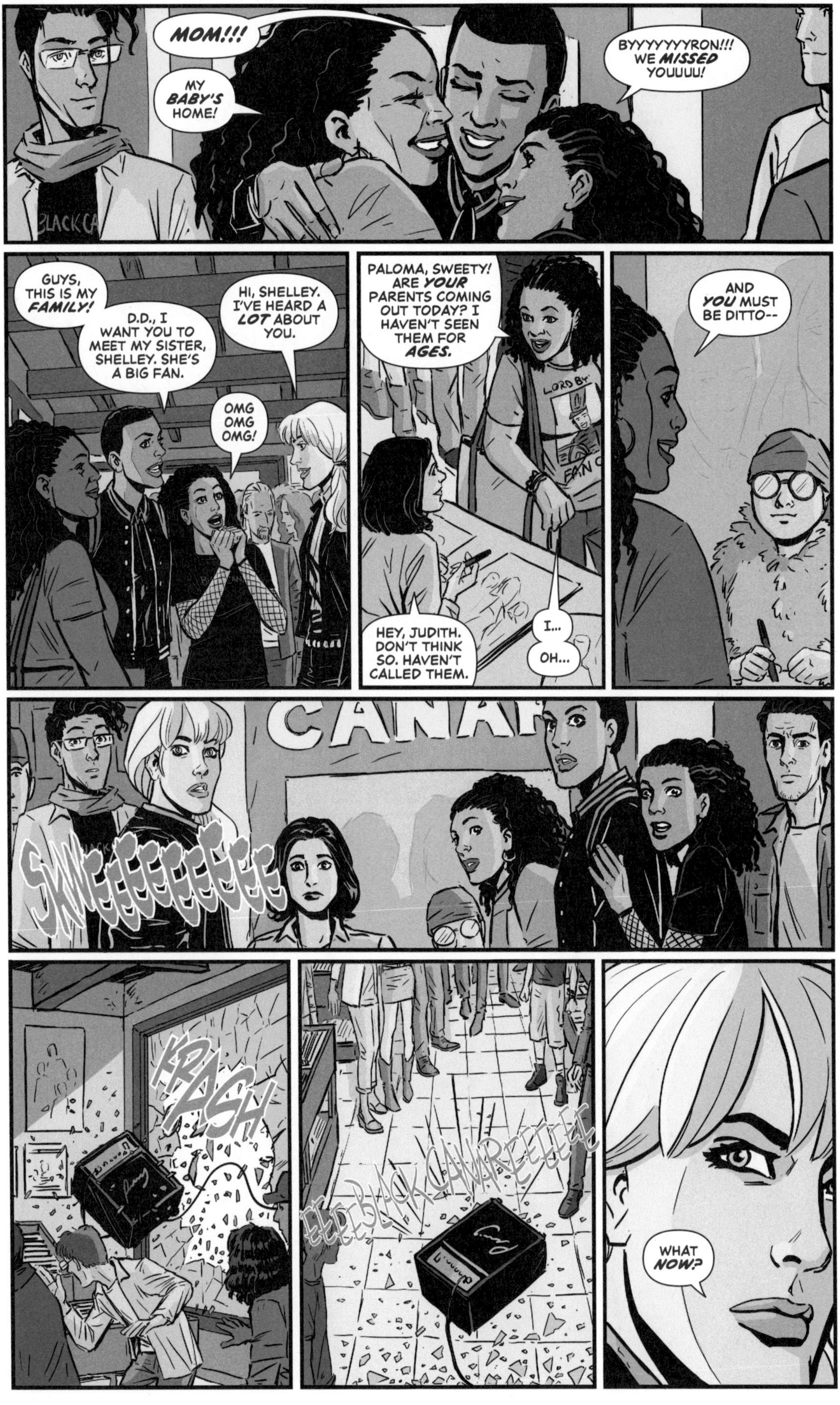
MOM!!!
MY BABY'S HOME!
BYYYYYYYRON!!! WE MISSED YOUUUU!
GUYS, THIS IS MY FAMILY!
D.D., I WANT YOU TO MEET MY SISTER, SHELLEY. SHE'S A BIG FAN.
HI, SHELLEY. I'VE HEARD A LOT ABOUT YOU.
OMG OMG OMG!
PALOMA, SWEETY! ARE YOUR PARENTS COMING OUT TODAY? I HAVEN'T SEEN THEM FOR AGES.
HEY, JUDITH. DON'T THINK SO. HAVEN'T CALLED THEM.
I...
OH...
AND YOU MUST BE DITTO--
CANA
SKNEEEEEEEEEEE
KRASH
EEEEBLACK CANAREEEEEEEE
WHAT NOW?

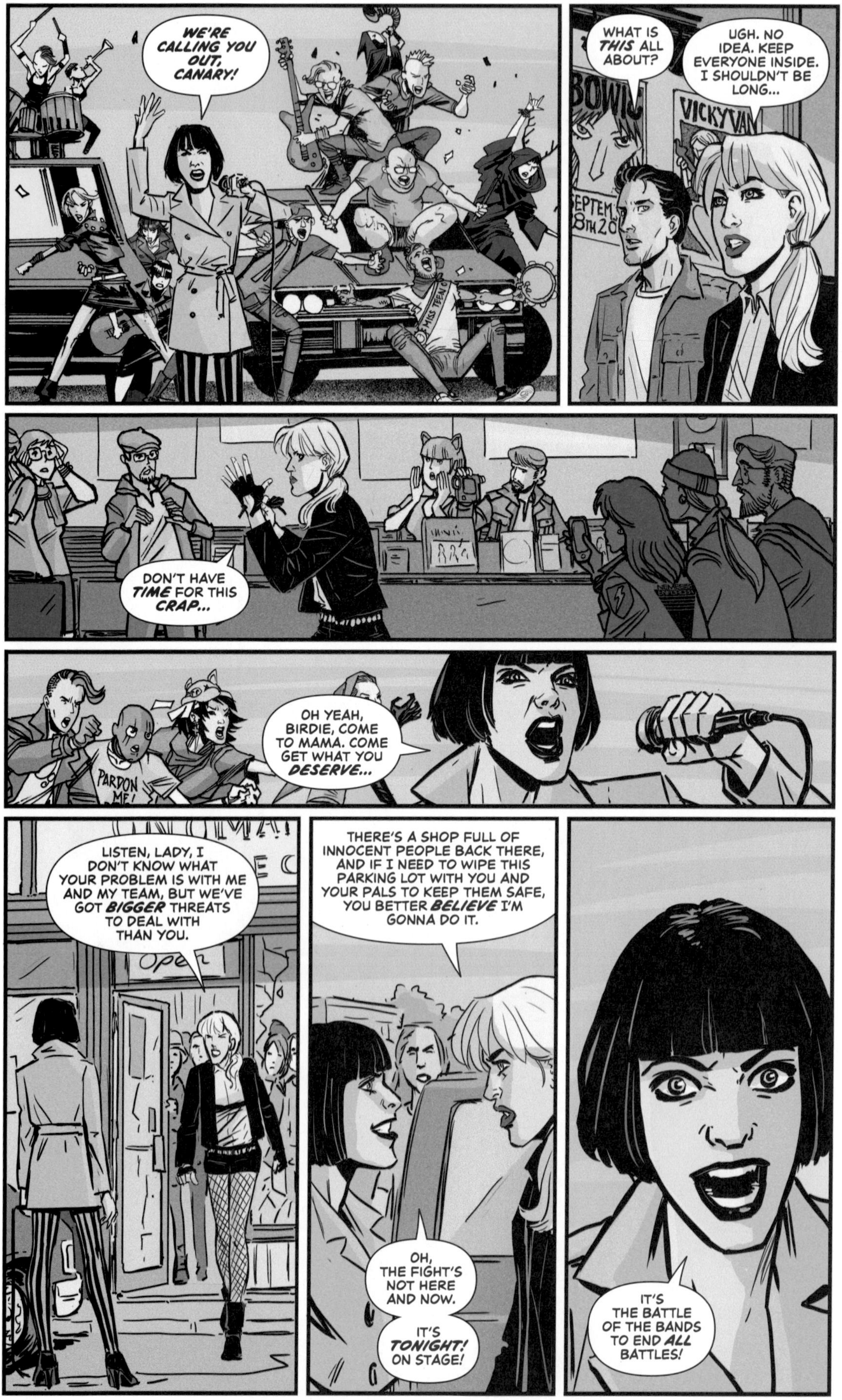

WE'RE CALLING YOU OUT, CANARY!
WHAT IS THIS ALL ABOUT?
UGH. NO IDEA. KEEP EVERYONE INSIDE. I SHOULDN'T BE LONG...
DON'T HAVE TIME FOR THIS CRAP...
PARDON ME!
OH YEAH, BIRDIE, COME TO MAMA. COME GET WHAT YOU DESERVE...
LISTEN, LADY, I DON'T KNOW WHAT YOUR PROBLEM IS WITH ME AND MY TEAM, BUT WE'VE GOT BIGGER THREATS TO DEAL WITH THAN YOU.
THERE'S A SHOP FULL OF INNOCENT PEOPLE BACK THERE, AND IF I NEED TO WIPE THIS PARKING LOT WITH YOU AND YOUR PALS TO KEEP THEM SAFE, YOU BETTER BELIEVE I'M GONNA DO IT.
OH, THE FIGHT'S NOT HERE AND NOW.
IT'S TONIGHT! ON STAGE!
IT'S THE BATTLE OF THE BANDS TO END ALL BATTLES!

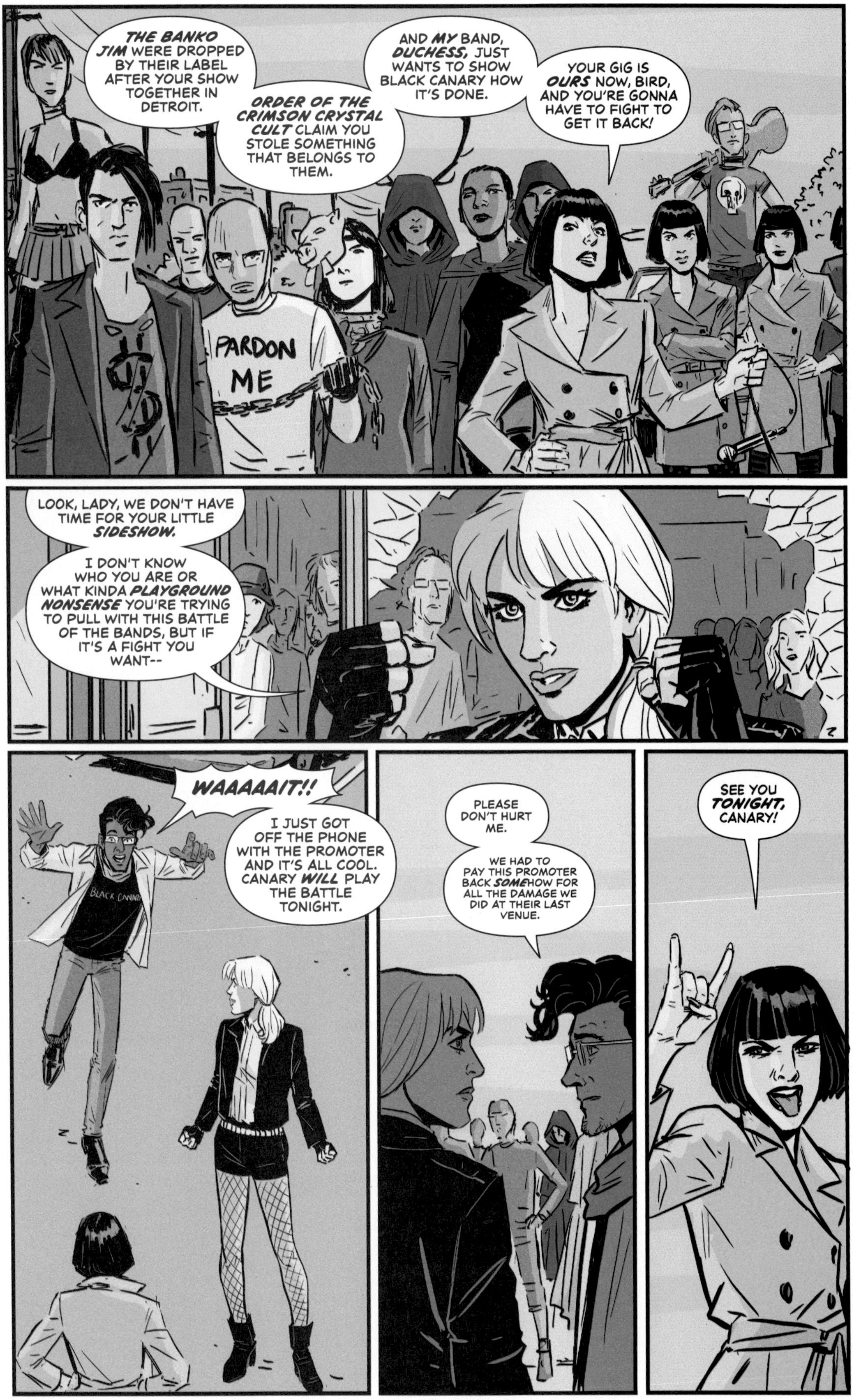
THE BANKO JIM WERE DROPPED BY THEIR LABEL AFTER YOUR SHOW TOGETHER IN DETROIT.
ORDER OF THE CRIMSON CRYSTAL CULT CLAIM YOU STOLE SOMETHING THAT BELONGS TO THEM.
AND MY BAND, DUCHESS, JUST WANTS TO SHOW BLACK CANARY HOW IT'S DONE.
YOUR GIG IS OURS NOW, BIRD, AND YOU'RE GONNA HAVE TO FIGHT TO GET IT BACK!
PARDON ME
LOOK, LADY, WE DON'T HAVE TIME FOR YOUR LITTLE SIDESHOW.
I DON'T KNOW WHO YOU ARE OR WHAT KINDA PLAYGROUND NONSENSE YOU'RE TRYING TO PULL WITH THIS BATTLE OF THE BANDS, BUT IF IT'S A FIGHT YOU WANT--
WAAAAAIT!!
I JUST GOT OFF THE PHONE WITH THE PROMOTER AND IT'S ALL COOL. CANARY WILL PLAY THE BATTLE TONIGHT.
PLEASE DON'T HURT ME.
WE HAD TO PAY THIS PROMOTER BACK SOMEHOW FOR ALL THE DAMAGE WE DID AT THEIR LAST VENUE.
SEE YOU TONIGHT, CANARY!

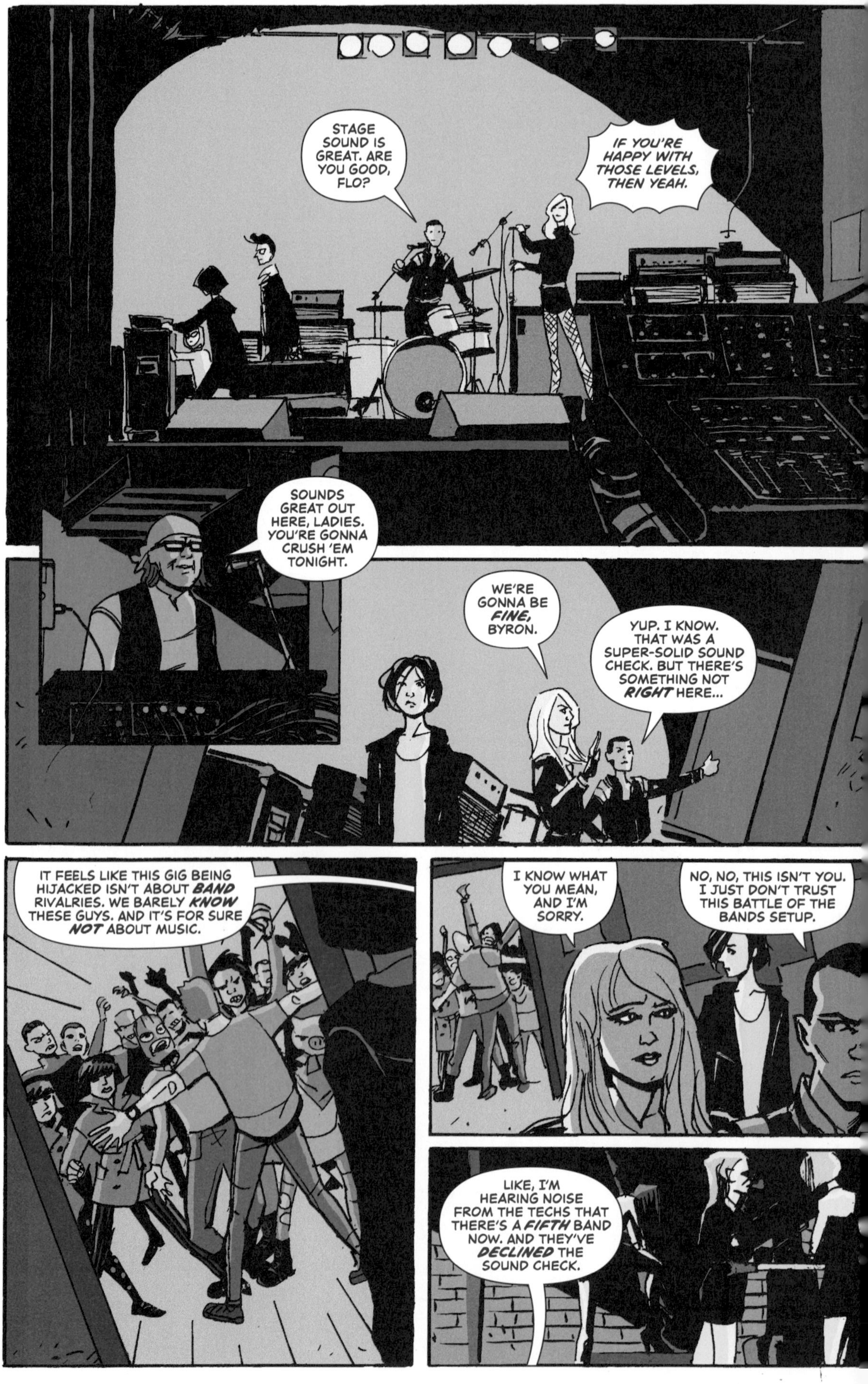
STAGE SOUND IS GREAT. ARE YOU GOOD, FLO?
IF YOU'RE HAPPY WITH THOSE LEVELS, THEN YEAH.
SOUNDS GREAT OUT HERE, LADIES. YOU'RE GONNA CRUSH 'EM TONIGHT.
WE'RE GONNA BE FINE, BYRON.
YUP. I KNOW. THAT WAS A SUPER-SOLID SOUND CHECK. BUT THERE'S SOMETHING NOT RIGHT HERE...
IT FEELS LIKE THIS GIG BEING HIJACKED ISN'T ABOUT BAND RIVALRIES. WE BARELY KNOW THESE GUYS. AND IT'S FOR SURE NOT ABOUT MUSIC.
I KNOW WHAT YOU MEAN, AND I'M SORRY.
NO, NO, THIS ISN'T YOU. I JUST DON'T TRUST THIS BATTLE OF THE BANDS SETUP.
LIKE, I'M HEARING NOISE FROM THE TECHS THAT THERE'S A FIFTH BAND NOW. AND THEY'VE DECLINED THE SOUND CHECK.

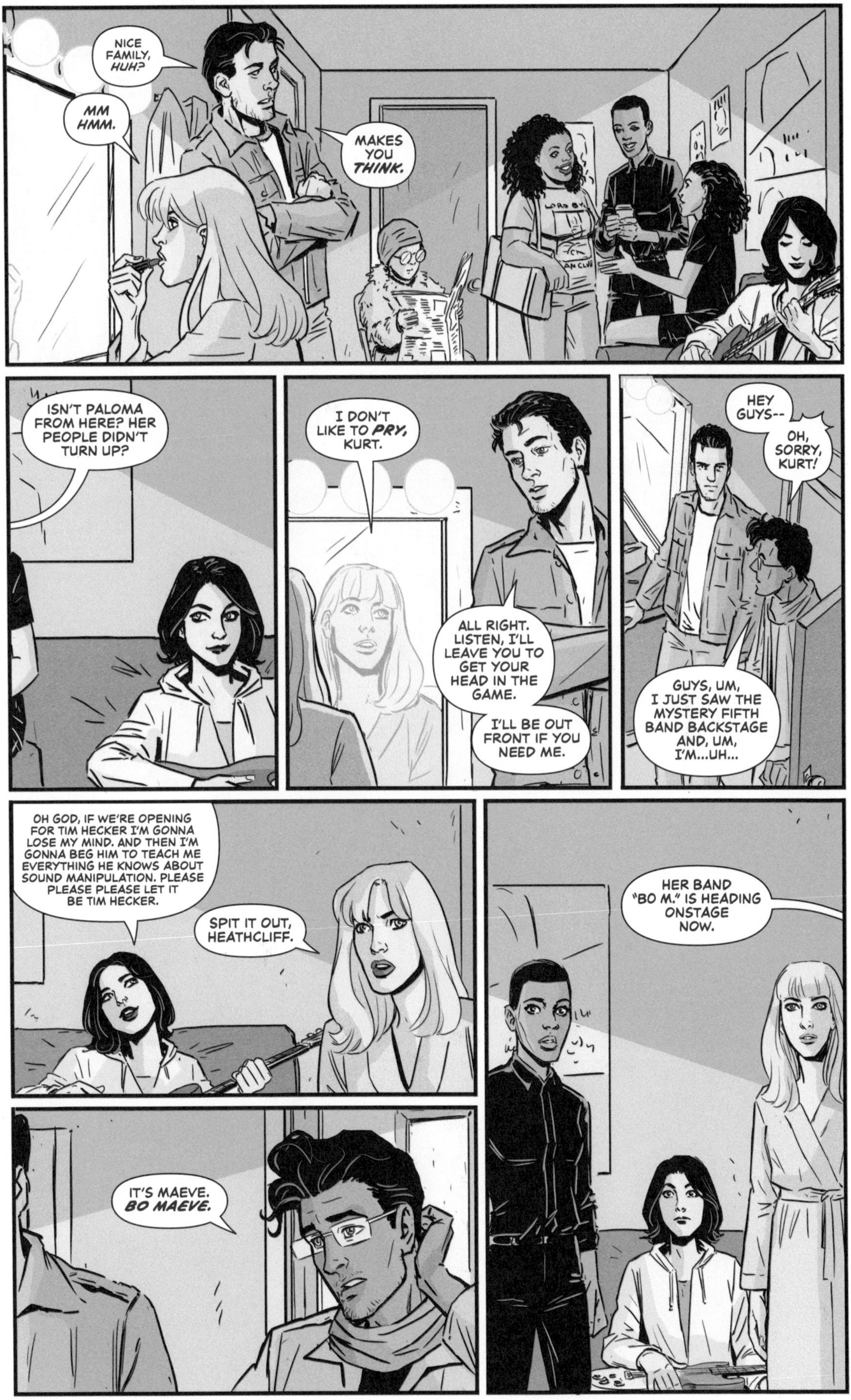
NICE FAMILY, HUH?
MM HMM.
MAKES YOU THINK.
ISN'T PALOMA FROM HERE? HER PEOPLE DIDN'T TURN UP?
I DON'T LIKE TO PRY, KURT.
ALL RIGHT. LISTEN, I'LL LEAVE YOU TO GET YOUR HEAD IN THE GAME.
I'LL BE OUT FRONT IF YOU NEED ME.
HEY GUYS--
OH, SORRY, KURT!
GUYS, UM, I JUST SAW THE MYSTERY FIFTH BAND BACKSTAGE AND, UM, I'M...UH...
OH GOD, IF WE'RE OPENING FOR TIM HECKER I'M GONNA LOSE MY MIND. AND THEN I'M GONNA BEG HIM TO TEACH ME EVERYTHING HE KNOWS ABOUT SOUND MANIPULATION. PLEASE PLEASE PLEASE LET IT BE TIM HECKER.
SPIT IT OUT, HEATHCLIFF.
IT'S MAEVE. BO MAEVE.
HER BAND "BO M." IS HEADING ONSTAGE NOW.

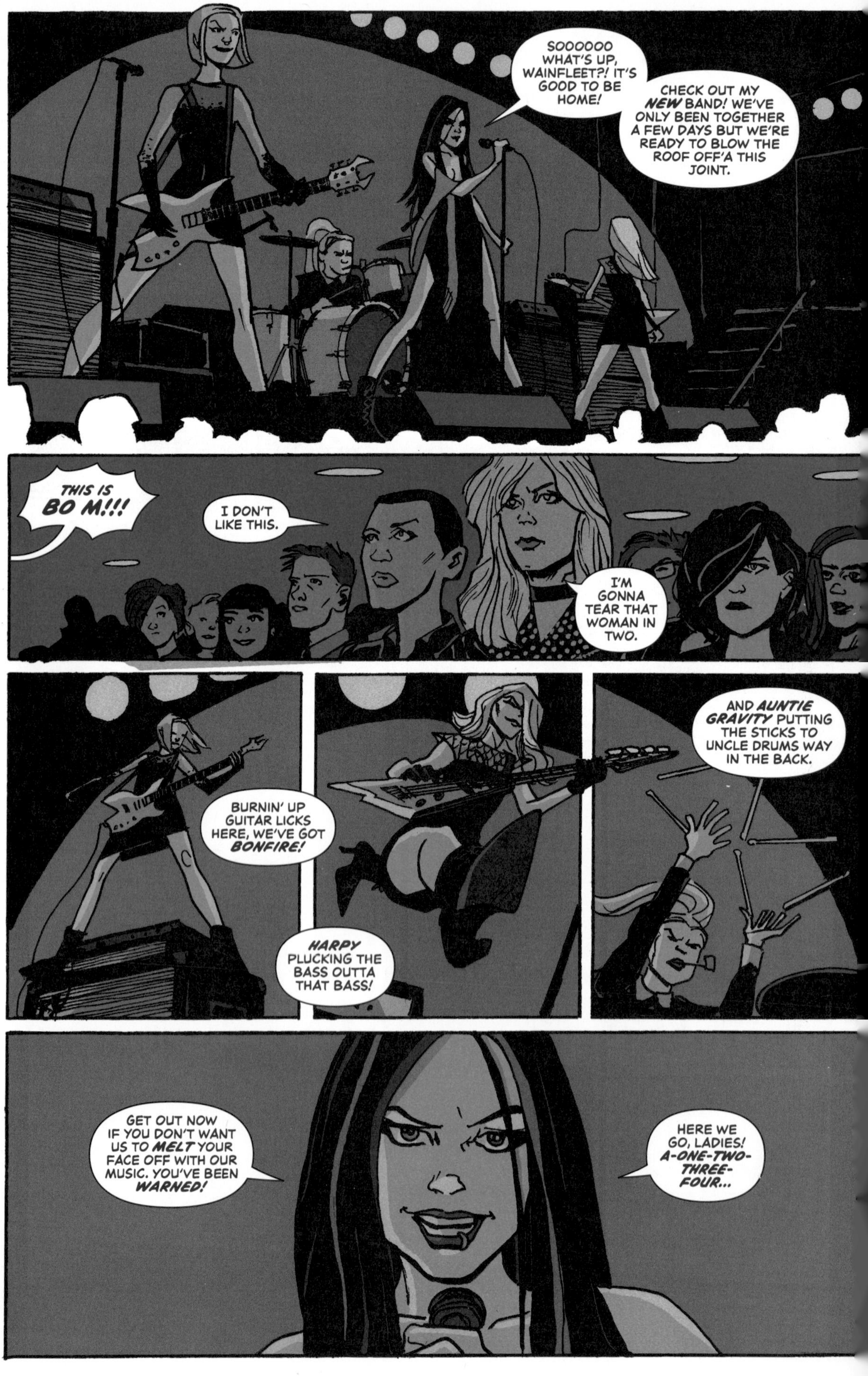
SOOOOOO WHAT'S UP, WAINFLEET?! IT'S GOOD TO BE HOME!
CHECK OUT MY NEW BAND! WE'VE ONLY BEEN TOGETHER A FEW DAYS BUT WE'RE READY TO BLOW THE ROOF OFF'A THIS JOINT.
THIS IS BO M!!!
I DON'T LIKE THIS.
I'M GONNA TEAR THAT WOMAN IN TWO.
BURNIN' UP GUITAR LICKS HERE, WE'VE GOT BONFIRE!
HARPY PLUCKING THE BASS OUTTA THAT BASS!
AND AUNTIE GRAVITY PUTTING THE STICKS TO UNCLE DRUMS WAY IN THE BACK.
GET OUT NOW IF YOU DON'T WANT US TO MELT YOUR FACE OFF WITH OUR MUSIC. YOU'VE BEEN WARNED!
HERE WE GO, LADIES! A-ONE-TWO-THREE-FOUR...

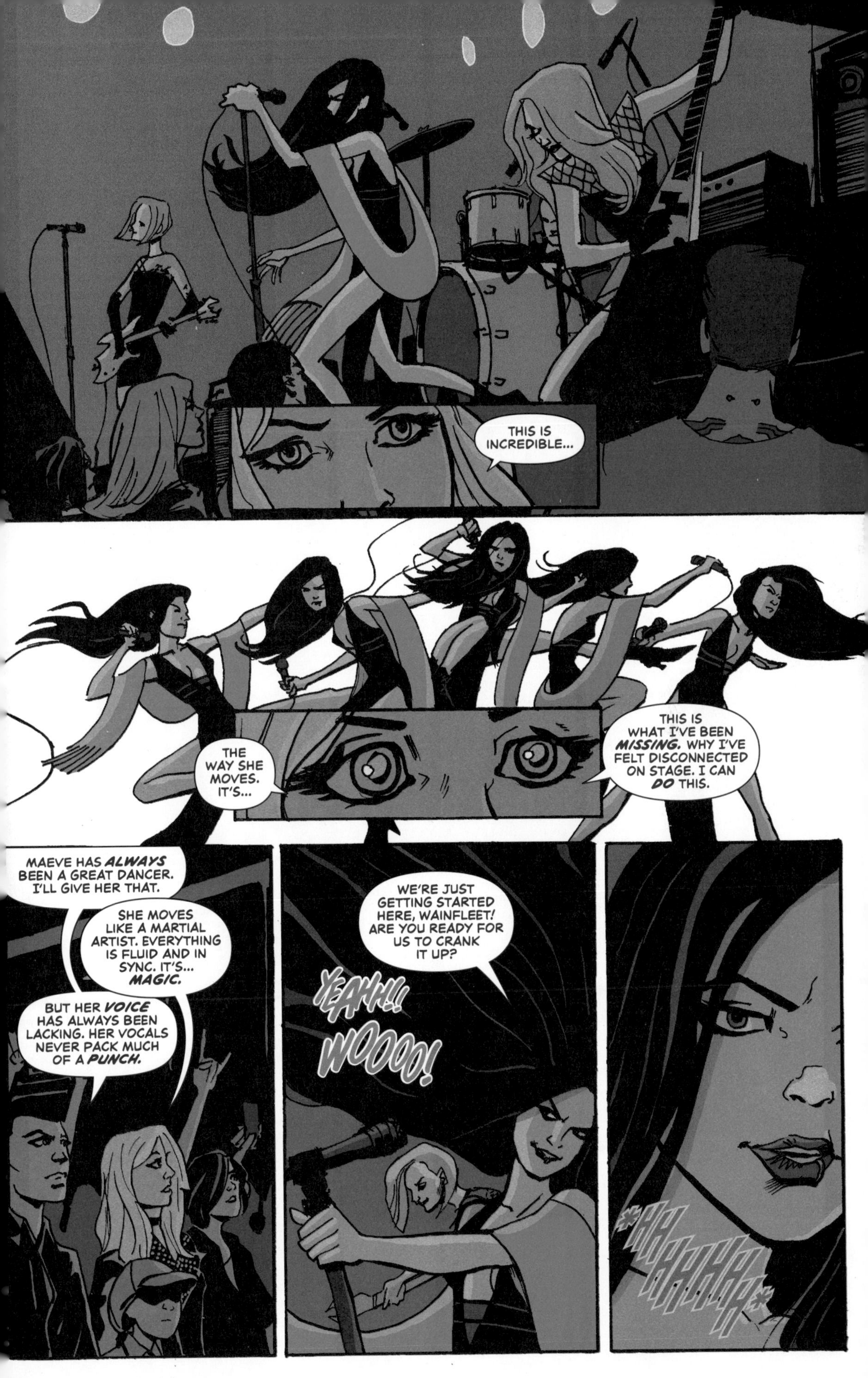
THIS IS INCREDIBLE...
THE WAY SHE MOVES. IT'S...
THIS IS WHAT I'VE BEEN MISSING. WHY I'VE FELT DISCONNECTED ON STAGE. I CAN DO THIS.
MAEVE HAS ALWAYS BEEN A GREAT DANCER. I'LL GIVE HER THAT.
SHE MOVES LIKE A MARTIAL ARTIST. EVERYTHING IS FLUID AND IN SYNC. IT'S... MAGIC.
BUT HER VOICE HAS ALWAYS BEEN LACKING. HER VOCALS NEVER PACK MUCH OF A PUNCH.
WE'RE JUST GETTING STARTED HERE, WAINFLEET! ARE YOU READY FOR US TO CRANK IT UP?
YEAHH!!
WOOOO!
HHHHHHH

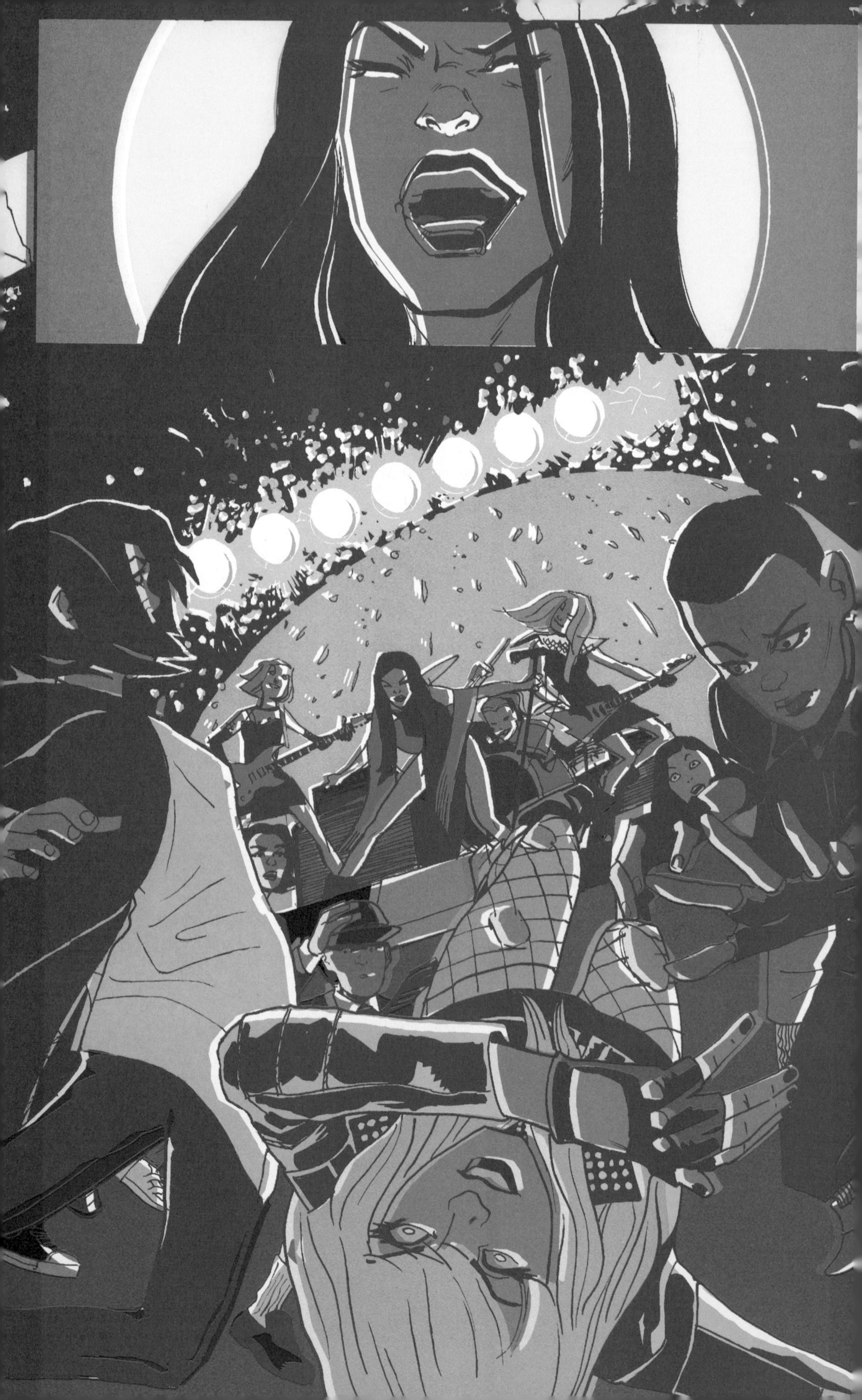

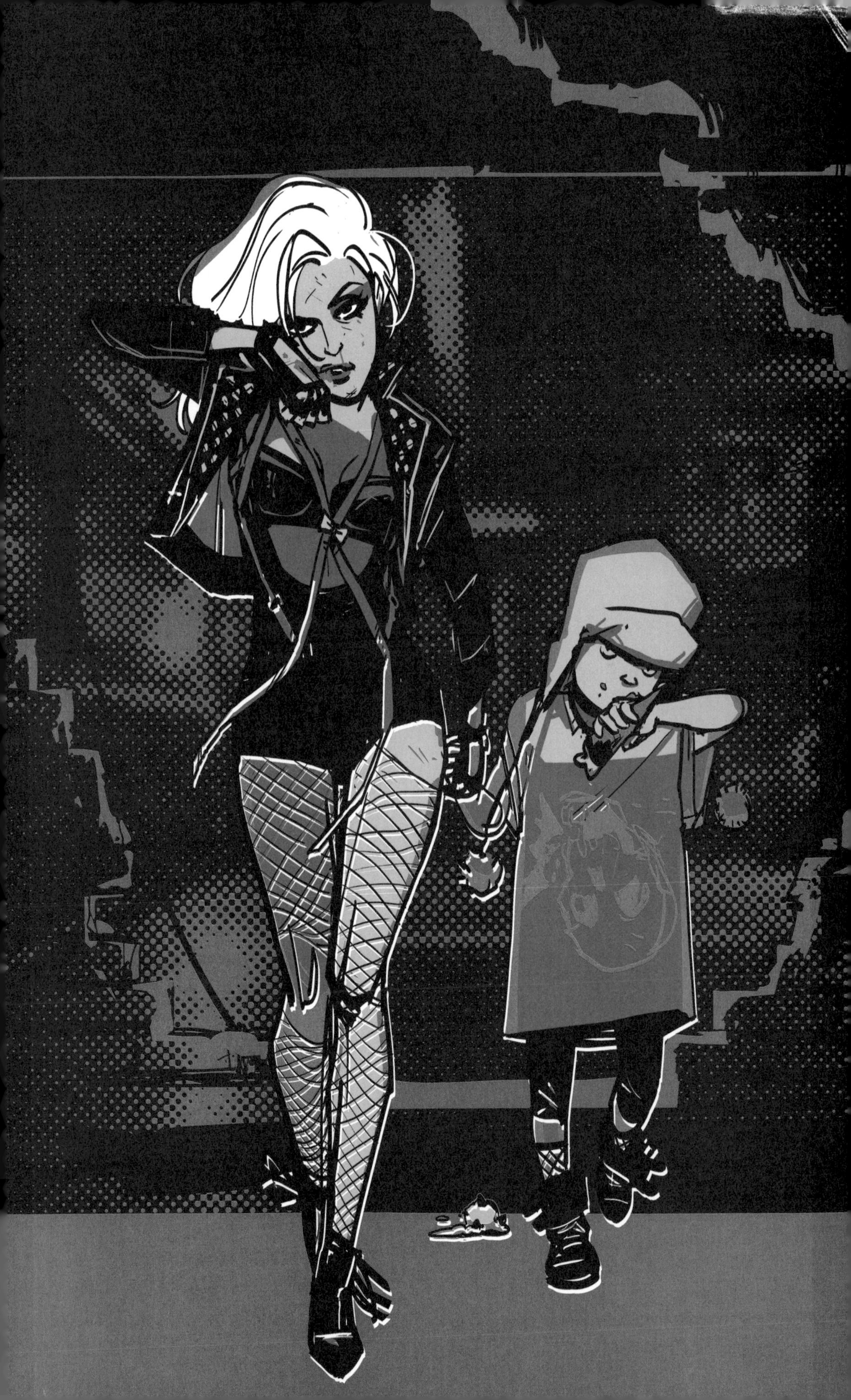

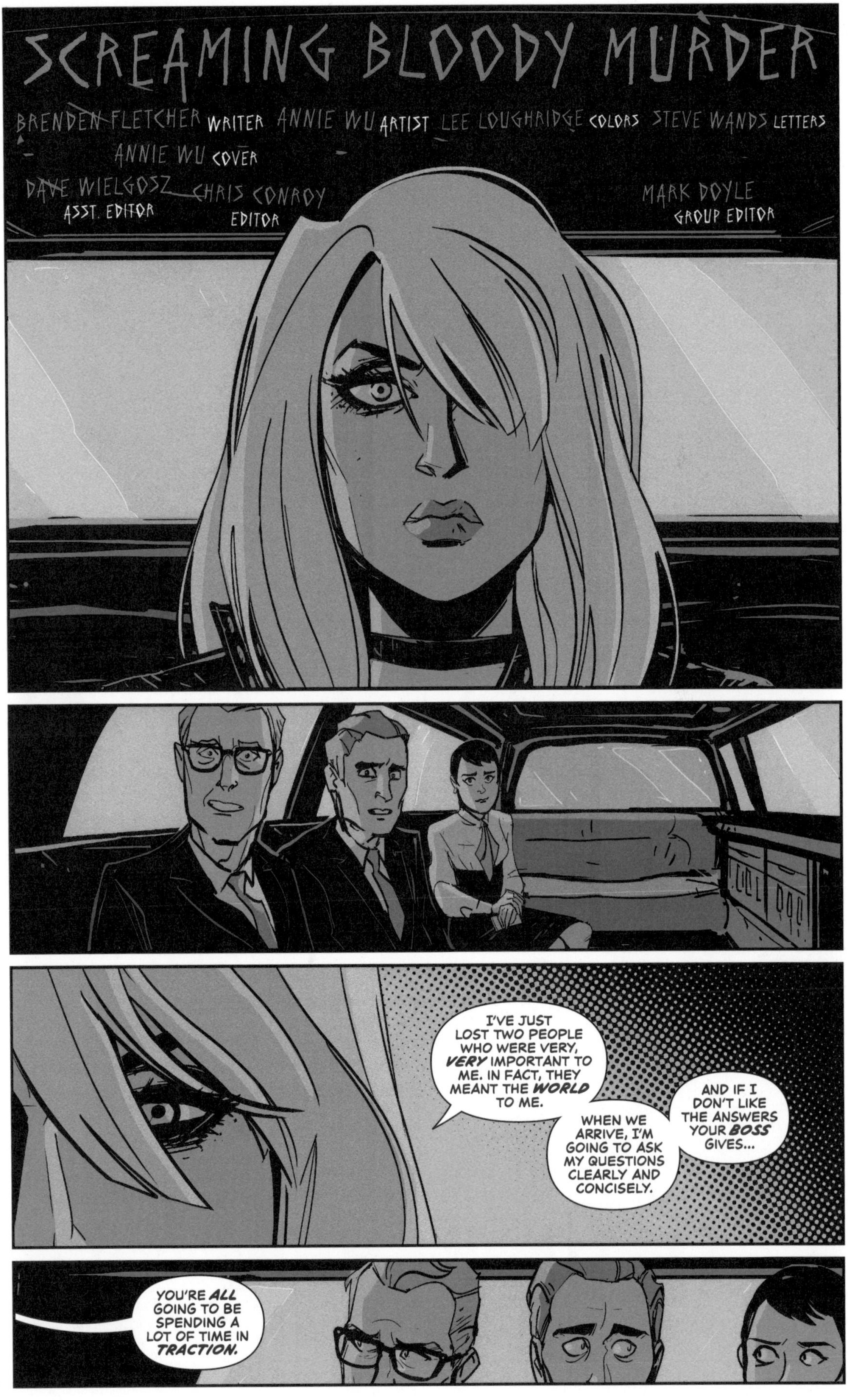
SCREAMING BLOODY MURDER
BRENDEN FLETCHER WRITER ANNIE WU ARTIST LEE LOUGHRIDGE COLORS STEVE WANDS LETTERS
ANNIE WU COVER
DAVE WIELGOSZ ASST. EDITOR CHRIS CONROY EDITOR MARK DOYLE GROUP EDITOR
I'VE JUST LOST TWO PEOPLE WHO WERE VERY, VERY IMPORTANT TO ME. IN FACT, THEY MEANT THE WORLD TO ME.
WHEN WE ARRIVE, I'M GOING TO ASK MY QUESTIONS CLEARLY AND CONCISELY.
AND IF I DON'T LIKE THE ANSWERS YOUR BOSS GIVES...
YOU'RE ALL GOING TO BE SPENDING A LOT OF TIME IN TRACTION.

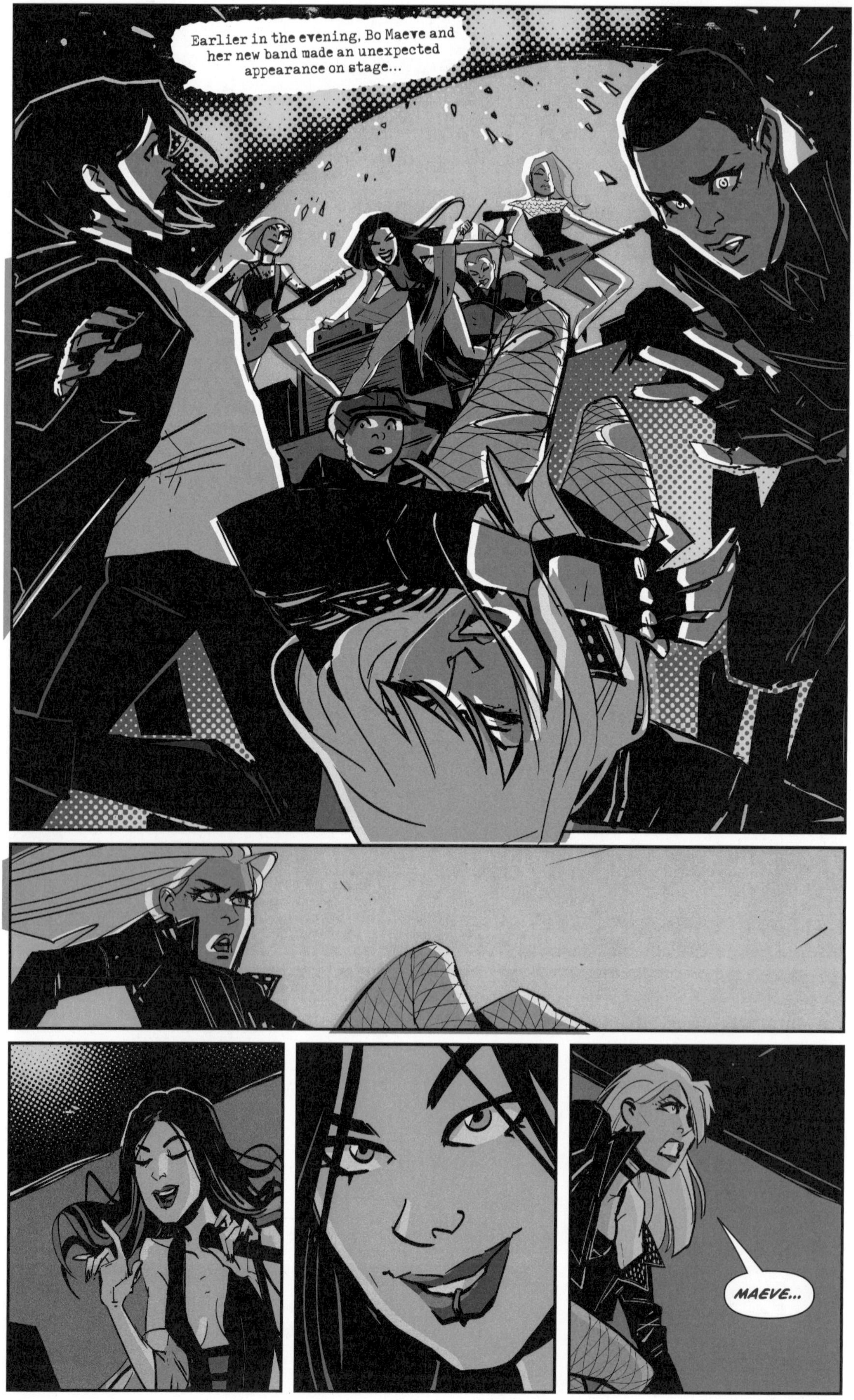
Earlier in the evening, Bo Maeve and her new band made an unexpected appearance on stage...
MAEVE...

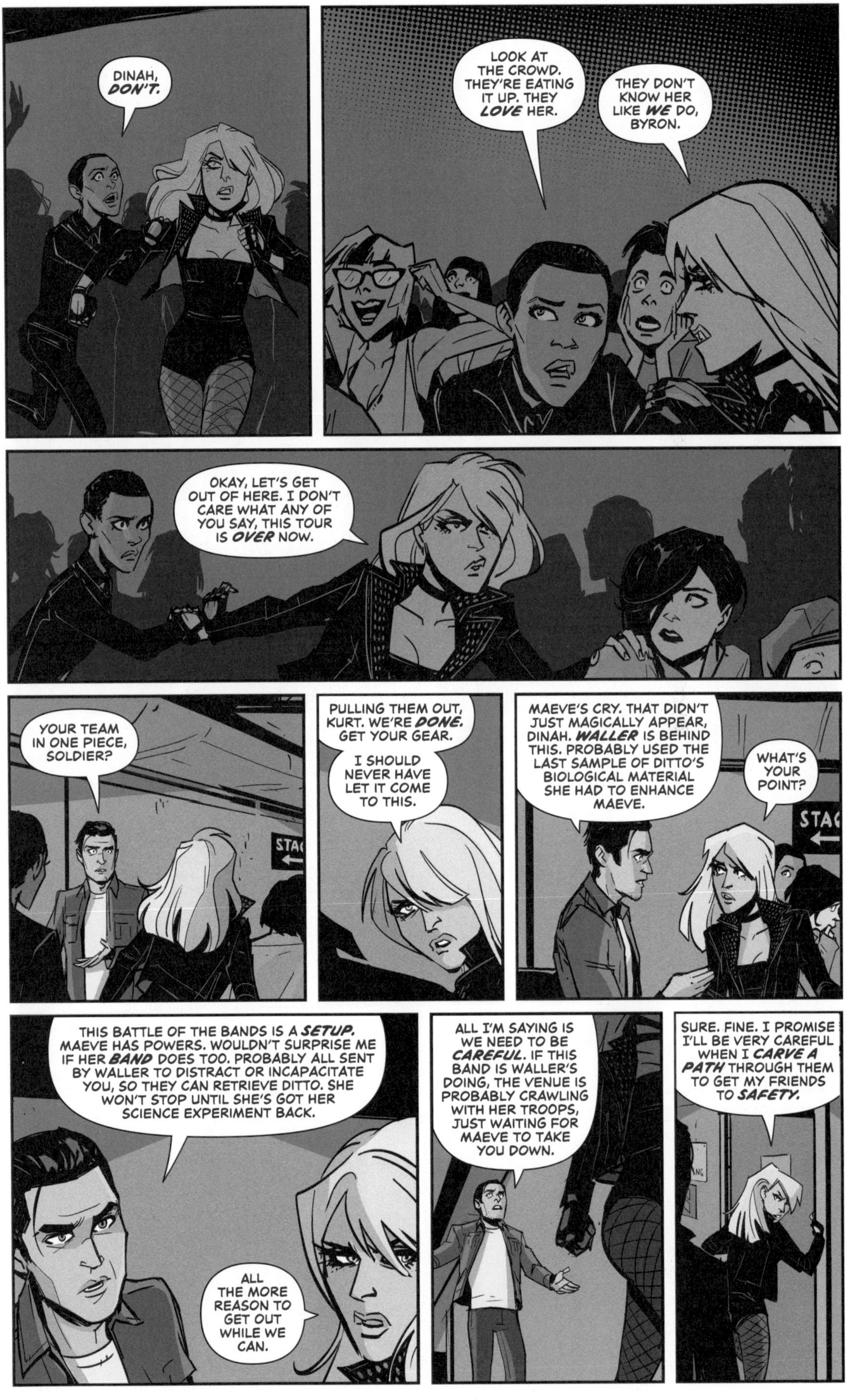
DINAH, DON'T.
LOOK AT THE CROWD. THEY'RE EATING IT UP. THEY LOVE HER.
THEY DON'T KNOW HER LIKE WE DO, BYRON.
OKAY, LET'S GET OUT OF HERE. I DON'T CARE WHAT ANY OF YOU SAY, THIS TOUR IS OVER NOW.
YOUR TEAM IN ONE PIECE, SOLDIER?
PULLING THEM OUT, KURT. WE'RE DONE. GET YOUR GEAR.
I SHOULD NEVER HAVE LET IT COME TO THIS.
MAEVE'S CRY. THAT DIDN'T JUST MAGICALLY APPEAR, DINAH. WALLER IS BEHIND THIS. PROBABLY USED THE LAST SAMPLE OF DITTO'S BIOLOGICAL MATERIAL SHE HAD TO ENHANCE MAEVE.
WHAT'S YOUR POINT?
THIS BATTLE OF THE BANDS IS A SETUP. MAEVE HAS POWERS. WOULDN'T SURPRISE ME IF HER BAND DOES TOO. PROBABLY ALL SENT BY WALLER TO DISTRACT OR INCAPACITATE YOU, SO THEY CAN RETRIEVE DITTO. SHE WON'T STOP UNTIL SHE'S GOT HER SCIENCE EXPERIMENT BACK.
ALL THE MORE REASON TO GET OUT WHILE WE CAN.
ALL I'M SAYING IS WE NEED TO BE CAREFUL. IF THIS BAND IS WALLER'S DOING, THE VENUE IS PROBABLY CRAWLING WITH HER TROOPS, JUST WAITING FOR MAEVE TO TAKE YOU DOWN.
SURE. FINE. I PROMISE I'LL BE VERY CAREFUL WHEN I CARVE A PATH THROUGH THEM TO GET MY FRIENDS TO SAFETY.

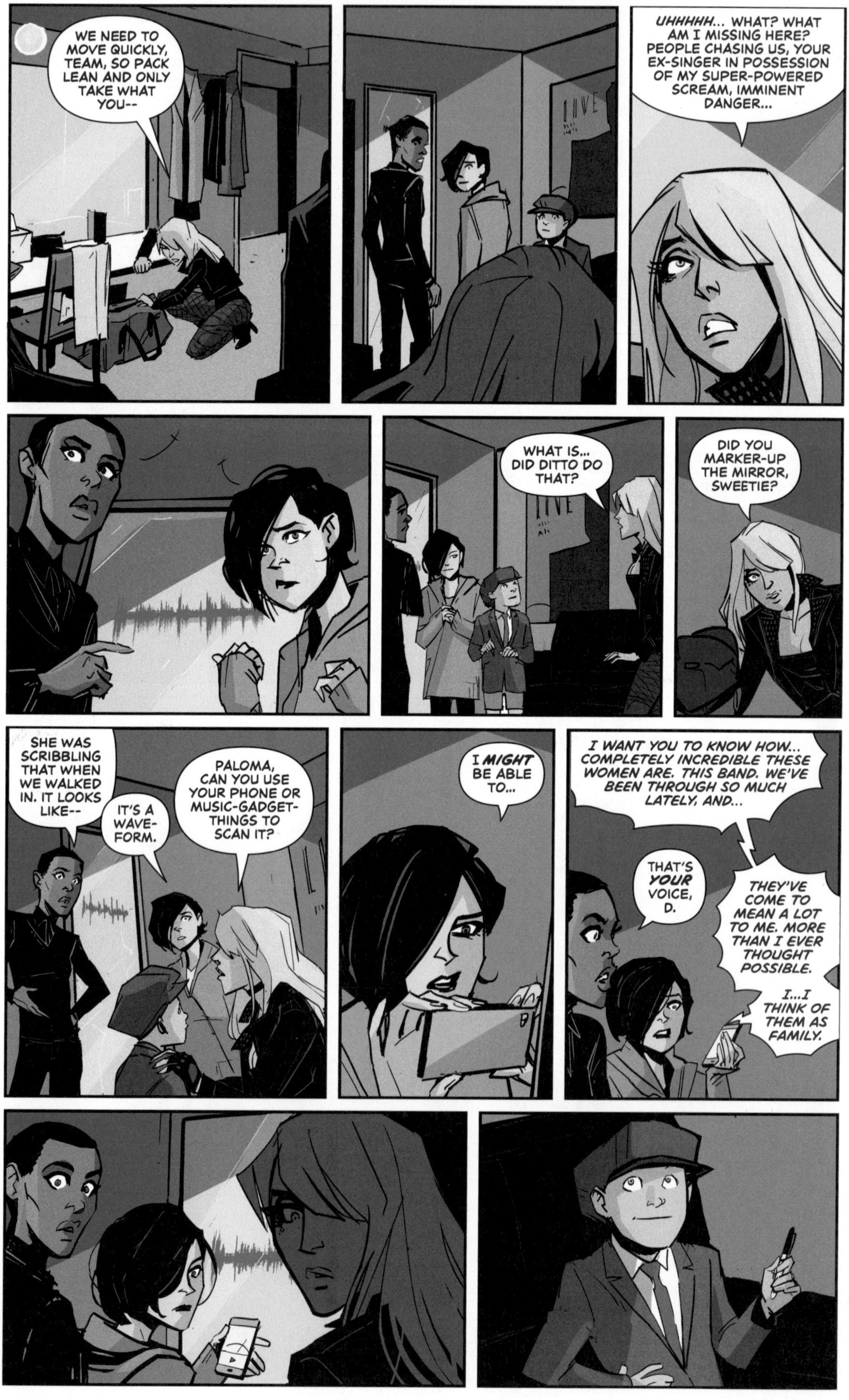
WE NEED TO MOVE QUICKLY, TEAM, SO PACK LEAN AND ONLY TAKE WHAT YOU--
UHHHHH... WHAT? WHAT AM I MISSING HERE? PEOPLE CHASING US, YOUR EX-SINGER IN POSSESSION OF MY SUPER-POWERED SCREAM, IMMINENT DANGER...
WHAT IS... DID DITTO DO THAT?
DID YOU MARKER-UP THE MIRROR, SWEETIE?
SHE WAS SCRIBBLING THAT WHEN WE WALKED IN. IT LOOKS LIKE--
IT'S A WAVE-FORM.
PALOMA, CAN YOU USE YOUR PHONE OR MUSIC-GADGET-THINGS TO SCAN IT?
I *MIGHT* BE ABLE TO...
I WANT YOU TO KNOW HOW... COMPLETELY INCREDIBLE THESE WOMEN ARE. THIS BAND. WE'VE BEEN THROUGH SO MUCH LATELY, AND...
THAT'S *YOUR* VOICE, D.
THEY'VE COME TO MEAN A LOT TO ME. MORE THAN I EVER THOUGHT POSSIBLE.
I...I THINK OF THEM AS FAMILY.

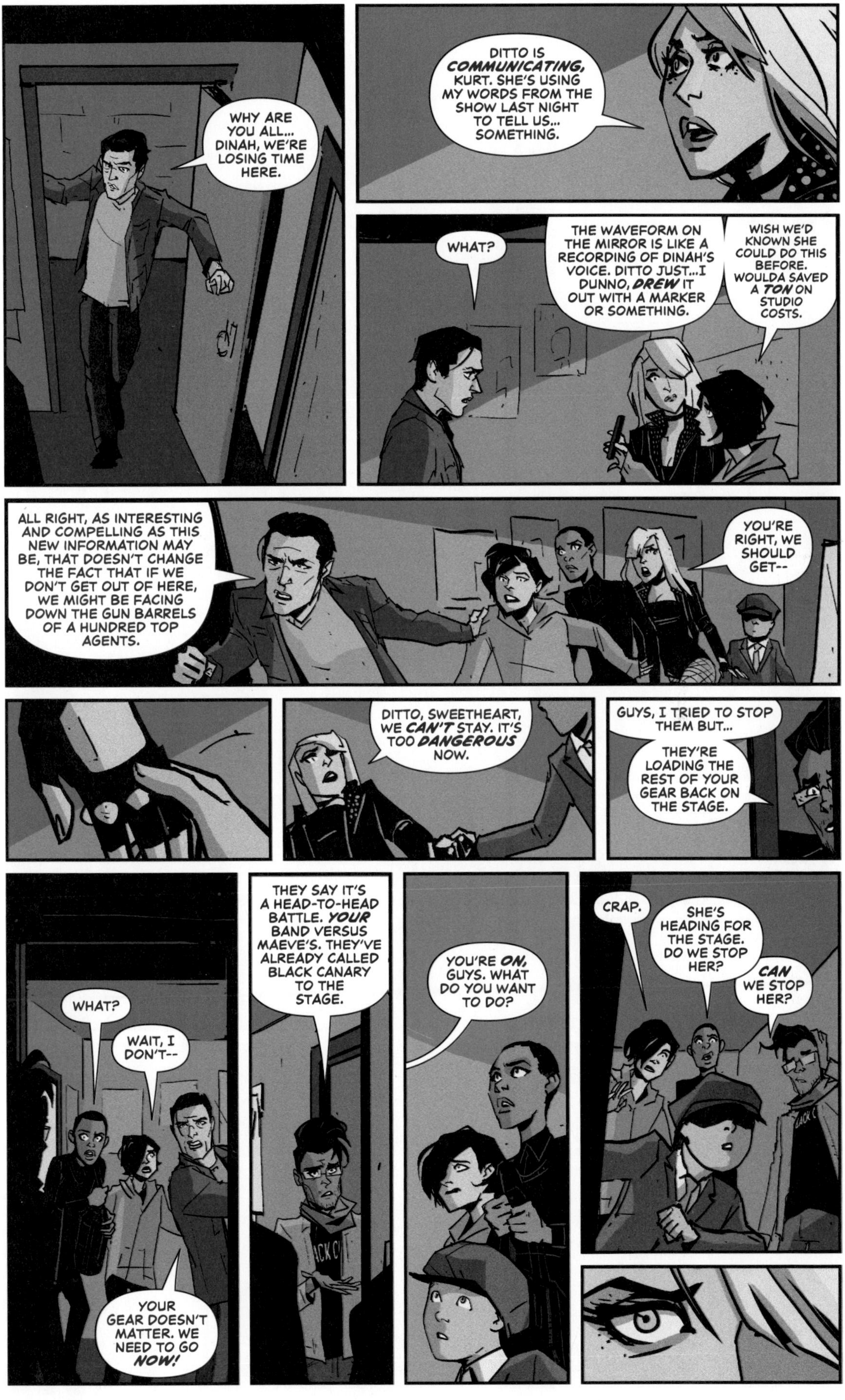
WHY ARE YOU ALL... DINAH, WE'RE LOSING TIME HERE.
DITTO IS *COMMUNICATING,* KURT. SHE'S USING MY WORDS FROM THE SHOW LAST NIGHT TO TELL US... SOMETHING.
WHAT?
THE WAVEFORM ON THE MIRROR IS LIKE A RECORDING OF DINAH'S VOICE. DITTO JUST...I DUNNO, *DREW* IT OUT WITH A MARKER OR SOMETHING.
WISH WE'D KNOWN SHE COULD DO THIS BEFORE. WOULDA SAVED A *TON* ON STUDIO COSTS.
ALL RIGHT, AS INTERESTING AND COMPELLING AS THIS NEW INFORMATION MAY BE, THAT DOESN'T CHANGE THE FACT THAT IF WE DON'T GET OUT OF HERE, WE MIGHT BE FACING DOWN THE GUN BARRELS OF A HUNDRED TOP AGENTS.
YOU'RE RIGHT, WE SHOULD GET--
DITTO, SWEETHEART, WE *CAN'T* STAY. IT'S TOO *DANGEROUS* NOW.
GUYS, I TRIED TO STOP THEM BUT...
THEY'RE LOADING THE REST OF YOUR GEAR BACK ON THE STAGE.
WHAT?
WAIT, I DON'T--
YOUR GEAR DOESN'T MATTER. WE NEED TO GO *NOW!*
THEY SAY IT'S A HEAD-TO-HEAD BATTLE. *YOUR* BAND VERSUS MAEVE'S. THEY'VE ALREADY CALLED BLACK CANARY TO THE STAGE.
YOU'RE *ON,* GUYS. WHAT DO YOU WANT TO DO?
CRAP.
SHE'S HEADING FOR THE STAGE. DO WE STOP HER?
CAN WE STOP HER?

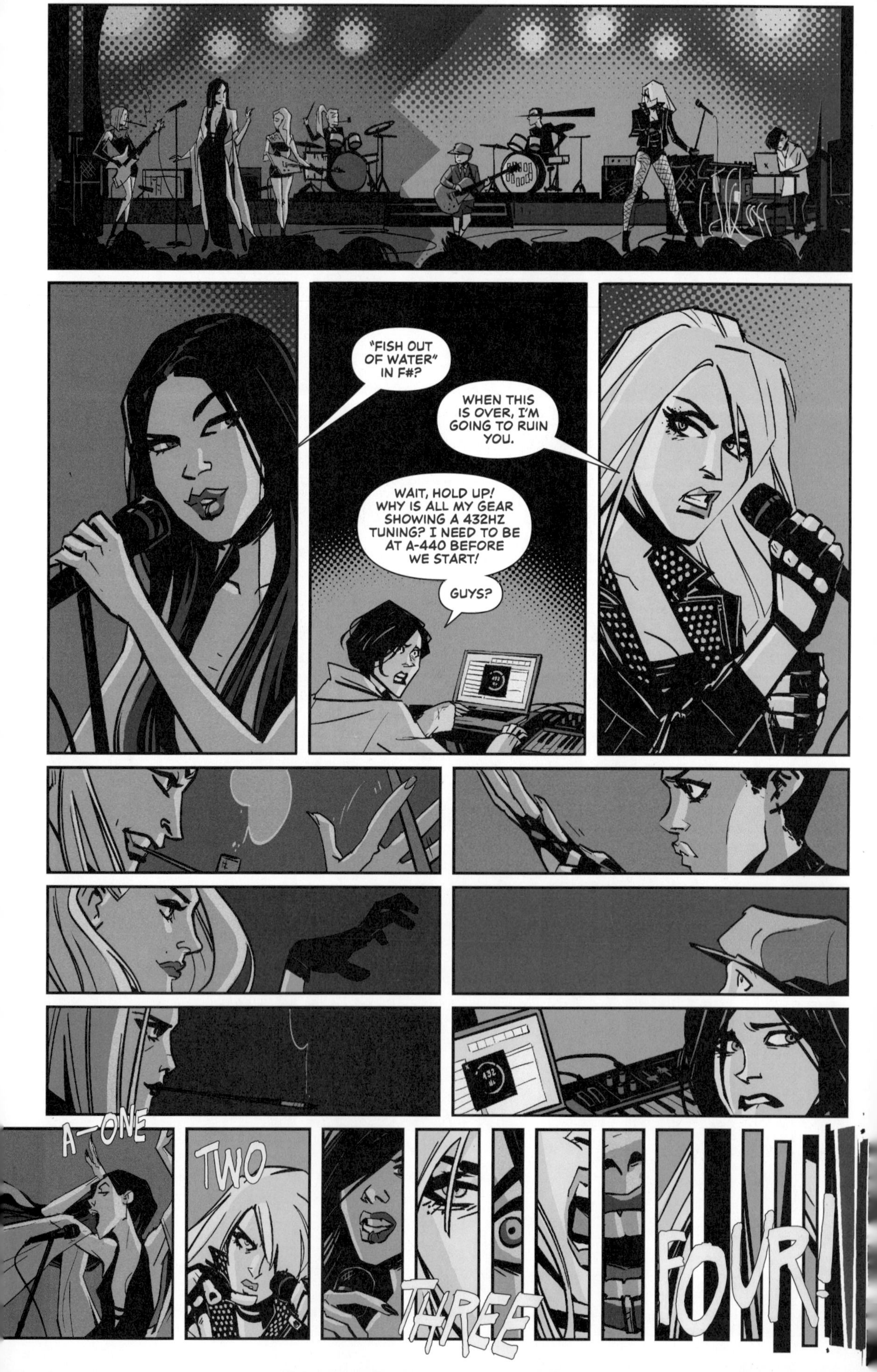
"FISH OUT OF WATER" IN F#?
WHEN THIS IS OVER, I'M GOING TO RUIN YOU.
WAIT, HOLD UP! WHY IS ALL MY GEAR SHOWING A 432HZ TUNING? I NEED TO BE AT A-440 BEFORE WE START!
GUYS?
A-ONE
TWO
THREE
FOUR!

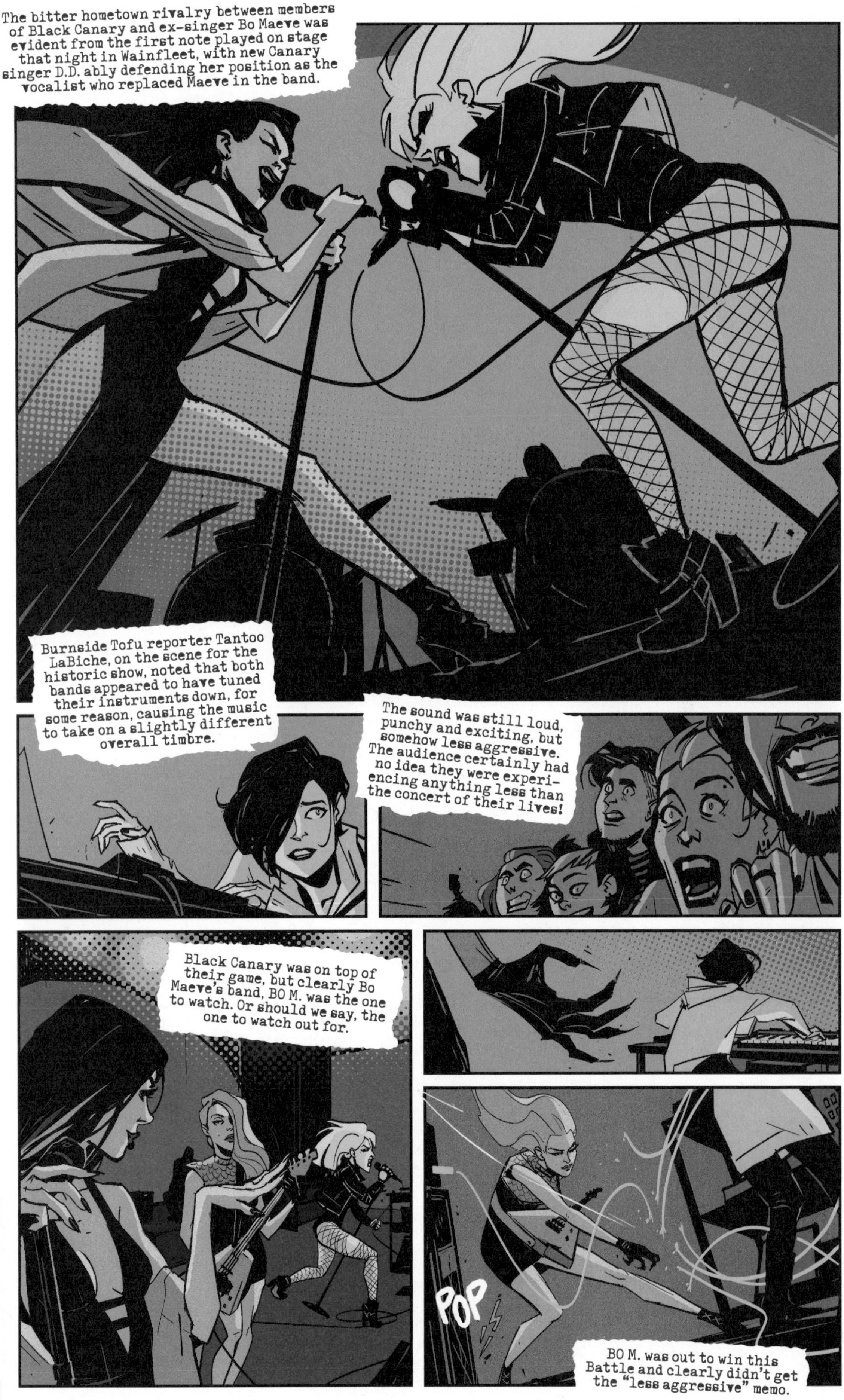
The bitter hometown rivalry between members of Black Canary and ex-singer Bo Maeve was evident from the first note played on stage that night in Wainfleet, with new Canary singer D.D. ably defending her position as the vocalist who replaced Maeve in the band.
Burnside Tofu reporter Tantoo LaBiche, on the scene for the historic show, noted that both bands appeared to have tuned their instruments down, for some reason, causing the music to take on a slightly different overall timbre.
The sound was still loud, punchy and exciting, but somehow less aggressive. The audience certainly had no idea they were experiencing anything less than the concert of their lives!
Black Canary was on top of their game, but clearly Bo Maeve's band, BO M. was the one to watch. Or should we say, the one to watch out for.
POP
BO M. was out to win this Battle and clearly didn't get the "less aggressive" memo.

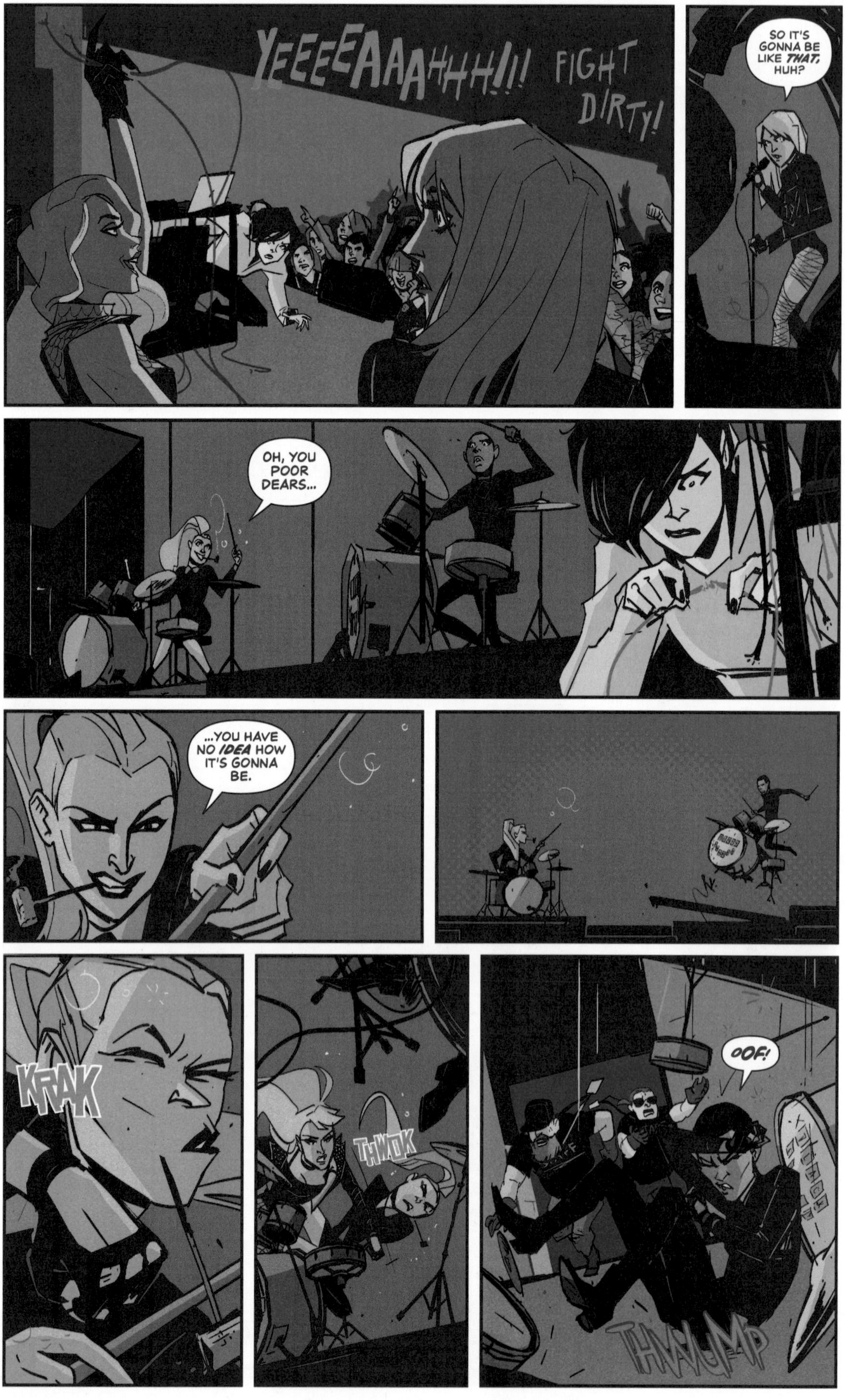
YEEEEAAAHHH!!!
FIGHT DIRTY!
SO IT'S GONNA BE LIKE *THAT,* HUH?
OH, YOU POOR DEARS...
...YOU HAVE NO *IDEA* HOW IT'S GONNA BE.
KRAK
THWOK
OOF!
THWUMP

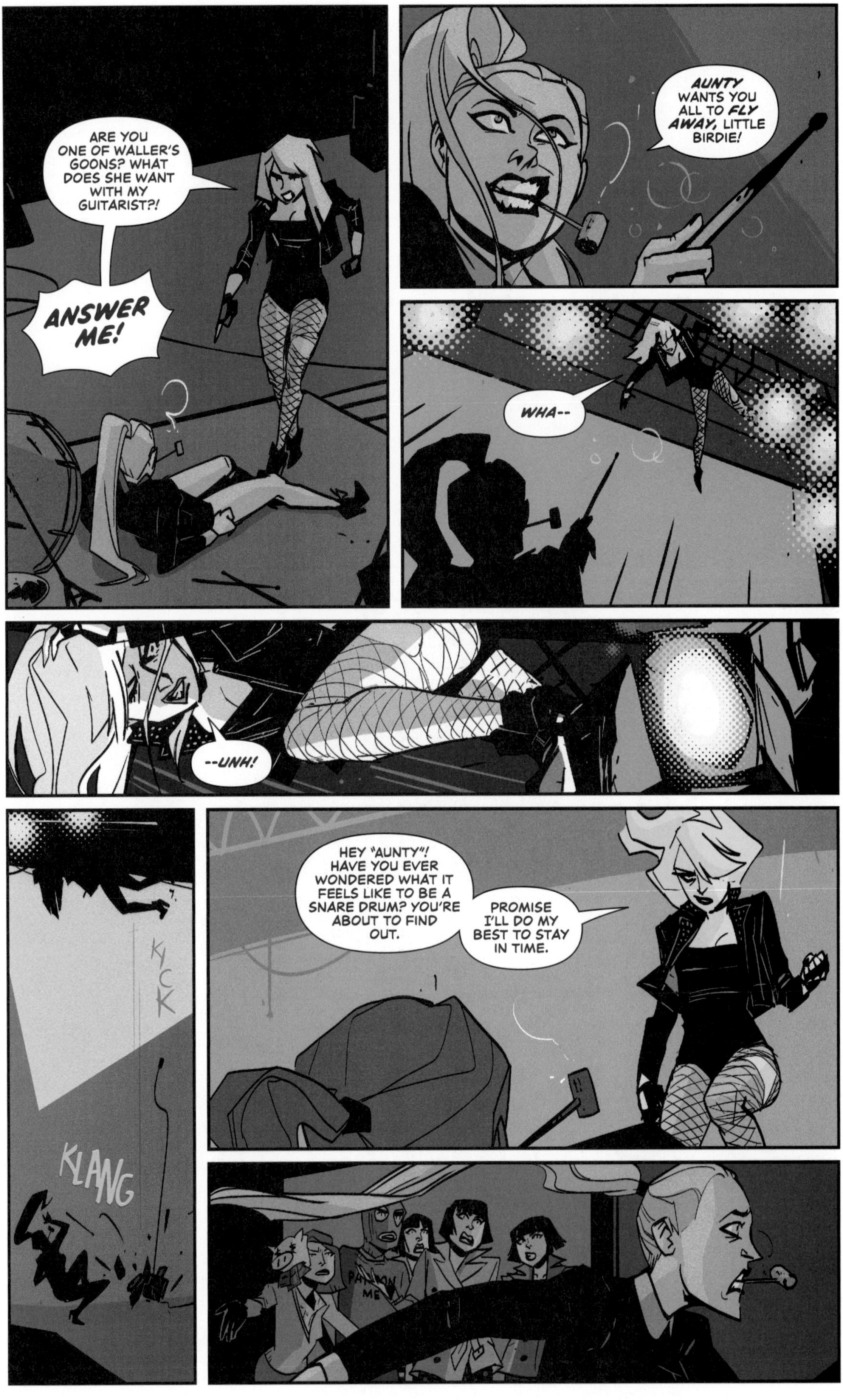
ARE YOU ONE OF WALLER'S GOONS? WHAT DOES SHE WANT WITH MY GUITARIST?!
ANSWER ME!
AUNTY WANTS YOU ALL TO FLY AWAY, LITTLE BIRDIE!
WHA--
--UNH!
KICK
KLANG
HEY "AUNTY"! HAVE YOU EVER WONDERED WHAT IT FEELS LIKE TO BE A SNARE DRUM? YOU'RE ABOUT TO FIND OUT.
PROMISE I'LL DO MY BEST TO STAY IN TIME.

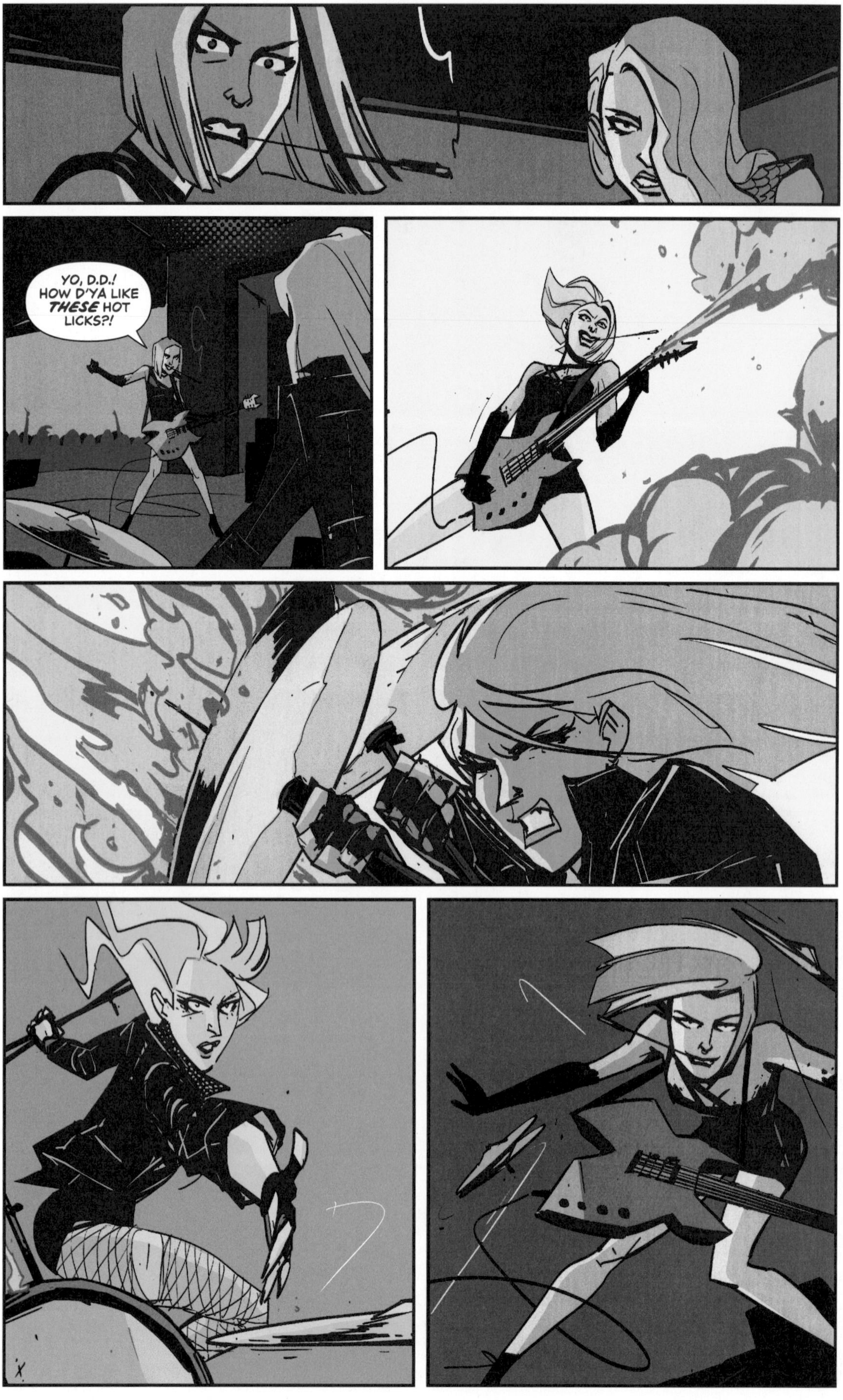
YO, D.D.! HOW D'YA LIKE *THESE* HOT LICKS?!

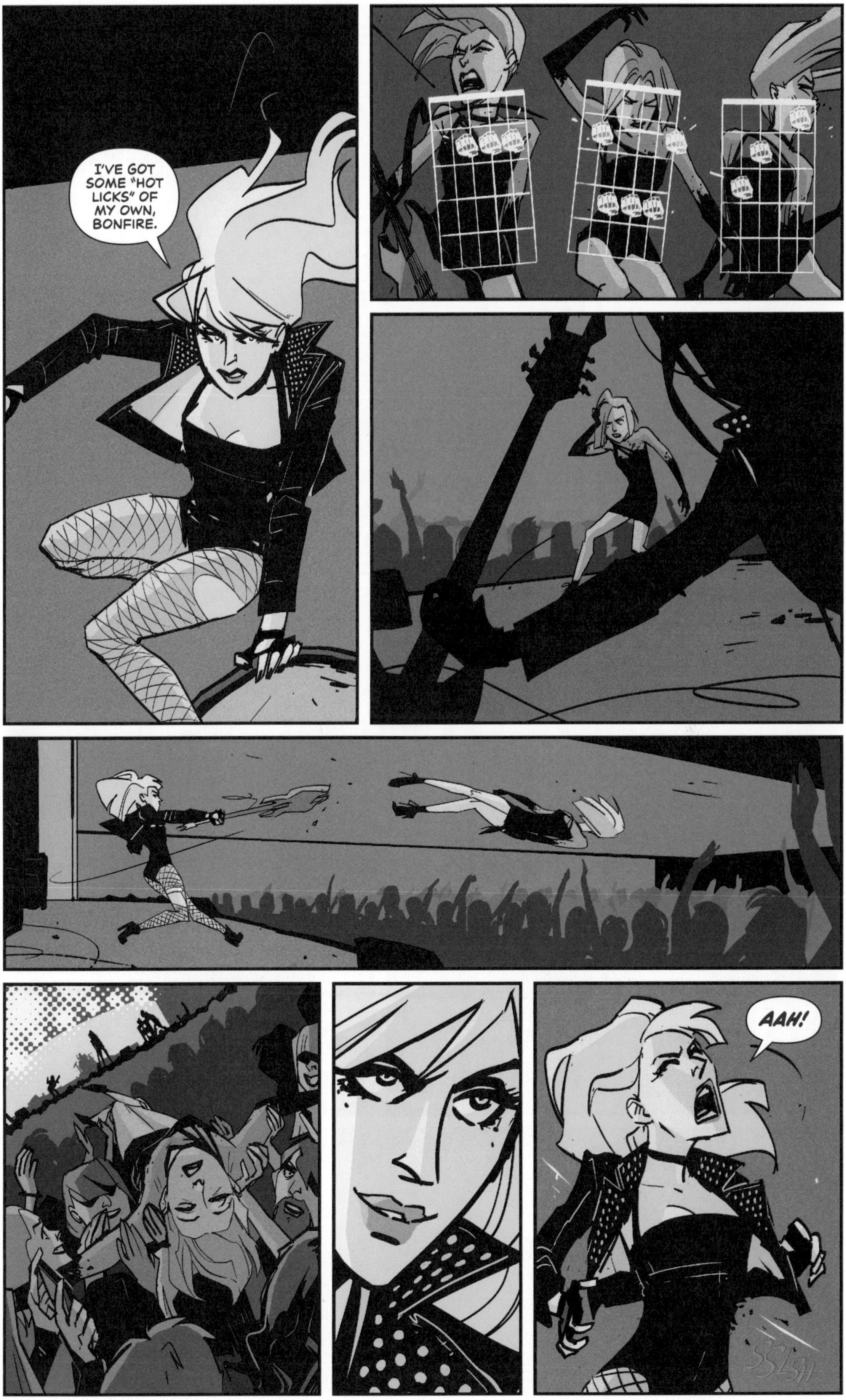
I'VE GOT SOME "HOT LICKS" OF MY OWN, BONFIRE.
AAH!
SSLSH

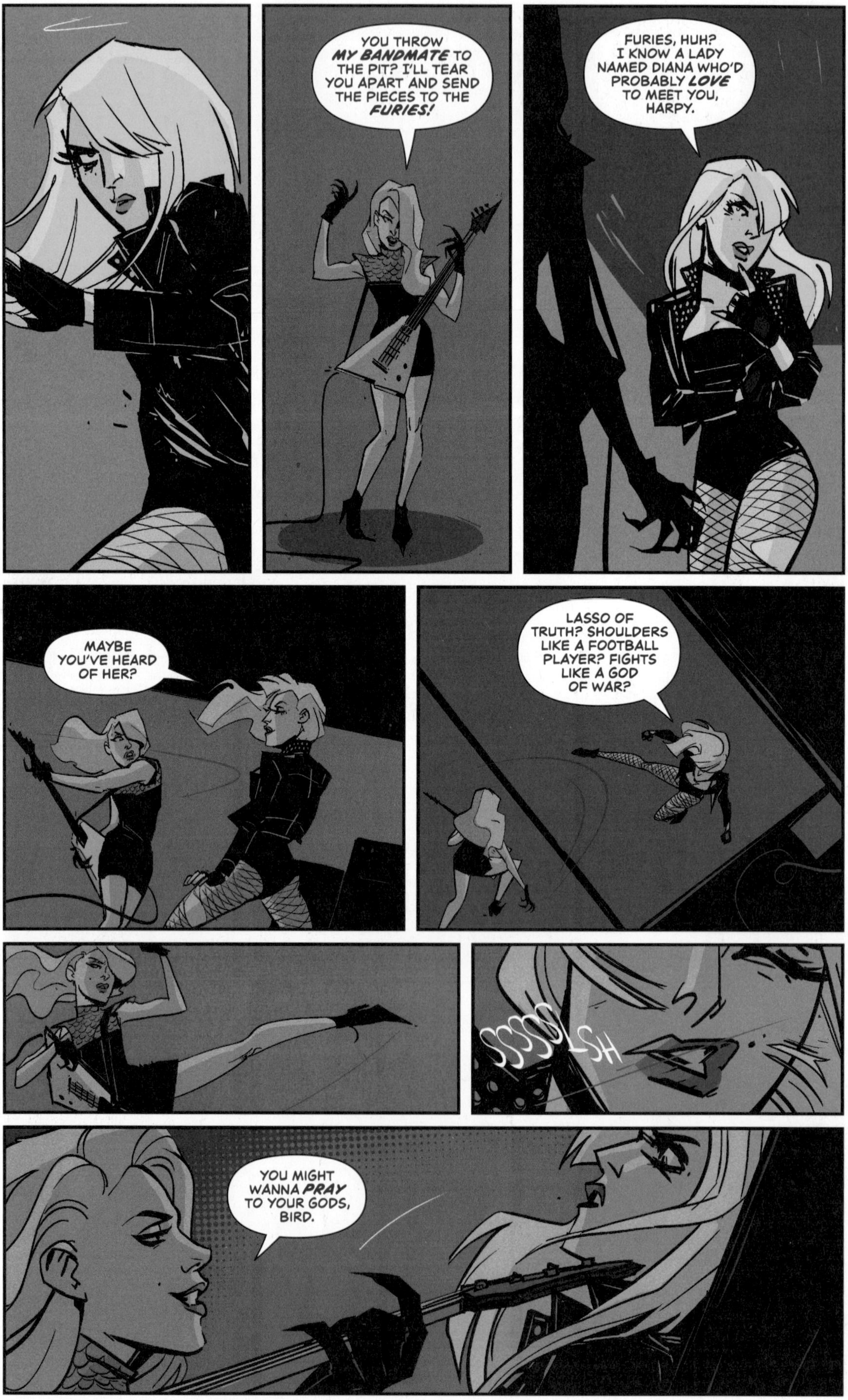
YOU THROW *MY BANDMATE* TO THE PIT? I'LL TEAR YOU APART AND SEND THE PIECES TO THE *FURIES!*
FURIES, HUH? I KNOW A LADY NAMED DIANA WHO'D PROBABLY *LOVE* TO MEET YOU, HARPY.
MAYBE YOU'VE HEARD OF HER?
LASSO OF TRUTH? SHOULDERS LIKE A FOOTBALL PLAYER? FIGHTS LIKE A GOD OF WAR?
SSSSSLSH
YOU MIGHT WANNA *PRAY* TO YOUR GODS, BIRD.

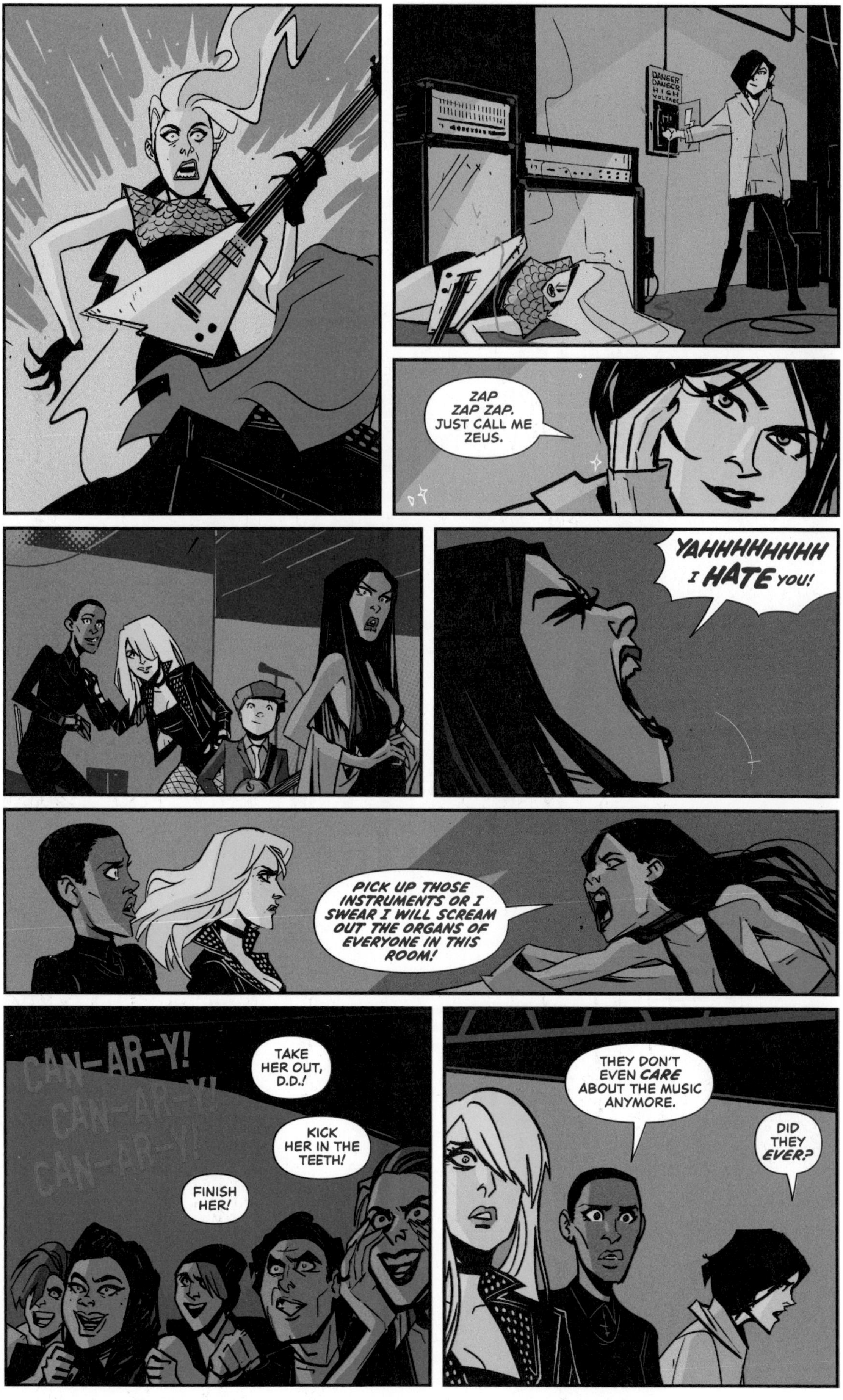
DANGER DANGER HIGH VOLTAGE
ZAP ZAP ZAP. JUST CALL ME ZEUS.
YAHHHHHHHH I HATE YOU!
PICK UP THOSE INSTRUMENTS OR I SWEAR I WILL SCREAM OUT THE ORGANS OF EVERYONE IN THIS ROOM!
CAN-AR-Y! CAN-AR-Y! CAN-AR-Y!
TAKE HER OUT, D.D.!
KICK HER IN THE TEETH!
FINISH HER!
THEY DON'T EVEN CARE ABOUT THE MUSIC ANYMORE.
DID THEY EVER?

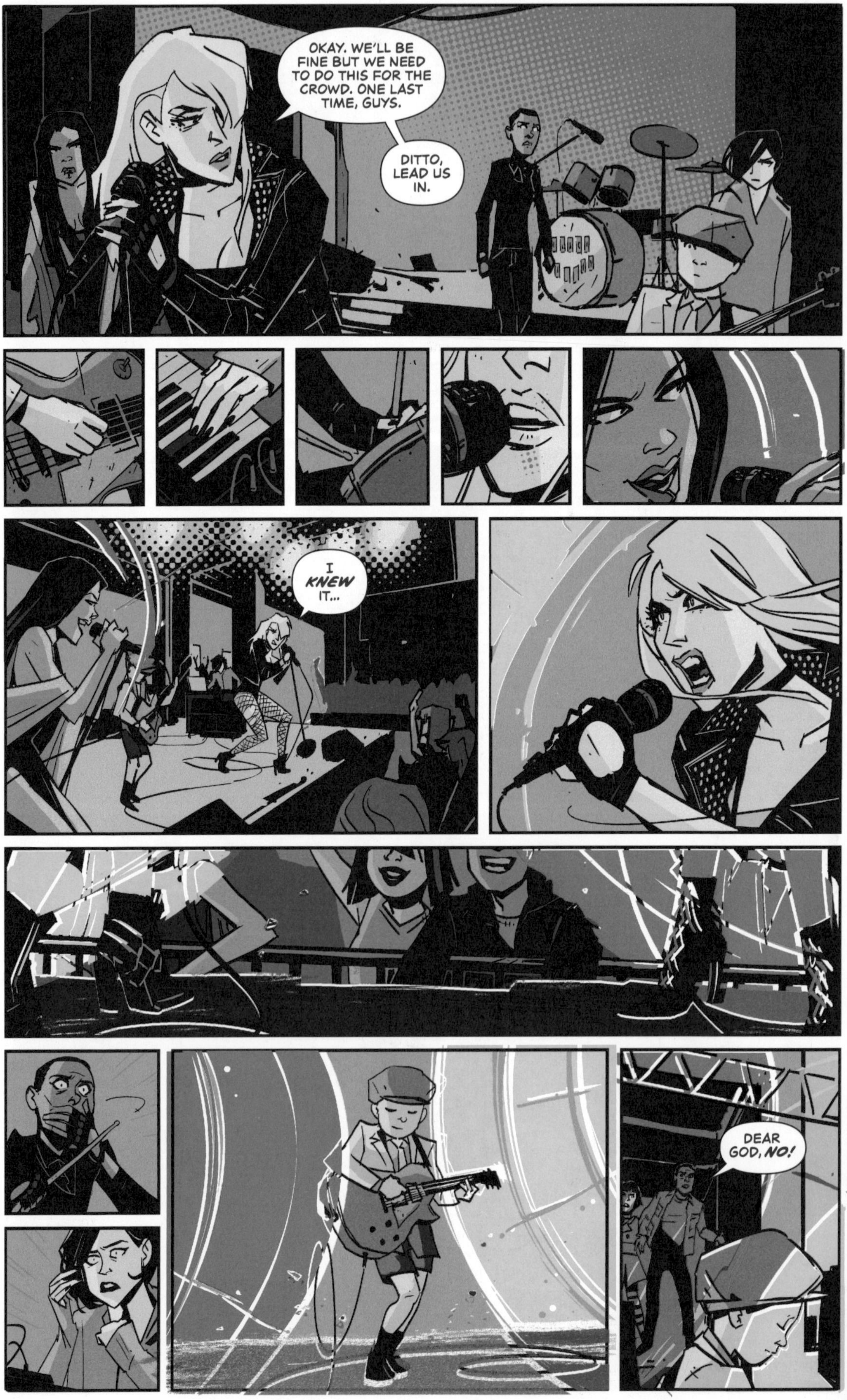
OKAY. WE'LL BE FINE BUT WE NEED TO DO THIS FOR THE CROWD. ONE LAST TIME, GUYS.
DITTO, LEAD US IN.
I KNEW IT...
DEAR GOD, NO!

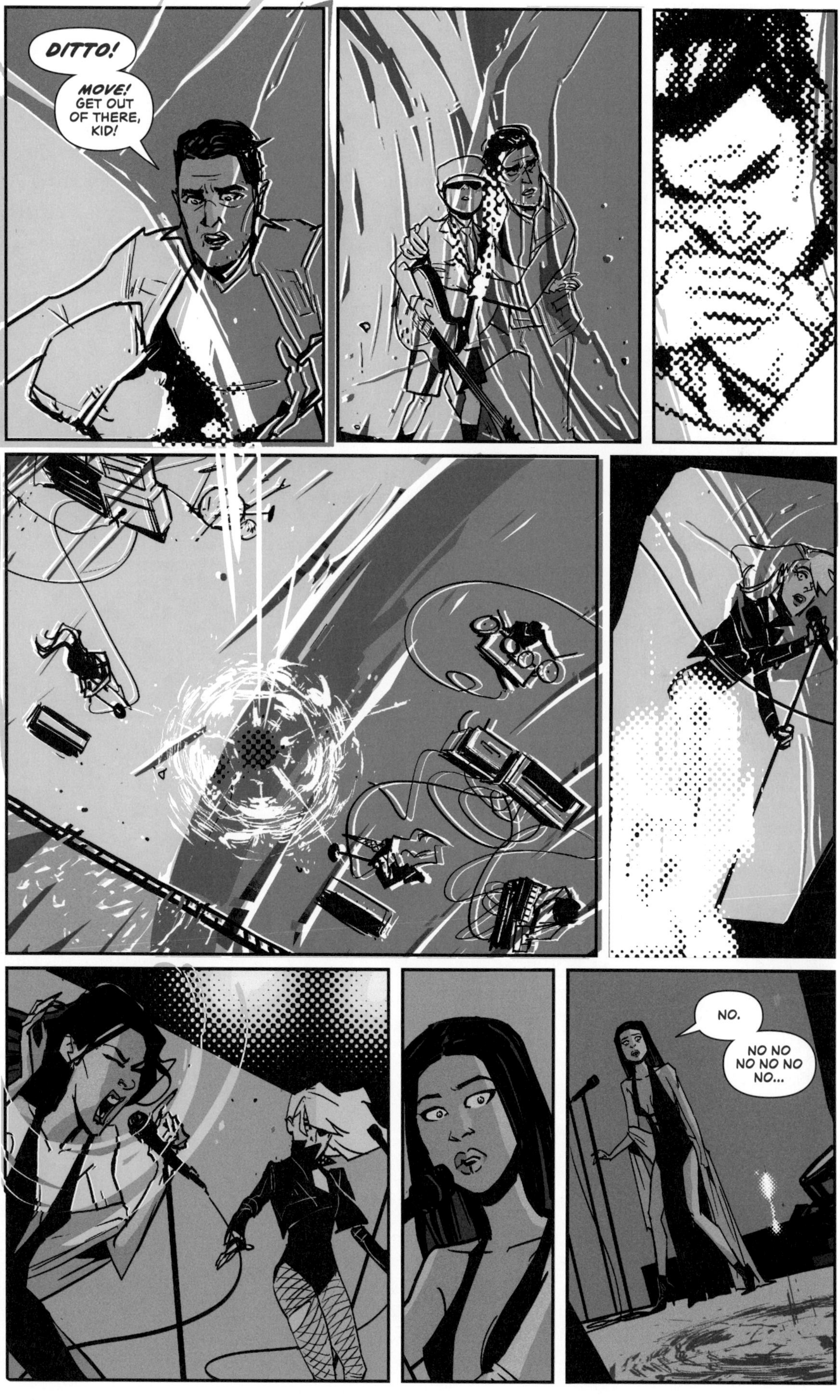
DITTO!
MOVE! GET OUT OF THERE, KID!
NO.
NO NO NO NO NO NO...

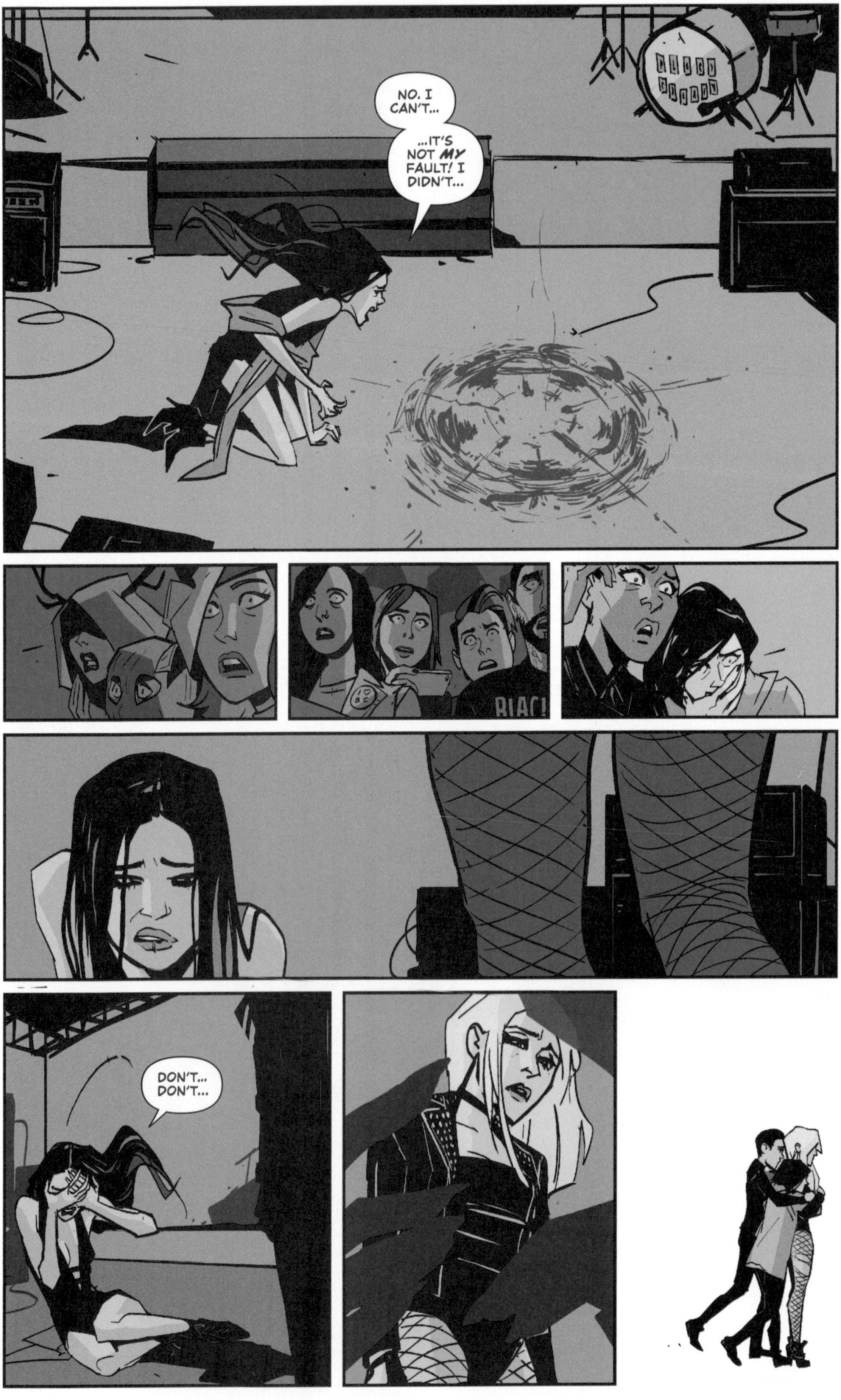
NO. I CAN'T...
...IT'S NOT *MY* FAULT! I DIDN'T...
DON'T... DON'T...

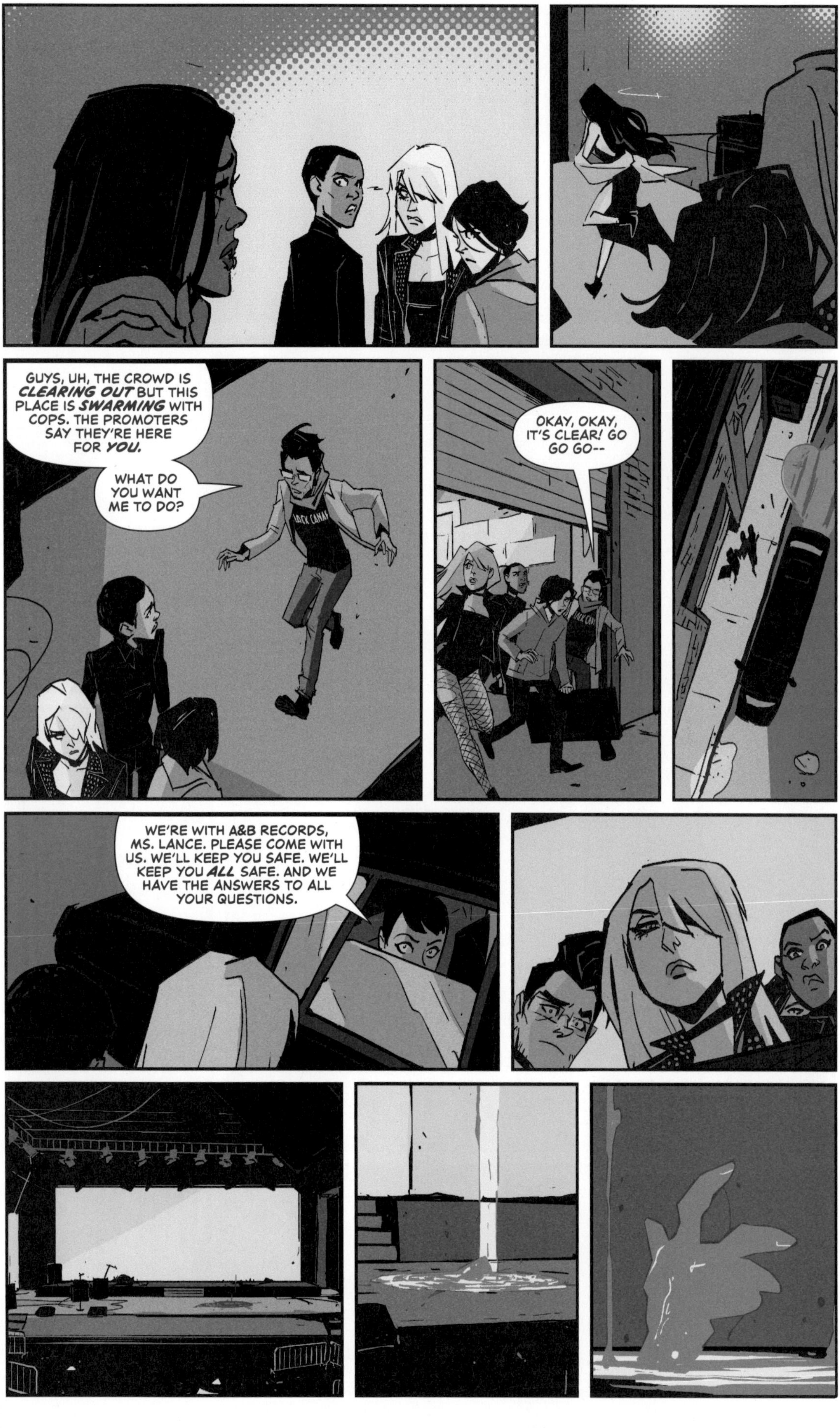
GUYS, UH, THE CROWD IS CLEARING OUT BUT THIS PLACE IS SWARMING WITH COPS. THE PROMOTERS SAY THEY'RE HERE FOR YOU.
WHAT DO YOU WANT ME TO DO?
OKAY, OKAY, IT'S CLEAR! GO GO GO--
WE'RE WITH A&B RECORDS, MS. LANCE. PLEASE COME WITH US. WE'LL KEEP YOU SAFE. WE'LL KEEP YOU ALL SAFE. AND WE HAVE THE ANSWERS TO ALL YOUR QUESTIONS.

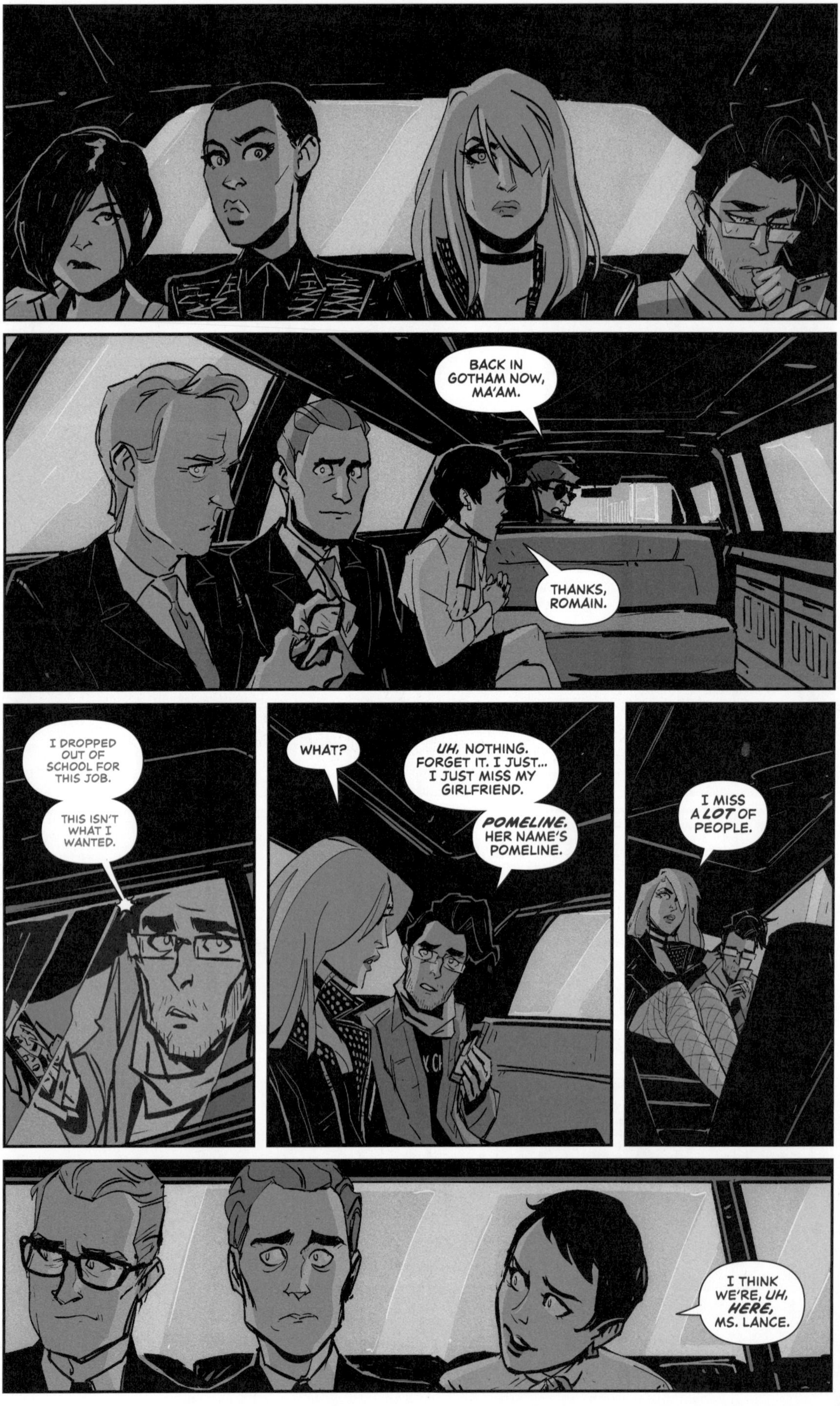
BACK IN GOTHAM NOW, MA'AM.
THANKS, ROMAIN.
I DROPPED OUT OF SCHOOL FOR THIS JOB.
THIS ISN'T WHAT I WANTED.
WHAT?
UH, NOTHING. FORGET IT. I JUST... I JUST MISS MY GIRLFRIEND.
POMELINE. HER NAME'S POMELINE.
I MISS A LOT OF PEOPLE.
I THINK WE'RE, UH, HERE, MS. LANCE.

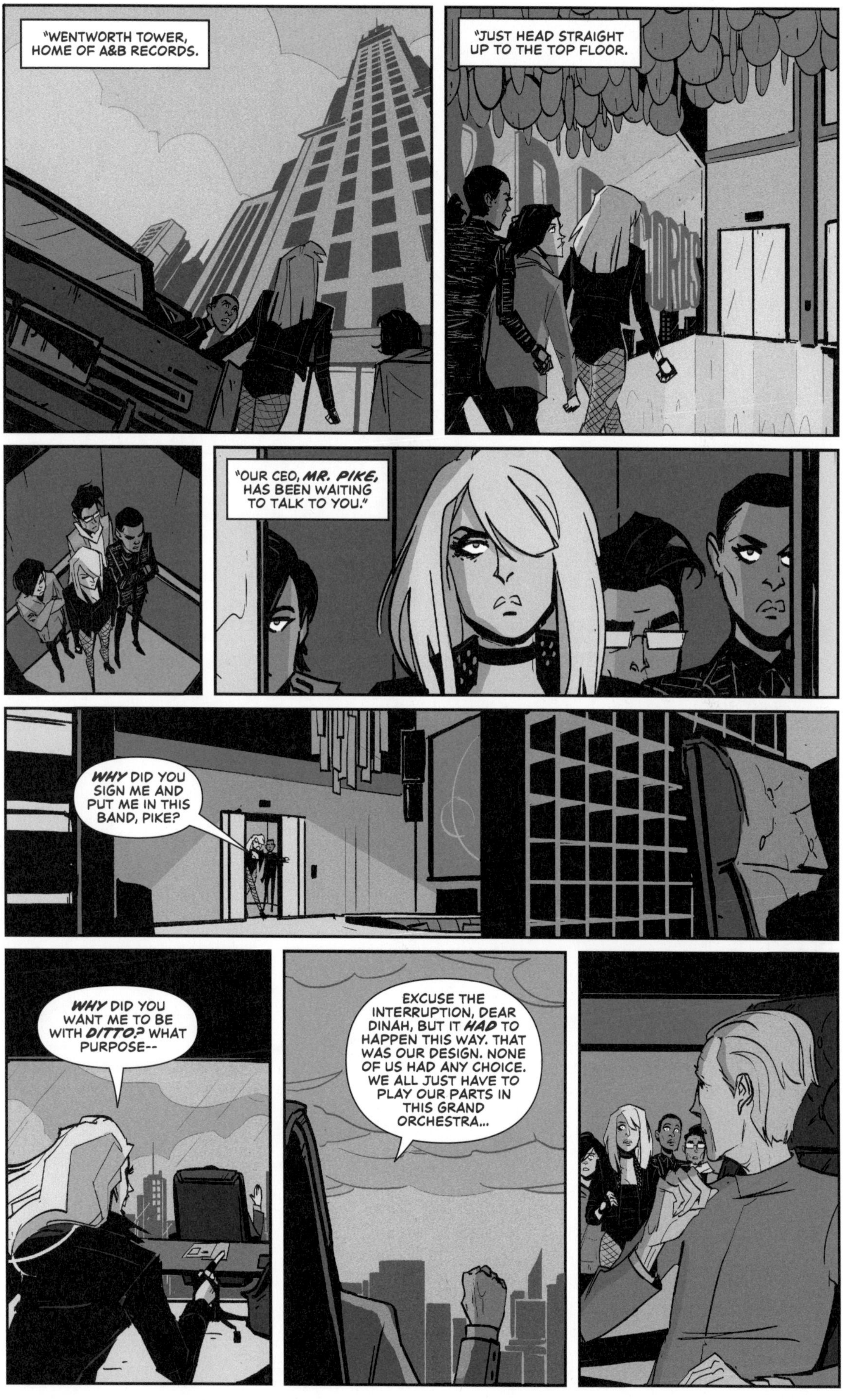

"WENTWORTH TOWER, HOME OF A&B RECORDS.
"JUST HEAD STRAIGHT UP TO THE TOP FLOOR.
"OUR CEO, MR. PIKE, HAS BEEN WAITING TO TALK TO YOU."
WHY DID YOU SIGN ME AND PUT ME IN THIS BAND, PIKE?
WHY DID YOU WANT ME TO BE WITH DITTO? WHAT PURPOSE--
EXCUSE THE INTERRUPTION, DEAR DINAH, BUT IT HAD TO HAPPEN THIS WAY. THAT WAS OUR DESIGN. NONE OF US HAD ANY CHOICE. WE ALL JUST HAVE TO PLAY OUR PARTS IN THIS GRAND ORCHESTRA...

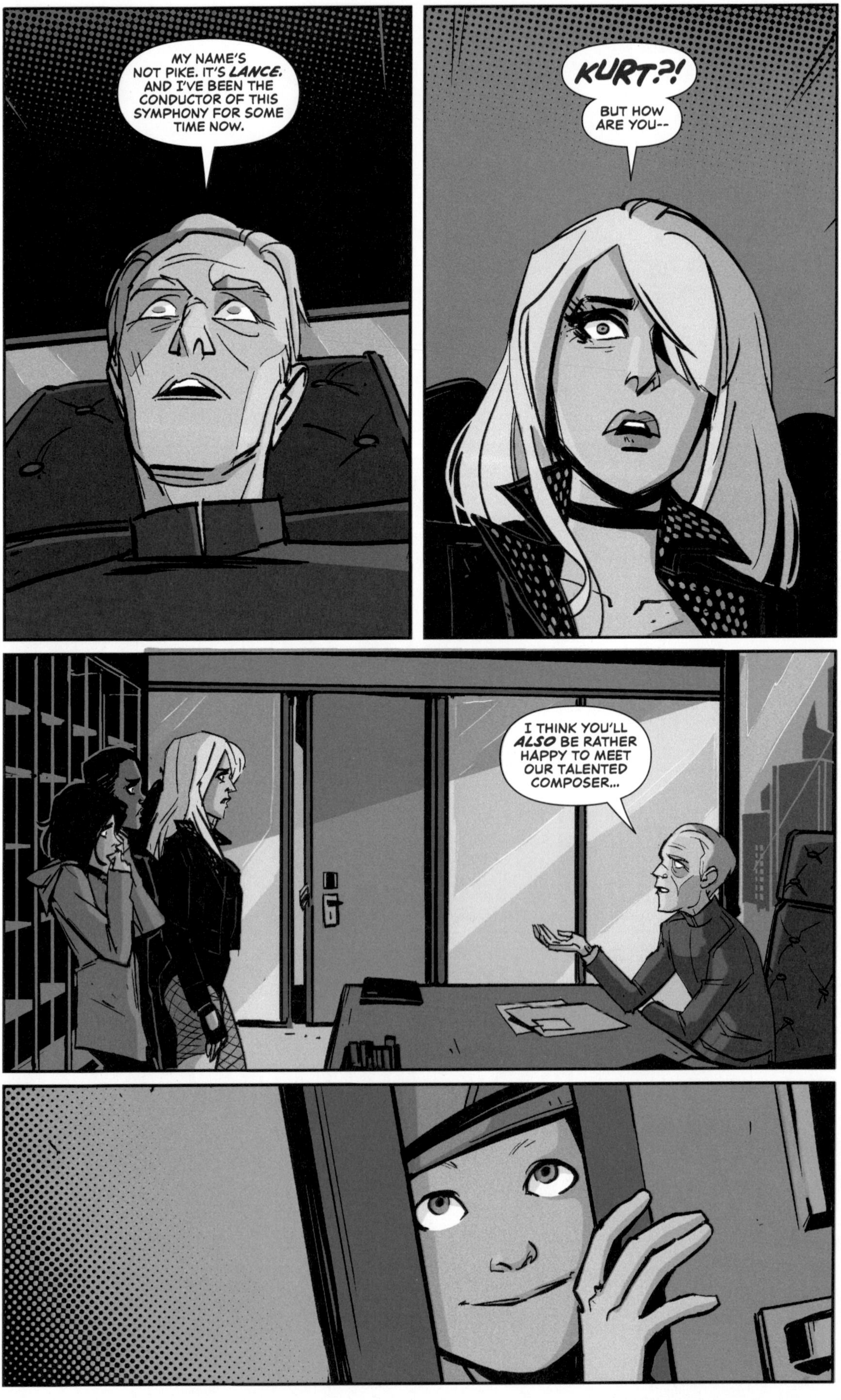
MY NAME'S NOT PIKE. IT'S LANCE. AND I'VE BEEN THE CONDUCTOR OF THIS SYMPHONY FOR SOME TIME NOW.
KURT?!
BUT HOW ARE YOU--
I THINK YOU'LL ALSO BE RATHER HAPPY TO MEET OUR TALENTED COMPOSER...

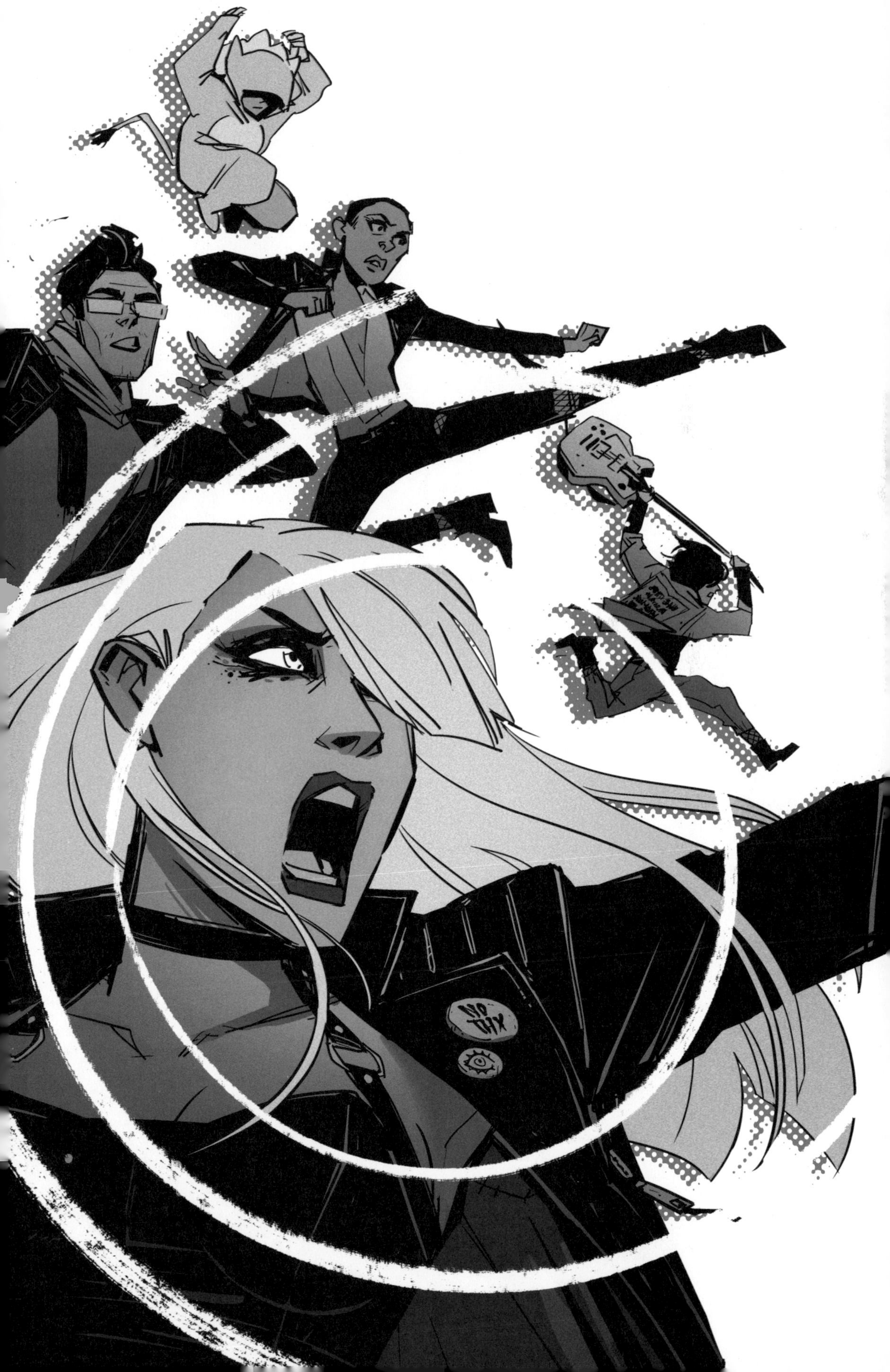
NO THX

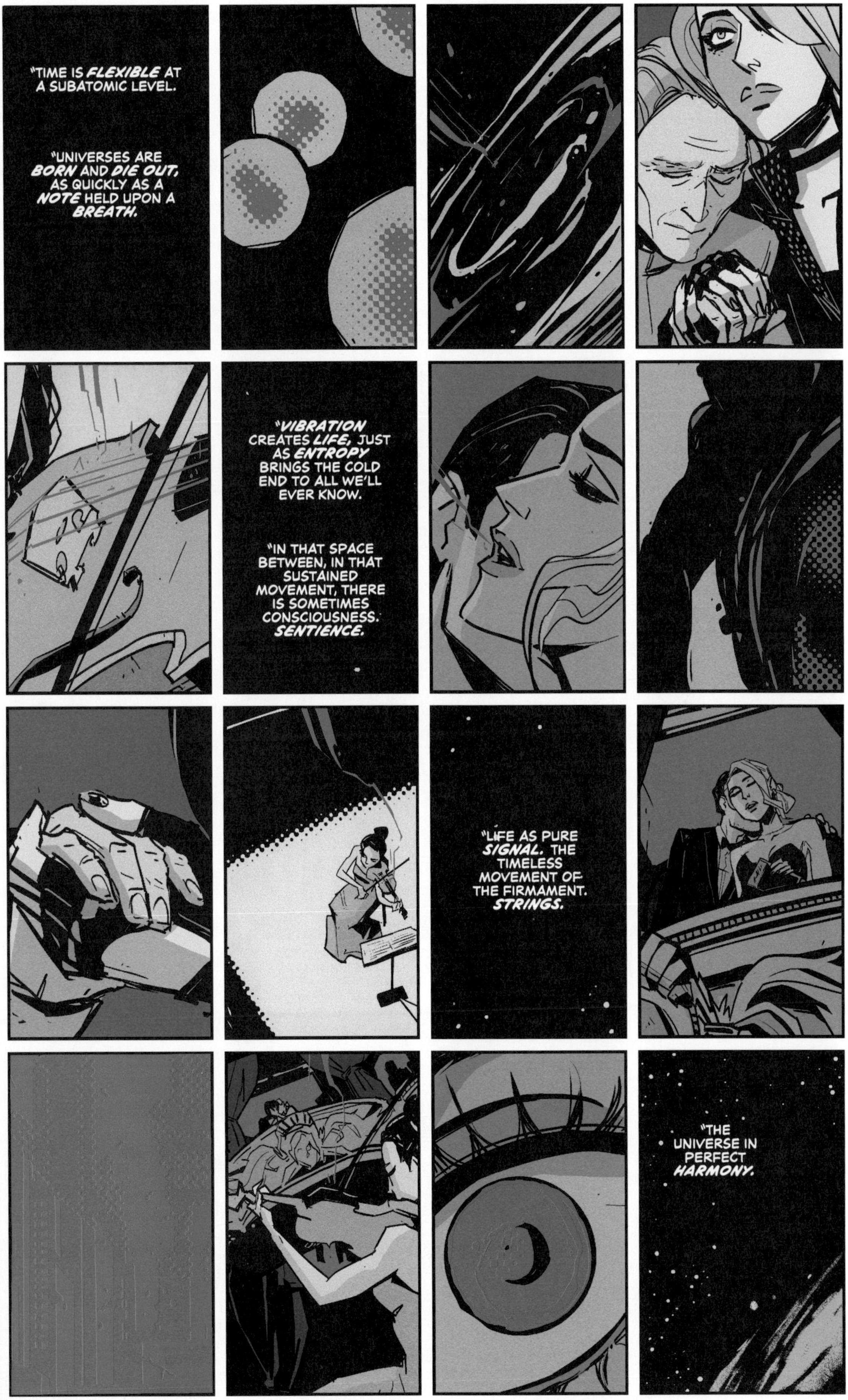
"TIME IS FLEXIBLE AT A SUBATOMIC LEVEL.
"UNIVERSES ARE BORN AND DIE OUT, AS QUICKLY AS A NOTE HELD UPON A BREATH.
"VIBRATION CREATES LIFE, JUST AS ENTROPY BRINGS THE COLD END TO ALL WE'LL EVER KNOW.
"IN THAT SPACE BETWEEN, IN THAT SUSTAINED MOVEMENT, THERE IS SOMETIMES CONSCIOUSNESS. SENTIENCE.
"LIFE AS PURE SIGNAL. THE TIMELESS MOVEMENT OF THE FIRMAMENT. STRINGS.
"THE UNIVERSE IN PERFECT HARMONY.

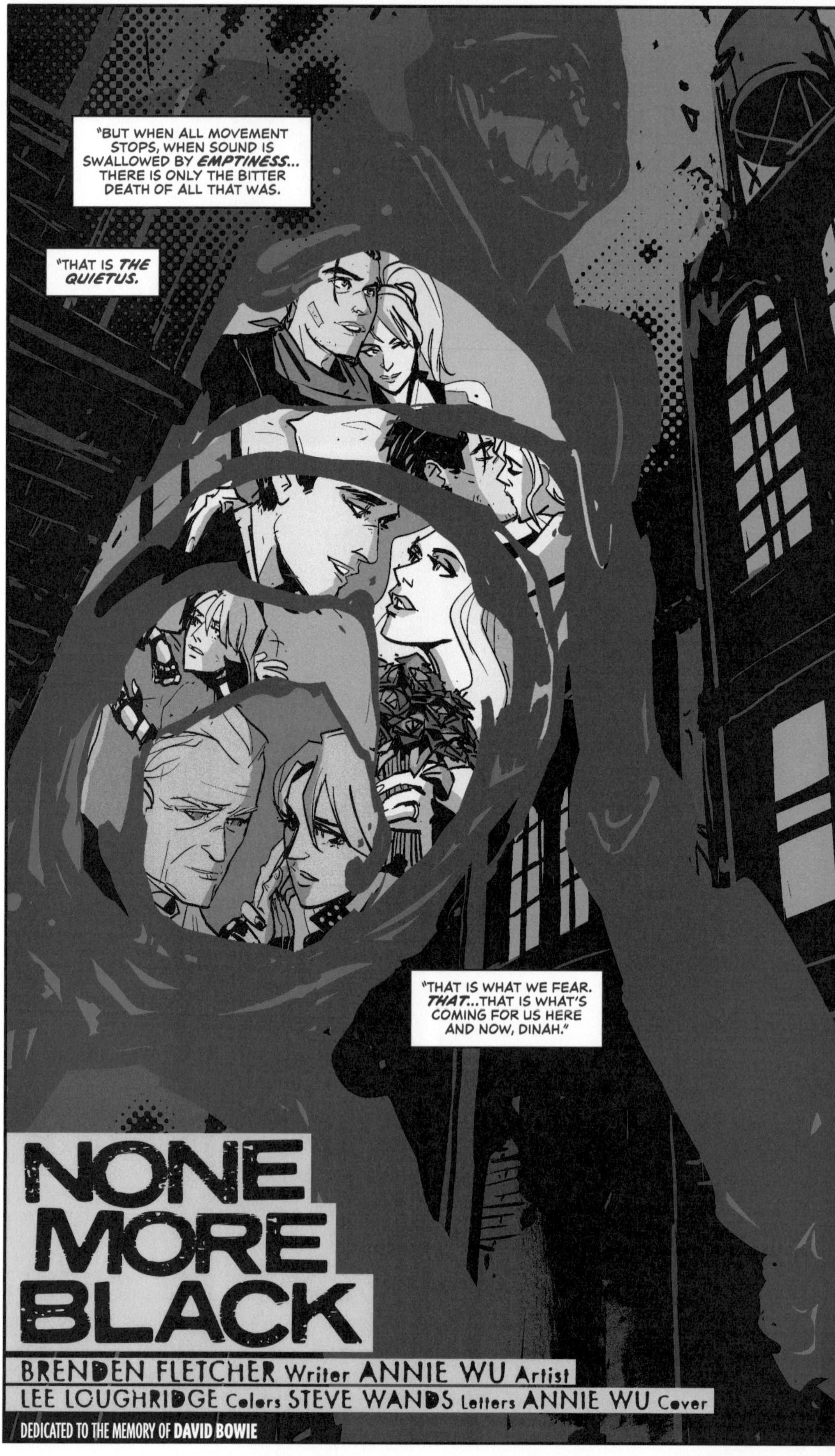
"BUT WHEN ALL MOVEMENT STOPS, WHEN SOUND IS SWALLOWED BY EMPTINESS... THERE IS ONLY THE BITTER DEATH OF ALL THAT WAS.
"THAT IS THE QUIETUS.
"THAT IS WHAT WE FEAR. THAT...THAT IS WHAT'S COMING FOR US HERE AND NOW, DINAH."
NONE MORE BLACK
BRENDEN FLETCHER Writer ANNIE WU Artist
LEE LOUGHRIDGE Colors STEVE WANDS Letters ANNIE WU Cover
DEDICATED TO THE MEMORY OF DAVID BOWIE

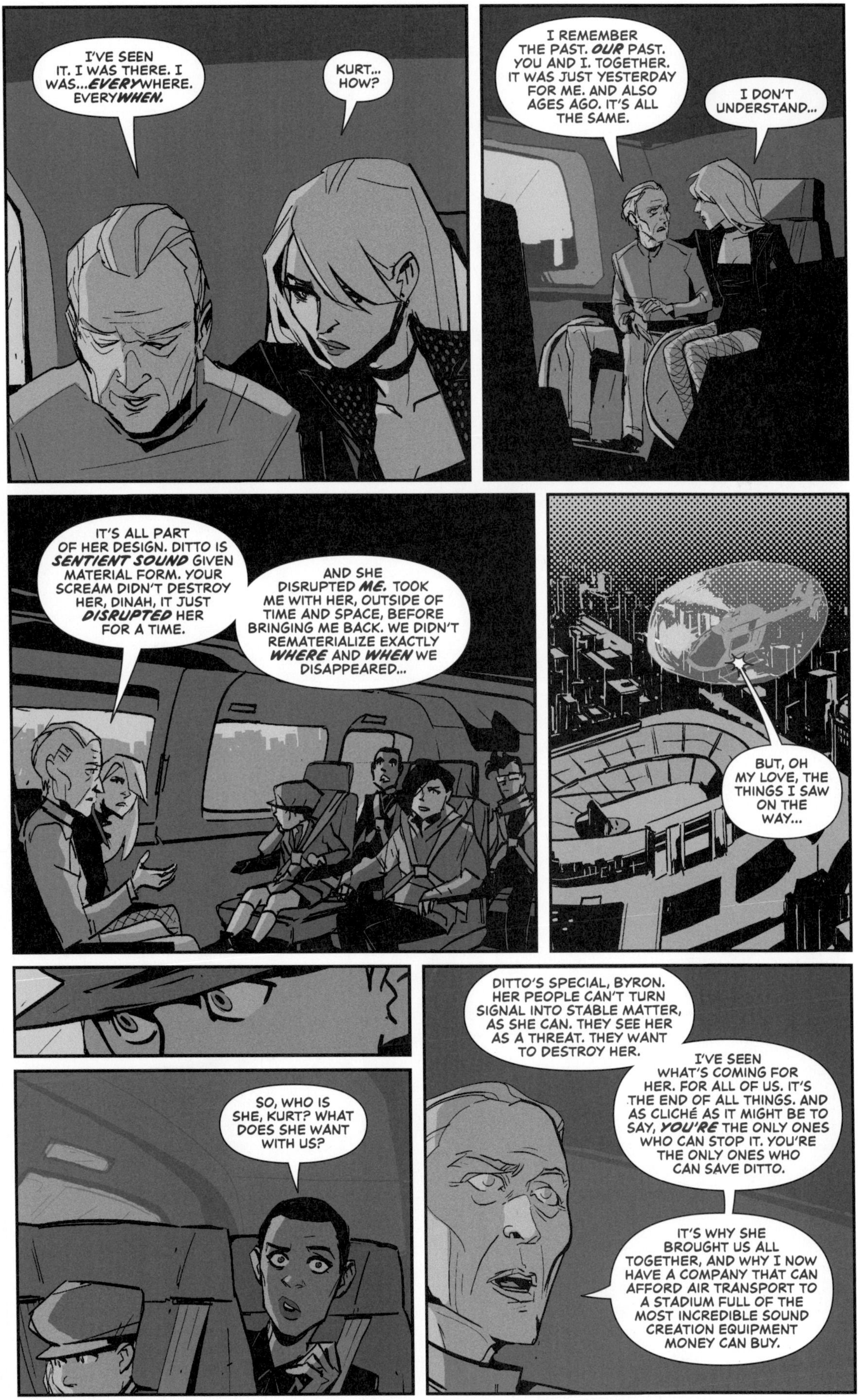
I'VE SEEN IT. I WAS THERE. I WAS...EVERYWHERE. EVERYWHEN.
KURT... HOW?
I REMEMBER THE PAST. OUR PAST. YOU AND I. TOGETHER. IT WAS JUST YESTERDAY FOR ME. AND ALSO AGES AGO. IT'S ALL THE SAME.
I DON'T UNDERSTAND...
IT'S ALL PART OF HER DESIGN. DITTO IS SENTIENT SOUND GIVEN MATERIAL FORM. YOUR SCREAM DIDN'T DESTROY HER, DINAH, IT JUST DISRUPTED HER FOR A TIME.
AND SHE DISRUPTED ME. TOOK ME WITH HER, OUTSIDE OF TIME AND SPACE, BEFORE BRINGING ME BACK. WE DIDN'T REMATERIALIZE EXACTLY WHERE AND WHEN WE DISAPPEARED...
BUT, OH MY LOVE, THE THINGS I SAW ON THE WAY...
SO, WHO IS SHE, KURT? WHAT DOES SHE WANT WITH US?
DITTO'S SPECIAL, BYRON. HER PEOPLE CAN'T TURN SIGNAL INTO STABLE MATTER, AS SHE CAN. THEY SEE HER AS A THREAT. THEY WANT TO DESTROY HER.
I'VE SEEN WHAT'S COMING FOR HER. FOR ALL OF US. IT'S THE END OF ALL THINGS. AND AS CLICHÉ AS IT MIGHT BE TO SAY, YOU'RE THE ONLY ONES WHO CAN STOP IT. YOU'RE THE ONLY ONES WHO CAN SAVE DITTO.
IT'S WHY SHE BROUGHT US ALL TOGETHER, AND WHY I NOW HAVE A COMPANY THAT CAN AFFORD AIR TRANSPORT TO A STADIUM FULL OF THE MOST INCREDIBLE SOUND CREATION EQUIPMENT MONEY CAN BUY.

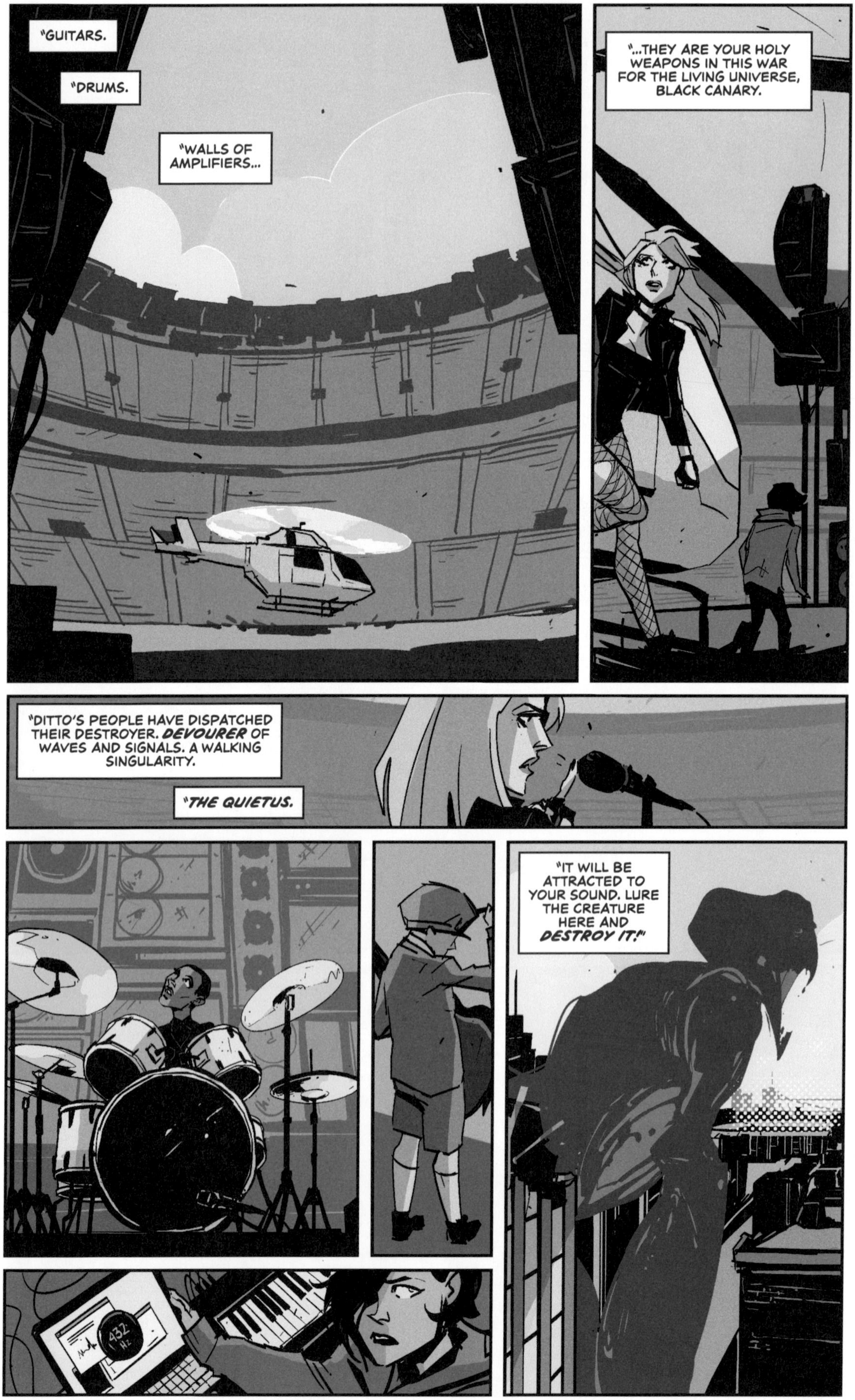
"GUITARS.
"DRUMS.
"WALLS OF AMPLIFIERS...
"...THEY ARE YOUR HOLY WEAPONS IN THIS WAR FOR THE LIVING UNIVERSE, BLACK CANARY.
"DITTO'S PEOPLE HAVE DISPATCHED THEIR DESTROYER. *DEVOURER* OF WAVES AND SIGNALS. A WALKING SINGULARITY.
"*THE QUIETUS.*
"IT WILL BE ATTRACTED TO YOUR SOUND. LURE THE CREATURE HERE AND *DESTROY IT!*"
432 Hz

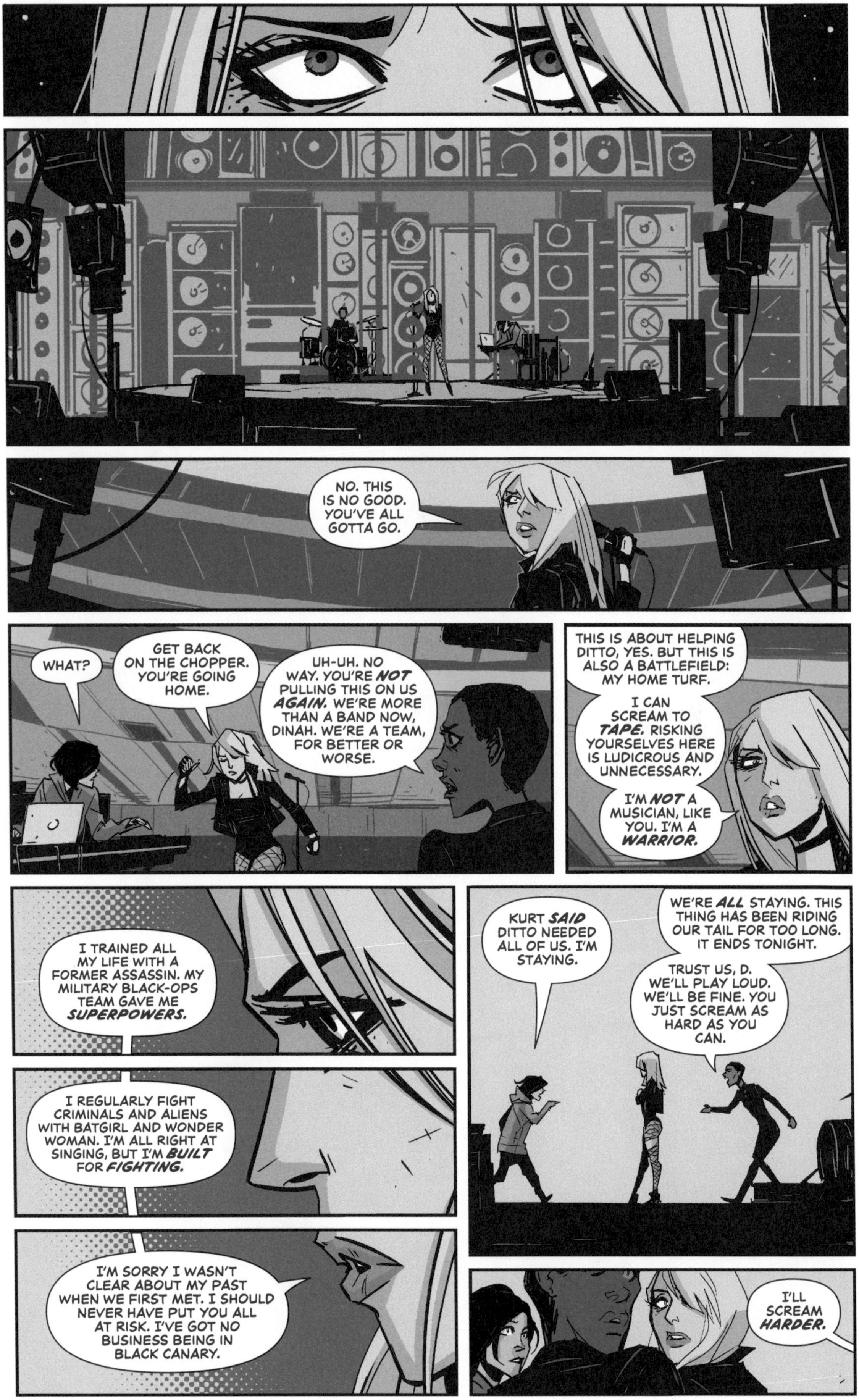

NO. THIS IS NO GOOD. YOU'VE ALL GOTTA GO.
WHAT?
GET BACK ON THE CHOPPER. YOU'RE GOING HOME.
UH-UH. NO WAY. YOU'RE *NOT* PULLING THIS ON US *AGAIN.* WE'RE MORE THAN A BAND NOW, DINAH. WE'RE A TEAM, FOR BETTER OR WORSE.
THIS IS ABOUT HELPING DITTO, YES. BUT THIS IS ALSO A BATTLEFIELD: MY HOME TURF.
I CAN SCREAM TO *TAPE.* RISKING YOURSELVES HERE IS LUDICROUS AND UNNECESSARY.
I'M *NOT* A MUSICIAN, LIKE YOU. I'M A *WARRIOR.*
I TRAINED ALL MY LIFE WITH A FORMER ASSASSIN. MY MILITARY BLACK-OPS TEAM GAVE ME *SUPERPOWERS.*
I REGULARLY FIGHT CRIMINALS AND ALIENS WITH BATGIRL AND WONDER WOMAN. I'M ALL RIGHT AT SINGING, BUT I'M *BUILT* FOR *FIGHTING.*
I'M SORRY I WASN'T CLEAR ABOUT MY PAST WHEN WE FIRST MET. I SHOULD NEVER HAVE PUT YOU ALL AT RISK. I'VE GOT NO BUSINESS BEING IN BLACK CANARY.
KURT *SAID* DITTO NEEDED ALL OF US. I'M STAYING.
WE'RE *ALL* STAYING. THIS THING HAS BEEN RIDING OUR TAIL FOR TOO LONG. IT ENDS TONIGHT.
TRUST US, D. WE'LL PLAY LOUD. WE'LL BE FINE. YOU JUST SCREAM AS HARD AS YOU CAN.
I'LL SCREAM *HARDER.*

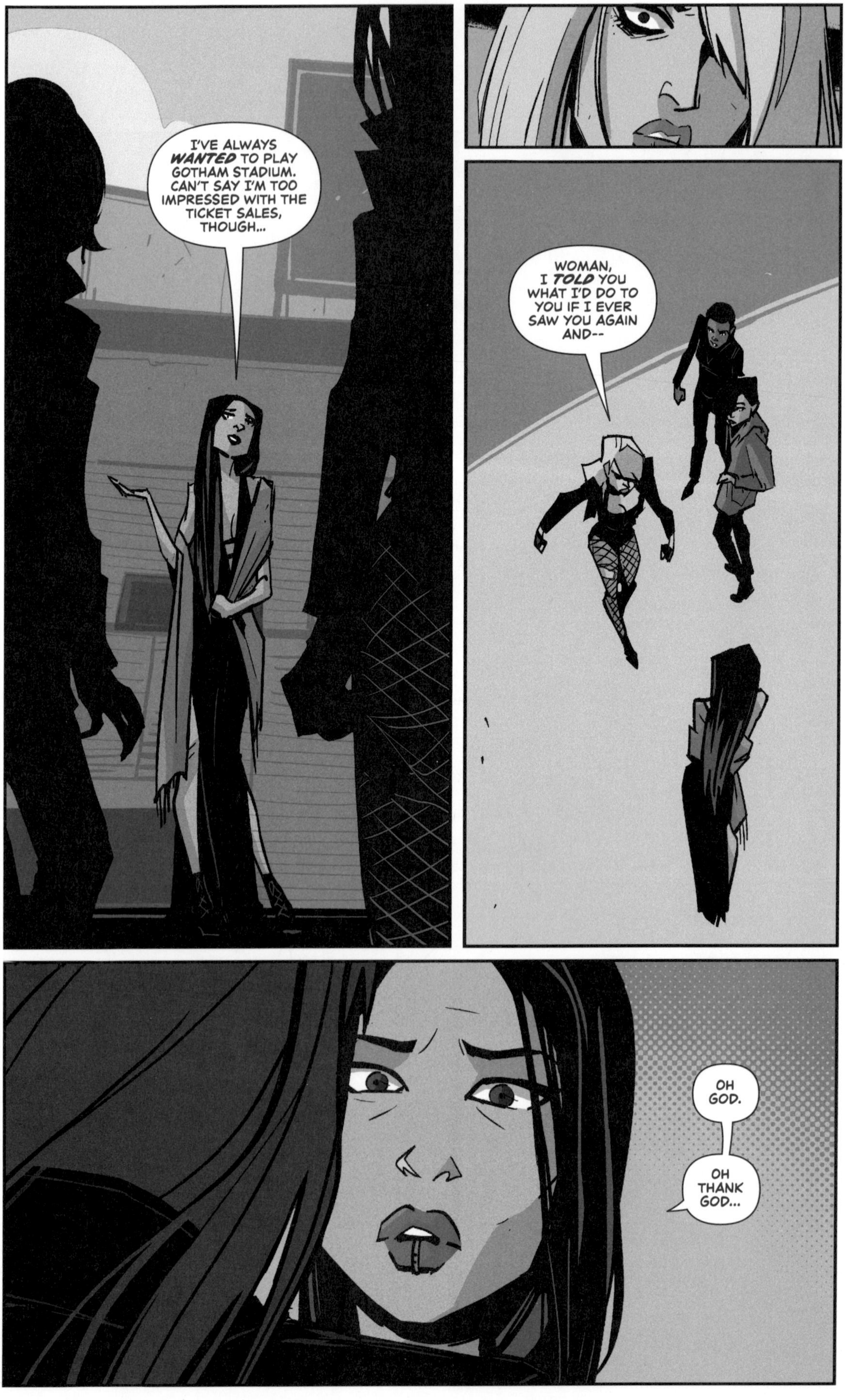
I'VE ALWAYS WANTED TO PLAY GOTHAM STADIUM. CAN'T SAY I'M TOO IMPRESSED WITH THE TICKET SALES, THOUGH...
WOMAN, I TOLD YOU WHAT I'D DO TO YOU IF I EVER SAW YOU AGAIN AND--
OH GOD.
OH THANK GOD...

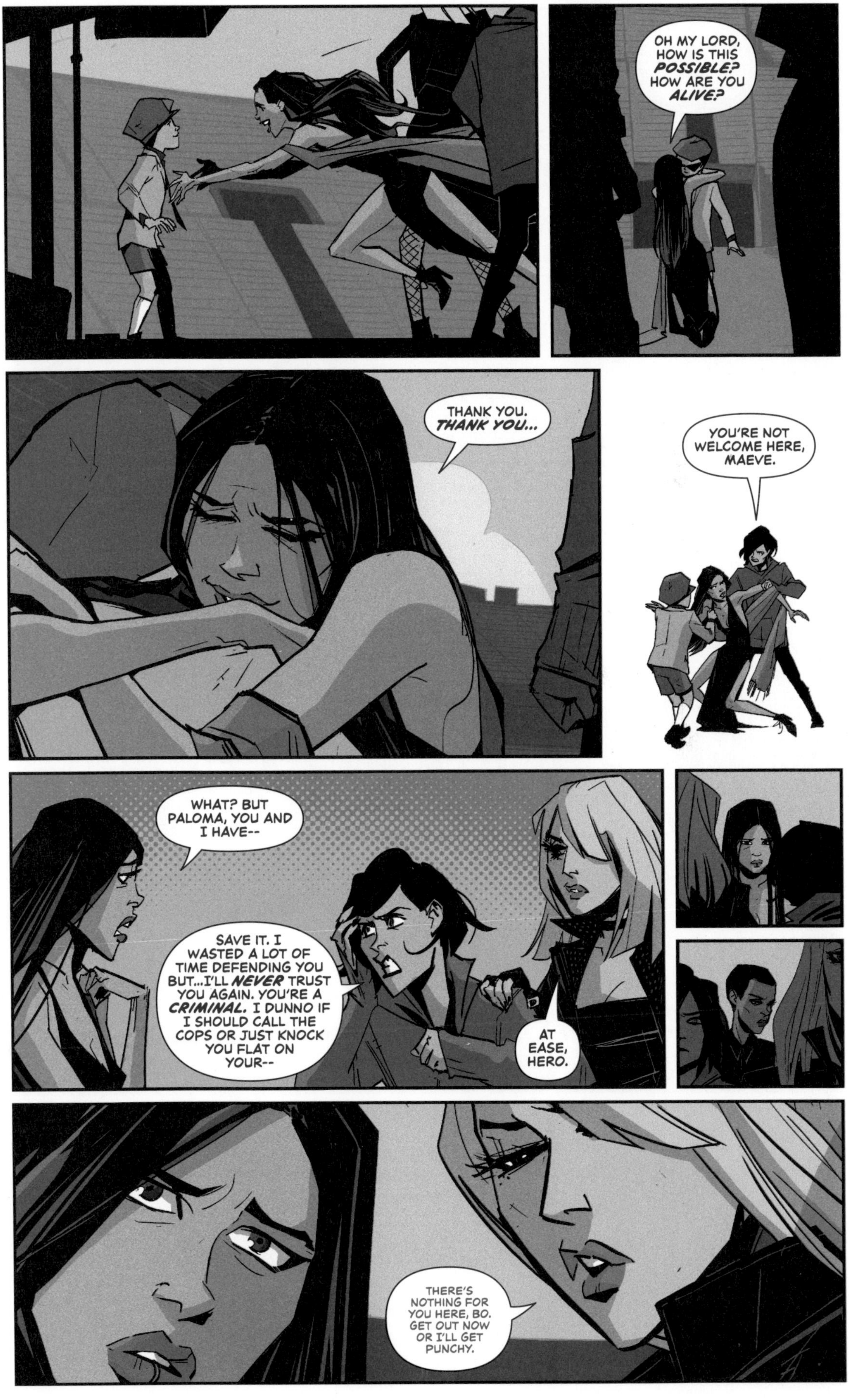
OH MY LORD, HOW IS THIS POSSIBLE? HOW ARE YOU ALIVE?
THANK YOU. THANK YOU...
YOU'RE NOT WELCOME HERE, MAEVE.
WHAT? BUT PALOMA, YOU AND I HAVE--
SAVE IT. I WASTED A LOT OF TIME DEFENDING YOU BUT...I'LL NEVER TRUST YOU AGAIN. YOU'RE A CRIMINAL. I DUNNO IF I SHOULD CALL THE COPS OR JUST KNOCK YOU FLAT ON YOUR--
AT EASE, HERO.
THERE'S NOTHING FOR YOU HERE, BO. GET OUT NOW OR I'LL GET PUNCHY.

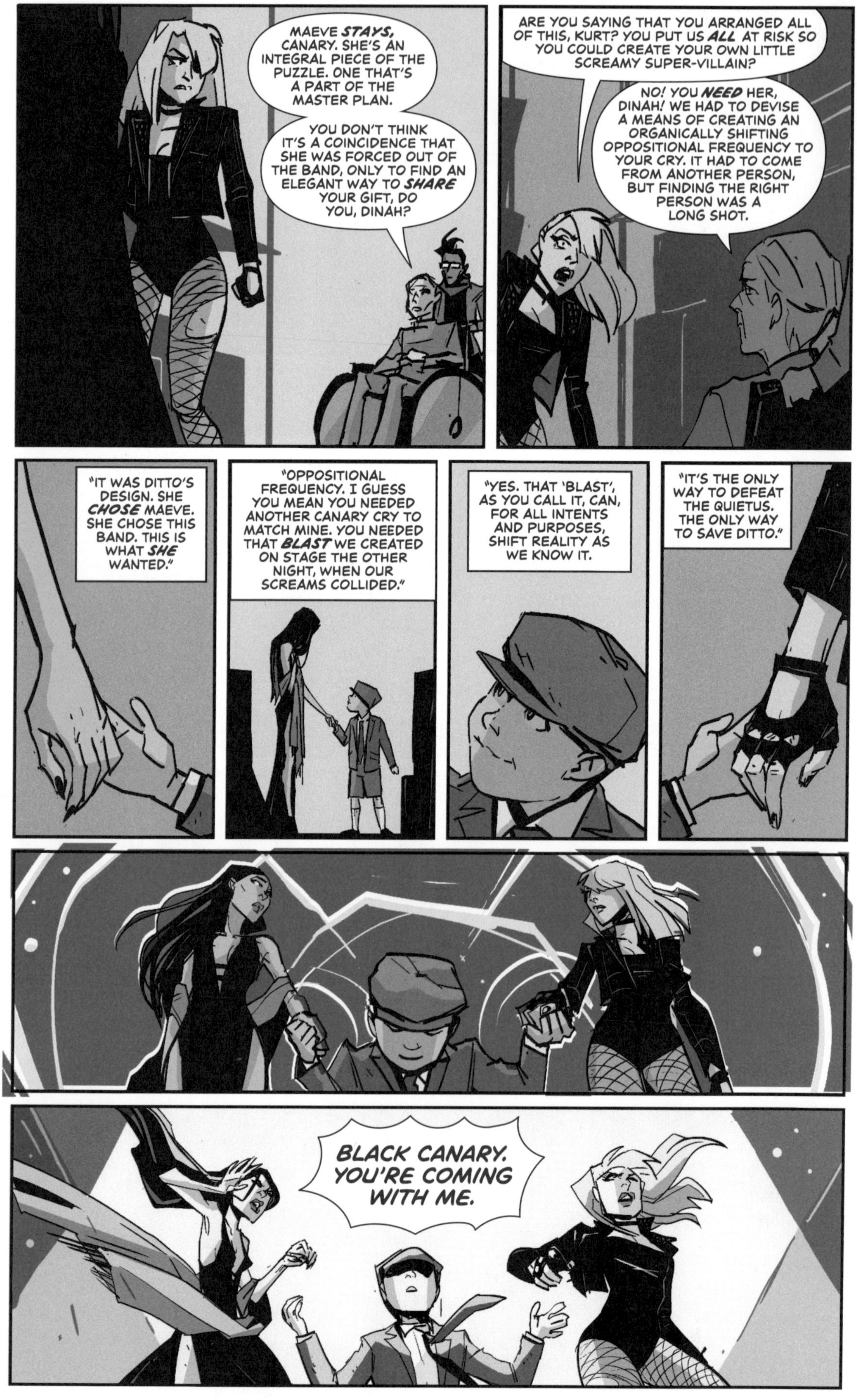

MAEVE STAYS, CANARY. SHE'S AN INTEGRAL PIECE OF THE PUZZLE. ONE THAT'S A PART OF THE MASTER PLAN.
YOU DON'T THINK IT'S A COINCIDENCE THAT SHE WAS FORCED OUT OF THE BAND, ONLY TO FIND AN ELEGANT WAY TO SHARE YOUR GIFT, DO YOU, DINAH?
ARE YOU SAYING THAT YOU ARRANGED ALL OF THIS, KURT? YOU PUT US ALL AT RISK SO YOU COULD CREATE YOUR OWN LITTLE SCREAMY SUPER-VILLAIN?
NO! YOU NEED HER, DINAH! WE HAD TO DEVISE A MEANS OF CREATING AN ORGANICALLY SHIFTING OPPOSITIONAL FREQUENCY TO YOUR CRY. IT HAD TO COME FROM ANOTHER PERSON, BUT FINDING THE RIGHT PERSON WAS A LONG SHOT.
"IT WAS DITTO'S DESIGN. SHE CHOSE MAEVE. SHE CHOSE THIS BAND. THIS IS WHAT SHE WANTED."
"OPPOSITIONAL FREQUENCY. I GUESS YOU MEAN YOU NEEDED ANOTHER CANARY CRY TO MATCH MINE. YOU NEEDED THAT BLAST WE CREATED ON STAGE THE OTHER NIGHT, WHEN OUR SCREAMS COLLIDED."
"YES. THAT 'BLAST', AS YOU CALL IT, CAN, FOR ALL INTENTS AND PURPOSES, SHIFT REALITY AS WE KNOW IT.
"IT'S THE ONLY WAY TO DEFEAT THE QUIETUS. THE ONLY WAY TO SAVE DITTO."
BLACK CANARY. YOU'RE COMING WITH ME.

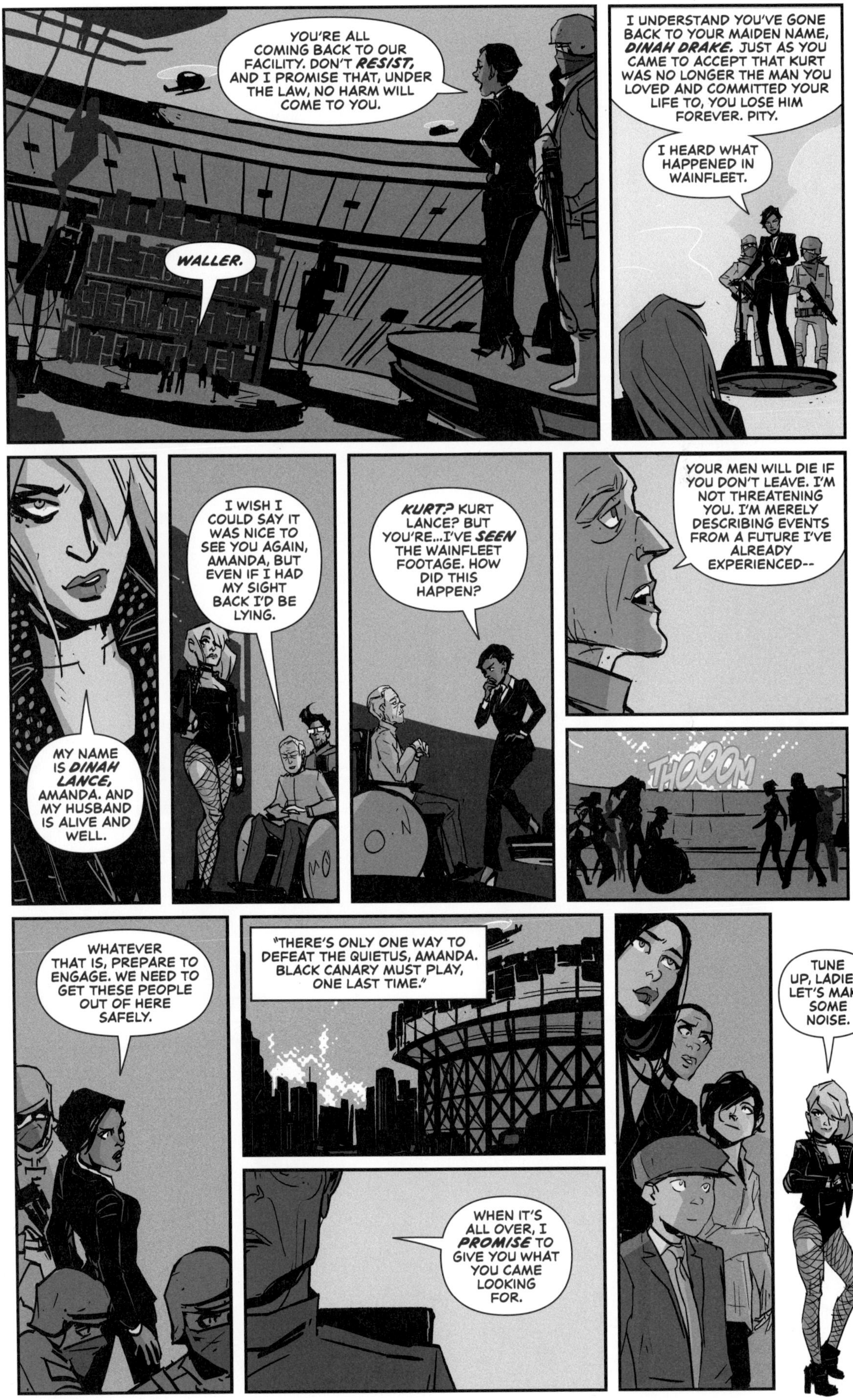

YOU'RE ALL COMING BACK TO OUR FACILITY. DON'T RESIST, AND I PROMISE THAT, UNDER THE LAW, NO HARM WILL COME TO YOU.
WALLER.
I UNDERSTAND YOU'VE GONE BACK TO YOUR MAIDEN NAME, DINAH DRAKE. JUST AS YOU CAME TO ACCEPT THAT KURT WAS NO LONGER THE MAN YOU LOVED AND COMMITTED YOUR LIFE TO, YOU LOSE HIM FOREVER. PITY.
I HEARD WHAT HAPPENED IN WAINFLEET.
MY NAME IS DINAH LANCE, AMANDA. AND MY HUSBAND IS ALIVE AND WELL.
I WISH I COULD SAY IT WAS NICE TO SEE YOU AGAIN, AMANDA, BUT EVEN IF I HAD MY SIGHT BACK I'D BE LYING.
KURT? KURT LANCE? BUT YOU'RE...I'VE SEEN THE WAINFLEET FOOTAGE. HOW DID THIS HAPPEN?
YOUR MEN WILL DIE IF YOU DON'T LEAVE. I'M NOT THREATENING YOU. I'M MERELY DESCRIBING EVENTS FROM A FUTURE I'VE ALREADY EXPERIENCED--
THOOOM
WHATEVER THAT IS, PREPARE TO ENGAGE. WE NEED TO GET THESE PEOPLE OUT OF HERE SAFELY.
"THERE'S ONLY ONE WAY TO DEFEAT THE QUIETUS, AMANDA. BLACK CANARY MUST PLAY, ONE LAST TIME."
WHEN IT'S ALL OVER, I PROMISE TO GIVE YOU WHAT YOU CAME LOOKING FOR.
TUNE UP, LADIES. LET'S MAKE SOME NOISE.

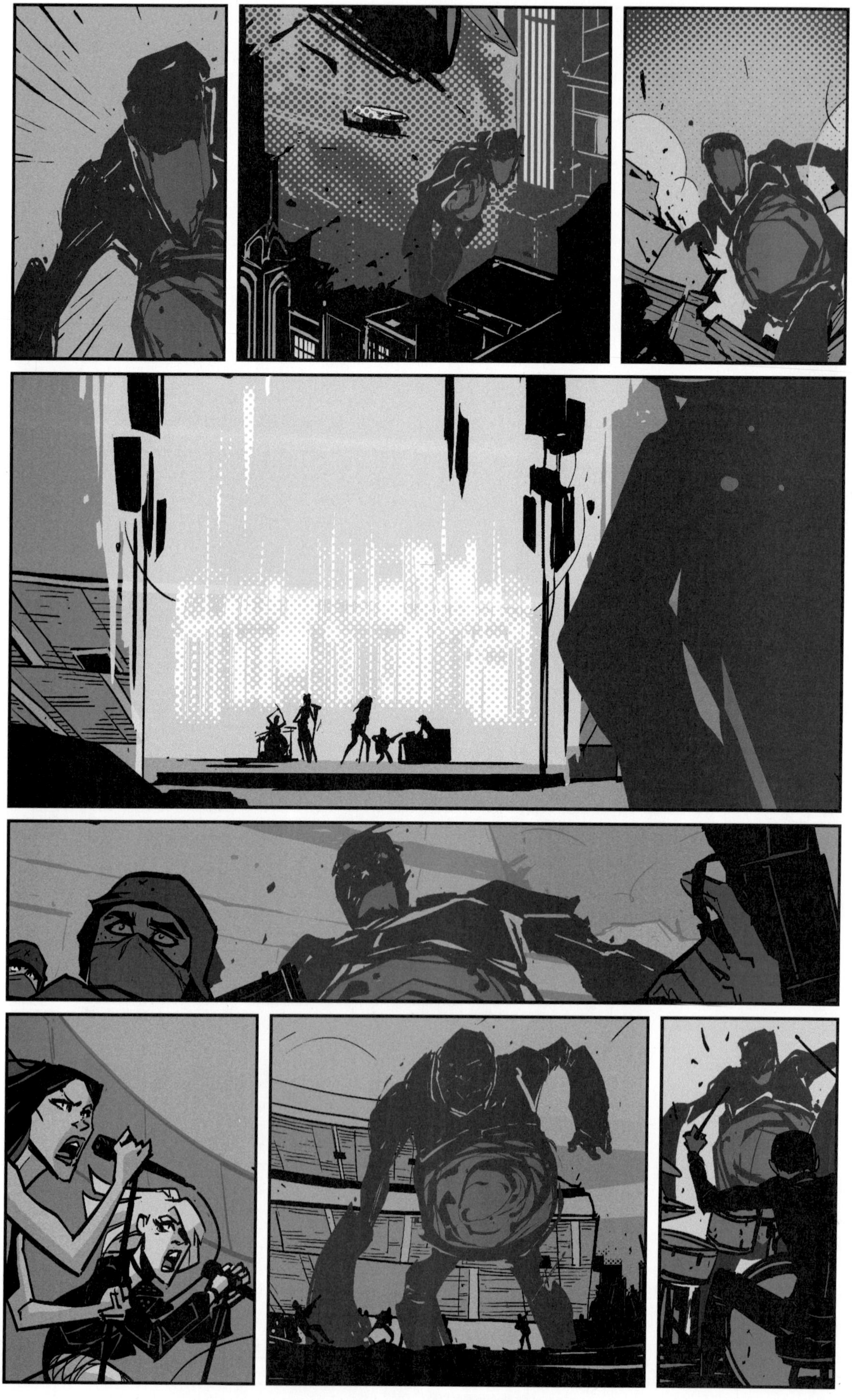

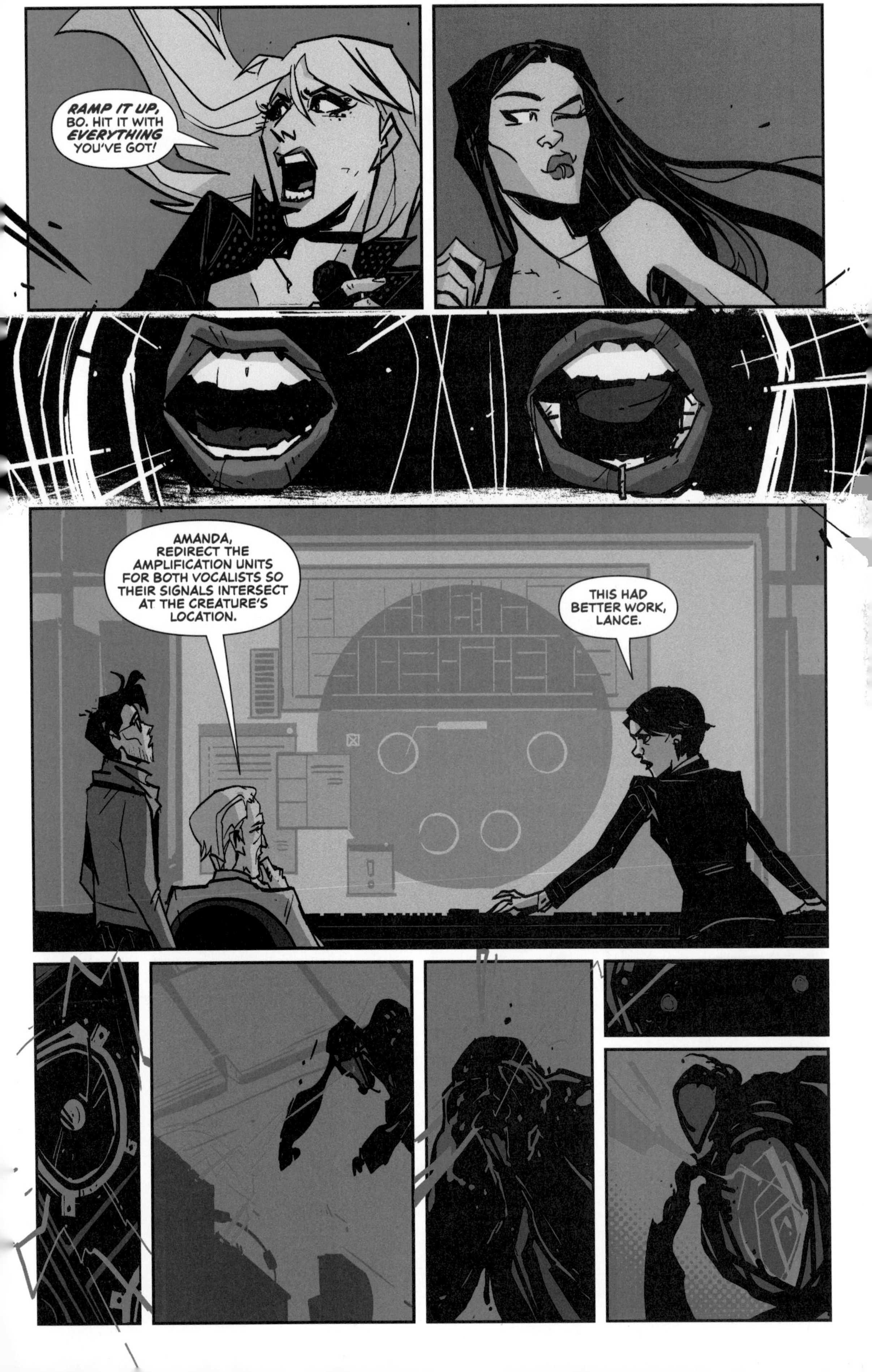

RAMP IT UP, BO. HIT IT WITH EVERYTHING YOU'VE GOT!
AMANDA, REDIRECT THE AMPLIFICATION UNITS FOR BOTH VOCALISTS SO THEIR SIGNALS INTERSECT AT THE CREATURE'S LOCATION.
THIS HAD BETTER WORK, LANCE.

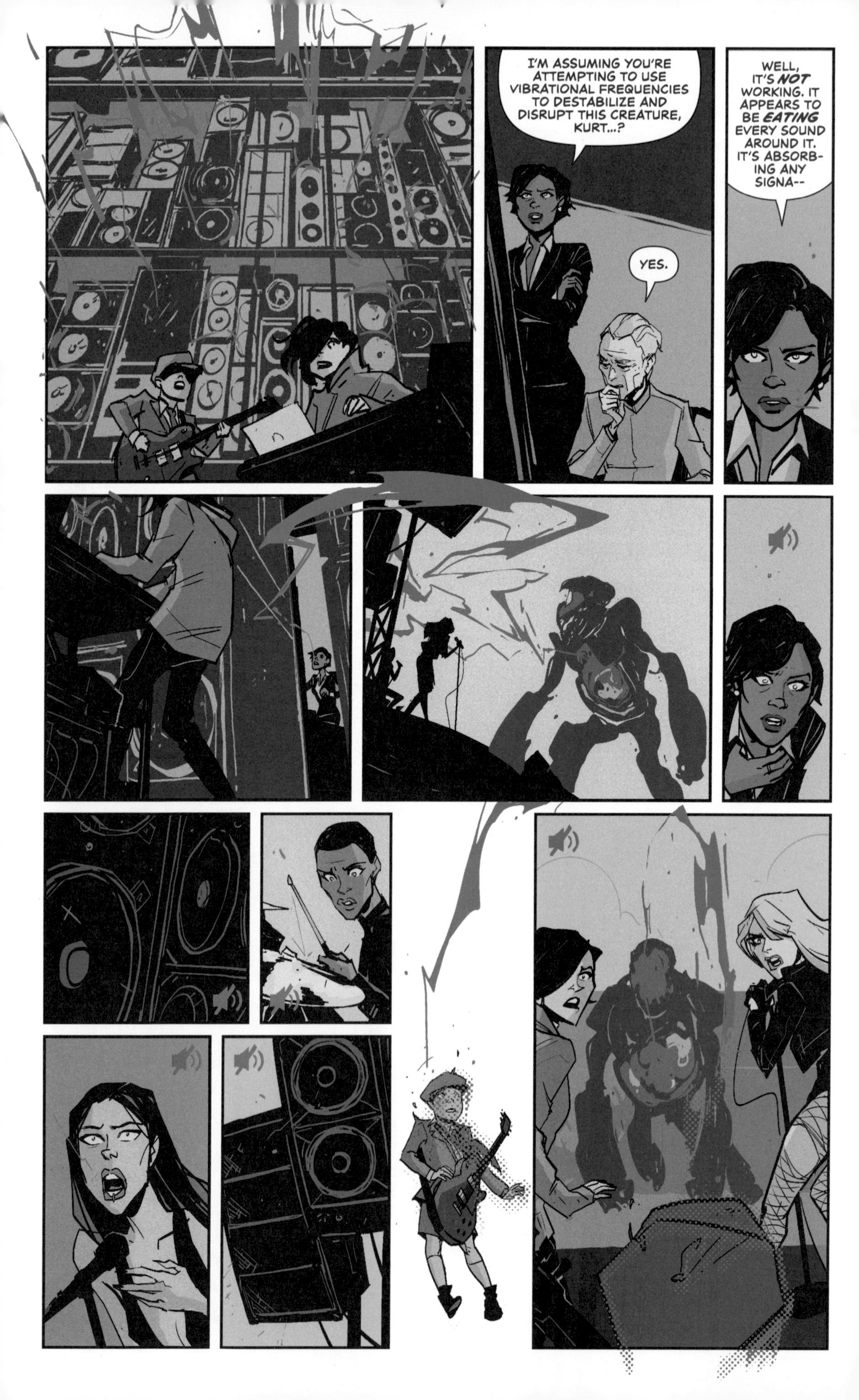
I'M ASSUMING YOU'RE ATTEMPTING TO USE VIBRATIONAL FREQUENCIES TO DESTABILIZE AND DISRUPT THIS CREATURE, KURT...?
YES.
WELL, IT'S *NOT* WORKING. IT APPEARS TO BE *EATING* EVERY SOUND AROUND IT. IT'S ABSORBING ANY SIGNA--

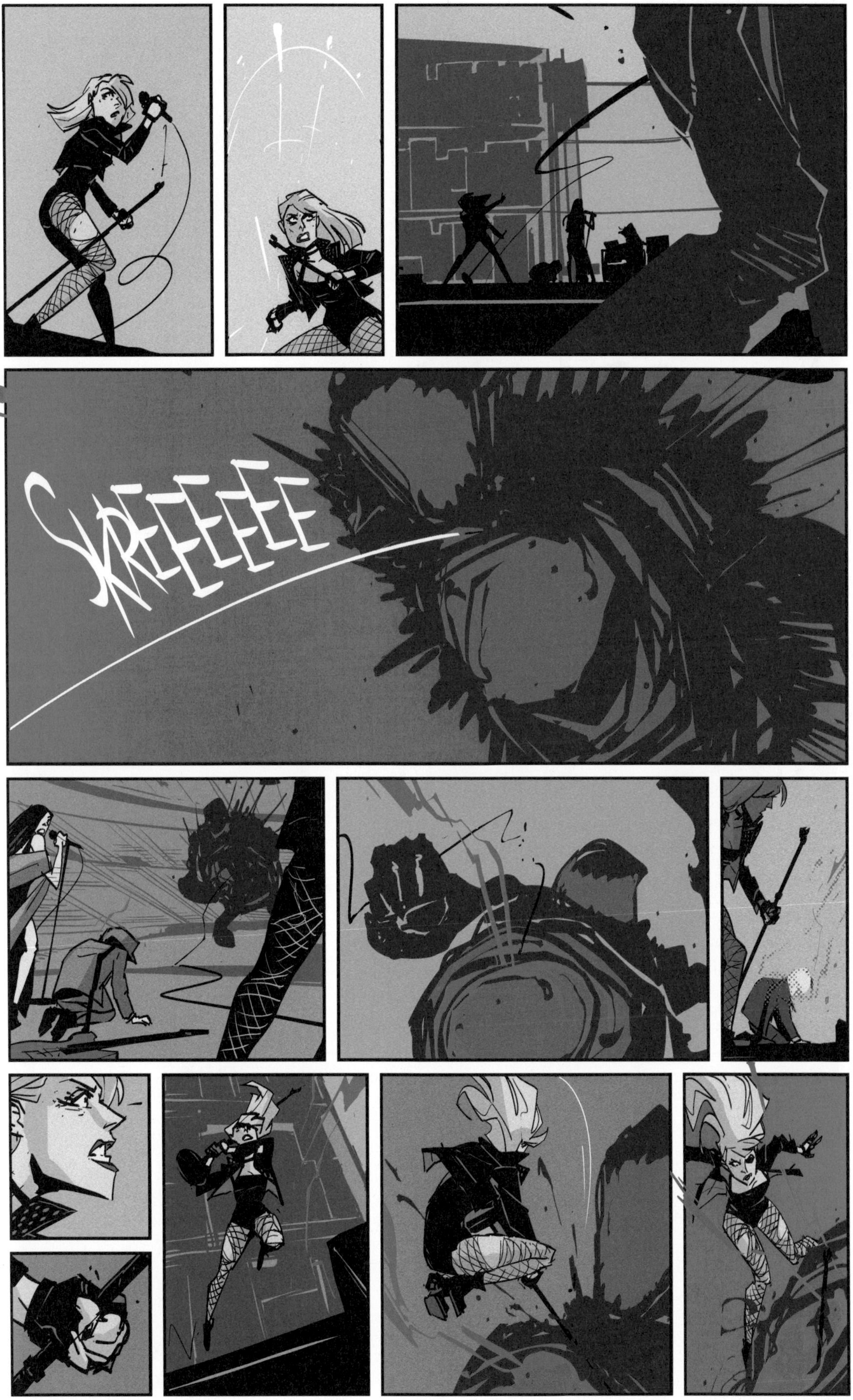
SKREEEEEEE

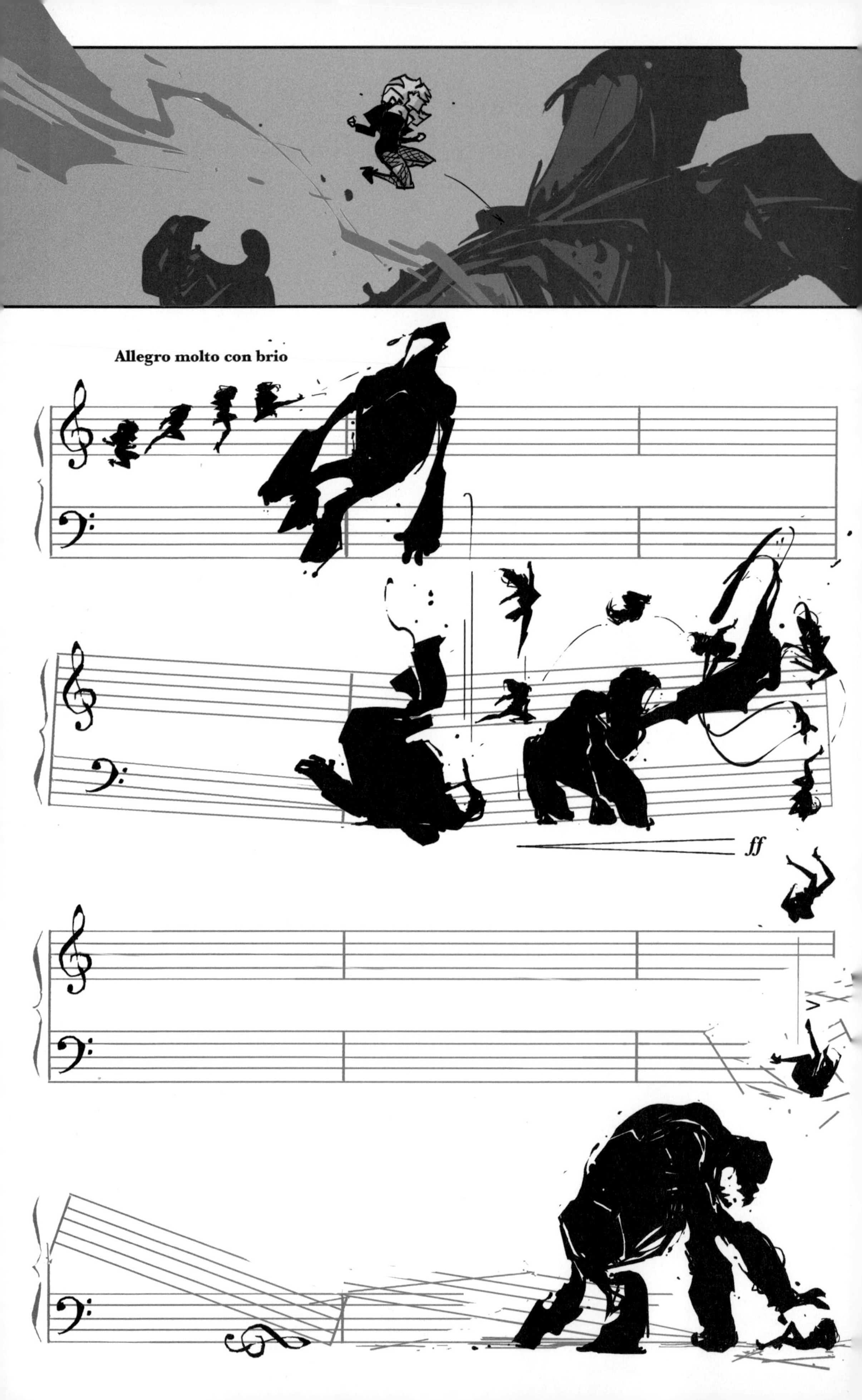
Allegro molto con brio
ff

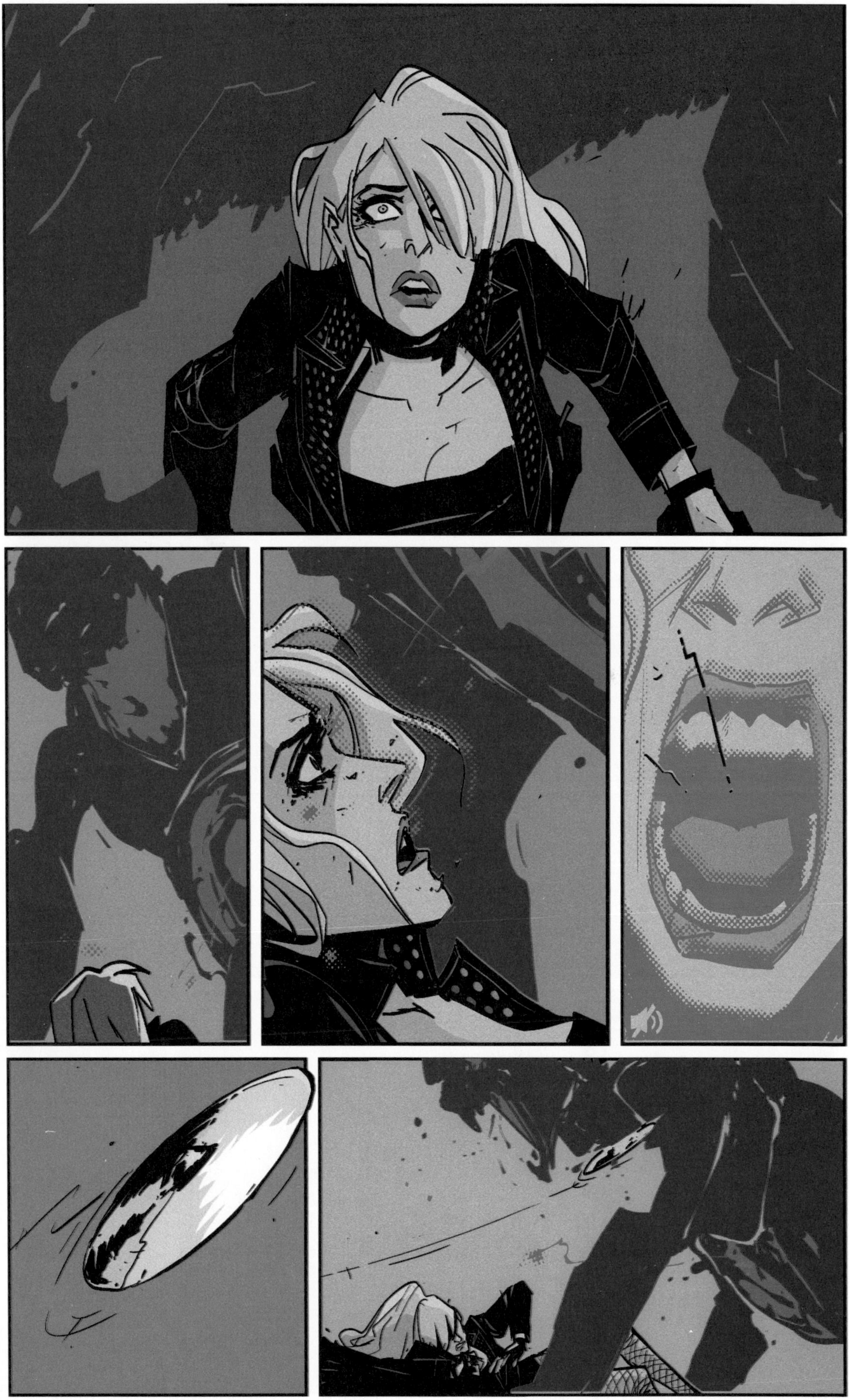

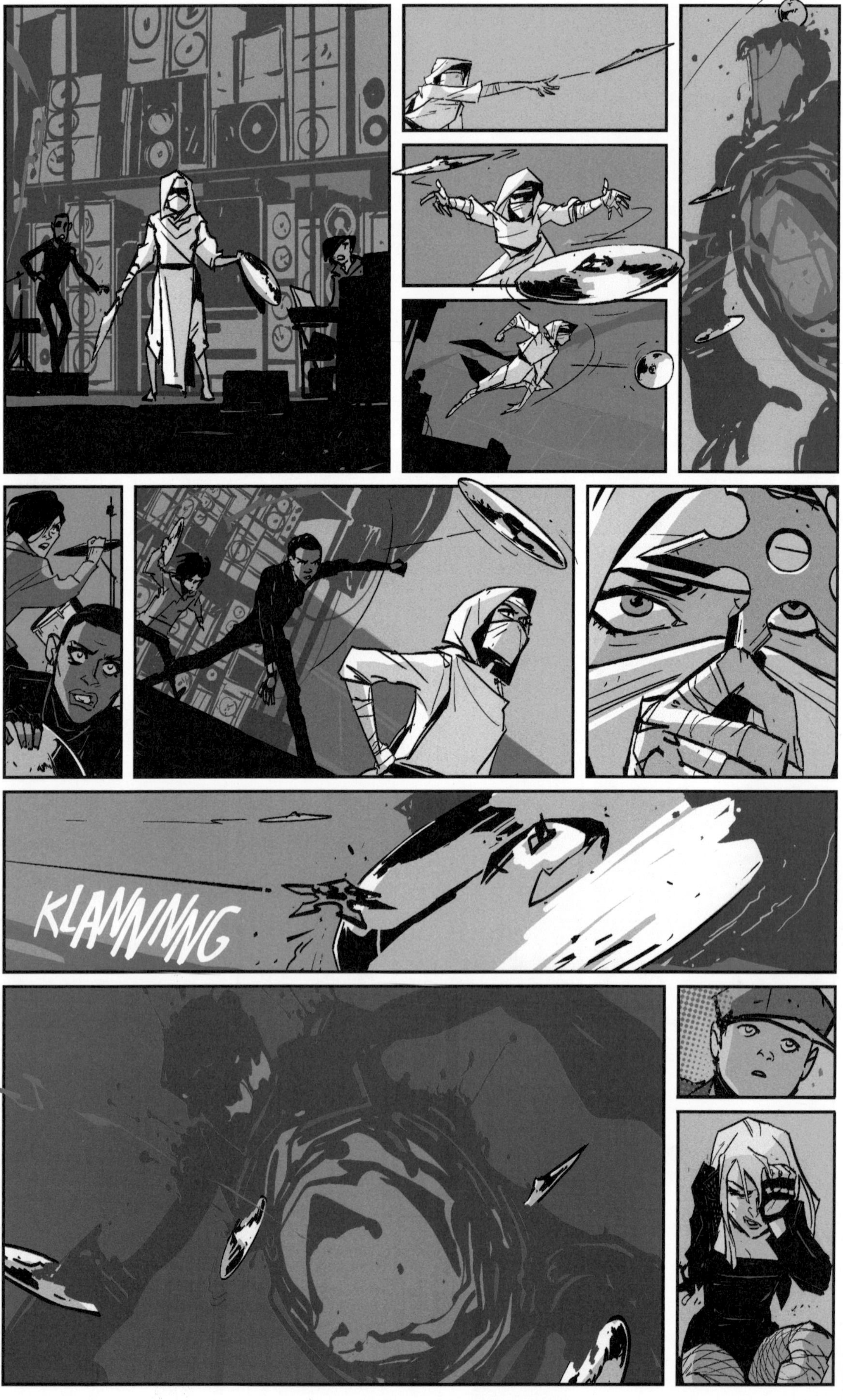
KLANNNNG

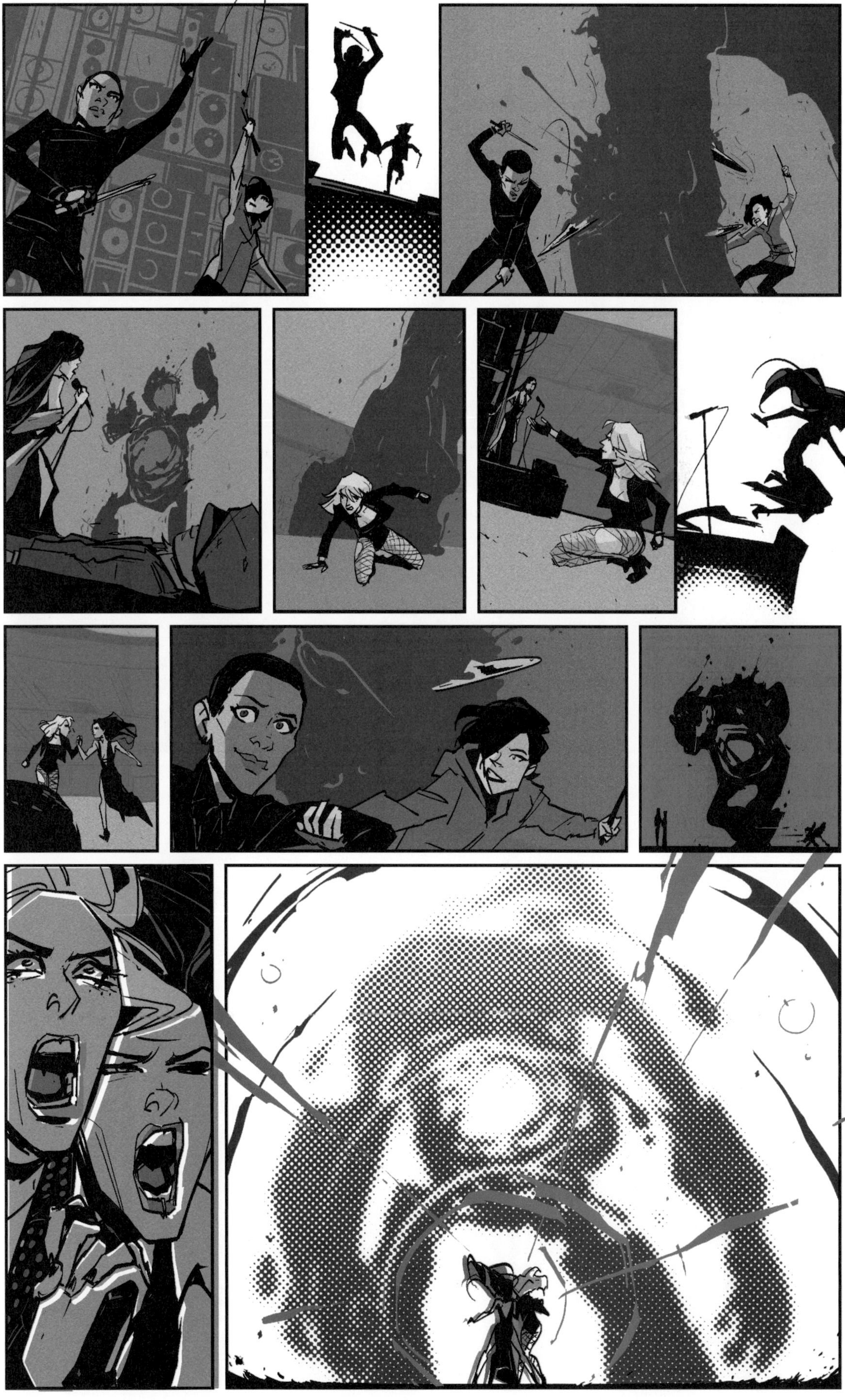

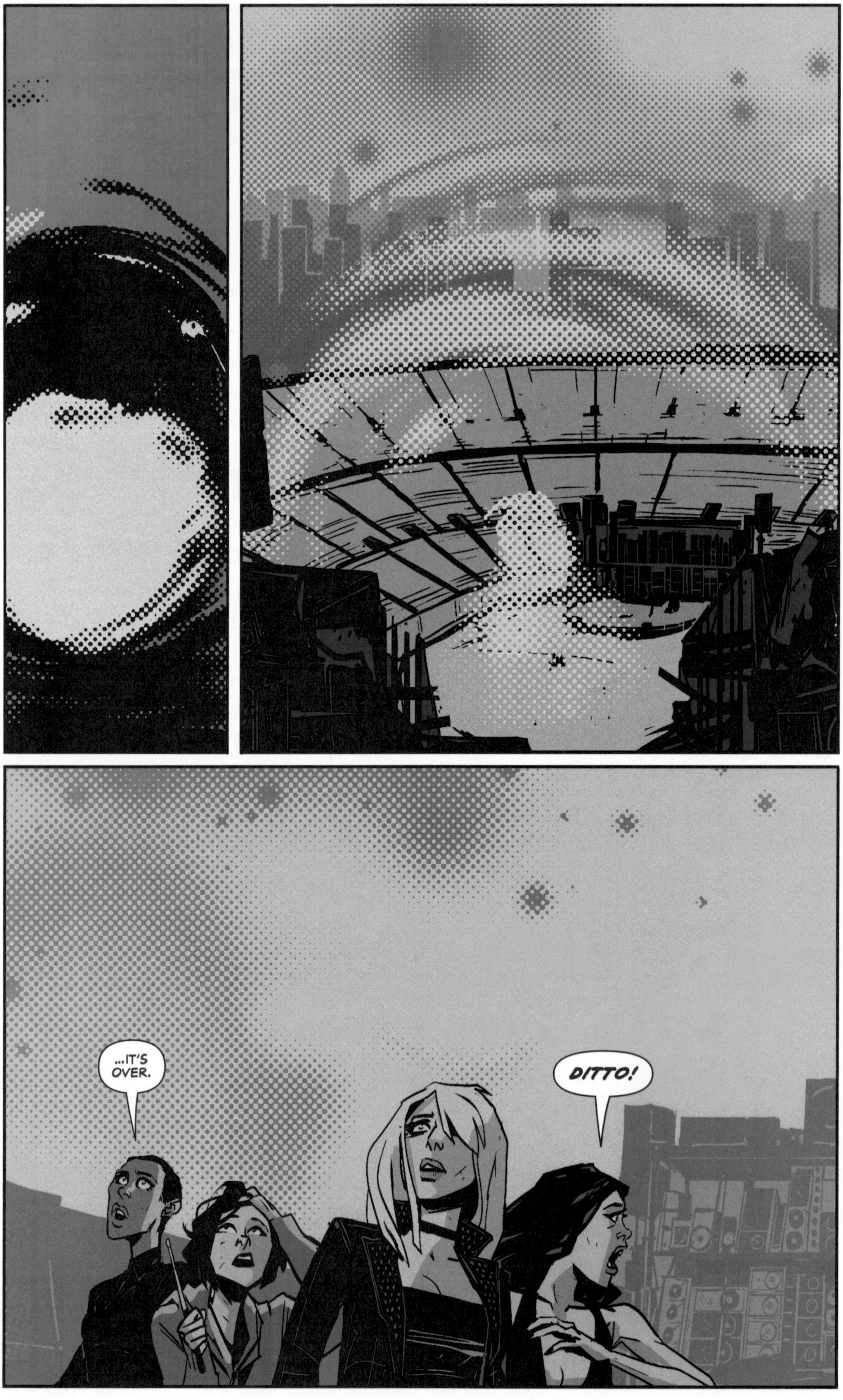
...IT'S
OVER.
DITTO!

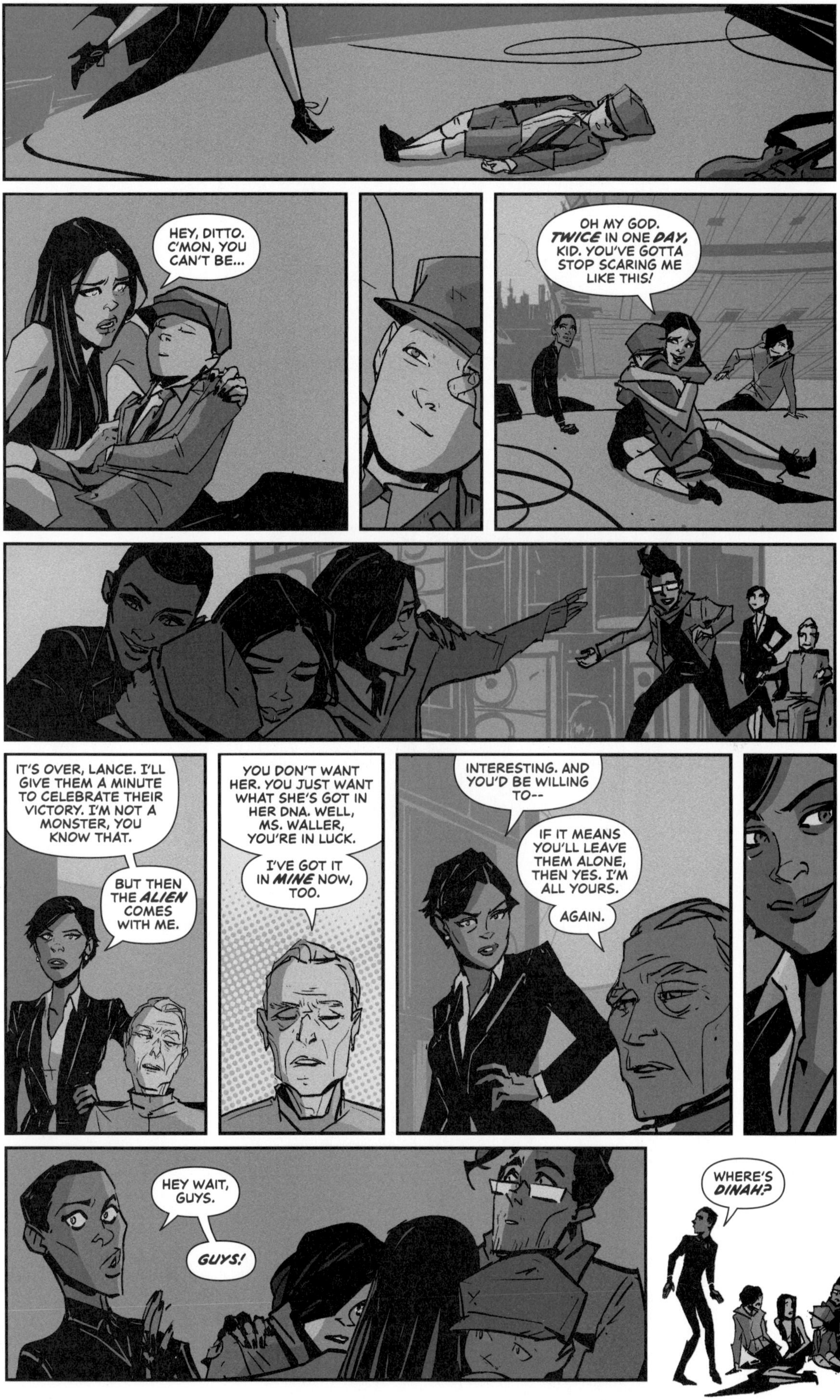
HEY, DITTO. C'MON, YOU CAN'T BE...
OH MY GOD. TWICE IN ONE DAY, KID. YOU'VE GOTTA STOP SCARING ME LIKE THIS!
IT'S OVER, LANCE. I'LL GIVE THEM A MINUTE TO CELEBRATE THEIR VICTORY. I'M NOT A MONSTER, YOU KNOW THAT.
BUT THEN THE ALIEN COMES WITH ME.
YOU DON'T WANT HER. YOU JUST WANT WHAT SHE'S GOT IN HER DNA. WELL, MS. WALLER, YOU'RE IN LUCK.
I'VE GOT IT IN MINE NOW, TOO.
INTERESTING. AND YOU'D BE WILLING TO--
IF IT MEANS YOU'LL LEAVE THEM ALONE, THEN YES. I'M ALL YOURS.
AGAIN.
HEY WAIT, GUYS.
GUYS!
WHERE'S DINAH?

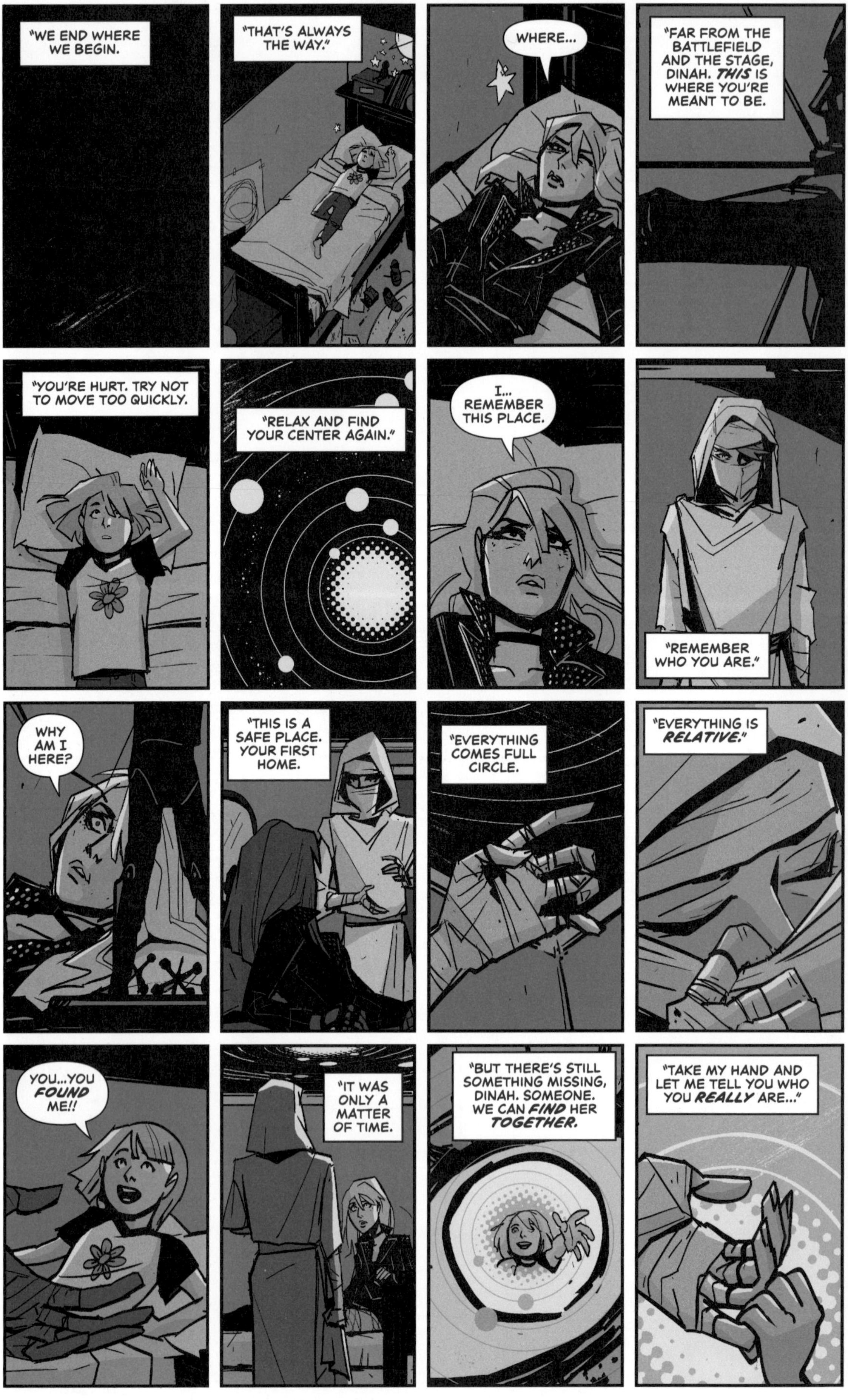

"WE END WHERE WE BEGIN.
"THAT'S ALWAYS THE WAY."
WHERE...
"FAR FROM THE BATTLEFIELD AND THE STAGE, DINAH. *THIS* IS WHERE YOU'RE MEANT TO BE.
"YOU'RE HURT. TRY NOT TO MOVE TOO QUICKLY.
"RELAX AND FIND YOUR CENTER AGAIN."
I... REMEMBER THIS PLACE.
"REMEMBER WHO YOU ARE."
WHY AM I HERE?
"THIS IS A SAFE PLACE. YOUR FIRST HOME.
"EVERYTHING COMES FULL CIRCLE.
"EVERYTHING IS *RELATIVE.*"
YOU...YOU *FOUND* ME!!
"IT WAS ONLY A MATTER OF TIME.
"BUT THERE'S STILL SOMETHING MISSING, DINAH. SOMEONE. WE CAN *FIND* HER *TOGETHER.*
"TAKE MY HAND AND LET ME TELL YOU WHO YOU *REALLY* ARE..."

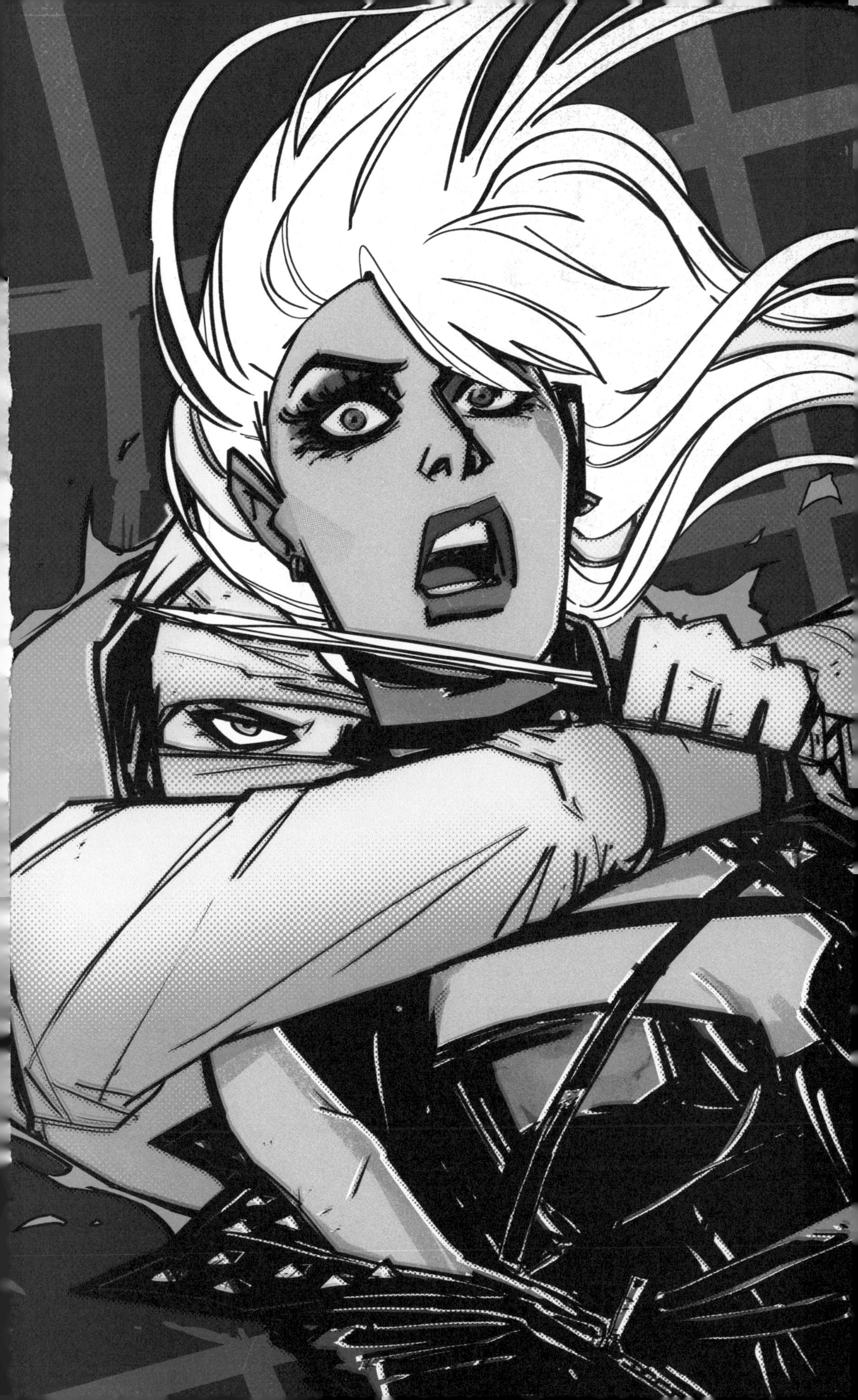

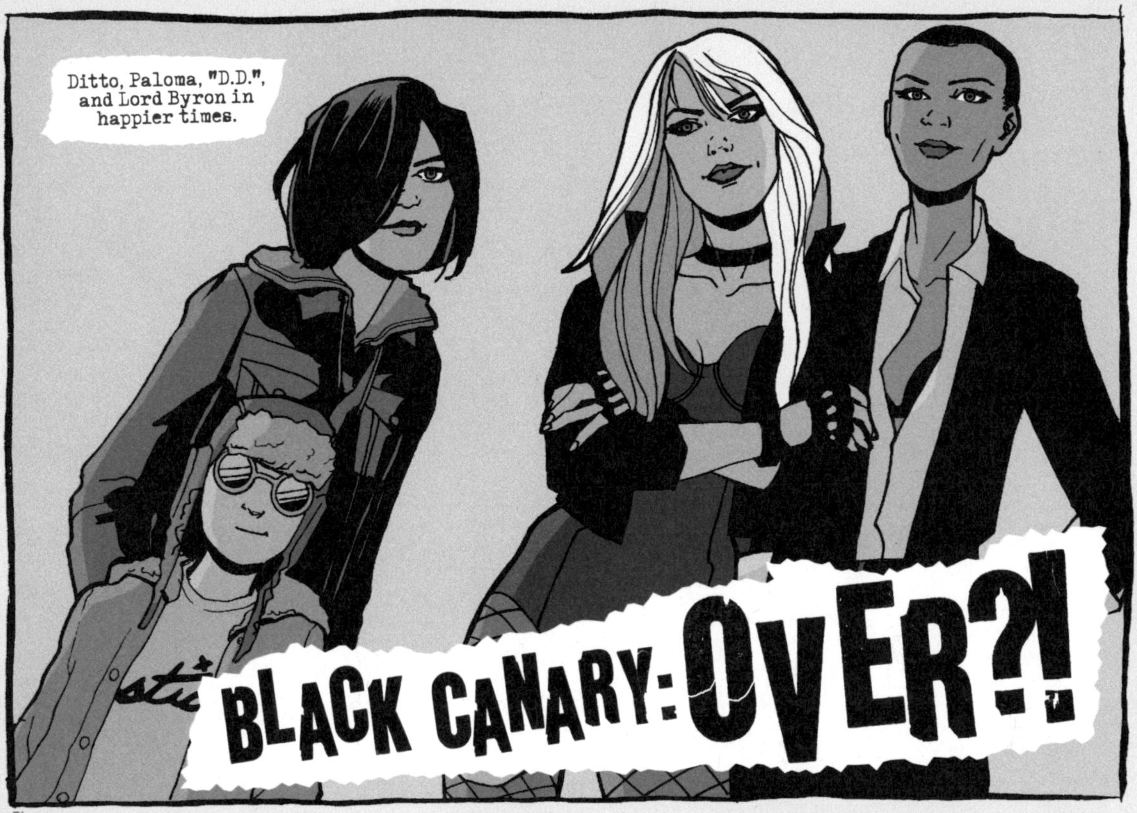
Ditto, Paloma, "D.D.", and Lord Byron in happier times.
BLACK CANARY: OVER?!

TWO MISSING SINCE ONSTAGE ACCIDENT DURING TRAGIC BATTLE OF THE BANDS, INCLUDING CANARY GUITARIST—A BURNSIDE TOFU EXCLUSIVE BY TANTOO LA BICHE

Some might call it fate. Some might say it was an act of God. But for those, like us, who watched Black Canary's meteoric rise to stardom amongst the spilled blood and broken bones of each and every one of their debut tour gigs, it seemed the band could have no other end but this, the saddest and most tragic of finales.

With their lead singer missing, their guitarist presumed dead, and authorities hunting for answers from remaining members of the band and their record label, it seems Black Canary is all but done.

Full story on page 2

"THIS IS *RIDICULOUS.* WE'VE BEEN INTERVIEWING YOU ALL FOR TWO WEEKS NOW AND YOU SAY YOU *STILL* HAVE NO IDEA WHAT HAPPENED TO YOUR LEAD SINGER? THIS, UH, *"D.D."* WOMAN?"

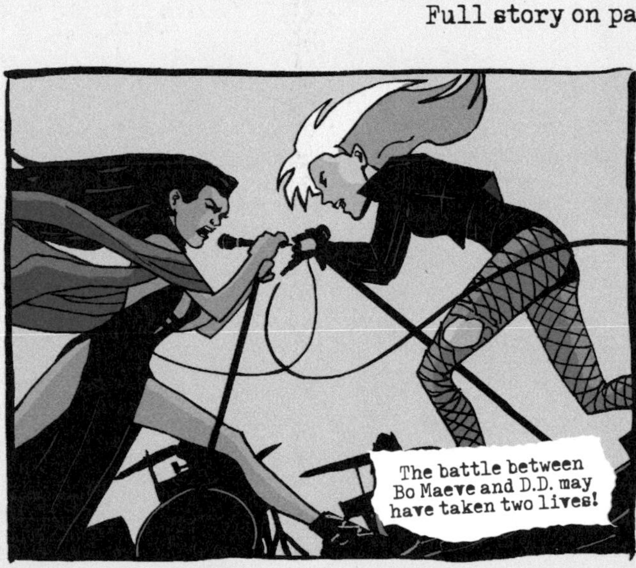
The battle between Bo Maeve and D.D. may have taken two lives!

BURNSIDE TOFU
The zine for people with the right kind of taste

BRENDEN FLETCHER Writer
SANDY JARRELL Artist
LEE LOUGHRIDGE Colors
STEVE WANDS Letters
ANNIE WU Cover
DAVE WIELGOSZ Asst. Editor
CHRIS CONROY Editor
MARK DOYLE Group Editor

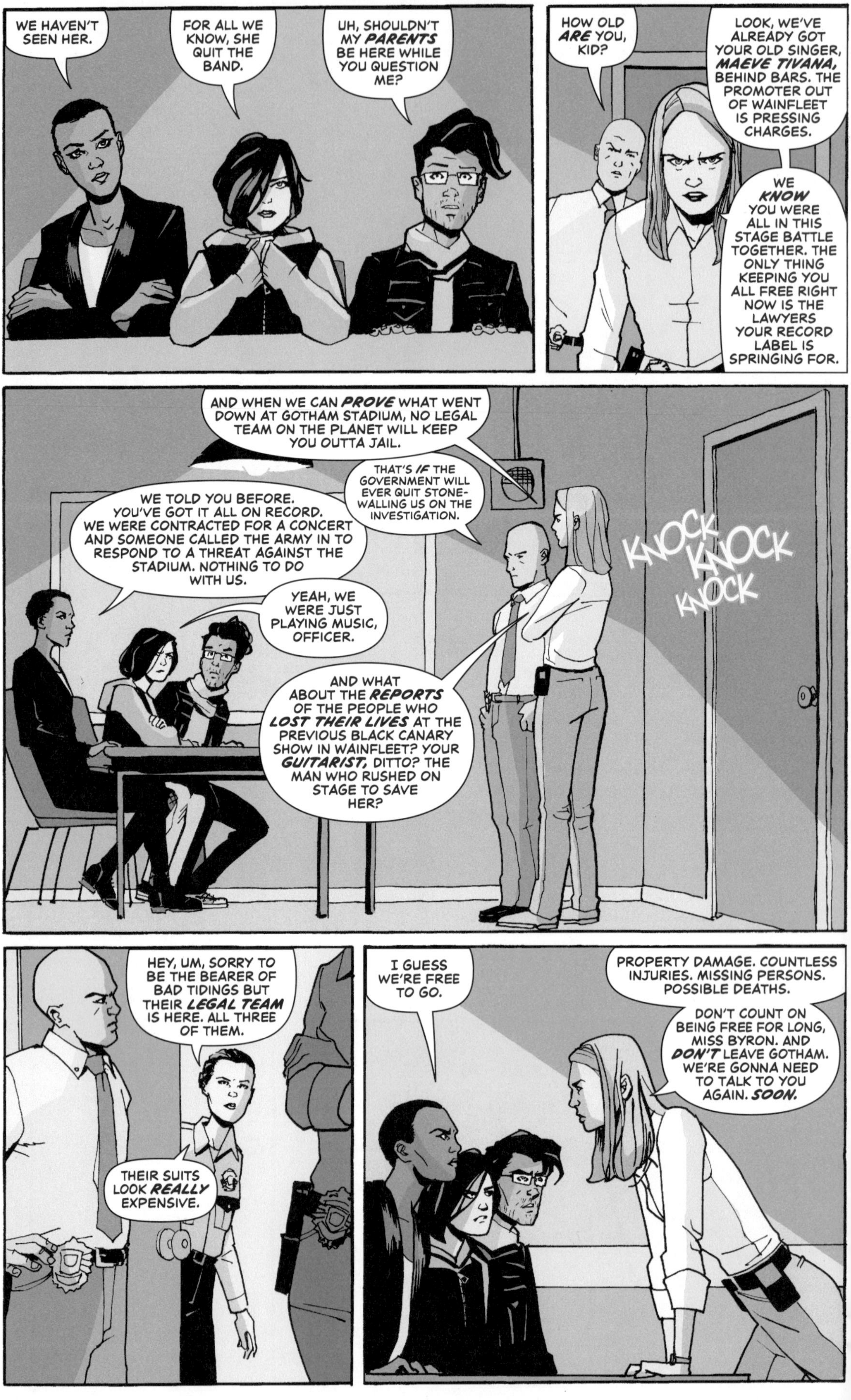
WE HAVEN'T SEEN HER.
FOR ALL WE KNOW, SHE QUIT THE BAND.
UH, SHOULDN'T MY PARENTS BE HERE WHILE YOU QUESTION ME?
HOW OLD ARE YOU, KID?
LOOK, WE'VE ALREADY GOT YOUR OLD SINGER, MAEVE TIVANA, BEHIND BARS. THE PROMOTER OUT OF WAINFLEET IS PRESSING CHARGES.
WE KNOW YOU WERE ALL IN THIS STAGE BATTLE TOGETHER. THE ONLY THING KEEPING YOU ALL FREE RIGHT NOW IS THE LAWYERS YOUR RECORD LABEL IS SPRINGING FOR.
AND WHEN WE CAN PROVE WHAT WENT DOWN AT GOTHAM STADIUM, NO LEGAL TEAM ON THE PLANET WILL KEEP YOU OUTTA JAIL.
THAT'S IF THE GOVERNMENT WILL EVER QUIT STONE-WALLING US ON THE INVESTIGATION.
WE TOLD YOU BEFORE. YOU'VE GOT IT ALL ON RECORD. WE WERE CONTRACTED FOR A CONCERT AND SOMEONE CALLED THE ARMY IN TO RESPOND TO A THREAT AGAINST THE STADIUM. NOTHING TO DO WITH US.
YEAH, WE WERE JUST PLAYING MUSIC, OFFICER.
AND WHAT ABOUT THE REPORTS OF THE PEOPLE WHO LOST THEIR LIVES AT THE PREVIOUS BLACK CANARY SHOW IN WAINFLEET? YOUR GUITARIST, DITTO? THE MAN WHO RUSHED ON STAGE TO SAVE HER?
KNOCK KNOCK KNOCK
HEY, UM, SORRY TO BE THE BEARER OF BAD TIDINGS BUT THEIR LEGAL TEAM IS HERE. ALL THREE OF THEM.
THEIR SUITS LOOK REALLY EXPENSIVE.
I GUESS WE'RE FREE TO GO.
PROPERTY DAMAGE. COUNTLESS INJURIES. MISSING PERSONS. POSSIBLE DEATHS.
DON'T COUNT ON BEING FREE FOR LONG, MISS BYRON. AND DON'T LEAVE GOTHAM. WE'RE GONNA NEED TO TALK TO YOU AGAIN. SOON.

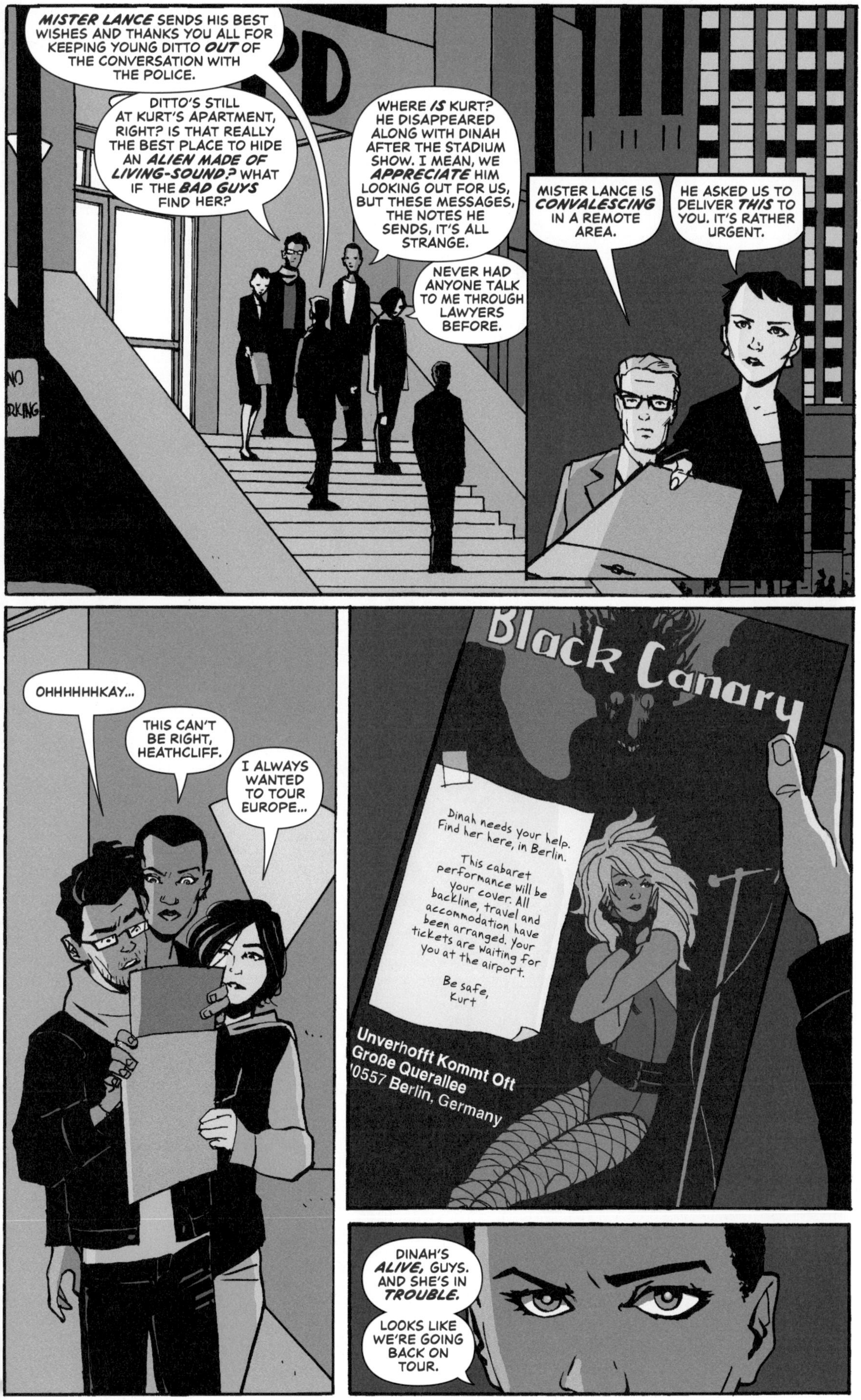
MISTER LANCE SENDS HIS BEST WISHES AND THANKS YOU ALL FOR KEEPING YOUNG DITTO OUT OF THE CONVERSATION WITH THE POLICE.
DITTO'S STILL AT KURT'S APARTMENT, RIGHT? IS THAT REALLY THE BEST PLACE TO HIDE AN ALIEN MADE OF LIVING-SOUND? WHAT IF THE BAD GUYS FIND HER?
WHERE IS KURT? HE DISAPPEARED ALONG WITH DINAH AFTER THE STADIUM SHOW. I MEAN, WE APPRECIATE HIM LOOKING OUT FOR US, BUT THESE MESSAGES, THE NOTES HE SENDS, IT'S ALL STRANGE.
NEVER HAD ANYONE TALK TO ME THROUGH LAWYERS BEFORE.
MISTER LANCE IS CONVALESCING IN A REMOTE AREA.
HE ASKED US TO DELIVER THIS TO YOU. IT'S RATHER URGENT.
OHHHHHHKAY...
THIS CAN'T BE RIGHT, HEATHCLIFF.
I ALWAYS WANTED TO TOUR EUROPE...
Black Canary
Dinah needs your help. Find her here, in Berlin.
This cabaret performance will be your cover. All backline, travel and accommodation have been arranged. Your tickets are waiting for you at the airport.
Be safe, Kurt
Unverhofft Kommt Oft
Große Querallee
10557 Berlin, Germany
DINAH'S ALIVE, GUYS. AND SHE'S IN TROUBLE.
LOOKS LIKE WE'RE GOING BACK ON TOUR.

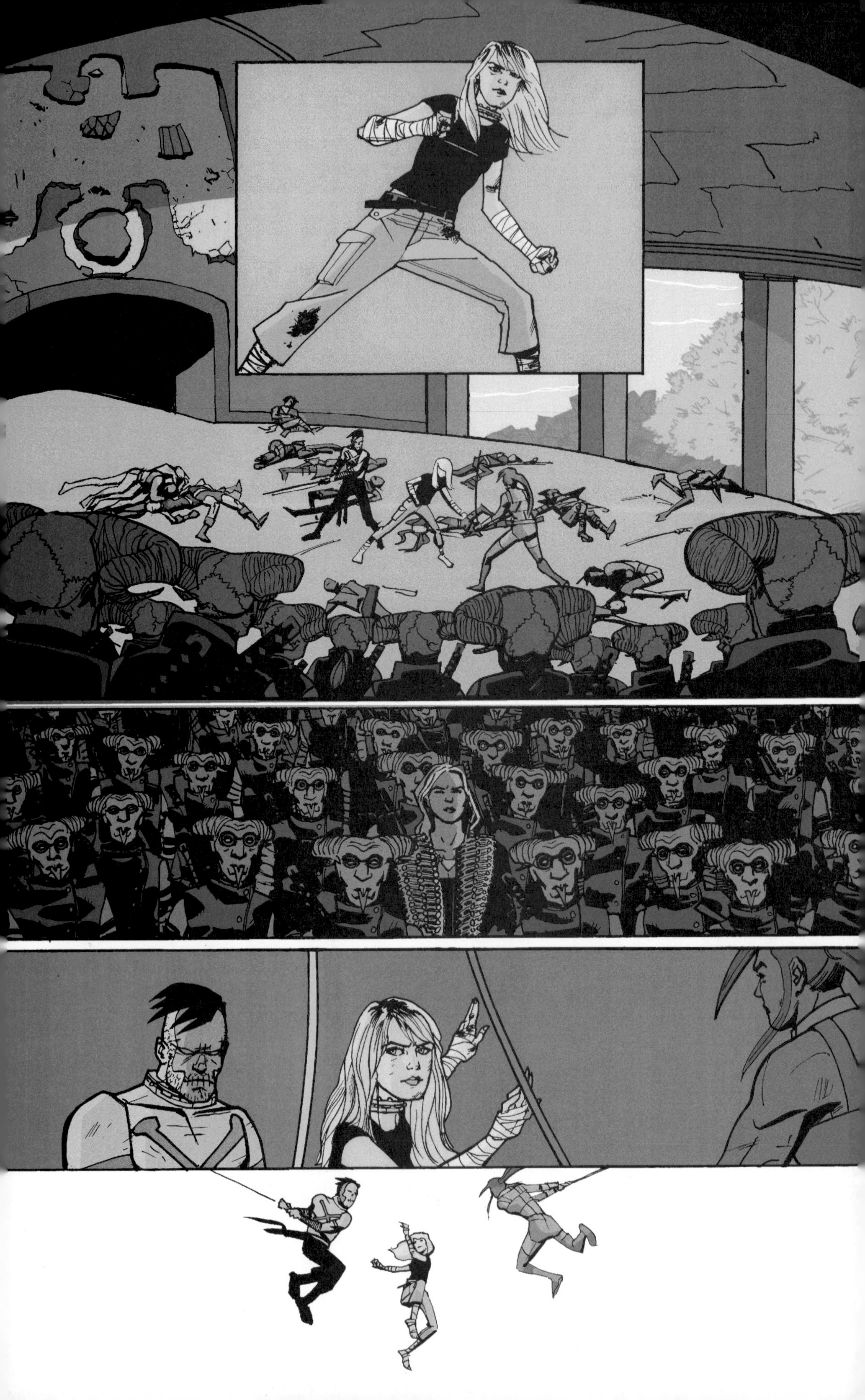

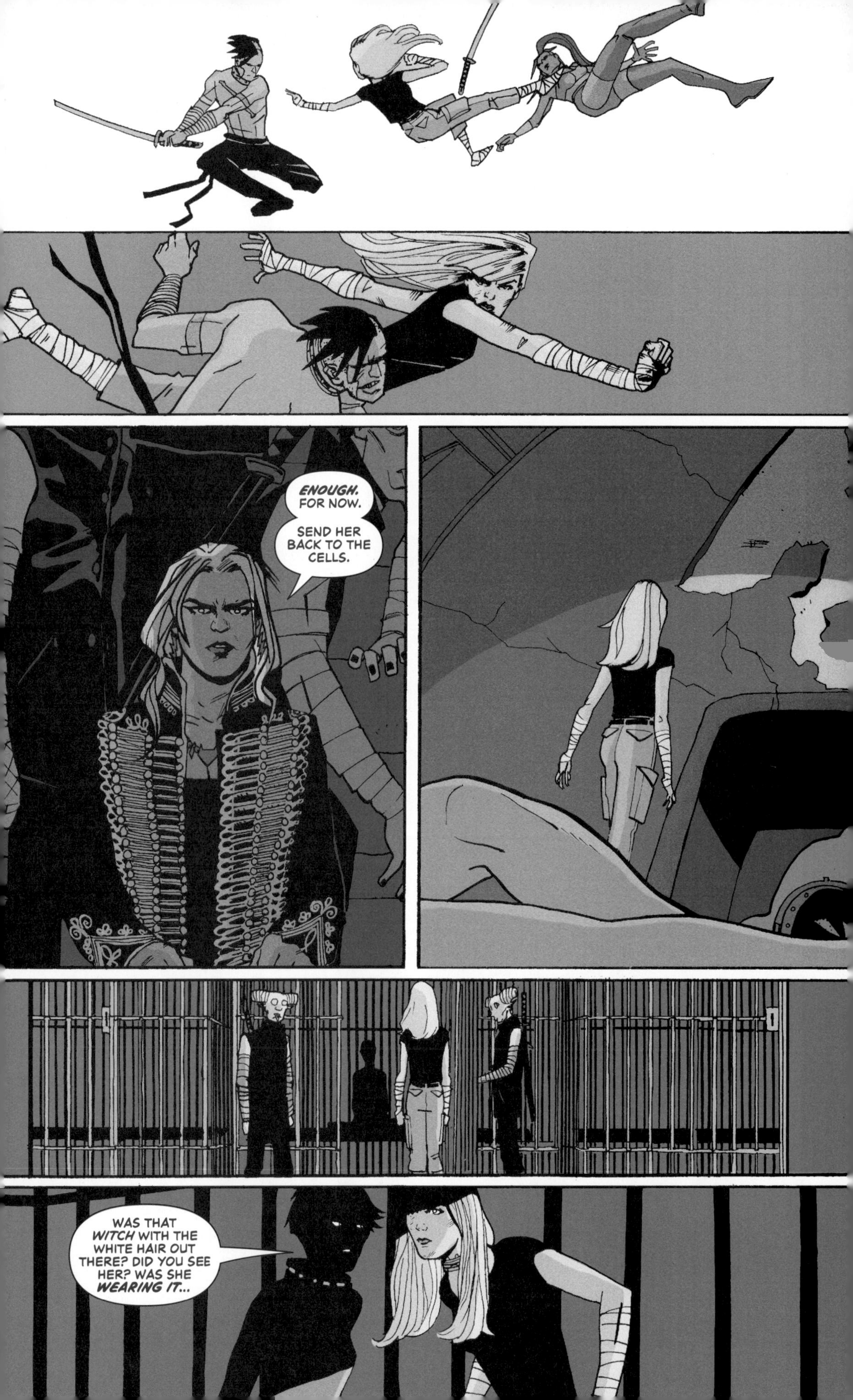
ENOUGH. FOR NOW.
SEND HER BACK TO THE CELLS.
WAS THAT WITCH WITH THE WHITE HAIR OUT THERE? DID YOU SEE HER? WAS SHE WEARING IT...

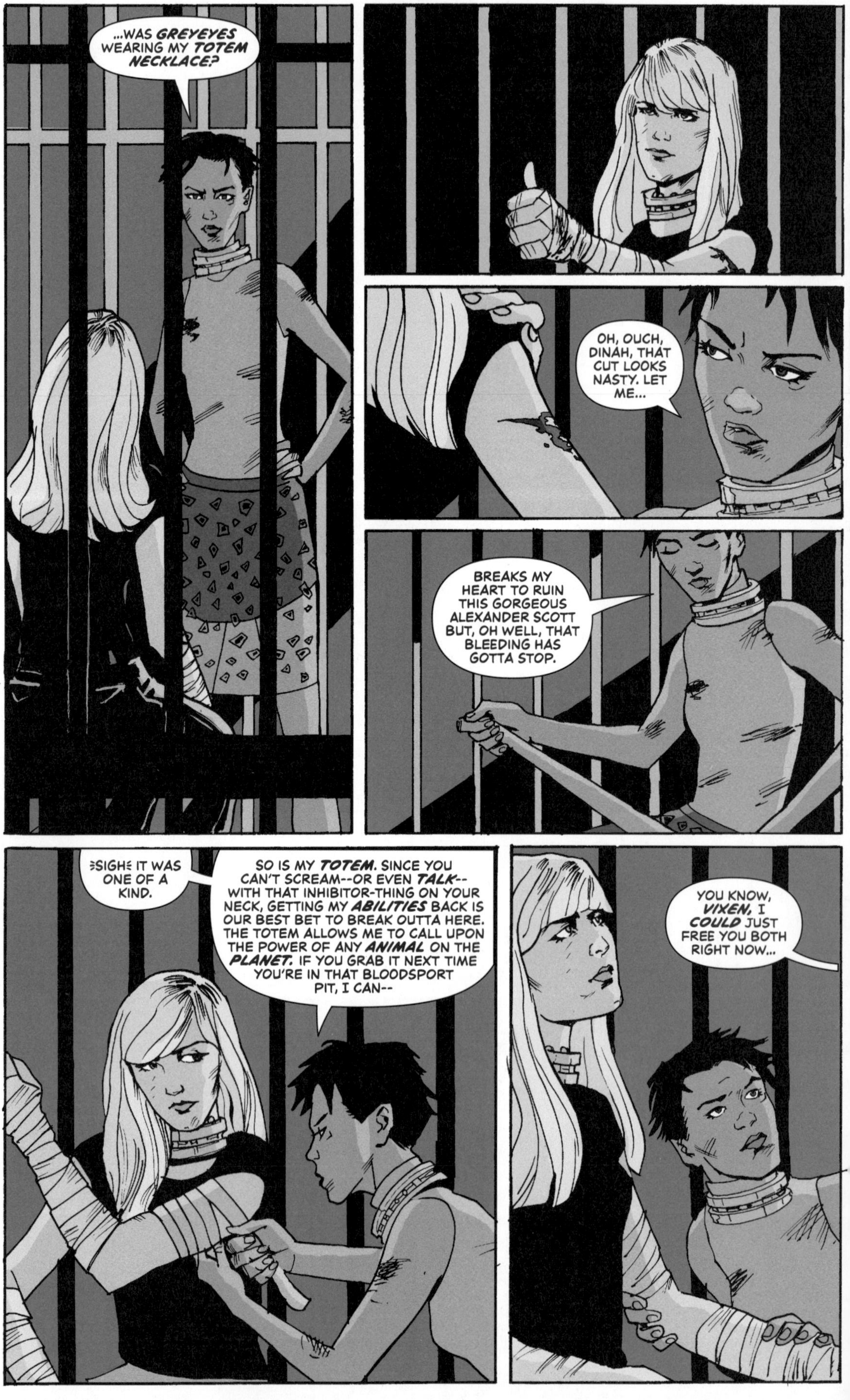
...WAS GREYEYES WEARING MY TOTEM NECKLACE?
OH, OUCH, DINAH, THAT CUT LOOKS NASTY. LET ME...
BREAKS MY HEART TO RUIN THIS GORGEOUS ALEXANDER SCOTT BUT, OH WELL, THAT BLEEDING HAS GOTTA STOP.
≡SIGH≡ IT WAS ONE OF A KIND.
SO IS MY TOTEM. SINCE YOU CAN'T SCREAM--OR EVEN TALK--WITH THAT INHIBITOR-THING ON YOUR NECK, GETTING MY ABILITIES BACK IS OUR BEST BET TO BREAK OUTTA HERE. THE TOTEM ALLOWS ME TO CALL UPON THE POWER OF ANY ANIMAL ON THE PLANET. IF YOU GRAB IT NEXT TIME YOU'RE IN THAT BLOODSPORT PIT, I CAN--
YOU KNOW, VIXEN, I COULD JUST FREE YOU BOTH RIGHT NOW...

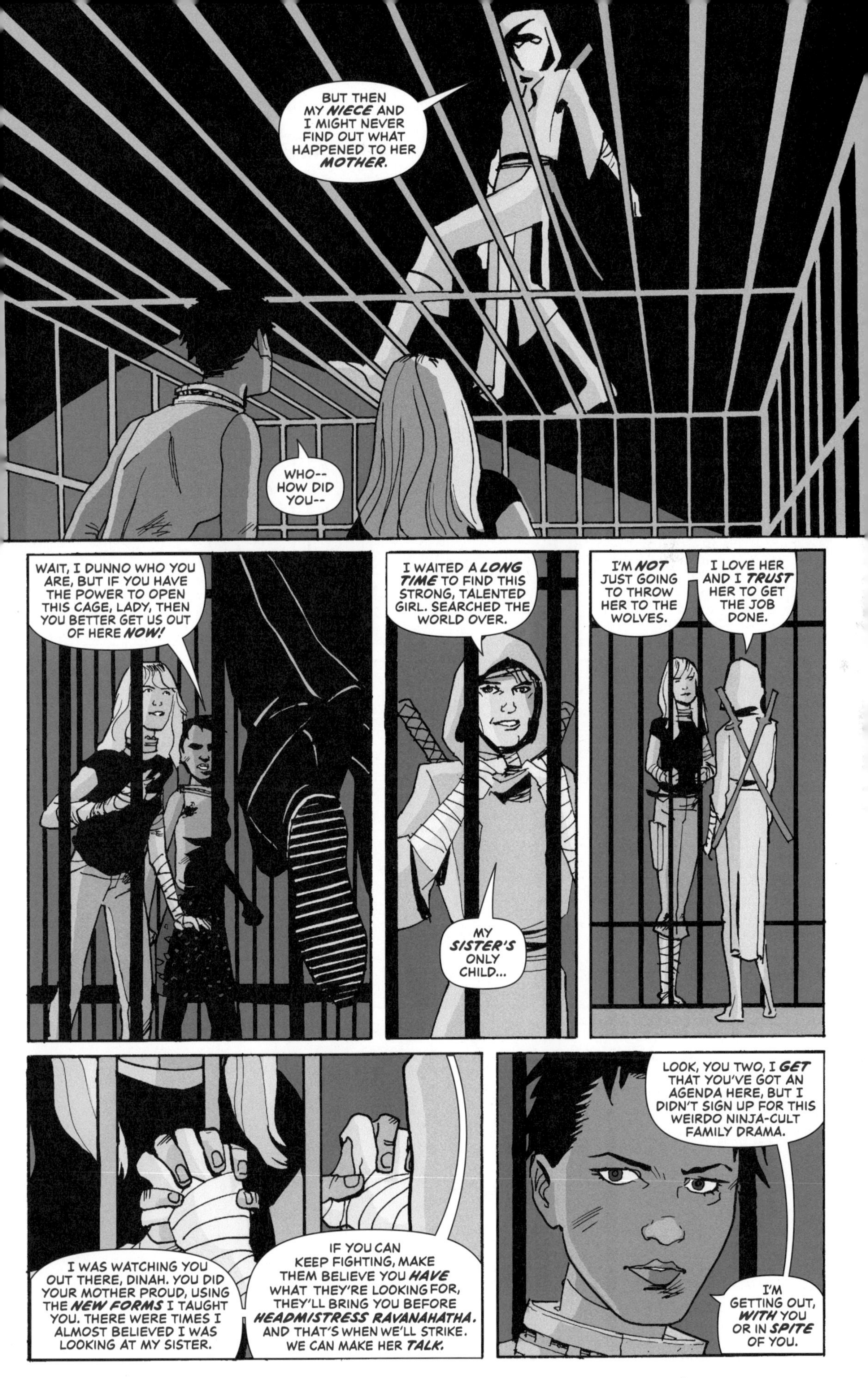

BUT THEN MY *NIECE* AND I MIGHT NEVER FIND OUT WHAT HAPPENED TO HER *MOTHER*.
WHO-- HOW DID YOU--
WAIT, I DUNNO WHO YOU ARE, BUT IF YOU HAVE THE POWER TO OPEN THIS CAGE, LADY, THEN YOU BETTER GET US OUT OF HERE *NOW!*
I WAITED A *LONG TIME* TO FIND THIS STRONG, TALENTED GIRL. SEARCHED THE WORLD OVER.
MY *SISTER'S* ONLY CHILD...
I'M *NOT* JUST GOING TO THROW HER TO THE WOLVES.
I LOVE HER AND I *TRUST* HER TO GET THE JOB DONE.
I WAS WATCHING YOU OUT THERE, DINAH. YOU DID YOUR MOTHER PROUD, USING THE *NEW FORMS* I TAUGHT YOU. THERE WERE TIMES I ALMOST BELIEVED I WAS LOOKING AT MY SISTER.
IF YOU CAN KEEP FIGHTING, MAKE THEM BELIEVE YOU *HAVE* WHAT THEY'RE LOOKING FOR, THEY'LL BRING YOU BEFORE *HEADMISTRESS RAVANAHATHA*. AND THAT'S WHEN WE'LL STRIKE. WE CAN MAKE HER *TALK*.
LOOK, YOU TWO, I *GET* THAT YOU'VE GOT AN AGENDA HERE, BUT I DIDN'T SIGN UP FOR THIS WEIRDO NINJA-CULT FAMILY DRAMA.
I'M GETTING OUT, *WITH* YOU OR IN *SPITE* OF YOU.

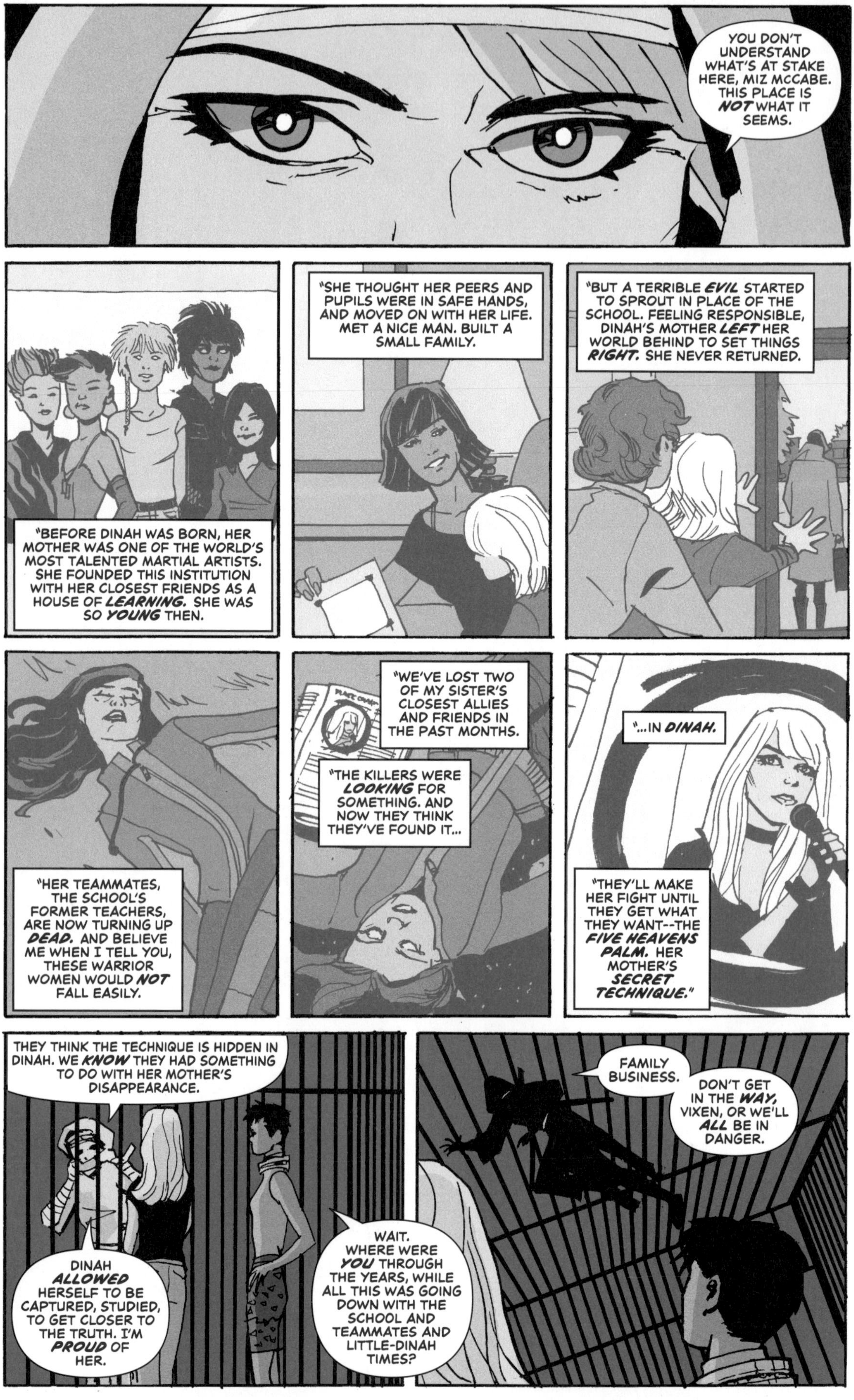
YOU DON'T UNDERSTAND WHAT'S AT STAKE HERE, MIZ McCABE. THIS PLACE IS NOT WHAT IT SEEMS.
"BEFORE DINAH WAS BORN, HER MOTHER WAS ONE OF THE WORLD'S MOST TALENTED MARTIAL ARTISTS. SHE FOUNDED THIS INSTITUTION WITH HER CLOSEST FRIENDS AS A HOUSE OF LEARNING. SHE WAS SO YOUNG THEN.
"SHE THOUGHT HER PEERS AND PUPILS WERE IN SAFE HANDS, AND MOVED ON WITH HER LIFE. MET A NICE MAN. BUILT A SMALL FAMILY.
"BUT A TERRIBLE EVIL STARTED TO SPROUT IN PLACE OF THE SCHOOL. FEELING RESPONSIBLE, DINAH'S MOTHER LEFT HER WORLD BEHIND TO SET THINGS RIGHT. SHE NEVER RETURNED.
"HER TEAMMATES, THE SCHOOL'S FORMER TEACHERS, ARE NOW TURNING UP DEAD. AND BELIEVE ME WHEN I TELL YOU, THESE WARRIOR WOMEN WOULD NOT FALL EASILY.
"WE'VE LOST TWO OF MY SISTER'S CLOSEST ALLIES AND FRIENDS IN THE PAST MONTHS.
"THE KILLERS WERE LOOKING FOR SOMETHING. AND NOW THEY THINK THEY'VE FOUND IT...
"...IN DINAH.
"THEY'LL MAKE HER FIGHT UNTIL THEY GET WHAT THEY WANT--THE FIVE HEAVENS PALM. HER MOTHER'S SECRET TECHNIQUE."
THEY THINK THE TECHNIQUE IS HIDDEN IN DINAH. WE KNOW THEY HAD SOMETHING TO DO WITH HER MOTHER'S DISAPPEARANCE.
DINAH ALLOWED HERSELF TO BE CAPTURED, STUDIED, TO GET CLOSER TO THE TRUTH. I'M PROUD OF HER.
WAIT. WHERE WERE YOU THROUGH THE YEARS, WHILE ALL THIS WAS GOING DOWN WITH THE SCHOOL AND TEAMMATES AND LITTLE-DINAH TIMES?
FAMILY BUSINESS.
DON'T GET IN THE WAY, VIXEN, OR WE'LL ALL BE IN DANGER.

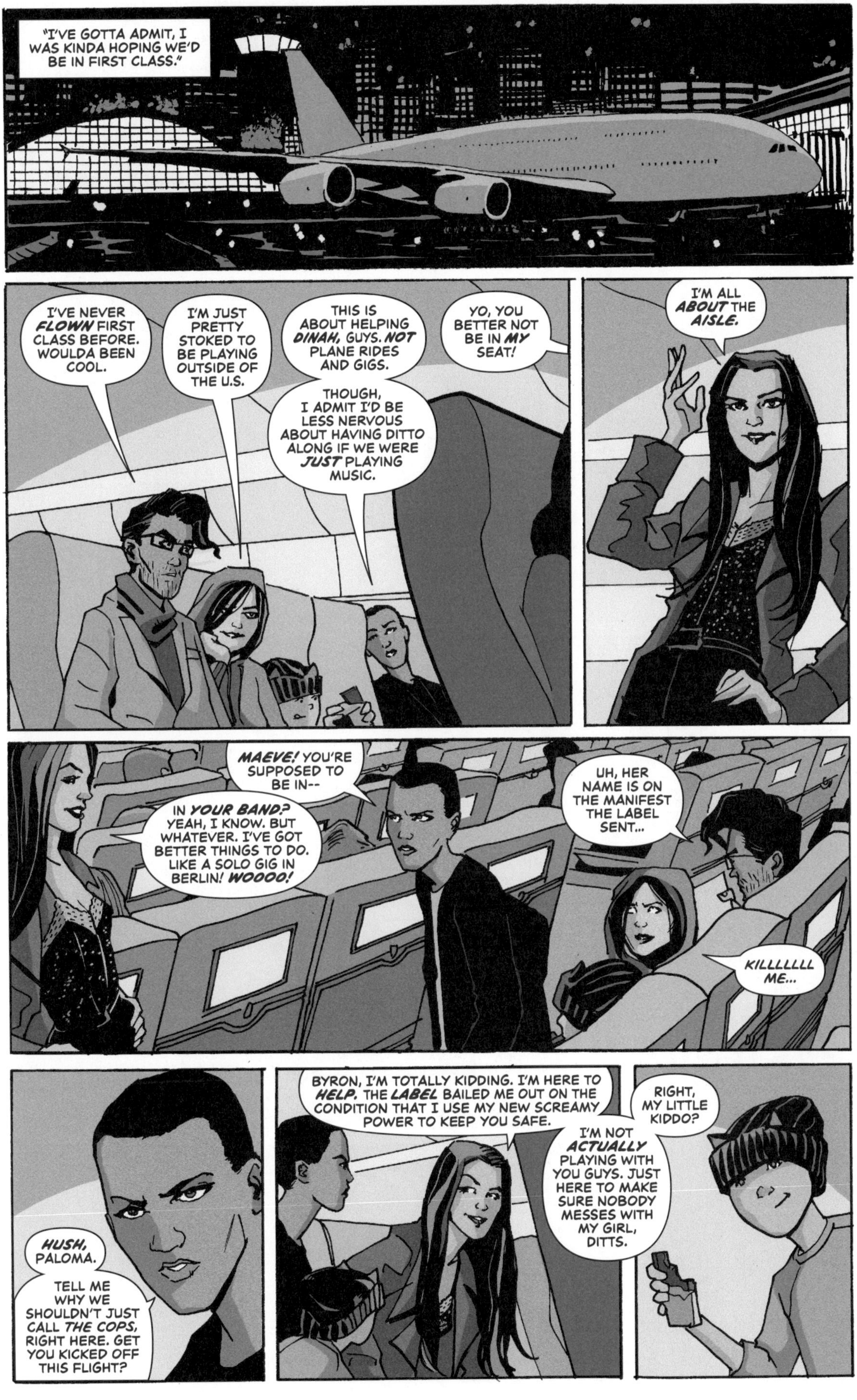
"I'VE GOTTA ADMIT, I WAS KINDA HOPING WE'D BE IN FIRST CLASS."
I'VE NEVER *FLOWN* FIRST CLASS BEFORE. WOULDA BEEN COOL.
I'M JUST PRETTY STOKED TO BE PLAYING OUTSIDE OF THE U.S.
THIS IS ABOUT HELPING *DINAH,* GUYS. *NOT* PLANE RIDES AND GIGS.
THOUGH, I ADMIT I'D BE LESS NERVOUS ABOUT HAVING DITTO ALONG IF WE WERE *JUST* PLAYING MUSIC.
YO, YOU BETTER NOT BE IN *MY* SEAT!
I'M ALL *ABOUT* THE *AISLE.*
MAEVE! YOU'RE SUPPOSED TO BE IN--
IN *YOUR BAND?* YEAH, I KNOW. BUT WHATEVER. I'VE GOT BETTER THINGS TO DO. LIKE A SOLO GIG IN BERLIN! *WOOOO!*
UH, HER NAME IS ON THE MANIFEST THE LABEL SENT...
KILLLLLLL ME...
HUSH, PALOMA.
TELL ME WHY WE SHOULDN'T JUST CALL *THE COPS,* RIGHT HERE. GET YOU KICKED OFF THIS FLIGHT?
BYRON, I'M TOTALLY KIDDING. I'M HERE TO *HELP.* THE *LABEL* BAILED ME OUT ON THE CONDITION THAT I USE MY NEW SCREAMY POWER TO KEEP YOU SAFE.
I'M NOT *ACTUALLY* PLAYING WITH YOU GUYS. JUST HERE TO MAKE SURE NOBODY MESSES WITH MY GIRL, DITTS.
RIGHT, MY LITTLE KIDDO?

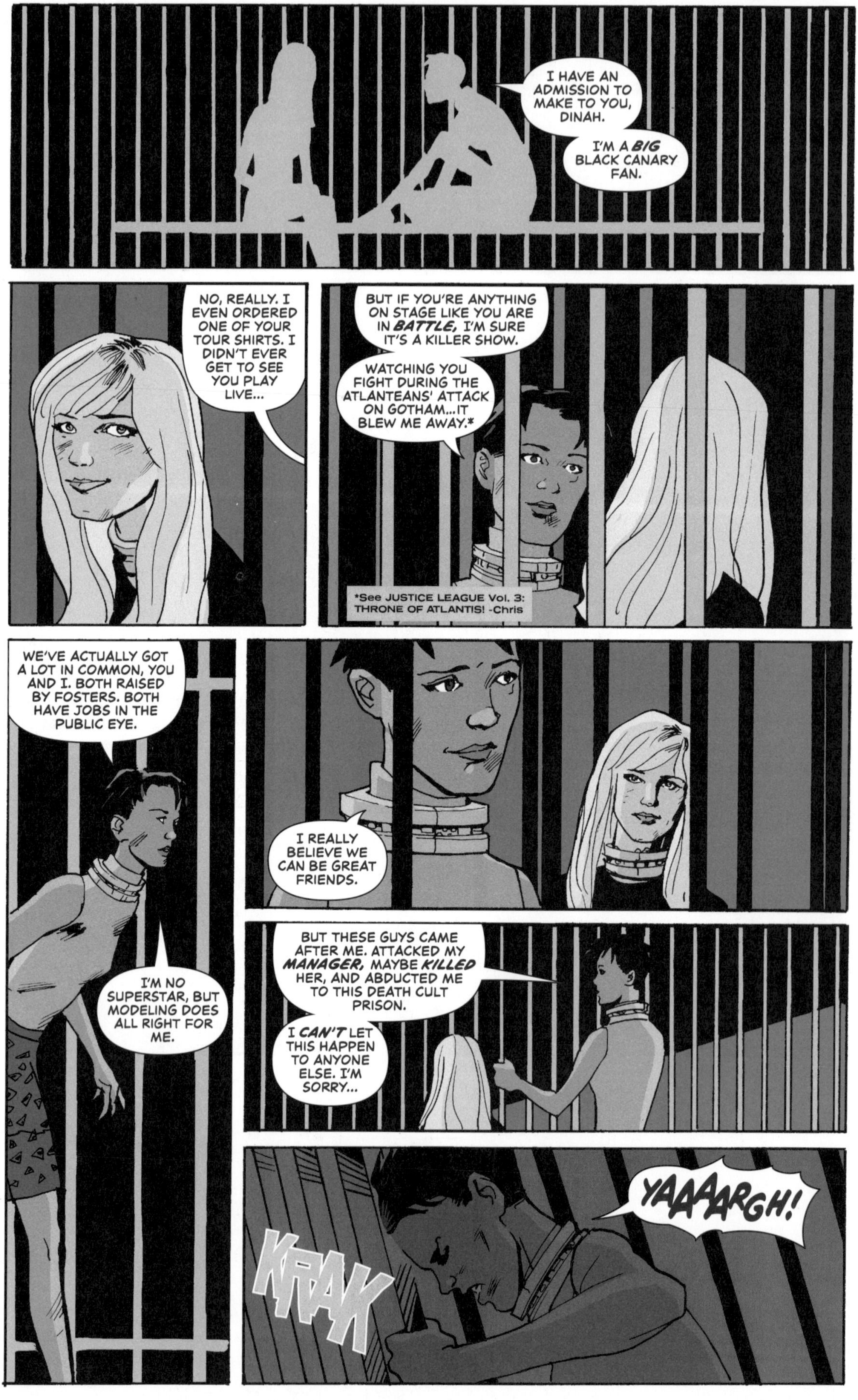
I HAVE AN ADMISSION TO MAKE TO YOU, DINAH.
I'M A BIG BLACK CANARY FAN.
NO, REALLY. I EVEN ORDERED ONE OF YOUR TOUR SHIRTS. I DIDN'T EVER GET TO SEE YOU PLAY LIVE...
BUT IF YOU'RE ANYTHING ON STAGE LIKE YOU ARE IN BATTLE, I'M SURE IT'S A KILLER SHOW.
WATCHING YOU FIGHT DURING THE ATLANTEANS' ATTACK ON GOTHAM...IT BLEW ME AWAY.*
*See JUSTICE LEAGUE Vol. 3: THRONE OF ATLANTIS! -Chris
WE'VE ACTUALLY GOT A LOT IN COMMON, YOU AND I. BOTH RAISED BY FOSTERS. BOTH HAVE JOBS IN THE PUBLIC EYE.
I'M NO SUPERSTAR, BUT MODELING DOES ALL RIGHT FOR ME.
I REALLY BELIEVE WE CAN BE GREAT FRIENDS.
BUT THESE GUYS CAME AFTER ME. ATTACKED MY MANAGER, MAYBE KILLED HER, AND ABDUCTED ME TO THIS DEATH CULT PRISON.
I CAN'T LET THIS HAPPEN TO ANYONE ELSE. I'M SORRY...
YAAAARGH!
KRAK

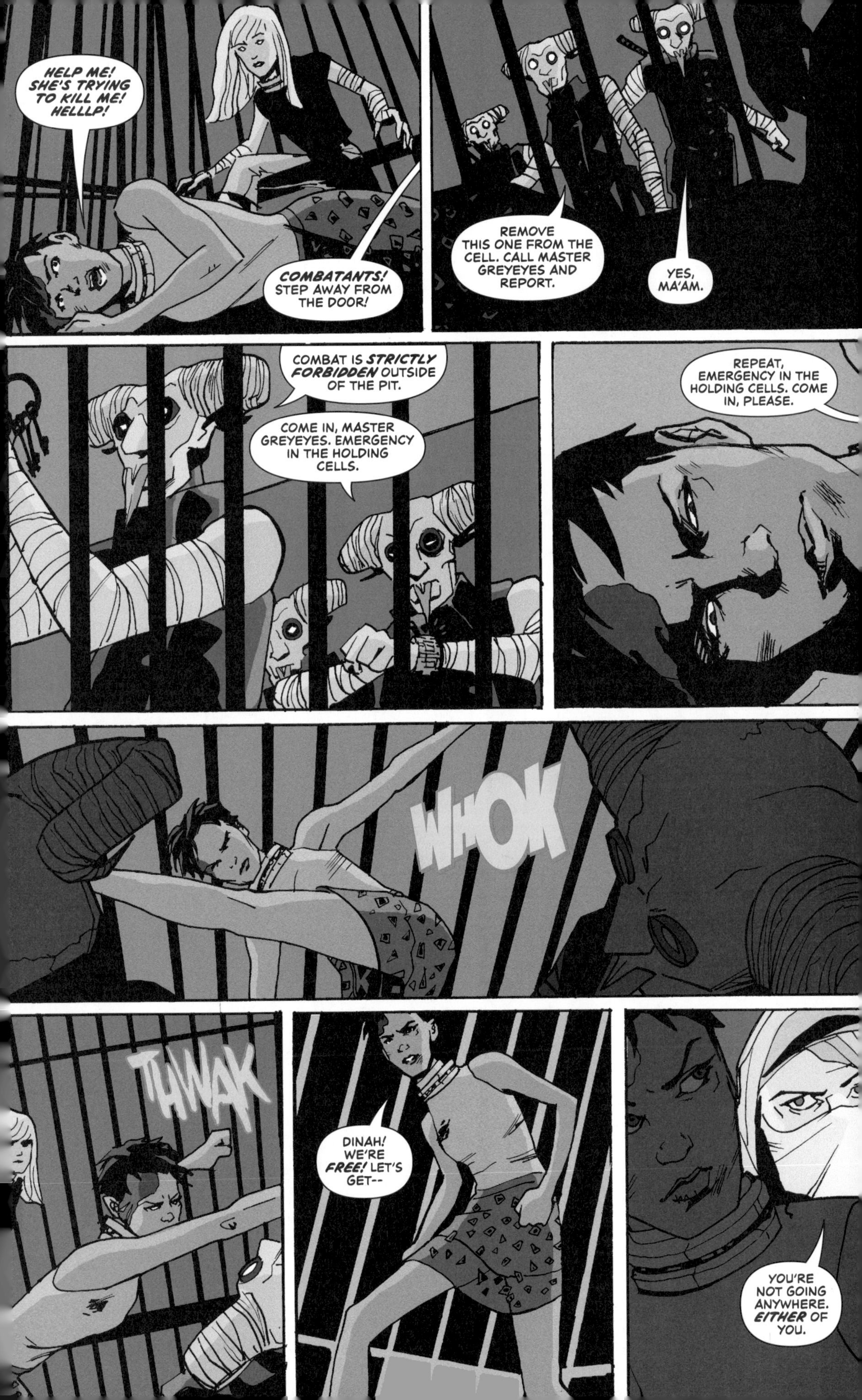
HELP ME! SHE'S TRYING TO KILL ME! HELLLP!
COMBATANTS! STEP AWAY FROM THE DOOR!
REMOVE THIS ONE FROM THE CELL. CALL MASTER GREYEYES AND REPORT.
YES, MA'AM.
COMBAT IS STRICTLY FORBIDDEN OUTSIDE OF THE PIT.
COME IN, MASTER GREYEYES. EMERGENCY IN THE HOLDING CELLS.
REPEAT, EMERGENCY IN THE HOLDING CELLS. COME IN, PLEASE.
WHOK
THWAK
DINAH! WE'RE FREE! LET'S GET--
YOU'RE NOT GOING ANYWHERE. EITHER OF YOU.

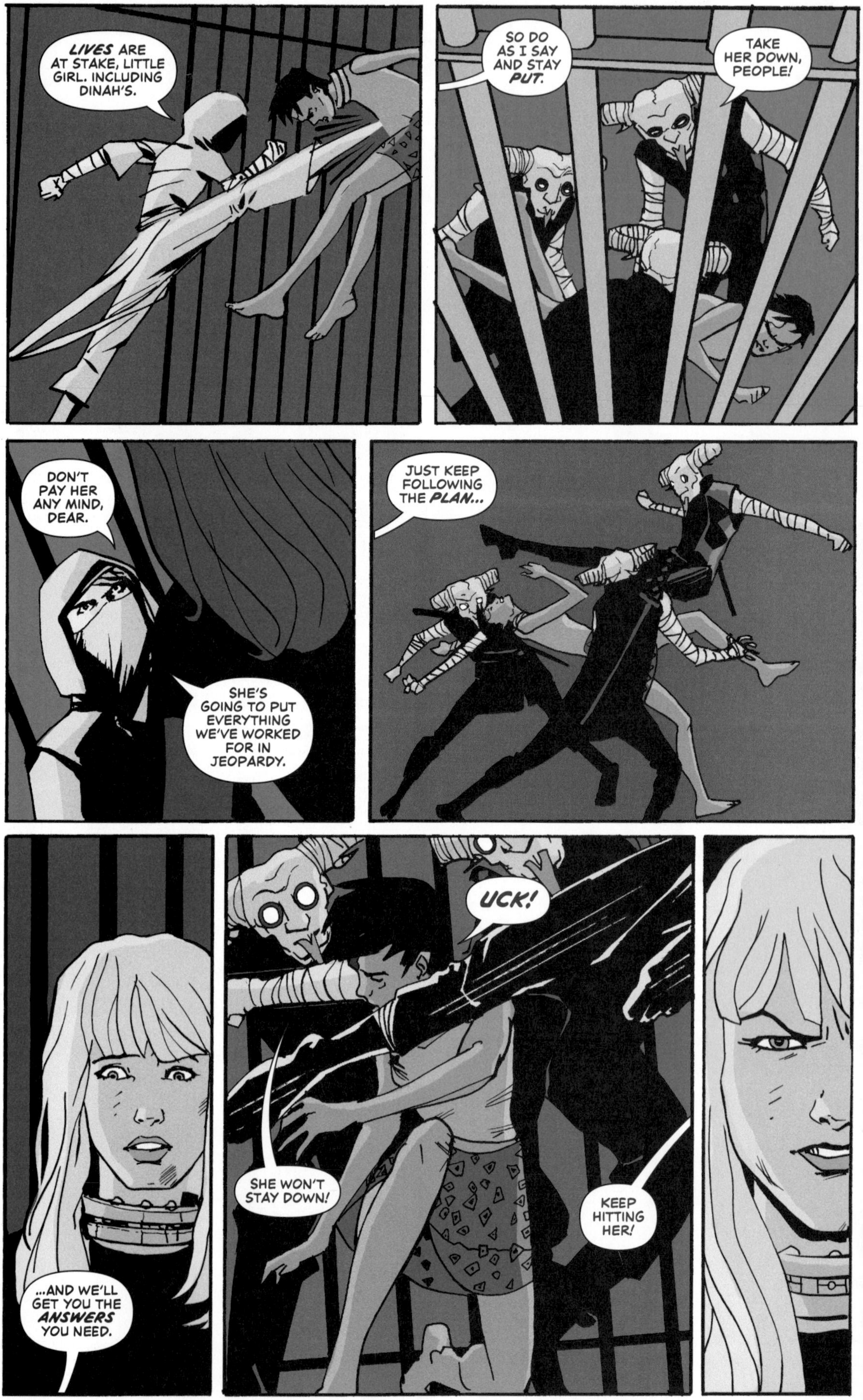
LIVES ARE AT STAKE, LITTLE GIRL. INCLUDING DINAH'S.
SO DO AS I SAY AND STAY PUT.
TAKE HER DOWN, PEOPLE!
DON'T PAY HER ANY MIND, DEAR.
SHE'S GOING TO PUT EVERYTHING WE'VE WORKED FOR IN JEOPARDY.
JUST KEEP FOLLOWING THE PLAN...
...AND WE'LL GET YOU THE ANSWERS YOU NEED.
UCK!
SHE WON'T STAY DOWN!
KEEP HITTING HER!

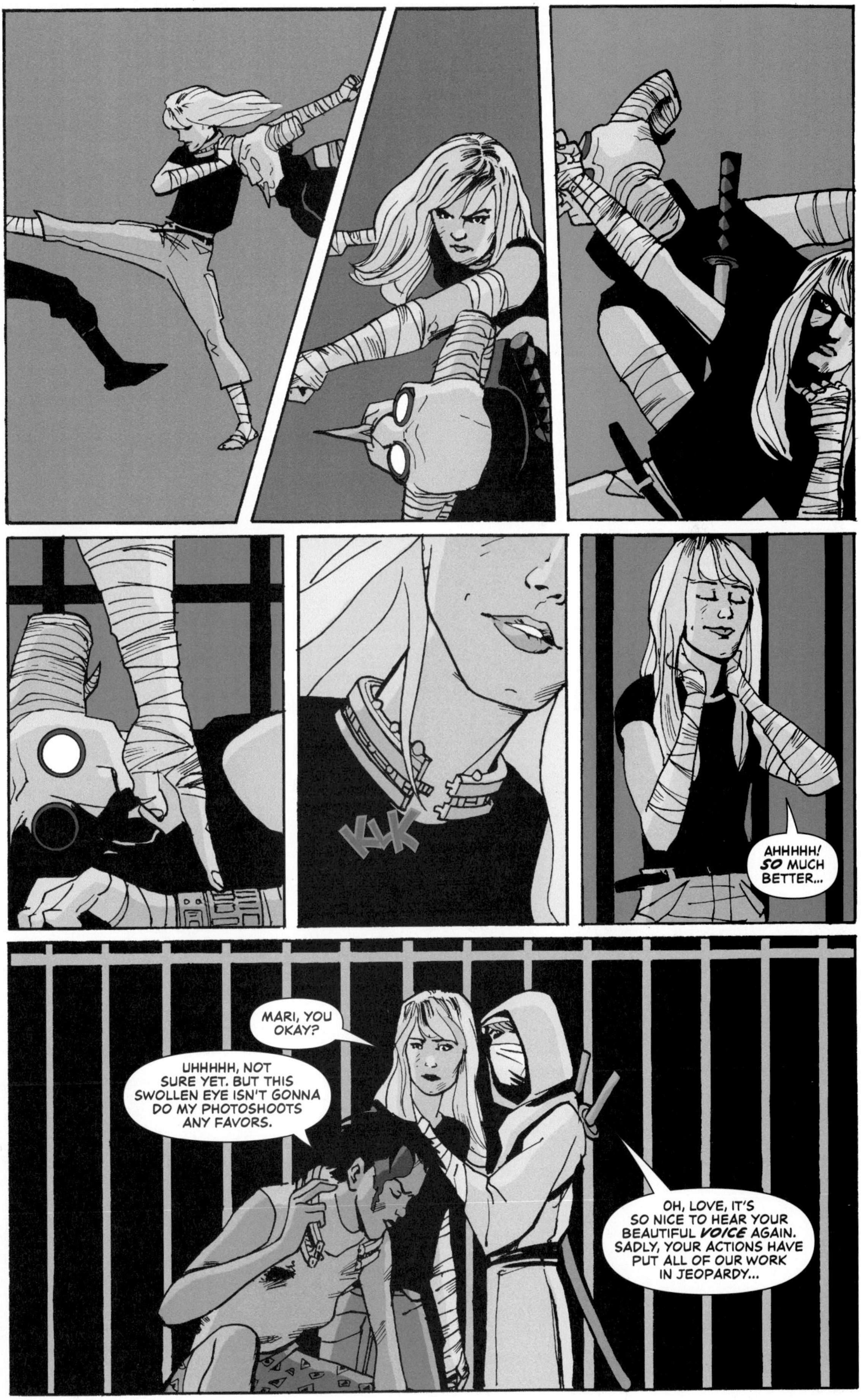
KLK
AHHHHH! SO MUCH BETTER...
MARI, YOU OKAY?
UHHHHH, NOT SURE YET. BUT THIS SWOLLEN EYE ISN'T GONNA DO MY PHOTOSHOOTS ANY FAVORS.
OH, LOVE, IT'S SO NICE TO HEAR YOUR BEAUTIFUL VOICE AGAIN. SADLY, YOUR ACTIONS HAVE PUT ALL OF OUR WORK IN JEOPARDY...

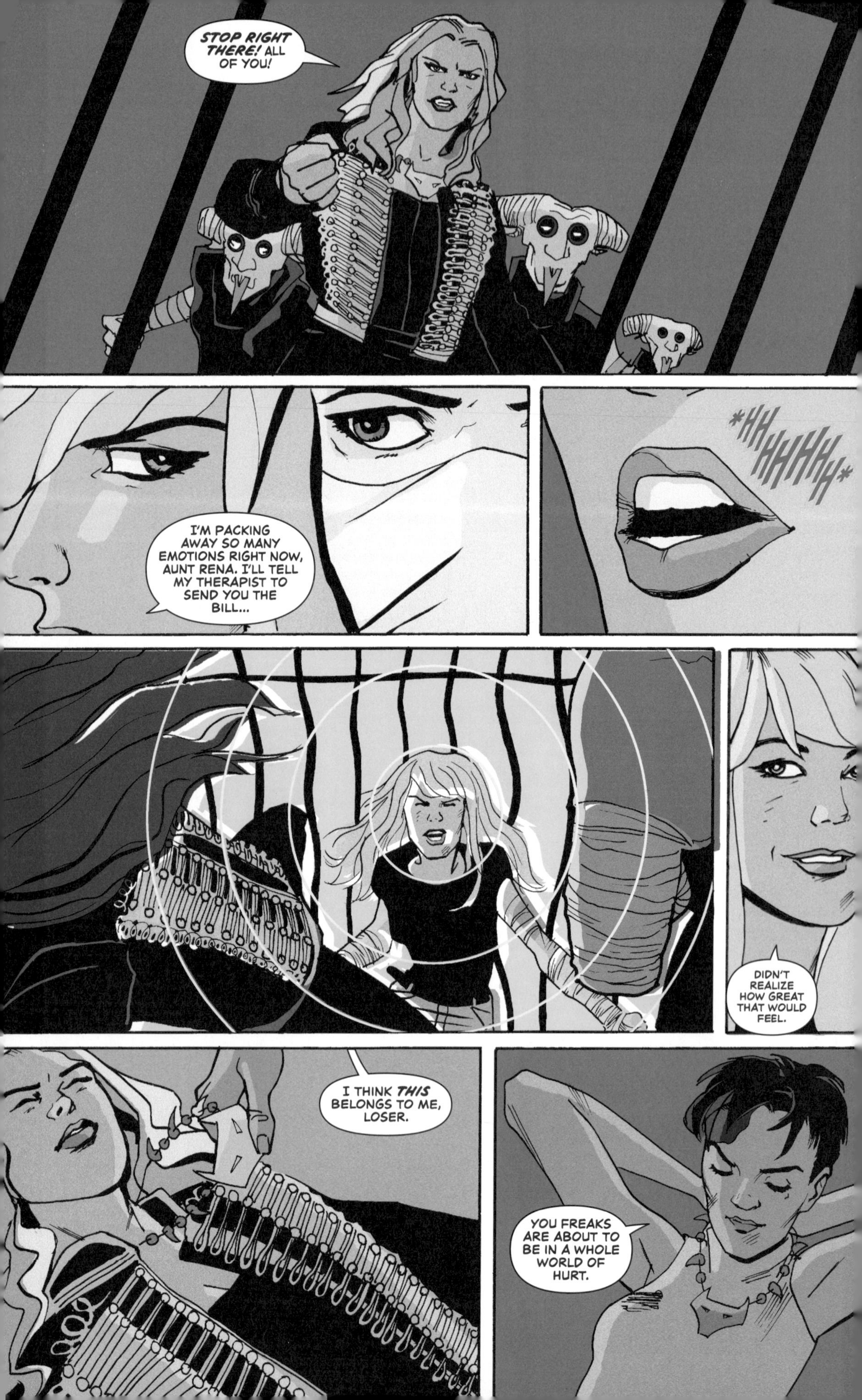
STOP RIGHT THERE! ALL OF YOU!
I'M PACKING AWAY SO MANY EMOTIONS RIGHT NOW, AUNT RENA. I'LL TELL MY THERAPIST TO SEND YOU THE BILL...
HHHHHHH
DIDN'T REALIZE HOW GREAT THAT WOULD FEEL.
I THINK THIS BELONGS TO ME, LOSER.
YOU FREAKS ARE ABOUT TO BE IN A WHOLE WORLD OF HURT.

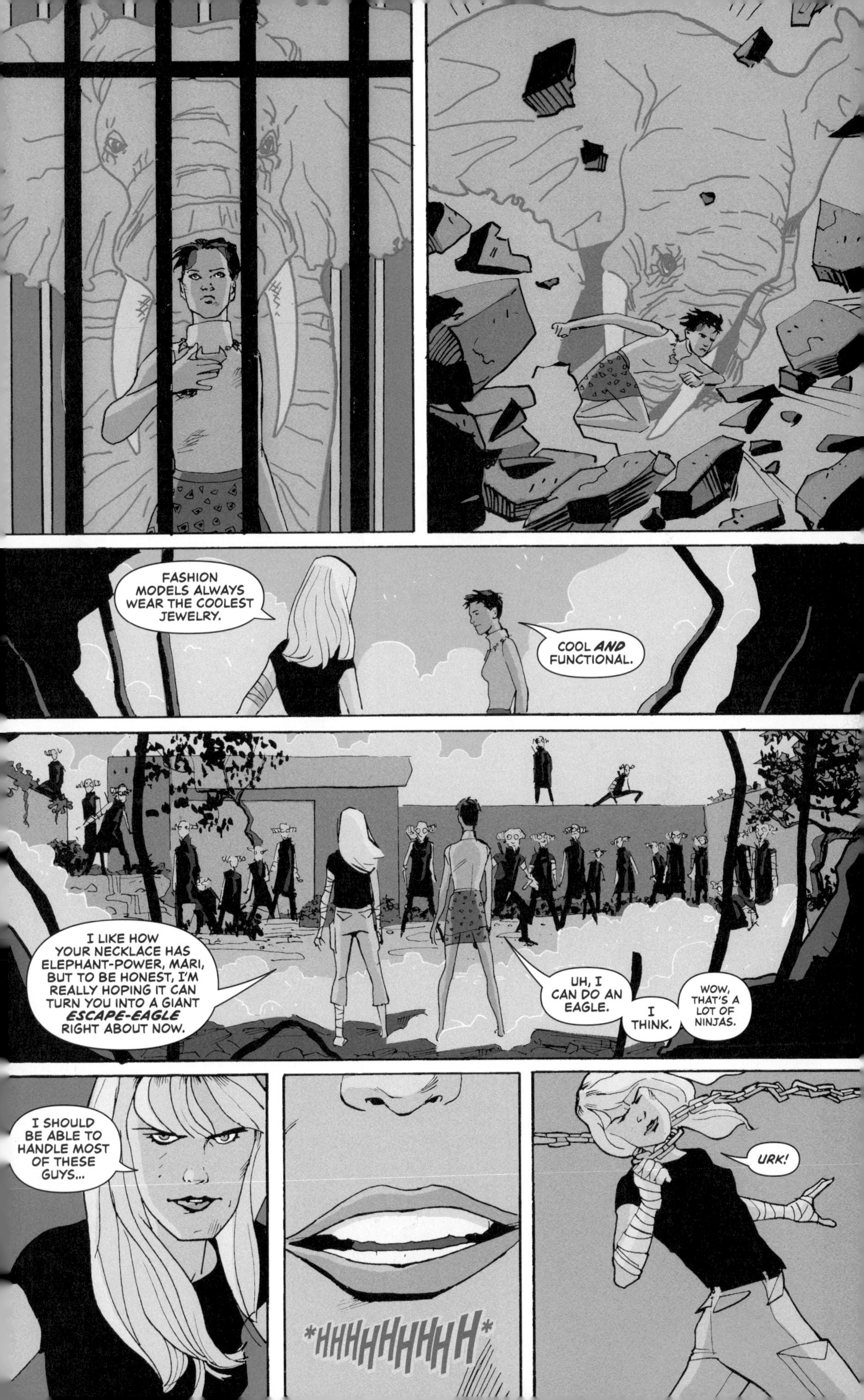
FASHION MODELS ALWAYS WEAR THE COOLEST JEWELRY.
COOL **AND** FUNCTIONAL.
I LIKE HOW YOUR NECKLACE HAS ELEPHANT-POWER, MARI, BUT TO BE HONEST, I'M REALLY HOPING IT CAN TURN YOU INTO A GIANT ***ESCAPE-EAGLE*** RIGHT ABOUT NOW.
UH, I CAN DO AN EAGLE.
I THINK.
WOW, THAT'S A LOT OF NINJAS.
I SHOULD BE ABLE TO HANDLE MOST OF THESE GUYS...
HHHHHHHHH
URK!

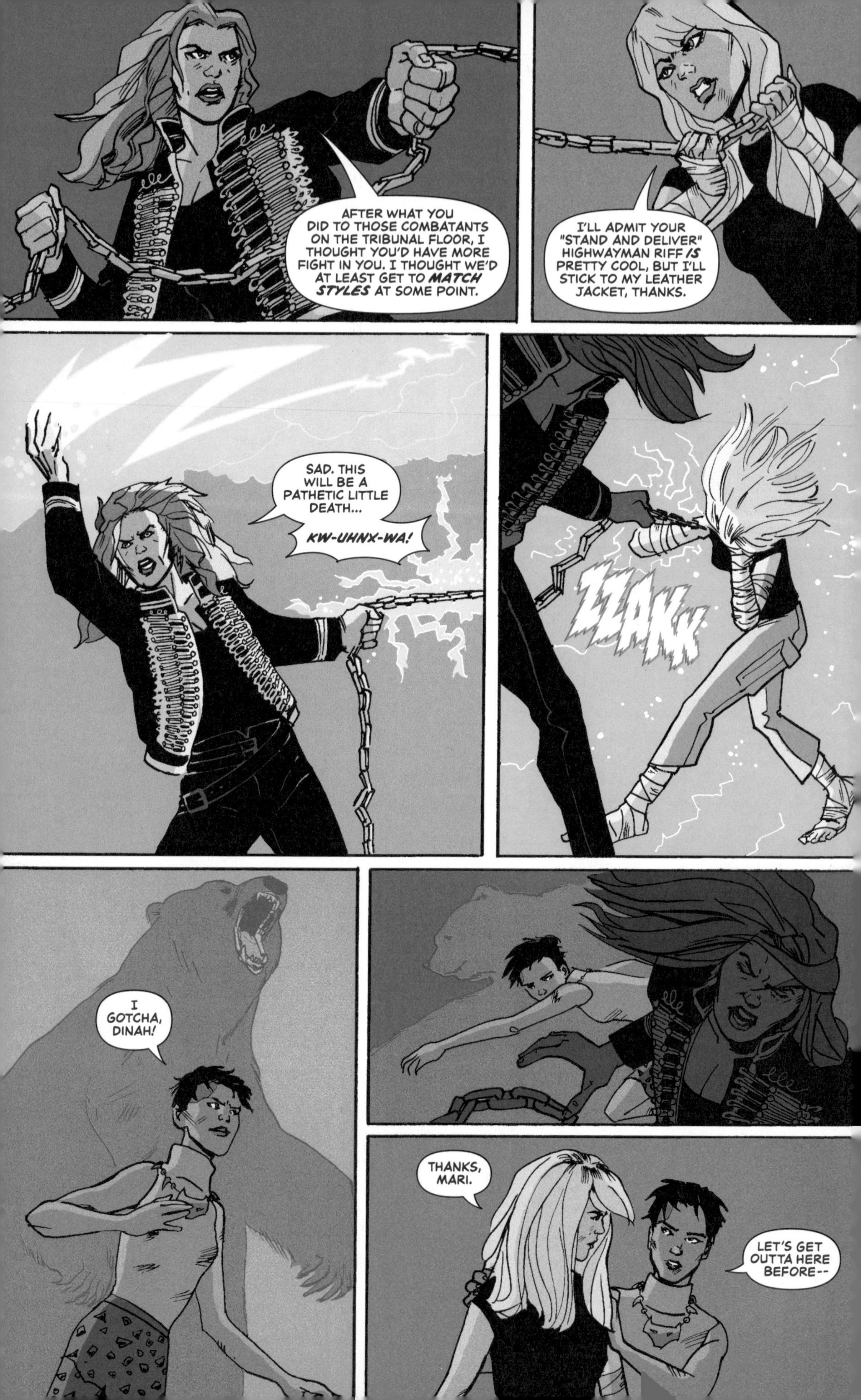
AFTER WHAT YOU DID TO THOSE COMBATANTS ON THE TRIBUNAL FLOOR, I THOUGHT YOU'D HAVE MORE FIGHT IN YOU. I THOUGHT WE'D AT LEAST GET TO MATCH STYLES AT SOME POINT.
I'LL ADMIT YOUR "STAND AND DELIVER" HIGHWAYMAN RIFF IS PRETTY COOL, BUT I'LL STICK TO MY LEATHER JACKET, THANKS.
SAD. THIS WILL BE A PATHETIC LITTLE DEATH...
KW-UHNX-WA!
ZZAKK
I GOTCHA, DINAH!
THANKS, MARI.
LET'S GET OUTTA HERE BEFORE--

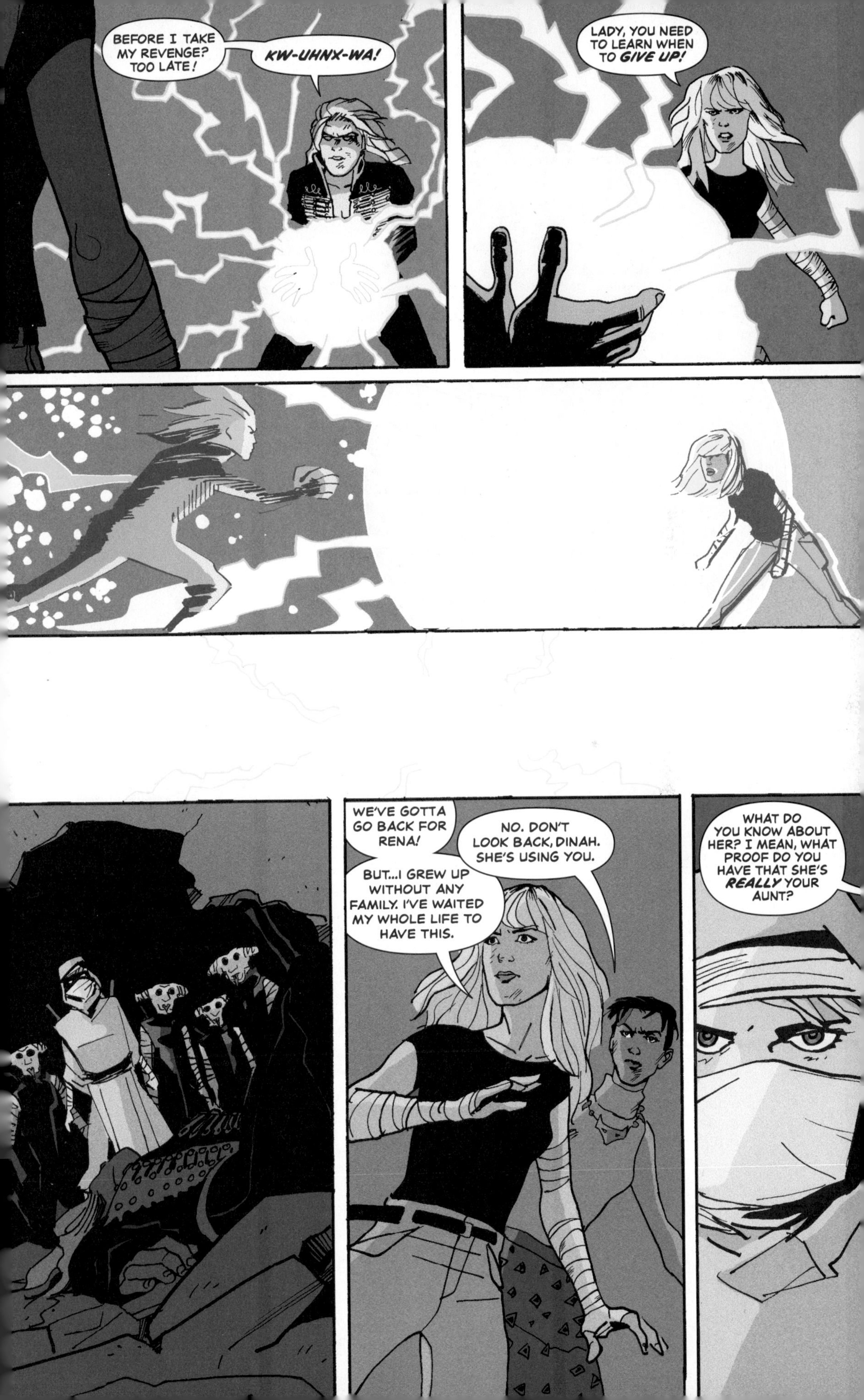
BEFORE I TAKE MY REVENGE? TOO LATE!
KW-UHNX-WA!
LADY, YOU NEED TO LEARN WHEN TO GIVE UP!
WE'VE GOTTA GO BACK FOR RENA!
NO. DON'T LOOK BACK, DINAH. SHE'S USING YOU.
BUT...I GREW UP WITHOUT ANY FAMILY. I'VE WAITED MY WHOLE LIFE TO HAVE THIS.
WHAT DO YOU KNOW ABOUT HER? I MEAN, WHAT PROOF DO YOU HAVE THAT SHE'S REALLY YOUR AUNT?

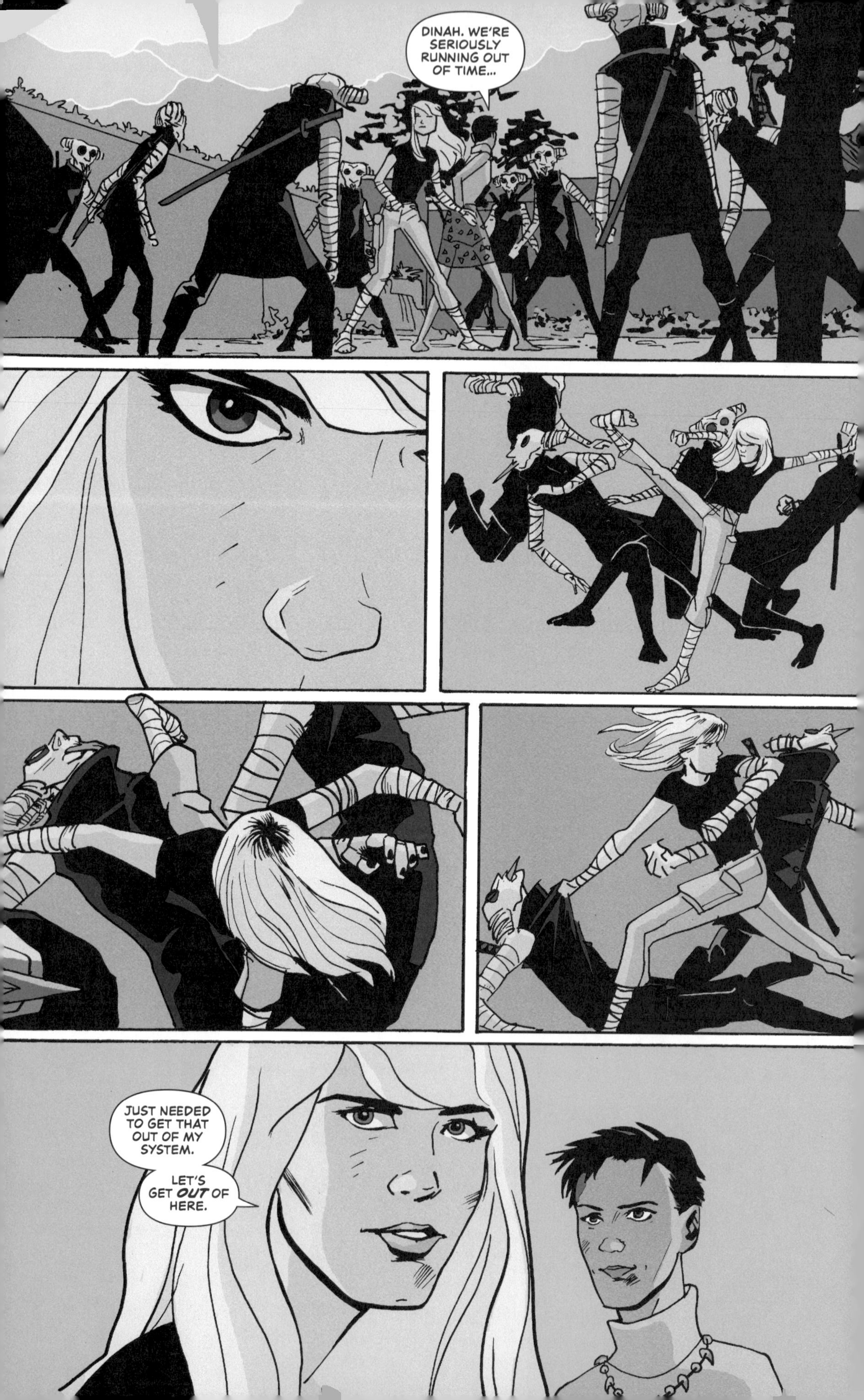
DINAH. WE'RE SERIOUSLY RUNNING OUT OF TIME...
JUST NEEDED TO GET THAT OUT OF MY SYSTEM.
LET'S GET OUT OF HERE.

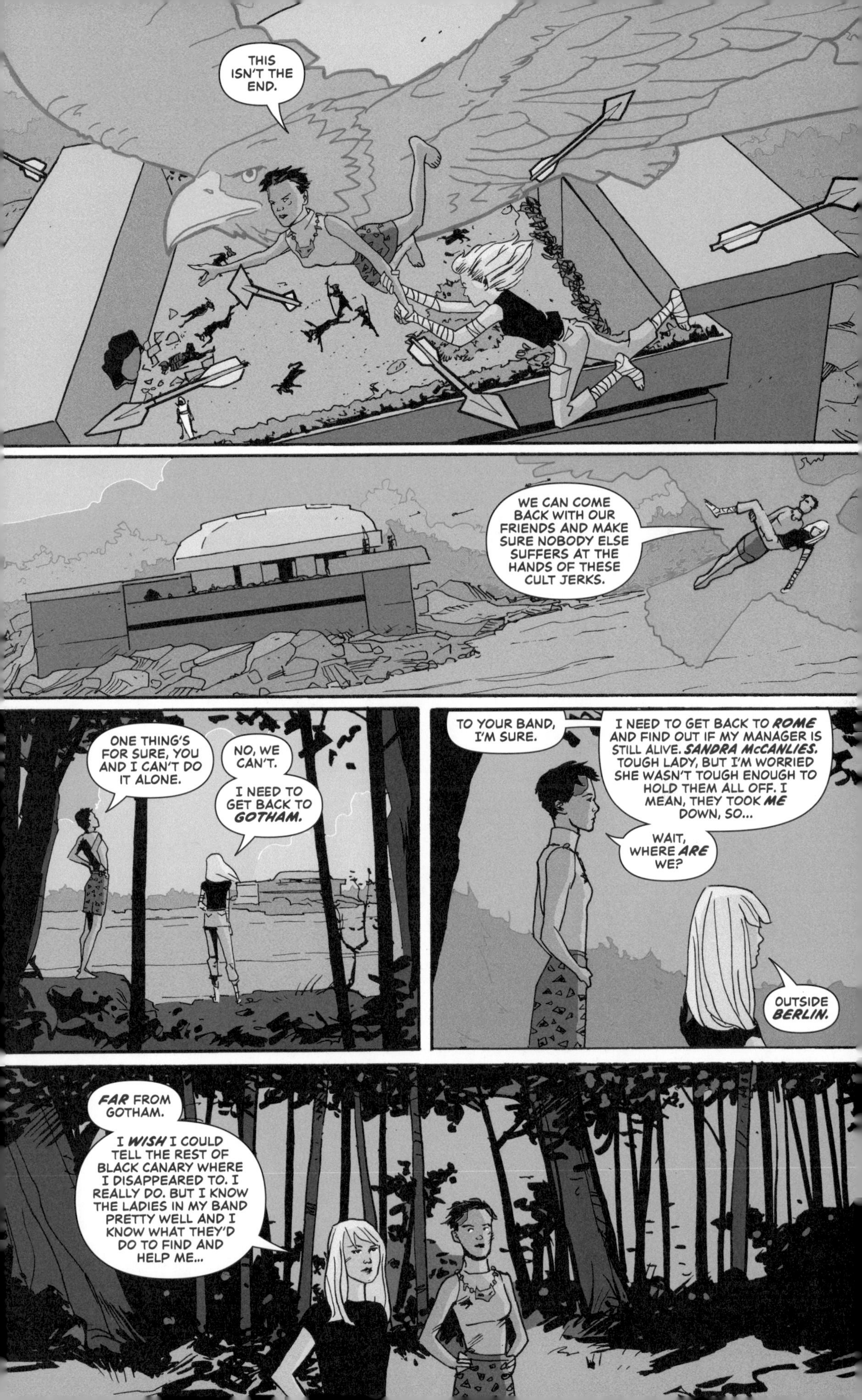
THIS ISN'T THE END.
WE CAN COME BACK WITH OUR FRIENDS AND MAKE SURE NOBODY ELSE SUFFERS AT THE HANDS OF THESE CULT JERKS.
ONE THING'S FOR SURE, YOU AND I CAN'T DO IT ALONE.
NO, WE CAN'T.
I NEED TO GET BACK TO GOTHAM.
TO YOUR BAND, I'M SURE.
I NEED TO GET BACK TO ROME AND FIND OUT IF MY MANAGER IS STILL ALIVE. SANDRA McCANLIES. TOUGH LADY, BUT I'M WORRIED SHE WASN'T TOUGH ENOUGH TO HOLD THEM ALL OFF. I MEAN, THEY TOOK ME DOWN, SO...
WAIT, WHERE ARE WE?
OUTSIDE BERLIN.
FAR FROM GOTHAM.
I WISH I COULD TELL THE REST OF BLACK CANARY WHERE I DISAPPEARED TO. I REALLY DO. BUT I KNOW THE LADIES IN MY BAND PRETTY WELL AND I KNOW WHAT THEY'D DO TO FIND AND HELP ME...

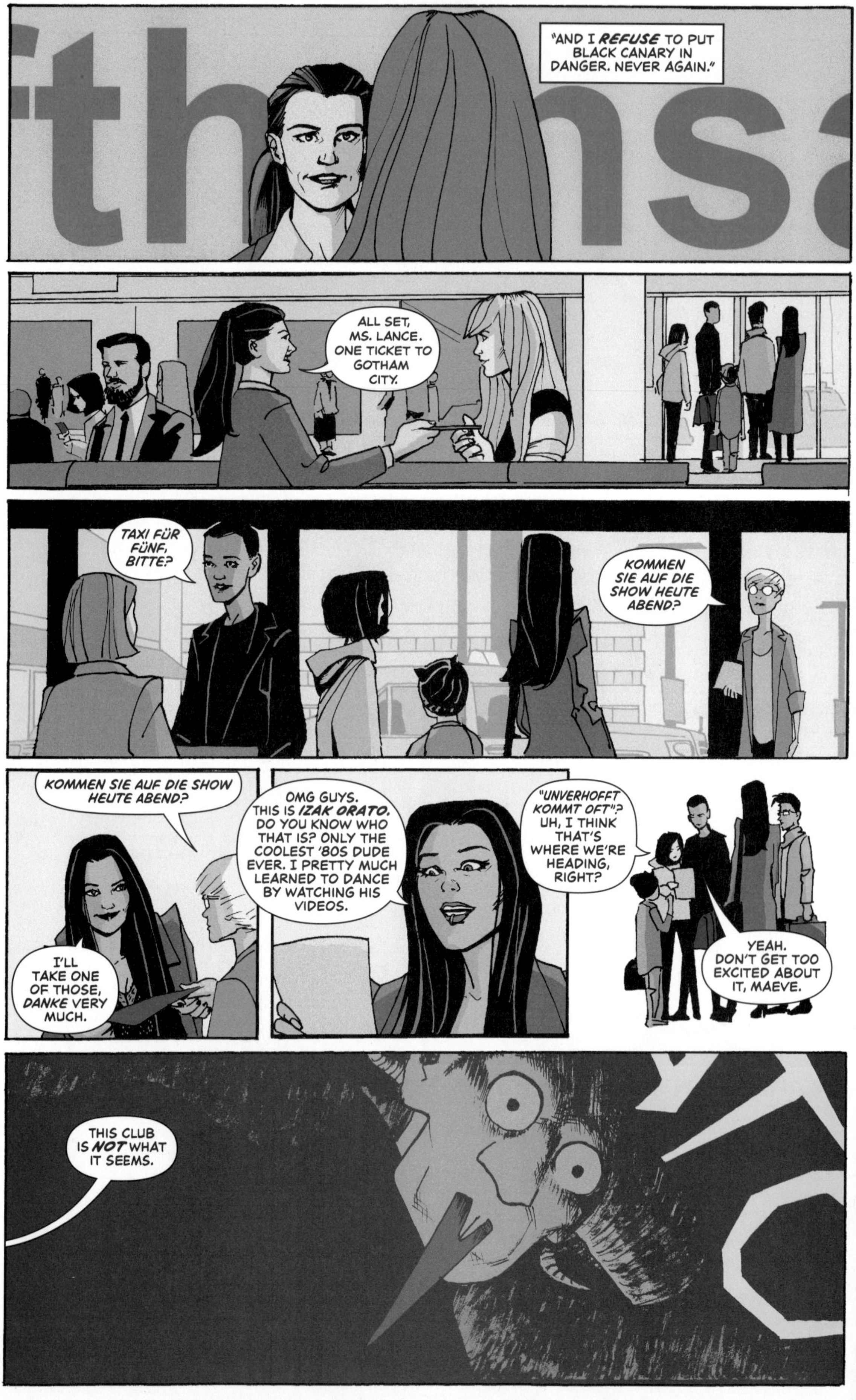
"AND I *REFUSE* TO PUT BLACK CANARY IN DANGER. NEVER AGAIN."
ALL SET, MS. LANCE. ONE TICKET TO GOTHAM CITY.
TAXI FÜR FÜNF, BITTE?
KOMMEN SIE AUF DIE SHOW HEUTE ABEND?
KOMMEN SIE AUF DIE SHOW HEUTE ABEND?
I'LL TAKE ONE OF THOSE, *DANKE* VERY MUCH.
OMG GUYS. THIS IS *IZAK ORATO.* DO YOU KNOW WHO THAT IS? ONLY THE COOLEST '80S DUDE EVER. I PRETTY MUCH LEARNED TO DANCE BY WATCHING HIS VIDEOS.
"UNVERHOFFT KOMMT OFT"? UH, I THINK THAT'S WHERE WE'RE HEADING, RIGHT?
YEAH. DON'T GET TOO EXCITED ABOUT IT, MAEVE.
THIS CLUB IS *NOT* WHAT IT SEEMS.

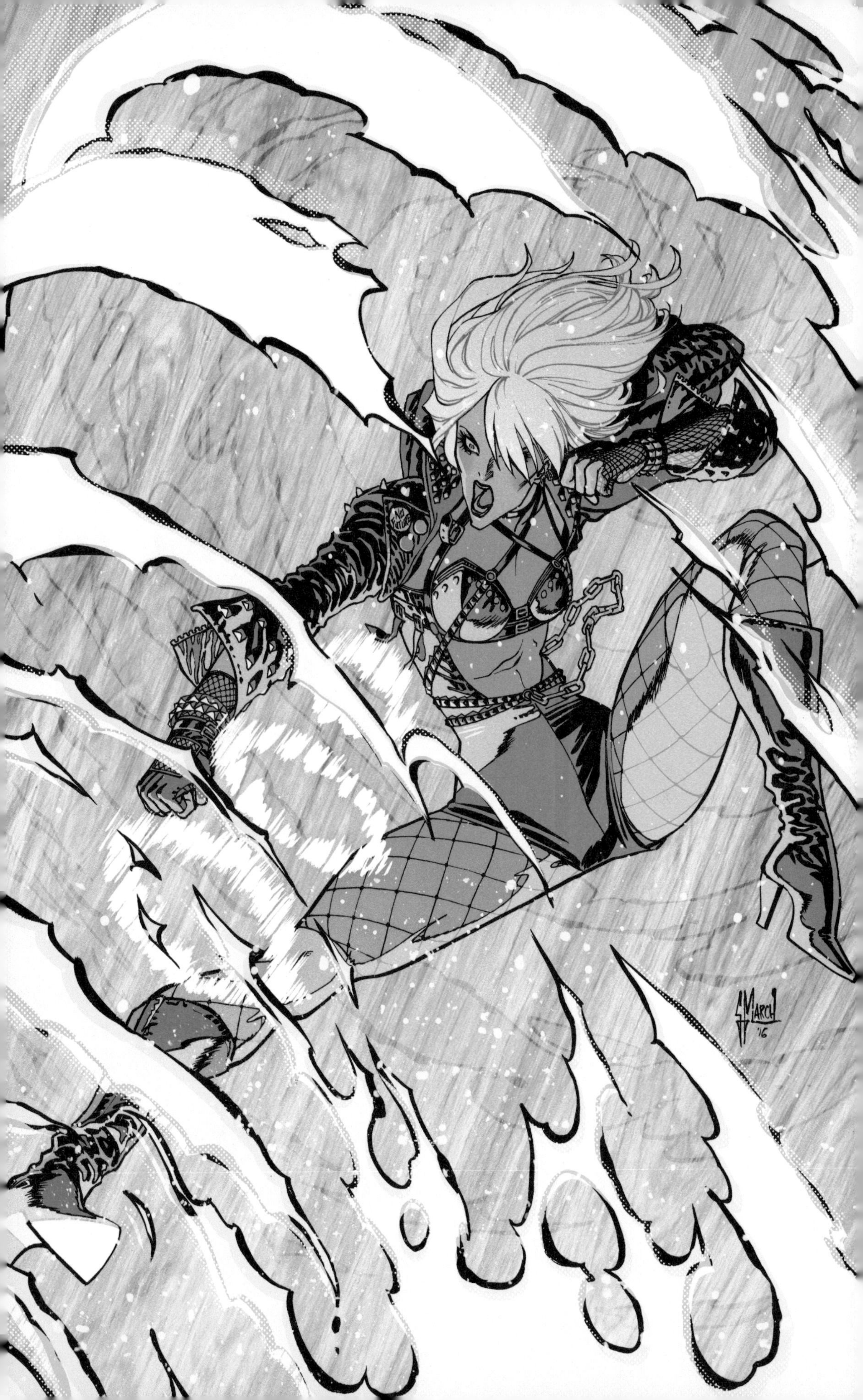

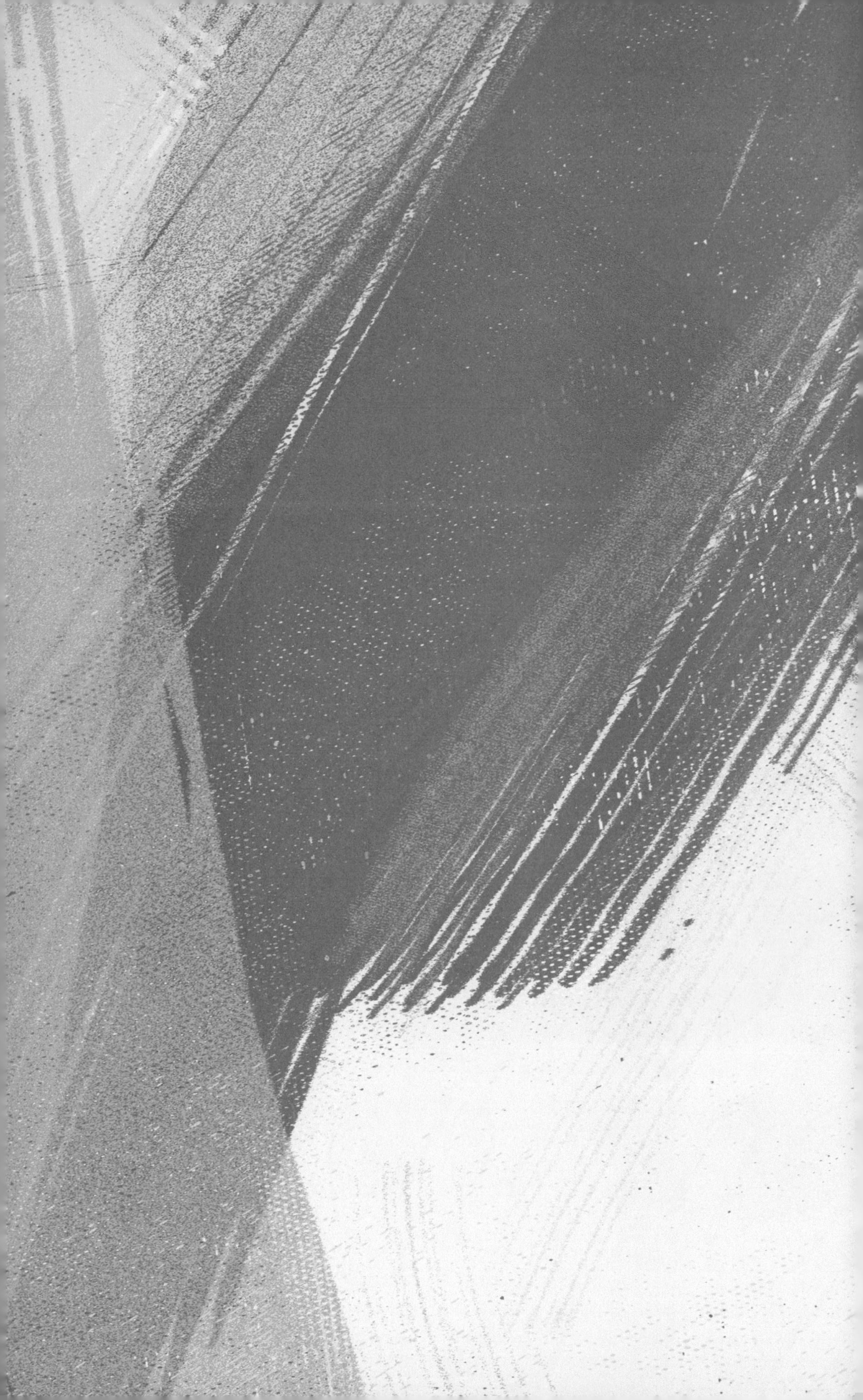

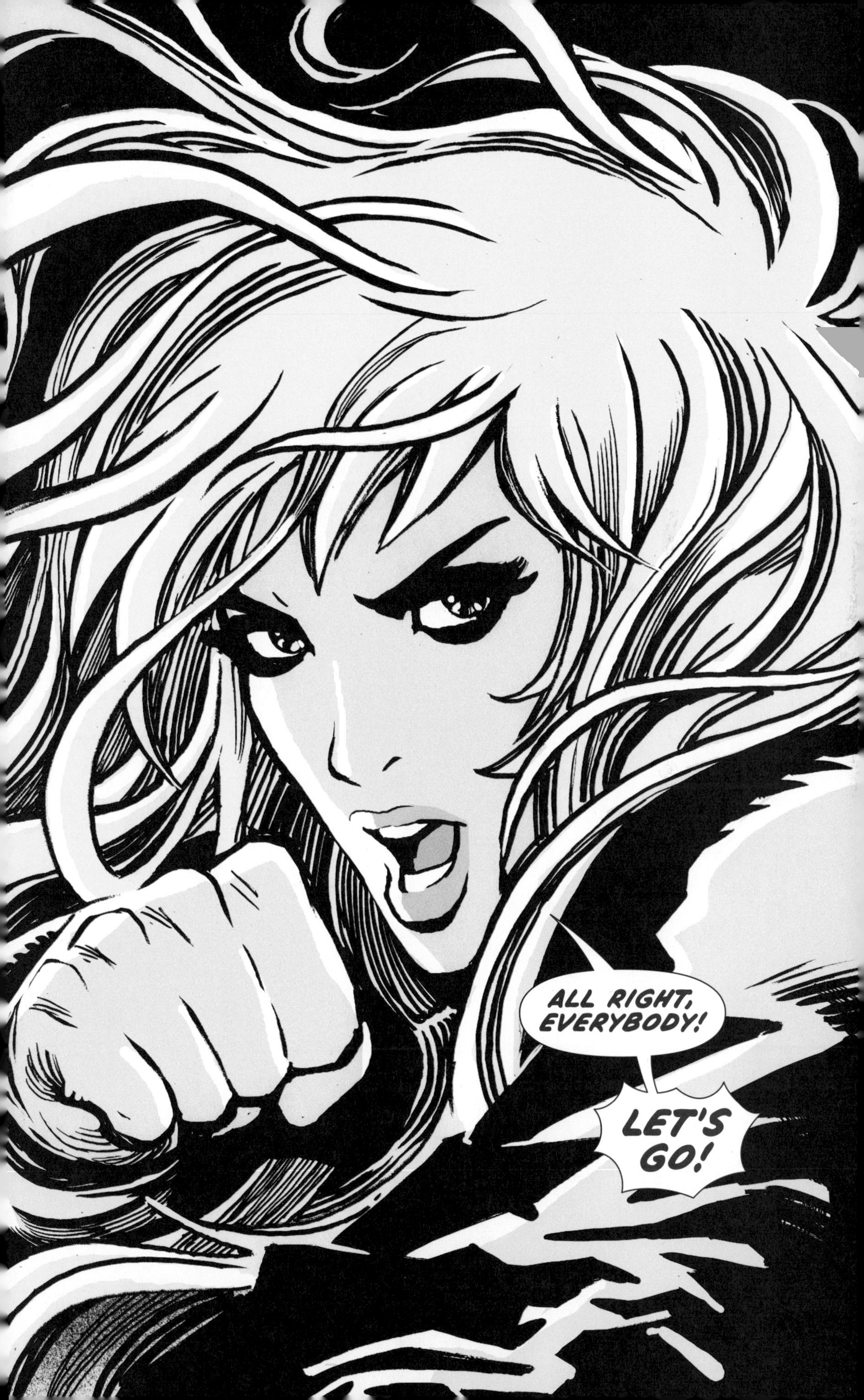
ALL RIGHT, EVERYBODY!
LET'S GO!

TWO HOURS EARLIER.

We're bringing you the never-before-seen story of an unpublicized secret show from Black Canary's debut tour—a concert played before their lives went completely bonkers with aliens, and spies, and living sound creatures, and etc. etc. etc.! Even in those early days, though, it was never easy...

MADDEN

KNOCK
KNOCK

THIS SUUUUUCKS.

STOP BEING SUCH A DOWNER.

YES?

WE'RE THE BAND.

YOU'RE RIGHT, BYRON. THIS DOESN'T SUCK. AT ALL.

GOOD SECURITY IS...

OBNOXIOUS?

IMPORTANT. THIS WHAT WE DO, PALOMA.

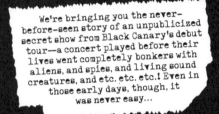
WE PLAY IN A BAND. TO MAKE FANS.

AND MONEY.

AND MONEY.

OH, YOU MUST BE THE BAND. I'M ALLEGRA MADDEN.

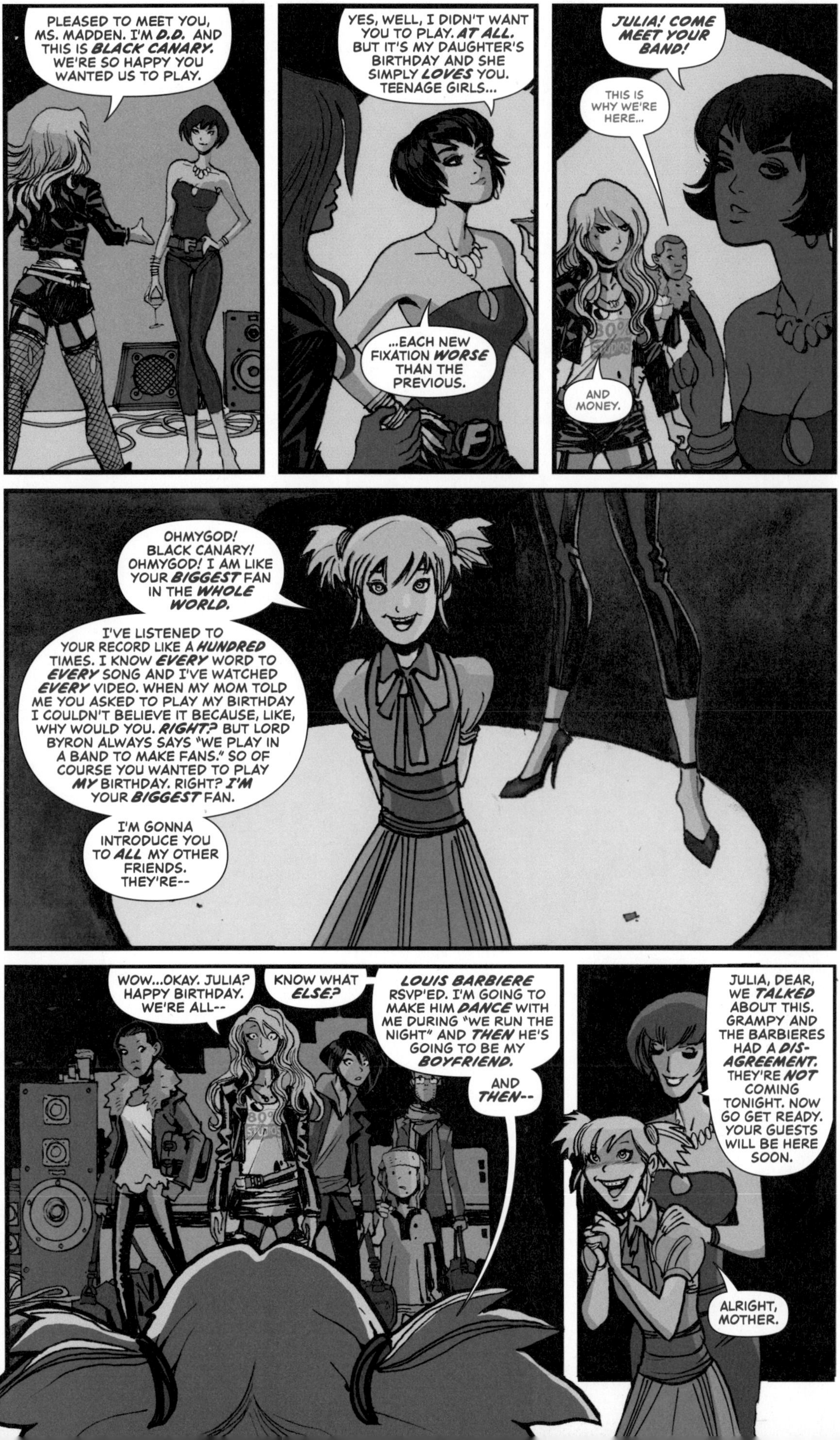
PLEASED TO MEET YOU, MS. MADDEN. I'M D.D. AND THIS IS BLACK CANARY. WE'RE SO HAPPY YOU WANTED US TO PLAY.
YES, WELL, I DIDN'T WANT YOU TO PLAY. AT ALL. BUT IT'S MY DAUGHTER'S BIRTHDAY AND SHE SIMPLY LOVES YOU. TEENAGE GIRLS...
...EACH NEW FIXATION WORSE THAN THE PREVIOUS.
JULIA! COME MEET YOUR BAND!
THIS IS WHY WE'RE HERE...
AND MONEY.
OHMYGOD! BLACK CANARY! OHMYGOD! I AM LIKE YOUR BIGGEST FAN IN THE WHOLE WORLD.
I'VE LISTENED TO YOUR RECORD LIKE A HUNDRED TIMES. I KNOW EVERY WORD TO EVERY SONG AND I'VE WATCHED EVERY VIDEO. WHEN MY MOM TOLD ME YOU ASKED TO PLAY MY BIRTHDAY I COULDN'T BELIEVE IT BECAUSE, LIKE, WHY WOULD YOU. RIGHT? BUT LORD BYRON ALWAYS SAYS "WE PLAY IN A BAND TO MAKE FANS." SO OF COURSE YOU WANTED TO PLAY MY BIRTHDAY. RIGHT? I'M YOUR BIGGEST FAN.
I'M GONNA INTRODUCE YOU TO ALL MY OTHER FRIENDS. THEY'RE--
WOW...OKAY. JULIA? HAPPY BIRTHDAY. WE'RE ALL--
KNOW WHAT ELSE?
LOUIS BARBIERE RSVP'ED. I'M GOING TO MAKE HIM DANCE WITH ME DURING "WE RUN THE NIGHT" AND THEN HE'S GOING TO BE MY BOYFRIEND.
AND THEN--
JULIA, DEAR, WE TALKED ABOUT THIS. GRAMPY AND THE BARBIERES HAD A DIS-AGREEMENT. THEY'RE NOT COMING TONIGHT. NOW GO GET READY. YOUR GUESTS WILL BE HERE SOON.
ALRIGHT, MOTHER.

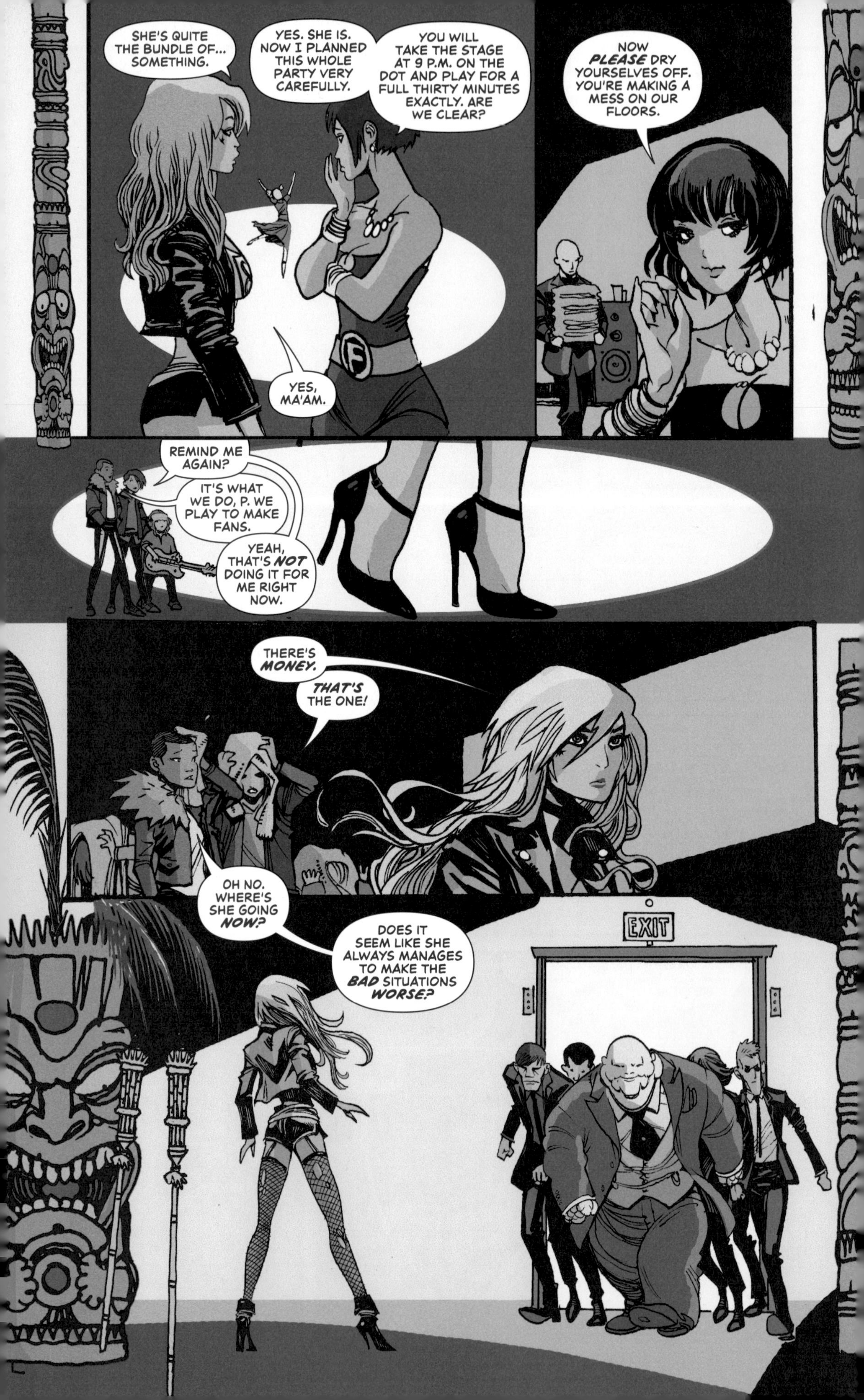
SHE'S QUITE THE BUNDLE OF... SOMETHING.
YES. SHE IS. NOW I PLANNED THIS WHOLE PARTY VERY CAREFULLY.
YOU WILL TAKE THE STAGE AT 9 P.M. ON THE DOT AND PLAY FOR A FULL THIRTY MINUTES EXACTLY. ARE WE CLEAR?
YES, MA'AM.
NOW *PLEASE* DRY YOURSELVES OFF. YOU'RE MAKING A MESS ON OUR FLOORS.
REMIND ME AGAIN?
IT'S WHAT WE DO, P. WE PLAY TO MAKE FANS.
YEAH, THAT'S *NOT* DOING IT FOR ME RIGHT NOW.
THERE'S *MONEY.*
THAT'S THE ONE!
OH NO. WHERE'S SHE GOING *NOW?*
DOES IT SEEM LIKE SHE ALWAYS MANAGES TO MAKE THE *BAD* SITUATIONS *WORSE?*
EXIT

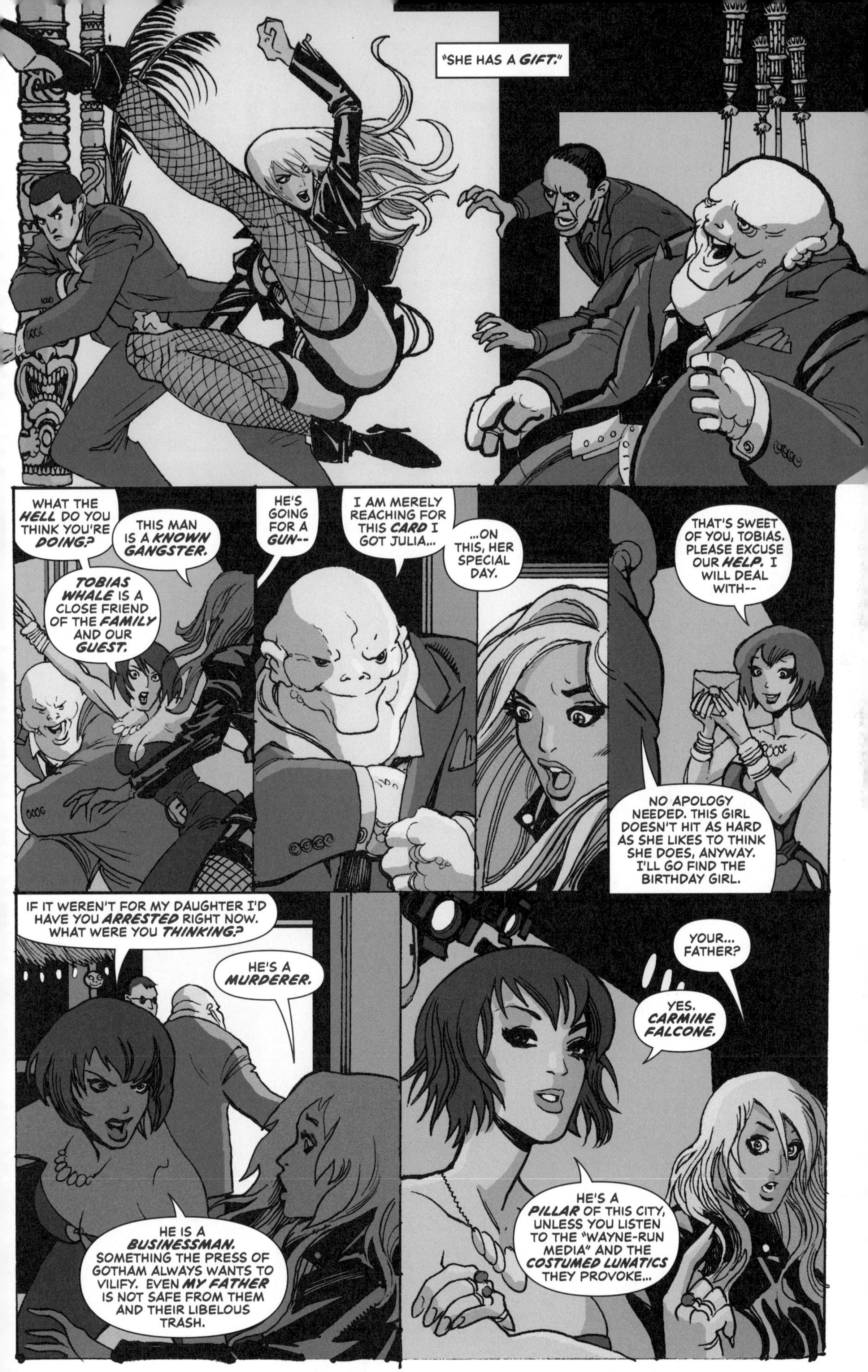
"SHE HAS A GIFT."
WHAT THE HELL DO YOU THINK YOU'RE DOING?
THIS MAN IS A KNOWN GANGSTER.
TOBIAS WHALE IS A CLOSE FRIEND OF THE FAMILY AND OUR GUEST.
HE'S GOING FOR A GUN--
I AM MERELY REACHING FOR THIS CARD I GOT JULIA...
...ON THIS, HER SPECIAL DAY.
THAT'S SWEET OF YOU, TOBIAS. PLEASE EXCUSE OUR HELP. I WILL DEAL WITH--
NO APOLOGY NEEDED. THIS GIRL DOESN'T HIT AS HARD AS SHE LIKES TO THINK SHE DOES, ANYWAY. I'LL GO FIND THE BIRTHDAY GIRL.
IF IT WEREN'T FOR MY DAUGHTER I'D HAVE YOU ARRESTED RIGHT NOW. WHAT WERE YOU THINKING?
HE'S A MURDERER.
HE IS A BUSINESSMAN. SOMETHING THE PRESS OF GOTHAM ALWAYS WANTS TO VILIFY. EVEN MY FATHER IS NOT SAFE FROM THEM AND THEIR LIBELOUS TRASH.
YOUR... FATHER?
YES. CARMINE FALCONE.
HE'S A PILLAR OF THIS CITY, UNLESS YOU LISTEN TO THE "WAYNE-RUN MEDIA" AND THE COSTUMED LUNATICS THEY PROVOKE...

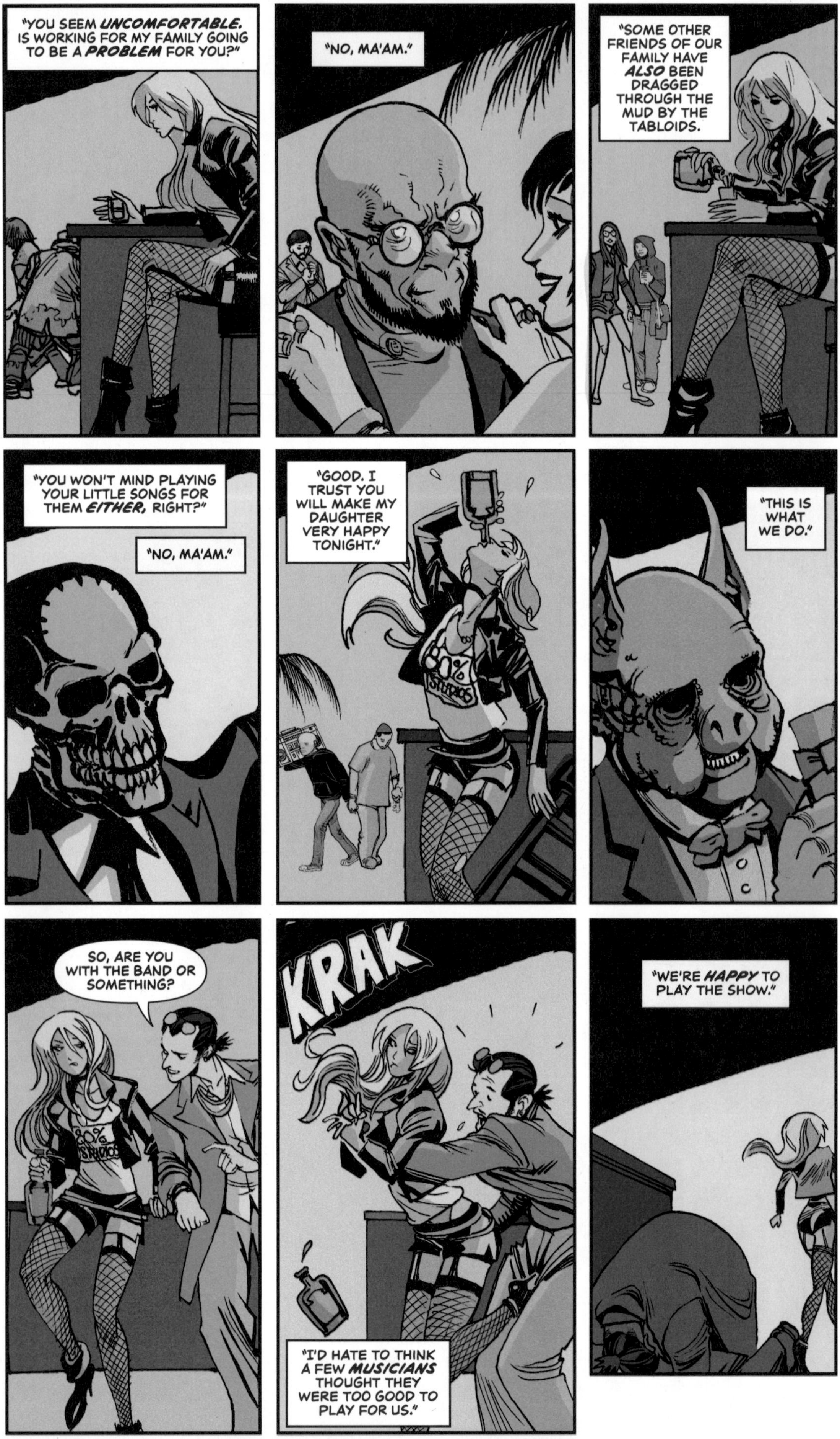
"YOU SEEM UNCOMFORTABLE. IS WORKING FOR MY FAMILY GOING TO BE A PROBLEM FOR YOU?"
"NO, MA'AM."
"SOME OTHER FRIENDS OF OUR FAMILY HAVE ALSO BEEN DRAGGED THROUGH THE MUD BY THE TABLOIDS.
"YOU WON'T MIND PLAYING YOUR LITTLE SONGS FOR THEM EITHER, RIGHT?"
"NO, MA'AM."
"GOOD. I TRUST YOU WILL MAKE MY DAUGHTER VERY HAPPY TONIGHT."
"THIS IS WHAT WE DO."
SO, ARE YOU WITH THE BAND OR SOMETHING?
KRAK
"I'D HATE TO THINK A FEW MUSICIANS THOUGHT THEY WERE TOO GOOD TO PLAY FOR US."
"WE'RE HAPPY TO PLAY THE SHOW."

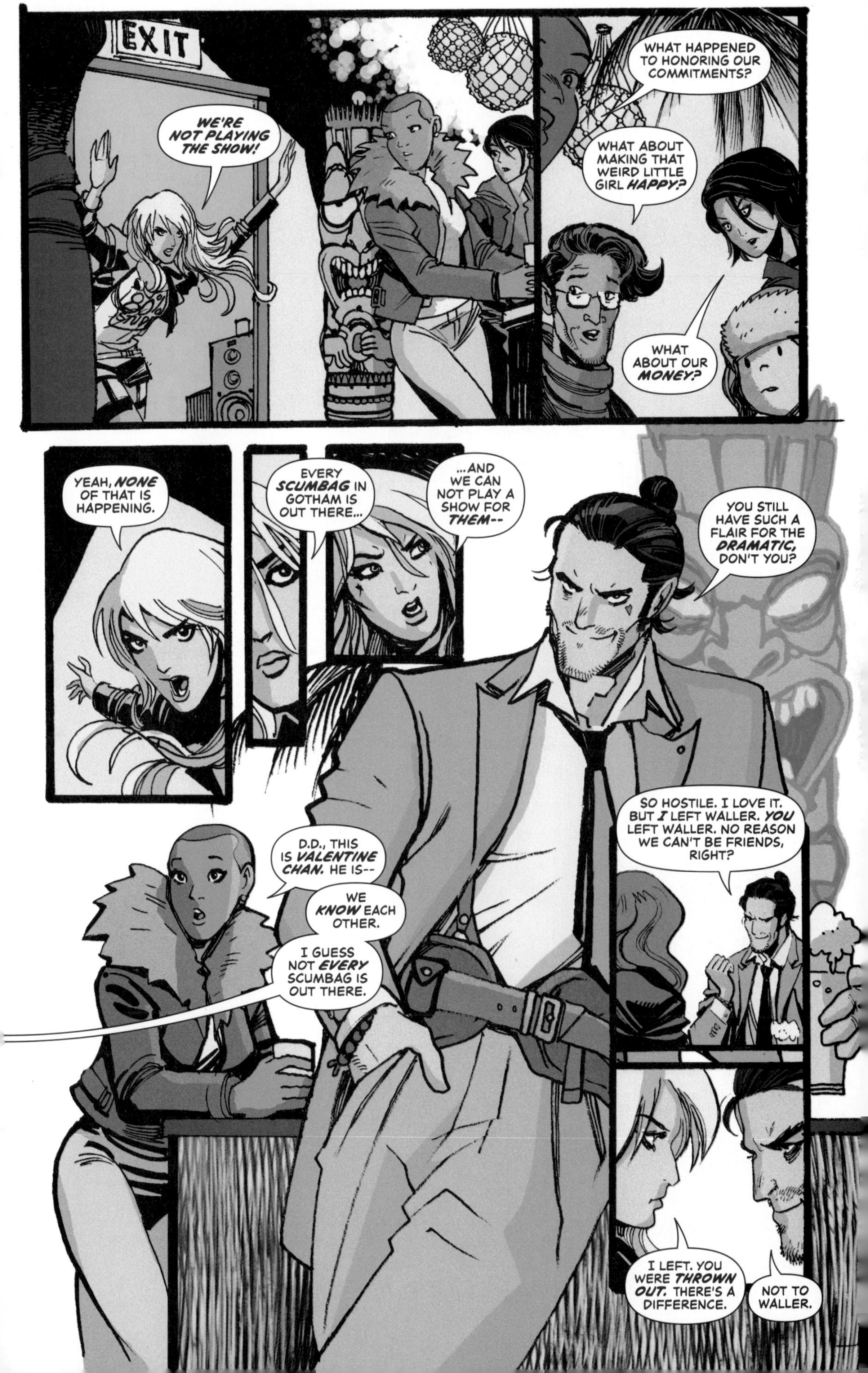

EXIT
WE'RE NOT PLAYING THE SHOW!
WHAT HAPPENED TO HONORING OUR COMMITMENTS?
WHAT ABOUT MAKING THAT WEIRD LITTLE GIRL HAPPY?
WHAT ABOUT OUR MONEY?
YEAH, NONE OF THAT IS HAPPENING.
EVERY SCUMBAG IN GOTHAM IS OUT THERE...
...AND WE CAN NOT PLAY A SHOW FOR THEM--
YOU STILL HAVE SUCH A FLAIR FOR THE DRAMATIC, DON'T YOU?
D.D., THIS IS VALENTINE CHAN. HE IS--
WE KNOW EACH OTHER.
I GUESS NOT EVERY SCUMBAG IS OUT THERE.
SO HOSTILE. I LOVE IT. BUT I LEFT WALLER. YOU LEFT WALLER. NO REASON WE CAN'T BE FRIENDS, RIGHT?
I LEFT. YOU WERE THROWN OUT. THERE'S A DIFFERENCE.
NOT TO WALLER.

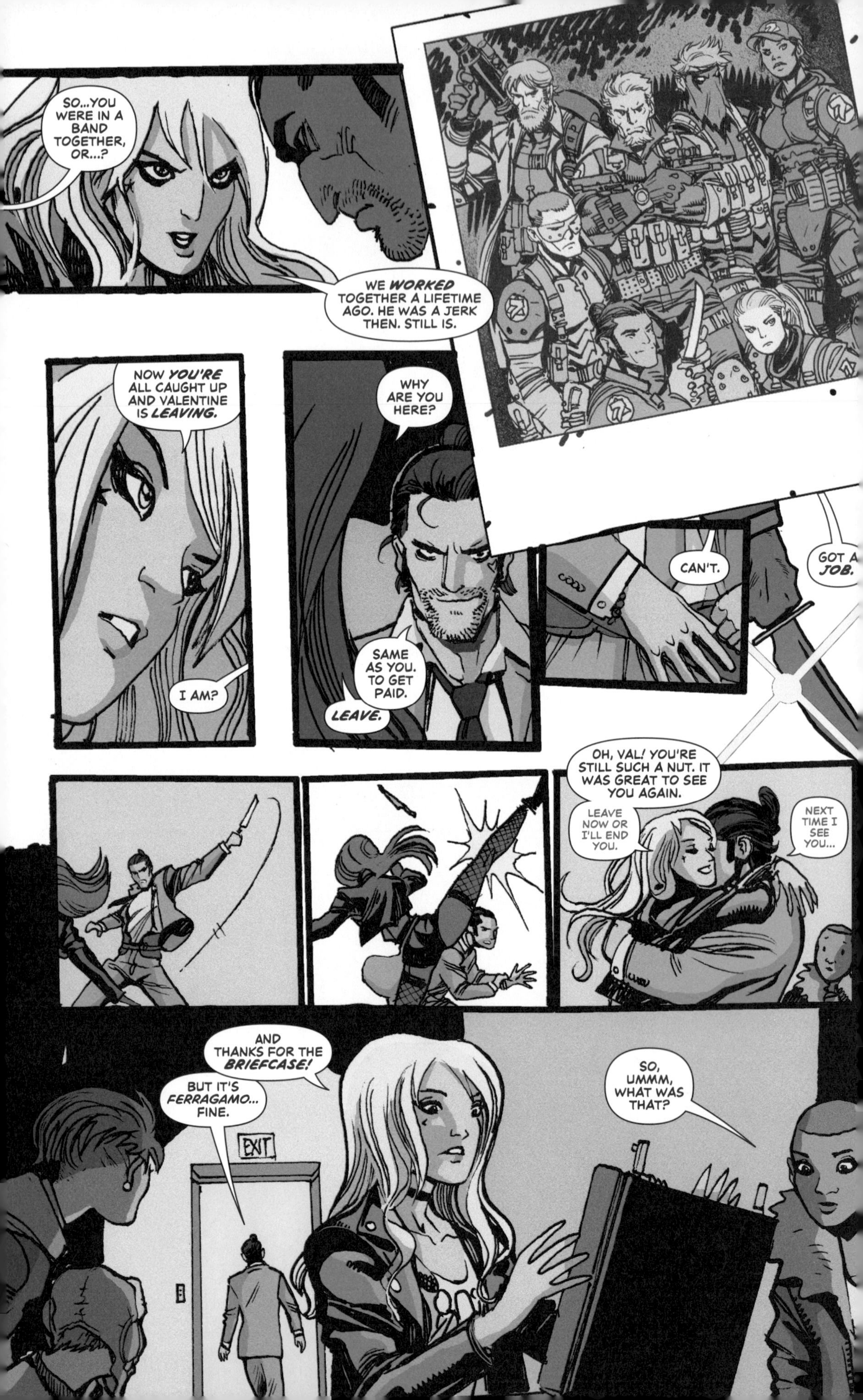
SO...YOU WERE IN A BAND TOGETHER, OR...?
WE *WORKED* TOGETHER A LIFETIME AGO. HE WAS A JERK THEN. STILL IS.
NOW *YOU'RE* ALL CAUGHT UP AND VALENTINE IS *LEAVING.*
I AM?
WHY ARE YOU HERE?
SAME AS YOU. TO GET PAID.
LEAVE.
CAN'T.
GOT A *JOB.*
OH, VAL! YOU'RE STILL SUCH A NUT. IT WAS GREAT TO SEE YOU AGAIN.
LEAVE NOW OR I'LL END YOU.
NEXT TIME I SEE YOU...
AND THANKS FOR THE *BRIEFCASE!*
BUT IT'S *FERRAGAMO...* FINE.
EXIT
SO, UMMM, WHAT WAS THAT?

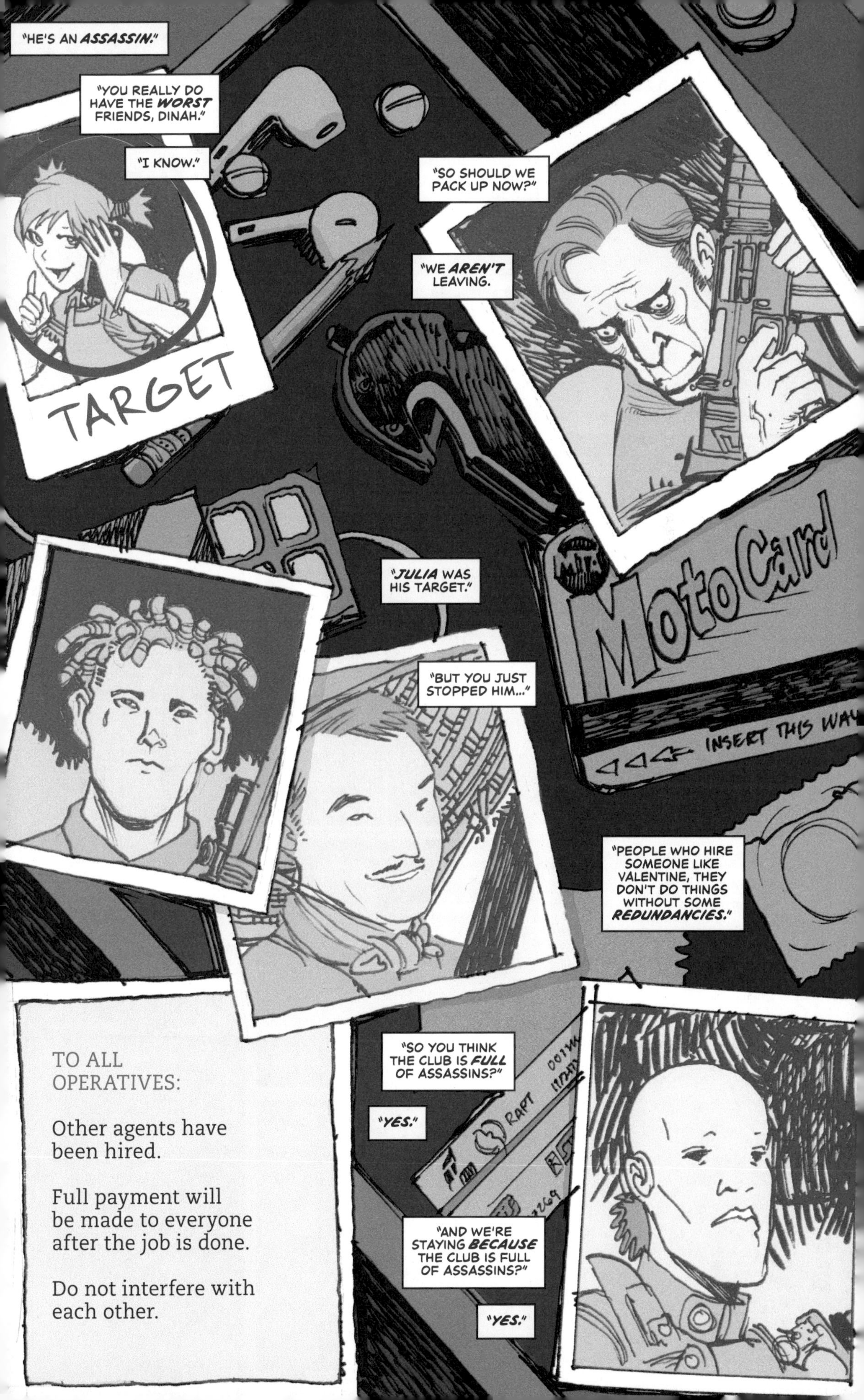
"HE'S AN ASSASSIN."
"YOU REALLY DO HAVE THE WORST FRIENDS, DINAH."
"I KNOW."
TARGET
"SO SHOULD WE PACK UP NOW?"
"WE AREN'T LEAVING.
MotoCard
"JULIA WAS HIS TARGET."
"BUT YOU JUST STOPPED HIM..."
"PEOPLE WHO HIRE SOMEONE LIKE VALENTINE, THEY DON'T DO THINGS WITHOUT SOME REDUNDANCIES."
TO ALL OPERATIVES:
Other agents have been hired.
Full payment will be made to everyone after the job is done.
Do not interfere with each other.
"SO YOU THINK THE CLUB IS FULL OF ASSASSINS?"
"YES."
"AND WE'RE STAYING BECAUSE THE CLUB IS FULL OF ASSASSINS?"
"YES."

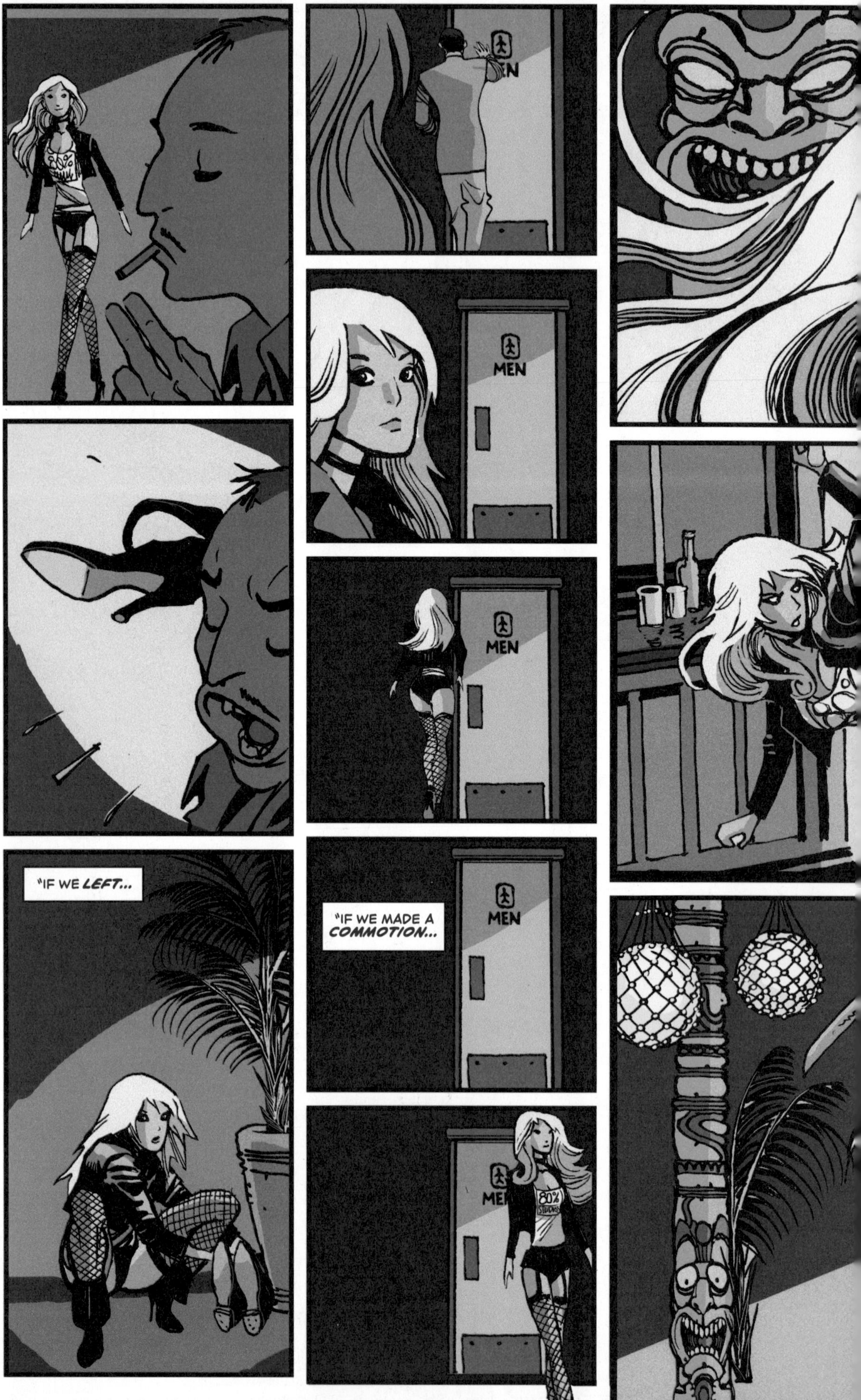
MEN
MEN
MEN
"IF WE LEFT...
"IF WE MADE A COMMOTION...
MEN
80%

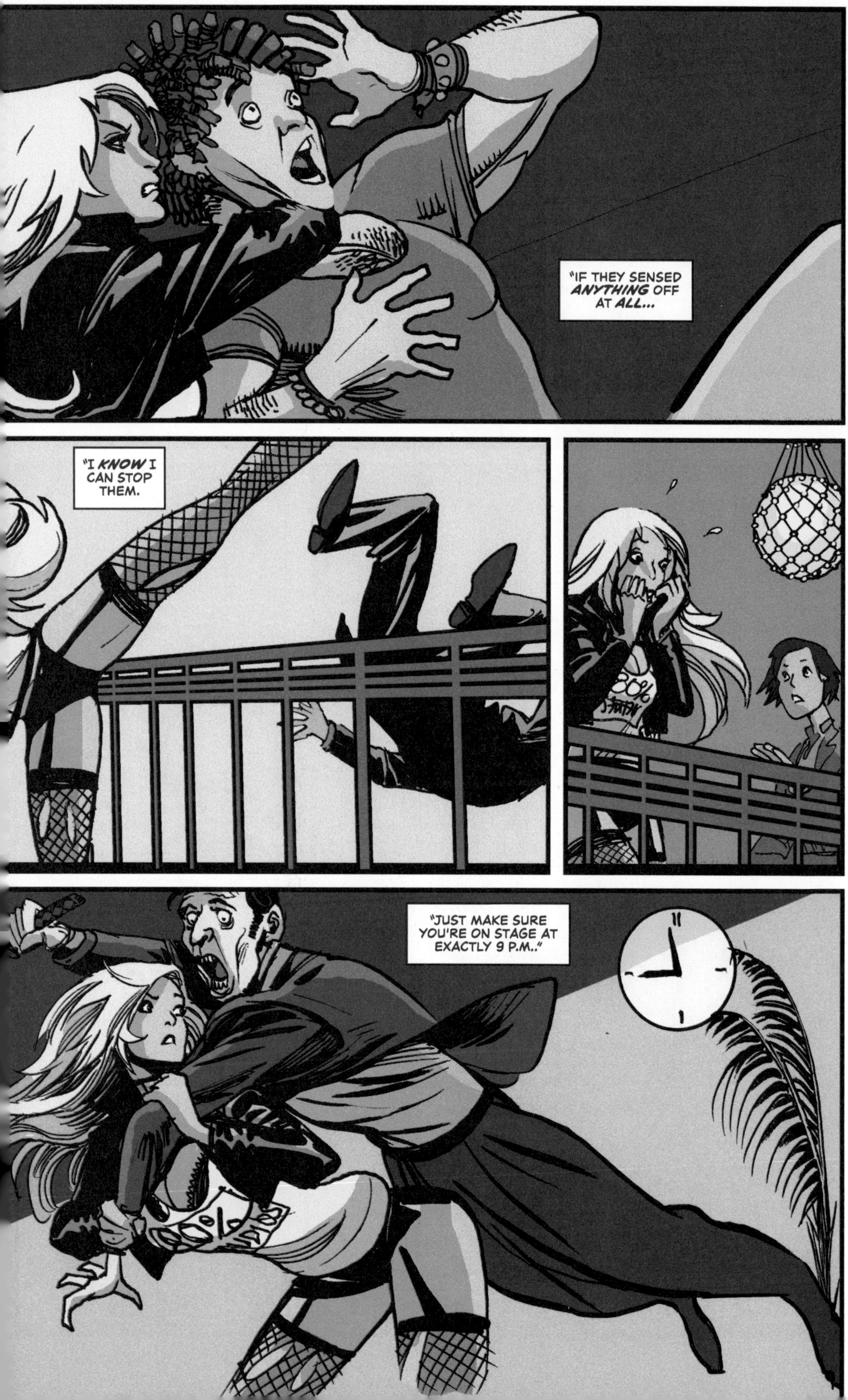
"IF THEY SENSED ANYTHING OFF AT ALL...
"I KNOW I CAN STOP THEM.
"JUST MAKE SURE YOU'RE ON STAGE AT EXACTLY 9 P.M.."

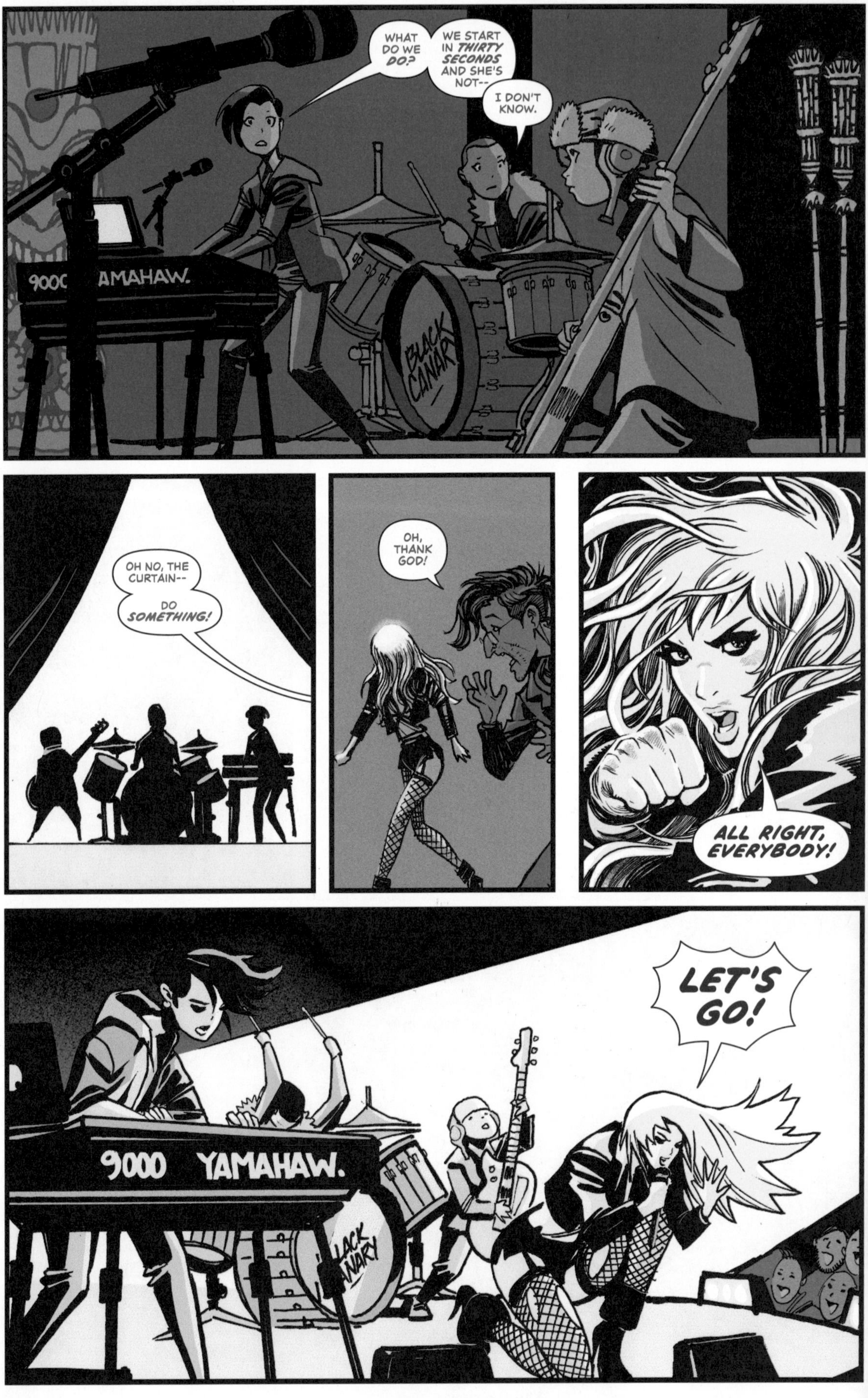
WHAT DO WE DO?
WE START IN THIRTY SECONDS AND SHE'S NOT--
I DON'T KNOW.
9000 YAMAHAW.
BLACK CANAR
OH NO, THE CURTAIN--
DO SOMETHING!
OH, THANK GOD!
ALL RIGHT, EVERYBODY!
LET'S GO!
9000 YAMAHAW.
LACK ANARY

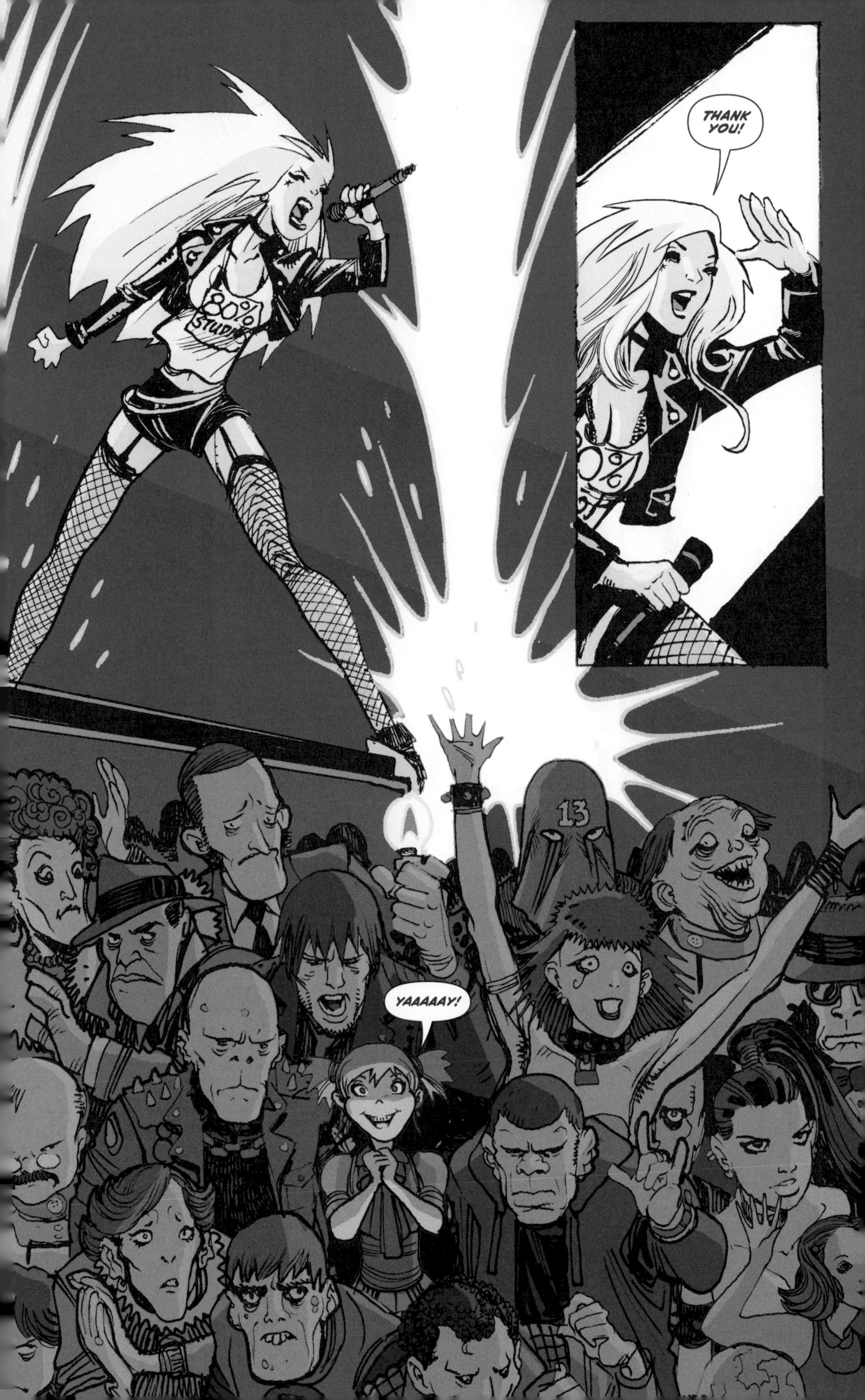
THANK YOU!
YAAAAAY!

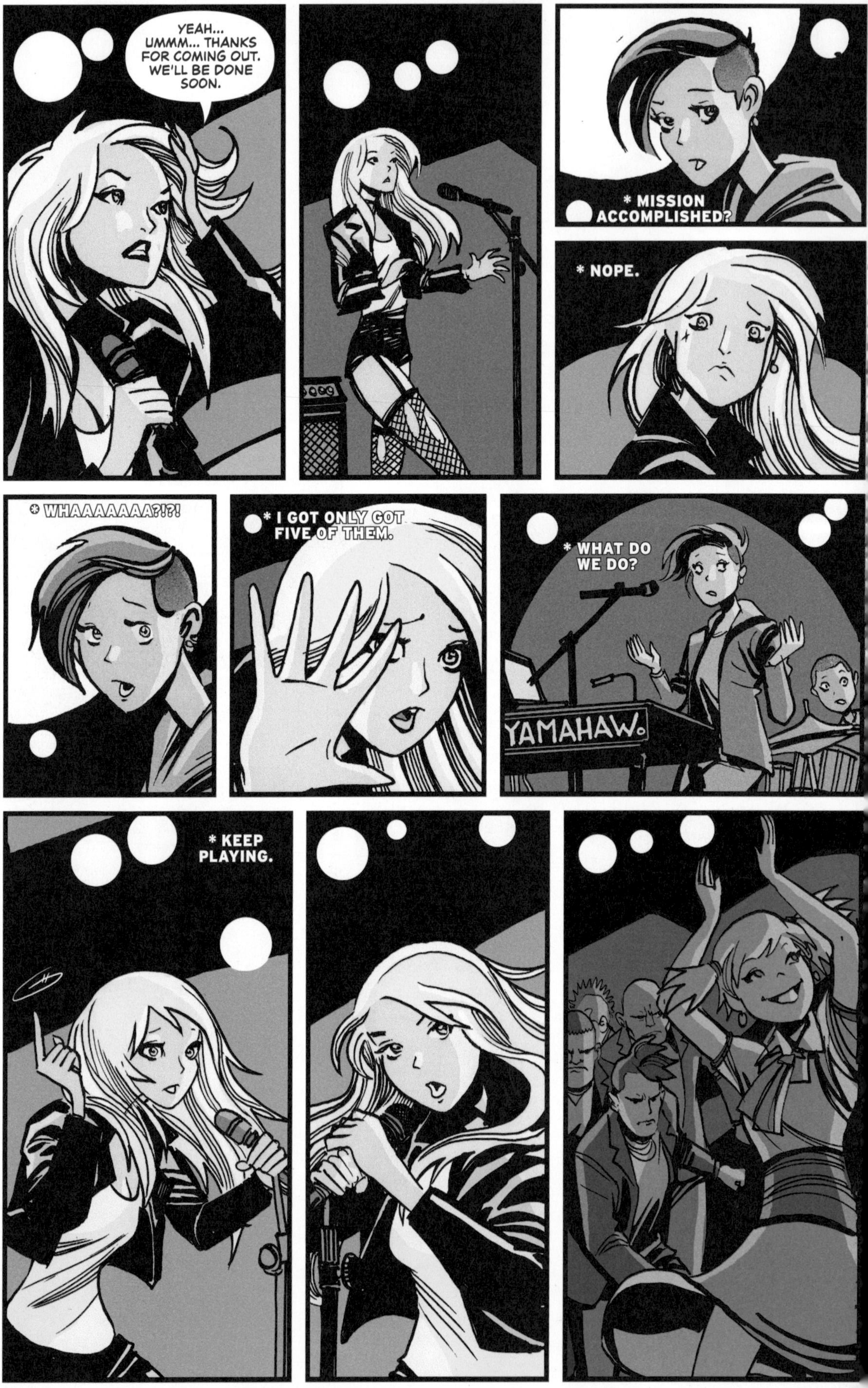
YEAH... UMMM... THANKS FOR COMING OUT. WE'LL BE DONE SOON.
* MISSION ACCOMPLISHED?
* NOPE.
* WHAAAAAAA?!?!
* I GOT ONLY GOT FIVE OF THEM.
* WHAT DO WE DO?
YAMAHAW.
* KEEP PLAYING.

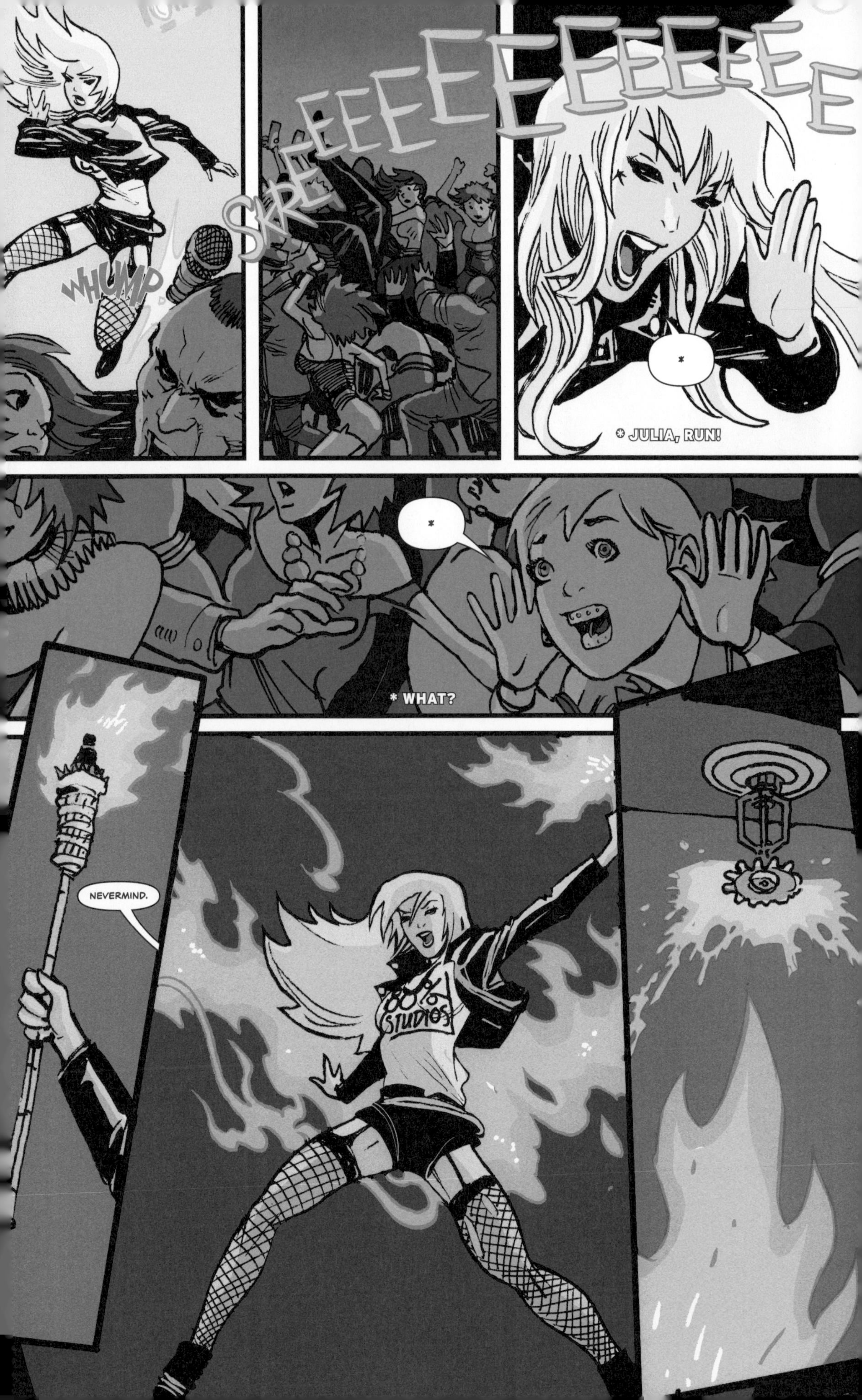
WHUMP
SKREEEEEEEEEEEEEEE
*
* JULIA, RUN!
*
* WHAT?
NEVERMIND.
80% STUDIOS

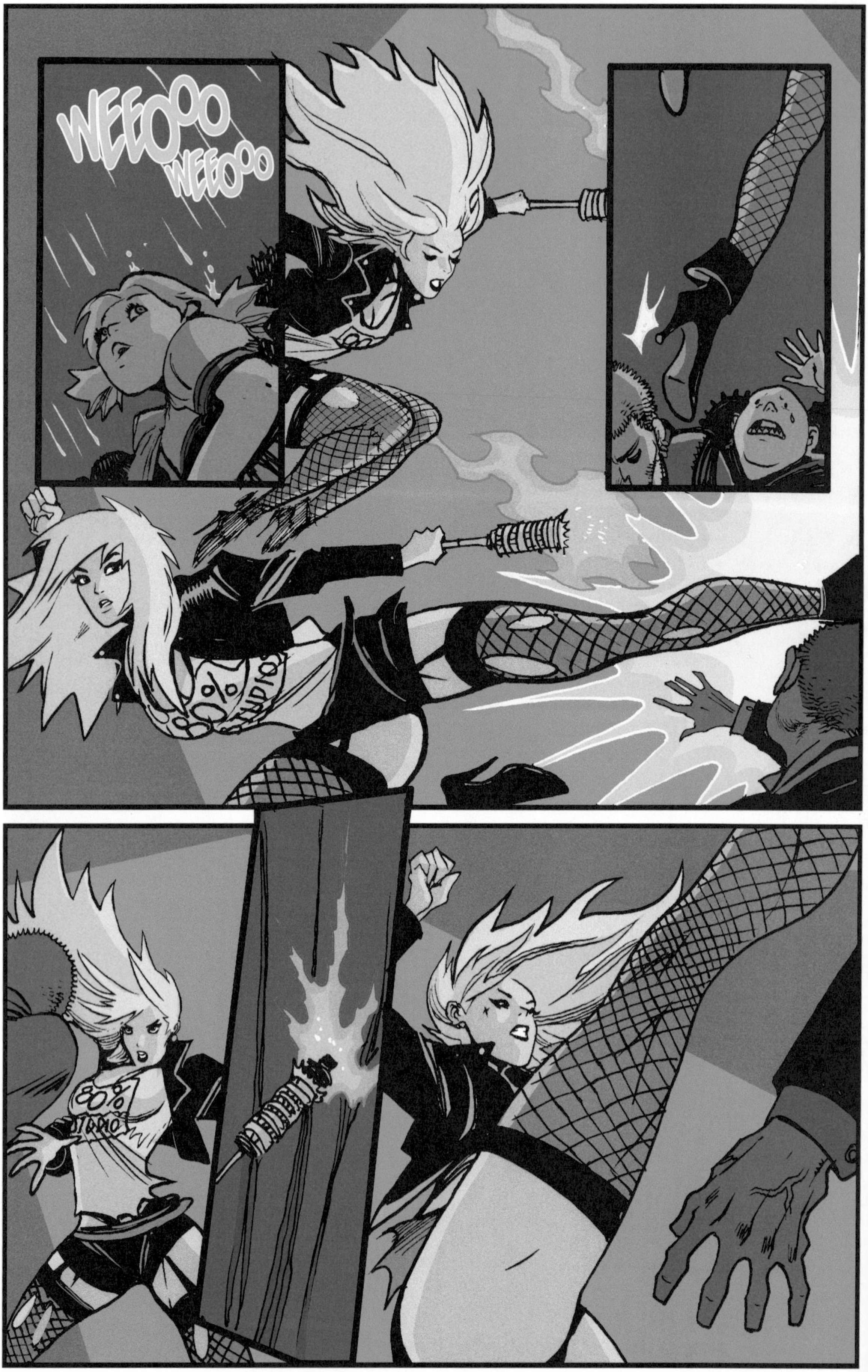
WEEOoo
WEEOoo

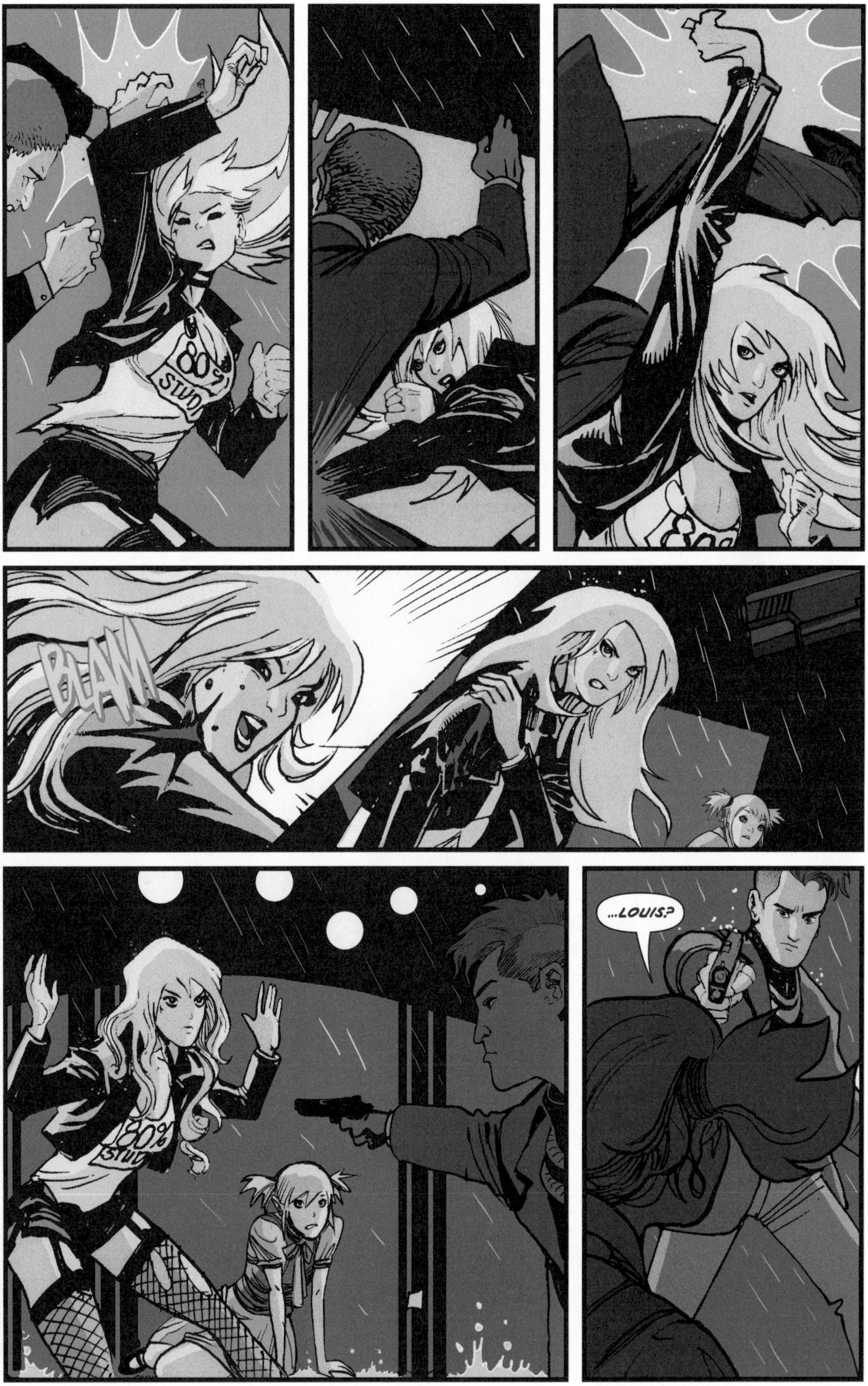

BLAM
...LOUIS?

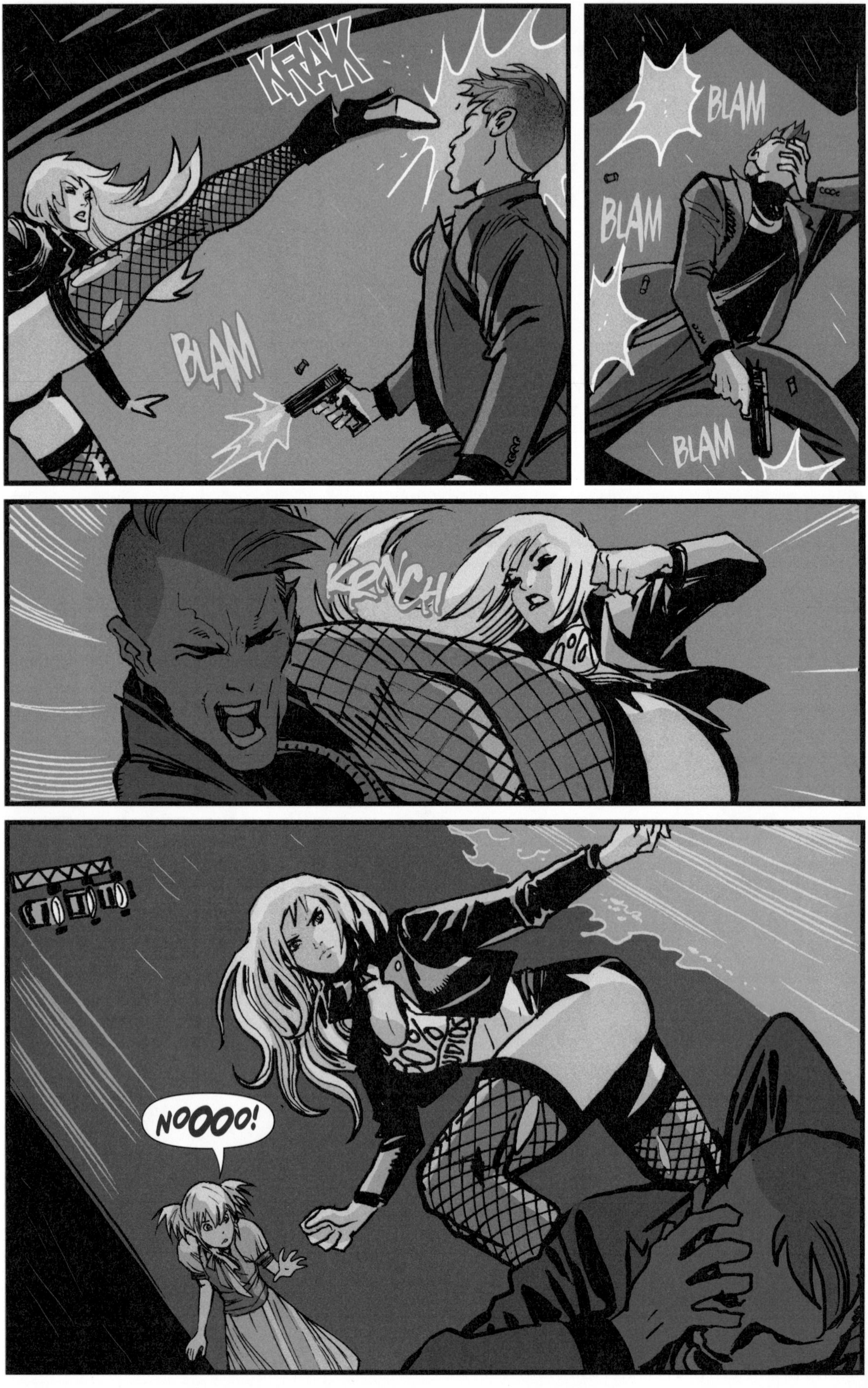
KRAK
BLAM
BLAM
BLAM
BLAM
KRNCH
NOOOO!

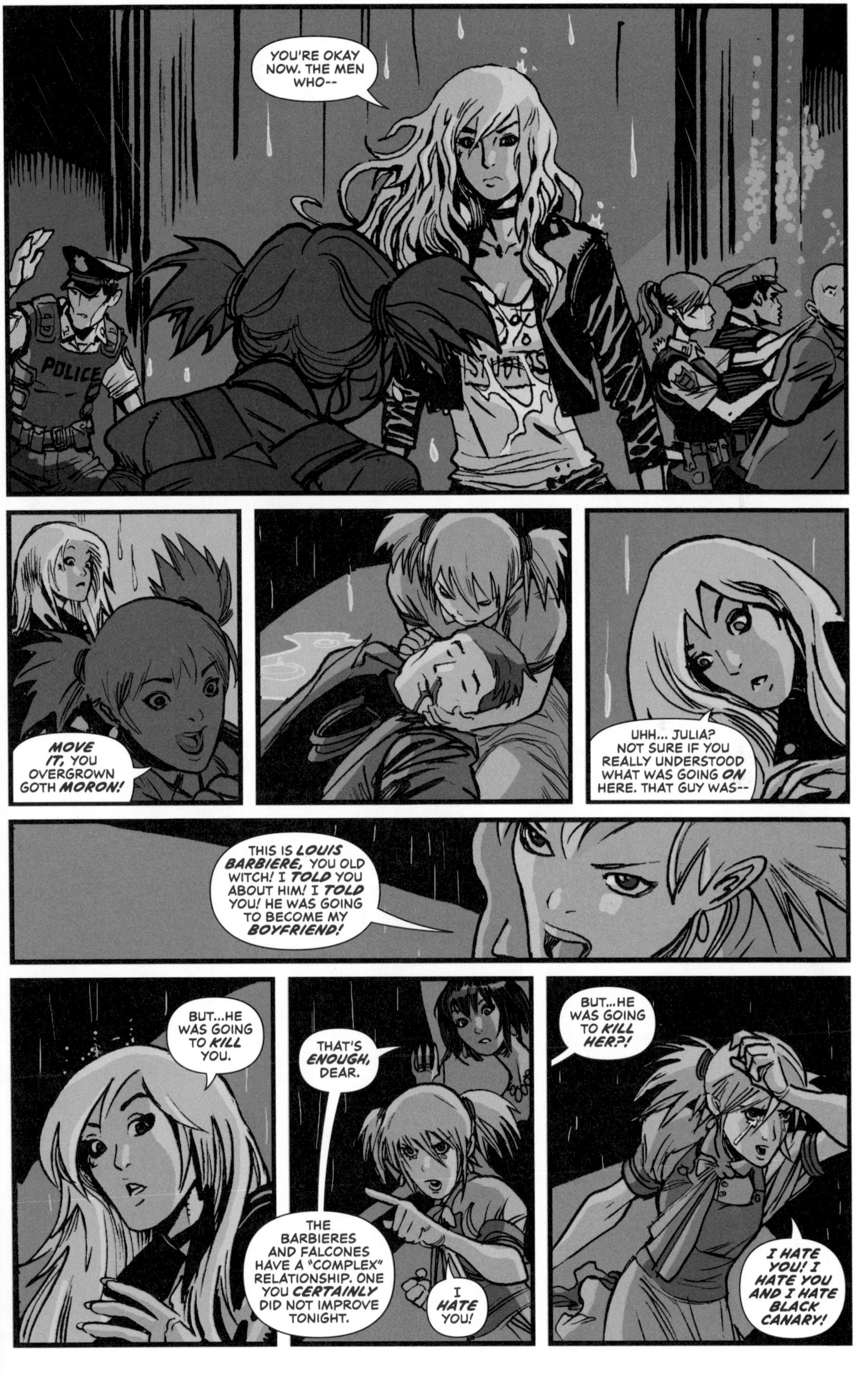
YOU'RE OKAY NOW. THE MEN WHO--
MOVE IT, YOU OVERGROWN GOTH MORON!
UHH... JULIA? NOT SURE IF YOU REALLY UNDERSTOOD WHAT WAS GOING ON HERE. THAT GUY WAS--
THIS IS LOUIS BARBIERE, YOU OLD WITCH! I TOLD YOU ABOUT HIM! I TOLD YOU! HE WAS GOING TO BECOME MY BOYFRIEND!
BUT...HE WAS GOING TO KILL YOU.
THAT'S ENOUGH, DEAR.
THE BARBIERES AND FALCONES HAVE A "COMPLEX" RELATIONSHIP. ONE YOU CERTAINLY DID NOT IMPROVE TONIGHT.
I HATE YOU!
BUT...HE WAS GOING TO KILL HER?!
I HATE YOU! I HATE YOU AND I HATE BLACK CANARY!

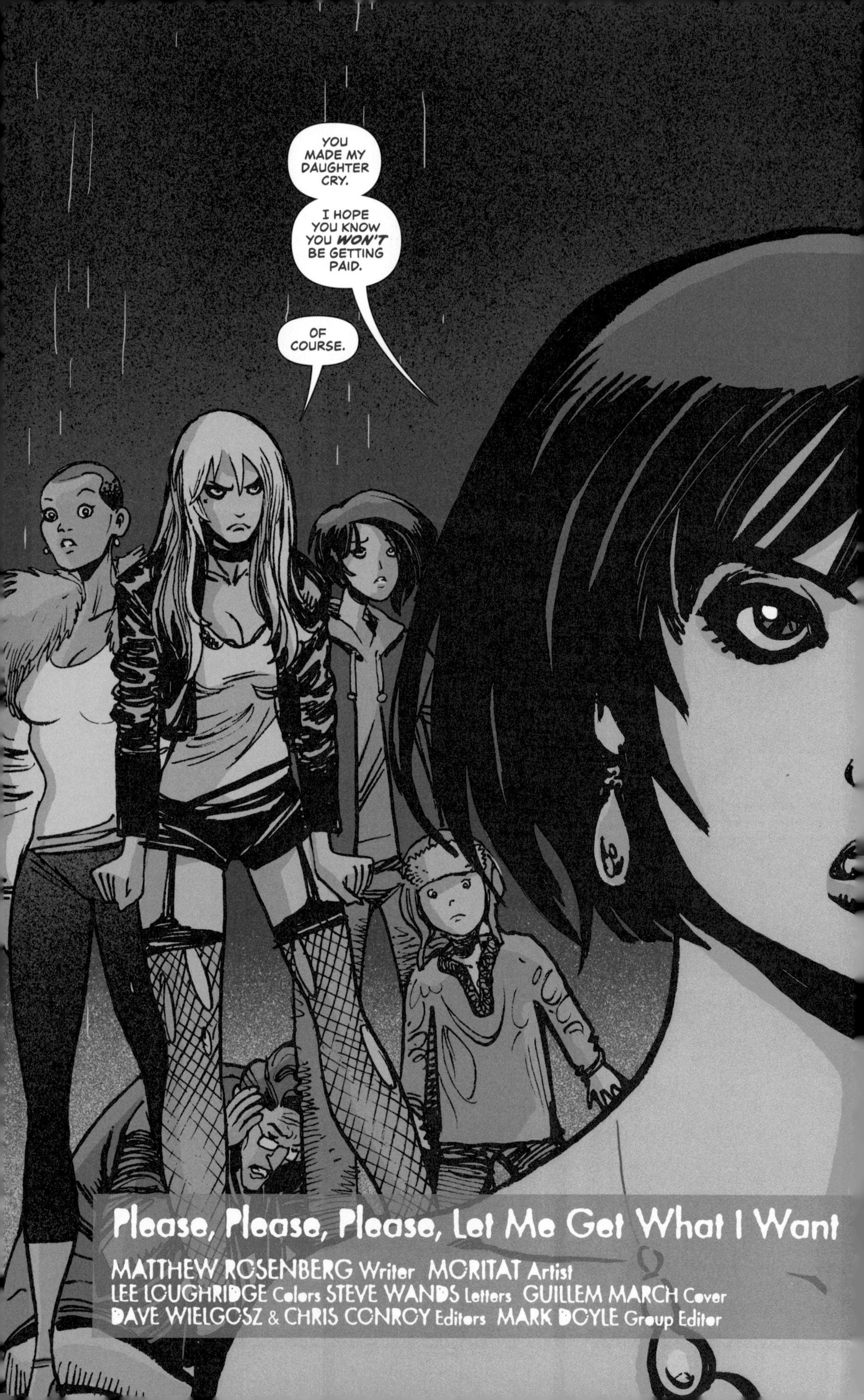
YOU MADE MY DAUGHTER CRY.
I HOPE YOU KNOW YOU WON'T BE GETTING PAID.
OF COURSE.
Please, Please, Please, Let Me Get What I Want
MATTHEW ROSENBERG Writer MORITAT Artist
LEE LOUGHRIDGE Colors STEVE WANDS Letters GUILLEM MARCH Cover
DAVE WIELGOSZ & CHRIS CONROY Editors MARK DOYLE Group Editor

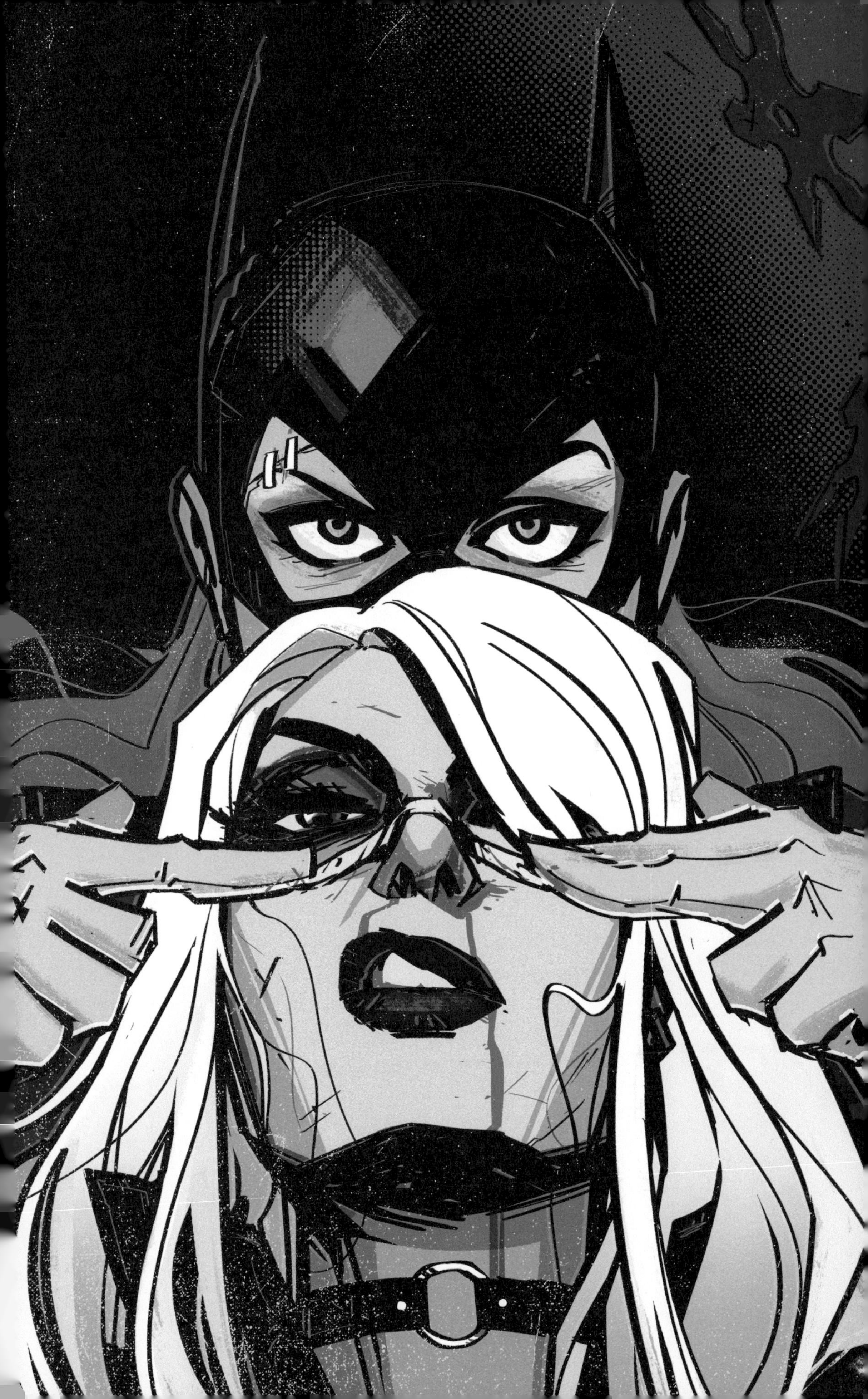

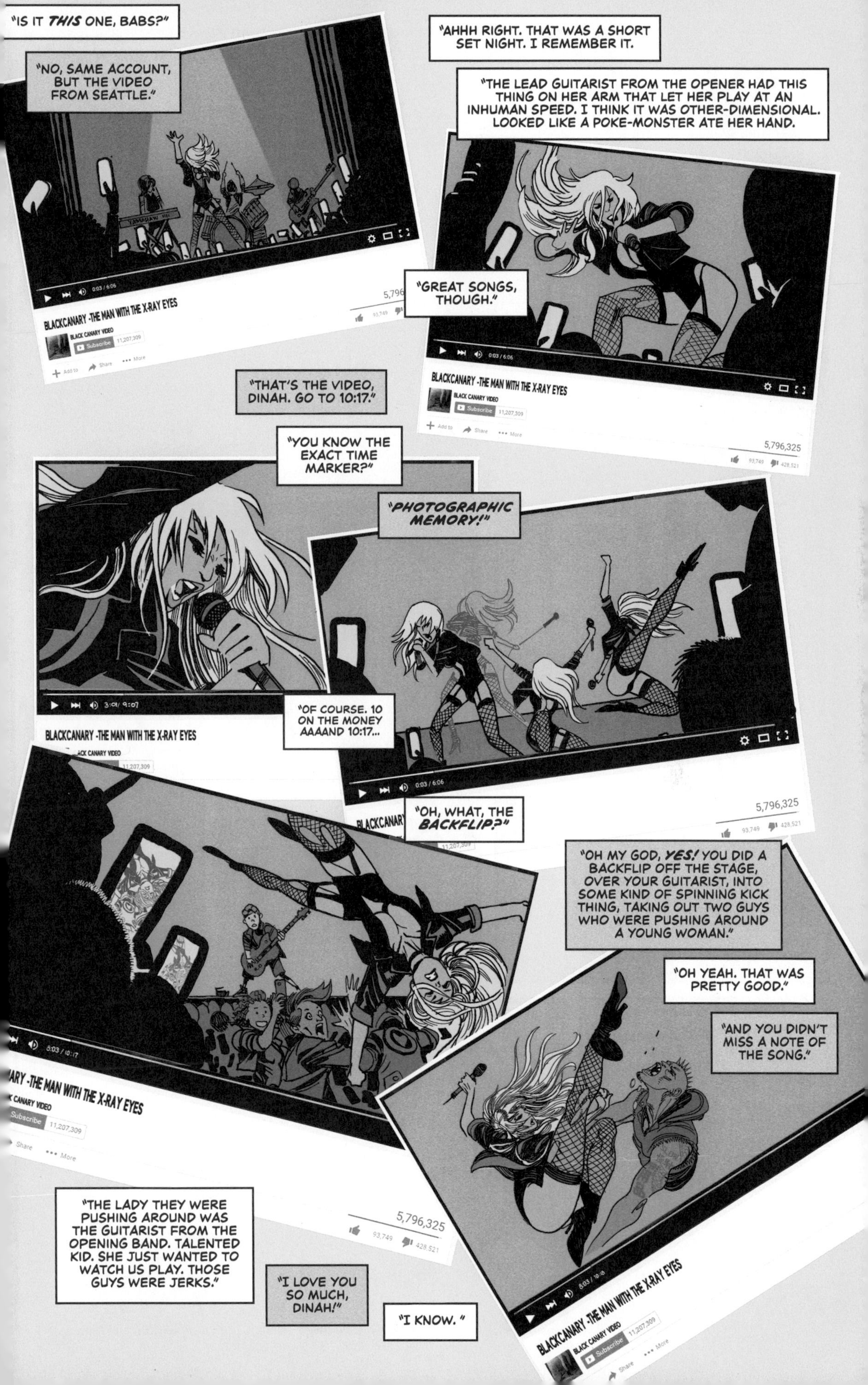
"IS IT *THIS* ONE, BABS?"
"NO, SAME ACCOUNT, BUT THE VIDEO FROM SEATTLE."
BLACKCANARY -THE MAN WITH THE X-RAY EYES
"AHHH RIGHT. THAT WAS A SHORT SET NIGHT. I REMEMBER IT.
"THE LEAD GUITARIST FROM THE OPENER HAD THIS THING ON HER ARM THAT LET HER PLAY AT AN INHUMAN SPEED. I THINK IT WAS OTHER-DIMENSIONAL. LOOKED LIKE A POKE-MONSTER ATE HER HAND.
"GREAT SONGS, THOUGH."
BLACKCANARY -THE MAN WITH THE X-RAY EYES
5,796,325
"THAT'S THE VIDEO, DINAH. GO TO 10:17."
"YOU KNOW THE EXACT TIME MARKER?"
"PHOTOGRAPHIC MEMORY!"
BLACKCANARY -THE MAN WITH THE X-RAY EYES
"OF COURSE. 10 ON THE MONEY AAAAND 10:17...
5,796,325
"OH, WHAT, THE *BACKFLIP?*"
"OH MY GOD, *YES!* YOU DID A BACKFLIP OFF THE STAGE, OVER YOUR GUITARIST, INTO SOME KIND OF SPINNING KICK THING, TAKING OUT TWO GUYS WHO WERE PUSHING AROUND A YOUNG WOMAN."
"OH YEAH. THAT WAS PRETTY GOOD."
"AND YOU DIDN'T MISS A NOTE OF THE SONG."
5,796,325
"THE LADY THEY WERE PUSHING AROUND WAS THE GUITARIST FROM THE OPENING BAND. TALENTED KID. SHE JUST WANTED TO WATCH US PLAY. THOSE GUYS WERE JERKS."
"I LOVE YOU SO MUCH, DINAH!"
"I KNOW."
BLACKCANARY -THE MAN WITH THE X-RAY EYES

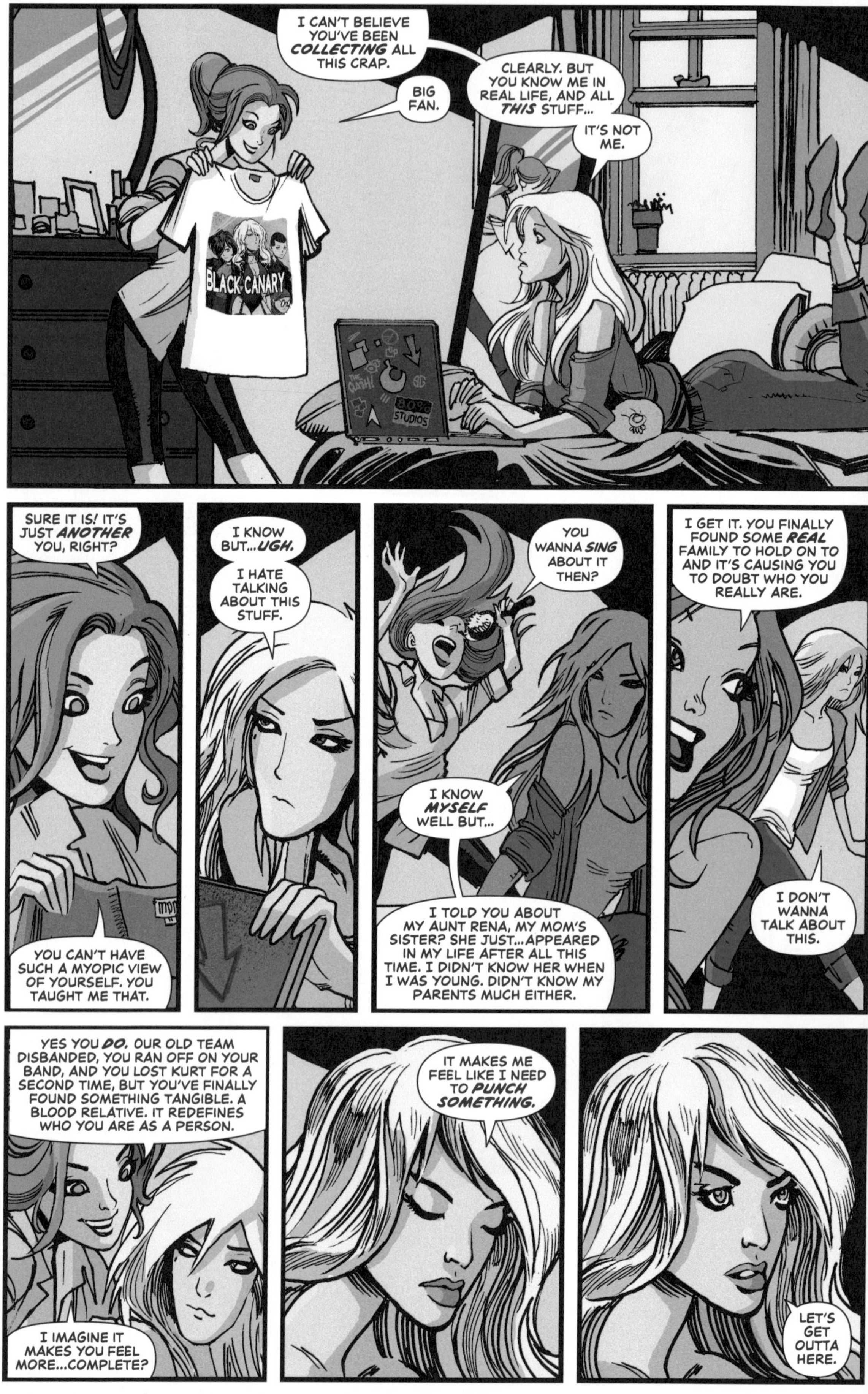
I CAN'T BELIEVE YOU'VE BEEN COLLECTING ALL THIS CRAP.
BIG FAN.
CLEARLY. BUT YOU KNOW ME IN REAL LIFE, AND ALL THIS STUFF...
IT'S NOT ME.
BLACK CANARY
80% STUDIOS
SURE IT IS! IT'S JUST ANOTHER YOU, RIGHT?
YOU CAN'T HAVE SUCH A MYOPIC VIEW OF YOURSELF. YOU TAUGHT ME THAT.
I KNOW BUT...UGH.
I HATE TALKING ABOUT THIS STUFF.
YOU WANNA SING ABOUT IT THEN?
I KNOW MYSELF WELL BUT...
I TOLD YOU ABOUT MY AUNT RENA, MY MOM'S SISTER? SHE JUST...APPEARED IN MY LIFE AFTER ALL THIS TIME. I DIDN'T KNOW HER WHEN I WAS YOUNG. DIDN'T KNOW MY PARENTS MUCH EITHER.
I GET IT. YOU FINALLY FOUND SOME REAL FAMILY TO HOLD ON TO AND IT'S CAUSING YOU TO DOUBT WHO YOU REALLY ARE.
I DON'T WANNA TALK ABOUT THIS.
YES YOU DO. OUR OLD TEAM DISBANDED, YOU RAN OFF ON YOUR BAND, AND YOU LOST KURT FOR A SECOND TIME, BUT YOU'VE FINALLY FOUND SOMETHING TANGIBLE. A BLOOD RELATIVE. IT REDEFINES WHO YOU ARE AS A PERSON.
I IMAGINE IT MAKES YOU FEEL MORE...COMPLETE?
IT MAKES ME FEEL LIKE I NEED TO PUNCH SOMETHING.
LET'S GET OUTTA HERE.

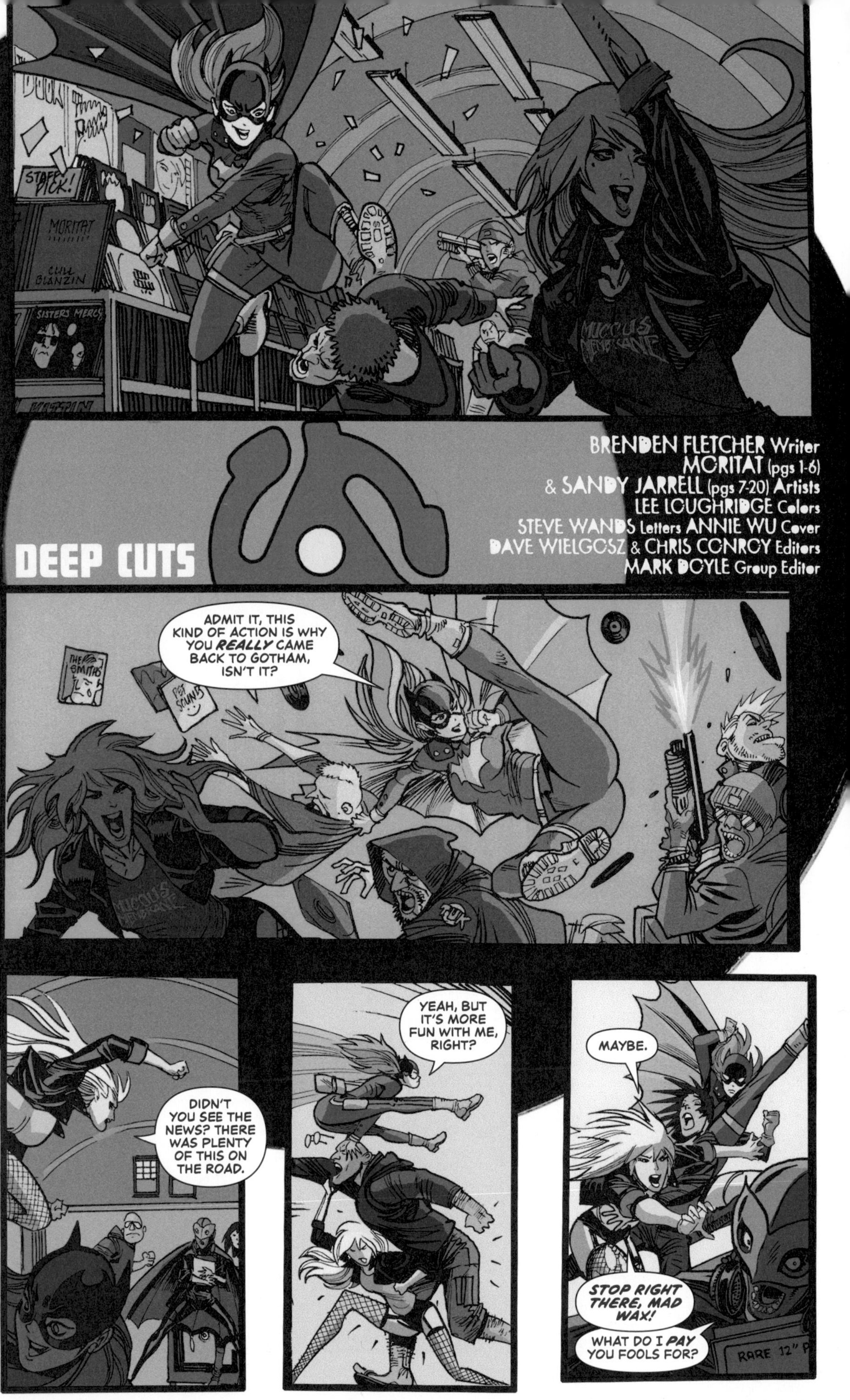
STAFF PICK!
MORITAT
DEEP CUTS
BRENDEN FLETCHER Writer
MORITAT (pgs 1-6)
& SANDY JARRELL (pgs 7-20) Artists
LEE LOUGHRIDGE Colors
STEVE WANDS Letters ANNIE WU Cover
DAVE WIELGOSZ & CHRIS CONROY Editors
MARK DOYLE Group Editor
ADMIT IT, THIS KIND OF ACTION IS WHY YOU REALLY CAME BACK TO GOTHAM, ISN'T IT?
DIDN'T YOU SEE THE NEWS? THERE WAS PLENTY OF THIS ON THE ROAD.
YEAH, BUT IT'S MORE FUN WITH ME, RIGHT?
MAYBE.
STOP RIGHT THERE, MAD WAX!
WHAT DO I PAY YOU FOOLS FOR?

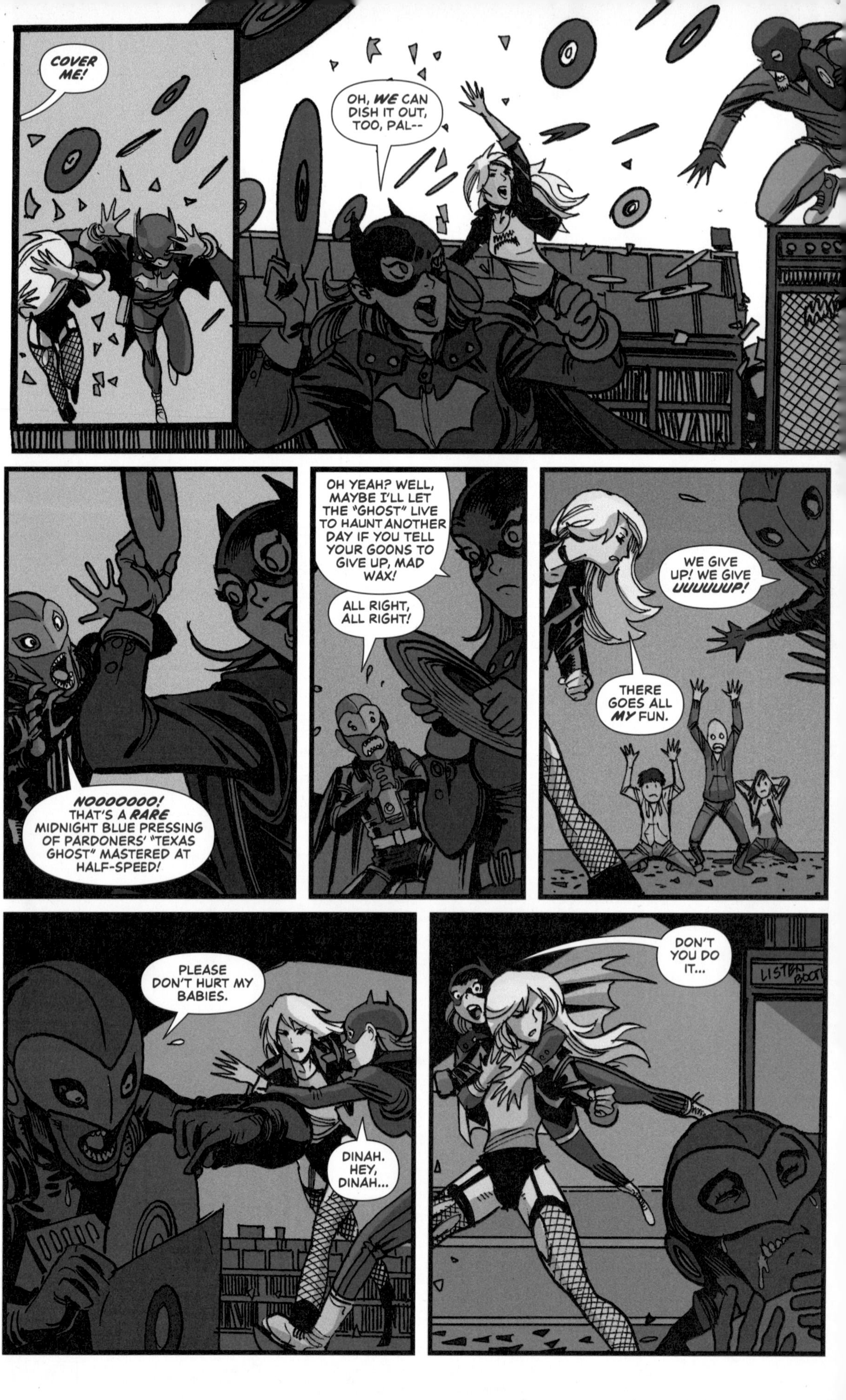
COVER ME!
OH, *WE* CAN DISH IT OUT, TOO, PAL--
NOOOOOOO! THAT'S A *RARE* MIDNIGHT BLUE PRESSING OF PARDONERS' "TEXAS GHOST" MASTERED AT HALF-SPEED!
OH YEAH? WELL, MAYBE I'LL LET THE "GHOST" LIVE TO HAUNT ANOTHER DAY IF YOU TELL YOUR GOONS TO GIVE UP, MAD WAX!
ALL RIGHT, ALL RIGHT!
WE GIVE UP! WE GIVE *UUUUUUP!*
THERE GOES ALL *MY* FUN.
PLEASE DON'T HURT MY BABIES.
DINAH. HEY, DINAH...
DON'T YOU DO IT...
LISTEN BOOT

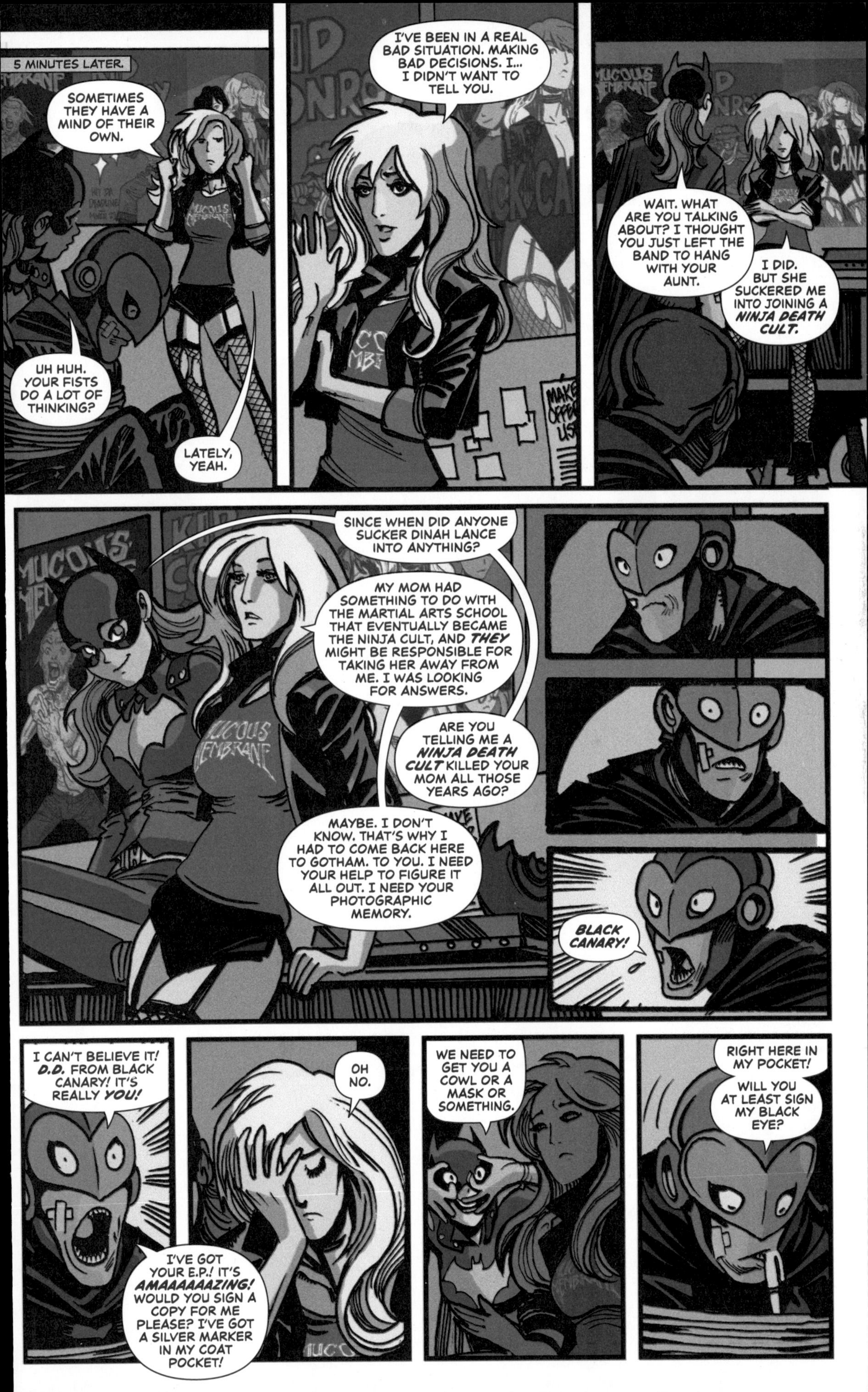
5 MINUTES LATER.
SOMETIMES THEY HAVE A MIND OF THEIR OWN.
UH HUH. YOUR FISTS DO A LOT OF THINKING?
LATELY, YEAH.
I'VE BEEN IN A REAL BAD SITUATION. MAKING BAD DECISIONS. I... I DIDN'T WANT TO TELL YOU.
WAIT. WHAT ARE YOU TALKING ABOUT? I THOUGHT YOU JUST LEFT THE BAND TO HANG WITH YOUR AUNT.
I DID. BUT SHE SUCKERED ME INTO JOINING A *NINJA DEATH CULT.*
SINCE WHEN DID ANYONE SUCKER DINAH LANCE INTO ANYTHING?
MY MOM HAD SOMETHING TO DO WITH THE MARTIAL ARTS SCHOOL THAT EVENTUALLY BECAME THE NINJA CULT, AND *THEY* MIGHT BE RESPONSIBLE FOR TAKING HER AWAY FROM ME. I WAS LOOKING FOR ANSWERS.
ARE YOU TELLING ME A *NINJA DEATH CULT* KILLED YOUR MOM ALL THOSE YEARS AGO?
MAYBE. I DON'T KNOW. THAT'S WHY I HAD TO COME BACK HERE TO GOTHAM. TO YOU. I NEED YOUR HELP TO FIGURE IT ALL OUT. I NEED YOUR PHOTOGRAPHIC MEMORY.
BLACK CANARY!
I CAN'T BELIEVE IT! *D.D.* FROM BLACK CANARY! IT'S REALLY *YOU!*
OH NO.
I'VE GOT YOUR E.P.! IT'S *AMAAAAAAZING!* WOULD YOU SIGN A COPY FOR ME PLEASE? I'VE GOT A SILVER MARKER IN MY COAT POCKET!
WE NEED TO GET YOU A COWL OR A MASK OR SOMETHING.
RIGHT HERE IN MY POCKET!
WILL YOU AT LEAST SIGN MY BLACK EYE?

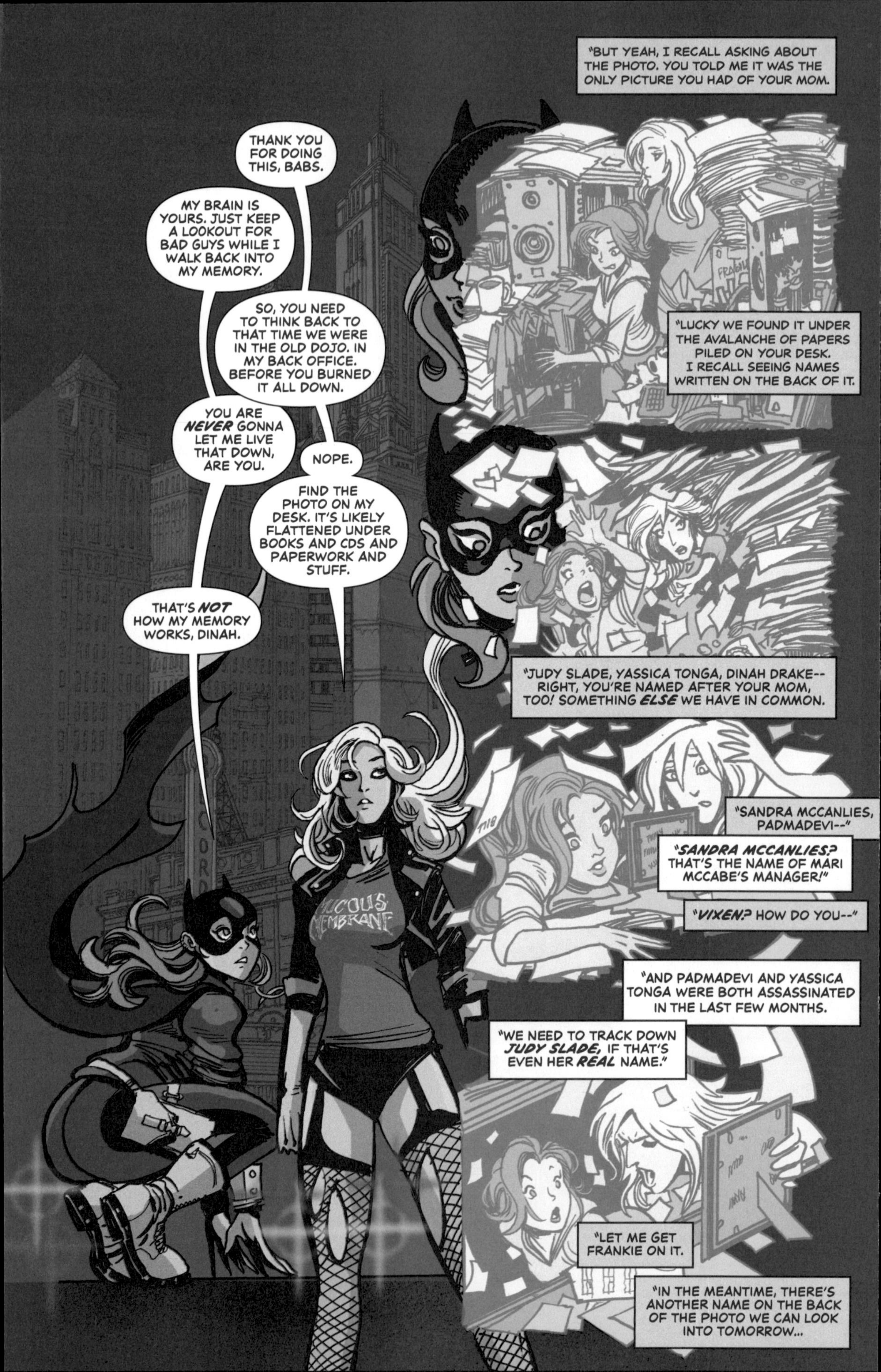

"BUT YEAH, I RECALL ASKING ABOUT THE PHOTO. YOU TOLD ME IT WAS THE ONLY PICTURE YOU HAD OF YOUR MOM.
THANK YOU FOR DOING THIS, BABS.
MY BRAIN IS YOURS. JUST KEEP A LOOKOUT FOR BAD GUYS WHILE I WALK BACK INTO MY MEMORY.
SO, YOU NEED TO THINK BACK TO THAT TIME WE WERE IN THE OLD DOJO. IN MY BACK OFFICE. BEFORE YOU BURNED IT ALL DOWN.
YOU ARE NEVER GONNA LET ME LIVE THAT DOWN, ARE YOU.
NOPE.
FIND THE PHOTO ON MY DESK. IT'S LIKELY FLATTENED UNDER BOOKS AND CDS AND PAPERWORK AND STUFF.
THAT'S NOT HOW MY MEMORY WORKS, DINAH.
"LUCKY WE FOUND IT UNDER THE AVALANCHE OF PAPERS PILED ON YOUR DESK. I RECALL SEEING NAMES WRITTEN ON THE BACK OF IT.
"JUDY SLADE, YASSICA TONGA, DINAH DRAKE-- RIGHT, YOU'RE NAMED AFTER YOUR MOM, TOO! SOMETHING ELSE WE HAVE IN COMMON.
"SANDRA MCCANLIES, PADMADEVI--"
"SANDRA MCCANLIES? THAT'S THE NAME OF MARI MCCABE'S MANAGER!"
"VIXEN? HOW DO YOU--"
"AND PADMADEVI AND YASSICA TONGA WERE BOTH ASSASSINATED IN THE LAST FEW MONTHS.
"WE NEED TO TRACK DOWN JUDY SLADE, IF THAT'S EVEN HER REAL NAME."
"LET ME GET FRANKIE ON IT.
"IN THE MEANTIME, THERE'S ANOTHER NAME ON THE BACK OF THE PHOTO WE CAN LOOK INTO TOMORROW...
MUCOUS MEMBRANE

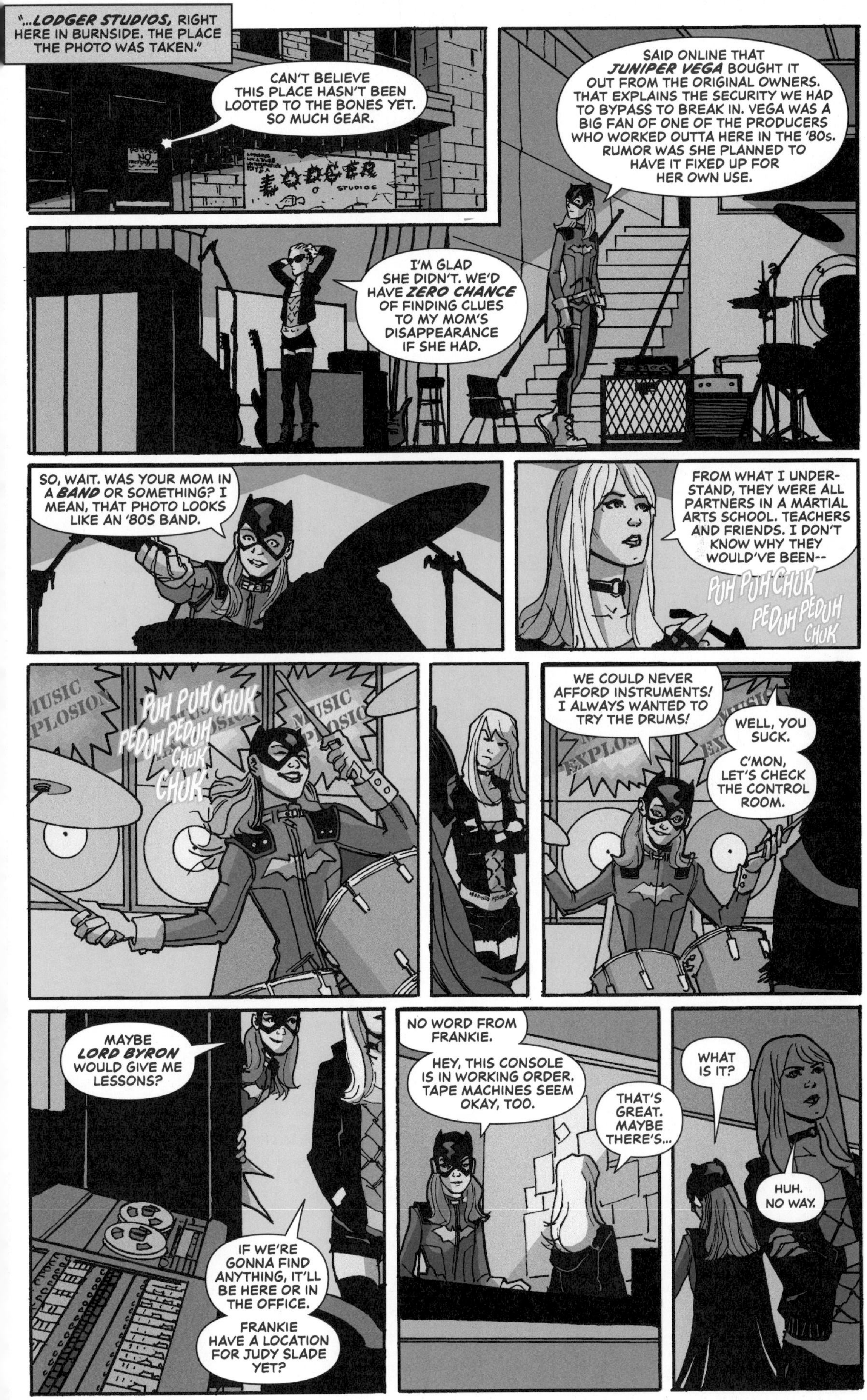
"...LODGER STUDIOS, RIGHT HERE IN BURNSIDE. THE PLACE THE PHOTO WAS TAKEN."
CAN'T BELIEVE THIS PLACE HASN'T BEEN LOOTED TO THE BONES YET. SO MUCH GEAR.
LODGER STUDIOS
SAID ONLINE THAT JUNIPER VEGA BOUGHT IT OUT FROM THE ORIGINAL OWNERS. THAT EXPLAINS THE SECURITY WE HAD TO BYPASS TO BREAK IN. VEGA WAS A BIG FAN OF ONE OF THE PRODUCERS WHO WORKED OUTTA HERE IN THE '80s. RUMOR WAS SHE PLANNED TO HAVE IT FIXED UP FOR HER OWN USE.
I'M GLAD SHE DIDN'T. WE'D HAVE ZERO CHANCE OF FINDING CLUES TO MY MOM'S DISAPPEARANCE IF SHE HAD.
SO, WAIT. WAS YOUR MOM IN A BAND OR SOMETHING? I MEAN, THAT PHOTO LOOKS LIKE AN '80S BAND.
FROM WHAT I UNDERSTAND, THEY WERE ALL PARTNERS IN A MARTIAL ARTS SCHOOL. TEACHERS AND FRIENDS. I DON'T KNOW WHY THEY WOULD'VE BEEN--
PUH PUH CHUK PEDUH PEDUH CHUK
PUH PUH CHUK PEDUH PEDUH CHUK CHUK
WE COULD NEVER AFFORD INSTRUMENTS! I ALWAYS WANTED TO TRY THE DRUMS!
WELL, YOU SUCK.
C'MON, LET'S CHECK THE CONTROL ROOM.
MAYBE LORD BYRON WOULD GIVE ME LESSONS?
IF WE'RE GONNA FIND ANYTHING, IT'LL BE HERE OR IN THE OFFICE.
FRANKIE HAVE A LOCATION FOR JUDY SLADE YET?
NO WORD FROM FRANKIE.
HEY, THIS CONSOLE IS IN WORKING ORDER. TAPE MACHINES SEEM OKAY, TOO.
THAT'S GREAT. MAYBE THERE'S...
WHAT IS IT?
HUH. NO WAY.

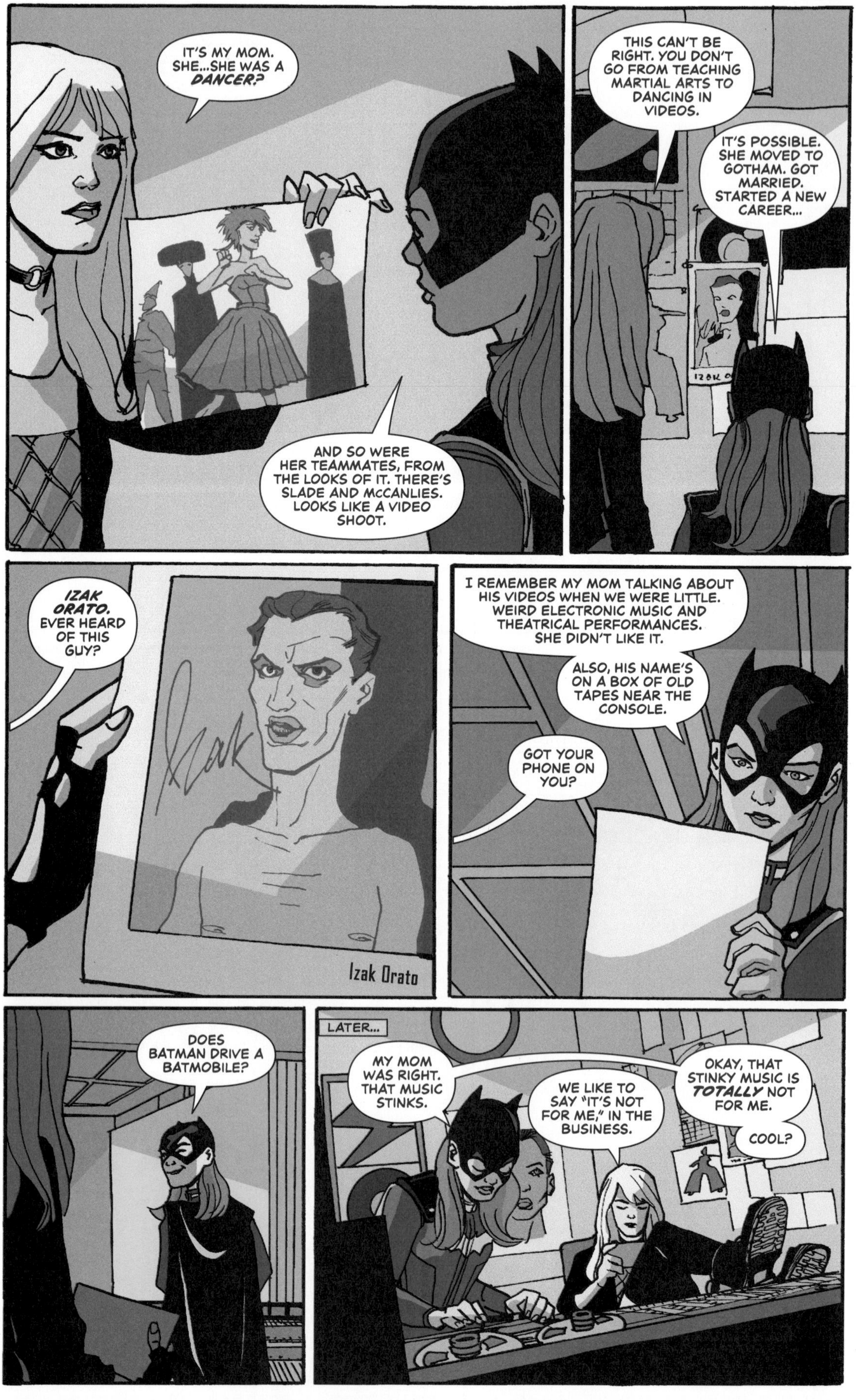
IT'S MY MOM. SHE...SHE WAS A *DANCER?*
AND SO WERE HER TEAMMATES, FROM THE LOOKS OF IT. THERE'S SLADE AND McCANLIES. LOOKS LIKE A VIDEO SHOOT.
THIS CAN'T BE RIGHT. YOU DON'T GO FROM TEACHING MARTIAL ARTS TO DANCING IN VIDEOS.
IT'S POSSIBLE. SHE MOVED TO GOTHAM. GOT MARRIED. STARTED A NEW CAREER...
IZAK ORATO. EVER HEARD OF THIS GUY?
Izak Orato
I REMEMBER MY MOM TALKING ABOUT HIS VIDEOS WHEN WE WERE LITTLE. WEIRD ELECTRONIC MUSIC AND THEATRICAL PERFORMANCES. SHE DIDN'T LIKE IT.
ALSO, HIS NAME'S ON A BOX OF OLD TAPES NEAR THE CONSOLE.
GOT YOUR PHONE ON YOU?
DOES BATMAN DRIVE A BATMOBILE?
LATER...
MY MOM WAS RIGHT. THAT MUSIC STINKS.
OKAY, THAT STINKY MUSIC IS *TOTALLY* NOT FOR ME.
WE LIKE TO SAY "IT'S NOT FOR ME," IN THE BUSINESS.
COOL?

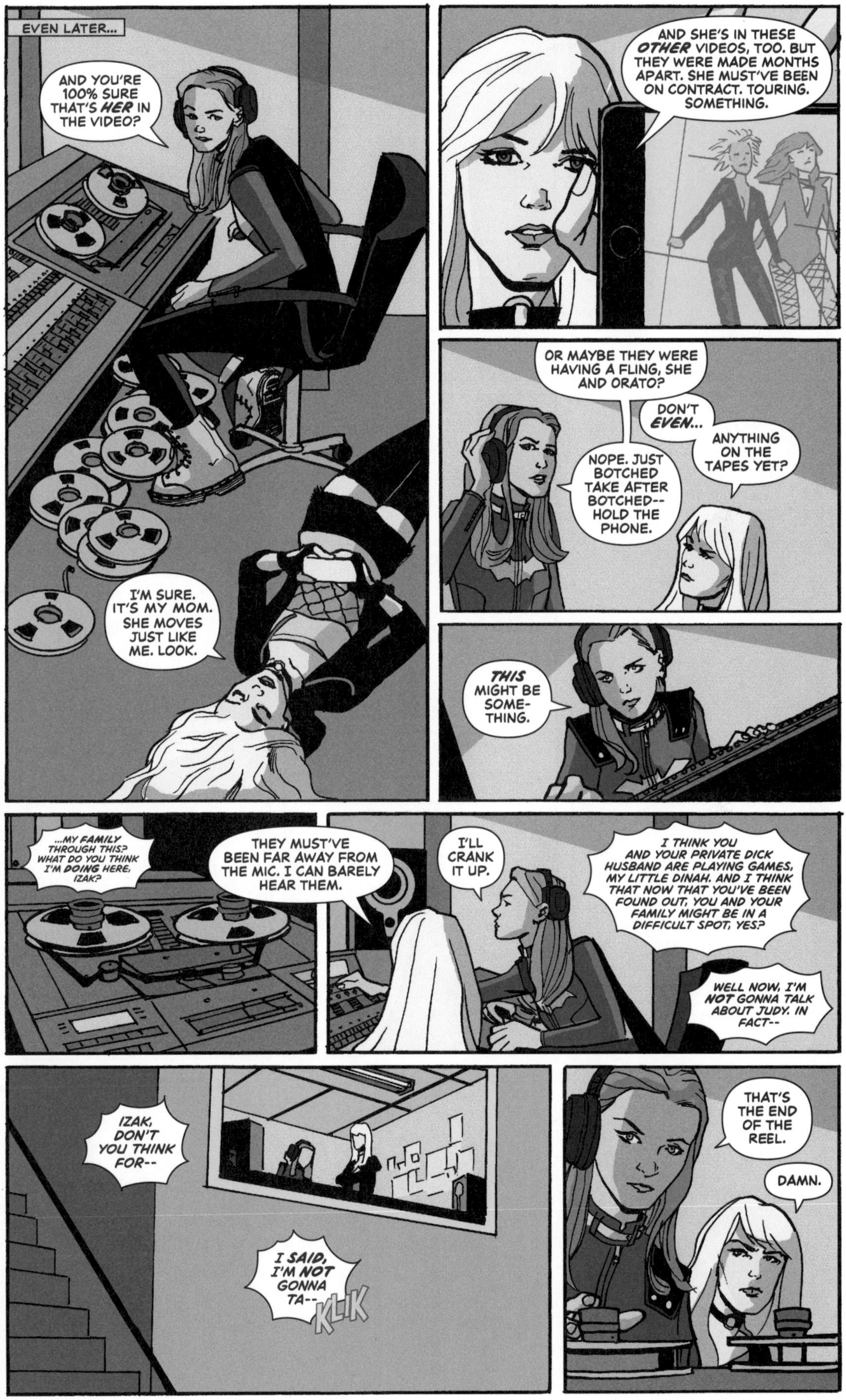
EVEN LATER...
AND YOU'RE 100% SURE THAT'S *HER* IN THE VIDEO?
I'M SURE. IT'S MY MOM. SHE MOVES JUST LIKE ME. LOOK.
AND SHE'S IN THESE *OTHER* VIDEOS, TOO. BUT THEY WERE MADE MONTHS APART. SHE MUST'VE BEEN ON CONTRACT. TOURING. SOMETHING.
OR MAYBE THEY WERE HAVING A FLING, SHE AND ORATO?
DON'T *EVEN*...
ANYTHING ON THE TAPES YET?
NOPE. JUST BOTCHED TAKE AFTER BOTCHED-- HOLD THE PHONE.
THIS MIGHT BE SOME-THING.
...MY *FAMILY* THROUGH THIS? WHAT DO YOU THINK I'M *DOING* HERE, IZAK?
THEY MUST'VE BEEN FAR AWAY FROM THE MIC. I CAN BARELY HEAR THEM.
I'LL CRANK IT UP.
I THINK YOU AND YOUR PRIVATE DICK HUSBAND ARE PLAYING GAMES, MY LITTLE DINAH. AND I THINK THAT NOW THAT YOU'VE BEEN FOUND OUT, YOU AND YOUR FAMILY MIGHT BE IN A DIFFICULT SPOT, YES?
WELL NOW, I'M *NOT* GONNA TALK ABOUT JUDY. IN FACT--
IZAK, DON'T YOU THINK FOR--
I *SAID*, I'M *NOT* GONNA TA--
KLIK
THAT'S THE END OF THE REEL.
DAMN.

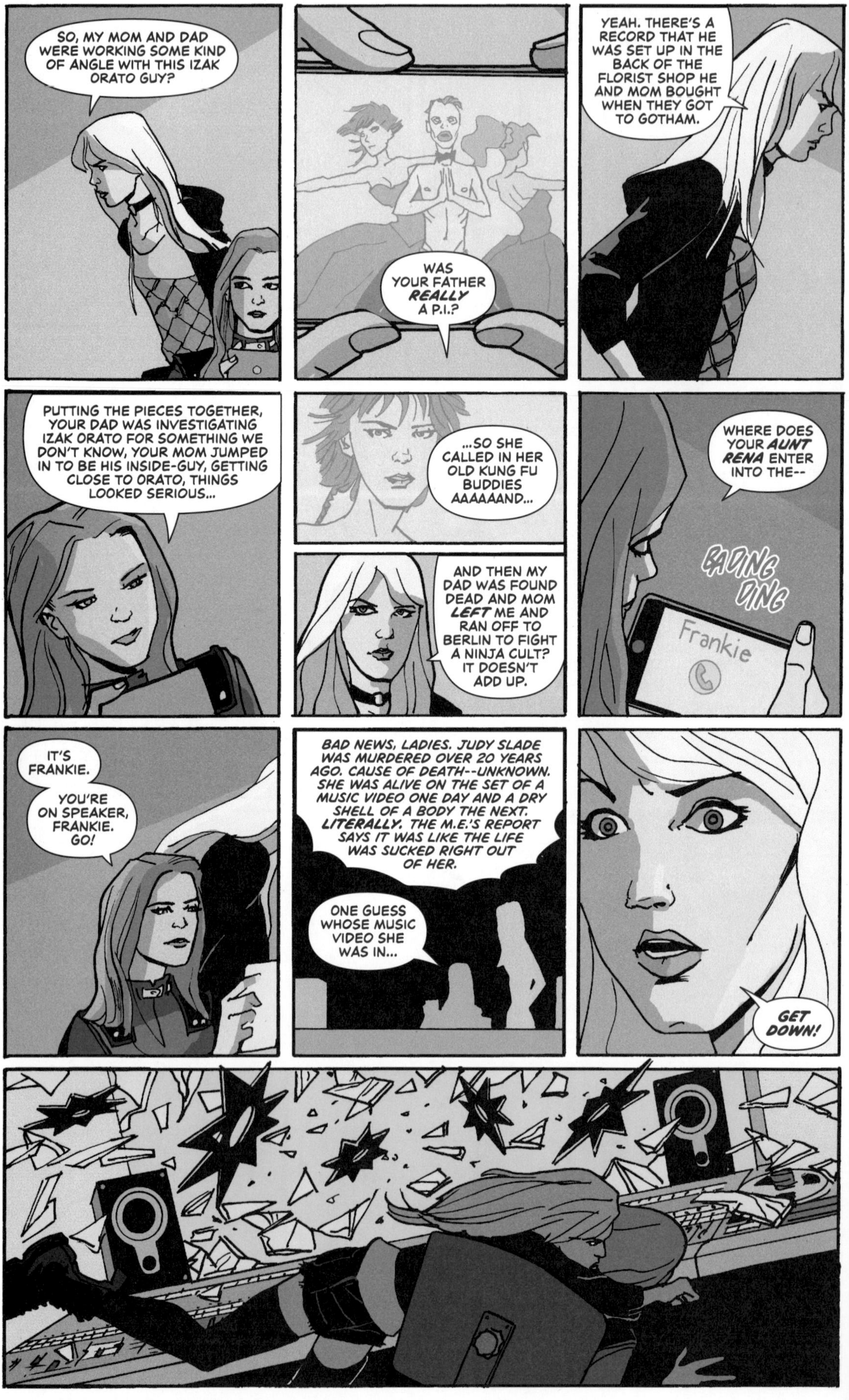
SO, MY MOM AND DAD WERE WORKING SOME KIND OF ANGLE WITH THIS IZAK ORATO GUY?
WAS YOUR FATHER REALLY A P.I.?
YEAH. THERE'S A RECORD THAT HE WAS SET UP IN THE BACK OF THE FLORIST SHOP HE AND MOM BOUGHT WHEN THEY GOT TO GOTHAM.
PUTTING THE PIECES TOGETHER, YOUR DAD WAS INVESTIGATING IZAK ORATO FOR SOMETHING WE DON'T KNOW, YOUR MOM JUMPED IN TO BE HIS INSIDE-GUY, GETTING CLOSE TO ORATO, THINGS LOOKED SERIOUS...
...SO SHE CALLED IN HER OLD KUNG FU BUDDIES AAAAAAND...
AND THEN MY DAD WAS FOUND DEAD AND MOM LEFT ME AND RAN OFF TO BERLIN TO FIGHT A NINJA CULT? IT DOESN'T ADD UP.
WHERE DOES YOUR AUNT RENA ENTER INTO THE--
BADING DING
Frankie
IT'S FRANKIE.
YOU'RE ON SPEAKER, FRANKIE. GO!
BAD NEWS, LADIES. JUDY SLADE WAS MURDERED OVER 20 YEARS AGO. CAUSE OF DEATH--UNKNOWN. SHE WAS ALIVE ON THE SET OF A MUSIC VIDEO ONE DAY AND A DRY SHELL OF A BODY THE NEXT. LITERALLY. THE M.E.'S REPORT SAYS IT WAS LIKE THE LIFE WAS SUCKED RIGHT OUT OF HER.
ONE GUESS WHOSE MUSIC VIDEO SHE WAS IN...
GET DOWN!

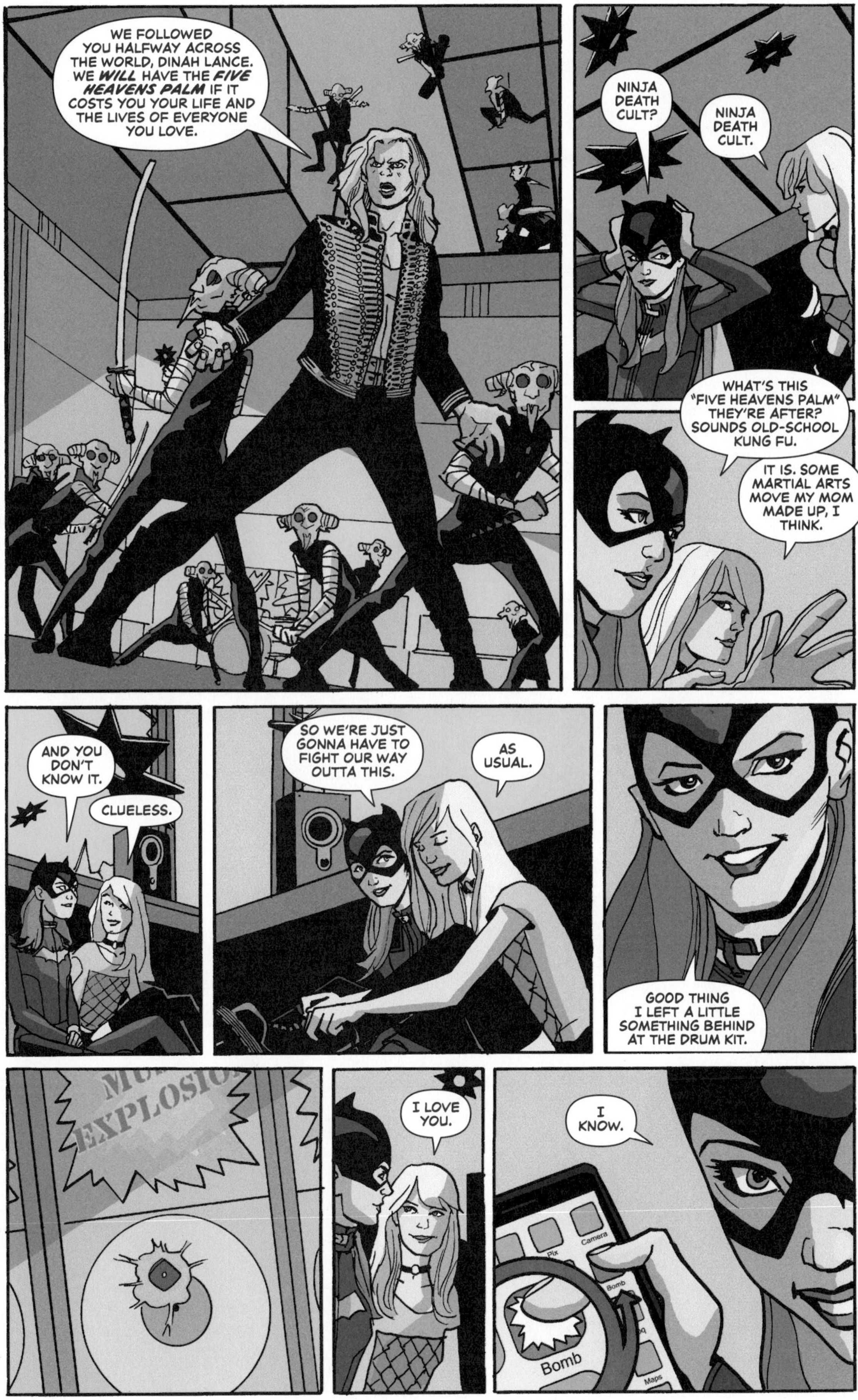
WE FOLLOWED YOU HALFWAY ACROSS THE WORLD, DINAH LANCE. WE *WILL* HAVE THE ***FIVE HEAVENS PALM*** IF IT COSTS YOU YOUR LIFE AND THE LIVES OF EVERYONE YOU LOVE.
NINJA DEATH CULT?
NINJA DEATH CULT.
WHAT'S THIS "FIVE HEAVENS PALM" THEY'RE AFTER? SOUNDS OLD-SCHOOL KUNG FU.
IT IS. SOME MARTIAL ARTS MOVE MY MOM MADE UP, I THINK.
AND YOU DON'T KNOW IT.
CLUELESS.
SO WE'RE JUST GONNA HAVE TO FIGHT OUR WAY OUTTA THIS.
AS USUAL.
GOOD THING I LEFT A LITTLE SOMETHING BEHIND AT THE DRUM KIT.
EXPLOSION
I LOVE YOU.
I KNOW.
Pix
Camera
Bomb
Bomb
Maps

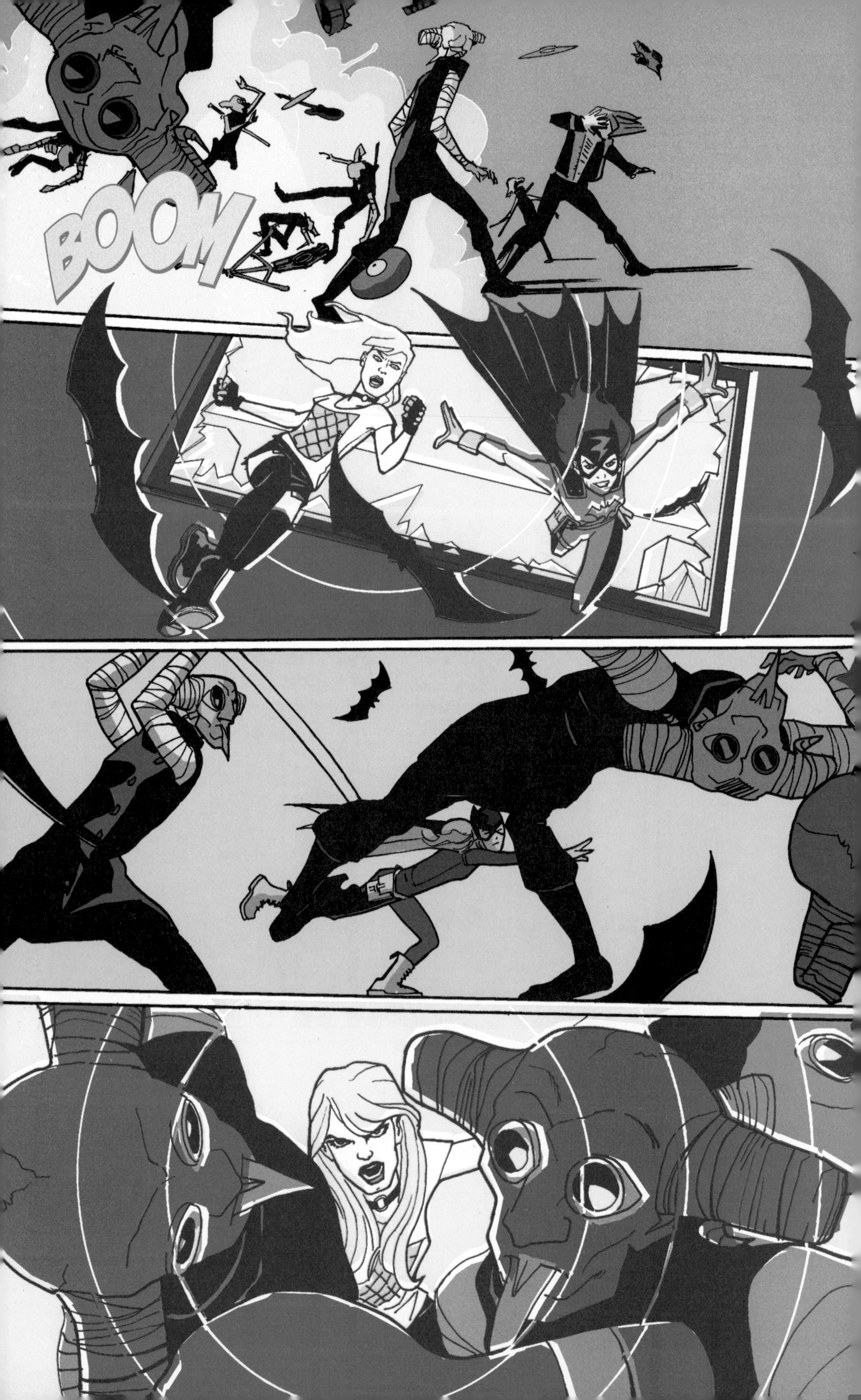
BOOM

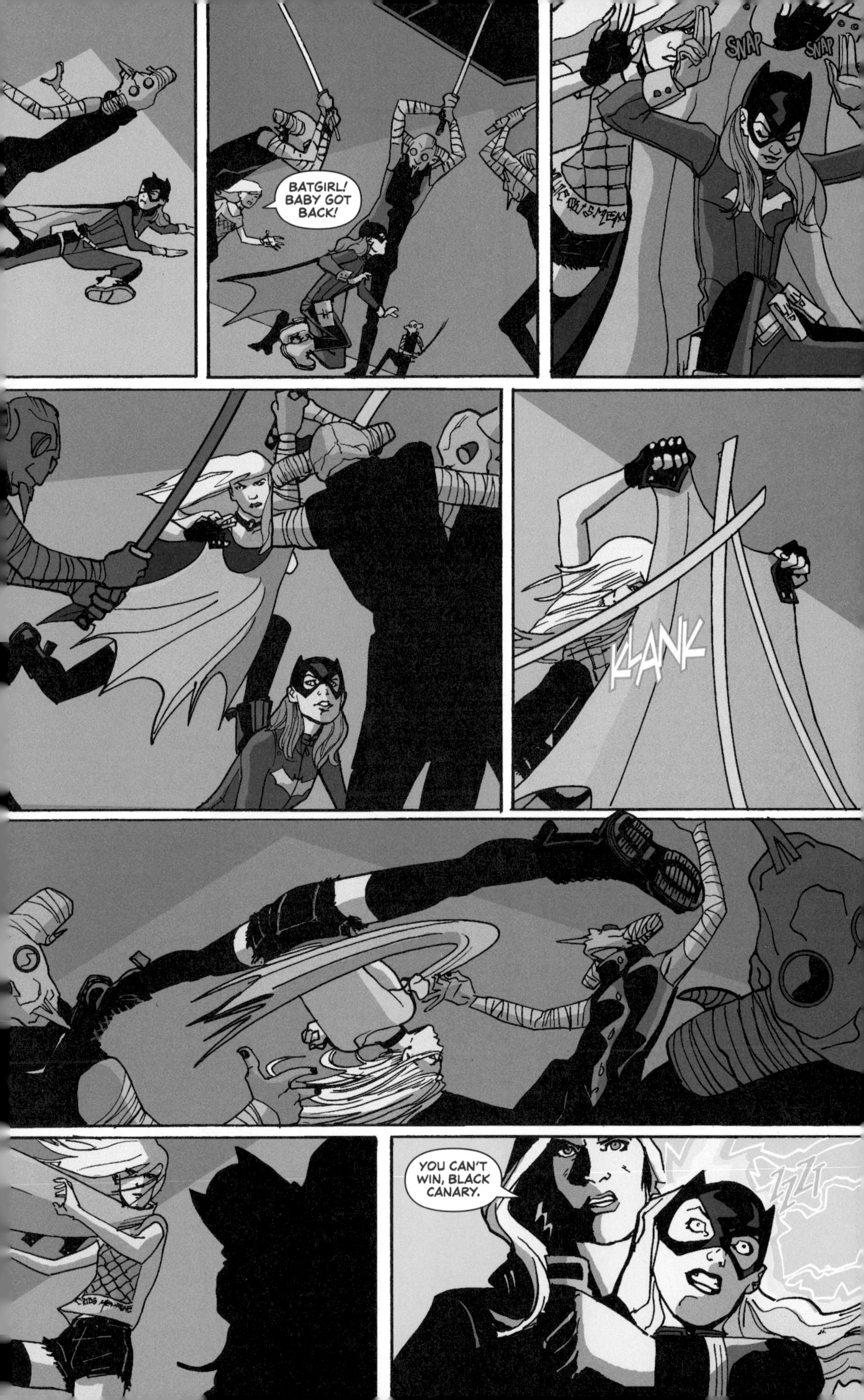
BATGIRL! BABY GOT BACK!
SNAP
SNAP
KLANK
YOU CAN'T WIN, BLACK CANARY.
ZZZT

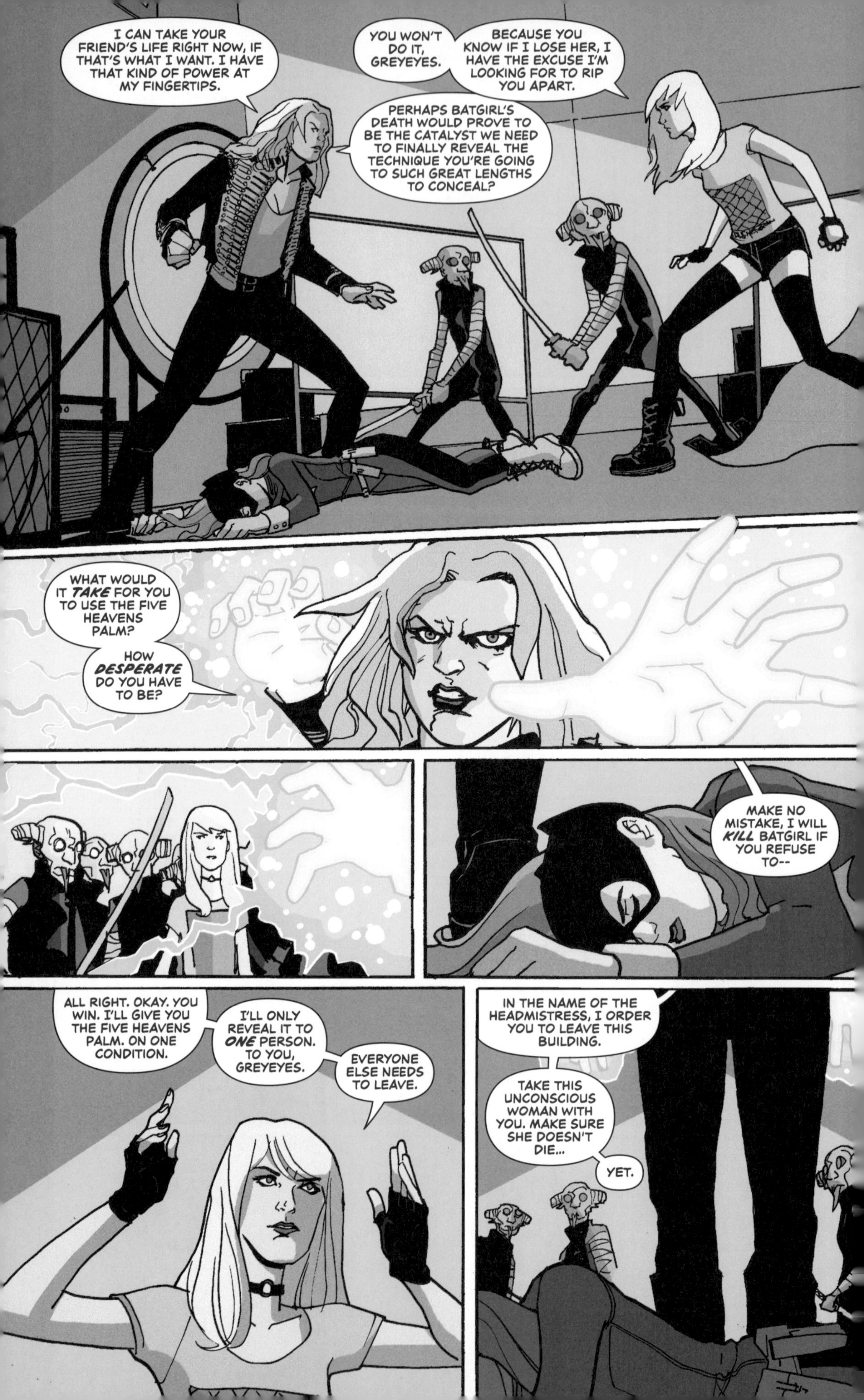
I CAN TAKE YOUR FRIEND'S LIFE RIGHT NOW, IF THAT'S WHAT I WANT. I HAVE THAT KIND OF POWER AT MY FINGERTIPS.
YOU WON'T DO IT, GREYEYES.
BECAUSE YOU KNOW IF I LOSE HER, I HAVE THE EXCUSE I'M LOOKING FOR TO RIP YOU APART.
PERHAPS BATGIRL'S DEATH WOULD PROVE TO BE THE CATALYST WE NEED TO FINALLY REVEAL THE TECHNIQUE YOU'RE GOING TO SUCH GREAT LENGTHS TO CONCEAL?
WHAT WOULD IT *TAKE* FOR YOU TO USE THE FIVE HEAVENS PALM?
HOW *DESPERATE* DO YOU HAVE TO BE?
MAKE NO MISTAKE, I WILL *KILL* BATGIRL IF YOU REFUSE TO--
ALL RIGHT. OKAY. YOU WIN. I'LL GIVE YOU THE FIVE HEAVENS PALM. ON ONE CONDITION.
I'LL ONLY REVEAL IT TO *ONE* PERSON. TO YOU, GREYEYES.
EVERYONE ELSE NEEDS TO LEAVE.
IN THE NAME OF THE HEADMISTRESS, I ORDER YOU TO LEAVE THIS BUILDING.
TAKE THIS UNCONSCIOUS WOMAN WITH YOU. MAKE SURE SHE DOESN'T DIE...
YET.

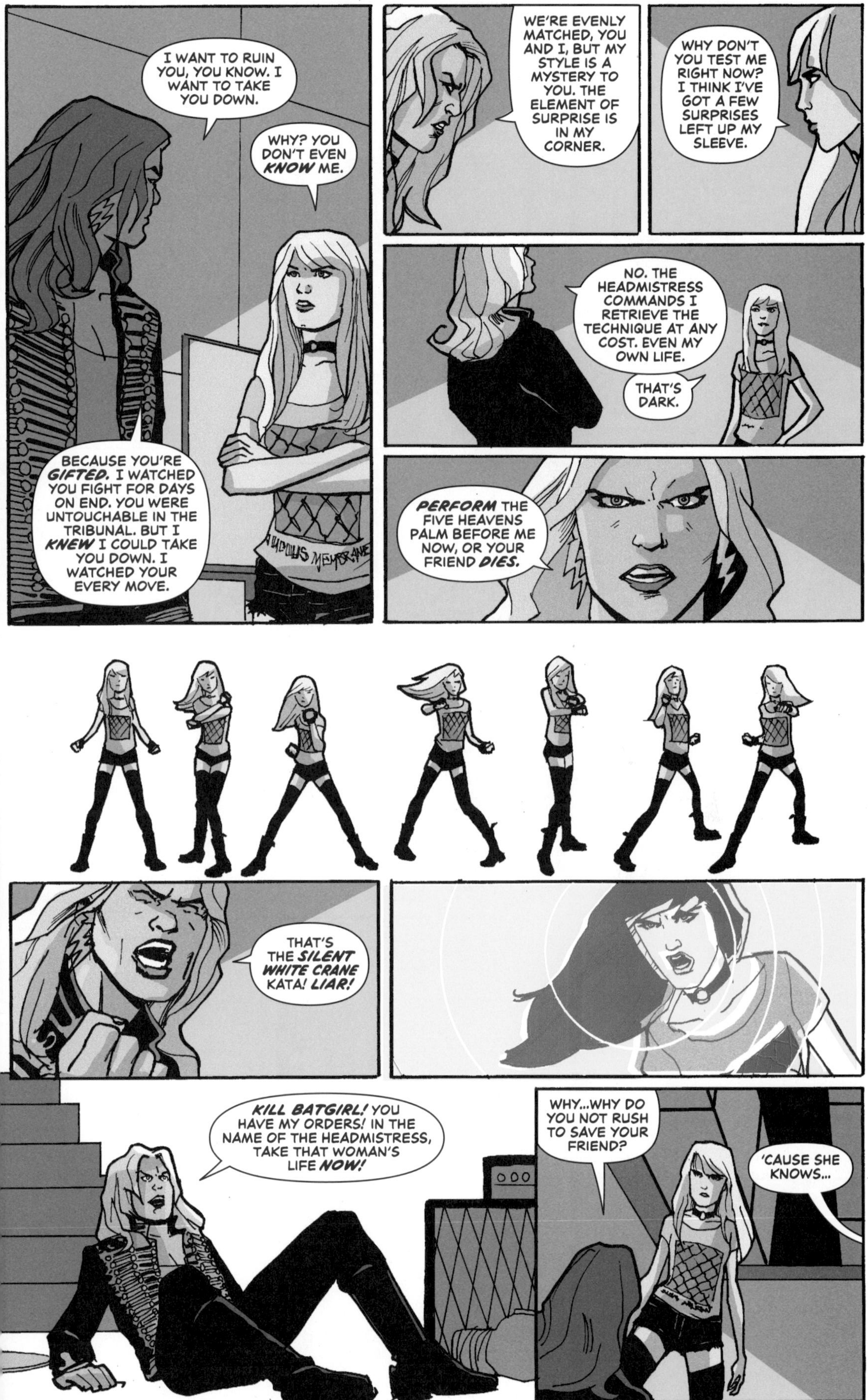
I WANT TO RUIN YOU, YOU KNOW. I WANT TO TAKE YOU DOWN.
WHY? YOU DON'T EVEN ***KNOW*** ME.
BECAUSE YOU'RE ***GIFTED.*** I WATCHED YOU FIGHT FOR DAYS ON END. YOU WERE UNTOUCHABLE IN THE TRIBUNAL. BUT I ***KNEW*** I COULD TAKE YOU DOWN. I WATCHED YOUR EVERY MOVE.
WE'RE EVENLY MATCHED, YOU AND I, BUT MY STYLE IS A MYSTERY TO YOU. THE ELEMENT OF SURPRISE IS IN MY CORNER.
WHY DON'T YOU TEST ME RIGHT NOW? I THINK I'VE GOT A FEW SURPRISES LEFT UP MY SLEEVE.
NO. THE HEADMISTRESS COMMANDS I RETRIEVE THE TECHNIQUE AT ANY COST. EVEN MY OWN LIFE.
THAT'S DARK.
PERFORM THE FIVE HEAVENS PALM BEFORE ME NOW, OR YOUR FRIEND ***DIES.***
THAT'S THE ***SILENT WHITE CRANE*** KATA! ***LIAR!***
KILL BATGIRL! YOU HAVE MY ORDERS! IN THE NAME OF THE HEADMISTRESS, TAKE THAT WOMAN'S LIFE ***NOW!***
WHY...WHY DO YOU NOT RUSH TO SAVE YOUR FRIEND?
'CAUSE SHE KNOWS...

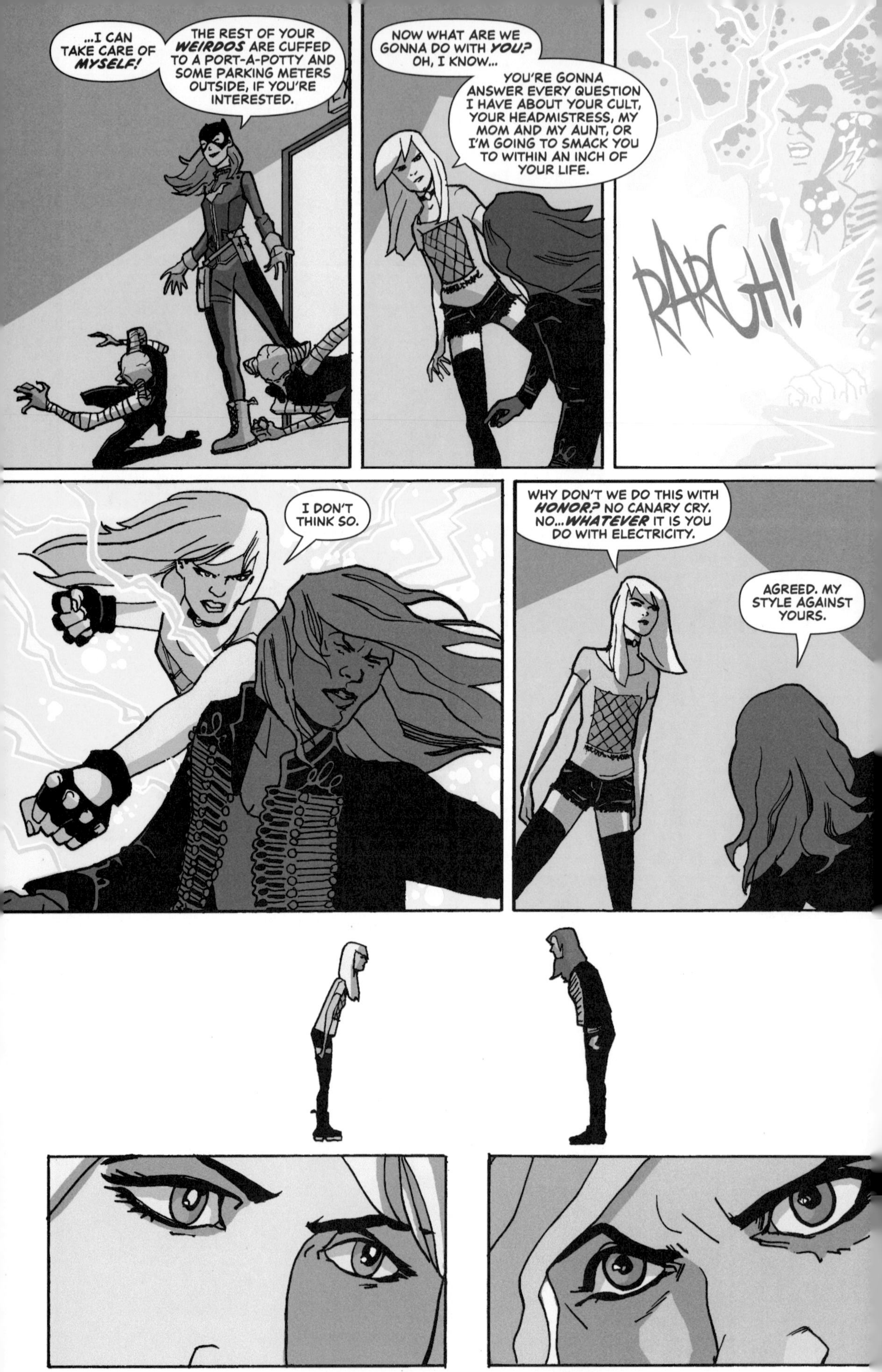
...I CAN TAKE CARE OF MYSELF!
THE REST OF YOUR WEIRDOS ARE CUFFED TO A PORT-A-POTTY AND SOME PARKING METERS OUTSIDE, IF YOU'RE INTERESTED.
NOW WHAT ARE WE GONNA DO WITH YOU? OH, I KNOW...
YOU'RE GONNA ANSWER EVERY QUESTION I HAVE ABOUT YOUR CULT, YOUR HEADMISTRESS, MY MOM AND MY AUNT, OR I'M GOING TO SMACK YOU TO WITHIN AN INCH OF YOUR LIFE.
RARGH!
I DON'T THINK SO.
WHY DON'T WE DO THIS WITH HONOR? NO CANARY CRY. NO...WHATEVER IT IS YOU DO WITH ELECTRICITY.
AGREED. MY STYLE AGAINST YOURS.

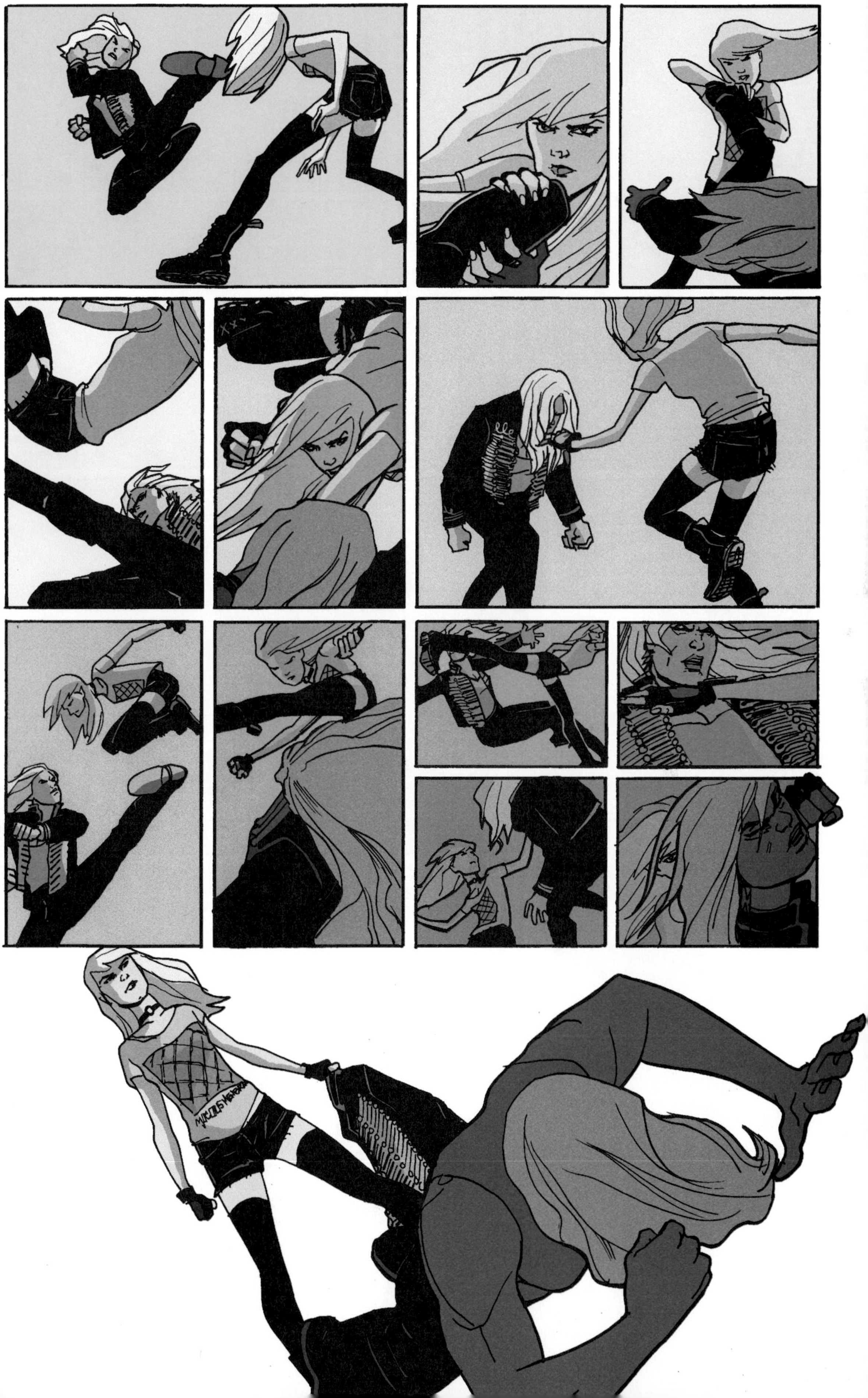

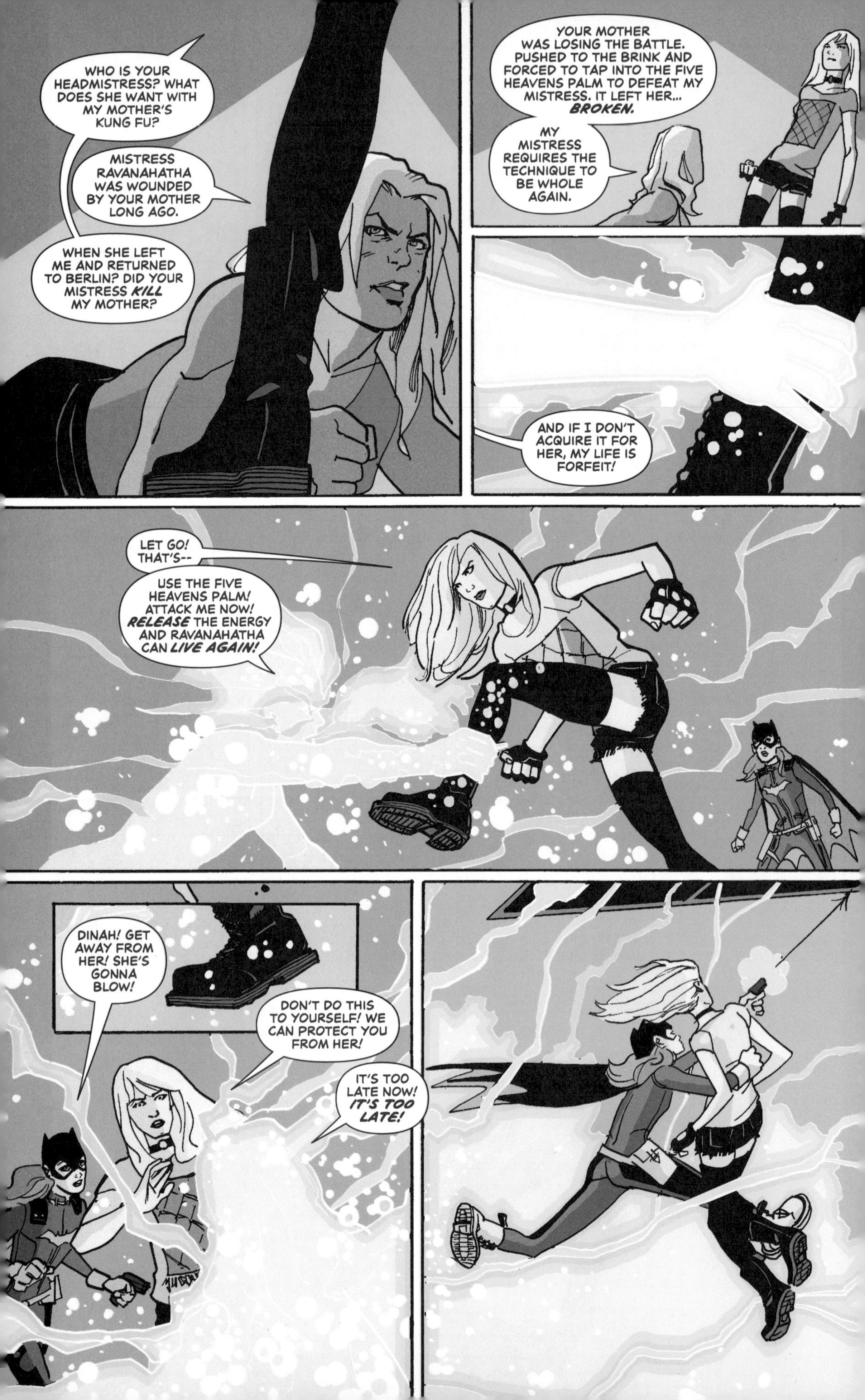
WHO IS YOUR HEADMISTRESS? WHAT DOES SHE WANT WITH MY MOTHER'S KUNG FU?
MISTRESS RAVANAHATHA WAS WOUNDED BY YOUR MOTHER LONG AGO.
WHEN SHE LEFT ME AND RETURNED TO BERLIN? DID YOUR MISTRESS KILL MY MOTHER?
YOUR MOTHER WAS LOSING THE BATTLE. PUSHED TO THE BRINK AND FORCED TO TAP INTO THE FIVE HEAVENS PALM TO DEFEAT MY MISTRESS. IT LEFT HER... BROKEN.
MY MISTRESS REQUIRES THE TECHNIQUE TO BE WHOLE AGAIN.
AND IF I DON'T ACQUIRE IT FOR HER, MY LIFE IS FORFEIT!
LET GO! THAT'S--
USE THE FIVE HEAVENS PALM! ATTACK ME NOW! RELEASE THE ENERGY AND RAVANAHATHA CAN LIVE AGAIN!
DINAH! GET AWAY FROM HER! SHE'S GONNA BLOW!
DON'T DO THIS TO YOURSELF! WE CAN PROTECT YOU FROM HER!
IT'S TOO LATE NOW! IT'S TOO LATE!

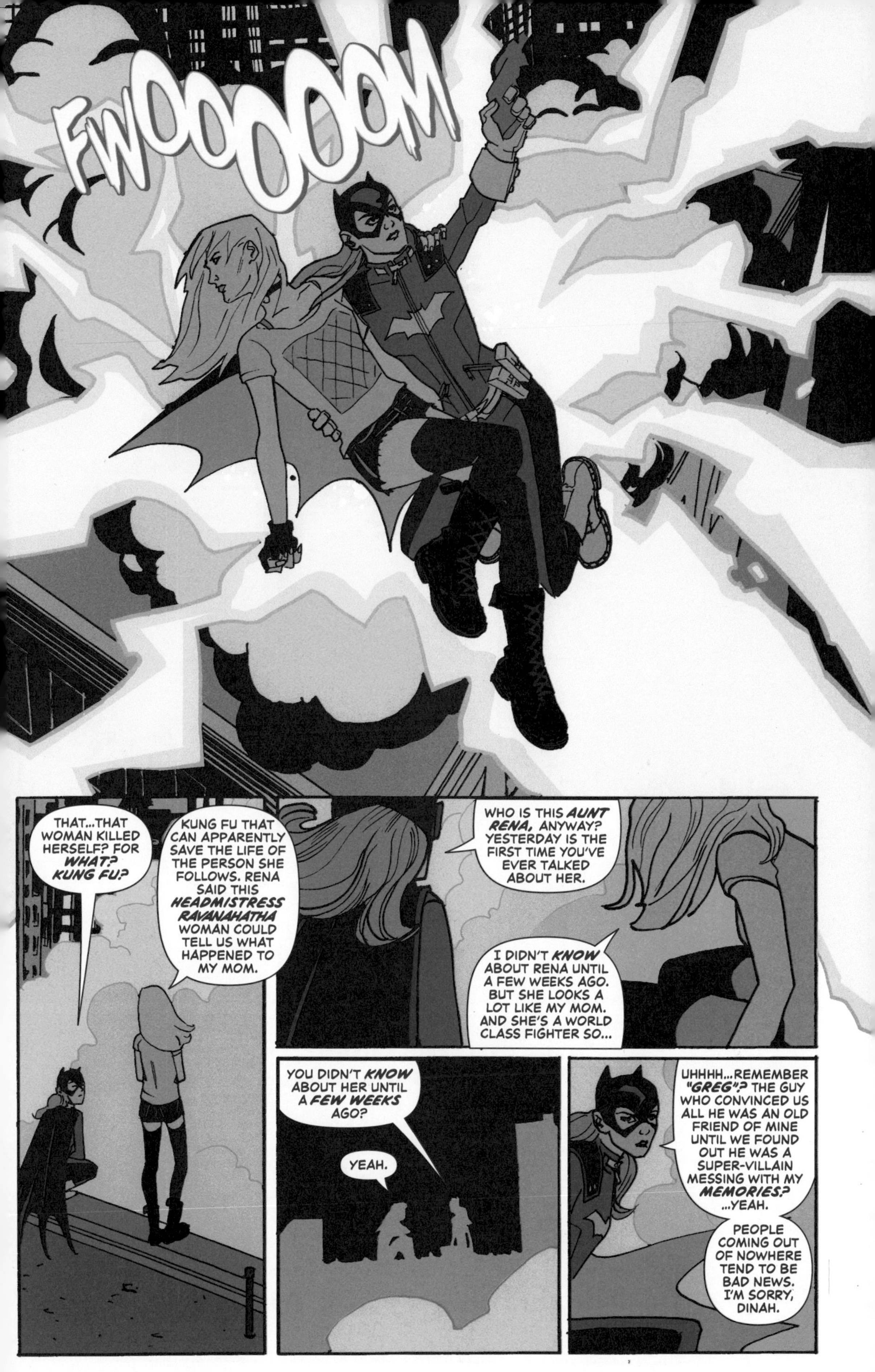
FWOOOOOM
THAT...THAT WOMAN KILLED HERSELF? FOR WHAT? KUNG FU?
KUNG FU THAT CAN APPARENTLY SAVE THE LIFE OF THE PERSON SHE FOLLOWS. RENA SAID THIS HEADMISTRESS RAVANAHATHA WOMAN COULD TELL US WHAT HAPPENED TO MY MOM.
WHO IS THIS AUNT RENA, ANYWAY? YESTERDAY IS THE FIRST TIME YOU'VE EVER TALKED ABOUT HER.
I DIDN'T KNOW ABOUT RENA UNTIL A FEW WEEKS AGO. BUT SHE LOOKS A LOT LIKE MY MOM. AND SHE'S A WORLD CLASS FIGHTER SO...
YOU DIDN'T KNOW ABOUT HER UNTIL A FEW WEEKS AGO?
YEAH.
UHHHH...REMEMBER "GREG"? THE GUY WHO CONVINCED US ALL HE WAS AN OLD FRIEND OF MINE UNTIL WE FOUND OUT HE WAS A SUPER-VILLAIN MESSING WITH MY MEMORIES? ...YEAH.
PEOPLE COMING OUT OF NOWHERE TEND TO BE BAD NEWS. I'M SORRY, DINAH.

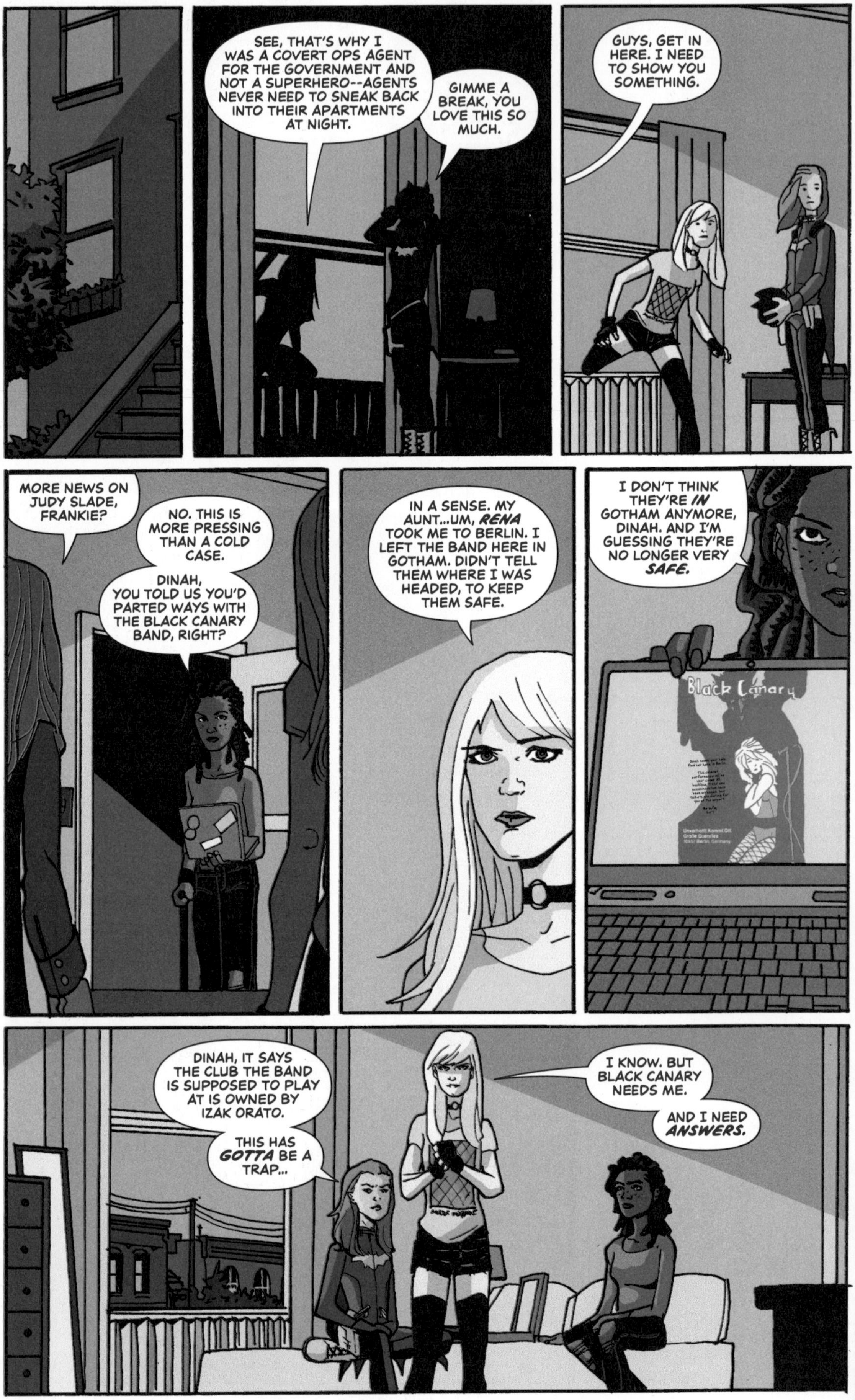
SEE, THAT'S WHY I WAS A COVERT OPS AGENT FOR THE GOVERNMENT AND NOT A SUPERHERO--AGENTS NEVER NEED TO SNEAK BACK INTO THEIR APARTMENTS AT NIGHT.
GIMME A BREAK, YOU LOVE THIS SO MUCH.
GUYS, GET IN HERE. I NEED TO SHOW YOU SOMETHING.
MORE NEWS ON JUDY SLADE, FRANKIE?
NO. THIS IS MORE PRESSING THAN A COLD CASE.
DINAH, YOU TOLD US YOU'D PARTED WAYS WITH THE BLACK CANARY BAND, RIGHT?
IN A SENSE. MY AUNT...UM, *RENA* TOOK ME TO BERLIN. I LEFT THE BAND HERE IN GOTHAM. DIDN'T TELL THEM WHERE I WAS HEADED, TO KEEP THEM SAFE.
I DON'T THINK THEY'RE *IN* GOTHAM ANYMORE, DINAH. AND I'M GUESSING THEY'RE NO LONGER VERY *SAFE.*
Black Canary
DINAH, IT SAYS THE CLUB THE BAND IS SUPPOSED TO PLAY AT IS OWNED BY IZAK ORATO.
THIS HAS *GOTTA* BE A TRAP...
I KNOW. BUT BLACK CANARY NEEDS ME.
AND I NEED *ANSWERS.*

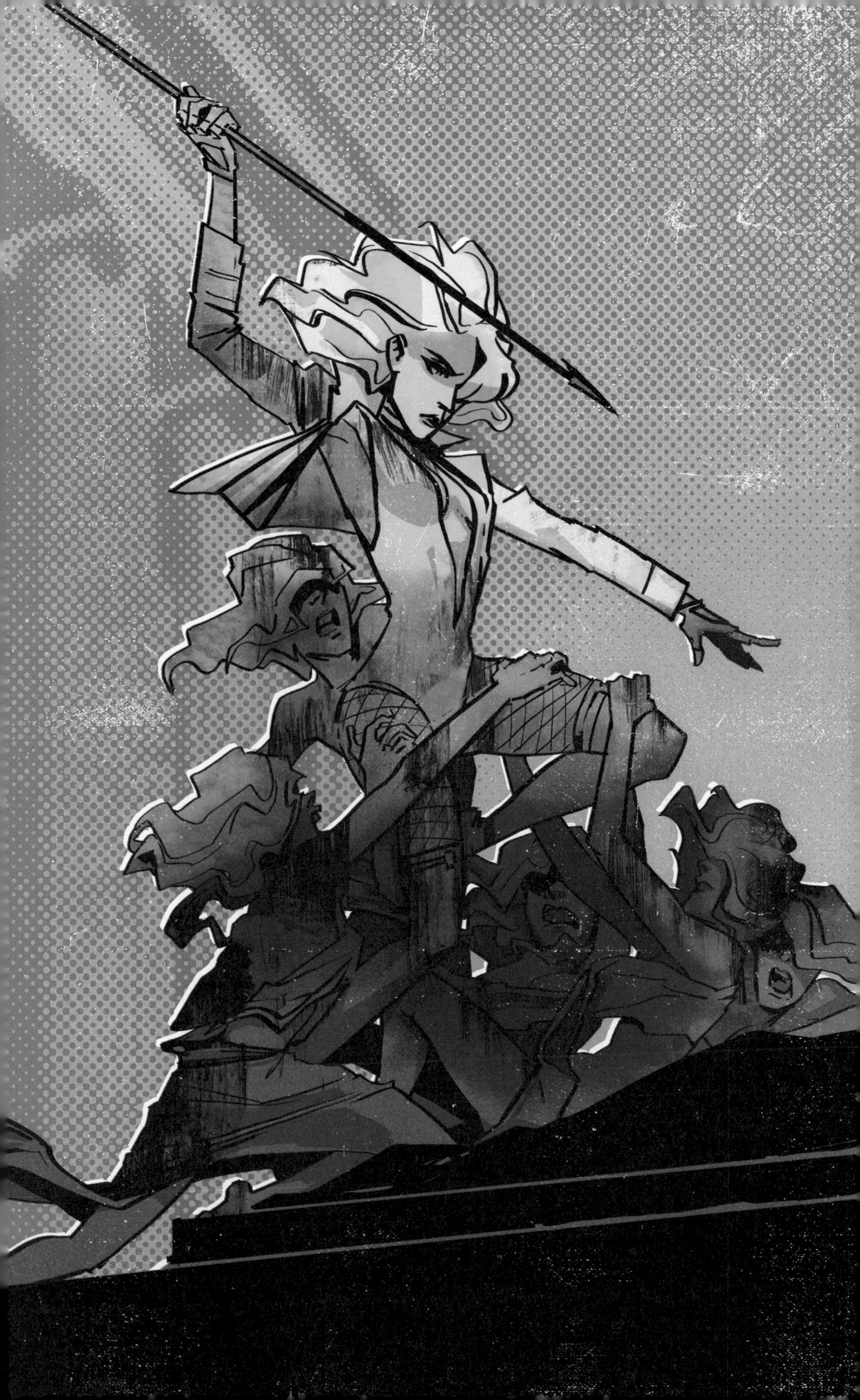

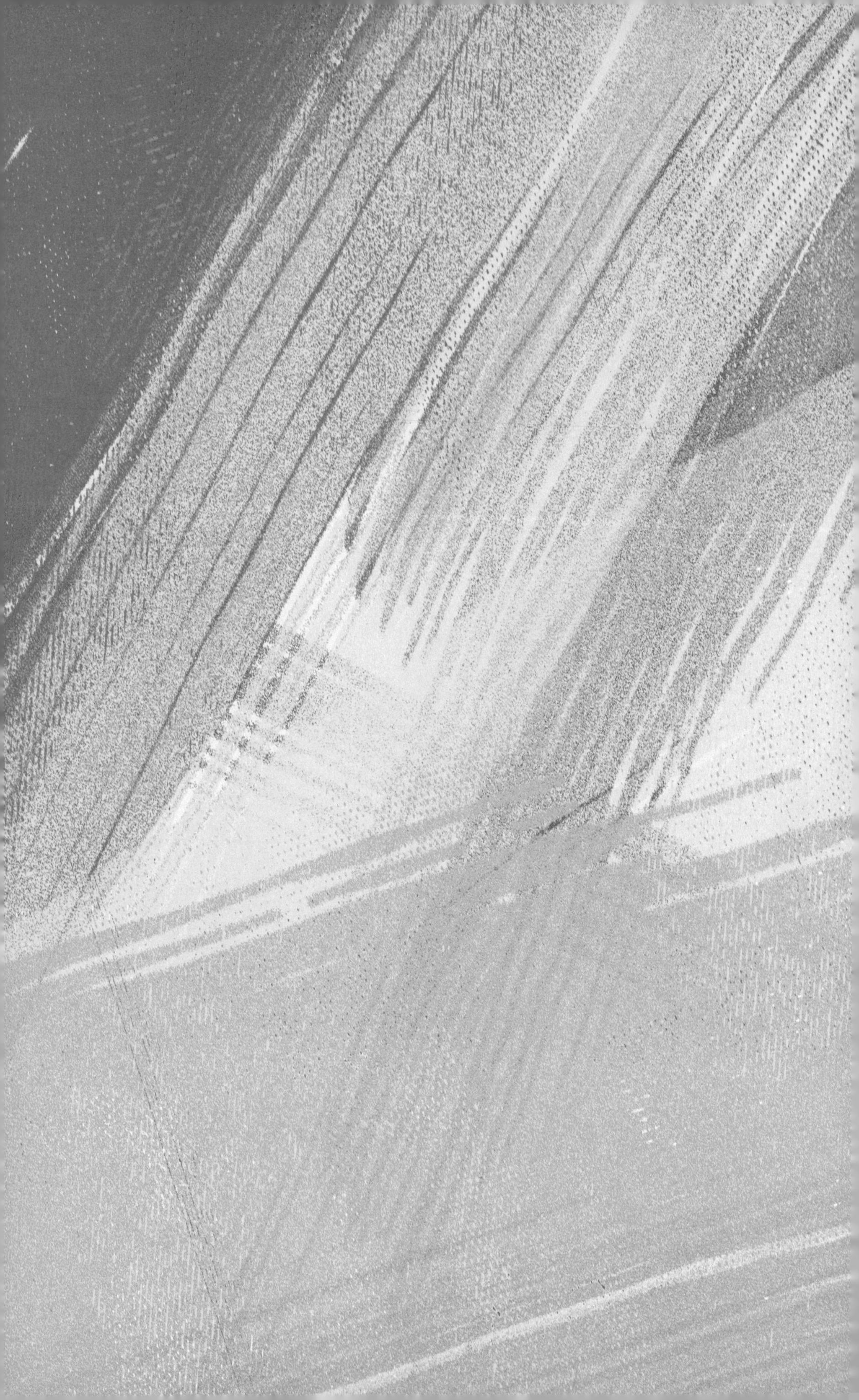

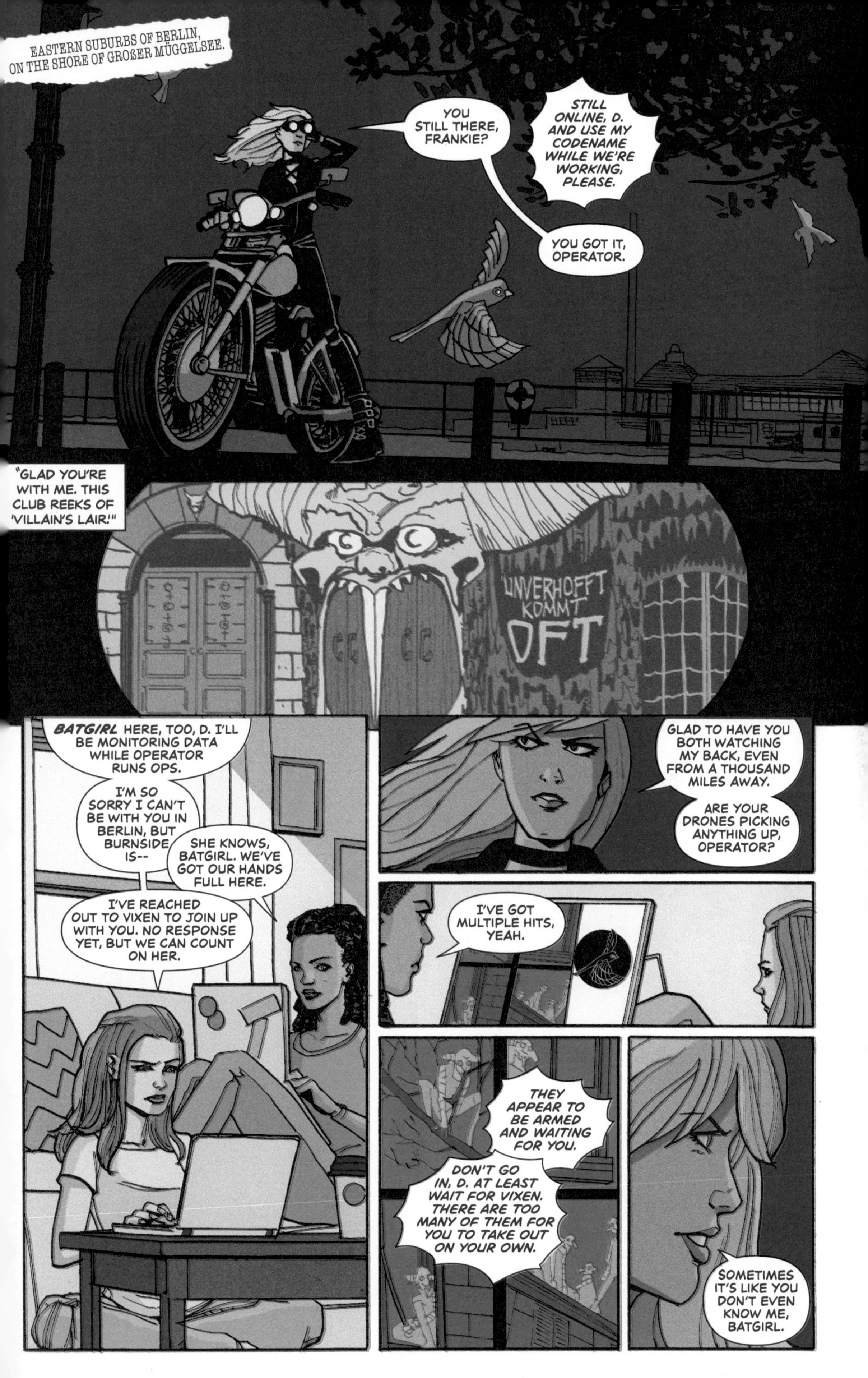
EASTERN SUBURBS OF BERLIN, ON THE SHORE OF GROßER MÜGGELSEE.
YOU STILL THERE, FRANKIE?
STILL ONLINE, D. AND USE MY CODENAME WHILE WE'RE WORKING, PLEASE.
YOU GOT IT, OPERATOR.
"GLAD YOU'RE WITH ME. THIS CLUB REEKS OF 'VILLAIN'S LAIR.'"
UNVERHOFFT KOMMT OFT
BATGIRL HERE, TOO, D. I'LL BE MONITORING DATA WHILE OPERATOR RUNS OPS.
I'M SO SORRY I CAN'T BE WITH YOU IN BERLIN, BUT BURNSIDE IS--
SHE KNOWS, BATGIRL. WE'VE GOT OUR HANDS FULL HERE.
I'VE REACHED OUT TO VIXEN TO JOIN UP WITH YOU. NO RESPONSE YET, BUT WE CAN COUNT ON HER.
GLAD TO HAVE YOU BOTH WATCHING MY BACK, EVEN FROM A THOUSAND MILES AWAY.
ARE YOUR DRONES PICKING ANYTHING UP, OPERATOR?
I'VE GOT MULTIPLE HITS, YEAH.
THEY APPEAR TO BE ARMED AND WAITING FOR YOU.
DON'T GO IN, D. AT LEAST WAIT FOR VIXEN. THERE ARE TOO MANY OF THEM FOR YOU TO TAKE OUT ON YOUR OWN.
SOMETIMES IT'S LIKE YOU DON'T EVEN KNOW ME, BATGIRL.

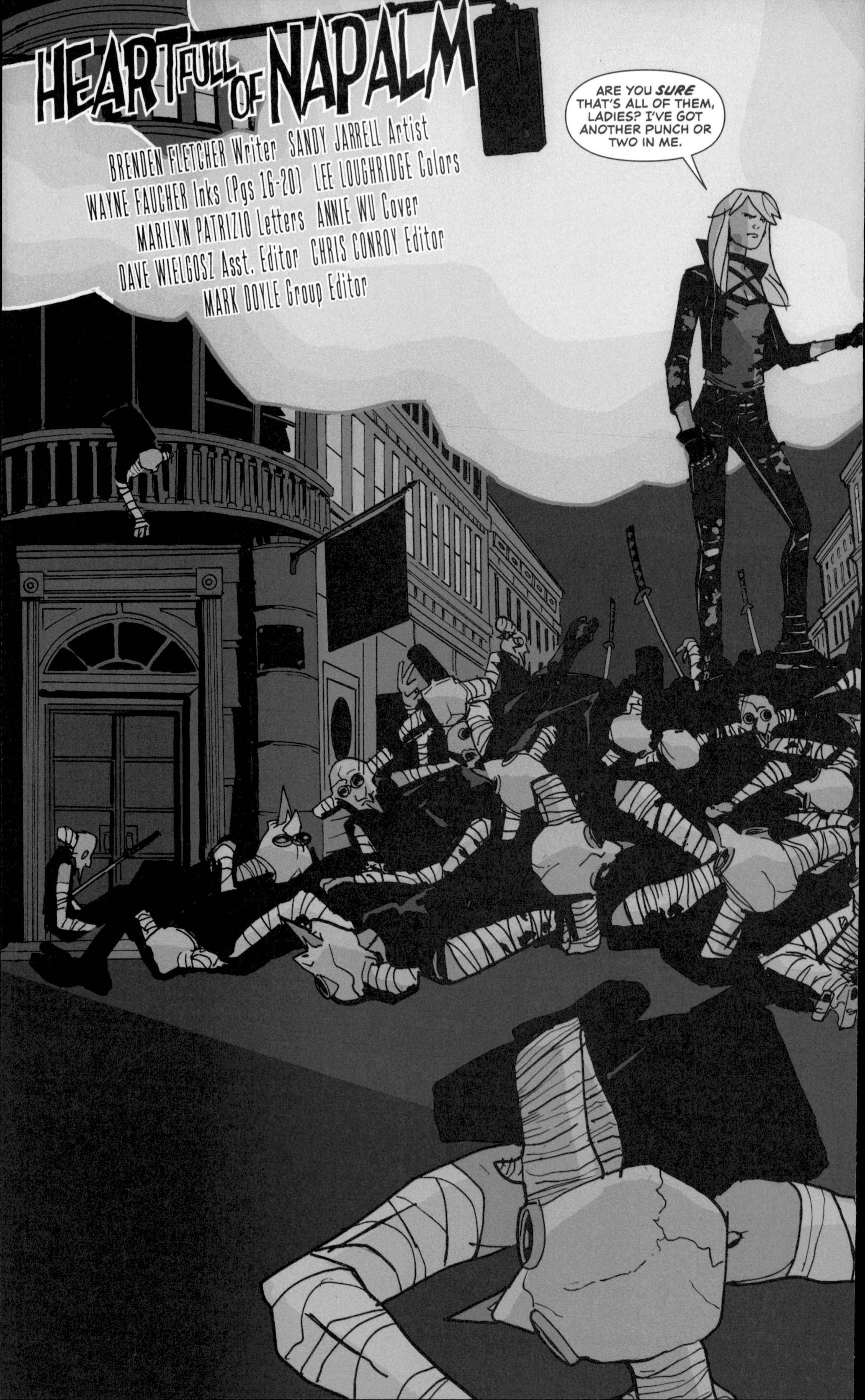
HEART FULL OF NAPALM
BRENDEN FLETCHER Writer SANDY JARRELL Artist
WAYNE FAUCHER Inks (Pgs 16-20) LEE LOUGHRIDGE Colors
MARILYN PATRIZIO Letters ANNIE WU Cover
DAVE WIELGOSZ Asst. Editor CHRIS CONROY Editor
MARK DOYLE Group Editor
ARE YOU SURE THAT'S ALL OF THEM, LADIES? I'VE GOT ANOTHER PUNCH OR TWO IN ME.

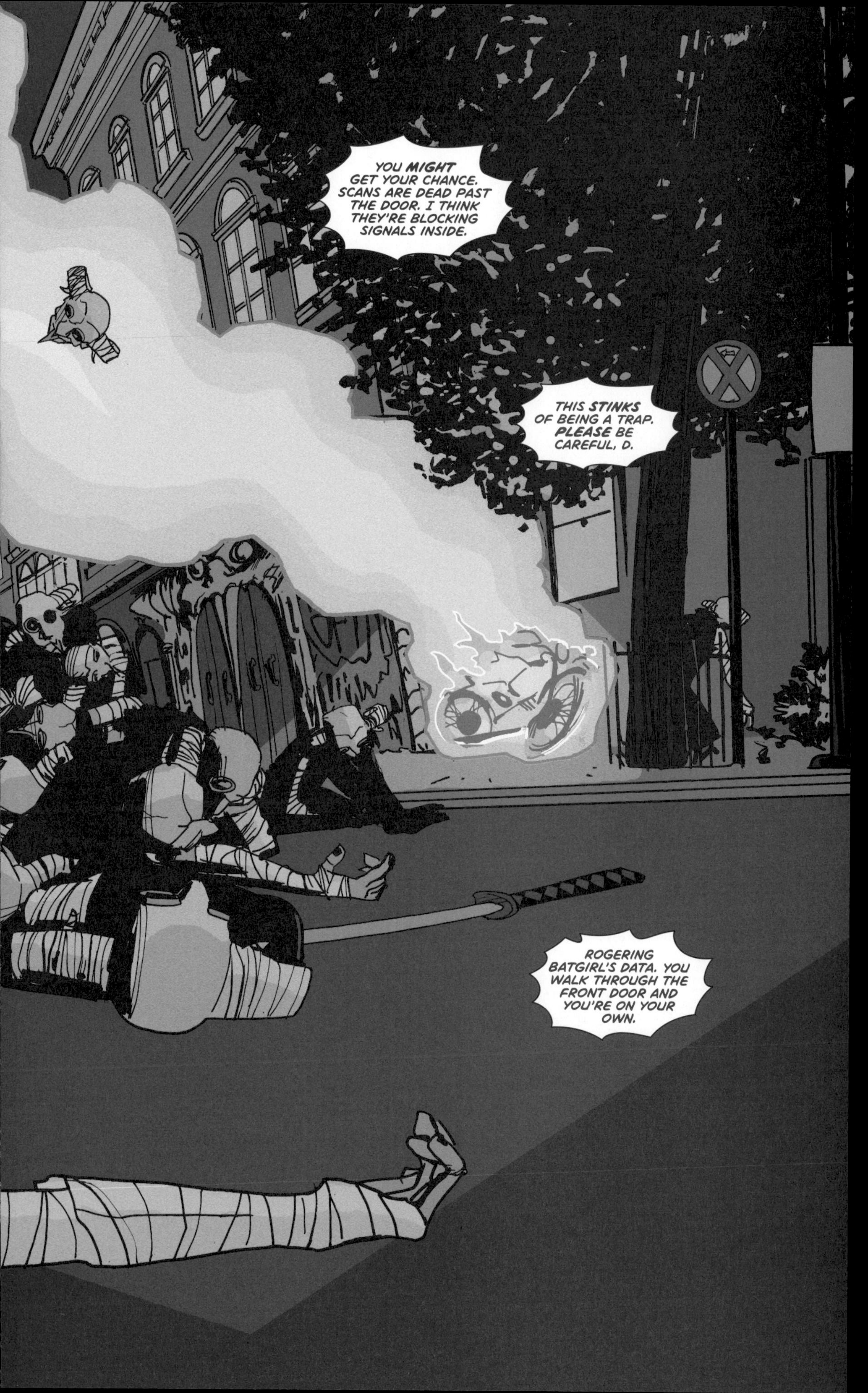
YOU MIGHT GET YOUR CHANCE. SCANS ARE DEAD PAST THE DOOR. I THINK THEY'RE BLOCKING SIGNALS INSIDE.
THIS STINKS OF BEING A TRAP. PLEASE BE CAREFUL, D.
ROGERING BATGIRL'S DATA. YOU WALK THROUGH THE FRONT DOOR AND YOU'RE ON YOUR OWN.

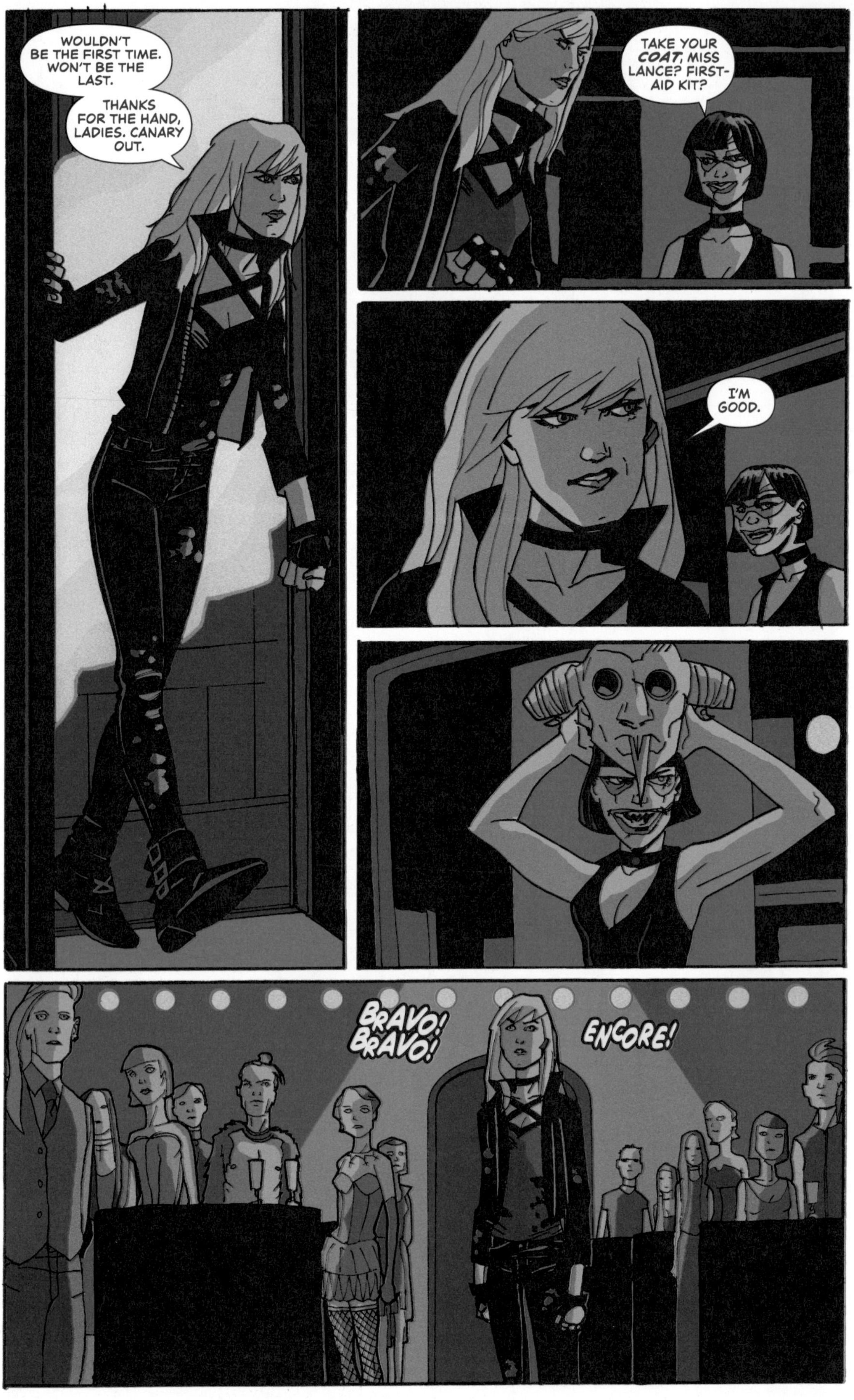
WOULDN'T BE THE FIRST TIME. WON'T BE THE LAST.
THANKS FOR THE HAND, LADIES. CANARY OUT.
TAKE YOUR COAT, MISS LANCE? FIRST-AID KIT?
I'M GOOD.
BRAVO! BRAVO!
ENCORE!

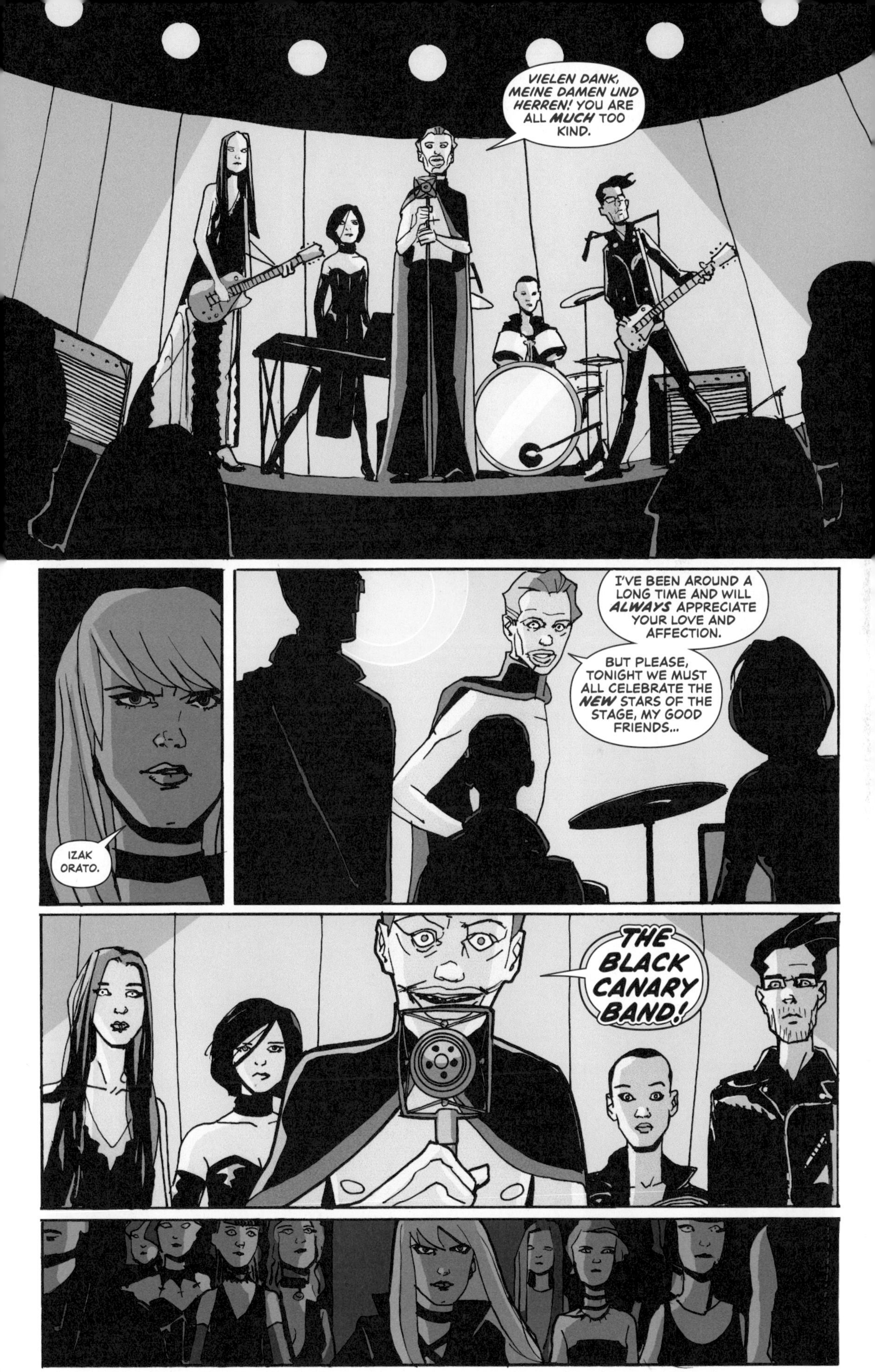

VIELEN DANK, MEINE DAMEN UND HERREN! YOU ARE ALL MUCH TOO KIND.
IZAK ORATO.
I'VE BEEN AROUND A LONG TIME AND WILL ALWAYS APPRECIATE YOUR LOVE AND AFFECTION.
BUT PLEASE, TONIGHT WE MUST ALL CELEBRATE THE NEW STARS OF THE STAGE, MY GOOD FRIENDS...
THE BLACK CANARY BAND!

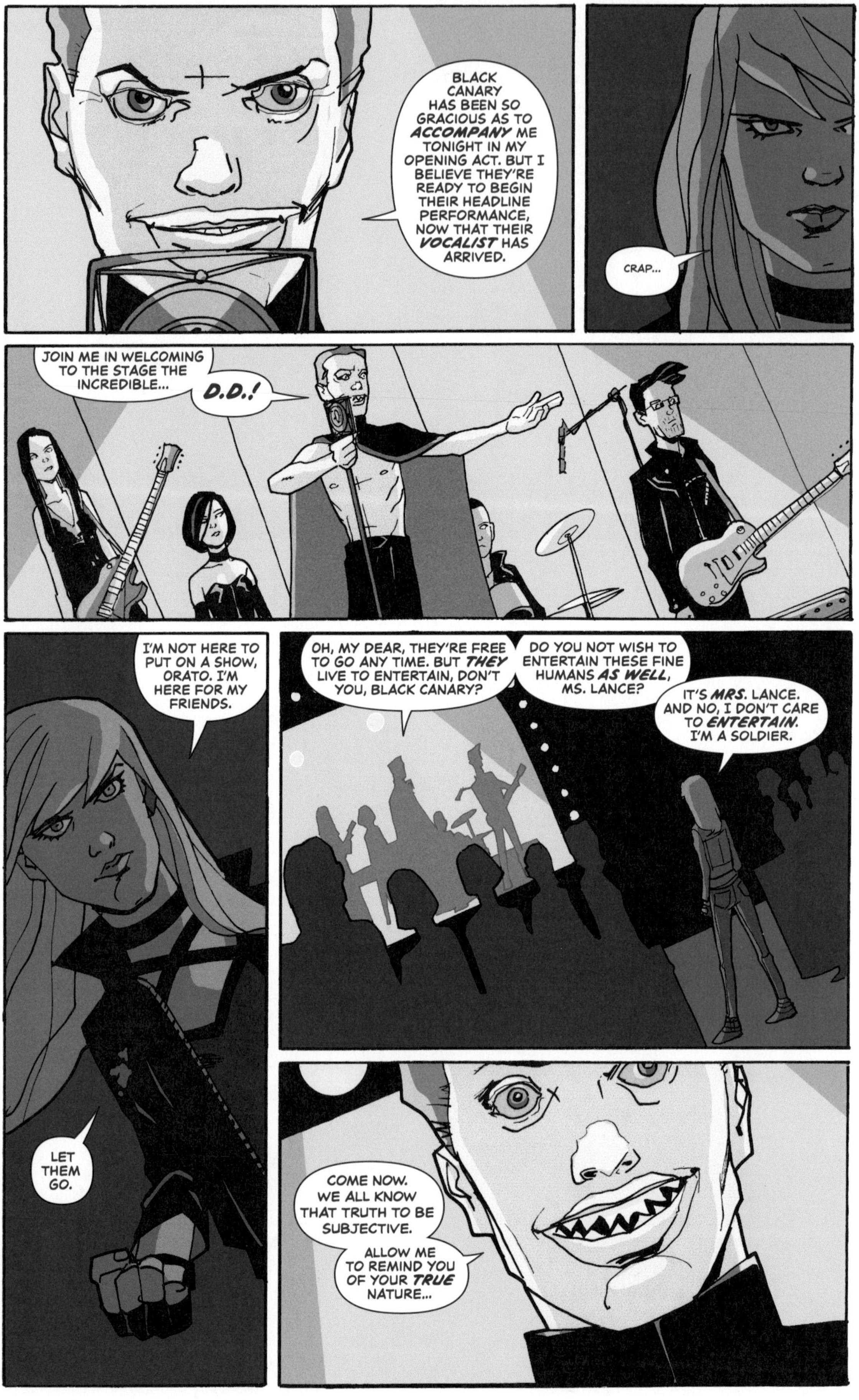
BLACK CANARY HAS BEEN SO GRACIOUS AS TO ACCOMPANY ME TONIGHT IN MY OPENING ACT. BUT I BELIEVE THEY'RE READY TO BEGIN THEIR HEADLINE PERFORMANCE, NOW THAT THEIR VOCALIST HAS ARRIVED.
CRAP...
JOIN ME IN WELCOMING TO THE STAGE THE INCREDIBLE...
D.D.!
I'M NOT HERE TO PUT ON A SHOW, ORATO. I'M HERE FOR MY FRIENDS.
LET THEM GO.
OH, MY DEAR, THEY'RE FREE TO GO ANY TIME. BUT THEY LIVE TO ENTERTAIN, DON'T YOU, BLACK CANARY?
DO YOU NOT WISH TO ENTERTAIN THESE FINE HUMANS AS WELL, MS. LANCE?
IT'S MRS. LANCE. AND NO, I DON'T CARE TO ENTERTAIN. I'M A SOLDIER.
COME NOW. WE ALL KNOW THAT TRUTH TO BE SUBJECTIVE.
ALLOW ME TO REMIND YOU OF YOUR TRUE NATURE...

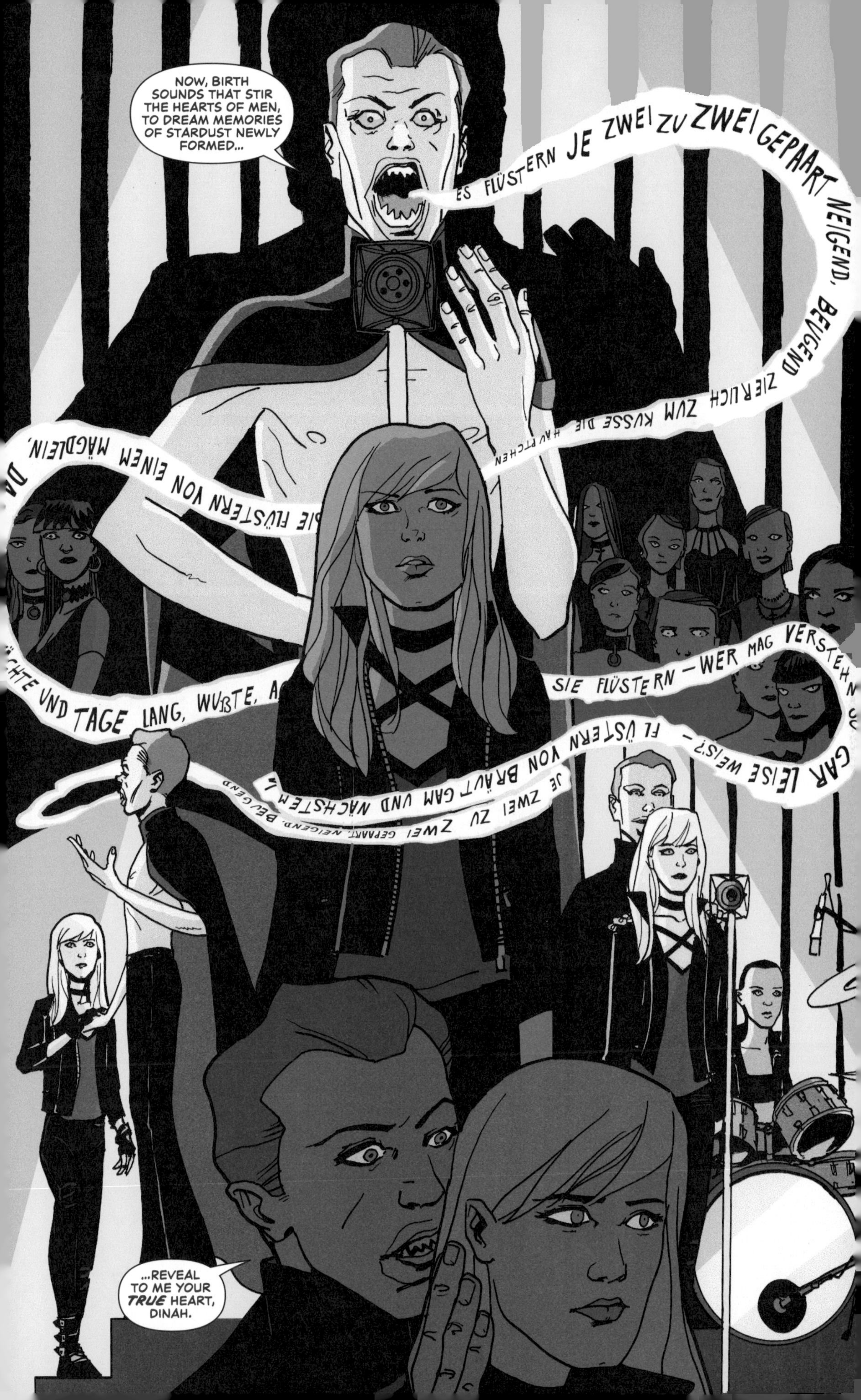
NOW, BIRTH SOUNDS THAT STIR THE HEARTS OF MEN, TO DREAM MEMORIES OF STARDUST NEWLY FORMED...
ES FLÜSTERN JE ZWEI ZU ZWEI GEPAART NEIGEND, BEUGEND ZIERLICH ZUM KUSSE DIE HÄUPTCHEN
SIE FLÜSTERN VON EINEM MÄGDLEIN, DA
CHTE UND TAGE LANG, WUßTE, A
SIE FLÜSTERN — WER MAG VERSTEHN
GAR LEISE WEIS'? — FLÜSTERN VON BRÄUTGAM UND NÄCHSTEM !,
JE ZWEI ZU ZWEI GEPAART, NEIGEND, BEUGEND
...REVEAL TO ME YOUR *TRUE* HEART, DINAH.

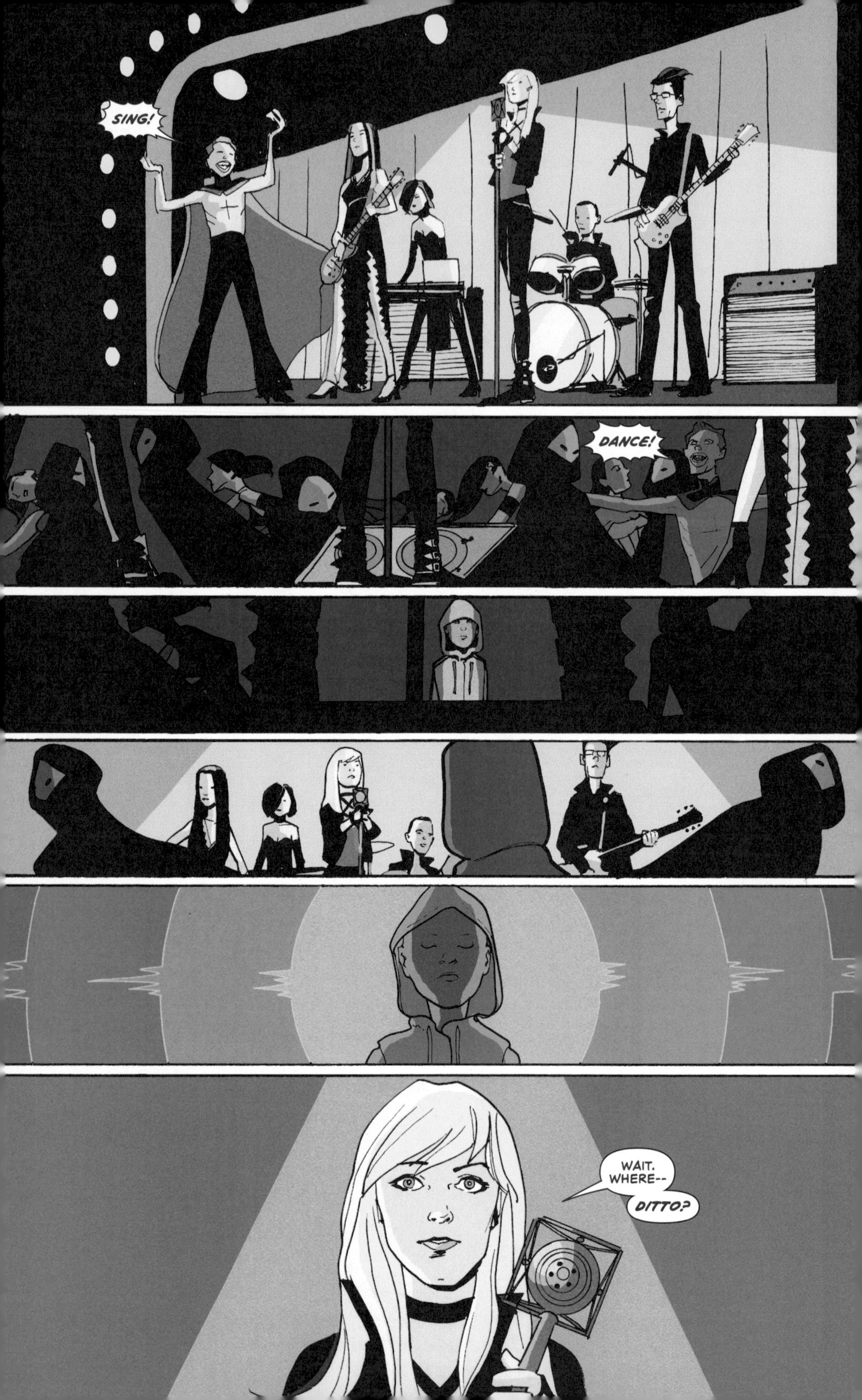
SING!
DANCE!
WAIT. WHERE--
DITTO?

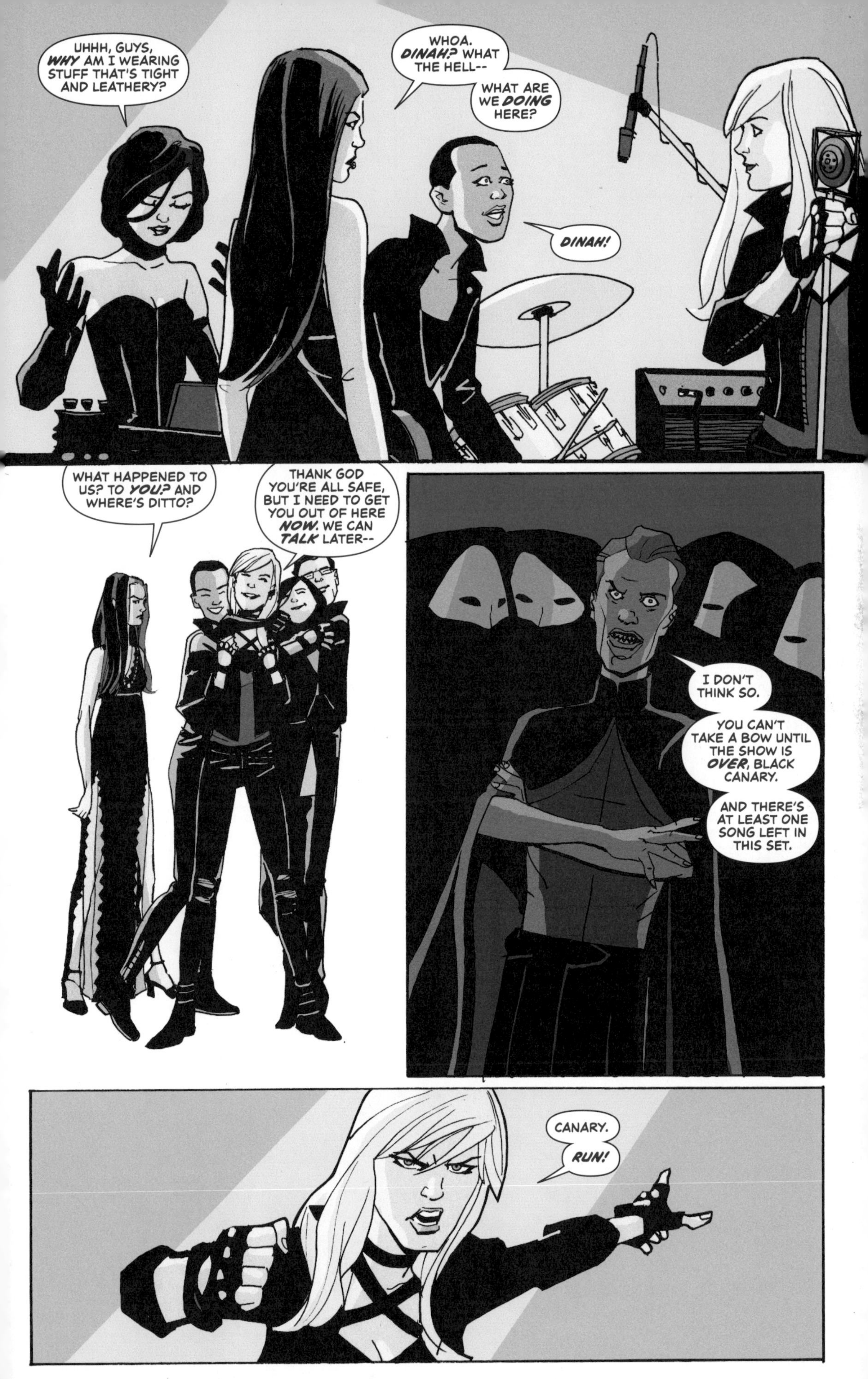
UHHH, GUYS, WHY AM I WEARING STUFF THAT'S TIGHT AND LEATHERY?
WHOA. DINAH? WHAT THE HELL--
WHAT ARE WE DOING HERE?
DINAH!
WHAT HAPPENED TO US? TO YOU? AND WHERE'S DITTO?
THANK GOD YOU'RE ALL SAFE, BUT I NEED TO GET YOU OUT OF HERE NOW. WE CAN TALK LATER--
I DON'T THINK SO.
YOU CAN'T TAKE A BOW UNTIL THE SHOW IS OVER, BLACK CANARY.
AND THERE'S AT LEAST ONE SONG LEFT IN THIS SET.
CANARY.
RUN!

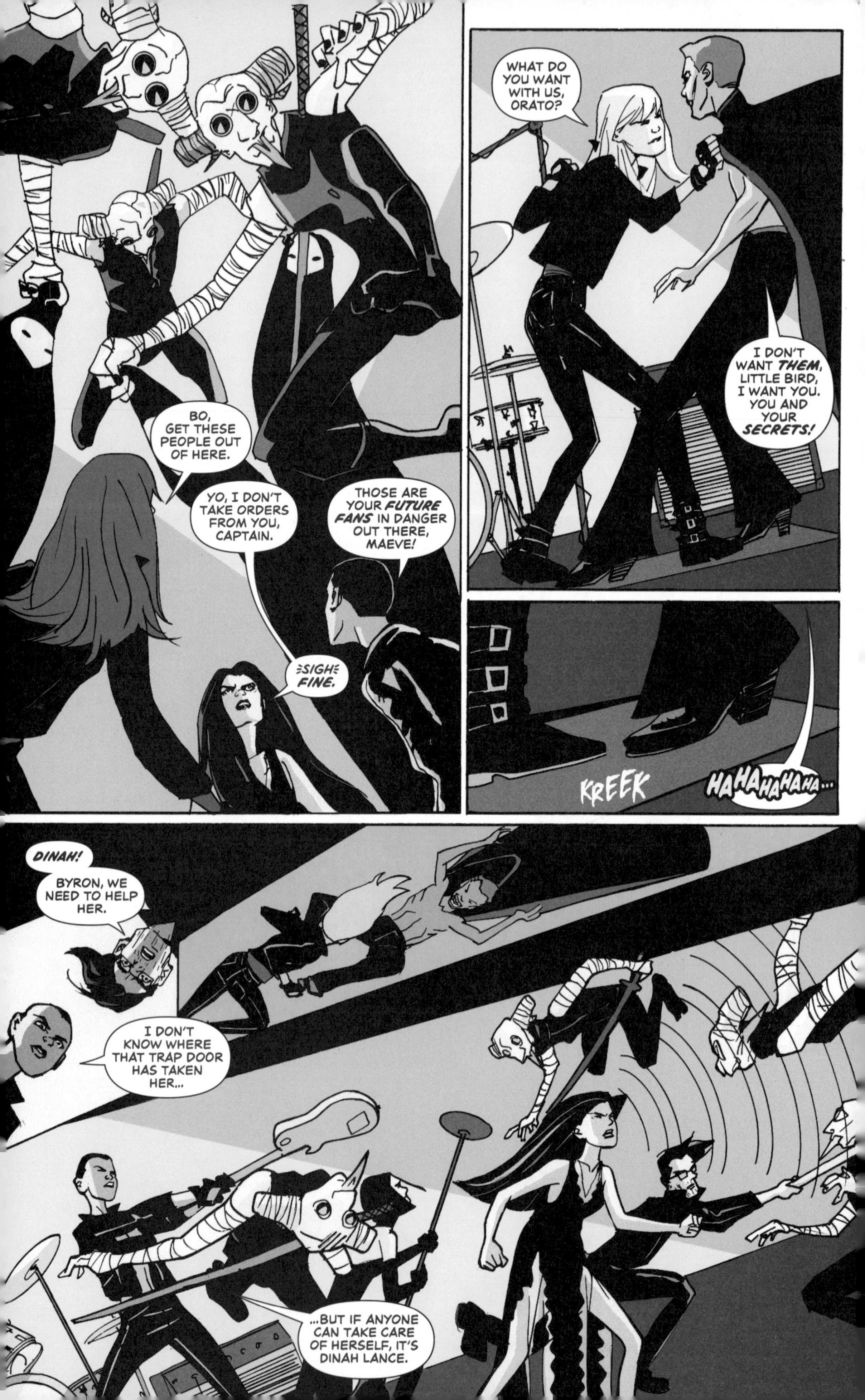
BO, GET THESE PEOPLE OUT OF HERE.
YO, I DON'T TAKE ORDERS FROM YOU, CAPTAIN.
THOSE ARE YOUR FUTURE FANS IN DANGER OUT THERE, MAEVE!
SIGH FINE.
WHAT DO YOU WANT WITH US, ORATO?
I DON'T WANT THEM, LITTLE BIRD, I WANT YOU. YOU AND YOUR SECRETS!
KREEK
HAHAHAHAHA...
DINAH!
BYRON, WE NEED TO HELP HER.
I DON'T KNOW WHERE THAT TRAP DOOR HAS TAKEN HER...
...BUT IF ANYONE CAN TAKE CARE OF HERSELF, IT'S DINAH LANCE.

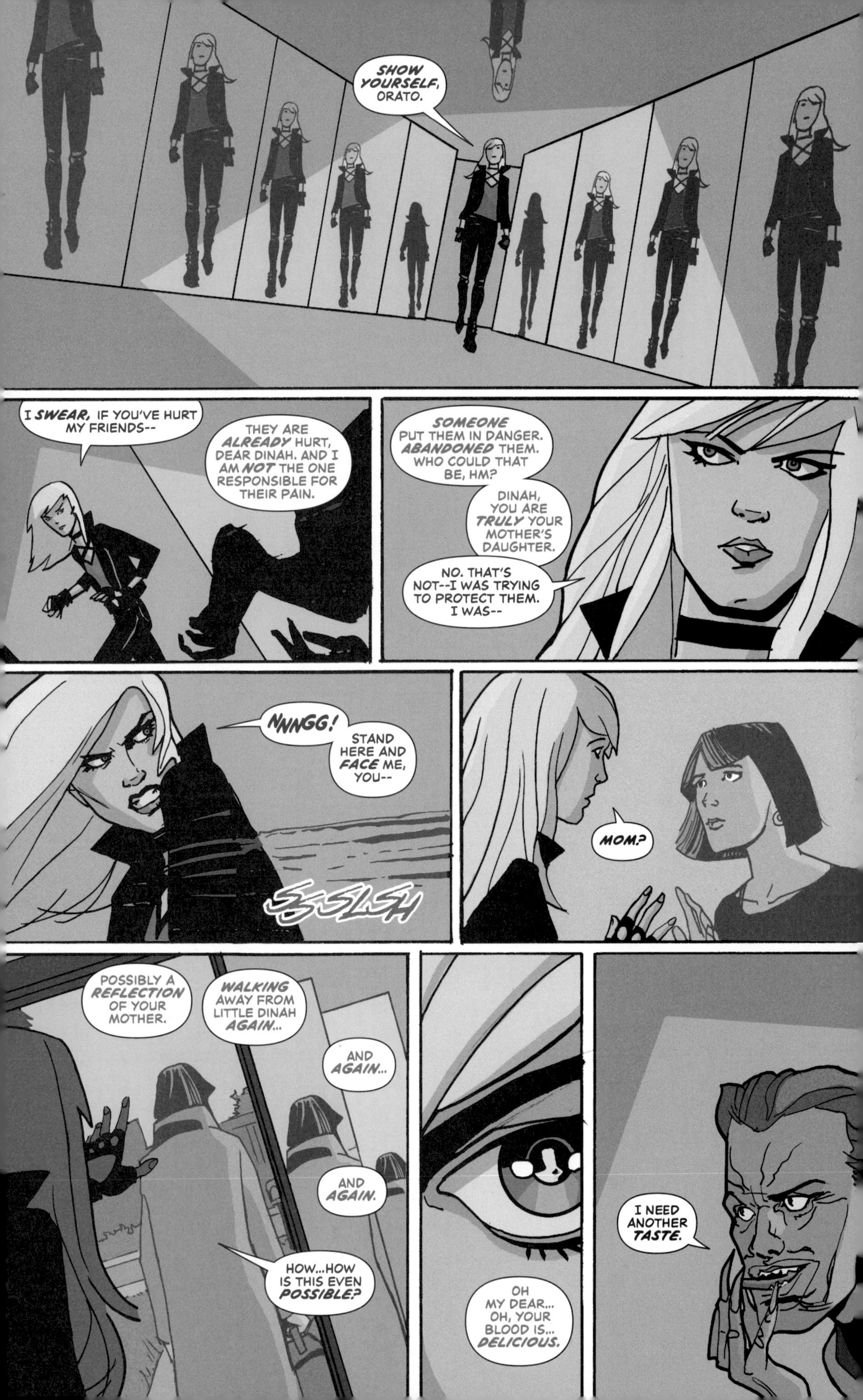
SHOW YOURSELF, ORATO.
I SWEAR, IF YOU'VE HURT MY FRIENDS--
THEY ARE ALREADY HURT, DEAR DINAH. AND I AM NOT THE ONE RESPONSIBLE FOR THEIR PAIN.
SOMEONE PUT THEM IN DANGER. ABANDONED THEM. WHO COULD THAT BE, HM?
DINAH, YOU ARE TRULY YOUR MOTHER'S DAUGHTER.
NO. THAT'S NOT--I WAS TRYING TO PROTECT THEM. I WAS--
NNNGG!
STAND HERE AND FACE ME, YOU--
SSSLSH
MOM?
POSSIBLY A REFLECTION OF YOUR MOTHER.
WALKING AWAY FROM LITTLE DINAH AGAIN...
AND AGAIN...
AND AGAIN.
HOW...HOW IS THIS EVEN POSSIBLE?
OH MY DEAR... OH, YOUR BLOOD IS... DELICIOUS.
I NEED ANOTHER TASTE.

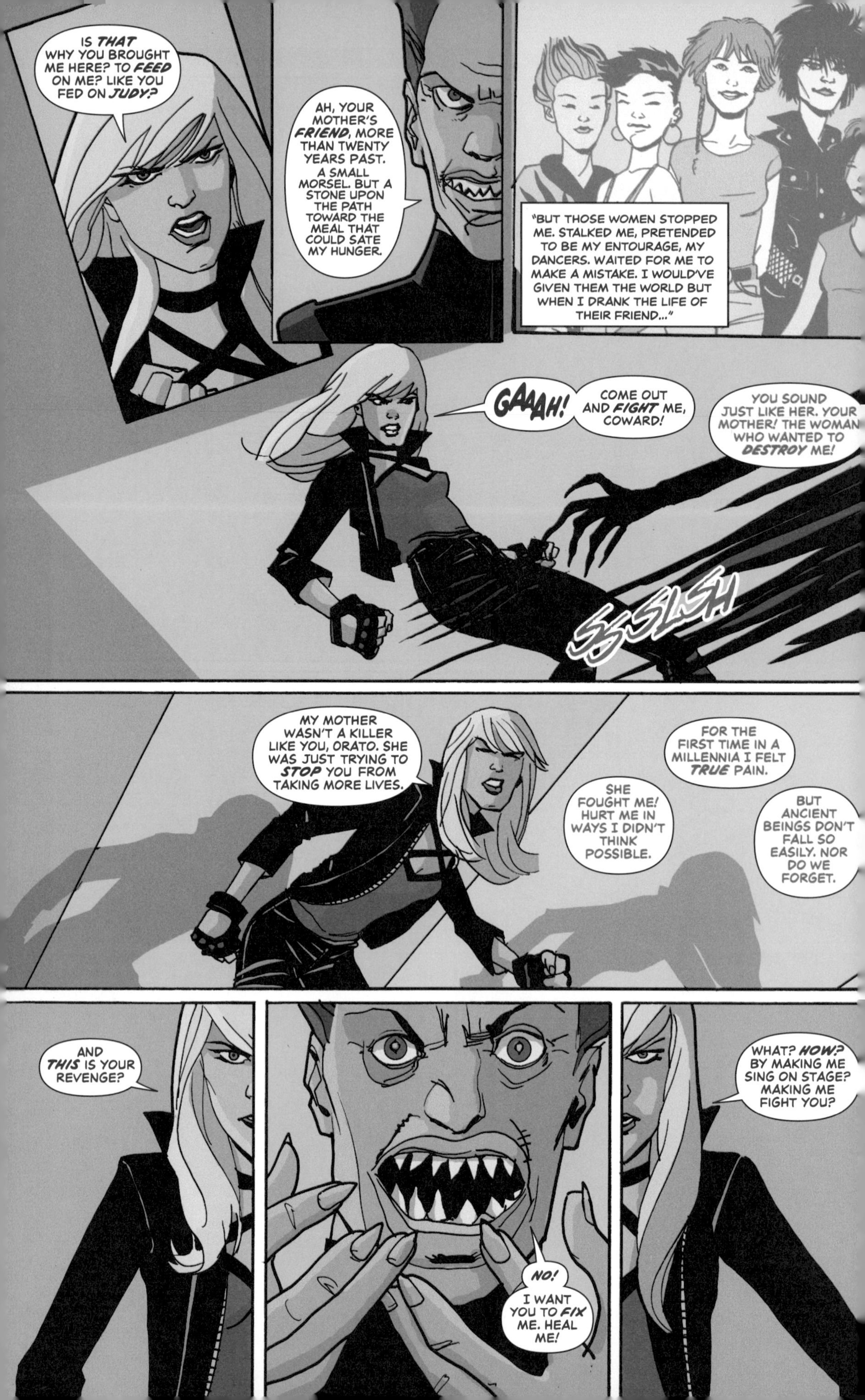
IS THAT WHY YOU BROUGHT ME HERE? TO FEED ON ME? LIKE YOU FED ON JUDY?
AH, YOUR MOTHER'S FRIEND, MORE THAN TWENTY YEARS PAST. A SMALL MORSEL. BUT A STONE UPON THE PATH TOWARD THE MEAL THAT COULD SATE MY HUNGER.
"BUT THOSE WOMEN STOPPED ME. STALKED ME, PRETENDED TO BE MY ENTOURAGE, MY DANCERS. WAITED FOR ME TO MAKE A MISTAKE. I WOULD'VE GIVEN THEM THE WORLD BUT WHEN I DRANK THE LIFE OF THEIR FRIEND..."
GAAAH!
COME OUT AND FIGHT ME, COWARD!
YOU SOUND JUST LIKE HER. YOUR MOTHER! THE WOMAN WHO WANTED TO DESTROY ME!
SSSLSH
MY MOTHER WASN'T A KILLER LIKE YOU, ORATO. SHE WAS JUST TRYING TO STOP YOU FROM TAKING MORE LIVES.
FOR THE FIRST TIME IN A MILLENNIA I FELT TRUE PAIN.
SHE FOUGHT ME! HURT ME IN WAYS I DIDN'T THINK POSSIBLE.
BUT ANCIENT BEINGS DON'T FALL SO EASILY. NOR DO WE FORGET.
AND THIS IS YOUR REVENGE?
WHAT? HOW? BY MAKING ME SING ON STAGE? MAKING ME FIGHT YOU?
NO! I WANT YOU TO FIX ME. HEAL ME!

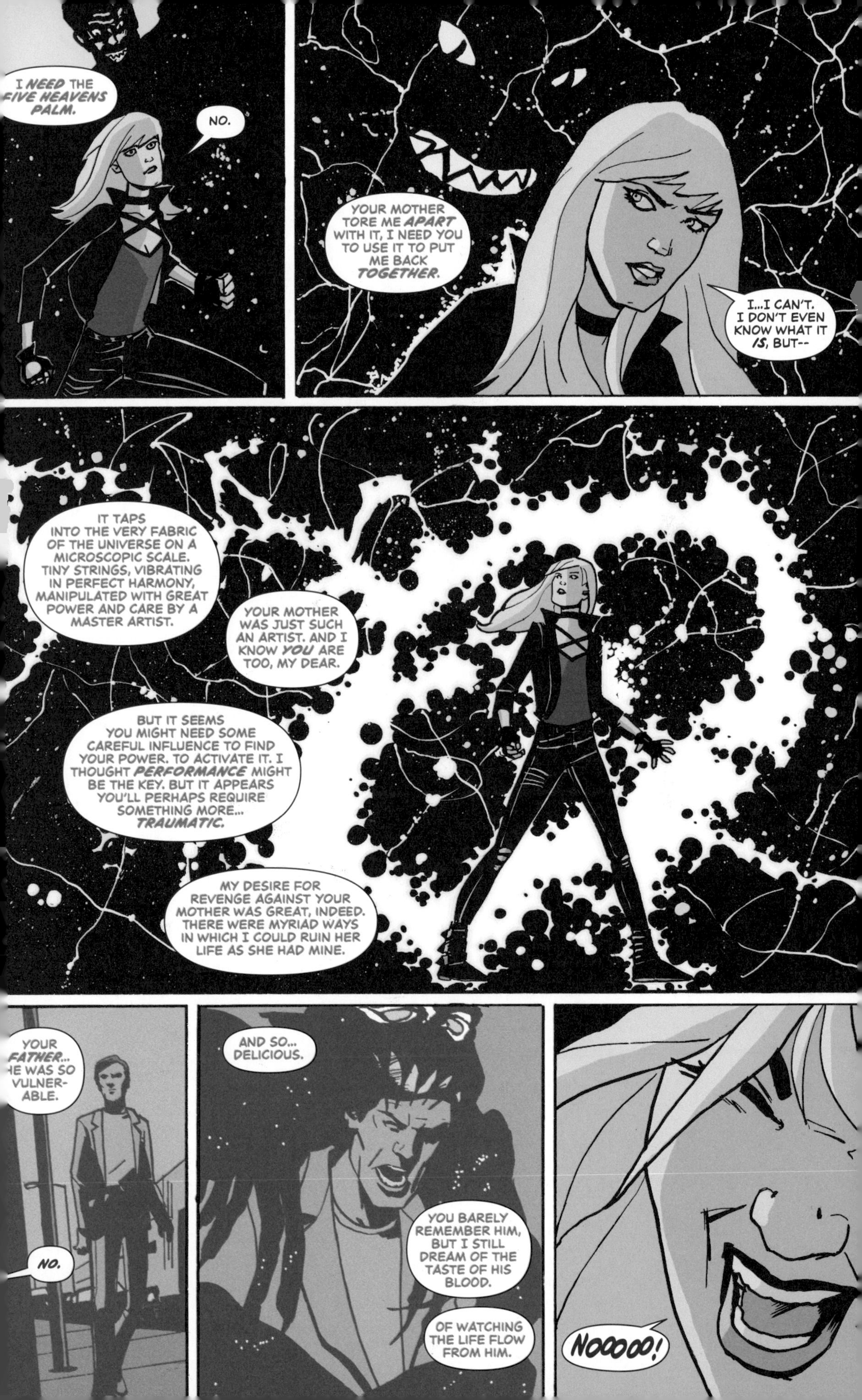
I NEED THE FIVE HEAVENS PALM.
NO.
YOUR MOTHER TORE ME APART WITH IT, I NEED YOU TO USE IT TO PUT ME BACK TOGETHER.
I...I CAN'T. I DON'T EVEN KNOW WHAT IT IS, BUT--
IT TAPS INTO THE VERY FABRIC OF THE UNIVERSE ON A MICROSCOPIC SCALE. TINY STRINGS, VIBRATING IN PERFECT HARMONY, MANIPULATED WITH GREAT POWER AND CARE BY A MASTER ARTIST.
YOUR MOTHER WAS JUST SUCH AN ARTIST. AND I KNOW YOU ARE TOO, MY DEAR.
BUT IT SEEMS YOU MIGHT NEED SOME CAREFUL INFLUENCE TO FIND YOUR POWER. TO ACTIVATE IT. I THOUGHT PERFORMANCE MIGHT BE THE KEY. BUT IT APPEARS YOU'LL PERHAPS REQUIRE SOMETHING MORE... TRAUMATIC.
MY DESIRE FOR REVENGE AGAINST YOUR MOTHER WAS GREAT, INDEED. THERE WERE MYRIAD WAYS IN WHICH I COULD RUIN HER LIFE AS SHE HAD MINE.
YOUR FATHER... HE WAS SO VULNER-ABLE.
NO.
AND SO... DELICIOUS.
YOU BARELY REMEMBER HIM, BUT I STILL DREAM OF THE TASTE OF HIS BLOOD.
OF WATCHING THE LIFE FLOW FROM HIM.
NOOOOO!

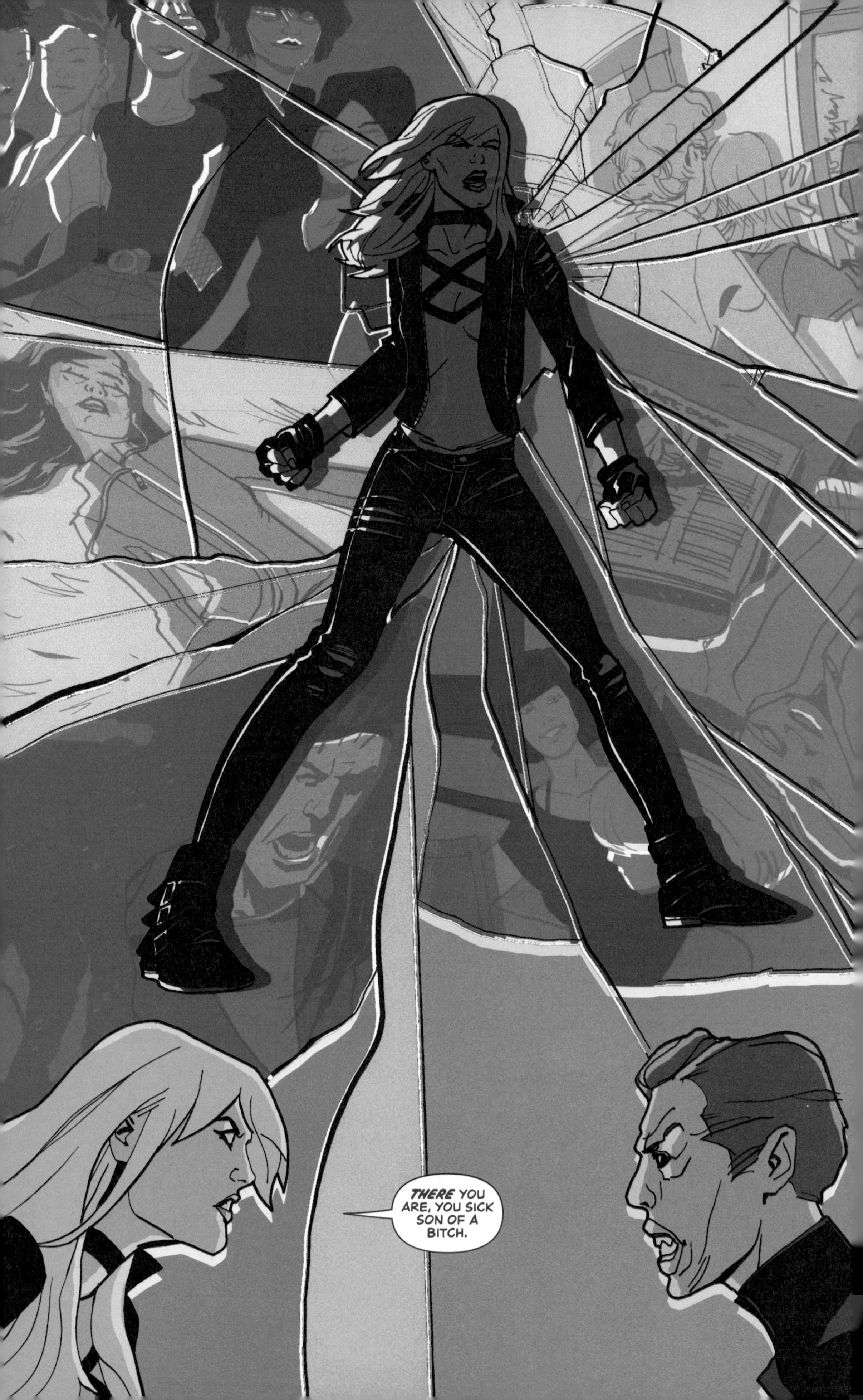

THERE YOU ARE, YOU SICK SON OF A BITCH.

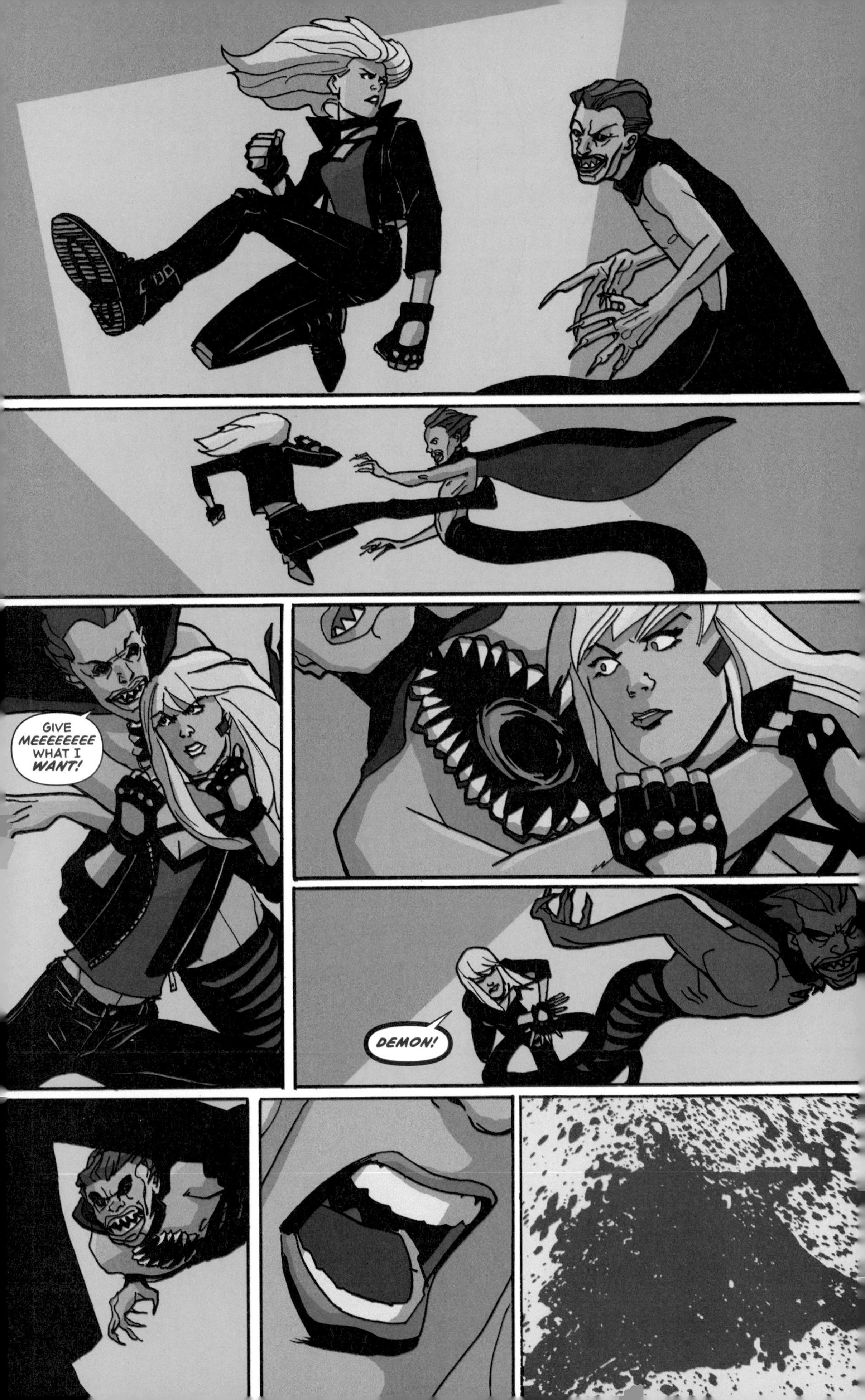
GIVE MEEEEEEEE WHAT I WANT!
DEMON!

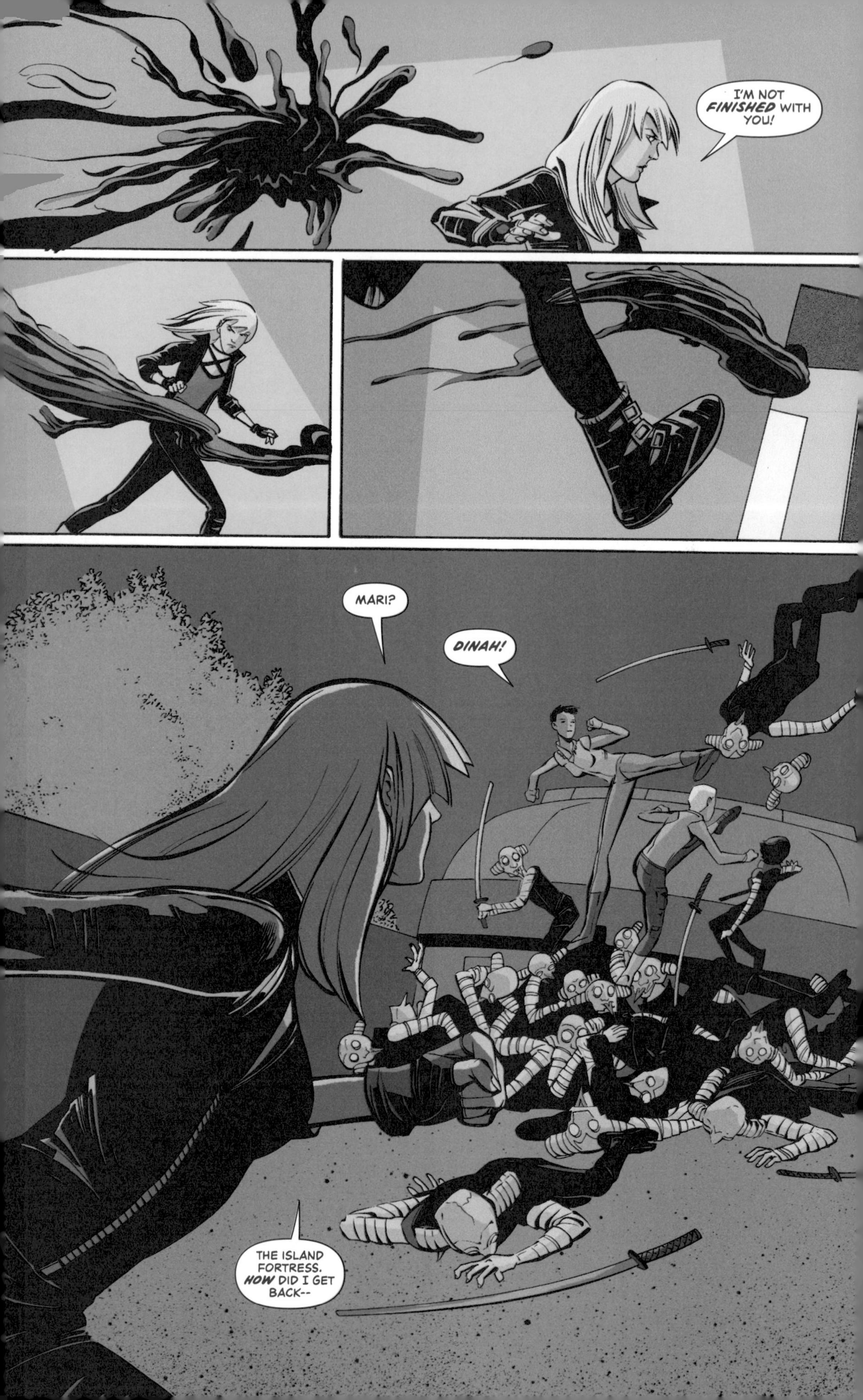
I'M NOT FINISHED WITH YOU!
MARI?
DINAH!
THE ISLAND FORTRESS. HOW DID I GET BACK--

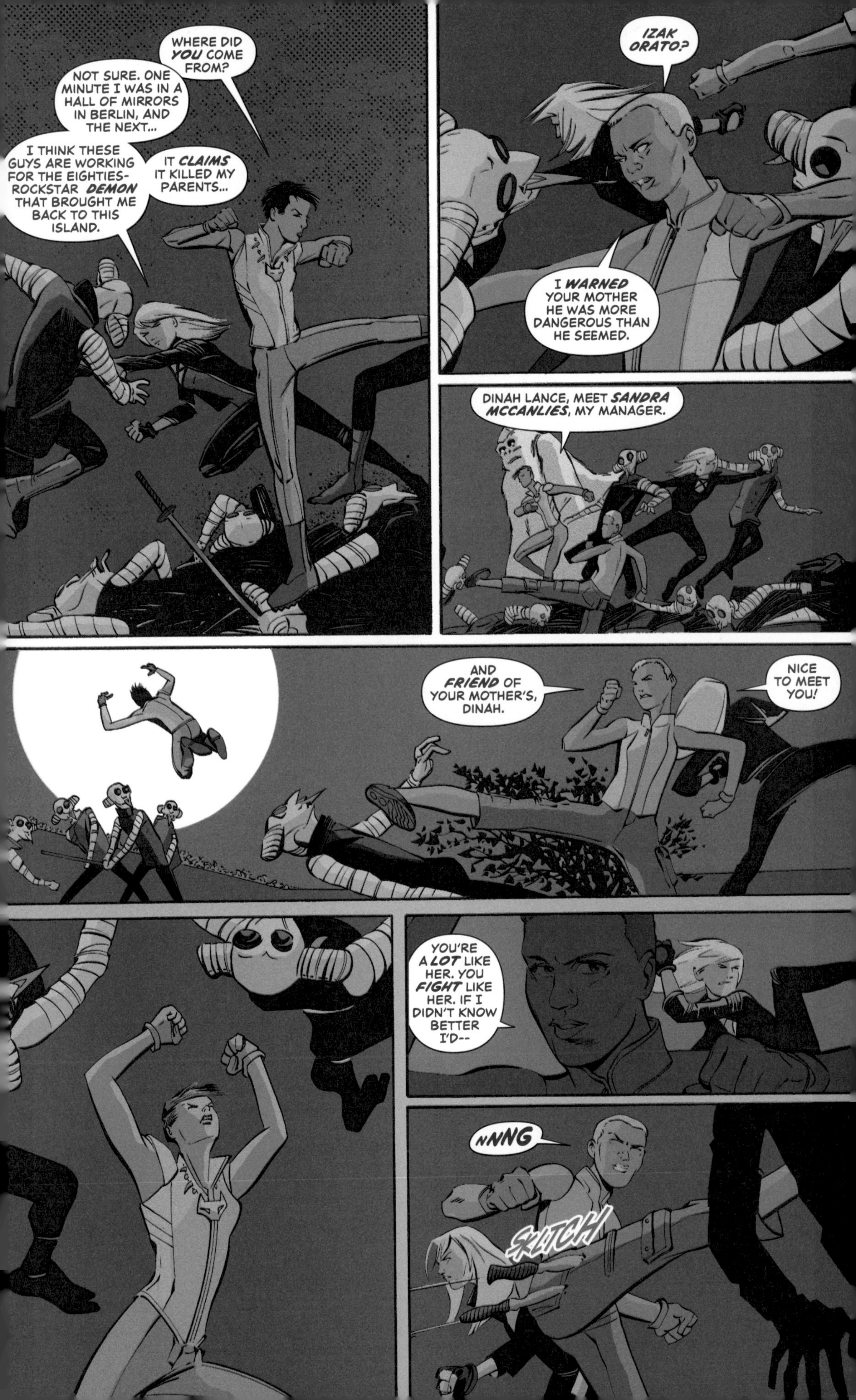
WHERE DID YOU COME FROM?
NOT SURE. ONE MINUTE I WAS IN A HALL OF MIRRORS IN BERLIN, AND THE NEXT...
I THINK THESE GUYS ARE WORKING FOR THE EIGHTIES-ROCKSTAR DEMON THAT BROUGHT ME BACK TO THIS ISLAND.
IT CLAIMS IT KILLED MY PARENTS...
IZAK ORATO?
I WARNED YOUR MOTHER HE WAS MORE DANGEROUS THAN HE SEEMED.
DINAH LANCE, MEET SANDRA MCCANLIES, MY MANAGER.
AND FRIEND OF YOUR MOTHER'S, DINAH.
NICE TO MEET YOU!
YOU'RE A LOT LIKE HER. YOU FIGHT LIKE HER. IF I DIDN'T KNOW BETTER I'D--
NNNG
SKLTCH

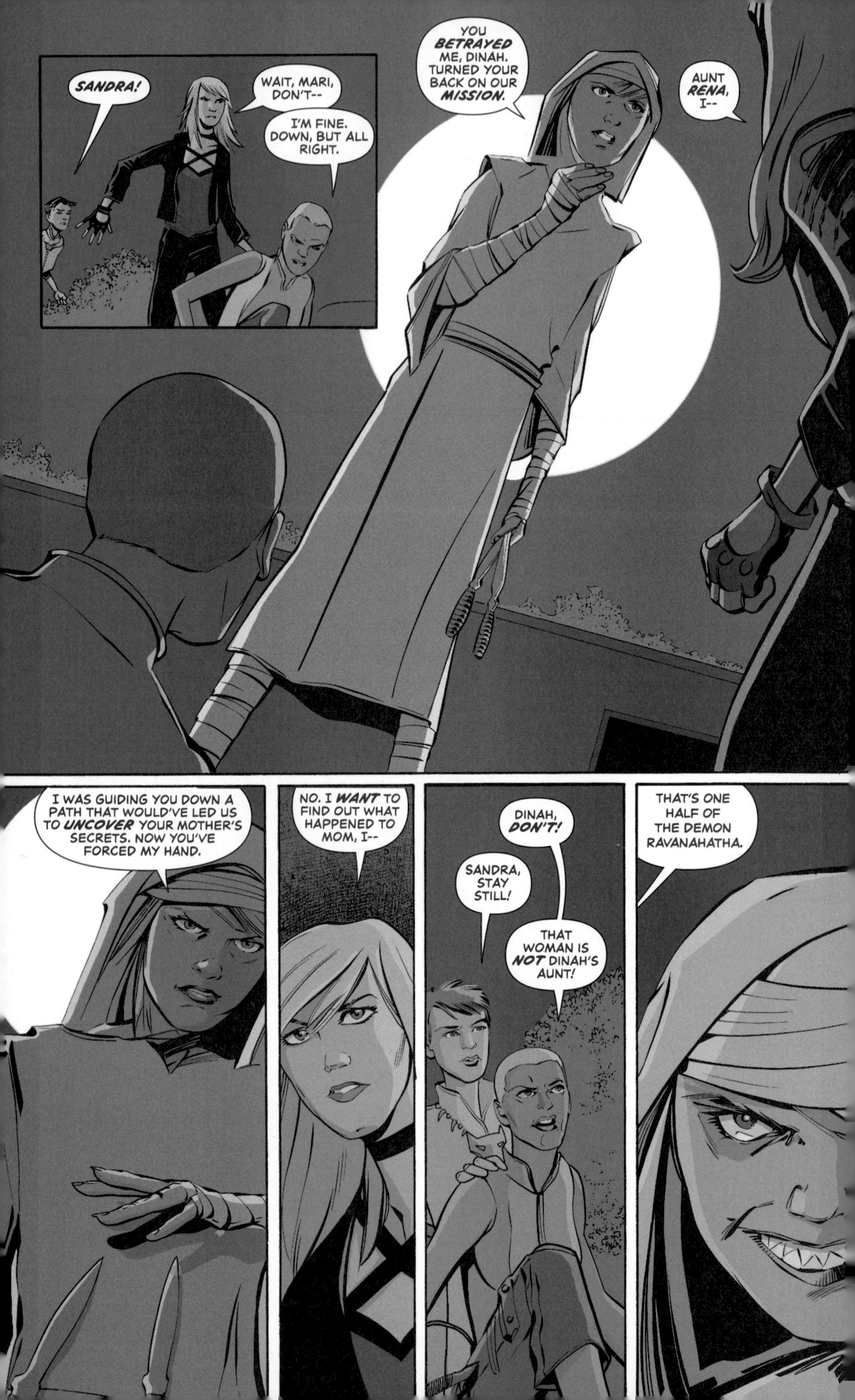
SANDRA!
WAIT, MARI, DON'T--
I'M FINE. DOWN, BUT ALL RIGHT.
YOU BETRAYED ME, DINAH. TURNED YOUR BACK ON OUR MISSION.
AUNT RENA, I--
I WAS GUIDING YOU DOWN A PATH THAT WOULD'VE LED US TO UNCOVER YOUR MOTHER'S SECRETS. NOW YOU'VE FORCED MY HAND.
NO. I WANT TO FIND OUT WHAT HAPPENED TO MOM, I--
DINAH, DON'T!
SANDRA, STAY STILL!
THAT WOMAN IS NOT DINAH'S AUNT!
THAT'S ONE HALF OF THE DEMON RAVANAHATHA.

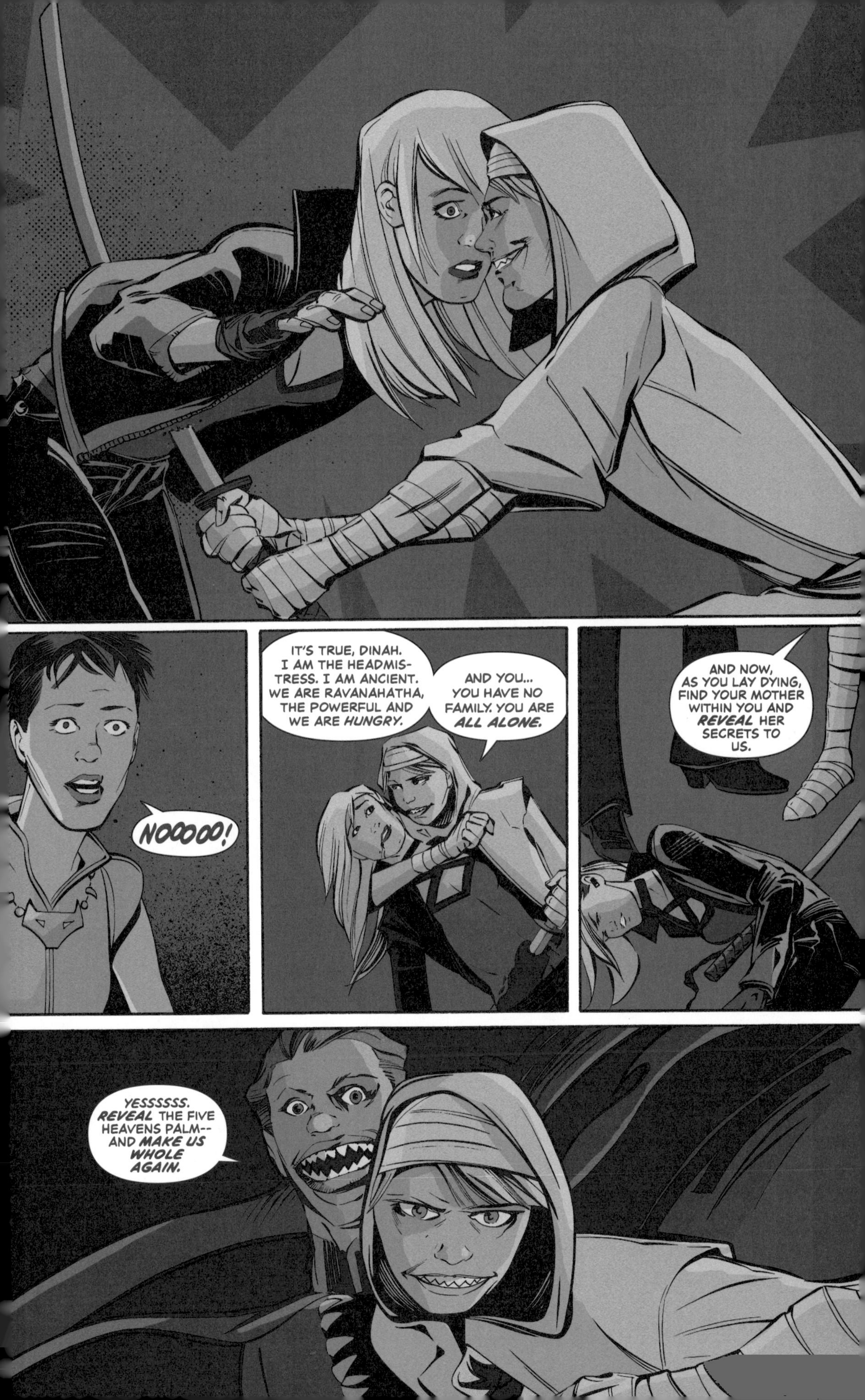
NOOOOO!
IT'S TRUE, DINAH. I AM THE HEADMIS-TRESS. I AM ANCIENT. WE ARE RAVANAHATHA, THE POWERFUL AND WE ARE HUNGRY.
AND YOU... YOU HAVE NO FAMILY. YOU ARE ALL ALONE.
AND NOW, AS YOU LAY DYING, FIND YOUR MOTHER WITHIN YOU AND REVEAL HER SECRETS TO US.
YESSSSSS. REVEAL THE FIVE HEAVENS PALM-- AND MAKE US WHOLE AGAIN.

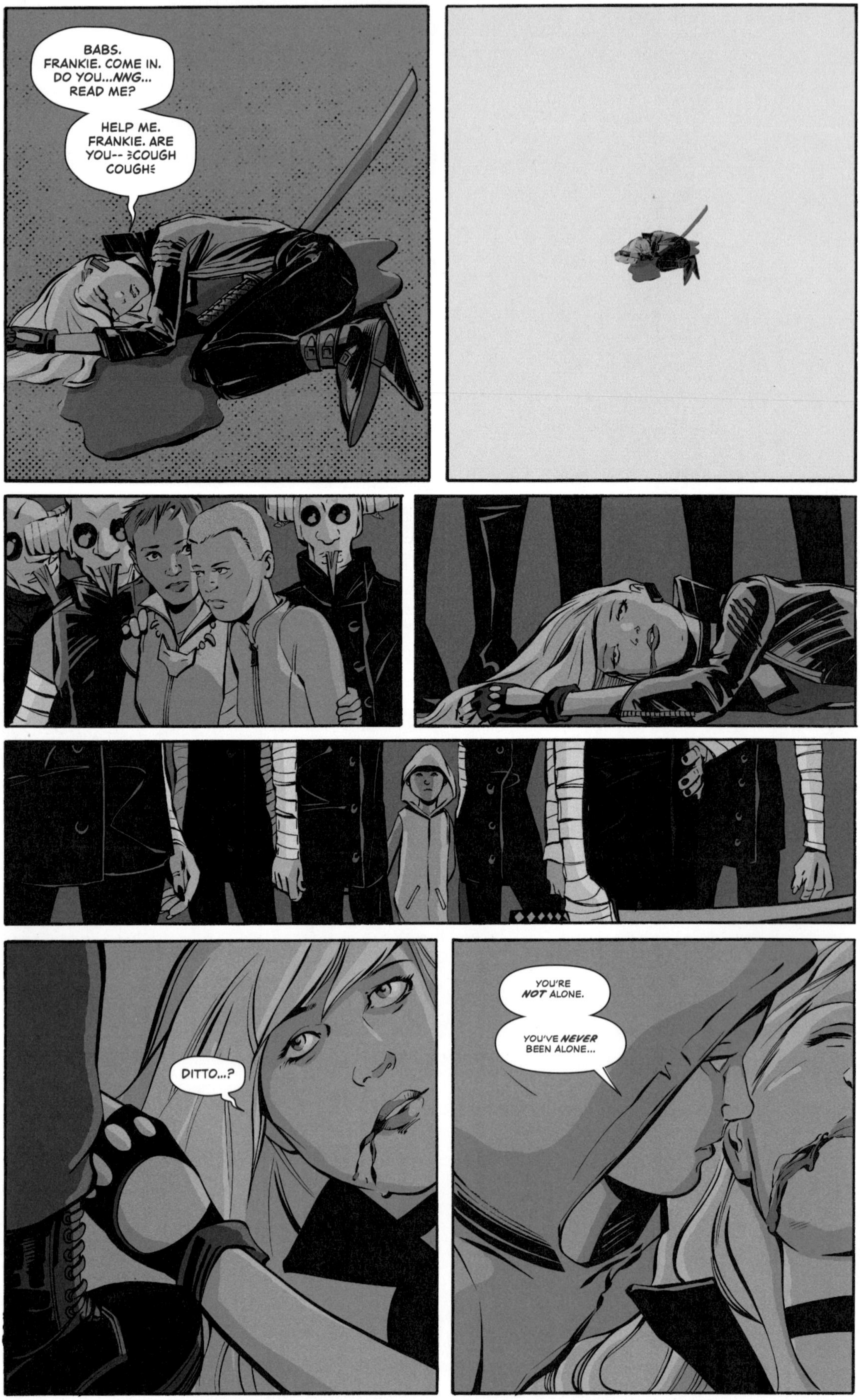
BABS. FRANKIE. COME IN. DO YOU...NNG... READ ME?
HELP ME. FRANKIE. ARE YOU-- ≡COUGH COUGH≡
DITTO...?
YOU'RE NOT ALONE.
YOU'VE NEVER BEEN ALONE...

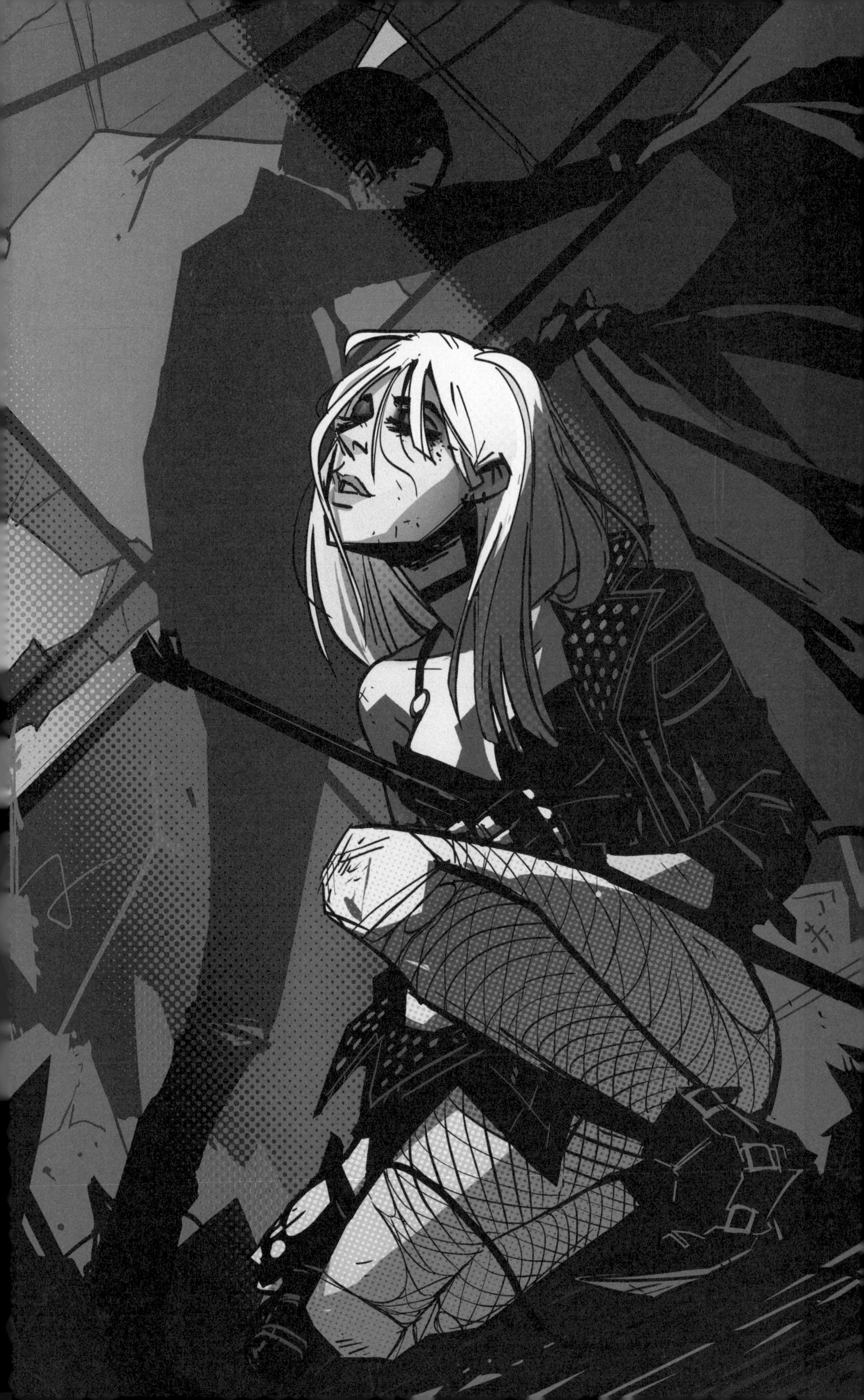

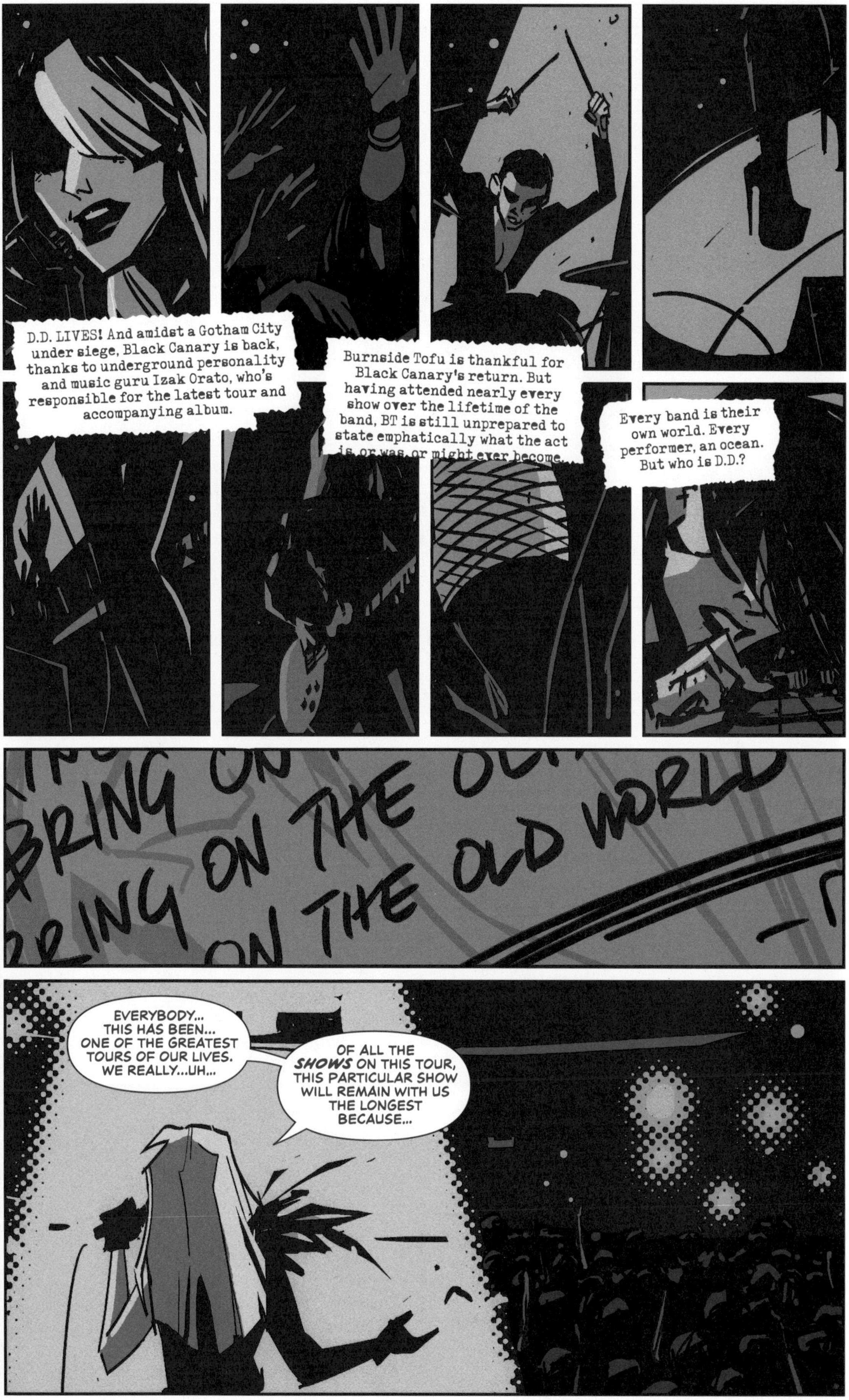
D.D. LIVES! And amidst a Gotham City under siege, Black Canary is back, thanks to underground personality and music guru Izak Orato, who's responsible for the latest tour and accompanying album.
Burnside Tofu is thankful for Black Canary's return. But having attended nearly every show over the lifetime of the band, BT is still unprepared to state emphatically what the act is, or was, or might ever become.
Every band is their own world. Every performer, an ocean. But who is D.D.?
BRING ON THE
BRING ON THE OLD WORLD
BRING ON THE OLD WORLD
EVERYBODY... THIS HAS BEEN... ONE OF THE GREATEST TOURS OF OUR LIVES. WE REALLY...UH...
OF ALL THE SHOWS ON THIS TOUR, THIS PARTICULAR SHOW WILL REMAIN WITH US THE LONGEST BECAUSE...

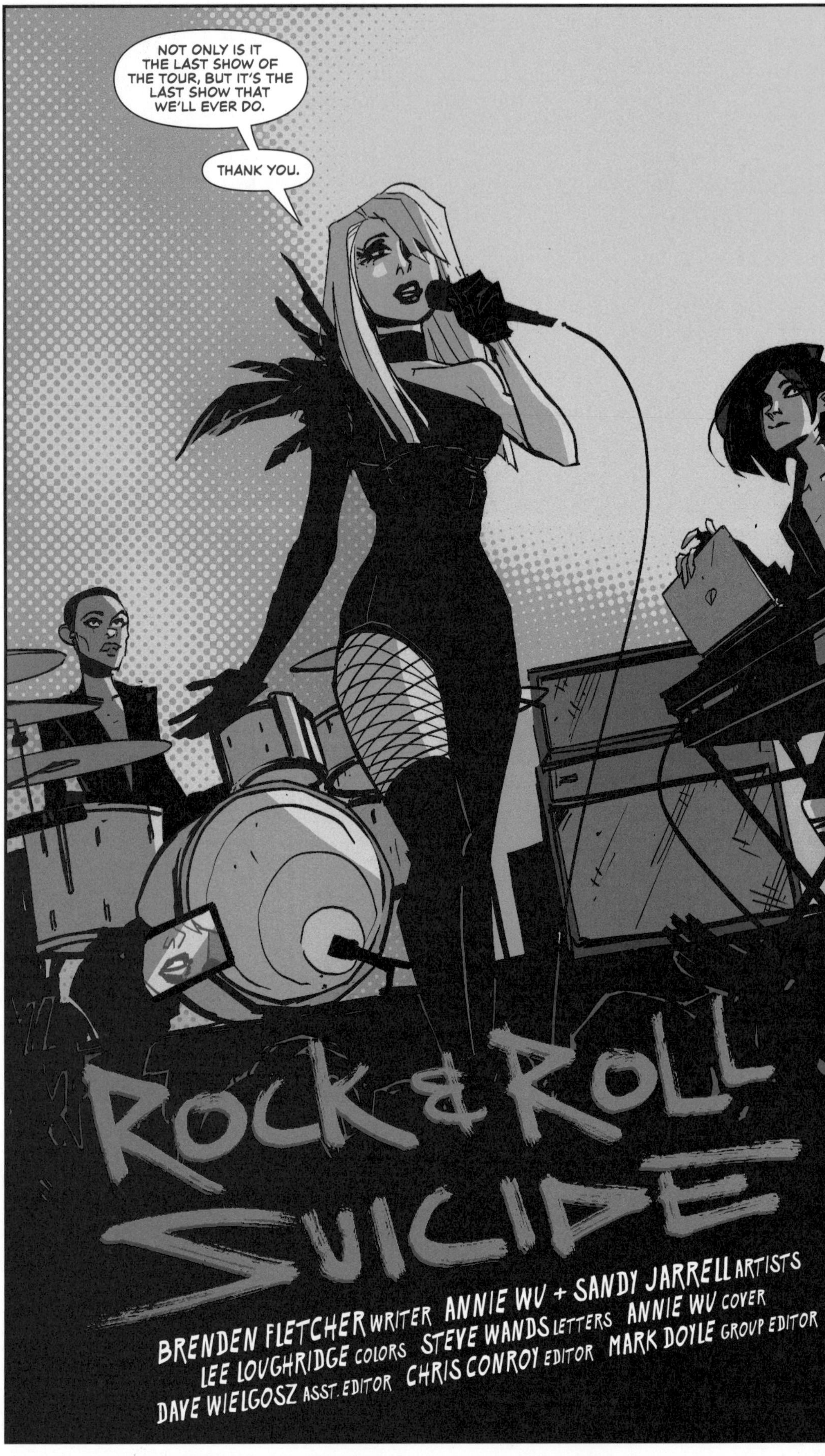
NOT ONLY IS IT THE LAST SHOW OF THE TOUR, BUT IT'S THE LAST SHOW THAT WE'LL EVER DO.
THANK YOU.
ROCK & ROLL SUICIDE
BRENDEN FLETCHER WRITER ANNIE WU + SANDY JARRELL ARTISTS
STEVE WANDS LETTERS ANNIE WU COVER
LEE LOUGHRIDGE COLORS
CHRIS CONROY EDITOR MARK DOYLE GROUP EDITOR
DAVE WIELGOSZ ASST. EDITOR

NE YEAR LATER -

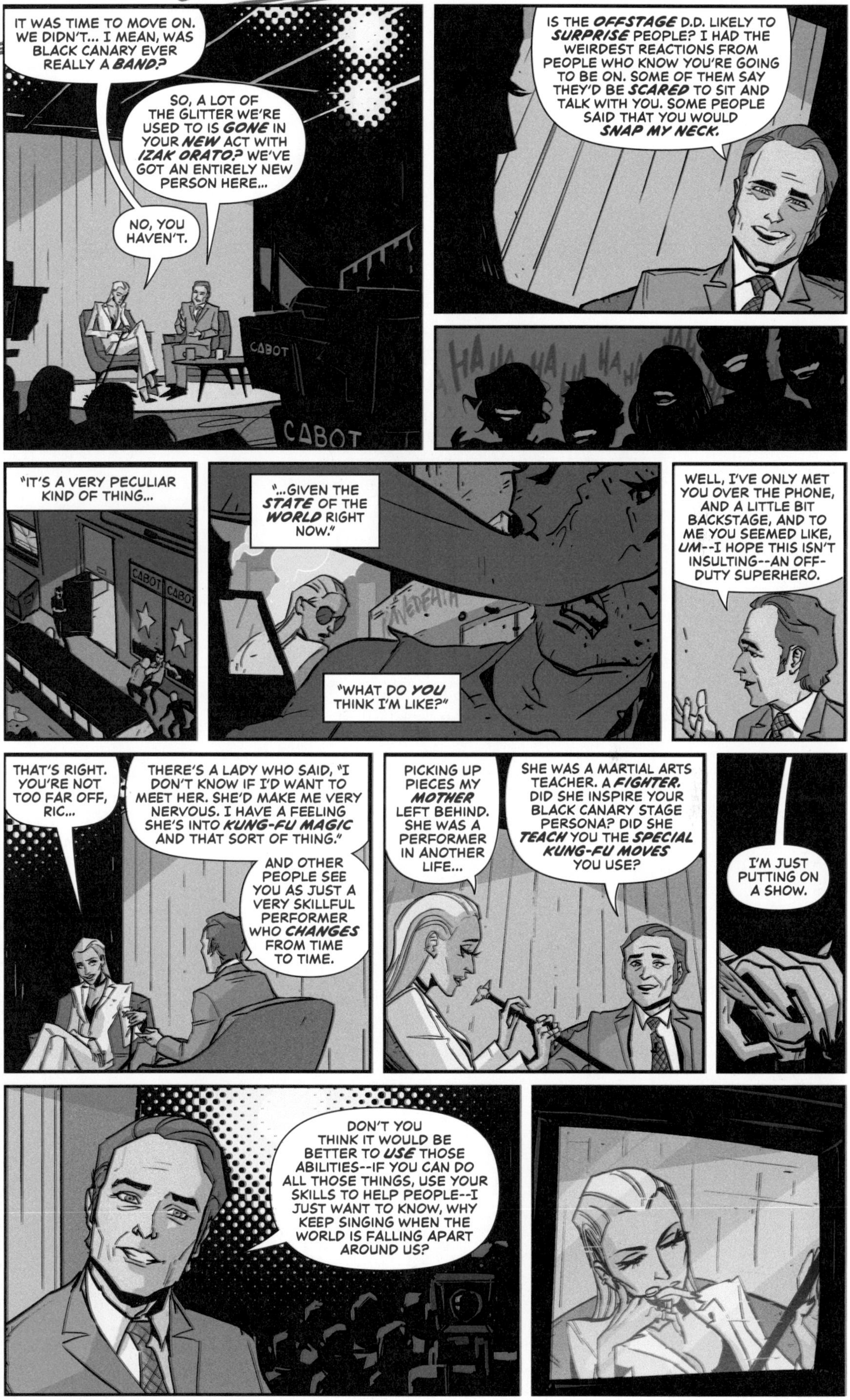

IT WAS TIME TO MOVE ON. WE DIDN'T... I MEAN, WAS BLACK CANARY EVER REALLY A BAND?
SO, A LOT OF THE GLITTER WE'RE USED TO IS GONE IN YOUR NEW ACT WITH IZAK ORATO? WE'VE GOT AN ENTIRELY NEW PERSON HERE...
NO, YOU HAVEN'T.
CABOT
CABOT
IS THE OFFSTAGE D.D. LIKELY TO SURPRISE PEOPLE? I HAD THE WEIRDEST REACTIONS FROM PEOPLE WHO KNOW YOU'RE GOING TO BE ON. SOME OF THEM SAY THEY'D BE SCARED TO SIT AND TALK WITH YOU. SOME PEOPLE SAID THAT YOU WOULD SNAP MY NECK.
"IT'S A VERY PECULIAR KIND OF THING...
CABOT
CABOT
"...GIVEN THE STATE OF THE WORLD RIGHT NOW."
"WHAT DO YOU THINK I'M LIKE?"
WELL, I'VE ONLY MET YOU OVER THE PHONE, AND A LITTLE BIT BACKSTAGE, AND TO ME YOU SEEMED LIKE, UM--I HOPE THIS ISN'T INSULTING--AN OFF-DUTY SUPERHERO.
THAT'S RIGHT. YOU'RE NOT TOO FAR OFF, RIC...
THERE'S A LADY WHO SAID, "I DON'T KNOW IF I'D WANT TO MEET HER. SHE'D MAKE ME VERY NERVOUS. I HAVE A FEELING SHE'S INTO KUNG-FU MAGIC AND THAT SORT OF THING."
AND OTHER PEOPLE SEE YOU AS JUST A VERY SKILLFUL PERFORMER WHO CHANGES FROM TIME TO TIME.
PICKING UP PIECES MY MOTHER LEFT BEHIND. SHE WAS A PERFORMER IN ANOTHER LIFE...
SHE WAS A MARTIAL ARTS TEACHER. A FIGHTER. DID SHE INSPIRE YOUR BLACK CANARY STAGE PERSONA? DID SHE TEACH YOU THE SPECIAL KUNG-FU MOVES YOU USE?
I'M JUST PUTTING ON A SHOW.
DON'T YOU THINK IT WOULD BE BETTER TO USE THOSE ABILITIES--IF YOU CAN DO ALL THOSE THINGS, USE YOUR SKILLS TO HELP PEOPLE--I JUST WANT TO KNOW, WHY KEEP SINGING WHEN THE WORLD IS FALLING APART AROUND US?

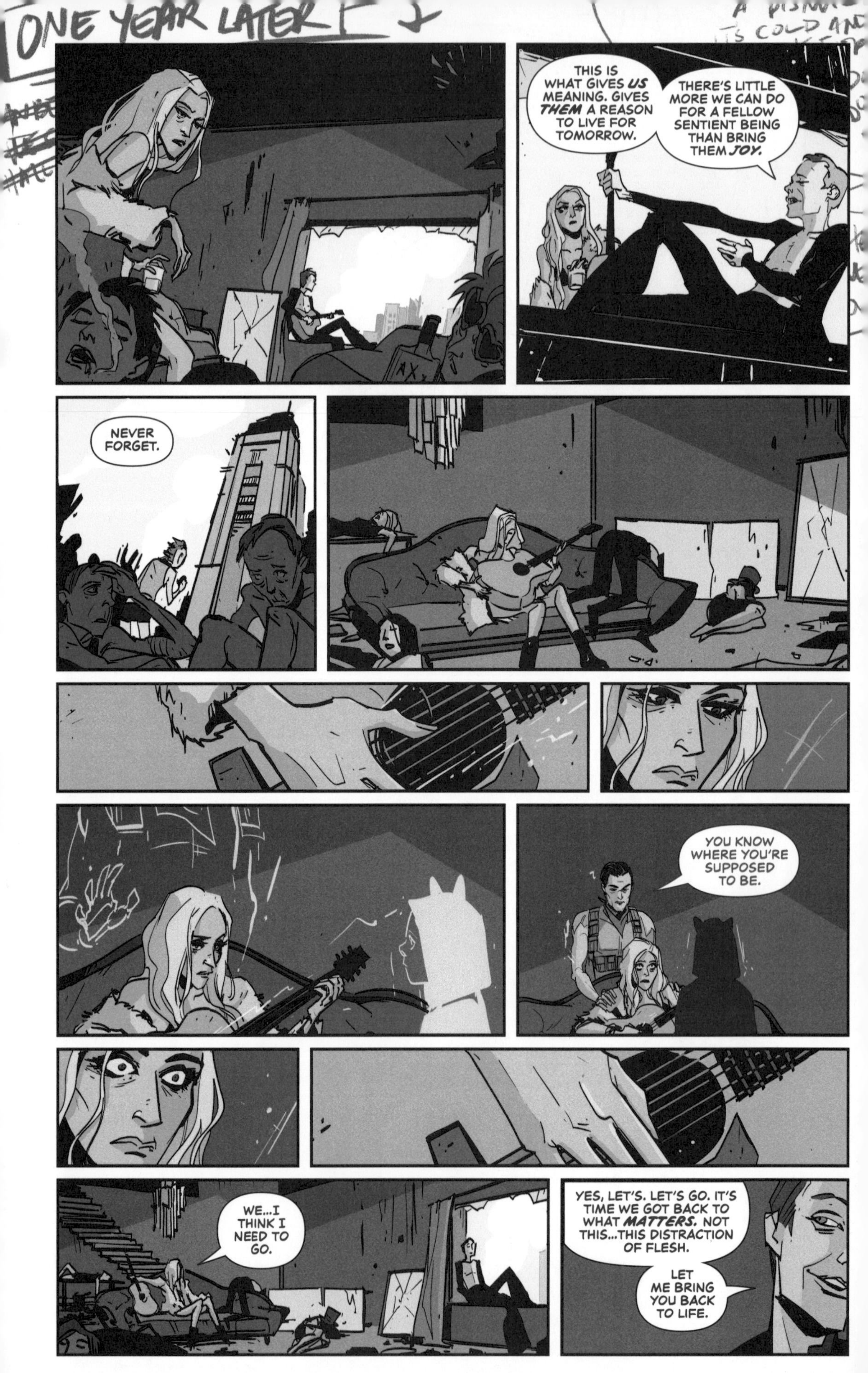
ONE YEAR LATER
THIS IS WHAT GIVES US MEANING. GIVES THEM A REASON TO LIVE FOR TOMORROW.
THERE'S LITTLE MORE WE CAN DO FOR A FELLOW SENTIENT BEING THAN BRING THEM JOY.
NEVER FORGET.
YOU KNOW WHERE YOU'RE SUPPOSED TO BE.
WE...I THINK I NEED TO GO.
YES, LET'S. LET'S GO. IT'S TIME WE GOT BACK TO WHAT MATTERS. NOT THIS...THIS DISTRACTION OF FLESH.
LET ME BRING YOU BACK TO LIFE.

TWO YEARS LATER

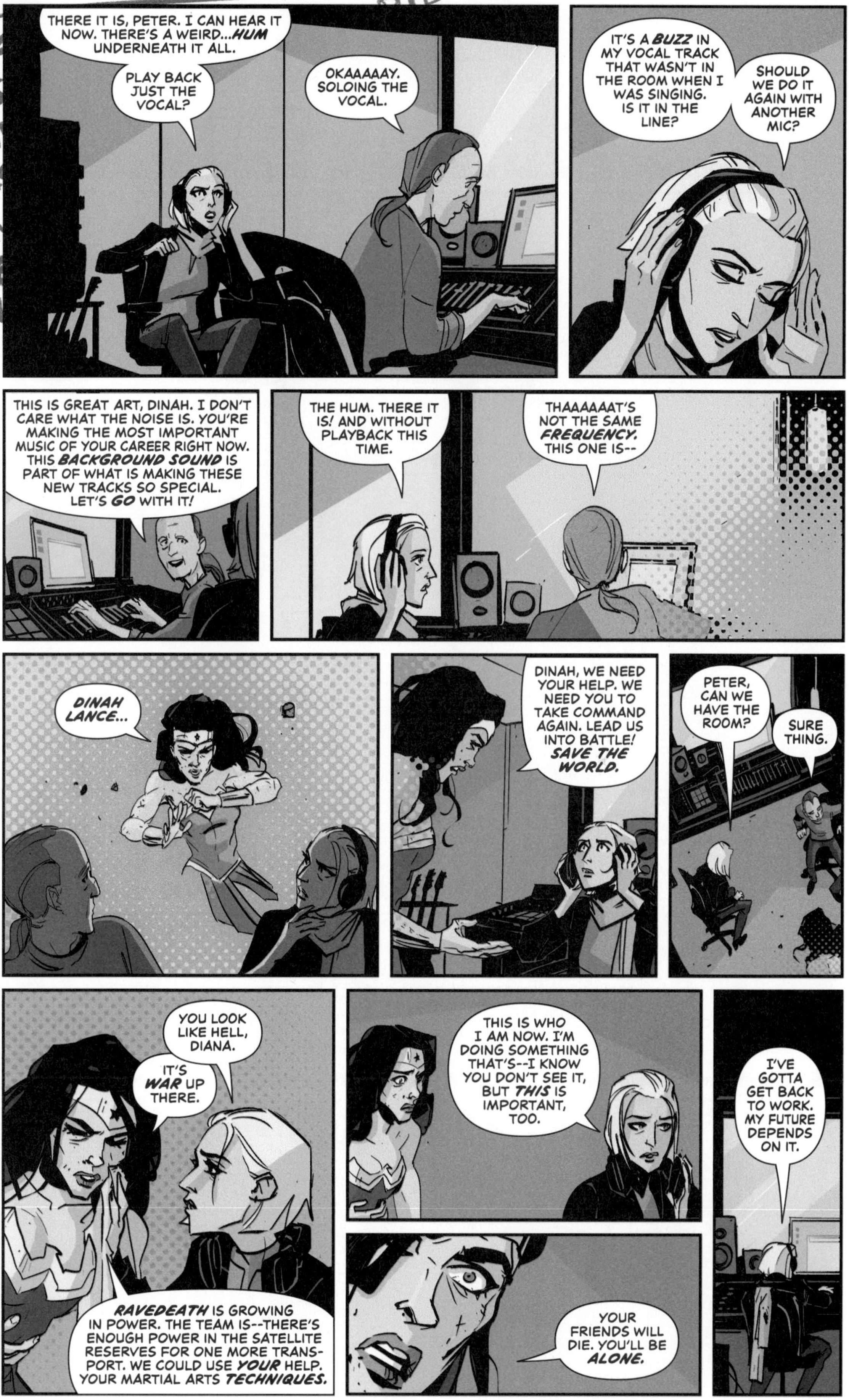

THERE IT IS, PETER. I CAN HEAR IT NOW. THERE'S A WEIRD...HUM UNDERNEATH IT ALL.
PLAY BACK JUST THE VOCAL?
OKAAAAAY. SOLOING THE VOCAL.
IT'S A BUZZ IN MY VOCAL TRACK THAT WASN'T IN THE ROOM WHEN I WAS SINGING. IS IT IN THE LINE?
SHOULD WE DO IT AGAIN WITH ANOTHER MIC?
THIS IS GREAT ART, DINAH. I DON'T CARE WHAT THE NOISE IS. YOU'RE MAKING THE MOST IMPORTANT MUSIC OF YOUR CAREER RIGHT NOW. THIS BACKGROUND SOUND IS PART OF WHAT IS MAKING THESE NEW TRACKS SO SPECIAL. LET'S GO WITH IT!
THE HUM. THERE IT IS! AND WITHOUT PLAYBACK THIS TIME.
THAAAAAAT'S NOT THE SAME FREQUENCY. THIS ONE IS--
DINAH LANCE...
DINAH, WE NEED YOUR HELP. WE NEED YOU TO TAKE COMMAND AGAIN. LEAD US INTO BATTLE! SAVE THE WORLD.
PETER, CAN WE HAVE THE ROOM?
SURE THING.
YOU LOOK LIKE HELL, DIANA.
IT'S WAR UP THERE.
RAVEDEATH IS GROWING IN POWER. THE TEAM IS--THERE'S ENOUGH POWER IN THE SATELLITE RESERVES FOR ONE MORE TRANSPORT. WE COULD USE YOUR HELP. YOUR MARTIAL ARTS TECHNIQUES.
THIS IS WHO I AM NOW. I'M DOING SOMETHING THAT'S--I KNOW YOU DON'T SEE IT, BUT THIS IS IMPORTANT, TOO.
YOUR FRIENDS WILL DIE. YOU'LL BE ALONE.
I'VE GOTTA GET BACK TO WORK. MY FUTURE DEPENDS ON IT.

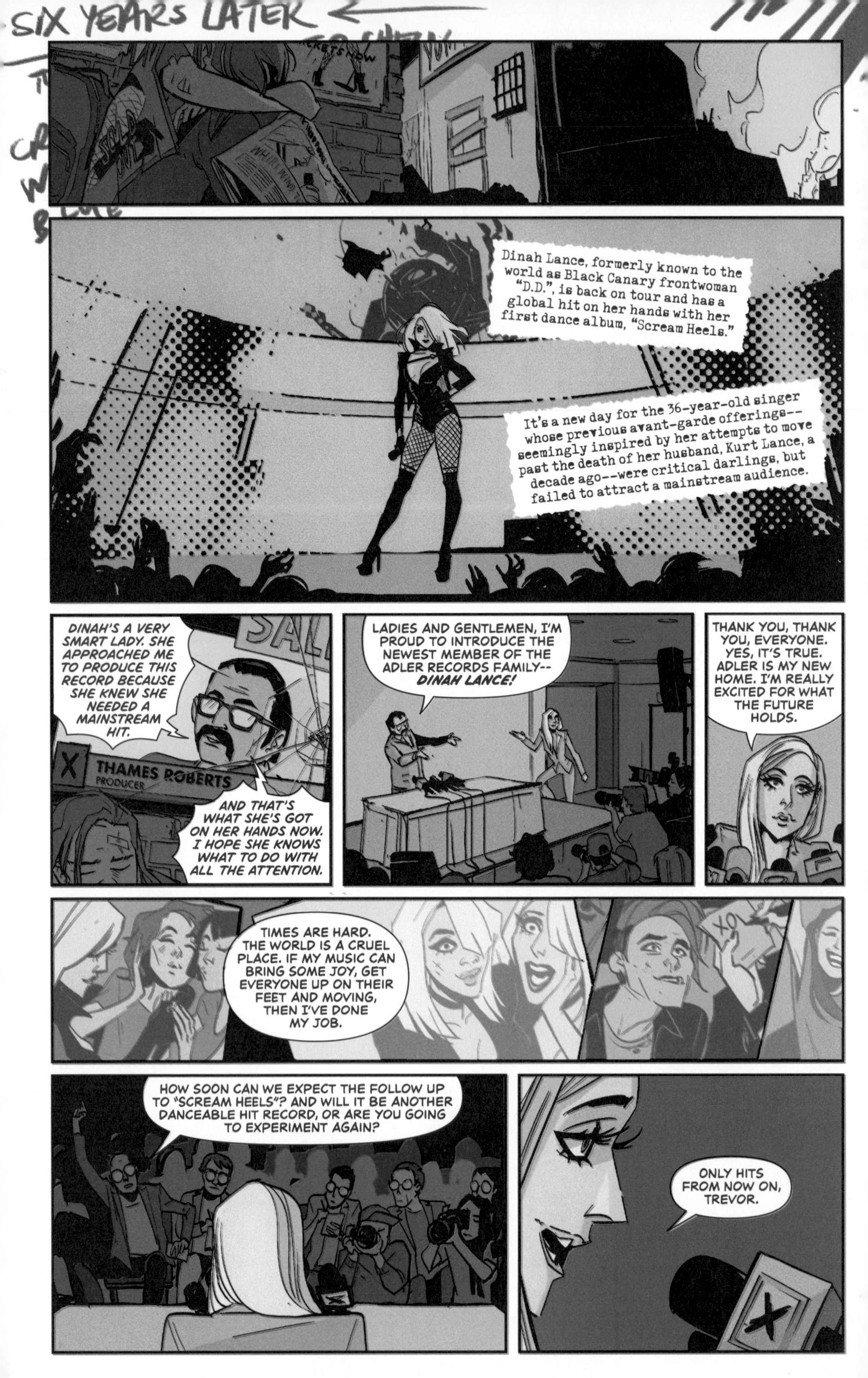
SIX YEARS LATER
SOLD OUT
Dinah Lance, formerly known to the world as Black Canary frontwoman "D.D.", is back on tour and has a global hit on her hands with her first dance album, "Scream Heels."
It's a new day for the 36-year-old singer--whose previous avant-garde offerings--seemingly inspired by her attempts to move past the death of her husband, Kurt Lance, a decade ago--were critical darlings, but failed to attract a mainstream audience.
DINAH'S A VERY SMART LADY. SHE APPROACHED ME TO PRODUCE THIS RECORD BECAUSE SHE KNEW SHE NEEDED A MAINSTREAM HIT.
THAMES ROBERTS
PRODUCER
AND THAT'S WHAT SHE'S GOT ON HER HANDS NOW. I HOPE SHE KNOWS WHAT TO DO WITH ALL THE ATTENTION.
LADIES AND GENTLEMEN, I'M PROUD TO INTRODUCE THE NEWEST MEMBER OF THE ADLER RECORDS FAMILY--DINAH LANCE!
THANK YOU, THANK YOU, EVERYONE. YES, IT'S TRUE. ADLER IS MY NEW HOME. I'M REALLY EXCITED FOR WHAT THE FUTURE HOLDS.
TIMES ARE HARD. THE WORLD IS A CRUEL PLACE. IF MY MUSIC CAN BRING SOME JOY, GET EVERYONE UP ON THEIR FEET AND MOVING, THEN I'VE DONE MY JOB.
HOW SOON CAN WE EXPECT THE FOLLOW UP TO "SCREAM HEELS"? AND WILL IT BE ANOTHER DANCEABLE HIT RECORD, OR ARE YOU GOING TO EXPERIMENT AGAIN?
ONLY HITS FROM NOW ON, TREVOR.

FOUR YEARS LATER:

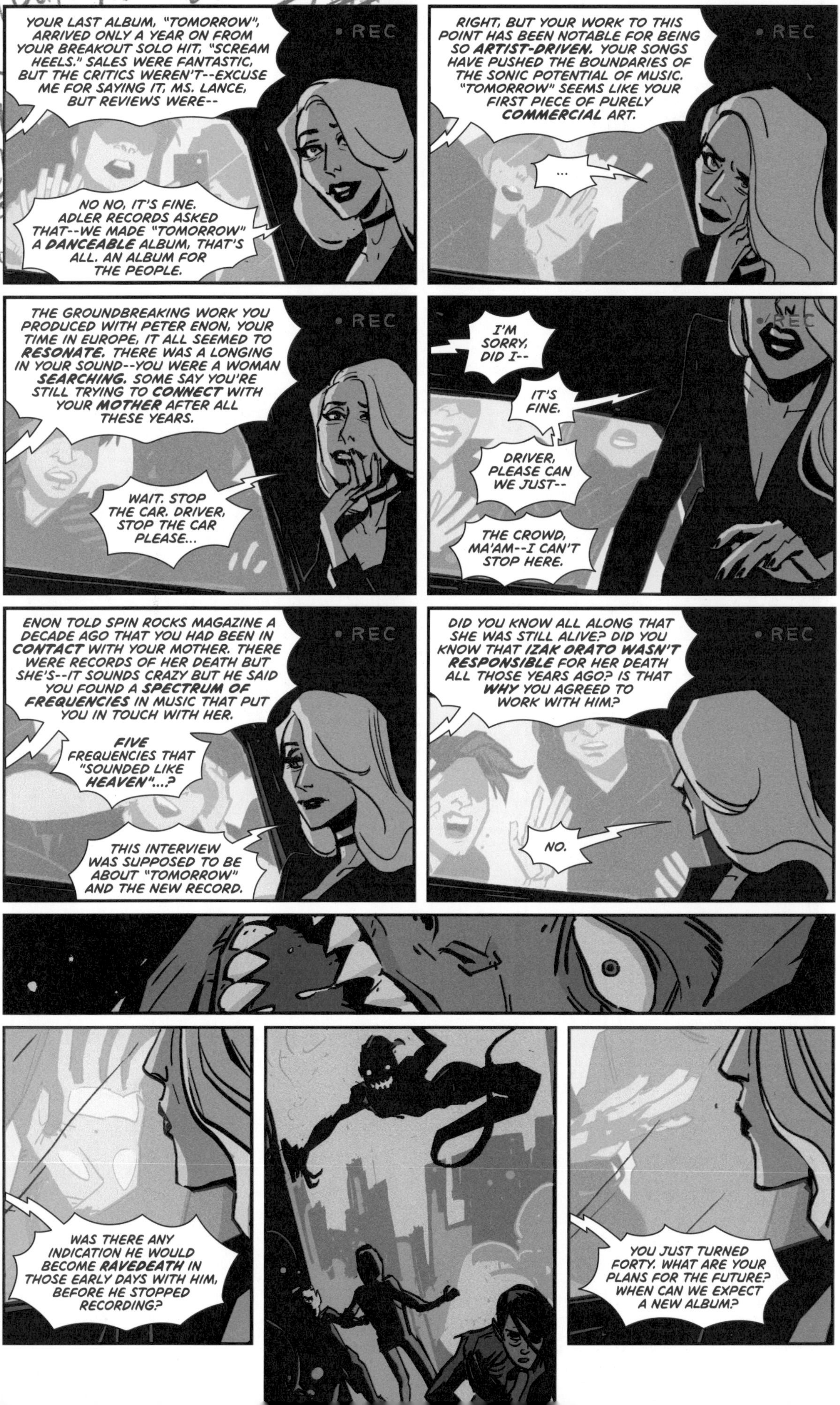
• REC
YOUR LAST ALBUM, "TOMORROW", ARRIVED ONLY A YEAR ON FROM YOUR BREAKOUT SOLO HIT, "SCREAM HEELS." SALES WERE FANTASTIC, BUT THE CRITICS WEREN'T--EXCUSE ME FOR SAYING IT, MS. LANCE, BUT REVIEWS WERE--
NO NO, IT'S FINE. ADLER RECORDS ASKED THAT--WE MADE "TOMORROW" A **DANCEABLE** ALBUM, THAT'S ALL. AN ALBUM FOR THE PEOPLE.
• REC
RIGHT, BUT YOUR WORK TO THIS POINT HAS BEEN NOTABLE FOR BEING SO **ARTIST-DRIVEN.** YOUR SONGS HAVE PUSHED THE BOUNDARIES OF THE SONIC POTENTIAL OF MUSIC. "TOMORROW" SEEMS LIKE YOUR FIRST PIECE OF PURELY **COMMERCIAL** ART.
...
• REC
THE GROUNDBREAKING WORK YOU PRODUCED WITH PETER ENON, YOUR TIME IN EUROPE, IT ALL SEEMED TO **RESONATE.** THERE WAS A LONGING IN YOUR SOUND--YOU WERE A WOMAN **SEARCHING.** SOME SAY YOU'RE STILL TRYING TO **CONNECT** WITH YOUR **MOTHER** AFTER ALL THESE YEARS.
WAIT. STOP THE CAR. DRIVER, STOP THE CAR PLEASE...
I'M SORRY, DID I--
IT'S FINE.
DRIVER, PLEASE CAN WE JUST--
THE CROWD, MA'AM--I CAN'T STOP HERE.
• REC
ENON TOLD SPIN ROCKS MAGAZINE A DECADE AGO THAT YOU HAD BEEN IN **CONTACT** WITH YOUR MOTHER. THERE WERE RECORDS OF HER DEATH BUT SHE'S--IT SOUNDS CRAZY BUT HE SAID YOU FOUND A **SPECTRUM OF FREQUENCIES** IN MUSIC THAT PUT YOU IN TOUCH WITH HER.
FIVE FREQUENCIES THAT "SOUNDED LIKE **HEAVEN**"...?
THIS INTERVIEW WAS SUPPOSED TO BE ABOUT "TOMORROW" AND THE NEW RECORD.
• REC
DID YOU KNOW ALL ALONG THAT SHE WAS STILL ALIVE? DID YOU KNOW THAT **IZAK ORATO WASN'T RESPONSIBLE** FOR HER DEATH ALL THOSE YEARS AGO? IS THAT **WHY** YOU AGREED TO WORK WITH HIM?
NO.
WAS THERE ANY INDICATION HE WOULD BECOME **RAVEDEATH** IN THOSE EARLY DAYS WITH HIM, BEFORE HE STOPPED RECORDING?
YOU JUST TURNED FORTY. WHAT ARE YOUR PLANS FOR THE FUTURE? WHEN CAN WE EXPECT A NEW ALBUM?

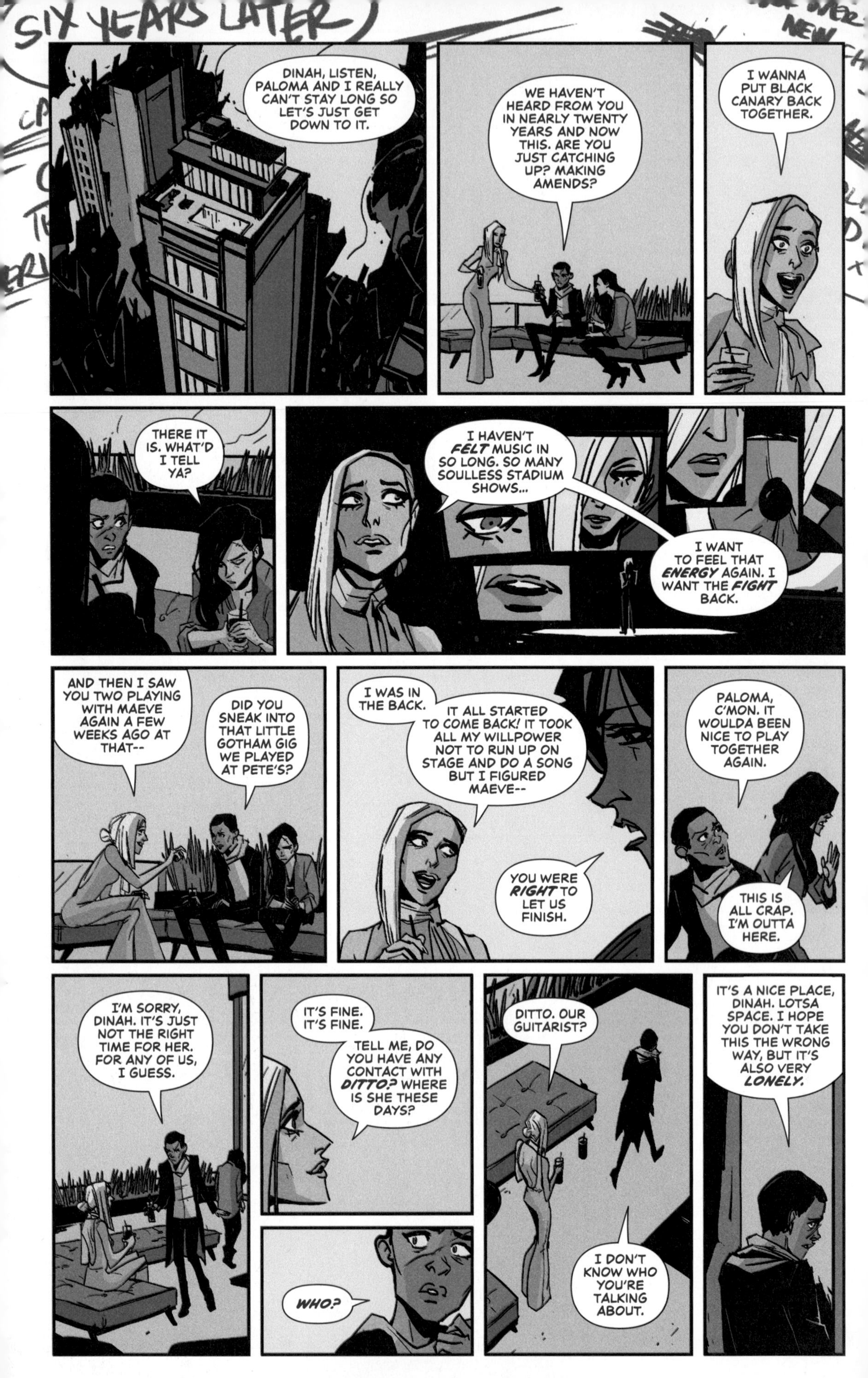
SIX YEARS LATER
DINAH, LISTEN, PALOMA AND I REALLY CAN'T STAY LONG SO LET'S JUST GET DOWN TO IT.
WE HAVEN'T HEARD FROM YOU IN NEARLY TWENTY YEARS AND NOW THIS. ARE YOU JUST CATCHING UP? MAKING AMENDS?
I WANNA PUT BLACK CANARY BACK TOGETHER.
THERE IT IS. WHAT'D I TELL YA?
I HAVEN'T FELT MUSIC IN SO LONG. SO MANY SOULLESS STADIUM SHOWS...
I WANT TO FEEL THAT ENERGY AGAIN. I WANT THE FIGHT BACK.
AND THEN I SAW YOU TWO PLAYING WITH MAEVE AGAIN A FEW WEEKS AGO AT THAT--
DID YOU SNEAK INTO THAT LITTLE GOTHAM GIG WE PLAYED AT PETE'S?
I WAS IN THE BACK.
IT ALL STARTED TO COME BACK! IT TOOK ALL MY WILLPOWER NOT TO RUN UP ON STAGE AND DO A SONG BUT I FIGURED MAEVE--
YOU WERE RIGHT TO LET US FINISH.
PALOMA, C'MON. IT WOULDA BEEN NICE TO PLAY TOGETHER AGAIN.
THIS IS ALL CRAP. I'M OUTTA HERE.
I'M SORRY, DINAH. IT'S JUST NOT THE RIGHT TIME FOR HER. FOR ANY OF US, I GUESS.
IT'S FINE. IT'S FINE.
TELL ME, DO YOU HAVE ANY CONTACT WITH DITTO? WHERE IS SHE THESE DAYS?
WHO?
DITTO. OUR GUITARIST?
I DON'T KNOW WHO YOU'RE TALKING ABOUT.
IT'S A NICE PLACE, DINAH. LOTSA SPACE. I HOPE YOU DON'T TAKE THIS THE WRONG WAY, BUT IT'S ALSO VERY LONELY.

SEVEN YEARS LATER

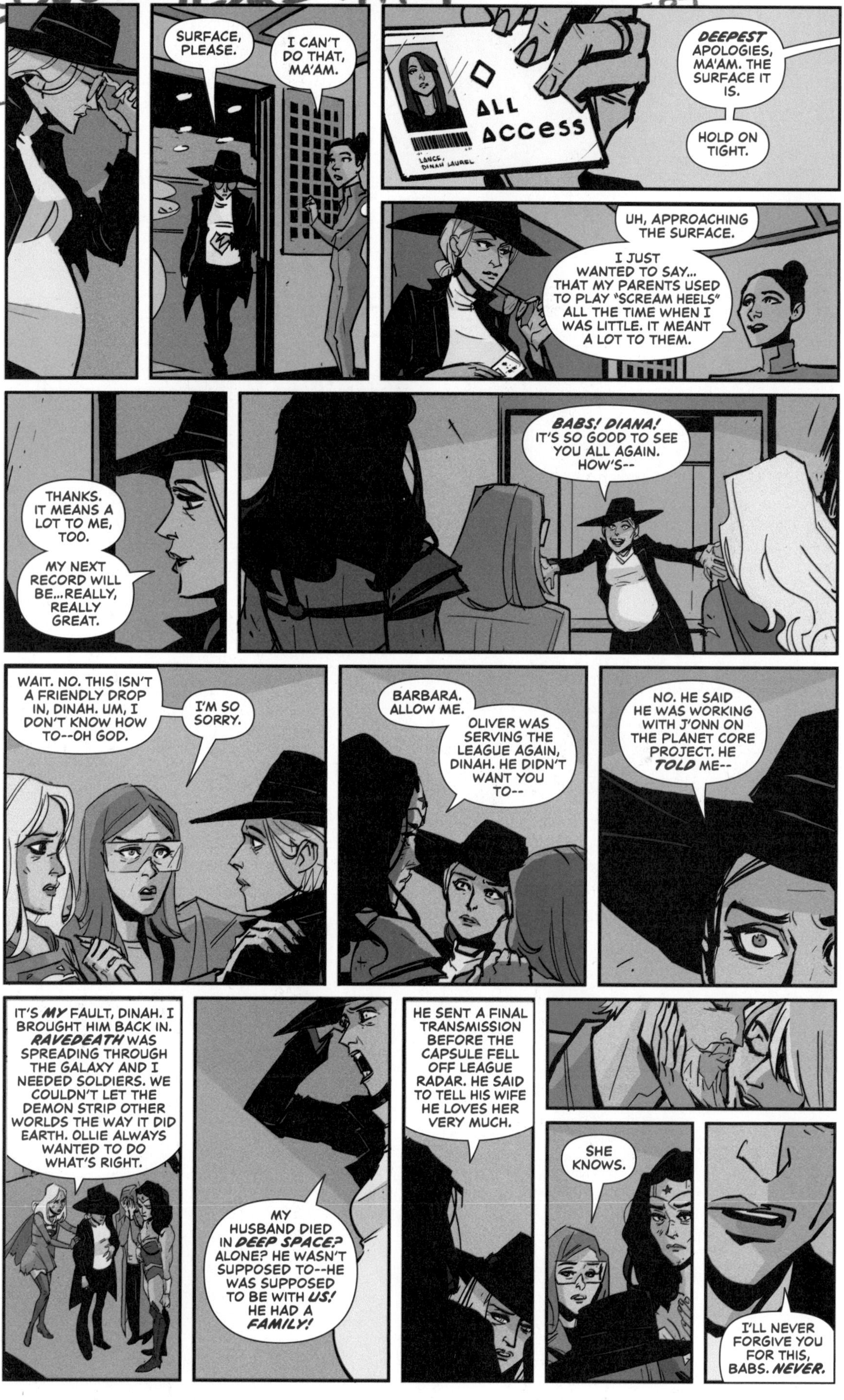
SURFACE, PLEASE.
I CAN'T DO THAT, MA'AM.
ALL ACCESS
LANCE, DINAH LAUREL
DEEPEST APOLOGIES, MA'AM. THE SURFACE IT IS.
HOLD ON TIGHT.
UH, APPROACHING THE SURFACE.
I JUST WANTED TO SAY... THAT MY PARENTS USED TO PLAY "SCREAM HEELS" ALL THE TIME WHEN I WAS LITTLE. IT MEANT A LOT TO THEM.
THANKS. IT MEANS A LOT TO ME, TOO.
MY NEXT RECORD WILL BE...REALLY, REALLY GREAT.
BABS! DIANA! IT'S SO GOOD TO SEE YOU ALL AGAIN. HOW'S--
WAIT. NO. THIS ISN'T A FRIENDLY DROP IN, DINAH. UM, I DON'T KNOW HOW TO--OH GOD.
I'M SO SORRY.
BARBARA. ALLOW ME.
OLIVER WAS SERVING THE LEAGUE AGAIN, DINAH. HE DIDN'T WANT YOU TO--
NO. HE SAID HE WAS WORKING WITH J'ONN ON THE PLANET CORE PROJECT. HE TOLD ME--
IT'S MY FAULT, DINAH. I BROUGHT HIM BACK IN. RAVEDEATH WAS SPREADING THROUGH THE GALAXY AND I NEEDED SOLDIERS. WE COULDN'T LET THE DEMON STRIP OTHER WORLDS THE WAY IT DID EARTH. OLLIE ALWAYS WANTED TO DO WHAT'S RIGHT.
MY HUSBAND DIED IN DEEP SPACE? ALONE? HE WASN'T SUPPOSED TO--HE WAS SUPPOSED TO BE WITH US! HE HAD A FAMILY!
HE SENT A FINAL TRANSMISSION BEFORE THE CAPSULE FELL OFF LEAGUE RADAR. HE SAID TO TELL HIS WIFE HE LOVES HER VERY MUCH.
SHE KNOWS.
I'LL NEVER FORGIVE YOU FOR THIS, BABS. NEVER.

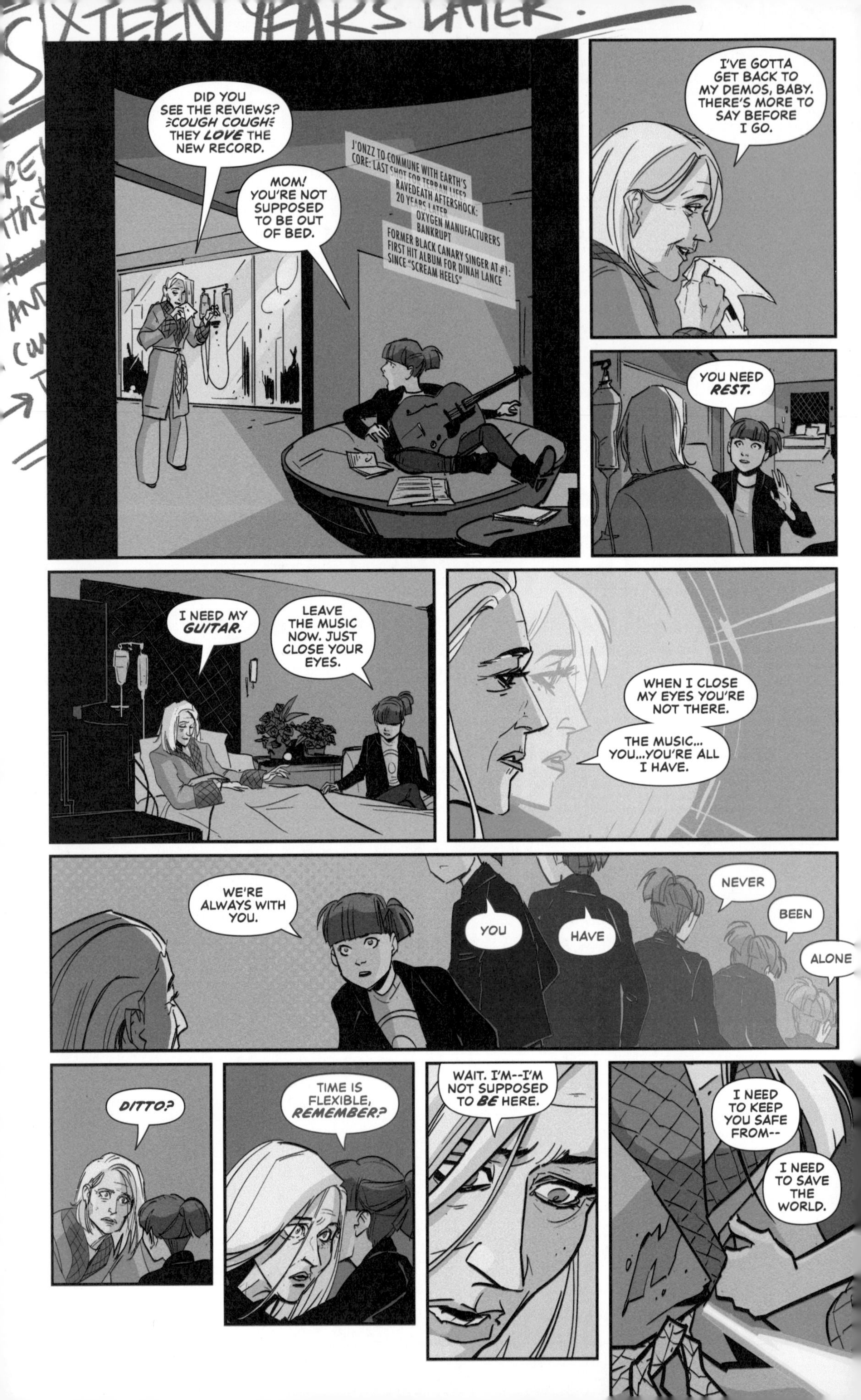
SIXTEEN YEARS LATER.
DID YOU SEE THE REVIEWS? *COUGH COUGH* THEY LOVE THE NEW RECORD.
MOM! YOU'RE NOT SUPPOSED TO BE OUT OF BED.
J'ONZZ TO COMMUNE WITH EARTH'S CORE: LAST SHOT FOR TERRAN LIFE?
RAVEDEATH AFTERSHOCK: 20 YEARS LATER
OXYGEN MANUFACTURERS BANKRUPT
FORMER BLACK CANARY SINGER AT #1: FIRST HIT ALBUM FOR DINAH LANCE SINCE "SCREAM HEELS"
I'VE GOTTA GET BACK TO MY DEMOS, BABY. THERE'S MORE TO SAY BEFORE I GO.
YOU NEED REST.
I NEED MY GUITAR.
LEAVE THE MUSIC NOW. JUST CLOSE YOUR EYES.
WHEN I CLOSE MY EYES YOU'RE NOT THERE.
THE MUSIC... YOU...YOU'RE ALL I HAVE.
WE'RE ALWAYS WITH YOU.
YOU
HAVE
NEVER
BEEN
ALONE
DITTO?
TIME IS FLEXIBLE, REMEMBER?
WAIT. I'M--I'M NOT SUPPOSED TO BE HERE.
I NEED TO KEEP YOU SAFE FROM--
I NEED TO SAVE THE WORLD.

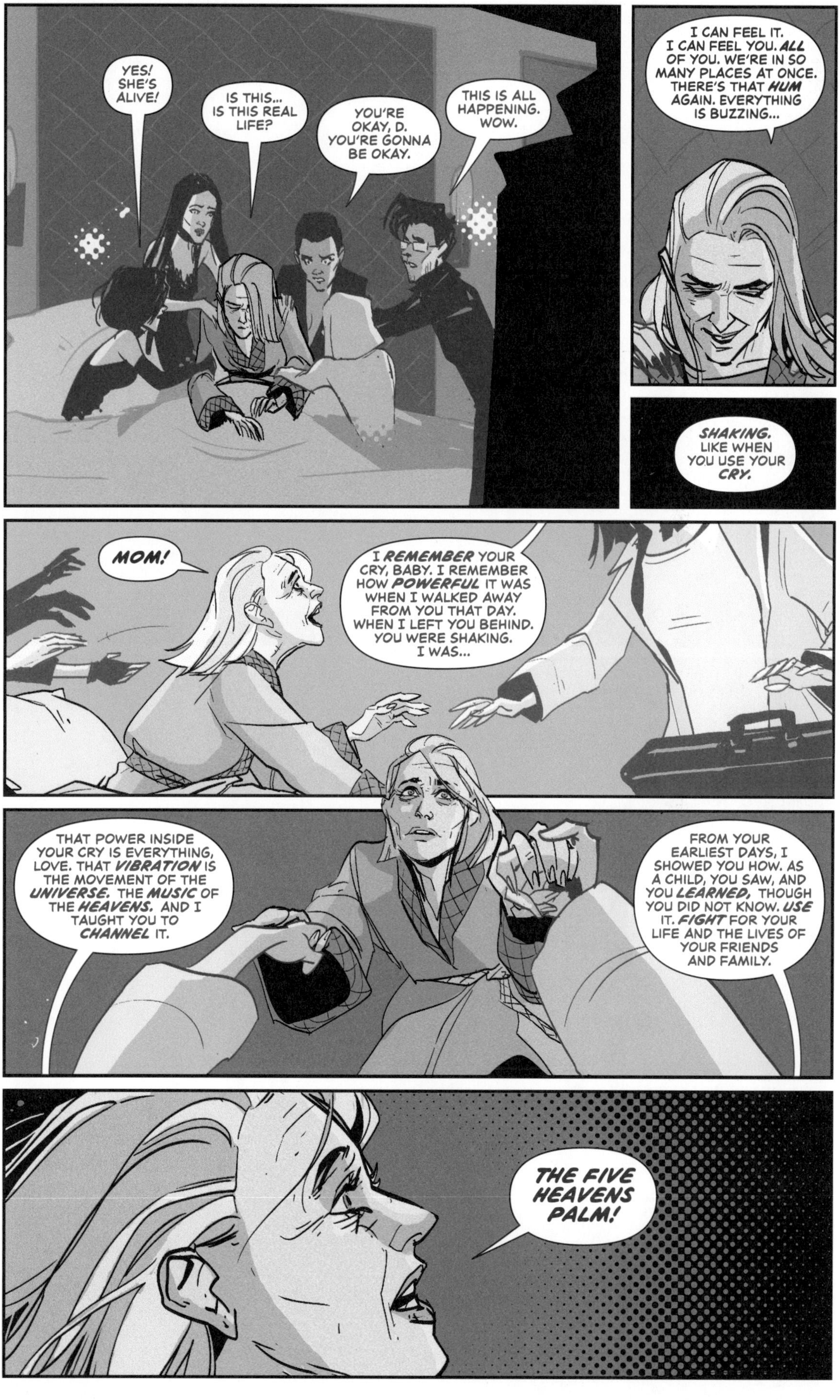
YES! SHE'S ALIVE!
IS THIS... IS THIS REAL LIFE?
YOU'RE OKAY, D. YOU'RE GONNA BE OKAY.
THIS IS ALL HAPPENING. WOW.
I CAN FEEL IT. I CAN FEEL YOU. ALL OF YOU. WE'RE IN SO MANY PLACES AT ONCE. THERE'S THAT HUM AGAIN. EVERYTHING IS BUZZING...
SHAKING. LIKE WHEN YOU USE YOUR CRY.
MOM!
I REMEMBER YOUR CRY, BABY. I REMEMBER HOW POWERFUL IT WAS WHEN I WALKED AWAY FROM YOU THAT DAY. WHEN I LEFT YOU BEHIND. YOU WERE SHAKING. I WAS...
THAT POWER INSIDE YOUR CRY IS EVERYTHING, LOVE. THAT VIBRATION IS THE MOVEMENT OF THE UNIVERSE. THE MUSIC OF THE HEAVENS. AND I TAUGHT YOU TO CHANNEL IT.
FROM YOUR EARLIEST DAYS, I SHOWED YOU HOW. AS A CHILD, YOU SAW, AND YOU LEARNED, THOUGH YOU DID NOT KNOW. USE IT. FIGHT FOR YOUR LIFE AND THE LIVES OF YOUR FRIENDS AND FAMILY.
THE FIVE HEAVENS PALM!

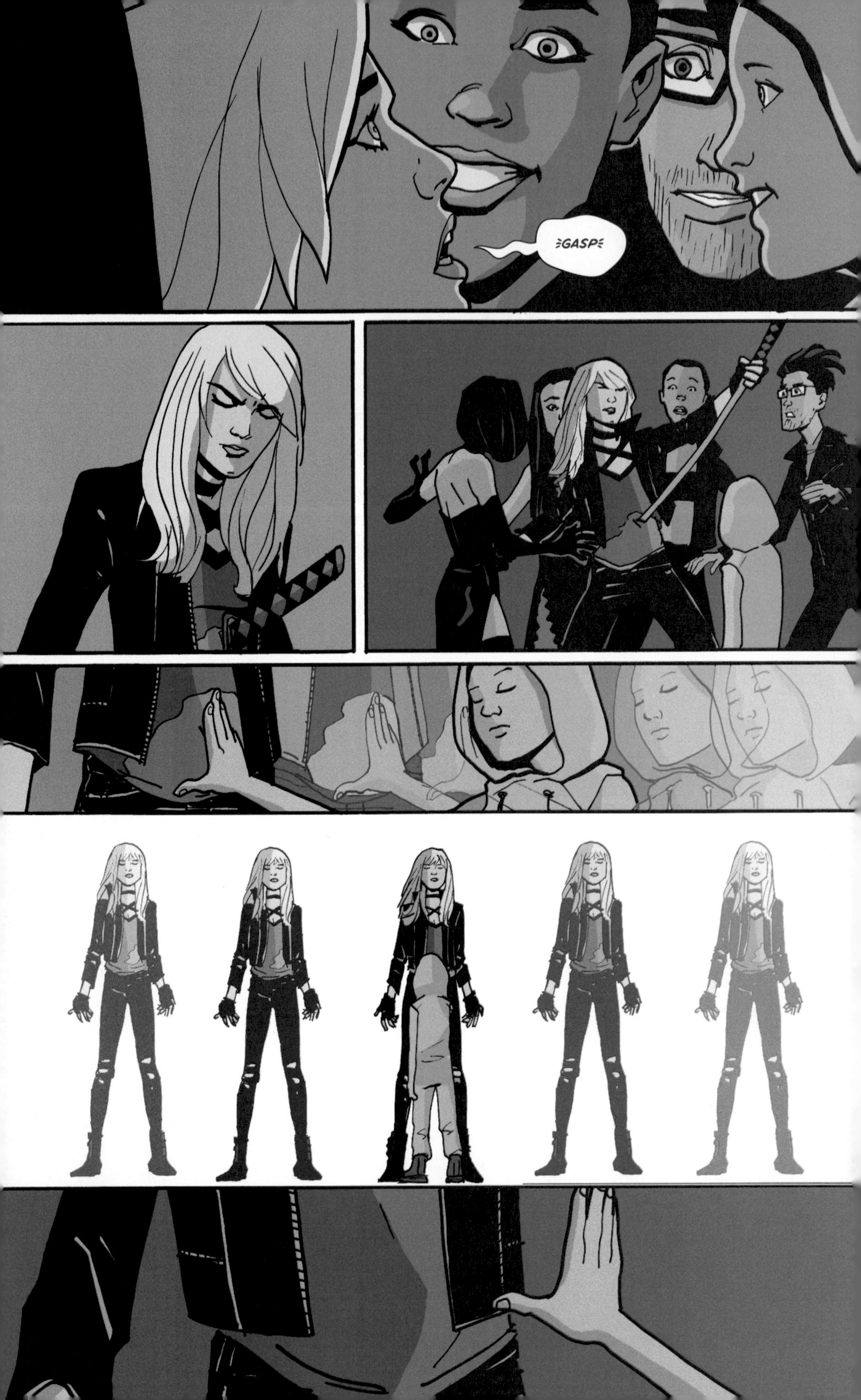
GASP

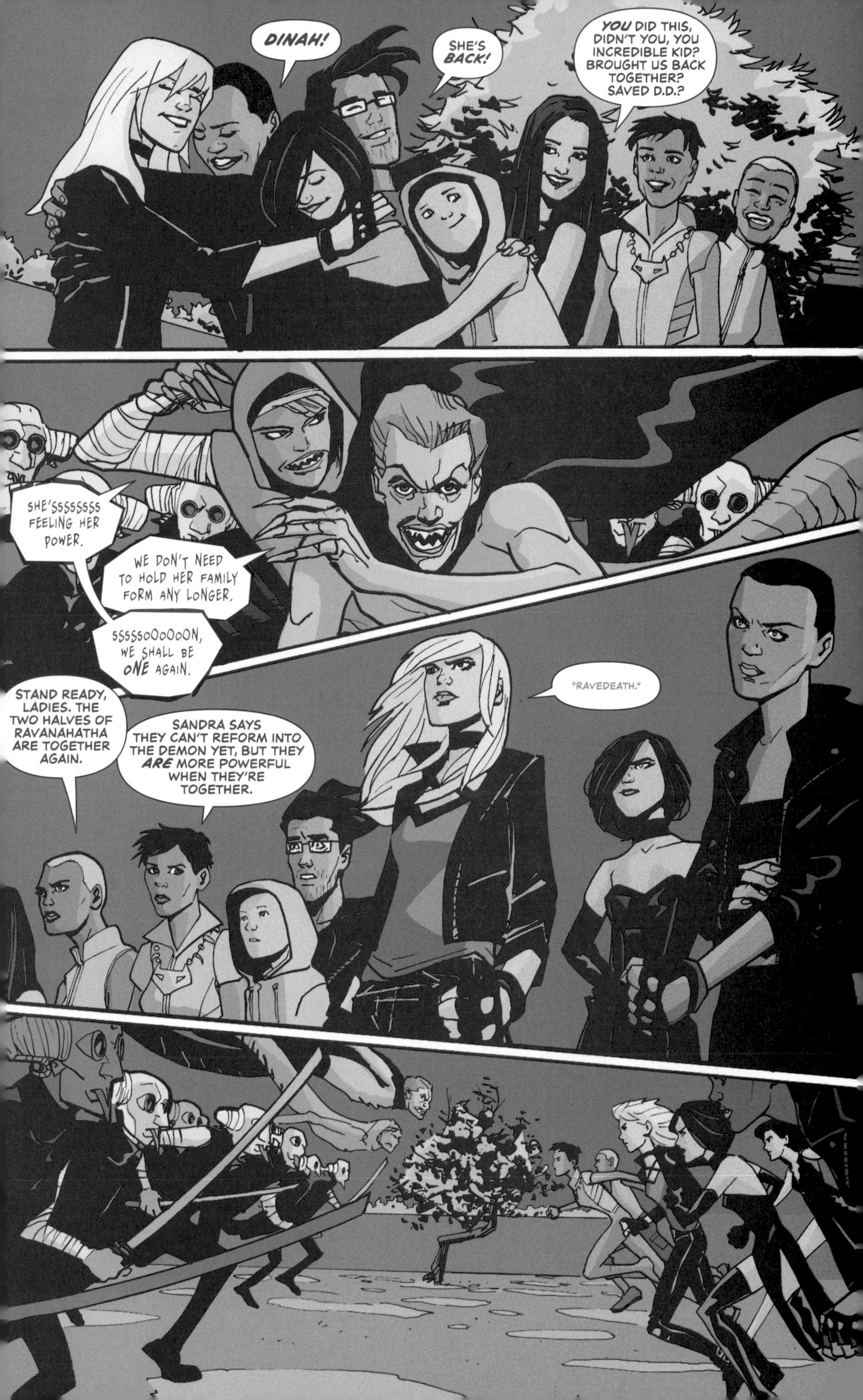
DINAH!
SHE'S BACK!
YOU DID THIS, DIDN'T YOU, YOU INCREDIBLE KID? BROUGHT US BACK TOGETHER? SAVED D.D.?
SHE'SSSSSSSS FEELING HER POWER.
WE DON'T NEED TO HOLD HER FAMILY FORM ANY LONGER.
SSSSSOOOOOON, WE SHALL BE ONE AGAIN.
STAND READY, LADIES. THE TWO HALVES OF RAVANAHATHA ARE TOGETHER AGAIN.
SANDRA SAYS THEY CAN'T REFORM INTO THE DEMON YET, BUT THEY ARE MORE POWERFUL WHEN THEY'RE TOGETHER.
"RAVEDEATH."

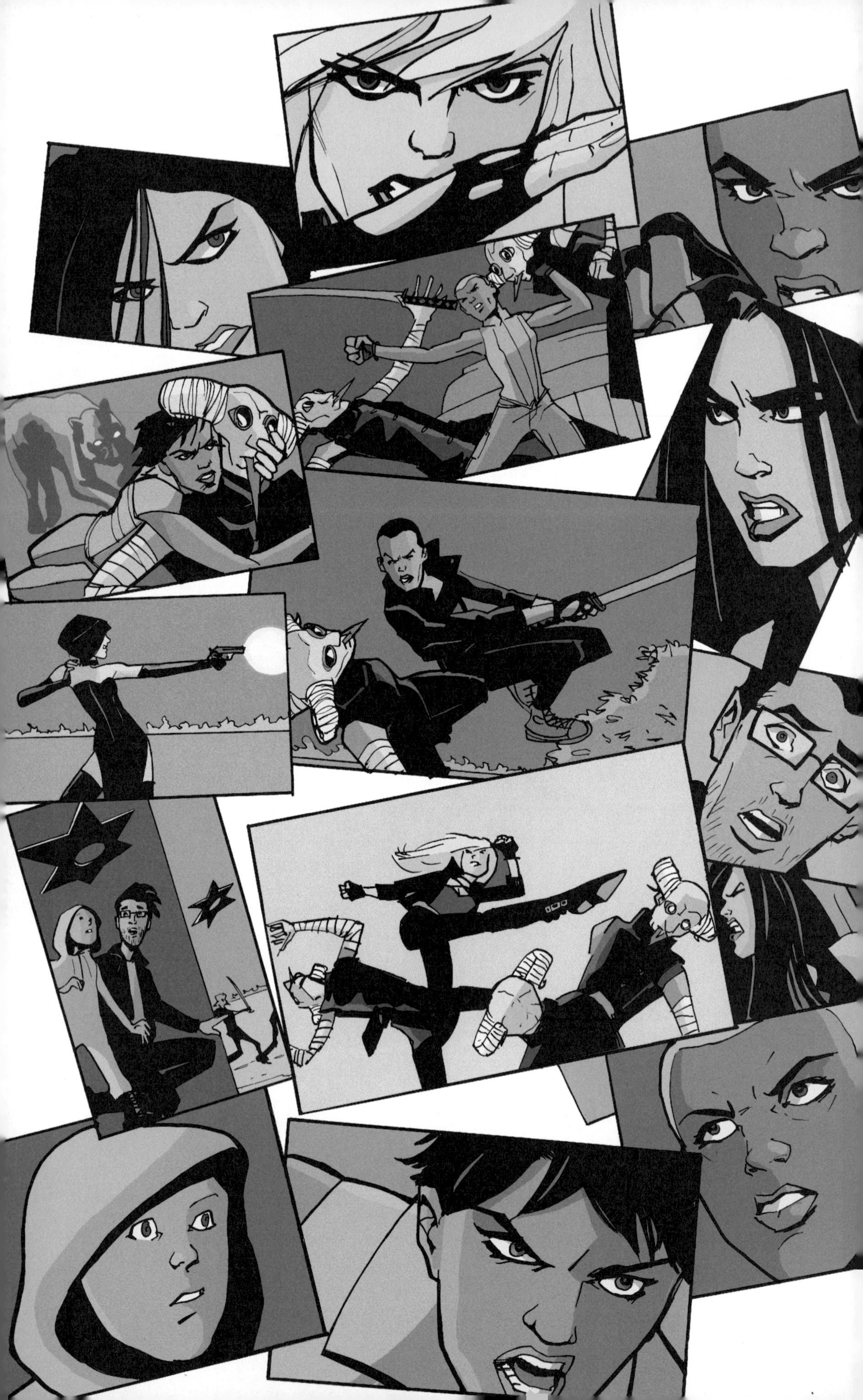

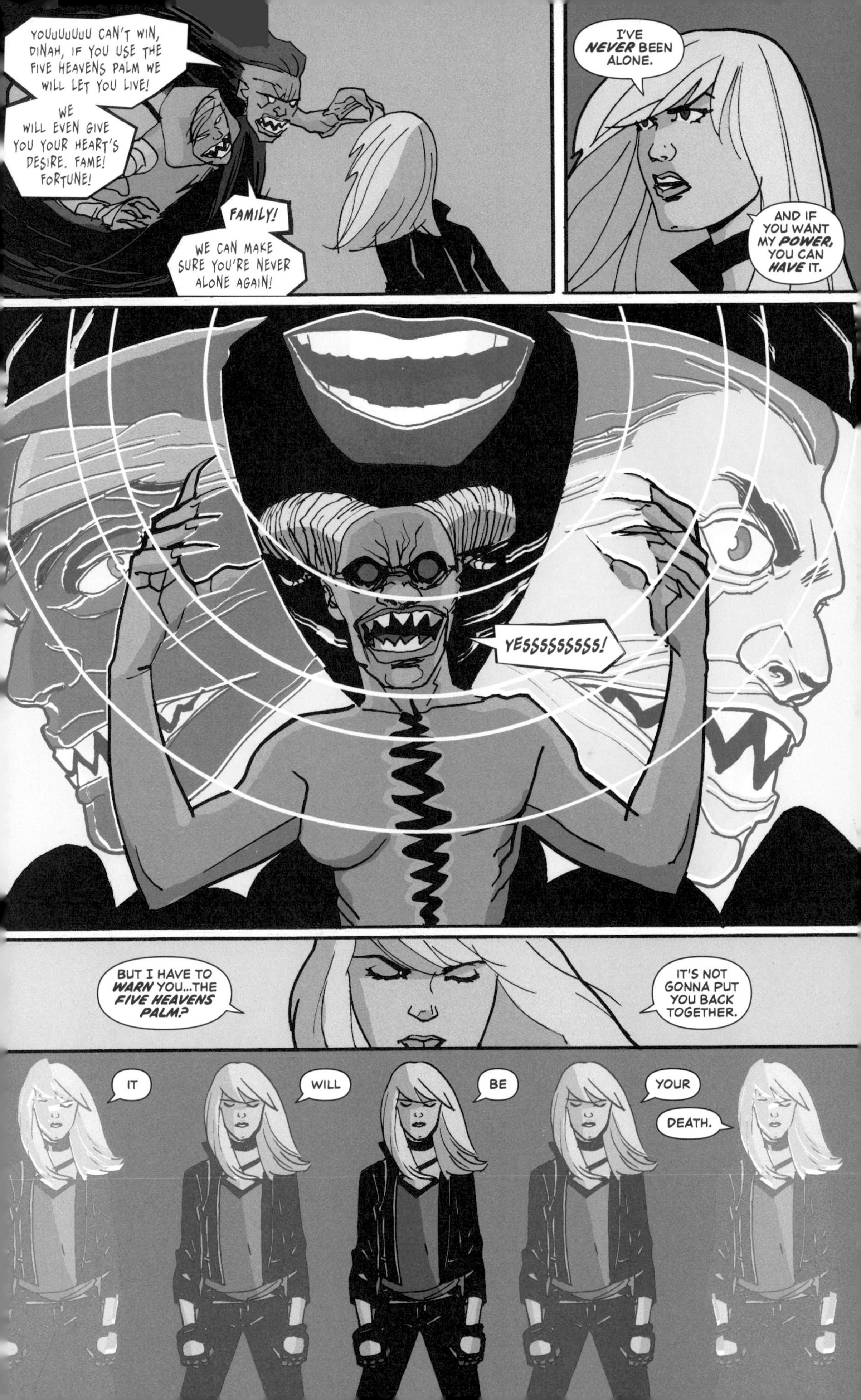
YOUUUUUUU CAN'T WIN, DINAH, IF YOU USE THE FIVE HEAVENS PALM WE WILL LET YOU LIVE!
WE WILL EVEN GIVE YOU YOUR HEART'S DESIRE. FAME! FORTUNE!
FAMILY!
WE CAN MAKE SURE YOU'RE NEVER ALONE AGAIN!
I'VE NEVER BEEN ALONE.
AND IF YOU WANT MY POWER, YOU CAN HAVE IT.
YESSSSSSSSS!
BUT I HAVE TO WARN YOU...THE FIVE HEAVENS PALM?
IT'S NOT GONNA PUT YOU BACK TOGETHER.
IT
WILL
BE
YOUR
DEATH.

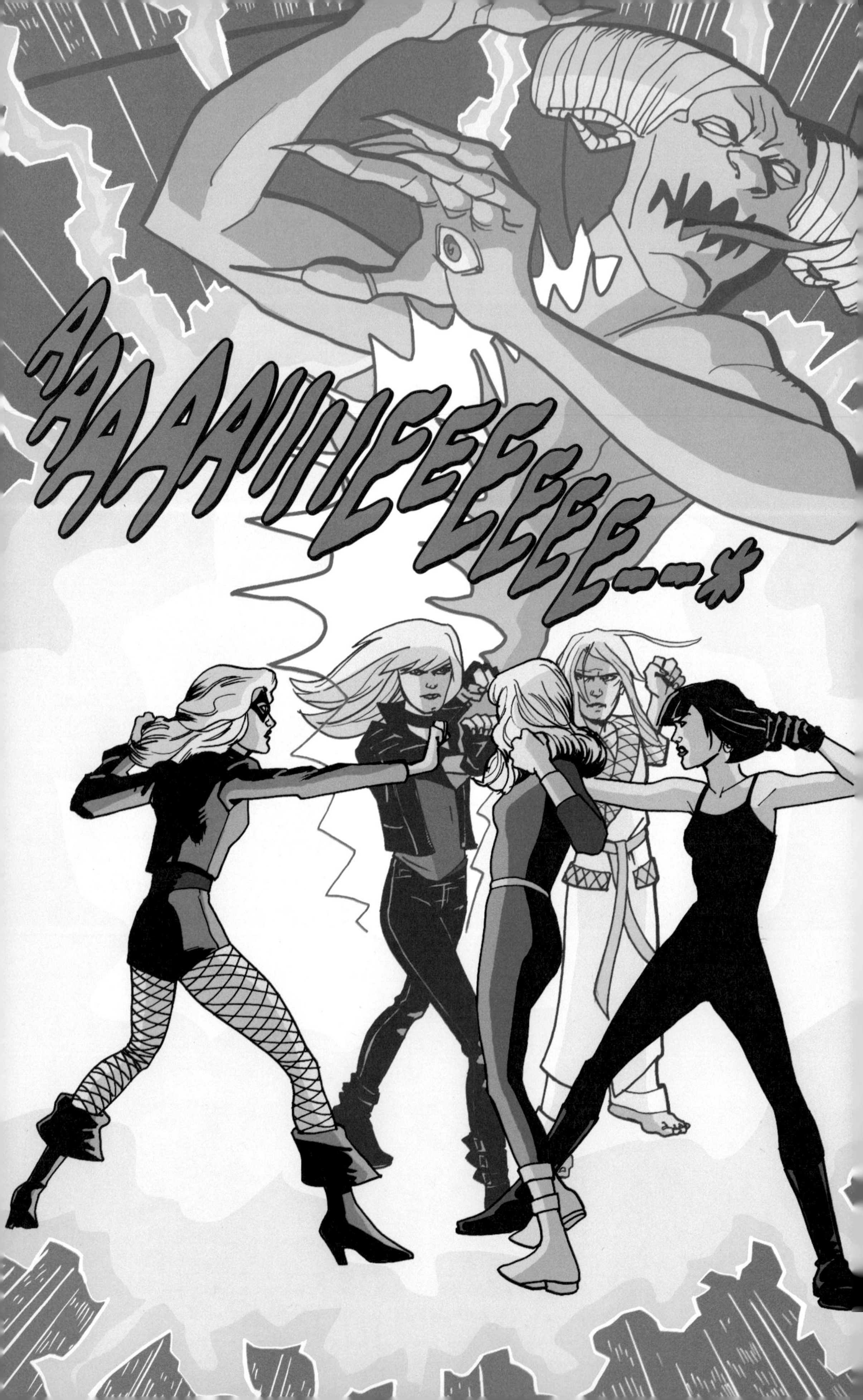
AAAAAIIIIEEEEEEE--*

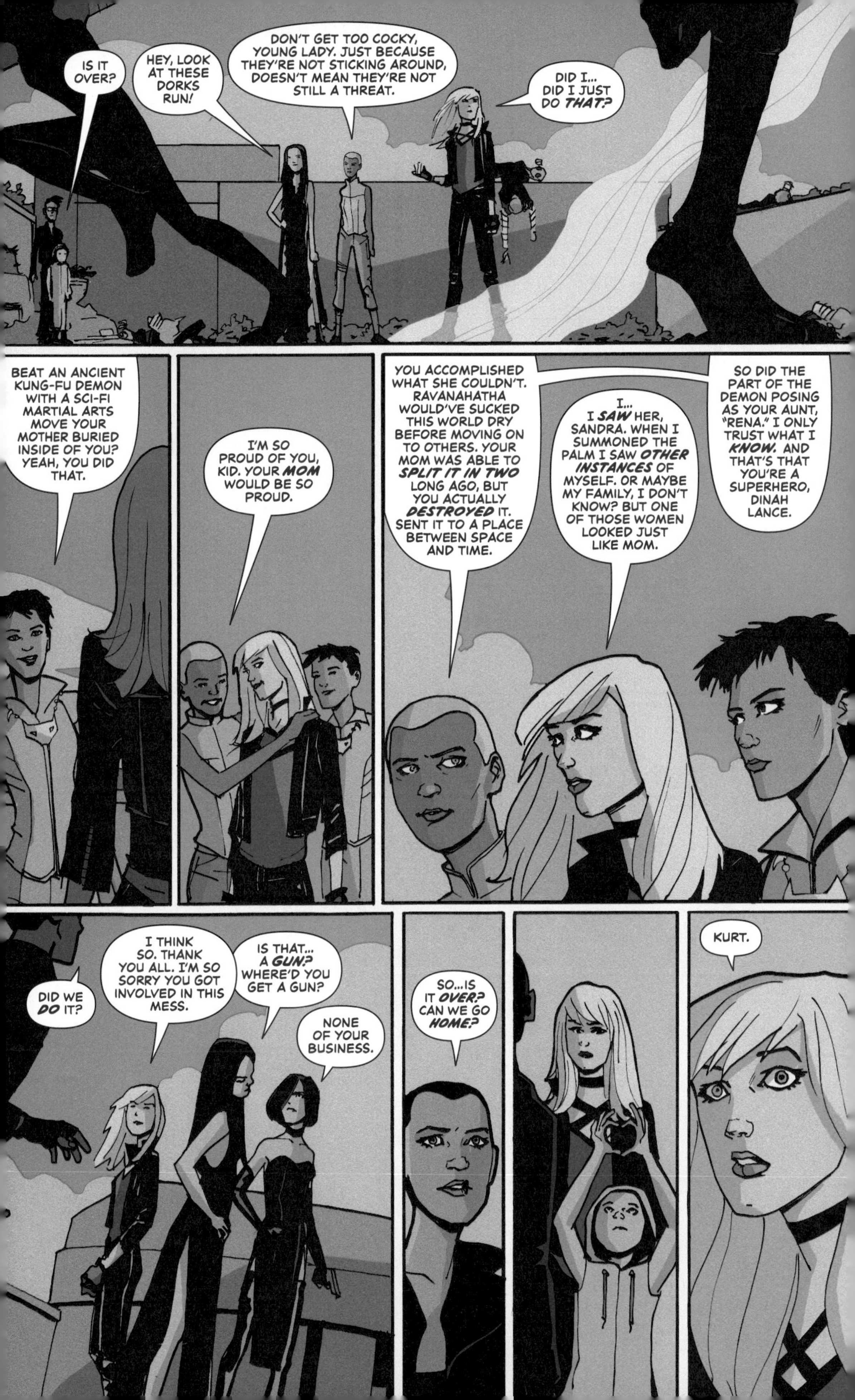

IS IT OVER?
HEY, LOOK AT THESE DORKS RUN!
DON'T GET TOO COCKY, YOUNG LADY. JUST BECAUSE THEY'RE NOT STICKING AROUND, DOESN'T MEAN THEY'RE NOT STILL A THREAT.
DID I... DID I JUST DO *THAT?*
BEAT AN ANCIENT KUNG-FU DEMON WITH A SCI-FI MARTIAL ARTS MOVE YOUR MOTHER BURIED INSIDE OF YOU? YEAH, YOU DID THAT.
I'M SO PROUD OF YOU, KID. YOUR *MOM* WOULD BE SO PROUD.
YOU ACCOMPLISHED WHAT SHE COULDN'T. RAVANAHATHA WOULD'VE SUCKED THIS WORLD DRY BEFORE MOVING ON TO OTHERS. YOUR MOM WAS ABLE TO *SPLIT IT IN TWO* LONG AGO, BUT YOU ACTUALLY *DESTROYED* IT. SENT IT TO A PLACE BETWEEN SPACE AND TIME.
I... I *SAW* HER, SANDRA. WHEN I SUMMONED THE PALM I SAW *OTHER INSTANCES* OF MYSELF. OR MAYBE MY FAMILY, I DON'T KNOW? BUT ONE OF THOSE WOMEN LOOKED JUST LIKE MOM.
SO DID THE PART OF THE DEMON POSING AS YOUR AUNT, "RENA." I ONLY TRUST WHAT I *KNOW.* AND THAT'S THAT YOU'RE A SUPERHERO, DINAH LANCE.
DID WE *DO* IT?
I THINK SO. THANK YOU ALL. I'M SO SORRY YOU GOT INVOLVED IN THIS MESS.
IS THAT... A *GUN?* WHERE'D YOU GET A GUN?
NONE OF YOUR BUSINESS.
SO...IS IT *OVER?* CAN WE GO *HOME?*
KURT.

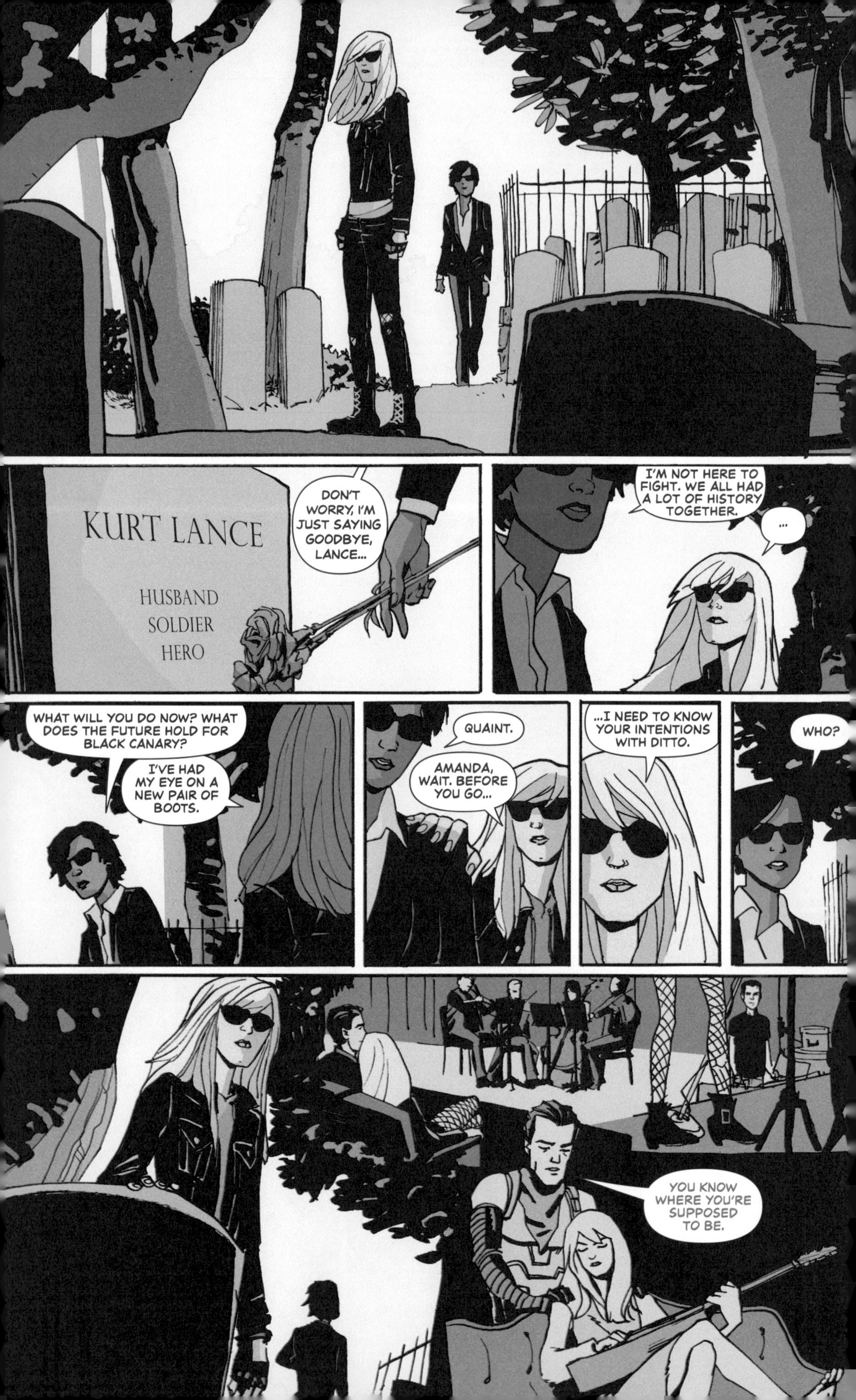
KURT LANCE
HUSBAND
SOLDIER
HERO
DON'T WORRY, I'M JUST SAYING GOODBYE, LANCE...
I'M NOT HERE TO FIGHT. WE ALL HAD A LOT OF HISTORY TOGETHER.
...
WHAT WILL YOU DO NOW? WHAT DOES THE FUTURE HOLD FOR BLACK CANARY?
I'VE HAD MY EYE ON A NEW PAIR OF BOOTS.
QUAINT.
AMANDA, WAIT. BEFORE YOU GO...
...I NEED TO KNOW YOUR INTENTIONS WITH DITTO.
WHO?
YOU KNOW WHERE YOU'RE SUPPOSED TO BE.

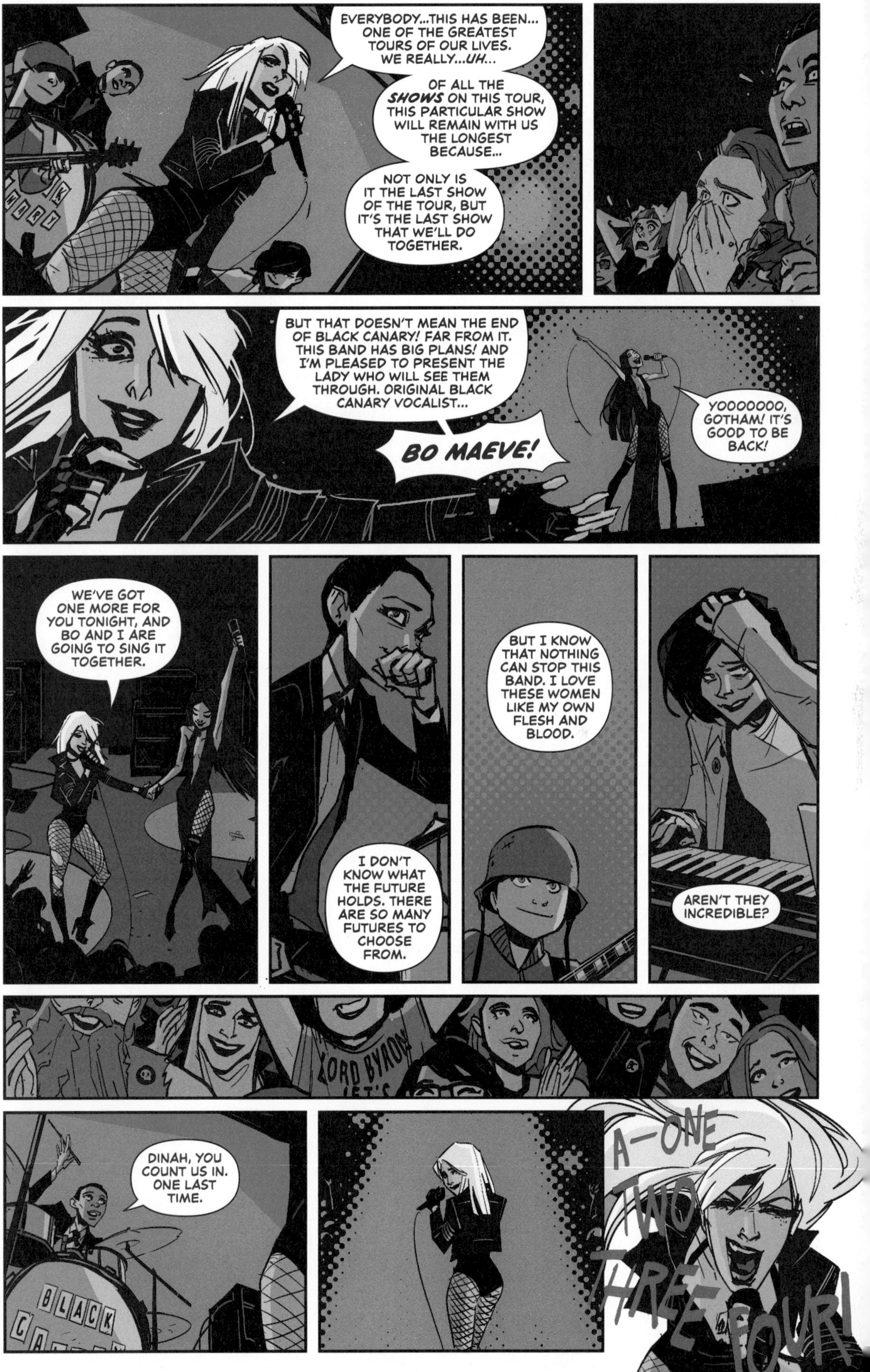
EVERYBODY...THIS HAS BEEN... ONE OF THE GREATEST TOURS OF OUR LIVES. WE REALLY...UH...
OF ALL THE SHOWS ON THIS TOUR, THIS PARTICULAR SHOW WILL REMAIN WITH US THE LONGEST BECAUSE...
NOT ONLY IS IT THE LAST SHOW OF THE TOUR, BUT IT'S THE LAST SHOW THAT WE'LL DO TOGETHER.
BUT THAT DOESN'T MEAN THE END OF BLACK CANARY! FAR FROM IT. THIS BAND HAS BIG PLANS! AND I'M PLEASED TO PRESENT THE LADY WHO WILL SEE THEM THROUGH. ORIGINAL BLACK CANARY VOCALIST...
BO MAEVE!
YOOOOOOO, GOTHAM! IT'S GOOD TO BE BACK!
WE'VE GOT ONE MORE FOR YOU TONIGHT, AND BO AND I ARE GOING TO SING IT TOGETHER.
I DON'T KNOW WHAT THE FUTURE HOLDS. THERE ARE SO MANY FUTURES TO CHOOSE FROM.
BUT I KNOW THAT NOTHING CAN STOP THIS BAND. I LOVE THESE WOMEN LIKE MY OWN FLESH AND BLOOD.
AREN'T THEY INCREDIBLE?
DINAH, YOU COUNT US IN. ONE LAST TIME.
A-ONE TWO THREE FOUR!

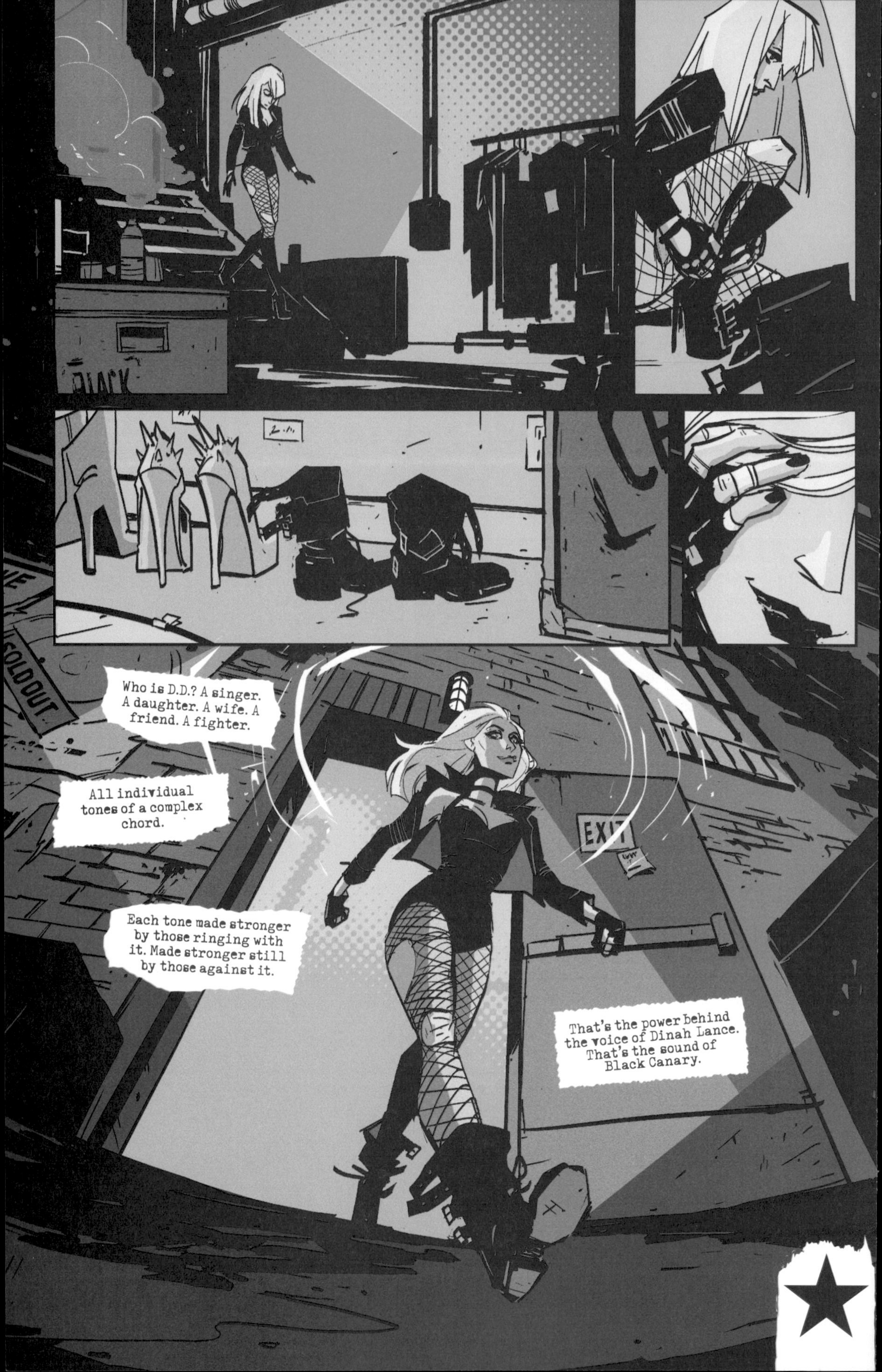
SOLD OUT
Who is D.D.? A singer. A daughter. A wife. A friend. A fighter.
All individual tones of a complex chord.
Each tone made stronger by those ringing with it. Made stronger still by those against it.
EXIT
That's the power behind the voice of Dinah Lance. That's the sound of Black Canary.

BURNSIDE TOFU
The zine for people with the right kind of taste

WHO IS BLACK CaNaRY?

BY TANTOO LA BICHE

presents a special PULL-OUT GUIDE!

PALOMA TERRIFIC.   DITTO.   D.D.   LORD BYRON.

Who is Black Canary? Good question. If you're an average music fan, you probably know that the band is a four-piece out of Gotham City with a recently released, critically celebrated three-song EP. You probably also know that hitting one of their gigs is a potentially dangerous endeavor for those not trained in the art of self-defense. What you might not know, however—unless you're an avid reader of Burnside Tofu (WHICH YOU TOTALLY SHOULD BE)—is that there's more to the ladies in this band than meets the eye. Burnside Tofu stole a few moments with Black Canary during load-out at a recent show in Fairfield. Here's what we learned:

1. DON'T MESS WITH D.D.:
Our reporter (ME!) was *maybe* waiting for the band outside the Liquid Room stage door, *maybe* hiding in a shadowy spot just around the corner from the dumpster by the bus. BIG MISTAKE! If you learn anything from this issue of Burnside Tofu let it be that you should never sneak up on D.D. even if it's in the interest of hard-hitting music journalism. You might end up on the painful end of a judo throw.

2. D.D. = "DINAH"???:
The former Ashes on Sunday singer was forthcoming with a truly sincere apology for the judo throw, but not with information about her past. As she came to the assistance of this reporter, her bandmate Lord Byron asked "Dinah" if everything was OK. When questioned about her real name, D.D. offered a playful wink and returned to the load-out.

"I go through a pair a day. It accounts for a quarter of the band's budget." - D.D. on her fishnet tights

3. LORD BYRON IS THE BAND:
Byron was kind enough to talk to Burnside Tofu about the origin of the band and her part in it. It turns out that Lord Byron is the mastermind behind Black Canary, pioneering their sound, co-writing every song and even handling some of the lighter aspects of the business. This band has been her life's ambition, and though she seems pleased with how quickly and sharply their star has risen, it's clear that the controversy surrounding Canary is a cause of some concern.

"Bass is my one true love. But this drum kit is my piece on the side." - Lord Byron

4. DITTO IS HOW OLD?:
According to Black Canary tour manager Heathcliff Ray–who, I might add, seems suspiciously young himself–guitar magician "Ditto" is a full 19 years of age (with a gland condition) and legally allowed to play the stage of most, if not all, music venues. Burnside Tofu was born only a short while ago, Heathcliff, but was not born yesterday. Ditto looks no older than 12. BT has reached out to the band's management and label for confirmation.

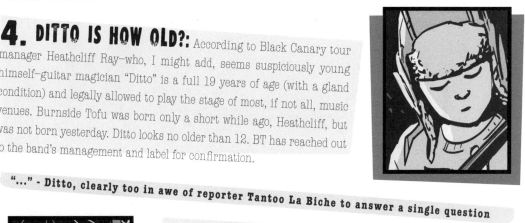

"..." - Ditto, clearly too in awe of reporter Tantoo La Biche to answer a single question

5. PALOMA IS REALLY TERRIFIC:
The Tofu-mobile broke down outside the Liquid Room. As the Canary tour bus drove away from the venue, it pulled up alongside and offered assistance. Paloma Terrific popped the hood, worked her magic and the Tofu-mobile was right as rain. In fact, the car hasn't required a tune-up since! Super terrific, Paloma!

"Confession: All of my keyboard lines are cribbed from old Franz Waxman film scores. Okay, maybe not all of them." - Paloma Terrific

6. D.D. IS NOT THE ORIGINAL SINGER:
Byron and Paloma started the band in college with a theater student named Maeve. The trio was quickly signed to a record deal and began working on their debut album, even going so far as to shoot a music video for their first single. And then Maeve was bought out, dropped from the contract and replaced by D.D. It was at this point that the band gained the name Black Canary. What happened to Maeve? And why the name Black Canary?

DEBUT TOUR IS THE FINAL TOUR:
There are strong hints that Black Canary might be a one-EP, one-tour band. Say it isn't so! More to come...

BURNSIDE TOFU The zine for people with the right kind of taste

BUILDING BLACK CANARY

BY TANTOO LA BICHE

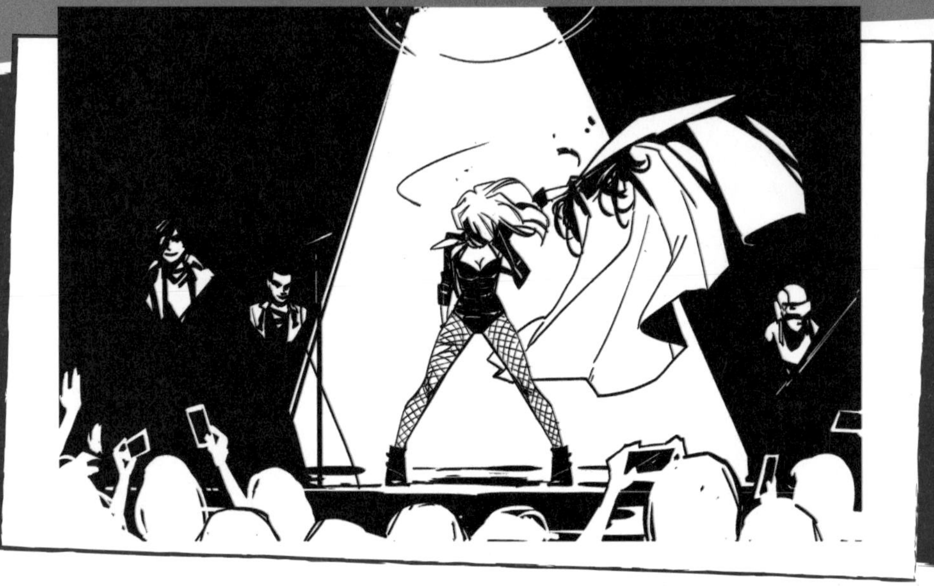

Most bands come together in an organic way. Friends join friends to make music, bond, have a good time. Not so with Black Canary. While the Gotham four-piece hit all the right notes with their debut EP, the shifty manner in which they became a band shows all the signs of being a manipulated third-party mash-up. Whose idea was it to throw them together? Where's the money coming from? Why this challenging, expensive tour? And just who are the people supporting Black Canary on the road?

Ace reporter Tantoo La Biche (YES, yours truly!) tracked down a representative of Canary label A&B Records who agreed to spill the beans (anonymously) about what they know of the band's formation.

The rep claims the order to disband the original group (with singer Bo Maeve) came from the top...as did the mandate to add D.D. to the lineup. With new guitarist Ditto in place, the label upped their financial commitment, putting their full weight behind breaking Black Canary big. That's where the tour came in.

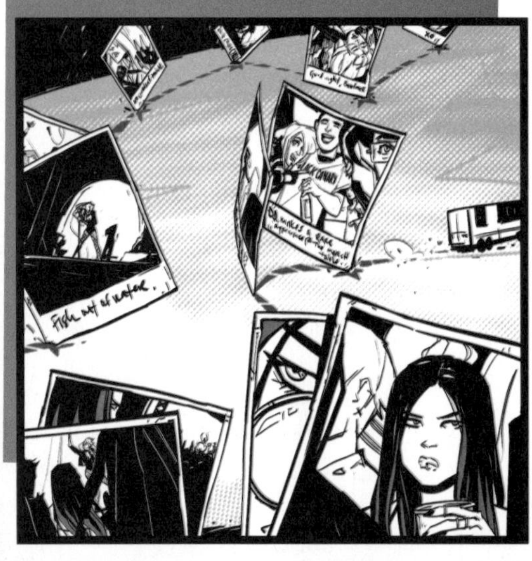

DREAM TOUR?

A&B Records has apparently never financed a tour this large for a band as green as Black Canary. Just under 30 dates in 30 days is a grueling schedule for even the most seasoned touring acts, but to thrust this on a group as fresh as this was just begging for disaster. Burnside Tofu has tabulated the top three most costly performances of the tour so far:

1. **WIZARD'S WAND** - Detroit: $50,000+ (Caved-in roof, destroyed PA system speaker, damaged flooring, walls, structural supports, etc.)
2. **RADIO THEATRE** - Metropolis: $8,400 (Damaged bar beyond repair, overloaded PA system, giant hole in parking lot [how did they manage that?])
3. **SUBCULTURE** - Central City: $3,800 (Stage floorboards demolished, lighting grid bent, general human suffering)

DREAM (TOUR) MANAGER

The job of keeping the band organized while on the road falls to the tour manager. Black Canary seems lucky that young Heathcliff Ray has agreed to stick it out with them in this capacity, given all he's had to go through to keep them on schedule (and alive) these past few weeks.

"I wasn't expecting the job to be so...action-packed," Ray admitted when we caught him selling shirts at the band's merch table before a recent show. Burnside Tofu wasn't able to find a record of employment for Ray before his job for Canary's management company. His last known position was at Gotham Academy...as a student.

DREAM MACHINE

Florence "Flo" Mandelbaum drives Black Canary from city to city, from gig to gig, in a 2003 MAGISTRATE EX2 ENTERTAINER BUS provided by the label (virtually unheard of for a breaking band like this!). This thing is wild, sleeping six comfortably with front and rear lounges for hangouts and jams. Flo handles the machine with precision and care, but confirms to Burnside Tofu that she was actually hired as the band's traveling sound professional, not their chauffeur. When questioned about a possibly compromising lack of sleep between mixing the band's live shows and driving them around, Flo clutched her large coffee and stared off into the distance.

D.D. REVEALED

Burnside Tofu believes we have uncovered some shocking and definitive answers about Canary's lead singer, "D.D."

Our contact at A&B slipped us heavily redacted documents from the U.S. military showing proof of marriage between a person by the name of Dinah Drake and one Kurt Lance. All other details are illegible, though there's a hint that seems to refer to both being members of something called "Team 7."

It's all starting to come together. If these documents are relevant and true, Black Canary's "D.D." is really ex-military operative Dinah Drake. The fact that she's been hiding her identity from fans and the press—and the redacted nature of the marriage docs—suggest her time in the military was most likely spent in a highly skilled, top-secret group. Has she been keeping secrets to ensure the safety of others—possibly her old teammates—or is she in hiding from the government? And what's her current marital status? Is Dinah still married to Kurt Lance? If so, where is he?

Burnside Tofu won't rest until these burning questions are answered!

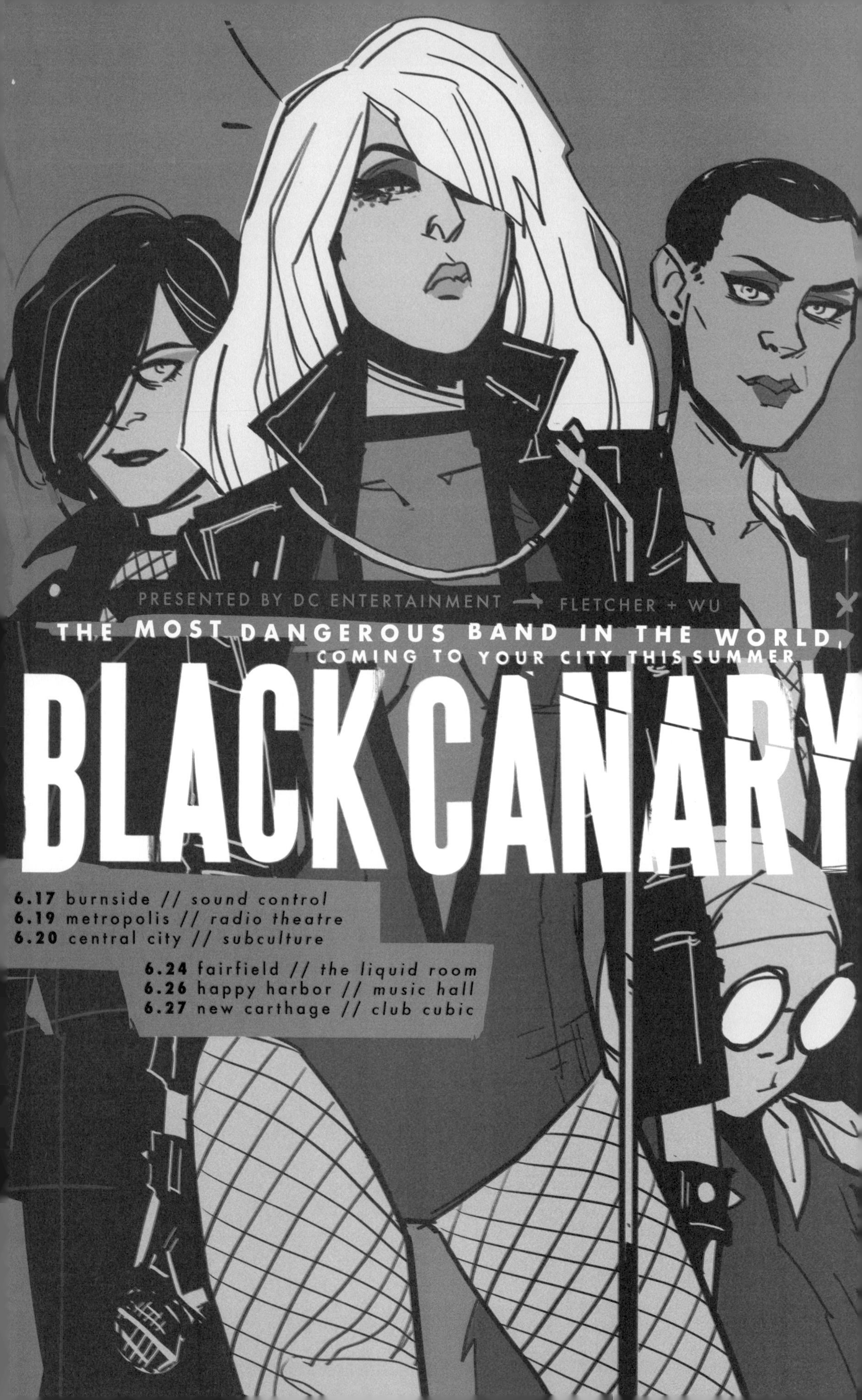
PRESENTED BY DC ENTERTAINMENT → FLETCHER + WU
THE MOST DANGEROUS BAND IN THE WORLD,
COMING TO YOUR CITY THIS SUMMER
BLACK CANARY
6.17 burnside // sound control
6.19 metropolis // radio theatre
6.20 central city // subculture
6.24 fairfield // the liquid room
6.26 happy harbor // music hall
6.27 new carthage // club cubic

BLACK CANARY #1
VARIANT COVER BY TULA LOTAY

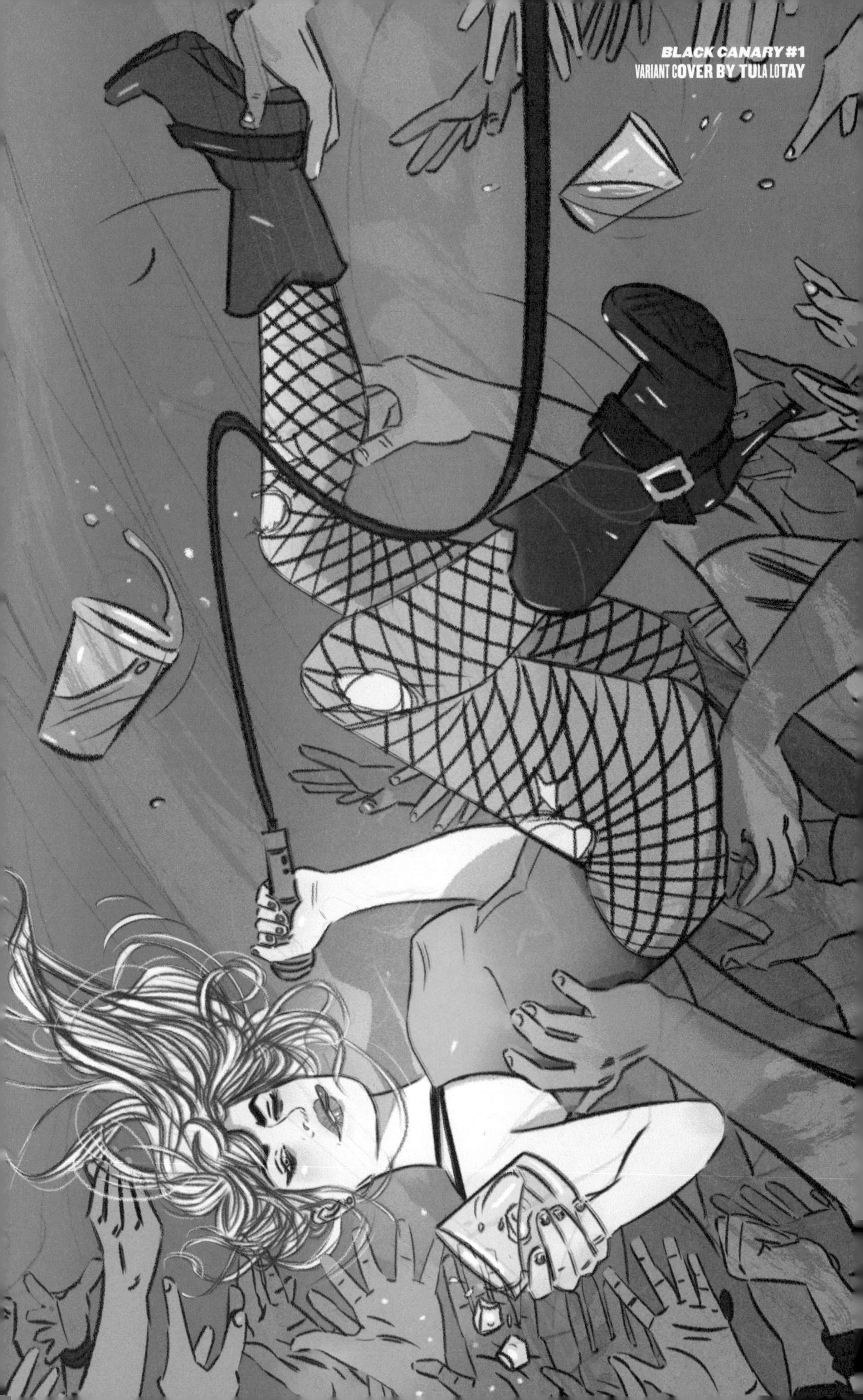

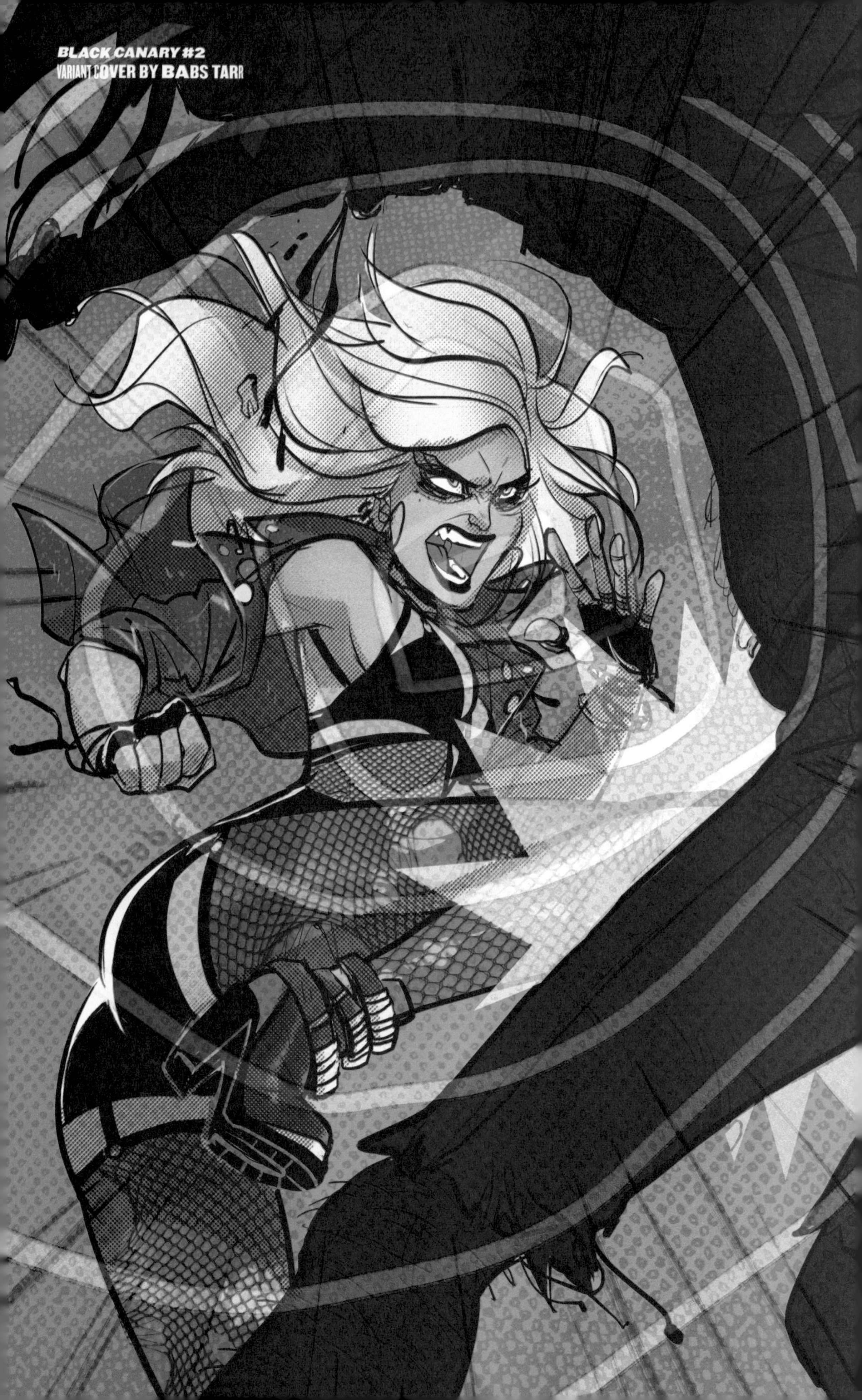

BLACK CANARY #2
VARIANT COVER BY BABS TARR

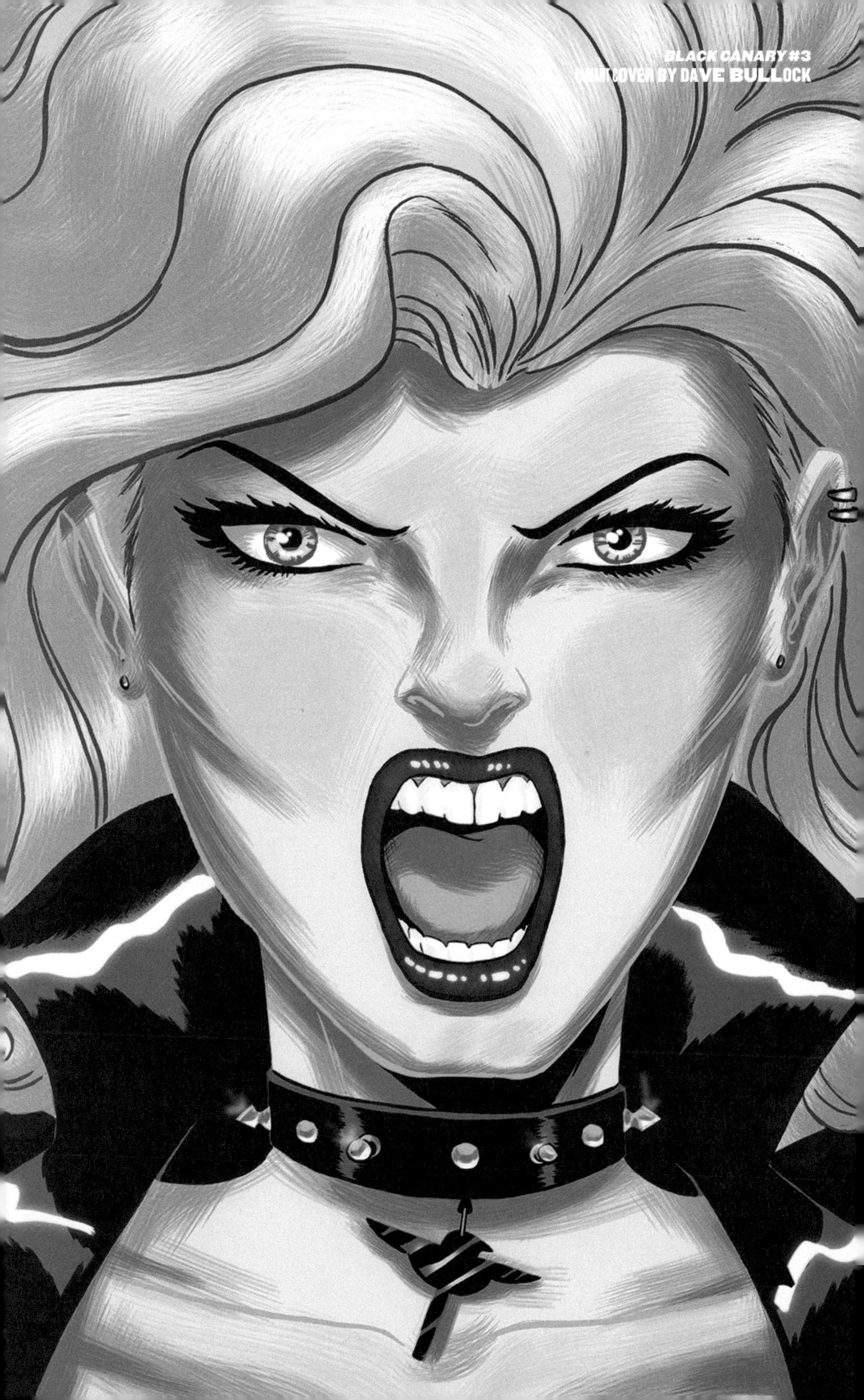

BLACK CANARY #3
VARIANT COVER BY DAVE BULLOCK

BLACK CANARY #4
GREEN LANTERN 75TH ANNIVERSARY
VARIANT COVER BY EVAN "DOC" SHANER

BLACK CANARY #5
MONSTER VARIANT COVER BY MICHAEL AND LAURA ALLRED

BLACK CANARY #6
LOONEY TUNES VARIANT COVER
BY PIA GUERRA AND SPIKE BRANDT

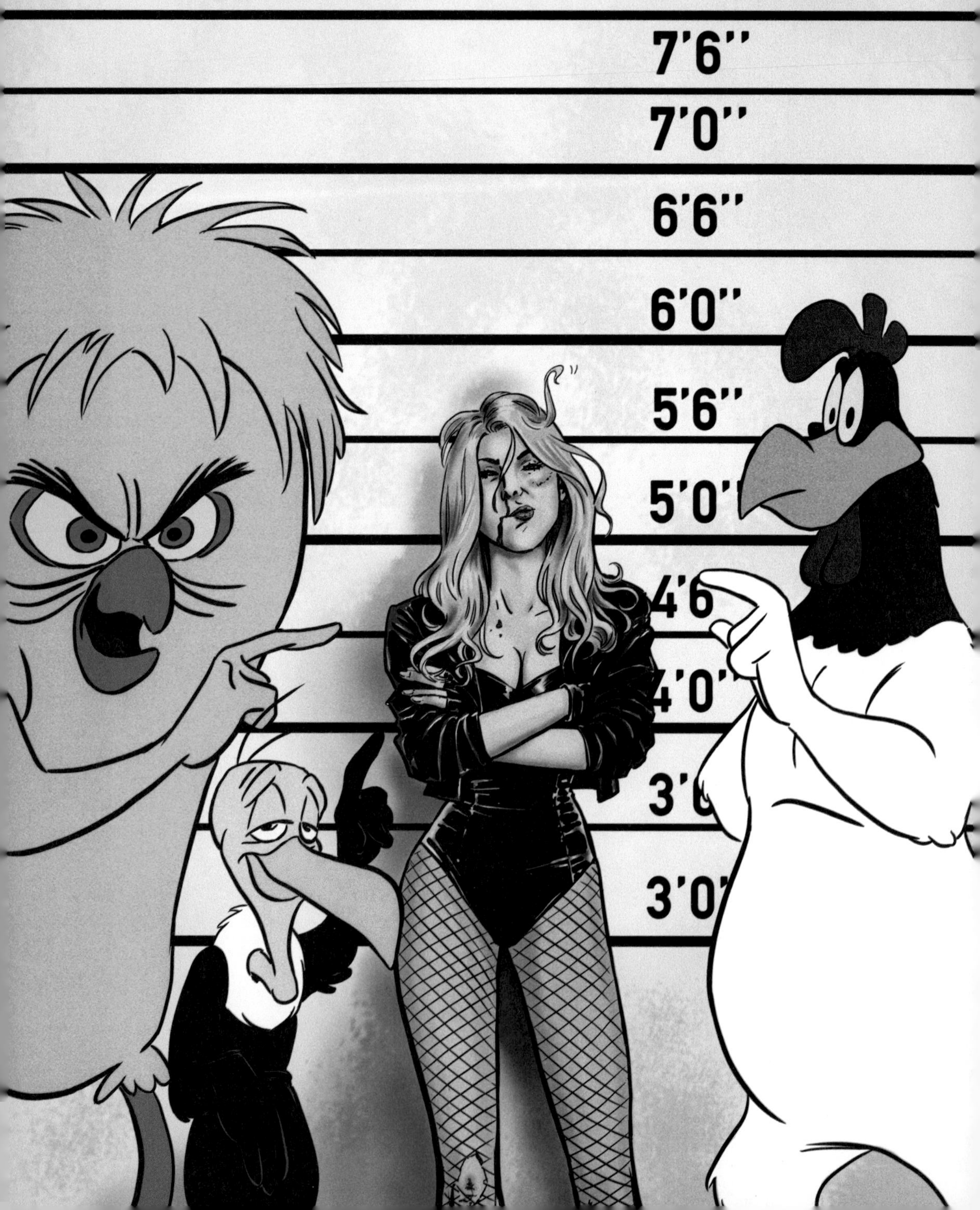
7'6''
7'0''
6'6''
6'0''
5'6''

BLACK CANARY
FLETCHER WU

BLACK
CANARY

Black
Canary,
1

BLACK
CANARY

BLACK
CANARY
FLETCHER WU

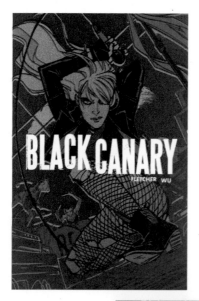

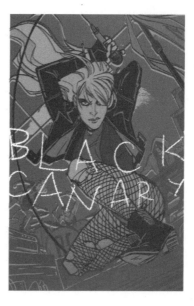

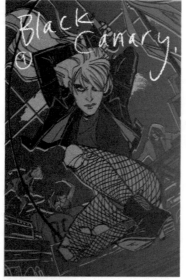

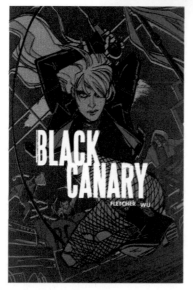

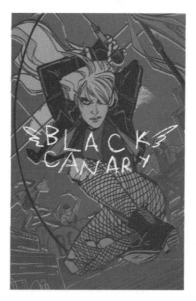

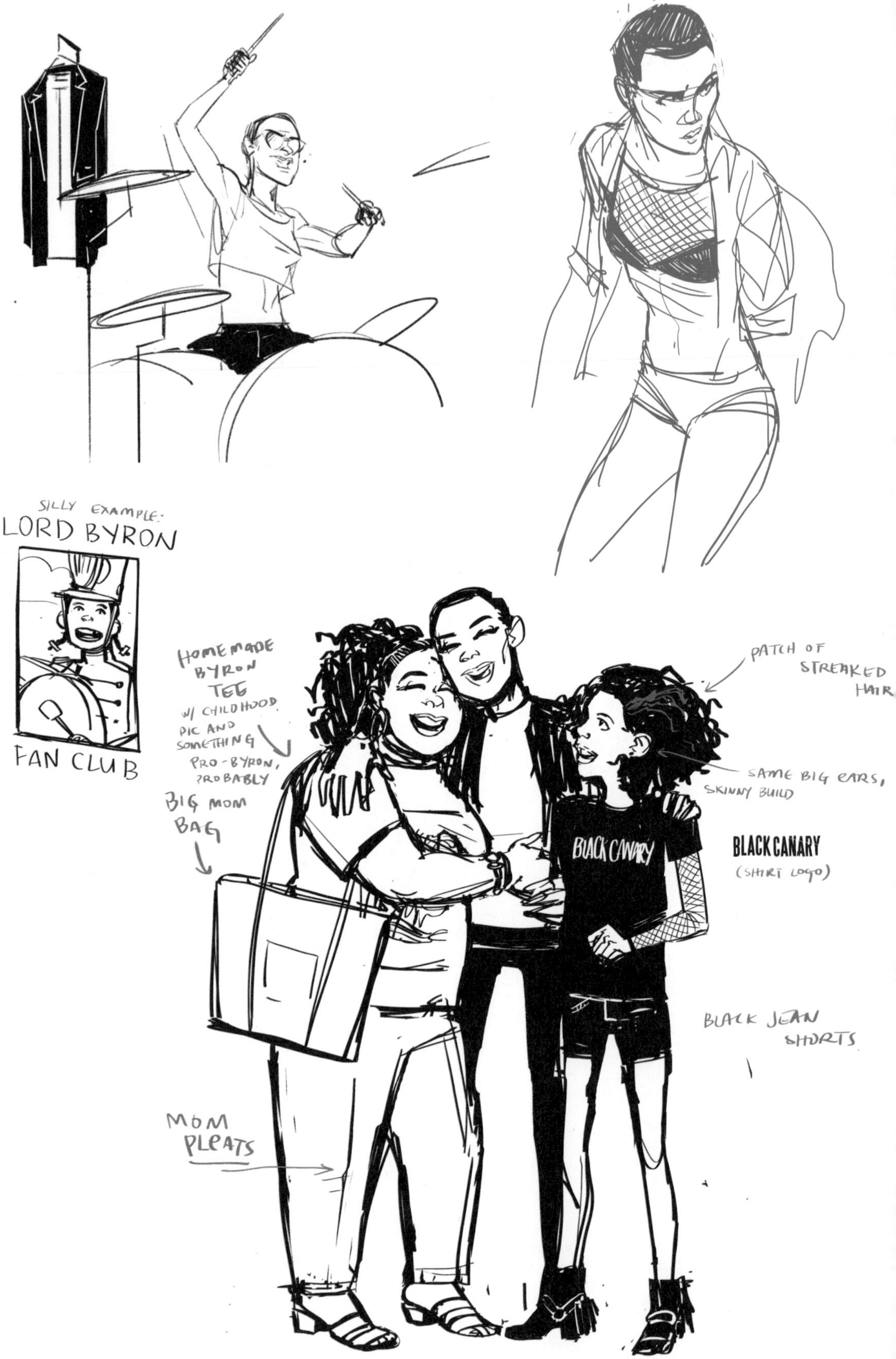
SILLY EXAMPLE:
LORD BYRON
FAN CLUB
HOMEMADE BYRON TEE W/ CHILDHOOD PIC AND SOMETHING PRO-BYRON, PROBABLY
BIG MOM BAG
MOM PLEATS
PATCH OF STREAKED HAIR
SAME BIG EARS, SKINNY BUILD
BLACK CANARY
BLACK CANARY
(SHIRT LOGO)
BLACK JEAN SHORTS

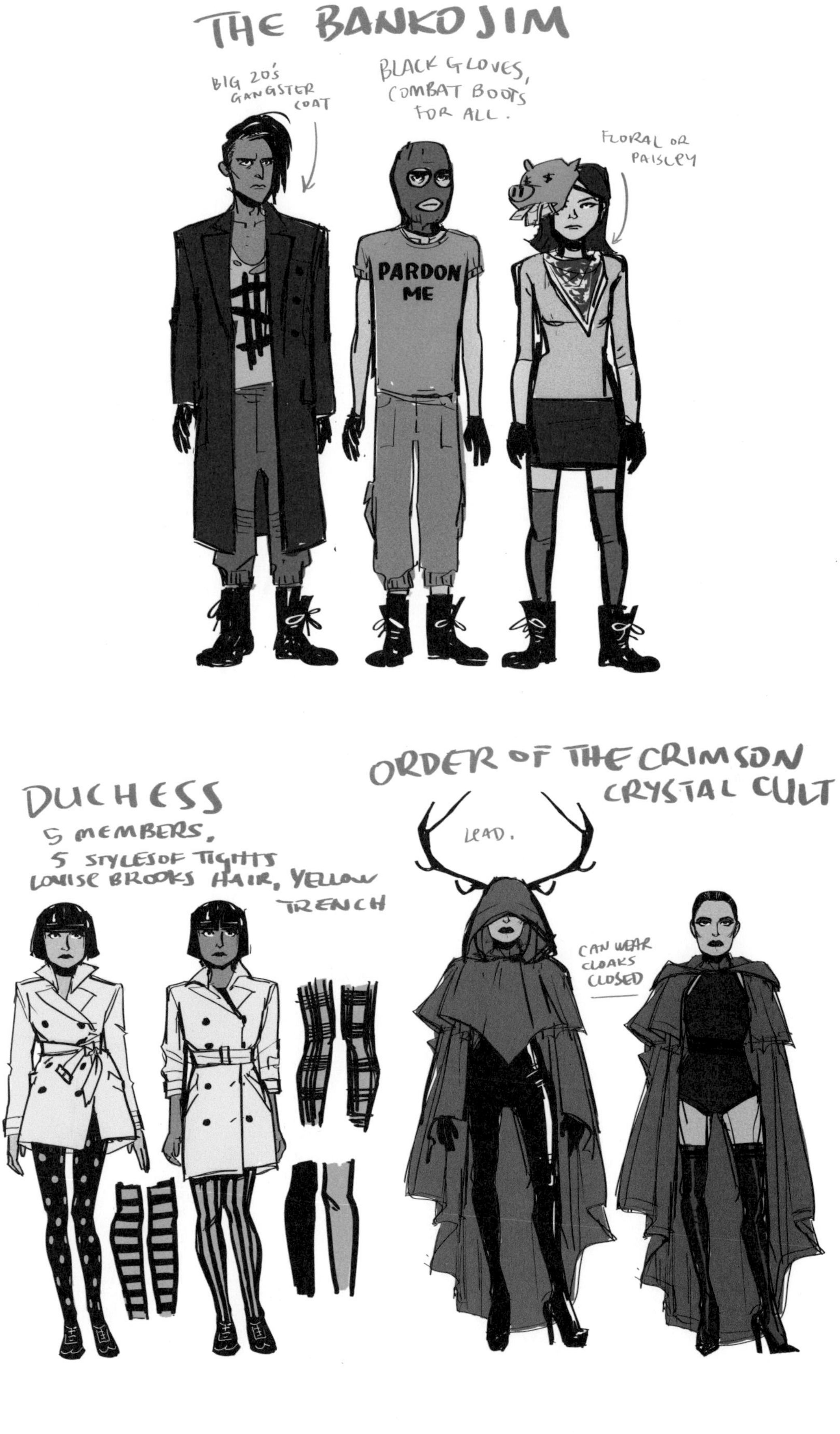
THE BANKOJIM
BIG 20's GANGSTER COAT
BLACK GLOVES, COMBAT BOOTS FOR ALL.
FLORAL OR PAISLEY
PARDON ME
DUCHESS
5 MEMBERS, 5 STYLES OF TIGHTS
LOUISE BROOKS HAIR, YELLOW TRENCH
ORDER OF THE CRIMSON CRYSTAL CULT
LEAD.
CAN WEAR CLOAKS CLOSED

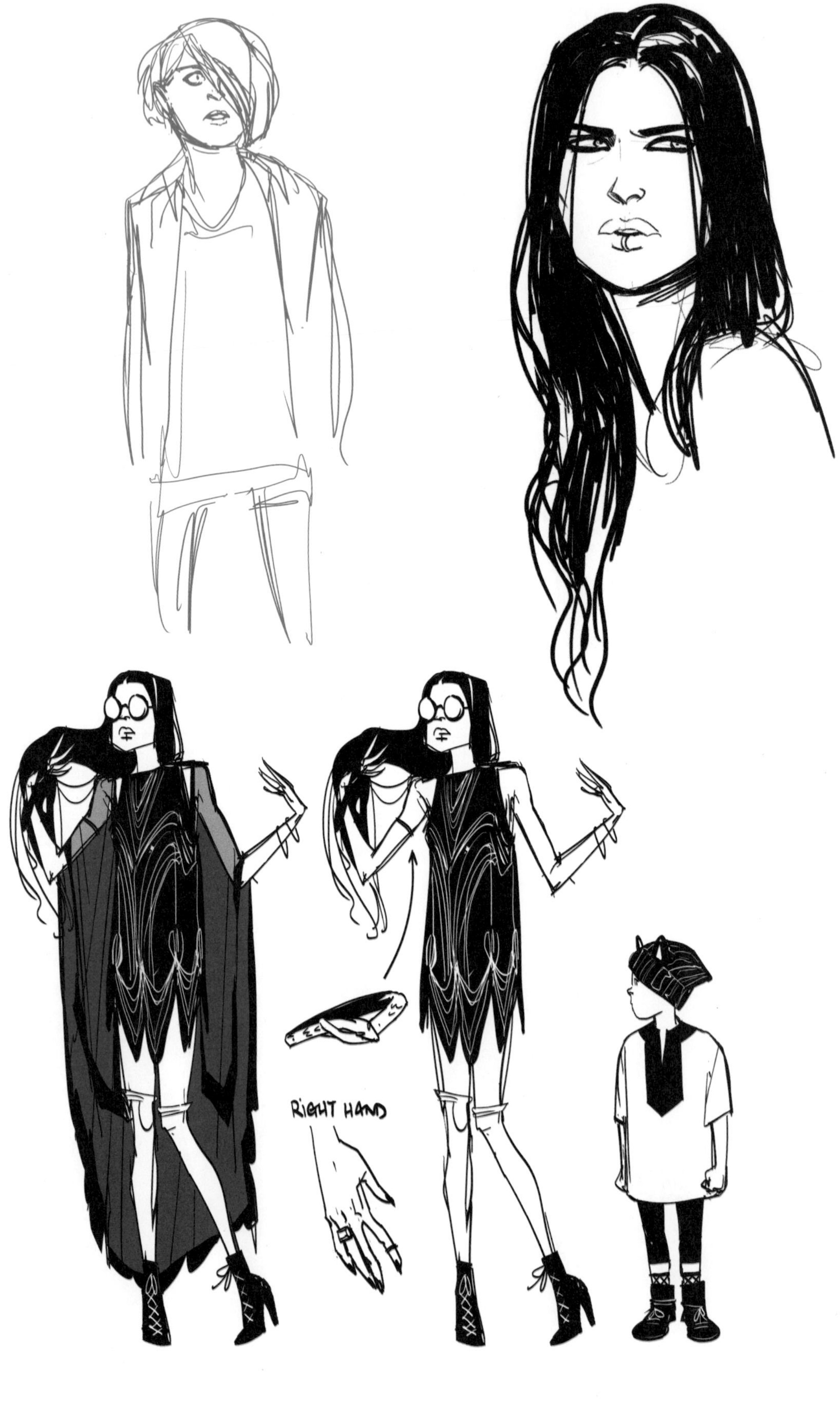
RIGHT HAND

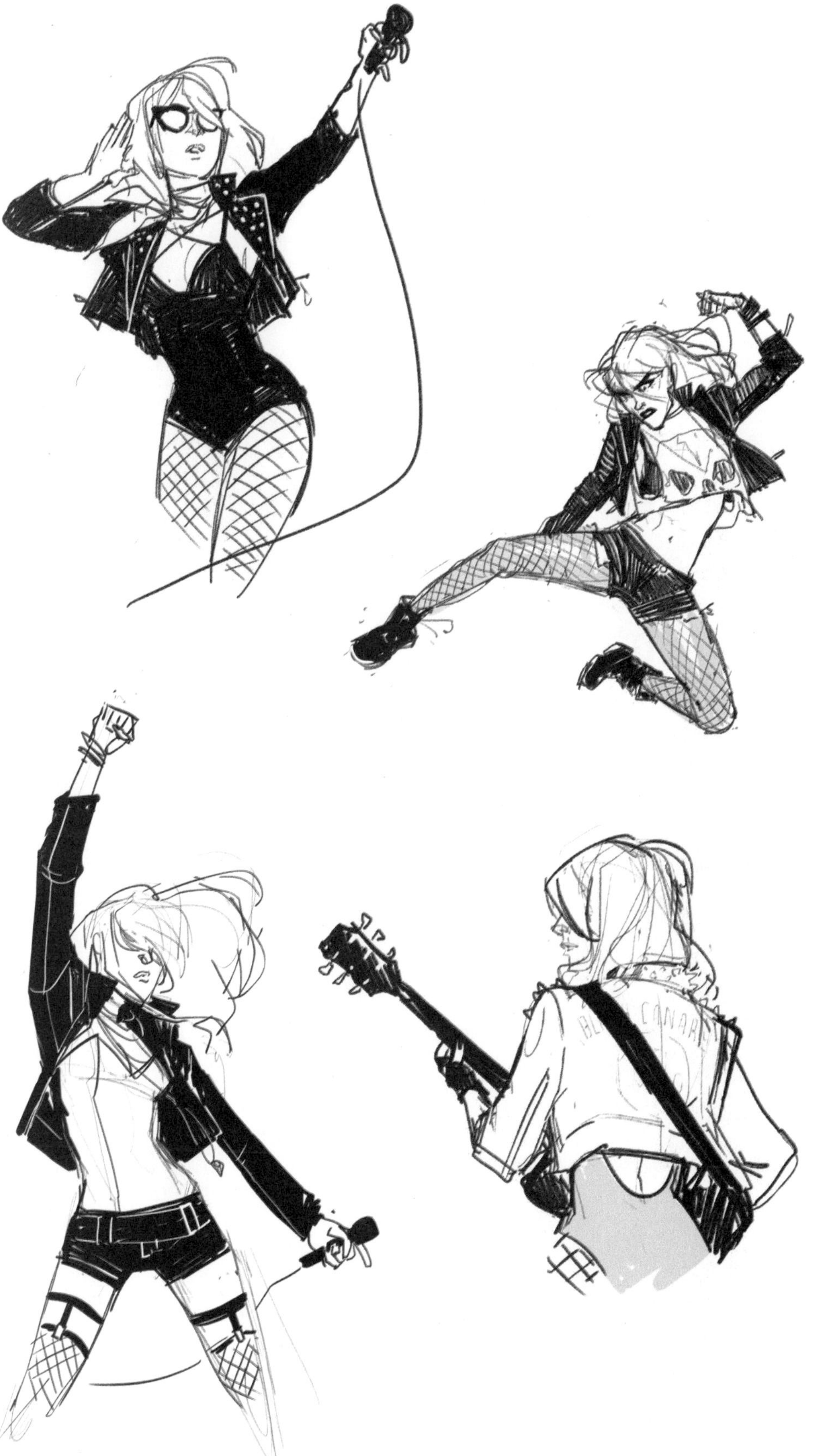

HARLEY QUINN

VOL. 1: HOT IN THE CITY
AMANDA CONNER
with JIMMY PALMIOTTI
& CHAD HARDIN

READ THE ENTIRE EPIC!

HARLEY QUINN VOL. 4:
A CALL TO ARMS

HARLEY QUINN VOL. 5:
THE JOKER'S LAST LAUGH

**HARLEY QUINN
VOL. 2: POWER OUTAGE**

**HARLEY QUINN
VOL. 3: KISS KISS BANG STAB**

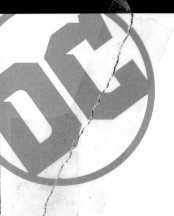

"A smart concept, snappy one-liners and a great twist to match a tag-team of talented artists."
—NEWSARAMA

"Every bit as chaotic and unabashedly fun as one would expect."
—IGN

HARLEY QUINN

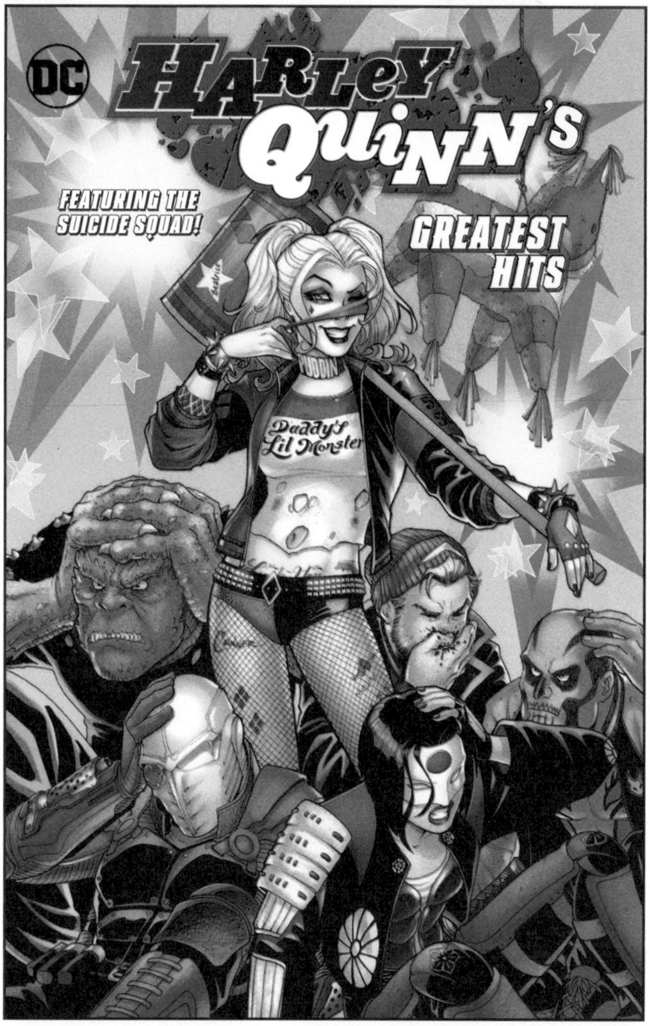

HARLEY QUINN'S
FEATURING THE SUICIDE SQUAD!
GREATEST HITS

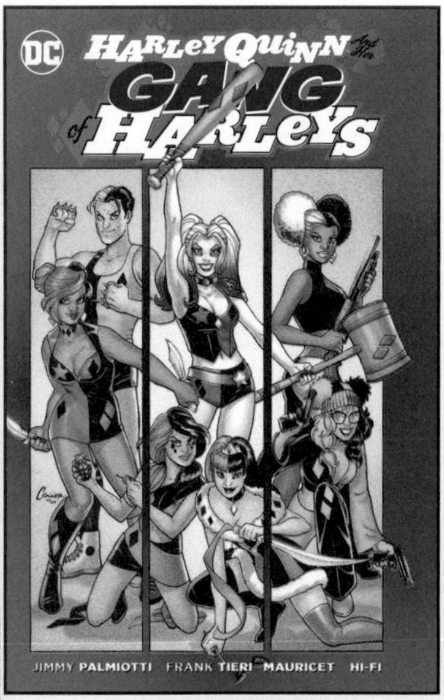

HARLEY QUINN And Her
GANG of HARLEYS
JIMMY PALMIOTTI FRANK TIERI MAURICET HI-FI

HARLEY QUINN AND HER GANG OF HARLEYS

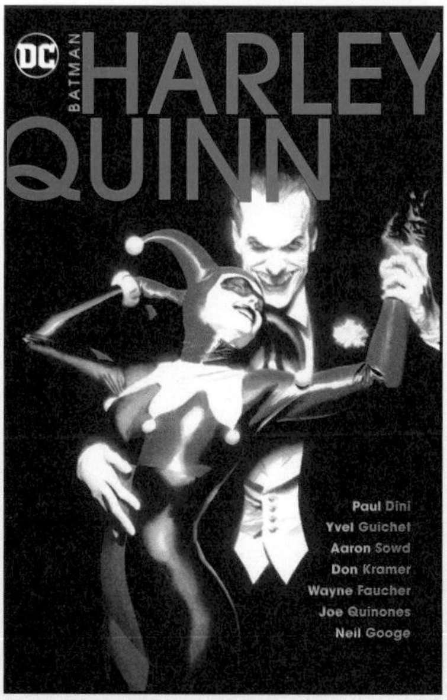

BATMAN
HARLEY QUINN
Paul Dini
Yvel Guichet
Aaron Sowd
Don Kramer
Wayne Faucher
Joe Quinones
Neil Googe

BATMAN HARLEY QUINN

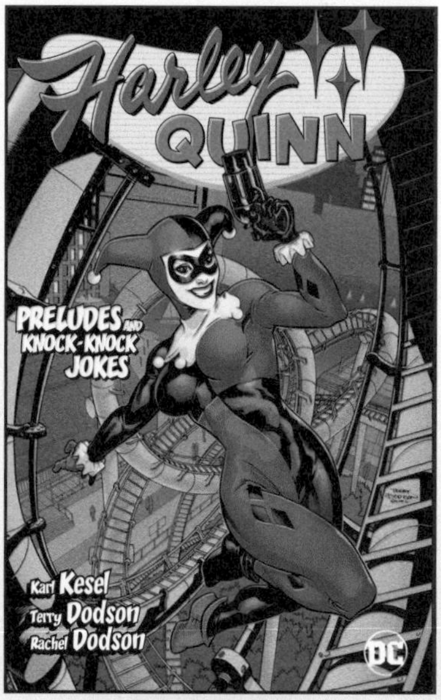

Harley QUINN
PRELUDES AND KNOCK-KNOCK JOKES
Karl Kesel
Terry Dodson
Rachel Dodson

HARLEY QUINN: PRELUDES AND KNOCK-KNOCK JOKES

Get more DC graphic novels wherever comics and books are sold!

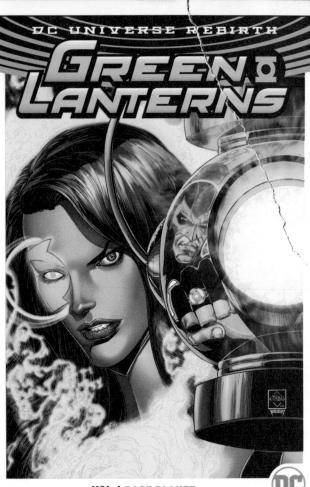